Persuasion in Society

Persuasion in Society, Third Edition introduces readers to the rich tapestry of persuasive technique and scholarship, interweaving rhetorical, critical theory, and social science traditions. This text examines current and classical theory through the lens of contemporary culture, encouraging readers to explore the nature of persuasion and to understand its impact in their lives. Employing a contemporary approach, authors Jean G. Jones and Herbert W. Simons draw from popular culture, mass media, and social media to help readers become informed creators and consumers of persuasive messages.

This introductory persuasion text offers:

- A broad-based approach to the scope of persuasion, expanding students' understanding of what persuasion is and how it is effected.

- Insights on the diversity of persuasion in action, through such contexts as advertising, marketing, political campaigns, activism and social movements, and negotiation in social conflicts.

- The inclusion of "sender" and "receiver" perspectives, enhancing understanding of persuasion in practice.

- Extended treatment of the ethics of persuasion, featuring opposing views on handling controversial issues in the college classroom for enhanced instruction.

- Case studies showing how and why people fall for persuasive messages, demonstrating how persuasion works at a cognitive level.

- Discussion questions, exercises, and key terms for very nearly every chapter.

The core of this book is that persuasion is about winning beliefs and not arguments and that communicators who want to win that belief need to communicate with their audiences. This new edition of *Persuasion in Society* continues to bring this core message to readers with updated case studies, examples, and sources.

Jean G. Jones is professor of communication at Edinboro University of Pennsylvania and has over two decades' experience studying, teaching, and writing about rhetoric and persuasion. Named Edinboro University's "Educator of the Year" in 2006, Jones also has an active life in politics, having run for office and served on her city council.

Herbert W. Simons taught persuasion and related topics in communication at Temple University from 1960 until his retirement in 2007. A frequent media commentator, visiting professor, and guest lecturer, he directed Temple's London Study Abroad program, lectured at Peking University and at other institutions in China, and served as a Fulbright Senior Specialist in Hong Kong and Jakarta.

Persuasion in Society

Third Edition

Jean G. Jones
Herbert W. Simons

Routledge
Taylor & Francis Group

NEW YORK AND LONDON

Third edition published 2017
by Routledge
711 Third Avenue, New York, NY 10017

and by Routledge
2 Park Square, Milton Park, Abingdon, Oxon, OX14 4RN

Routledge is an imprint of the Taylor & Francis Group, an *informa* business

First edition published by SAGE 2001
Second edition published by Routledge 2011

Library of Congress Cataloging in Publication Data
A catalog record for this book has been requested

ISBN: 978-1-138-82565-9 (hbk)
ISBN: 978-1-138-82566-6 (pbk)
ISBN: 978-1-315-73981-6 (ebk)

Typeset in Stone Serif
by Saxon Graphics Ltd, Derby

MIX
Paper from
responsible sources
FSC FSC® C013056
www.fsc.org

Printed and bound in Great Britain by
TJ International Ltd, Padstow, Cornwall

CONTENTS

ACKNOWLEDGMENTS

This book has been a labor of many years. We wish to thank each other and our spouses, and those who helped shape the book through two editions. Special thanks to past contributors Bruce Gronbeck and Joanne Morreale, to Routledge Publisher Linda Bathgate and Editorial Assistant Stephanie Gorman, to Herb's past editors at Sage, to Routledge's anonymous reviewers and to colleagues who volunteered reviews of selected chapters. These included Michael Barzelay (LSE), Maxim Fetissenko (Northeastern), David Hoffman (Baruch), and Kathleen Reardon (USC). Thanks also to editorial assistants Melissa Hennen and Allison Hendrich at Edinboro and Temple's Erin Schlessing. *Muchas gracias* to Jean's classes in persuasion and to Herb's at Temple and at the Osher Lifelong Learning Institute. You were our guinea pigs.

PREFACE

This book is the third in a series of textbooks on persuasion, each one building on the last, incorporating new knowledge and new theory about persuasion while adapting to social and cultural changes in our increasingly globalized world. Some things have not changed in this edition, including its core convictions: that persuasion is about winning beliefs, not arguments; that communicators who seek to win belief need to communicate with their audiences, not at them; and that persuasion at its best is a matter of giving and not just getting, recognizing that they are most likely to give you what you want if they are convinced that what you propose also gives them what they want. This is the essence of the book's *coactive* approach to persuasion.

Persuasion in Society also remains focused on clear-cut instances of attempted persuasion—called *paradigm cases*—but gives increased attention to cases in which intent to persuade is not so obvious. We have become convinced, for example, that popular entertainment programming does more to shape American values—indeed, the media-connected *world's* values—than do sermons and editorials, political oratory, and parental advice. Yet seldom do people think of entertainment as persuasion. Also occupying a place in what we call the *gray areas* of persuasion's domain are newscasts, scientific reports, classroom teaching, and, yes, textbooks such as this one—all rendered especially credible by appearing in the guise of objectivity.

This edition of *Persuasion in Society* has been significantly updated to incorporate new theory and research on such topics as priming, subliminal persuasion, framing, political campaigning, and negotiation. New case studies on such topics as mind control, the animal rights controversy, and the ethics of faculty advocacy should be of interest, prompting readers to search for more information that can be readily obtained by way of links on the book's website, including speech and debate transcripts, video clips, Internet sources, and Taylor and Francis's own compendium of published materials. The website's code-accessible instructor's manual includes for each chapter sample test questions and PowerPoint lectures.

PART I

Understanding Persuasion

The Study of Persuasion

Today's practice of **persuasion** is mired in controversies that mirror those in ancient Greece almost 2,500 years ago, and they are unlikely to go away any time soon. At issue still are questions of truth, justice, ethics, and power. These issues still matter, as we can see in *The Daily Show's* Jon Stewart's dogged pursuit of CNBC's Jim Cramer on March 12, 2009. The interview, rated by *The Week* in the number one slot when ranking Jon Stewart's five most hard-hitting interviews, took place at the height of the worldwide financial meltdown. In it Stewart confronts Cramer about his role in contributing to the situation as Cramer seeks to evade responsibility for knowingly offering bad investment advice to his viewers for the sake of personal gain:

Thinking It Through

To watch the full video on the Daily Show site, go to:
http://thedailyshow.cc.com/videos/fttmoj/exclusive---jim-cramer-extended-interview-pt--1

FIGURE 1.1   *Stewart and Cramer.*

STEWART: This is the promo for your show:

—*"In Cramer We Trust" promo plays*—

STEWART: Isn't there a problem with selling snake oil and labeling it as vitamin tonic and saying that it cures impetigo.... Isn't that the difficulty here?

CRAMER: I think that there are two kinds of people. People come out and make good calls and bad calls that are financial professionals and there are people who say they only make good calls and they are liars. I try really hard to make as many good calls as I can.

STEWART: I think the difference is not good call/bad call. The difference is real market and unreal market.... CNBC could be an incredibly powerful tool of illumination for people that believe that there are two markets: One that has been sold to us as long term. Put your money in 401ks. Put your money in pensions and just leave it there. Don't worry about it. It's all doing fine. Then, there's this other market; this real market that is occurring in the back room. Where giant piles of money are going in and out and people are trading them and it's transactional and it's fast. But it's dangerous, it's ethically dubious and it hurts that long term market. So what it feels like to us—and I'm talking purely as a layman—it feels like we are capitalizing your adventure by our pension and our hard earned money. And that it is a game that you know.... That you know is going on. But you go on television as a financial network and pretend isn't happening.

CRAMER: Let me say this: I am trying to expose this stuff. Exactly what you guys do and I am trying to get the regulators to look at it.

STEWART: No, no, no, no, no. I want desperately for that, but I feel like that's not what we're getting. What we're getting is ... [shows video clip]

> CRAMER: *I would encourage anyone who is in the hedge fund unit "do it" because it is legal. It is a very quick way to make the money and very satisfying. By the way, no one else in the world would ever admit that but I don't care.*
> UNKNOWN: *That's right and you can say that here.*
> CRAMER: *I'm not going to say it on TV.*

CRAMER: It's on TV now.

STEWART: I want the Jim Cramer on CNBC to protect me from that Jim Cramer.

STEWART: I gotta tell you. I understand that you want to make finance entertaining, but it's not an f—ing game. When I watch that I get, I can't tell you how angry it makes me, because it says to me, you all know. You all know what's going on. You can draw a straight line from those shenanigans to the stuff that was being pulled at Bear and at AIG and all this derivative market stuff that is this weird Wall Street side bet.

CRAMER: But Jon, don't you want guys like me that have been in it to show the shenanigans? What else can I do? I mean, last night's show—

STEWART: No, no, no, no, no. I want desperately for that, but I feel like that's not what we're getting. What we're getting is.... Listen, you knew what the banks were doing and yet were touting it for months and months. The entire network was and so now to pretend that this was some sort of crazy, once-in-a-lifetime tsunami that nobody could have seen coming is disingenuous at best and criminal at worst.

[...]

CRAMER: Well, I think that your goal should always be to try to expose the fact that there is no easy money.

STEWART: But there are literally shows called Fast Money.

CRAMER: I think that people.... *[Audience laughs]* There's a market for it and you give it to them.

STEWART: There's a market for cocaine and hookers. What is the responsibility of the people who cover Wall Street? Who are you responsible to? The people with the 401ks and the pensions and the general public, or the Wall Street traders?

There is a name for discourse of this kind. It's called "sophistic," after the **sophists** of ancient Greece and Rome. As their name continues to suggest, the sophists tended to be seen as sophisticated or worldly wise, but also, in some quarters, as "sophistic" in the negative sense of putting rhetorical power and effectiveness above truth and justice. The sophists made considerable fortunes for the coaching they offered to Athenians in the arts of oratory, but they got mixed reviews for their ethics. No Athenian was more scathing in his criticism than Plato, a student of Socrates who had earned a reputation in his own right as the "father" of Western philosophy.

Plato's primary way of sharing his views was through his Socratic Dialogues, a series of scripted conversations in which the respected Socrates is cast as the questioner. In the dialogue on persuasion bearing the sophist Gorgias's name, the conversation centers upon the issue of whether **rhetoric**, the art of persuasion, is corrupt (Plato, 2006). Gorgias evokes Socrates' ire when he observes that the ability to impress an audience is the surest path to power:

> By the exercise of the ability [to persuade], you will have the doctor and the trainer as your slaves, and your man of business will turn out to be making money for another; for you, in fact, who have the ability to speak and convince the masses.
> (Gorgias, 452c; see also *Americanrhetoric.com/platoonrhetoric.htm;*
> L'Etang & Pieczka, 2006).

Gorgias's student, Polus, adds that power is the greatest good. Socrates affects surprise at these seemingly superficial claims. Is there not, he asks, a difference between true knowledge and mere belief? Socrates does get Gorgias to concede that power can be used for both good and ill, but Gorgias and his fellow sophists continue to argue that ultimate success comes through knowledge of persuasion. They even boast at one point that knowledge of anything else is unnecessary, arguing for the position that it is a worthy goal to simply create the appearance of knowing more than the experts.

The discussion continues, and Socrates will have none of it. Sophistic rhetoric, he maintains, is an art of hoodwinking the ignorant about the justice or injustice of a matter, without imparting any real knowledge. This kind of rhetoric does great damage in the law tribunal by making the worse appear the better argument and allowing the guilty to go free (Plato, 2006).

Years later, Plato's student, Aristotle, would offer a defense of rhetoric (Aristotle, 2004). Aristotle's response to Plato (and to Socrates) concedes the dangers of rhetoric but rejects their alleged inevitability. His arguments can be summarizes as follows: Rhetoric can be—indeed, often is—an instrument for giving effectiveness to truth. And truth is not always easy to come by. Still, those debating about issues of policy need eventually to come to a conclusion, and those brought before the court of law have the right to defend themselves. While philosophers like Socrates and Plato have the luxury of suspending judgment until they have arrived at universal principles, ordinary citizens will need help in their roles as decision makers in assessing alternative courses of action. In addition, as persuaders ordinary citizens will benefit from guidance in determining the best available means of persuasion for a particular audience or occasion. A solid understanding of rhetoric is therefore useful.

Both Plato's critique of rhetoric and Aristotle's defense of it contain a good deal of wisdom. Plato's analysis paved the way for critiques of today's sophistic practices in our corporate, legal, and political world that Plato himself could not have possibly imagined. Still, as you might have anticipated, this book gives Aristotle the edge in the debate with Plato. To be sure, persuasive speech can be used to deceive, mislead, exploit, and oppress. Clever persuaders can exploit what Aristotle called the "defects of their hearers." Unwise actions can be made to appear wise by use of sham arguments, known as *fallacies,* which appear reasonable on first impression but fall apart on close examination. All this is possible, as Plato claimed in the *Gorgias,* but it is not inevitable. Persuaders can serve the interests of their audiences at the same time as they serve their own interests; they can achieve power *with* others and not simply power *over* others (Burke, 1969; Grunig, et al., 2002).

Insufficiently appreciated by Plato was Aristotle's key insight: Persuasion deals in matters of judgment, rather than matters of certainty. Matters of judgment cannot be settled by fact alone or by sheer calculation. On controversial issues, we expect honest differences of opinion. Even experts can legitimately disagree on what the facts are, which facts are most relevant, and, most important, what should be made of them.

Box 1.1 *Jon Stewart: Philosopher or Sophist?*

FIGURE 1.2   *Jon Stewart.*
Reprinted with permission of AP Images Inc.

Had he practiced his brand of serious comedy in ancient Athens, where would Jon Stewart have stood in the sophist/Platonist debate? A modern-day Socrates but with a better sense of humor, he would surely have appreciated the importance of skillful questioning. However, it was the sophists, particularly Protagoras, who most influenced today's courtroom practices, including the practice of cross-examination.

But then again the sophists were relativists on questions of truth. Protagoras is well known for his view that we humans "are the measure of all things"; we decide what counts, or measures up as "truth." When Stewart turns serious, as he did in the Cramer interview there is little question but that truth to him is not simply a human invention, or, as discussed in Chapter Three, a social construction. Stewart gives evidence of having been influenced by all sides in this three-cornered debate and to have taken the best from each.

For example, when researching the effect of sun exposure on humans, scientific studies often take diametrically opposed positions. One concludes that due to the links between sun exposure and skin cancer, we should not to leave the house without sunscreen on. At the same time, other studies show that we need to be exposed to the sun to be able to allow our bodies to absorb vitamin D (Jio, 2014). Or consider calcium in our diets. On the one hand, scientific studies proclaim that calcium is considered essential for maintaining strong bones and avoiding fractures, especially for older people. On the other hand, new studies are finding that calcium supplements may increase the risk of cardiovascular disease deaths (Kim, 2013).

As these examples demonstrate, the scientists offer judgments, and in these cases, conflicting judgments. There are at least two sides to most stories, a point repeatedly emphasized by the sophists. This is surely true of the sophist-Platonist controversy and it is no less true today than in ancient Greece. Now as then, say public relations experts L'Etang and Pieczka, "There is no simple way of providing moral and intellectual comfort to practitioners. Consequently, the fundamental ethical questions have to be confronted daily in routine practice" (2006).

But just because persuasion deals in matters of judgment rather than certainty, Aristotle did not view this as an invitation to impulsive or random decision making or to perpetual indecision. Nor was Aristotle of the opinion that any decision was as good as any other, any argument as good as any other. As much as audiences might be taken in by clever deceivers, for Aristotle truth still had a natural advantage over falsehood, and logic a natural advantage over illogic—all other things being equal. The power of truth and logic is best appreciated when we agree to them reluctantly, as in the following case:

> At an inner-city junior high school for troubled students who had been booted out of other schools, an eighth-grade English class came to life when a student proposed that the school be put on trial for unfair rules. But the student who proposed the mock trial found himself in the role of the defense attorney for the administration, and he could not resist doing a convincing job in its behalf. Witness 1 for the prosecution was destroyed on cross-examination as he was caught over-generalizing. No, he admitted, the milk at the school is not always spoiled. In fact, it rarely is. Witness 2 was forced to concede that the school doesn't really enforce its rule against bringing candy to class. Then the defense attorney caught the prosecution off guard by pressing an objection: The prosecution had been leading the witness. And so it went. When the deliberations were concluded, the seven student judges voted 6 to 1 for the administration.
>
> (Michie, 1998).

WHY STUDY PERSUASION?

The study of persuasion has grown exponentially since Aristotle's day—from oral communication to written communication, from the verbal to the non-verbal, from the unmediated to the mediated, from the obviously intended to the non-obvious, and from the public arena to the study of all or virtually all symbolic action or interaction, including the study of persuasion about persuasion. Persuasion's increased scope places increased demands on practicing, analyzing, and understanding of persuasion. Let us consider each in turn.

Practice

Effective persuasion is a crucial component of personal and career success. But, complains business and political consultant, Frank Luntz:

> The average CEO cannot communicate their way out of a paper bag. The average CEO only knows facts, figures, statistics and what to say on a balance sheet. And so there's no resonance. There's no empathy. There's no understanding of the anger and frustration that some Americans feel towards corporate America.... The CEOs, they just speak from their head and it's not coming from their heart.
>
> (*NOW*, 2004)

And how important is persuasion in business? As Allied Signal's CEO recently explained,

> The day when you could yell and scream and beat people into good performance is over. Today you have to appeal to them by helping them to see how they can get from here to there, by establishing some credibility, and by giving them some reason and help to get there. Do all those things, and they'll knock down doors.
>
> (Conger, 1999)

Now, more than ever, persuasion is "the language of business leadership" (Conger, 1999).

The same is true of the professions. The "people professions"—law, sales, social work, etc.—could just as well be called "persuasion professions." Moreover, virtually all professional associations require persuasion consultants. Within colleges and universities, the interdisciplinary nature of the subject is reflected by the variety of courses in different academic departments that bear upon it: "Public Opinion and Propaganda," "Argumentation and Debate," "Rhetoric and Composition," "Media Literacy," "Rules of Evidence in Criminal Law," "Strategic Communication," "Homiletics," "Perception Management," "Community Organizing," and many others.

Beyond the private and professional levels, you may be interested in working for social and political betterment. Alone or in groups, you may be seeking more funding for environmental issues, intervention in areas where famine and genocide are occurring, racial and gender equality, or greater participation by students in university governance.

Having a solid understanding of how persuasion functions helps you determine the means that are most appropriate for achieving your goals. It helps you evaluate situations and weigh options. For example, if you are seeking donations for Doctors Without Borders, you are confronted with a dilemma. Should you ask potential donors for much more than you expect them to give in the hopes of getting what you bargain for? Or, conversely, if you ask for a larger donation than you need, would you be risking outright rejection? And what if it is societal change you are after? Should you be a moderate who signs petitions or a militant who stages confrontations? Too often, these decisions are made purely on a gut level, without sober analysis of their consequences, and the study of persuasion aids you as you seek to make the better judgments.

Analysis

Persuading others is one side of the persuasion equation; the other is responding intelligently and discerningly to the armies of message makers who compete for your attention, your agreement, your involvement, and your money. Much as we may practice persuasion, most of us spend more time on the receiving end of persuasive messages. We are literally bombarded by them from the moment we are awakened by the alarm to the instant we fall asleep before the television set.

Think about the last time you visited a department store or even a supermarket. Virtually every object there was market tested, advertised, and merchandized to get you to buy it. The objects in these stores do more than service your material needs; they're also symbols, especially for new generations of consumption communities in the United States and abroad. How often do we define ourselves and our friends by what we wear and what music we listen to and what shows we watch on television? (Barber, 1996, 2007).

Persuasion is the engine of our market-driven global economy. In 1995, Deirdre McCloskey co-authored an influential study in the *American Economic Review* estimating that persuasion—by salespeople, teachers, politicians, lobbyists, lawyers, and others—made up a quarter of America's gross domestic product (McCloskey & Klamer, 1995). Since the publication of that influential study, that percentage has grown, as demonstrated when the same analysis was updated in 2013 by an Australian economist and showed that persuasion now makes up 30 percent of US GDP (Antioch, 2013). In McCloskey's mind, this is a fact not to be feared, but to be faced, in that "a free society is a 'rhetorical society' where speech is used to persuade people about what to buy or whom to vote for, rather than violence" (McCloskey, 2013). "People always say advertising is manipulation," says McCloskey. "But if the only alternative to persuasion is violence, how else are we going to decide what car to buy except by people trying to charm us?" (McCloskey, 2013).

In our increasingly smaller but more complicated world, being an intelligent consumer of persuasive messages is not easy. Part of the problem is what psychologists call the "not me" phenomenon—otherwise known as the "third person" effect (Golan, 2008). Here is what the author of *The Power of Persuasion* has to say about "not me":

> People tend to have a curious illusion of invulnerability to manipulation—a belief that we're not as vulnerable as others around us. In part this illusion derives from the subtlety of clever operators who make it hard to see that you're being manipulated. In part, it feeds off another "normal" illusion—that we're more capable and, so, better defended than other people. The illusion of invulnerability is a comforting notion for moving forward in an unpredictable and dangerous world. Unfortunately, however, the more immune we feel, the less likely we are to take precautions and, as a result, the more susceptible than ever we become.
>
> (Levine, 2003).

When we combine the "not me" phenomenon with the contemporary problem of message density, we see that the problem is compounded. Today, persuasive messages are presented to us at dizzying speeds. Gigabytes of information are available at the click of a mouse. If we believe we are invulnerable to the persuasive impact of the messages we receive, and combine that with the number of messages we take in each day, we see that without a solid understanding of how persuasion functions, we are vulnerable indeed.

Under the best of circumstances, persuasive messages present us with a dilemma. On the one side is the need for human connection, as we don't want to go through life cynically distrusting every communicative act we encounter. On the other hand, there is quite obviously a need for vigilance in the face of unscrupulous persuaders; there is every reason to weigh and evaluate controversial assertions even when they emanate from those we trust. The study of persuasion provides us with the analytic tools we need to find a balance.

Understanding

Thinking It Through

Consider for a moment the way institutions, belief systems, and cultural norms govern and guide us as we deal with our genders. From the moment a child is born, it is conditioned to live within gendered boundaries. Baby girls are dressed in pink, baby boys wear blue. As they grow, girls come to play with kitchen sets, baby dolls, and dress-up clothes, while boys play with work benches, trucks, and miniature sports equipment. By the time they are grown, most children have internalized their socially accepted gender roles and live within those boundaries without question, seeing them as unchangeable, "normal," and "natural." And they do that thinking that they are fully in charge of their lives.

Make a list of the things you've done today that are gender-specific. And then, imagine yourself as a member of the opposite sex, and make a list of what you would have done today in that instance. Most of all, notice how you've behaved in a gender-appropriate manner without even thinking about it. Notice how your "gender" is a central part of who you are.

We humans are both the creators and products of our societies in a never-ending cycle. The movements and campaigns of persuasion that our forbears once waged helped produce the very institutions, belief systems, and cultural norms that now govern or at least guide our thoughts and behaviors. To be sure, historical change does not occur through persuasion alone, and in fact, a recent study of presidential influence brought news of how often American presidents have ruled by decree (Howell, 2003). Most often it is by a combination of forms of influence that major change occurs, not least the power of the "carrot" (**inducements**) and the "stick" (**coercion**) (Simons, 1972). Still, it is primarily by persuasion that ideas are introduced and hearts and minds changed.

Among the cultural truisms that people take for granted are those which at one time or other were the subject of considerable controversy. Americans are no longer British colonists. What's more, as much as they would like to think of themselves as members of the world community, they find it difficult if not impossible to transcend their American identities. Their economic system, republican form of government, commitments to freedom of speech, conceptions of themselves as a special people, and even their idea of nationhood can be traced to efforts of persuasion from centuries past.

We can begin to understand how discourse functions to create new and accepted ways of viewing the world by examining our own era, noticing the political and social issues that we confront and the means we employ to deal with them. Looking back over the recent history of American politics, we can recall some of the rhetorical catchwords that persuaded us to create new realities:

- "change we can believe in" that led us to "hope" that the ouster of one political party would transform our world,

- "compassionate conservatism" that persuaded us to implement sweeping educational change so that "no child will be left behind,"

- the "war on terror" from which we did not "cut and run," because we wanted to have a "Mission Accomplished,"

- "global warming" fears that persuaded some of us to "go green," while others resisted the notion of "man-made climate change," and

- concerns about "illegal aliens," or should we say "undocumented workers," that persuaded us to change our attitudes toward immigration policy.

In all of these instances, the rhetoric is richly metaphorical, and each example takes on a reality as social truth. Each persuasive construction had real-world policy ramifications for the citizenry: the first African-American president was elected, soldiers were sent to fight in wars, our public schools were transformed as they incorporated regular testing to measure student progress, car manufacturers thrived or declined as buyers sought cars that made lesser impacts on the environment, and we constructed walls on our borders to manage issues of immigration.

But it is not just in issues of public policy that rhetoric has had an influence. Rhetorical constructions also helped us understand the changes in our day-to-day lives. Americans have become far more cosmopolitan, and increasingly dependent on the new information technologies. "Spanglish" is now a de facto American language, social networks are flourishing on the Internet, the "blogosphere" has proliferated, and nearly everyone has "friended" somebody else.

Thinking It Through

Consider how you have been persuaded to think differently about communication over just the last few years. What does it mean to have "friends" on social networking sites like Facebook? How has the definition of "friend" been transformed? How have you been persuaded to think differently about friendship?

Further, how has your communication changed thanks to your laptop computer, your cell phone, and your wi-fi connection? How would you feel, emotionally and physically, if you had to live for a day without your phone or your connection to the Internet? Would you be nervous and uncomfortable? How have you been persuaded that is necessary to maintain constant connection through technology, and how does this impact your life?

Then, as if unnoticed, "predatory lenders" have caused various "bubbles" to burst, leading to a worldwide "meltdown," with calls for a "bailout," antagonism between "Wall Street" and "Main Street," prompting most Americans to vote for "change."

In addition to knowledge of the role of persuasion in society, there is considerable benefit in coming to grips with the psychological dynamics of persuasion. From an examination of persuasion at work, one gets a better understanding of how human beings attend to stimuli, how they order their environment, how thought and emotion interact. Psychological theories of attention, perception, learning, motivation, emotion, etc., have in turn contributed greatly to our understanding of persuasion. Several chapters in this book bring psychological theories to bear upon the subject.

Synthesis: Putting Together Rhetorical Practice, Analysis, and Understanding

Understanding, practice, and analysis are closely interrelated. In order to become a discriminating consumer of persuasive messages, you need to be aware of the techniques that others may use to influence you. In order to persuade effectively, you need to anticipate how consumers of persuasive messages are likely to respond. And in order to respond perceptively or persuade effectively, you need to have a general understanding of the nature of the persuasive process and the role of persuasion in society. By the same token, our experiences as persuaders and persuadees may help us to understand in small ways how persuasion has shaped human choices and destinies during the major events of history, and we may also come to a better understanding of the contemporary political process.

In some respects this text is a handbook. It provides principles by which you may better persuade or more critically react to persuasive communication by others. In addition, it is designed to provide insights about persuasion as it functions to shape your world, independent of whether these insights lead you to change your rhetorical practices or not. Finally, and perhaps most importantly, this book is designed to help you understand the ways in which you can make an impact on your world. Ultimately, to seek to correct injustice or improve the lives of others requires the ability to analyze rhetoric, to understand how persuasion works to create new socially constructed "truths," and to create ethically appropriate persuasive messages.

METHODS OF STUDYING PERSUASION

Depending on individual goals, the student of persuasion may choose among a wide variety of research methods. Although scholars these days rely heavily on social-scientific methodologies, for almost all of its long history, the field of persuasion has been the province of the humanities. The ancient Athenians' initial method of instruction remains helpful to this day; it involved learning from role models and practice, practice, practice. Every Athenian citizen knew Pericles' funeral oration by heart. They also knew the legend of Demosthenes' struggle to overcome a stuttering affliction by practicing aloud with pebbles in his mouth. Out of practice came theory, the systematizing of lessons learned into generalized concepts and principles. Drawing on the experiences of those who practiced the art, and on the critical judgments of trained observers, Aristotle and others fashioned rhetorical principles that have withstood the test of time remarkably well.

Method One: Rhetorical Criticism

Contemporary **rhetorical criticism** grew out of classical rhetorical theory, but has moved well beyond it to include studies of forms and genres unimagined by the ancients. Consider these sample research questions about rhetorical artifacts:

What made Lincoln's Gettysburg Address so memorable? Why is one blog so much more persuasive than another? If I were to give a speech all over again, how would I do it differently? If I could have my choice, which celebrity would I most like to have representing my anti-bullying campaign? When is faculty advocacy in the classroom legitimate and when is it unethical?

Or consider these questions concerning the words individuals speak: Since stylistic simplicity is so highly valued in our culture, how is it that Martin Luther King, Jr. is considered such a memorable speaker while having used a highly ornate style? Why are most college course catalog descriptions so uninspiring and what can be done to improve them? Why is being a "liberal" viewed by most Americans as an elite lifestyle? What are the discursive dilemmas presidents face in trying to instill public confidence in a shaky economy and which of their strategic alternatives is likely to work best in this recession?

Each of these questions and thousands more like them constitute legitimate starting points for critical analyses of rhetorical happenings. Critics or analysts (we use the terms interchangeably) may be motivated by outrage at an apparent misuse of language or logic or a pretension to objectivity that is belied by the facts. Their critical impulse may spring from a pragmatic interest in persuading others or in determining how others attempt to persuade them. They may have an irreverent streak and thus be inclined to debunk claims and claimants to universal truth. They may appreciate a rhetorical effort and want to know why it was so admirable. Or they may simply be puzzle-solvers by temperament who enjoy unraveling some of the mysteries of persuasion. In each case, they will attempt to make sense of the rhetorical act or event, either as an object of interest in its own right or because it helps illuminate some larger issue, problem, or theoretical question. Criticism serves consummatory functions when it stops at evaluation or explanation of a rhetorical effort. It performs instrumental functions when it focuses on persuasive discourse as case-study material in service of a larger end such as theory building or theory testing. Like the objects of their analyses, critics are themselves persuaders with cases to present and defend. We may not entirely agree with the analysis, but we must respect it if the case has been well argued.

This book provides numerous examples of rhetorical criticism. Today, analysis of persuasion often is incorporated within a more inclusive term, critical studies, to refer to criticism of all kinds bearing on persuasion. Studies of recurrent forms or patterns of discourse by linguists and sociologists, semiotic analyses of language-like objects and symbolic actions, studies in non-verbal communication, analysis by feminist theorists and scholars examining the intersections of race and culture, and more all contribute to our understanding of persuasion. Here we provide two examples of rhetorical criticism, the first of a course catalog description, the second an illustration of dilemma-centered analysis focused on the task of sounding confident about a shaky economy but not overconfident.

Case #1 A rhetorical analysis of the college catalog

Catalog Description

> **COM 390R Seminar in Contemporary Rhetorical Criticism.** *May be repeated for credit when topics vary. Semester topics have included dramatistic criticism, content analysis, and methodologies for movement studies. Prerequisite: Upper-Division Standing.*

Hart (1997) analyzed this seemingly ordinary message to make two points. First, we are all experts of a sort on persuasion, having been exposed each day to a sea of rhetoric. As voracious consumers of messages, we develop *implicit* knowledge of their hidden meanings, undisclosed motives, and subtle strategies. We know, says Hart, that this is a catalog description; we would recognize it anywhere and be able to distinguish it from a chili recipe or a love letter or the lyrics to a rock song. We know, too, that descriptions such as these aren't always trustworthy. The prose bears the marks of having been funneled through a bureaucracy. Before signing up for COM 390R, perhaps we ought to check with peers or with the instructor who will actually teach the course.

Hart's (1997) second point is that even so simple a message repays close examination. For example, a good deal about persuasion can be learned by attending to its style. For one thing, the course description is telegraphic: Incomplete sentences and abnormal punctuation patterns suggest a hurried, businesslike tone, a message totally uninterested in wooing its reader. So, too, are its reasoning patterns telegraphic. Concepts such as "seminar," "credit," and "prerequisite" are never explained. The language is also formidable: excessive use of jargon, polysyllabic words, and opaque phrases (e.g., COM 390R).

Also revealing is what is not found in the text. Nobody runs or jumps here. No *doing* has been done. The absence of verbs suggests institutionalization, hardly what one would expect from what is essentially a piece of advertising. But this is a special sort of advertising, advertising without adjectives. And much else is missing. There are no extended examples to help the reader see what the course will be like, no powerful imagery to sustain the student's visions of wonder while standing in the registration line, no personal disclosure by the author to build identification with the reader. It is almost as if this message did not care about its reader, or, for that matter, even care about itself. It does nothing to invite or entice or intrigue (Hart, 2004).

As Hart's analysis demonstrates, rhetorical criticism is not simply about studying great speeches or persuasive essays, and the humanistic study of persuasive discourse is no longer the exclusive province of self-styled rhetoricians.

Case #2 A rhetorical analysis of discourse: shaky economy

Introduced here is a dilemma-centered framework for rhetorical criticism called the **Requirements-Problems-Strategies (RPS) approach** (Simons, 2007, 2000, 1996, 1994, 1970; Lu & Simons, 2006). These in brief are its basic concepts and principles:

Requirements (R)
By dint of their roles and of the situations they confront, persuaders are rarely free agents. The "demands" or "pressures" on persuaders constitute rhetorical *requirements*.

Problems (P)
Oftentimes these requirements come in the form of cross-pressures, necessitating difficult rhetorical choices. To the extent that these conflicting requirements are recurrent and predictable, they can assist the critic in understanding the persuader's rhetorical *problems*.

Strategies (S)
In response to problems, and in an effort to fulfill requirements, political actors devise rhetorical *strategies*. Not uncommonly, the strategies they devise create new problems even as they ameliorate others. Besides posing problems, situations may present political actors with *opportunities*. Strategizing involves calculations about how to realize goals, minimize problems, and exploit opportunities.

Particularly as persuaders seek to thread their way through difficult dilemmas, they must be practiced at what Lyne (1990) calls the "art of the sayable." Consider, for example, the difficulties the Obama administration faced when it inherited a recession that threatened to become a full-fledged depression. No one in the administration wanted to fuel the pessimism that comes with loss of jobs, homes, and credit, because optimism about the future is key to lending and spending; it is essential in getting a market economy back on track. Neither did they want to paint too rosy a picture out of fear of a boomerang effect, as President Bush had done with Iraq in declaring "Mission Accomplished." So, as repairs were gradually introduced into the economy, the administration sought ways to bolster confidence incrementally. "Glimmers of hope" were upgraded to "signs of recovery." Warning that "real recovery is months, if not years, ahead," Obama reported that "the gears of our economic engine do appear to be slowly turning once again" (Sanger, 2009).

"There's a kind of artistry to this, isn't there?" said Robert Dallek, the presidential historian best known for chronicling how Lyndon Johnson, the consummate politician, never led the public out of its view that everything was falling apart. "You don't want to come out and say the recession is over. You want to do a version of

Churchill's line about how this isn't the end, or the beginning of the end, but rather the end of the beginning."

(Sanger, 2009)

Rhetorical criticism, ultimately, seeks to examine how symbols are used to shape the audience. As these two cases display, the scope of artifacts worthy of study is vast: a critic can study a political speech, but might just as likely study a billboard, a song, a work of art, or a film. For example, the rhetorical critic would find it worthwhile to study what is communicated to girls and boys in the Disney film *The Little Mermaid*, where the star is a beautiful female who cannot walk, one who can only find love and mobility by giving up her voice. Given all of the possibilities, we strongly urge that you try your hand at doing rhetorical criticism, if for no other reason than that the act of applying principles covered in this book will help you to better assimilate them.

Method Two: Social-Scientific Approach

While the humanities in general and rhetorical analysis in particular contribute a great deal to our understanding of rhetoric, the more dominant approach to scholarly research on persuasion today involves the use of social-scientific methods. Although the contributions of **humanists** and social scientists are in many ways complementary, important differences may also be noted. First, many of the issues of concern to humanists are outside the pale of scientific inquiry. Questions of ethics, beauty, rhetorical artistry, etc., may be deemed important by social scientists, but they recognize also that such questions are not answerable by scientific methods. Second, whereas humanists retain faith in the subjective impressions of sensitive observers, social scientists attempt to replace personal judgments with impersonal, objective methods. Using what is sometimes referred to as the behavioral approach, social scientists subject theories and hypotheses to rigorous empirical tests. Third, humanists tend to regard persuasion as a highly individualized art and tend to be suspicious of extrapolations from scientific research to judgments about how human beings ought to persuade. Social scientists, by contrast, insist that their methods yield reliable generalizations which can be used with profit by would-be persuaders.

Social scientists have developed an array of methodologies useful in the study of persuasion, including focus group interviews, surveys, polls, and quantitative content analysis. Campaign decisions are often made based on focus group research and then tested for their effectiveness based on polls and surveys. These days, participants in the test-marketing of a newly designed campaign advertisement may be hooked up to a brain scanner the better to trace reactions to the ad through the brain's predominantly cognitive and emotional neural pathways (Heath & Heath 2007; Thaler & Sunstein, 2008; Westen, 2007).

For example, in one study, a group of 38 military veterans or active duty military who were now students at two different Nevada colleges participated in focus groups that have been designed to examine the college experiences and the attitudes of this population, with a goal toward creating a college climate that would enhance the success rates for military students. The groups were held over a number of sessions, with no more than eight participants per group, and the results brought varied perspectives that would likely not have come up through other forms of feedback-seeking activities such as surveys. While some of the results were to be expected (e.g., the older veteran students felt they had less in common with traditional, non-military students), there were some unexpected findings. Perhaps most interesting was that the veterans expressed a preference for anonymity, not wearing their uniforms on campus or identifying themselves as being part of the military. In fact, they did not want special attention:

> Several students reported that they were often singled out by faculty (once they knew of their military background) to speak for veterans in general or that they were called upon to make comments or be used as an example. The majority of student veterans said these in-class experiences made them very uncomfortable and made a bad impression on their non-veteran student counterparts by making them appear to be seeking attention and by highlighting how different they were from other students.
>
> (Gonzales, 2013)

Thanks to the military focus groups, the colleges were able to develop policies that were cost effective and useful, including things such as special training for faculty and special orientations that did not cause military members to spend time considering things that are useful to 18-year-olds, but not to experienced soldiers (Gonzales 2013).

In developing generalizations about the effectiveness of various types of persuasion, social scientists rely for the most part on research experiments conducted under carefully controlled conditions. This approach is *behavioral* in the sense of treating human judgments and actions as in some sense akin to the predictable, controllable behavior of lower-order animals in the laboratory. Social scientists systematically investigate variations in source (that is, the persuader), message, medium, audience, and context—in who says what to whom, when, where, and how. These communication factors are known as *independent variables*.

Determining their effects on dependent variables is the object of research. As McGuire has put it,

> The independent variables have to do with the communication process; these are the variables we can manipulate in order to see what happens.... The dependent variables ... are the variables that we expect will change when we manipulate the independent variables. Taken together, the independent and dependent variables define what we might call the "communication-persuasion matrix."
>
> (McGuire, 1978)

Consider, by way of illustration, the following generalizations about the psychology of persuasion. Which do you think are true? Which are false? Which are so muddled or so simplistic that you simply cannot judge their veracity?

1   The best way to persuade people to stop a practice harmful to their health is to combine strong fear appeals with concrete and convincing recommendations.

2   It is generally effective to present both sides of an issue, making sure to indicate why you think the weight of the evidence supports your position.

3   Because opposites attract, it is generally best when using testimonials in advertisements to present sources as unlike the intended audience as possible.

4   The more you pay people to argue publicly for a position contrary to their own values, the more likely they are to change their values.

5   Very intelligent people are more likely to be persuaded upon hearing an argument than are people of very low or moderate intelligence.

6   Vivid descriptions of a single problem are nearly always more impressive than comprehensive statistics.

7   The only rule about how to persuade is that there are no rules.

Not all the generalizations can be true, for if Rule 7 is correct, the others are not, and if any of the others are true, then Rule 7 is not.

There is something to be said for Rule 7. It could be argued that persuasion is too much an individual thing. It is too subject to variations in goals, media, contexts, audiences, and subject matter. Although persuasion may be fun to speculate about, it is impossible to generalize about with any degree of reliability. Many humanists subscribe to Rule 7. Rule 7 is probably wrong, however, or at least in need of modification.

Although there are no ironclad rules that apply to all individuals in all situations, it is possible to formulate general guidelines for persuaders that typically apply. Often, it is necessary to factor in variations in goals, media, audiences, and the like in formulating generalizations. For example, Rule 1 is generally on target, except that people with low self-esteem tend to become overwhelmed by strong fear appeals—at least until they are repeatedly assured that help for their problem is truly available. Especially for them, clear, specific, and optimistic instruction on how, when, and where to take action is essential (Leventhal, et al., 2005).

For reasons that will be discussed in subsequent chapters, Rule 2 is generally accurate, at least as applied to intelligent, well-educated audiences, especially those who are undecided or in disagreement with your position. Rule 3 should probably be marked false. Sources perceived as similar to their audiences tend to be regarded as far more attractive (e.g., likable, friendly, and warm) than sources seen as dissimilar. Rule 4 is generally false, and for reasons that may seem counterintuitive (see Chapter

2). Rule 5 is generally false as well; moderately intelligent people tend to be most persuadable. As for Rule 6, the generalization tends to hold for most message recipients, although the combination of vivid examples and comprehensive statistics tends to be even more powerful (Brock & Green, 2005).

But experiments testing for the effects of the independent variables in Rules 1 through 6 do not always yield the same results. Life is complicated, and persuasion is especially so. Fortunately, a statistical technique called *meta-analysis* can be used to compare studies of the same or similar variables and to reconcile apparent inconsistencies (Cooper, et al., 2009). Ensuing chapters summarize findings from a number of these meta-analyses and report on social-scientific theories that attempt to make sense of behavioral research findings and guide the search for new knowledge.

From research of this kind, scholars have become better able to understand the dynamics of persuasion and to provide useful advice to persuaders. Still, we would caution readers not to apply behavioral research findings formulaically, the way a cook uses a recipe. Our hope is not only that you will familiarize yourselves with these findings, but that you will also profit from personal practice and observation, from analysis of the communication of others, from reading humanistic studies of rhetorically significant public events, and from an examination of other social science research that may apply more specifically to the particular rhetorical problems you face. (There is, for example, an extensive body of sociological literature on techniques of community organizing, a body of political science research on electoral campaign strategies, and so on.)

Moreover, as you become more familiar with the procedures used in behavioral research on persuasion, we urge that you interpret findings critically. From time to time we have offered our own criticisms, especially of the tendency of behavioral researchers to ignore situational factors.

Finally, we urge once again that you immerse yourselves in the details of the unique situation confronting you, carefully analyzing your own goals, your audience, your subject matter, and the context in which you will be communicating. Behavioral research provides a rough guide to practice, but it is only one means for acquiring rhetorical sensitivity—and a limited one at that.

TOWARD A DEFINITION OF PERSUASION

How might we define persuasion and distinguish it from "non-persuasion"? How if at all does persuasion differ from **propaganda**?

A useful way to construct a definition is to look for common characteristics in what language specialists refer to as *paradigm cases*—examples from ordinary discourse that almost everyone would agree are instances of persuasion. Probably all of us would agree that the following are paradigm cases:

- a politician presenting a campaign speech to attract votes;

- an advertiser preparing a commercial for presentation on television;

- a legislator urging support for a bill;

- peaceful picketers displaying placards to passers-by;

- a trial lawyer's summing up a case to a jury;

- a parent advising a child to dress more neatly;

- a college representative recruiting student applicants;

- a newspaper editorial complaining about anti-inflationary measures;

- a minister imploring parishioners to respect human dignity;

- an essayist decrying American materialism;

- a student appealing to a professor for a makeup exam.

From the foregoing cases it is possible to identify common elements that constitute defining characteristics of persuasion.

Human Communication

Each of the above cases involves acts of human communication, whether verbal or non-verbal, oral or written, explicit or implicit, face-to-face or mediated through contemporary technology. Occasionally, "persuasion" is used metaphorically to refer to nonhuman acts, as when we say, "The severity of the blizzard persuaded me to go indoors." For the most part, however, the term is restricted to exchanges of messages between human beings.

Attempted Influence

To influence others is to make a difference in the way they think, feel, or act. All of the paradigm cases given above involved attempted influence. The politician attempted to attract votes; the legislator sought passage of a bill; the student sought permission to take a makeup exam. In some contexts it may be appropriate to refer to "persuasion" as an effect already produced by messages, whether intended or not. For example, we might say, "She persuaded me without even trying." So long as the context is made clear, this deviation from dominant usage need not bother us greatly. Our conception of persuasion remains virtually the same.

Modifying Judgments

Message recipients—otherwise referred to here as receivers, audiences, or persuadees—are invited to make a judgment of some sort. Is this politician trustworthy? Does that legislator's proposal warrant public support? Whom should I believe: the prosecution or the defense? Is it really so bad to want material comforts?

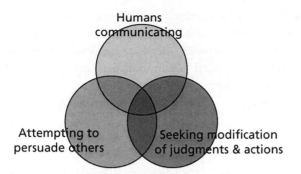

FIGURE 1.3 *Defining features of persuasion.*

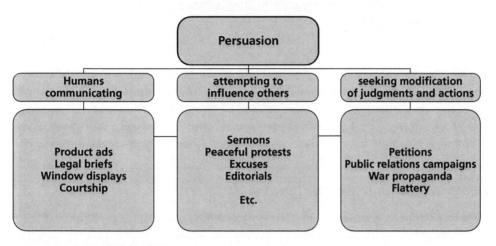

FIGURE 1.4 *Defining features.*

The cases of persuasion noted above involve no complex mixture of motives, no masking of persuasive intent, no questions about whether they are attempts at persuasion or some other form of influence. If persuasive intent is not apparent from the context, it is made obvious by what is said and how it is said. These paradigmatic examples of persuasion rely, at least in part, on linguistic or paralinguistic (language-like) messages to promote an image, a point of view, or a proposed action of some sort.

In general, when the term *persuasion* is used in this book, it is with the paradigm cases in mind. Persuasion is defined as *human communication designed to influence the judgments and actions of others*. In these respects it differs from other forms of influence. It is *not* the iron hand of torture, the stick-up, or other such forms of *coercion*. Nor, in its purest sense, is it the exchange of money or other such *material inducements* for actions performed by the person being influenced (see Box 1.2). Nor is it pressure to conform to the group or to the authority of the powerful.

Addressed as it is to choice-making individuals, persuasion *predisposes others but does not impose*. It affects their sense of what is true or false, probable or improbable; their evaluations of people, events, ideas, or proposals; their private and public commitments to take this or that action; and perhaps even their basic values and ideologies. All this is done by way of communication. According to St. Augustine more than 1,500 years ago, the fully influenced persuadee

> likes what you promise, fears what you say is imminent, hates what you censure, embraces what you command, regrets whatever you build up as regrettable, rejoices at whatever you say is cause for rejoicing, sympathizes with those whose wretchedness your words bring before his very eyes, shuns those whom you admonish him to shun … and in whatever other ways your high eloquence can affect the minds of your hearers, bringing them not merely to know what should be done, but to do what they know should be done.
>
> (Quoted in Burke, 1950/1969, p. 50)

As the above indicates, not all attempts at persuasion fall inside a neatly delineated core. There are many gray areas of persuasion, the so-called borderline cases in which the intent to persuade is not so clear. Seldom are persuaders fully aware of everything they are saying or doing when communicating a message, and what they communicate may have effects—welcomed or unwelcomed—beyond those the

---

Box 1.2 *Toy Truck: Persuasion, Inducements, Coercion*

To illustrate the differences between persuasion, material inducements, and coercion, consider the following nursery school situation. Olivia covets a toy truck that Caleb has been sitting on. Here are some of her options.

Persuasion
Aren't you tired of being on that truck?
That ball over there is fun. Why don't you play with it?

Inducements
If you let me play on that truck, I'll play with you.
I'll stop annoying you if you let me play with that truck.

Coercion
If you stay on that truck, I'll stop being your friend.
Get off the truck or I'll tell Miss Mary.

In her role as persuader, Olivia identifies the benefits or harms from the adoption or non-adoption of a proposal but does not claim to be the agent of those consequences. In the cases of inducements and coercion, she is the agent. Inducements promise positive consequences; coercion threatens negative consequences.

y intended. Moreover, the intent to influence another person's judgments is often masked, played down, or combined with other communication motives.

We should note that persuasion is not always aimed directly at modifying attitudes or altering overt behavior. On any one occasion, in fact, its aim may be to modify a single belief or value. Thus, the trial lawyer in our example had only one goal, and that was to modify the jury's beliefs about the defendant's guilt or innocence; the minister focused solely on the value of human dignity.

For the most part, our use of the term "persuasion" is confined in this book to paradigm cases. That being so, few should question our use of the term or the definition we assigned to it. But paradigm cases do not constitute the whole of persuasion. Persuasion is practiced by advertisers, lawyers, politicians, religious leaders, and their ilk, but also practiced by others who might not ordinarily be thought of as persuaders. Is it appropriate, for example, to refer to the activities of scientists addressing other scientists as "persuasion"? Can our definition be applied to newscasters and educators or to poets and dramatists? And if representatives of professions such as these are labeled as "persuaders," should this demean their status? We turn to questions of this kind in Chapter 3.

Persuasion versus Propaganda

Along with such terms as "rhetoric" and "persuasion," the use of the term "propaganda" tends to reflect the attitudes of the language user. All are emotionally loaded terms that figure in disputes of one sort or another, as when a critic of Martin Luther King, Jr.'s practice of civil disobedience said, "That's not persuasion; it's coercion." Propaganda differs from persuasion in that it is systematic, sustained, organized, and one-sided. Its aim is to win over large numbers of people.

But the same could be said of virtually all persuasive campaigns. What is missing from this list of defining features is the onus that "propaganda" has in contemporary culture. In an earlier age, "propaganda" was seen as a vehicle for carrying Truth to the masses (Pratkanis & Aronson, 2001). These days it tends to have more negative connotations. Propagandists are not seen as simply one-sided; they are also seen as manipulative, controlling, self-serving, and exploitative. On top of that their logic is seen as defective. Says Sproule, for example, propaganda "represents the work of large organizations or groups to win over the public for special interests through a massive orchestration of attractive conclusions packaged to conceal both their persuasive purposes and lack of supporting reasons" (Sproule, 1994).

Note in Sproule's definition the emphasis on concealment. In this view, propagandists operate in stealth. They masquerade as upstanding citizens. They achieve their aims not by direct expression but through innuendo, implication, suggestion, and planted disinformation. Thus has propaganda come to be regarded as unethical persuasion or, worse yet, as persuasion's evil twin (Bennett & O'Rourke, 2006; Pratkanis & Aronson, 2001).

But these characterizations have their own problems. If propaganda's aims and methods are always concealed, how are we to know it when we see it? Are we to trust in the discerning judgment of propaganda analysts? But they are not immune from propaganda in their analysis of propaganda and may, in the guise of objectivity, propagandize in their own right. How are we to know? Moreover, reason dictates that we not treat all propaganda as equivalently evil. Labels aside, we might even be able to identify cases that meet with our approval. Few among us, for example, would oppose the use of one-sided, somewhat manipulative mass persuasion in support of world peace.

Reason dictates that we need to differentiate between types of propaganda, weighing the flat-out objectionable against the relatively benign (Rogers, 2007). In doing so, however, we ought not to assume that our systems of classification are free of bias. In Western democracies, for example, public relations and commercial advertising have come in for a great deal of criticism as being nothing more than tools of corporate power that blunt the power of democracy in the guise of defending it (Carey 1997; Rampton & Stauber, 2003). The problem is, though, that critiques of this kind tend to come from outsiders rather than insiders to these professions. Those who are closely entwined in the situation more often value the work that they do.

By way of another example, we might assert that many Westerners find clearly unethical the Chinese government's propaganda in defense of its human rights abuses. But surveys of Chinese citizens find far greater satisfaction with their government than Americans express toward theirs (Osnos, 2008) and, from their point of view, Western criticisms of Chinese government practices are highly objectionable forms of propaganda in their own right.

And even when serious analysis is attempted, propaganda analysts often characterize the least objectionable propaganda as "white" and the most objectionable as "black" (Rogers, 2007; Jowett & O'Donnell, 2006) Isn't it time to evaluate those colorations and also inquire as to what prejudices lay behind the association of black with the negative and white with the positive?

These problems of classification are taken up again in later chapters. Suffice it to reiterate here the great lesson of contemporary critical studies of persuasion: that there is no escape from rhetoric, even in textbook pronouncements about the "nature" of rhetoric—or of propaganda, persuasion, and related terms (Billig, 2008). We return to this important principle in Chapter 3.

Ethical Perspectives of Persuasion

Imagine for a moment that you'd like to sell your car and you place an ad in the local newspaper. Three people respond to your ad and you make an appointment with each to show up at roughly the same time. You wanted all three to show up at the same time to persuade them that your car is a hot item, much in demand. This approach has a name: *stacked competition* (Cialdini, 2009). Is your approach ethical?

In the case of your approach to selling your car, a number of questions present themselves. What if one of the prospective customers loses patience and decides to leave? What if a second catches on to your game and expresses resentment? What if your car is really a clunker and you persuade the innocent third buyer to purchase it, only to have the individual sue you later for misrepresentation?

On the other hand, what if setting up a competition among prospective buyers nets you a good price? These considerations may not be irrelevant, but they should probably not form your entire judgment in the matter, either. What about your responsibility to the prospective buyers, or to agreed-on standards for doing business, or to your own conscience? And if you go on to focus on consequences, you might also ask yourself what the effects would be on society if practices such as these became the norm. Finally, because our self-concepts are formed from interaction with others, you might wish to consider what effect your actions are likely to have on you. Common to all these questions is a concern with the ethics of persuasion.

Each of us has at one time or another been victimized by persuaders. Politicians have pandered to us, advertisers have gulled us with their evasions and exaggerations, and even those we've loved and trusted have, on occasion, lied to us. When it has happened to us, we have generally deplored it, and often it has caused us great anguish.

Yet if we are honest, we would likely admit that there have been times when we have abused persuasion. We may have been deceptive or exaggerated the positive when it has seemed advantageous. That leads us to questions that go all the way back to Plato's critique of the sophists. Are pandering, evasions, exaggerations, and even outright lying always unethical, or does the morality or immorality of deception depend on the situation?

Ethics, at the most general level, is concerned with how people should act. In considering a situation from an ethical perspective, we are less interested in what a person actually did or might do. Understanding how people act is primarily a question for psychologists rather than ethicists. However, we can evaluate a person's actions, and try to determine if what they did do is what they should have done. It is the emphasis on the concepts of should and ought that distinguish the questions that arise when we look at persuasion from an ethical perspective.

Box 1.3 How Often Do You Attempt to Deceive Others?

How often do you attempt deception? Once a month? Once a week? All the time? Do males deceive more often than females? Do adults lie more often than children? Recent research shows that 60% of people lie at least once during a ten-minute conversation and told an average of two to three lies (Feldman, et al., 2002). But deception, according to Hopper and Bell (1984), can include not just outright, deliberate lying but also exaggerations, tall tales, bluffs, evasions, distortions, concealments, indirectness, and—a big category—self-deceptions. With this list in mind, how often do you attempt to deceive others?

THE ETHICS OF PERSUASION

In this concluding section of Chapter 1, we introduce several alternative perspectives on the ethics of persuasion. Here, as elsewhere in the book, our object is not to preach on ethical matters in persuasion but to provoke thought and inform your own choices. That's not to say that we'll pretend to neutrality on these matters. We've already tipped our hand on the sophist/Platonist controversy, and we've made clear our own activist inclinations. But we'd like nothing better than for readers to challenge our positions and make spirited defenses of their own. And so, we now turn to an introduction to the ethics in persuasion, one that will be engaged further in Chapter 15.

Utilitarianism

One way of dealing with ethical considerations and persuasion is to conclude that you are entitled to use questionable means only when your goals as a persuader are worthy beyond question. Thus, a medical doctor might feel justified in deceiving a patient for the patient's own good—for example, by exaggerating the negative consequences of what would happen if the patient does not get enough exercise, in order to persuade the patient to get off the sofa for health's sake. On similar grounds, a charitable organization might exaggerate its capacity to make a difference with the dollars its donors contribute. If these inflated estimates were exposed to the press, a spokesperson for the charity might respond that his group is exempted from responsibilities that fall on lesser entities because of all the good his charitable organization does in the world.

By the same token, if our ends are of dubious value, presumably we are obligated to refrain from using ethically questionable means. A former student reported that in his part-time job as a telemarketer to physicians, he could vastly improve his chances of getting through to them by posing as another doctor. But the student ultimately could not justify this deceit to himself and wound up getting another job.

Questions of this type arise repeatedly in the policy-making arena. During the congressional hearings in 1990 on whether the United States should take up arms to combat Iraqi aggression in Kuwait, a teenager testified to Congress that she saw Iraqi soldiers tear babies from incubators. That story was repeated many times in speeches by then President George H. W. Bush and was featured in the subsequent congressional debate on whether to support U.S. military action in the Gulf. The congressional committee was not told, however, that the teenager was the Kuwaiti ambassador's daughter; moreover, there is good reason to believe that the girl had not herself witnessed these alleged atrocities. Had he known she was the Kuwaiti ambassador's daughter, said Representative John Porter, the ranking Republican on the committee, he would not have allowed her to testify. But then again, he had heard other witnesses tell similar stories, and he thought there was strong evidence to support the charges (McArthur, 2003).

As in the above example, it is not uncommon that persuaders employ "the ends justify the means" as a rationale for achieving rhetorical success. But we only need to remember history to see the problems that can arise with this approach. The Nazi leadership believed in its ends and justified its use of hate campaigns that were built around polarizing symbols of identification and division. Politicians, public relations professionals, advertising executives, trial lawyers—and, yes, even some classroom speakers—are not above fabricating evidence or using misleading arguments. Once individuals have engaged in practices such as these, it is all too easy to rationalize them—to decide, for example, that a classroom speech is only an exercise and doesn't count in the real world or that fabricating evidence is justified because the speaker could always find evidence just like it if he had the time to dig it out of the library.

Moral standards for ethical persuasion can also be applied selectively and self-deceptively in conflicts between close friends and associates, and the tendency to apply moral standards inconsistently is all the more persistent because it is often done unconsciously. By deceiving ourselves about our own tendencies to deceive others, we manage both to protect our egos and to appear sincere to others.

Weighing ends against means, means against ends, and both against circumstances is most closely associated with the philosophical position on ethics known as **utilitarianism**. Its core principle is this: *Act to promote as much good as possible.* Given two or more alternatives, we should do what will provide the greatest good for the greatest number of people. Lying, ordinarily, does more harm than good, and so is presumed to be unethical. But there may be "white" lies that do little harm and a lot of good, in which case utilitarians would approve them.

Universalism

In contrast to **utilitarianism**, a second approach to the ethics of persuasion assumes that some practices are intrinsically virtuous and others are intrinsically objectionable, no matter what the objective or the circumstances. Universalist ethics may be derived from law or tradition or religion. For example, the Bible holds that we should *never* lie, slander, or bear false witness regardless of the good that might possibly come from such actions.

Philosopher Immanuel Kant held to the *categorical imperative,* the position that we should always act so that the principle of our actions is capable of being universalized. By that reasoning, lying is always wrong, even when it causes no harm in a particular situation, because if everyone were to lie, no one would believe anyone. Lying is wrong, in other words, because truth telling is a necessary condition of our having any meaningful verbal interaction at all (Solomon, 1984).

Of course, the issue with such an approach to the ethics of persuasion is that it does not entertain the circumstances of the particular situation, and instead gives privilege to the universal rule. Situations do intrude, though, and relationships matter. A universalist might have objected to the doctor who lied to his patient to promote her health on the grounds that the doctor has violated a universal injunction against lying. In fact, however, the doctor might have added years to his patient's life by persuading her to exercise. We can see how in some situations, the utilitarian and the universalist viewpoints would conflict.

Dialogic Ethics

A third approach to ethical persuasion may be derived from a view of communication as ideally *dialogic*. According to **dialogic ethics**, communication between two persons is facilitated when each treats the other as a *thou*, a person, rather than an *it*, an object to manipulate. Communication is imperiled, perhaps even destroyed, when the bonds of interpersonal trust are placed in question (Solomon, 1984). A list of ethical imperatives for the dialogic persuasive speaker or writer might include the following:

1 Practice inquiry before advocacy. Be open to a variety of points of view before you embrace any one of them.

2 Know your subject. If what you say isn't based on firsthand knowledge, get the information you need from the library or from the Internet.

3 Be honest about your identity. Don't purport to be an expert if you are not.

4 Try to tell the truth as you perceive it. Don't deliberately mislead audiences about your true opinions on a matter.

5 Avoid fabrications, misrepresentations, and distortions of evidence.

6 Don't oversimplify.

7 Acknowledge possible weaknesses, if any, in your position. Be honest about your own ambivalence or uncertainty.

8 Avoid irrelevant emotional appeals or diversionary tactics.

9 Appeal to the best motives in people, not their worst motives.

10 Be prepared to lose on occasion if winning means doing psychological harm to others and demeaning yourself in the bargain.

This, you might conclude, is a reasonable list, but as with any catalog of this sort, shouldn't there be exceptions to it? For example, doesn't politeness sometimes require a speaker to *not* tell an audience what he or she thinks of them? Given constraints of time and the situation at hand, isn't it often impossible to avoid oversimplification? Attorneys who are defending their clients in court may think it unwise to disclose the weaknesses in their positions, and when a client's future is a stake, can we blame them? And so we see, as with the other approaches to ethics, limitations exist with the dialogic approach. Things are not as tidy as they may first appear.

Situationalism

Finally, a fourth approach to the ethics of persuasion comes from those who take the position that the questions of ethics are role- or situation-specific, thus bolstering the case for exceptions to the above list of ethical imperatives. For example, the car you want to sell had been in an accident, but has since been fully repaired. Do you tell prospective buyers about it? Do you admit the problem if you're asked?

Assuming that ethical decisions should be role- or situation-specific, you might reason that evasion, and possibly even misrepresentation, are legitimate tactics for private car sales and even for business in general. A dialogic ethic is fine in the classroom or between friends, you reason, but it doesn't apply to strangers and certainly not if you eventually end up selling your car to a used car dealer. You might further assume that used car transactions are a form of *game* or *contest,* which is fair because both sides know, or at least should know, the rules. The game metaphor is consistent with the ethical position known as *situationalism.* This view of ethics enjoins us to pay particular attention to the special circumstances of a matter. Johannesen (2002) lists contextual factors as things like:

1   the role or function of the persuader for the audience;

2   the expectations held by receivers concerning such matters as appropriateness and reasonableness;

3   the degree of receiver awareness of the persuader's techniques;

4   the goals and values held by receivers;

5   the degree of urgency for implementation of the persuader's proposal; and

6   the ethical standards for communication held by receivers.

Situational ethics are often applied as a middle ground of communication ethics, between the poles of moral certainty on either side of it. In the case of the medical doctor who overstated the dangers of failing to comply with exercise recommendations, the situationalist might ask how dire is the situation for the patient and whether the doctor had tried a more honest and straightforward approach in the past. If the situation is dire and honesty hasn't worked, then exaggeration might possibly be justified.

Situational ethics also prompts consideration of the institutions of society: Do they place persuaders in situations where, try as they might, it is impossible for them to act honestly and forthrightly and still survive? In Mexico, bribes to local police to get out of traffic tickets is commonplace, and are considered akin to tips given to a restaurant server in the United States. Police are paid low wages because the expectation is that they will increase their income through such practices. What in the United States would be seen as a serious ethical lapse is considered as simple payment for services south of the border.

A situational ethic invites attention to other institutions as well. Which among our society's cultural, religious, and educational institutions prompt independent thinking, and which of them prompt conformist, cult-like thinking? Does persuasive product advertising prompt another type of mindless conformity, in this case to the insatiable demands of the economic marketplace? To paraphrase Bernard Barber (1996, 2007), have we become enchained by our department store chains, our food service chains, and, worse yet, by the irresistible impulses inside us to buy, buy, buy? Nevertheless, because it emphasizes the particulars of each situation rather than general principles, the situationalist perspective could very easily slide into little more than a rationalization of our actions in different situations, rather than a guide as to what we *should* do in those situations.

Putting It Together: Ethical Meta-Perspective

The four perspectives reviewed here are offered to provide a starting place for you to create your own perspective on the perspectives. As you begin, you should probably consider that the perspective that on first glance seems most appealing to you will probably depend on whether you see yourself primarily as a persuader or as a persuadee. If as a persuader, then you will probably be more inclined to utilitarianism or situationalism, as you will want to focus on finding ways to create rhetorical success. On the other hand, as a persuadee, you are likely to be more inclined toward universalism or dialogic ethics, where the rules for conduct are solid and you will be treated as a valued human being.

In formulating your ethical meta-perspective of persuasion, we advise you to first acknowledge your own biases and then we encourage you to avoid just following the crowd. You should not assume, for example, that what's commonly done *ought* to be done. Having an ethical perspective means moving beyond *description* (what is done) to *prescription* (what ought to be done), to formulating a clear sense of what's right.

Recognize, too, that it is possible—at least some of the time—to be ethical *and* effective. Finally, be aware that the perspectives are not mutually exclusive; hence, it is possible to borrow from each. For example, the utilitarian who seeks to do more good than harm might look to a nuanced situationalism for an idea of the good or to the universalist "Thou shalt nots" of the Ten Commandments for a conception of doing harm. Even the universalist might concede that there are circumstances justifying adultery or even murder while insisting that adultery and murder are intrinsically evil. Even the situationalist might concede that appeal to circumstances is too often an excuse for irresponsible behavior. Ultimately, with regards to the ethics of persuasion there is no court of last resort to resolve the outstanding issues once and for all. Nevertheless we are duty-bound to confront the issues and to act in good conscience with respect to them.

SUMMARY

Rhetoric, the study of persuasion, has had an uneven past. Conceived by the ancient Greeks as the prime instrument of democracy, it has at other times been fashioned for ignoble purposes. Few people are unambivalent in their feelings about persuasion; none can do without it.

The study of persuasion serves three vital functions. First, it informs persuasive practice, enabling would-be persuaders to maximize their opportunities for social control. Second, it enables us to become more intelligent and discriminating consumers of persuasive communications. Third, and most important, it adds to our understanding about human psychology and the individual's place in society and culture. A communication practice, persuasion is intended to influence the judgments and actions of others but always by giving them the power of decision. Thus, persuasion predisposes but does not impose.

In paradigm cases, the intent to persuade is clear-cut; in the gray areas of persuasion, it is not. Although in this text, persuasion may sometimes be treated as an effect, whether intended or not, for the most part, it is referred to as a practice. Thus, persuasion is defined as *human communication designed to influence the judgments and actions of others*.

Persuasion is of vital importance in any society but especially in a democratic, market-driven society. In an age of global economics and increasing democratization, it may be only a slight exaggeration to say that one fourth of the world's GDP is persuasion. Your most immediate interests in persuasion are probably in mastering the art and science of persuading and also in becoming a more savvy persuadee. For these purposes, *Persuasion in Society* shifts back and forth between the these two perspectives. It also seeks to prompt us to thoughtful consideration of the ethics of persuasion no matter which side of the persuasion equation we are on. It asks this question: should we be forgiving ourselves as persuaders for practices we would condemn as persuadees?

The study of persuasion benefits from its being a branch of the humanities (here known as *rhetoric*) and also from its being an area of research in the social sciences. The former brings together rhetorical scholars (rhetoricians), media analysts, and other close "readers" of persuasive acts and artifacts in a **critical studies approach** to the study of persuasion. From these critical analyses may come assessments of a persuader's rhetorical artistry, logic, or ethics. Criticism is also tied to theory building and theory testing.

In addition, behavioral research contributes a great deal to what is known about how to persuade. Using experiments, social scientists test hypotheses about what works under controlled conditions. Subjected to systematic investigation are variations in source, message, medium, audience, and context—in "who says what to whom, when, where, and how." Determining the effects of these independent variables on message recipients' judgments and actions is the object of the research.

Behavioral research of this type is linked to social-scientific theory in the same way that criticism both informs, and is guided by, rhetorical theory.

From the time of Socrates, and maybe even before, thoughtful people have debated about rhetoric and persuasion, some decrying it as inherently tainted, others seeing that it can serve purposes both good and ill. *Persuasion in Society* takes a middle road and features a *coactive* approach to the practice of persuasion. The central image is one of bridging differences, where persuaders move toward persuadees psychologically in hopes that persuadees will be moved toward acceptance of their ideas or proposals for action.

QUESTIONS FOR FURTHER STUDY

1   How would you define persuasion? Which of the following cases would you include, and which would you exclude?

- The blizzard persuaded me to go indoors.
- The puppy's sad look persuaded me to surrender choice pieces of filet mignon.
- The full moon persuaded us to make rapturous love.
- On seeing the t-shirt on a passer-by, I was persuaded to buy one just like it.
- The political candidate did her best but could not convince the voters to elect her.
- The burglar threatened us with his gun.

2   How, if at all, would you distinguish persuasion from coercion? From the use of force? From pressures toward conformity? From harassment? From teaching? From information giving? From spontaneous expression?

3   Think back to a situation in which you were turned down for a request that you thought should have been granted, considering it an instance where your attempts at persuasion failed. In your opinion, what factors may have influenced the negative outcome?

4   Recalling Aristotle's distinction between issues of judgment and issues of certainty, identify one issue of judgment on which you think reasonable individuals might legitimately differ and another for which you believe the arguments on one side clearly outweigh the arguments on the other. Defend your view.

5   Analyze a course description for one of your courses. Does it communicate interest in persuading? Whether it does so or not, is it persuasive?

6   What items have you purchased recently, and how were you persuaded to buy them? Did you buy them with your credit card, thereby being persuaded to purchase something even when you didn't at that moment have the money to pay for it?

7   How do twenty-first century marketing and advertising affect you? Are you a part of any consumption communities? What name-brand items do you have in your home, and what name-brand clothing do you wear? Why?

KEY TERMS

- Coercion
- Critical studies approach to persuasion
- Dependent Variables
- Dialogic Ethics
- Humanists
- Independent Variables
- Inducements
- Meta-Analysis
- Persuasion
- Propaganda
- Rhetoric
- Rhetorical Criticism
- Rhetorical approach to persuasion
- RPS model
- Situationalism
- Social-scientific approach to persuasion
- Sophists
- Universalism
- Utilitarianism

REFERENCES

Antioch, G. (2013). *Persuasion is now 30 percent of US GDP*. Economic Roundup Issue 1. Retrieved May 19, 2014, from www.treasury.gov.au/Publications AndMedia/Publications/2013/Economic-Roundup-Issue-1/Report/Persuasion-is-now-30-per-cent-of-US-GDP

Aristotle. (2004). *The rhetoric*. (W. Rhys Roberts, Trans.). New York: Dover. Retrieved July 8, 2009, from http://classics.mit.edu/Aristotle/rhetoric.html

Barber, B. (2007). *Consumed: How markets corrupt children, infantilize adults, and swallow citizens whole*. New York: W.W. Norton & Company.

Barber, B. R. (1996). *Jihad vs. McWorld: How globalism and tribalism are reshaping the world*. New York: Ballantine.

Bennett, S., & O'Rourke, S. P. (2006). A prologemenon to the future study of rhetoric and propaganda: critical foundations. In Jowett, G. E., and O'Donnell, V. (eds), *Readings in propaganda and persuasion: New and classic essays*. Thousand Oaks, CA: Sage, pp. 51–72.

Billig, M. (1996). *Arguing and thinking: A rhetorical approach to social psychology* (2nd ed.). Cambridge: Cambridge University Press.

Billig. M. (2008). The language of critical discourse analysis: The case of nominalization. *Discourse Society* 19(6), 783–800.

Brock, T. C., & Green, M. C. (2005). *Persuasion: Psychological insights and perspectives*. Thousand Oaks, CA: Sage Publications.

Burke, K. (1969). *A rhetoric of motives*. Berkeley: University of California Press. (Original work published 1950)

Carey, A. (1997). *Taking the risk out of democracy: Corporate propaganda vs. freedom and liberty*. Chicago: University of Illinois Press.

Cialdini, R. B. (2009). *Influence: Science and practice* (5th ed.). Boston: Pearson.

Conger, J. (1999). *Building leaders: How successful companies develop the next generation*. San Francisco: Jossey-Bass.

Cooper, H., Hedges, L. V., & Valentine, J. C. (2009). *The handbook of research synthesis and meta-analysis* (vol. 2). New York, NY: Russell Sage Foundation Publications.

Feldman, R. S., Forrest, J. A., & Happ, B. R. (2002). Self-presentation and verbal deception: Do self-presenters lie more? *Basic and Applied Social Psychology*, 24, 163–170.

Golan, G. (2008). Exploring a link between the third-person effect and the theory of reasoned action. *American Behavioral Scientist*, 208–224. Retrieved May 19, 2014, from http://abs.sagepub.com.proxy-edinboro.klnpa.org/content/52/2/208

Gonzalez, C. (2013). *Student veterans speak up: A focus group study*. University of Nevada, Reno (UNR). Reno: University Veterans Coalition. Retrieved May 22, 2014, from www.unr.edu/Documents/president/uvc/021313-Focus-Group-Report.pdg

Grunig, L., Grunig, J., & Dozier, D. (2002). Excellence in public relations and effective organizations. Mahwah, NJ: Lawrence Erlbaum.

Hart, R. P. (1997). *Modern rhetorical criticism* (2nd ed.). Needham Heights, MA: Allyn & Bacon.

Hart, R. P. (2004). *Modern rhetorical criticism* (3rd ed.). Needham Heights, MA: Allyn & Bacon.

Heath, C., & Heath D. (2007). *Made to stick: Why some ideas survive and others die*. New York: Random House.

Hopper, R., & Bell, R. (1984). Broadening the deception construct. *Quarterly Journal of Speech, 70, 288–302.*

Howell, W. (2003). *Power without persuasion: A theory of presidential action*. Princeton, NJ: Princeton University Press.

Jio, S. (2014). Making sense of conflicting health advice. *Woman's Day*. Retrieved May 19, 2014, from www.womansday.com/health-fitness/making-sense-of-conflicting-health-advice-114840

Johannesen, R. L. (2002). *Ethics in human communication* (5th ed.). Prospect Heights, IL: Waveland.

Jowett, G., & O'Donnell, V. (2006). *Propaganda and persuasion*. Thousand Oaks, CA: Sage.

Kim, L. (2013). USFC researcher make sense of conflicting advice on calcium intake. *UCSF*. Retrieved May 19, 2014, from www.ucsf.edu/news/2013/10/109826/making-sense-conflicting-advice-calcium-intake

L'Etang, J., & Pieczka, M. (2006). *Public relations: Critical debates and contemporary practice*. Mahwah, NJ: Lawrence Erlbaum Associates.

Leventhal, H., Cameron, L., Leventhal, E., & Ozakinci, G. (2005). *Persuasion: Psychological insights and perspectives*. New York: Sage Publications.

Levine, R. (2003). *The power of persuasion: How we're bought and sold*. Hoboken, NJ: John Wiley & Sons.

Lu, X., & Simons, H. W. (2006). Transitional rhetoric of Communist Party leaders in the Post-Mao Reform Period: Dilemmas and strategies, *Quarterly Journal of Speech, 92*, 262–268.

Luntz, F. (2004). Interview with David Broncaccio on *NOW*. Retrieved November 2, 2009, from www.pbs.org/now/politics/luntz.html

Lyne, J. (1990). Bio-rhetorics: Moralizing the life sciences. In Simons, H. W. (ed.), *The rhetorical turn: Invention and persuasion in the conduct of inquiry*. Chicago: University of Chicago Press, pp. 35–57.

Lyne, J. (1990). The culture of inquiry. *Quarterly Journal of Speech, 76*, 192–208.

McArthur, J. (2003). Remember Nayirah, witness for Kuwait? In Sifry, M., & Cerf, C. (eds), *The Gulf War Reader*. New York: Touchstone, pp. 135–162.

McCloskey, D. (2013). Persuasion is now 30 per cent of US GDP (L. Rowell, Interviewer). Retrieved May 19, 2014, from http://www.redark.com.au/blog/?p=1238

McCloskey, D., & Klamer. A. (1995). One quarter of GDP is persuasion. *American Economic Review, 85*, 191–195.

McGuire, W. (1978). Persuasion. In Miller, G. A. (ed.), *Communication, language and meaning*. New York: Harper.

Michie, G. (1998). Room to learn. *American Educator, 21*, 36–42.

Nelson, J., Megill, A., & McCloskey, D. (eds) (1987). *The rhetoric of the human sciences: Language and argument in scholarship and public affairs*. Madison: University of Wisconsin Press.

NOW (2004, July 2). PBS. Interview with Frank Luntz. Retrieved July 8, 2009, from http://www.pbs.org/now/transcript/transcript327_full.html#luntz

Osnos, E. (2008, July 28). Angry youth: The new generation's neocon nationalists. *New Yorker*. Retrieved July 8, 2009 from http://www.newyorker.com/reporting/2008/07/28/080728fa_fact_osnos

Plato. (2006). *Gorgias* (R. Waterfield, trans.). Oxford: Oxford University Press.

Pratkanis, A., & Aronson, E. (2001). *Age of propaganda: The everyday use and abuse of persuasion*. New York: Henry Holt.

Rampton, S., & Stauber, J. (2003). *Weapons of mass deception: The uses of propaganda in Bush's war on Iraq*. New York: Tarcher.

Rogers, W. (2007). *Persuasion: Messages, receivers, and contexts*. Lanham, MD: Rowman & Littlefield.

Sanger, D. Fine line for Obama on how to convey hope on economy. *New York Times*. Retrieved on July 8, 2009, from www.nytimes.com/2009/05/09/business/economy/09assess.html

Simons, H. W. (1970). Requirements, problems and strategies: A theory of persuasion for social movements, *Quarterly Journal of Speech*, 56, 1–11.

Simons, H. W. (1972). Persuasion in social conflicts: A critique of prevailing conceptions and a framework for future research. *Speech Monographs*, 39, 227–247.

Simons, H. W. (1994). "Going meta": Definition and political applications. *Quarterly Journal of Speech 80*, 468–481.

Simons, H. W. (1996). Judging a policy proposal by the company it keeps: The Gore-Perot NAFTA debate. *Quarterly Journal of Speech*, 82, 274–287.

Simons, H. W. (2000). A dilemma-centered analysis of Clinton's August 17th apologia: Implications for rhetorical theory and method. *Quarterly Journal of Speech*, 86, 438–453.

Simons, H. W. (2007). Race, ideology, and Barbiegate discourse: A dilemma-centered analysis. In Tracy, K., McDaniel, J. P., & Gronbeck, B. (eds). *The prettier doll: Rhetoric, discourse, and ordinary democracy*. Tuscaloosa: University of Alabama Press, pp. 45–69.

Solomon, R. C. (1984). *Ethics: A brief introduction*. New York: McGraw-Hill.

Sproule, J. M. (1994). *Propaganda and democracy: The American experience of media and mass persuasion*. Cambridge, MA: Cambridge University Press.

Thaler, R., & Sunstein, C. (2008). *Nudge: Improving decisions about health, wealth, and happiness*. New Haven, CT: Yale University Press.

Westen, Drew. (2007). *The political brain: The role of emotion in deciding the fate of the nation*. Cambridge, MA: PublicAffairs Publishing.

CHAPTER 2

The Psychology of Persuasion: Basic Concepts and Principles

In our post-9/11 world, the case of President Bill Clinton's extramarital affair, impeachment, acquittal, and legal disbarment almost seems like ancient history. So much has happened since, and our world has been transformed in so many ways. That being said, the Clinton episode is a benchmark historical moment. Only two presidents have been impeached, and in the language of the U.S. Constitution, impeachment is serious, involving removal from office due to "treason, bribery, or other high crimes and misdemeanors."

Today, emotions about the case have cooled, most people have sorted out how they feel about it, and we can examine the situation with a more objective eye.

President Clinton has worked to redeem himself though his charitable global initiatives, and it is his wife, Hillary Clinton, who is engaged in the politics of our day. But when the situation was happening, things were much more complex. During that time, the American people had absorbed a great deal of information about the scandal that formed the core of their *beliefs*. They learned, for example, that Clinton had misled them for several months about his illicit relationship with the White House intern and that he had probably misinformed his close aides as well in an effort to derail the investigation by Independent Counsel Kenneth Starr. Beginning with the revelations contained in surreptitiously taped phone conversations between White House intern Monica Lewinsky and her supposed friend, and concluding with DNA evidence on Lewinsky's dress, the facts of Clinton's sexual involvement with Lewinsky became well-nigh incontrovertible.

Yet Americans' *attitudes* toward President Clinton's job performance and toward whether he should be removed from office stemmed not just from their beliefs about sex, lies, and audiotapes, but also from their *values*. Were Clinton's transgressions important? Were they *as* important as the good job most people believed he had been doing in managing the economy and conducting foreign policy? Most Americans believed that President Clinton was untrustworthy, but placed a higher value on the job he was doing. They saw him as a "low virtue, high competence" president, and most liked what they saw (McGee, 1998).

Together, these beliefs and values strongly influenced Americans' attitudes toward President Clinton's performance and whether he should continue in office. Their attitudes, in turn, served as knowledge structures, called schemas, for the filtering of new information. These schemas performed, as it were, the work of a mental secretary, determining what new information would be allowed in the door, what importance it would be assigned, and how it would be interpreted.

Americans were polarized about the impeachment issue, making it unlikely that either side would be moved very much by new information or new arguments. Their attitudes toward the proposal to impeach ranged from hostile to enthusiastically supportive, with relatively few people on the fence. These attitudes influenced people's perceptions of the Senate trial as well as what they said to friends and co-workers.

But attitudes alone were not fully predictive of what people would say to their friends and co-workers about the Clinton affair. Another important predictor for many Americans (not all) was their **subjective norms**. Many persons' public actions (as opposed to their privately held attitudes) were influenced by what they believed was most socially acceptable: A great many Americans publicly dismissed the importance of the scandal even as they tuned in to CNN and MSNBC each night for the latest salacious details. Their public actions may have been attitude related, but their subjective norms played an important role as well.

Of course, some Americans thought hard about the Clinton–Lewinsky matter, whereas others were either unwilling or unable to perform the necessary mental labor. The former pursued what Petty and Cacioppo (1996) call the central route to judgment making; the latter pursued a peripheral route, mostly relying for their judgments on cognitive shorthands (Cialdini, 2009). These shorthands, which are the rules of thumb that enable people to get on with their lives without protracted deliberation, included conclusions like: "Everybody lies about sex, so what's the big deal?"

In the midst of all of this, we need to remember that being persuaded is a learning process, and that was certainly true in this situation. Americans learned to like or dislike Clinton on the basis of information, associations, and anticipated rewards and punishments. These constituents of the learning process were also at work as Americans contemplated the policy options of removal or continuation in office. And Americans not only learned information, but also learned whom they would trust. Typically, they tended to dismiss politicians as untrustworthy and, to some extent, trusted messages presented in the guise of entertainment (e.g., a late night comic's jokes about the scandal) or news (e.g., CNN's intensive coverage).

On August 17, 1998, President Clinton made a historic speech in which he admitted to the American people for the first time that he had misled them. It was Clinton's task in the speech to persuade his many longtime supporters, who had found news of the affair and subsequent cover-up troubling, to find ways of understanding and perhaps forgiving his transgressions. At the same time, when speaking to those who had made no secret of their dislike for Clinton and revulsion toward what he had done, he had to attempt to defuse some of their hostility and even create a sense of cognitive inconsistency between the Clinton they knew and despised and the Clinton they now saw on their television screens. To this day, scholars and critics are divided on whether or not Clinton succeeded at this dual task, but he did survive the trial, remain in office, and serve out his term.

The Clinton–Lewinsky scandal, then, has much to teach about the psychology of persuasion. Chapter 2 builds on this case study as it introduces psychological concepts and principles of persuasion.

BELIEFS, VALUES, AND ATTITUDES

Every field has its own jargon, and some fields use familiar terms in unfamiliar ways. In everyday life, "beliefs" range from religious faith to weather forecasts. Many people speak of their "values" as things they believe in. And "having an attitude" is sometimes used to mean being stubborn and hard to get along with. But persuasion specialists tend to treat these terms with more precision, and it is there we must begin.

Beliefs are what we each personally consider to be true or probable. We believe you will learn new things from this book, for example. We can't say that's true, but we believe it is highly probable. Furthermore, a distinction is made between *believing in* something (e.g., in the value of honesty) and *believing that* something (e.g., that your college football team is excellent). It is in the latter sense that belief is used in this book.

TABLE 2.1   *When seeking to persuade, we must adapt to the audience we are trying to reach*

	BELIEFS	VALUES	ATTITUDES
Focused on what is:	true vs. false probable vs. improbable	right vs. wrong judgments of worth	favorable vs. unfavorable
Example 1	• I believe that going to college will help me to get a better job. • I believe that college is expensive. • I believe that going to college will help me think and learn on my own.	• I value job advancement. • I think that college is worth the cost. • I value learning independently.	Therefore I have a strongly positive attitude toward getting in college.
Example 2	• I believe that studying abroad will make me a more well-rounded person. • I believe that travel is sometimes scary.	• I value encountering people from other cultures and becoming more well rounded. • I value taking risks.	Therefore, I have a strongly positive attitude toward studying abroad.
Example 3	• I believe that exercise is good for my health. • I believe that watching team sports on TV is dull. • I believe that I'm not good at team sports.	• I value good health. • I value excitement. • I value doing what I do best.	Therefore, I prefer working out on my own at a gym to watching or engaging in team sports.
Example 4	• I believe these Nikes are stylish, designed for jogging, a bit pricey, but well made.	• When I put sneakers on to play tennis, I'm indifferent to style, care not at all about jogging capability, am indifferent to cost, and, yes, want a well-made tennis sneaker.	On balance, I'd prefer some other sneakers than these, ones more consistent with my values when it comes to tennis.

Values are our ideals; they determine what we see as right or wrong, they contain our judgments about the worth of things, and they provide the principles that guide us in how to conduct our lives. It is not unusual to speak of our values in exclusively positive terms, but here and in other treatments of persuasion we argue that values can include judgments of negative worth as well—for example, most people *negatively value* adultery.

Attitudes are more than just our momentary emotional states or moods. In fact, they are general evaluations, whether favorable or unfavorable. Robert Gass and John Seiter (2013) define a number of characteristics of attitudes: first, they are learned and not innate. Second, they precede and consequently influence our behavior. They are the link between what we think and what we do. Third, they involve intensity of feeling: We characterize them as "strong," "weak," or "neutral." And they are directed toward a specific thing: A person, an event, an idea, a proposal for action, or an action itself.

Finally, the term *opinion* is used here in various ways. Is opinion the same as a belief, a value, or an attitude? Here, it is an all-purpose term for verbalized judgments of every type.

A PREVIEW OF THEORIES

Much of this chapter is taken up with psychological theories of persuasion. Theories of every type attempt to summarize and explain a phenomenon while directing the search for additional knowledge. The heart of any scientific theory is a set of assumptions, basic concepts, definitions of those concepts, and explanatory statements or theorems that relate the concepts in a condensed and organized way.

Psychological theories of persuasion include assumptions and explanatory statements about what goes on inside the head of the message recipient.

Opinions differ among persuasion theorists as to whether persuadees process messages rationally. Aristotle maintained that reason was the human being's most distinctive feature, and many theorists since have created *rational choice* models to explain how it is that humans calculate their own best interests. In general, say many of these theorists, our choices correspond to our expectations and values; hence, the name **expectancy-value theories**. For example, a proponent of this approach might argue that it's true, isn't it, that because most people value their lives they will choose lifestyles designed to prolong their lives.

Yet other theorists maintain that this is not the way choices are actually made (e.g., Bargh, 2006; Westen, 2007; Kahneman, 2011). These theorists point to the role of emotion in persuasion and of unconscious motives such as our propensity to rationalize after the event for decisions already made (e.g., Westen, 2007). They would only need to point to that quart of "chunky monkey" ice cream, filled with too many life-shortening and fat-filled calories, as evidence of the shortcomings of expectancy-value theories.

FIGURE 2.1 *Expectancy-value theories suggest that we will make rational choices: we will eat healthy foods to prolong our lives. These theories omit the role of emotions and unconscious motives in our decision-making process, which are powerful persuaders that, for example, cause us to choose to eat a delicious bowl of ice cream, even as we fully understand that it is not the healthiest choice.*

Skipping Class Rationalizations

FIGURE 2.2

Well now, it's about that time of the semester ... the time when students suddenly have the urge to disregard their boring lectures and frolic in the warm sunlight and fresh spring air. The hormones can't be helped, right?

We both know that's baloney. Anytime is a good time to skip class. You just need a good reason, right? Sure. You (or your parents, as the case may be) are spending boatloads of cash to go to this prestigious university, and it kind of hangs on your conscience that you don't feel like going. Behold, rationalizations to your rescue.

Here is your wonderful list of ways to skip class, and methods to rationalize them to yourself.

1 Sleep in

Rationalization: You are, in fact, recharging your mental batteries for the more demanding classes you will face later in the day/week/semester/life. Besides, your professor EXPECTS people to skip that 9:00 am lecture. The professor probably didn't even show up himself. Why trouble yourself to get out of bed, trudge across campus, and find out? You can always claim later to be doing sleep studies on yourself for your Psych 101 class.

2 Surf the Internet

Rationalization: It's educational. The Internet is the greatest source of information in the world. You're also improving your computer skills, vital to working in the real world. Hell, we have friends who get paid to surf the net all day ... of course their bosses don't know that. Is it really your fault if you happen to get sidetracked by less informative pages on the web? The web is built to do that. Grrr, damn web. (Raise your arm and shake your fist at the computer now, and grrrr along with me.)

3 Clean your room

Rationalization: Cleanliness is next to godliness. Godliness is definitely more important than linear algebra or Augustan literature. Besides, you can listen to music when you clean. Real loud. Loud music has been proven in frat house studies to be conducive to the learning process. And hey, you do need to dig that linear algebra textbook out from under the pile of dirty clothes anyway.

4 Wander about the more beautiful parts of campus

Rationalization: You're not paying this much to go to school just to sit in boring classes are you? Of course not! You've got to get out and see the beautiful portions of campus that your tuition dollars are paying so much to maintain. Hey, by the way, there are attractive men and women out there too! You might want to go take a gander at them while you're wandering.

5 Take a trip into town

Rationalization: You're at a college far away from home (or even near to home, bear with us here and ignore the little details) .... This may be your only chance to visit a local community you may never see again. Have fun. Meet the locals. Mingle. Claim you are studying for that sociology class you're gonna take next semester.

Source: http://Chainletters.net/chainletters/skipping-class-rationalizations/

Still other persuasion scholars find a place for reason and unreason, logic and emotion, the thoughtful, self-aware human and the seemingly robotic human. Increasingly popular these days are **two systems theories**, designed to account for vast differences in the way most of us respond to persuasive messages, depending, for example, on our willingness and ability in any given case to weigh arguments carefully or rely on emotional or cognitive shortcuts (Petty & Cacioppo, 1986, 1996; Thaler & Sunstein, 2008; Kahneman, 2011).

Their differences notwithstanding, all of these theories have a great deal to say to us about how to persuade and about how to make sense of persuasion by others.

PERSUASION BY DEGREES: ADAPTING TO DIFFERENT AUDIENCES

On any one occasion, a persuader might stop far short of producing wholesale changes in the thinking or behaviors of another and yet still consider the effort successful. Researchers tend to equate persuasion with attitude change, yet an exclusive focus on attitude change may obscure shifts in *degree* of attitude modification, *and* in underlying beliefs and values (Iyengar & McGrady, 2005). You may not persuade your friend to become a vegan, but you might persuade her to give up red meat by appealing to her love of animals, and that might be counted as a success.

Gerald Miller's (1980) threefold classification provides a useful way into understanding these phenomena but needs supplementation. Broadly speaking, he says, persuaders may succeed in (1) *shaping a response*, (2) *reinforcing a response*, and (3) *changing a response*.

1   **Response shaping** occurs when people acquire new beliefs on controversial matters or when they are socialized to learn new attitudes or acquire new values. Shaping may involve, for example, teaching a child to become a Lutheran, a Democrat, a capitalist, or a patriot. Political campaigns may shape voters' attitudes toward previously unknown candidates.

Colleges and universities are key sites for response shaping, as they introduce students to new concepts and ways of seeing that had never before been entertained. It is therefore not an understatement to proclaim that a college education can be life-changing, as students leave very different people than they were when they first arrived on campus. The key characteristic of such shaping is that it leads to the formation of new beliefs, values, and attitudes.

2   **Response reinforcing** consists of strengthening currently held convictions and making them more resistant to change. A campaign on behalf of a charity might begin by transforming lip service commitments into strongly felt commitments (*intensification*), then transforming those commitments into donations of time and money (*activation*), then working to maintain strong behavioral support

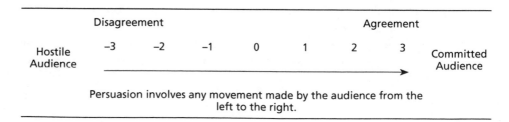

Persuasion involves any movement made by the audience from the left to the right.

FIGURE 2.3   *Persuasion takes place by degrees.*

and discouraging backsliding (*deterrence*). All these are forms of response reinforcing (Figure 2.4). Says Miller (1980):

> The response-reinforcing function underscores the fact that "being persuaded" is seldom, if ever, a one-message proposition; instead, people are constantly in the process of being persuaded. If an individual clings to an attitude (and the behaviors associated with it) more strongly after exposure to a communication, then persuasion has occurred as surely as if the individual has shifted from one set of responses to another. Moreover, those beliefs and behaviors most resistant to change are likely to be grounded in a long history of confirming messages, along with other positive reinforcers.

3   **Response changing** involves a wholesale shift of positions, more often in fits and starts than by way of a sudden, dramatic conversion. Tales of sudden conversions—whether from one political party to another, or one cigarette to another, or one religion to another—often neglect the processes leading up to them as well as lingering fondness for what we have given up. In reality, rather than undergoing dramatic conversions, humans are more likely to accept a range of possible options, all the while leaning toward one of them (Perloff, 2003). For example, many former opponents to gay marriage have completely changed their positions, but done so gradually, moving from opposition to first supporting civil unions, and then ultimately to accepting marriage equality. This process has occurred over time, and not without some discomfort, as these former opponents have come to meet and empathize with gay couples, seen more cultural acceptance of the LBGT community, and observed how changes in laws have not caused harm to heterosexual marriage.

If an audience is initially hostile, the first stage in response changing is *defusion* of their anger or suspicion. This may require a series of trust-building steps culminating only in their greater willingness to listen. Moving from left to right in Figure 2.5 is *neutralization*, bringing an audience from the point of moderate disagreement or dislike to a point of ambivalence or indecision. Yet a third stage on the way to response

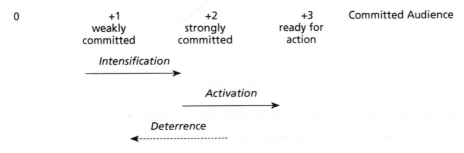

FIGURE 2.4 *Response reinforcement.*

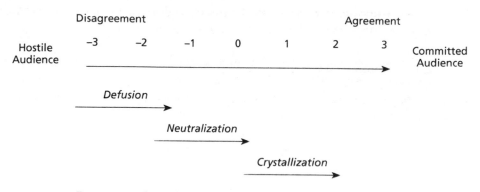

FIGURE 2.5   *Response changing.*

changing is *crystallization*, getting those persons who were uncommitted because of mixed feelings to join with the persuader in support of a position or proposal.

As discussed in subsequent chapters, each of these stages calls for different strategies of persuasion. Greatly complicating the task of the persuader is the mixed audience, where some message recipients are in agreement, others on the fence, still others in disagreement. Even among relatively homogeneous persuadees—e.g., a group of smokers who have sought help in quitting—the beliefs and values that undergird their favorable attitudes may differ widely, and hence need to be addressed by the persuader in different ways.

BVA THEORY: BELIEFS AND VALUES AS BUILDING BLOCKS OF ATTITUDES

Let's return to a fundamental premise of expectancy-value theories: that we humans act rationally in aligning our beliefs about the future with our values. Even if most humans fall far short of the ideal, isn't the assumption of rationality going to prove useful for persuaders in considering what Aristotle called the "available means of persuasion" for adapting to different audiences? For that, we turn to the **BVA theory**, which argues that beliefs and values are the building blocks of attitudes.

BVA theory is a relatively simple expectancy-value formulation of our own design, drawn from Fishbein and Ajzen's **theory of reasoned action** (1975) and theory of planned behavior (Ajzen, 1991). Its core postulates are as follows:

1   Beliefs (B) include judgments that a given object possesses certain attributes.

2   Values (V) include judgments of the worth of these perceived attributes (Ajzen & Fishbein, 1980).

3 Attitudes (A) combine our relevant beliefs (B) about an object with our value judgments (V) about the attributes that we associate with the object.

4 The stronger our beliefs about positively valued attributes, the more favorable should be our attitude toward that object.

5 The stronger our beliefs about negatively valued attributes, the less favorable our attitudes.

In shopping for a new car, for example, a buyer might be interested in things like efficiency, beauty, economy, speed, safety, and comfort. Car buyers typically have a variety of attributes in mind when considering different makes of cars, and the relative importance attached to each probably would not change much from one car to another.

Other car purchasers might assign different values to these attributes. According to BVA theory, prospective buyers' attitudes toward any given automobile would depend on both their beliefs about whether the object possesses particular attributes and the value weightings they assign to those attributes. These may vary considerably as we can see in relation to a fictitious attitude object—the new XL7 Zippo sedan.

Buyer A may believe that the XL7 Zippo sedan is great looking and fuel efficient and he has a highly favorable attitude toward the Zippo for just these reasons. Buyer B may agree that the Zippo possesses these attributes but views them neutrally or even negatively. Buyer C may value the attributes, but does not believe that the Zippo possesses them.

These variations in beliefs and values have great importance for persuaders. When shoppers enter a car lot, the first thing a salesperson seeks to do is "qualify" potential customers by figuring out what is important to them and, also, what might deter them from buying a particular car. This is because all good salespeople know that a sales pitch that might succeed with one customer could backfire with others. But a presentation specifically tailored to each prospective buyer could work wonders.

Thinking It Through

There's a somewhat vulgar but very funny motto in the car sales business, and it is this: "There's an ass for every seat." What that means is there is no car that is so ugly or distasteful that no one would buy it.

Jean knows of a car dealer who accidentally marked the wrong colors on his order form. The car that was delivered to the showroom was bright green with a flaming red interior. The salespeople feared that no one would ever buy it.

But, one day, a portly old man with a long beard entered the showroom and fell in love with the car. He worked as a mall Santa Claus, and he strongly identified with his role. And so, with great delight, he purchased his "Christmas tree car!"

FIGURE 2.6   *As this cartoon demonstrates, our beliefs, values, and attitudes are all important when it comes to purchasing a car.*
Cartoonist Group, Image #4119 by Nick Anderson.
Reprinted by permission of Cartoonist Group. www.cartoonistgroup.com

The *degree* to which beliefs are held and the *degree* to which values are positive or negative also enter into a buying decision. For example, in shopping around for a new sports car, a buyer might be drawn to the XL7 Zippo but have doubts about its fuel efficiency, because the fuel efficiency comes from making the car lighter and less safe. Or, the buyer might have second thoughts about whether to buy a car primarily because it is good looking.

This car-buying scenario presents an example of the practicality of expectancy-value theories in strategizing about persuasion. They can be very effective for those persuasive situations where we can and should plan our approach in advance, and they can aid us, as persuaders, in thinking through the persuasive situation from the perspective of the other.

Our trimmed-down BVA theory is useful for another reason: It has considerable generality and can be applied to almost any situation. It matters not a whole lot, says Babrow (2001), what sorts of attitudes (A) we are trying to mold or modify. The point is that attitude will have cognitive (B) and evaluative (V) components.

Thinking It Through

You need to write this down to make it work. Think about a situation in your life where you need to persuade someone of something. It can be big or small. Apply BVA to the task. List the beliefs you think the persuadee holds concerning the subject. Then move on to their values. Finally, consider their attitudes. Put it all together and write out your persuasive presentation, just so that you can see it for yourself.

How does this BVA-inspired presentation differ from what you would have said if you'd not done this exercise? Did BVA increase your chances of persuading successfully, and if so, how?

Yet BVA theory may achieve its generality by being too simple. As every car salesperson understands, the beliefs and values that enter into a car-buying decision are often linked to customers' more deep-seated beliefs and values. For example, imagine that on his last visit to the showroom, Buyer A invites his dear old Aunt Matilda to join him and she asks:

> Why do you want to invest so much money in a new car when so many people in Africa are starving? Can't you get by with a less expensive car? What does *Consumer Reports* say about this Zippo sedan? Isn't it more trustworthy than the word of that salesperson? I'll bet you've not even checked its consumer ratings out! And what is this obsession of yours with getting a sexy-looking car? Aren't you man enough to go without one? Where are your priorities?

As we can see, very quickly things can become complicated, and this is especially true when our elders decide to get involved! Thanks to Aunt Matilda, we can see that there are limits to the BVA theory. Some of the crucial questions that must be considered include the following:

1   Are people as aware as the theory suggests of their own beliefs, values, and attitudes, including small variations in degree of conviction?

2   Assuming that they are aware, are they as likely as the theory suggests to report candidly to others exactly what they're thinking and feeling?

3   Are people as calculating and organized in their decision making as BVA theory suggests?

4   Don't other attitudes come into play in a buying decision, including the buyer's trust in the salesperson? Are people as rational in their supposed calculations as this theory suggests?

FROM ATTITUDES TO ACTIONS AND THE ROLE OF SUBJECTIVE NORMS: THE THEORY OF REASONED ACTION

Fishbein and Ajzen's (1975) *Theory of Reasoned Action (TRA)* is a much more elaborate and highly quantified formulation of the problem posed earlier: How do beliefs about an object and evaluations of its attributes influence attitudes toward it? Also, what is the relationship between attitudes and actions, such as purchasing an XL7 Zippo sedan or using birth control pills?

One of the puzzles that Fishbein and Ajzen (1975) wrestled with in constructing their theory was evidence that a person's attitude toward an action or behavior (they used the terms interchangeably) did not always predict what action that person might eventually take. Buyer A might be favorably inclined toward purchasing the XL7 Zippo sedan and still not buy it. By contrast, a woman might have a negative attitude toward using birth control pills but still use them.

Fishbein and Ajzen (1975) concluded that the best predictor of behavior is *intentions*, which are a joint product of *attitudes toward behaviors* (AB) and *subjective norms* (SN). Just as AB has belief and value components, so SN is said to depend both on what we believe people whom we value highly would have us do and how desirous we are of complying with those norms.

Some of us are highly influenced by what other people we value would have us do; others are more self-reliant; still others of us vary in our willingness to accept the judgments of others. This might explain the case of the woman who had a negative attitude toward birth control pills but continued to use them; Fishbein and Ajzen's (1975) theory predicts that subjective norms were at work in that people around the woman whom she values would have her use them and so she does. The point here is this: When attitudes toward a contemplated behavior are put together with

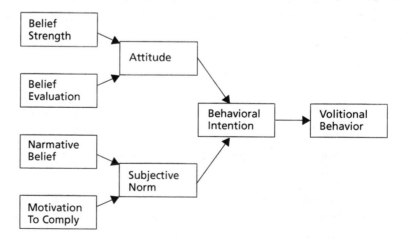

FIGURE 2.7   *Causal diagram of complete components of the theory of reasoned action.*
Reprinted by permission of Sage Publications.

subjective norms, the combination indicates more accurately how a person will act in a given situation.

> *Thinking It Through*
>
> How influenced are you by subjective norms? Can you think of a time when you followed them, and it worked out well for you? Conversely, when in your life have you followed those norms, only to see bad results?

THE ROLE OF EMOTION: WESTEN'S CRITIQUE OF EXPECTANCY-VALUE THEORIES

As with BVA theory, Fishbein and Ajzen's *Theory of Reasoned Action* assumes a rational actor (1975). But recent research on how we humans process information suggests otherwise. In the heat of the 2004 presidential contest, Drew Westen and his associates at Emory University confronted 30 Democrats and 30 Republicans with information about Democrat John Kerry and Republican George W. Bush at variance with the research subjects' beliefs (Westen, 2007). Rather than altering their beliefs, the subjects sought and found confirmatory evidence in support of their prior beliefs and ignored or reinterpreted counter-evidence.

Moreover, brain-imaging scans of the subjects as they participated in the questionnaire part of the study showed where in the brain these **confirmation biases** were coming from and how the biases were driven by emotions (Shermer, 2006). There was little activation of the parts of the brain normally engaged during reasoning, but the neural circuits hypothesized to be involved with emotion lit up.

Said Westen, "Essentially, it appears as if partisans twirl the cognitive kaleidoscope until they get the conclusions they want, and then they get massively reinforced for it, with the elimination of negative emotional states and activation of positive ones" (Emory University, 2006).

For Westen, a Democrat, this news had important political implications. It evidenced, as he saw it, a disturbing pattern where Democratic candidates, consistently trying to counter emotional appeals by Republican counterparts with well-reasoned rebuttals, too often went down in defeat. This stood in contrast to the Republican approach, where they would tell a story that appeals to people's emotions (positive and negative) and win.

> There have been exceptions—Bill Clinton understood it, Barack Obama seemed to. But the majority of progressives are still talking about policies and ideas hoping voters will see sense and vote accordingly. Barack Obama has fallen into this trap too. Progressives should be talking in stories that people can identify with and remember.
>
> (Porter 2013)

Thinking It Through

Westen's research took place in the first decade of the twenty-first century. How have things changed, if at all, since then? What role has emotion played in more presidential campaigns? How, if at all, have recent candidates tried to tap into voters at a deep emotional level?

Westen's most powerful example of the Democrats' rhetorical ineptitude was the first debate in 2000 between George Bush and Al Gore (2007).

Bush was seen as an emotional lightweight; Gore his intellectual better by far. Thus, when Bush lent his support to a Republican-sponsored Medicare bill in Congress that would place a greater share of the financial burden on senior citizens, Gore responded with an impressive array of statistics and a rather complex story about a man named George McKinney.

GORE: If I could respond to that. Under my plan I will put Medicare in an iron-clad lockbox and prevent the money from being used for anything other than Medicare. The governor has declined to endorse that idea even though the Republican as well as Democratic leaders in Congress have endorsed it. I would be interested to see if he would say this evening he'll put Medicare in a lockbox. $100 billion comes out of Medicare just for the wealthiest 1% in the tax cut. Now here is the difference. Some people who say the word reform actually mean cuts. Under the governor's plan, if you kept the same fee for service that you have now under Medicare, your premiums would go up by between 18% and 47%, and that is the study of the Congressional plan that he's modeled his proposal on by the Medicare actuaries.

   Let me give you one quick example. There is a man here tonight named George McKinney from Milwaukee. He's 70 years old, has high blood pressure, his wife has heart trouble. They have an income of $25,000 a year. They can't pay for their prescription drugs. They're some of the ones that go to Canada regularly in order to get their prescription drugs. Under my plan, half of their costs would be paid right away. Under Governor Bush's plan, they would get not one penny for four to five years and then they would be forced to go into an HMO or to an insurance company and ask them for coverage, but there would be no limit on the premiums or the deductibles or any of the terms and conditions.

BUSH: I cannot let this go by, the old-style Washington politics, if we're going to scare you in the voting booth. Under my plan the man gets immediate help with prescription drugs. It's called Immediate Helping Hand. Instead of squabbling and finger pointing, he gets immediate help. Let me say something.

MODERATOR: Your—

GORE: They get $25,000 a year income; that makes them ineligible.

FIGURE 2.8 *Westen found that Al Gore's cool and unemotional persuasive style contrasted poorly with George Bush's persona of a nice guy with a sense of humor.*
http://news.harvard.edu/gazette/2000/10.05/01-debate.html
Reprinted with permission of Harvard Public Affairs and Communications—Photo Sales.

BUSH: Look, this is a man who has great numbers. He talks about numbers. I'm beginning to think not only did he invent the Internet, but he invented the calculator. It's fuzzy math. It's a scaring—he's trying to scare people in the voting booth.

(Westen, 2007)

As Westen saw it, Bush's line about Gore claiming to invent the calculator was the memorable moment in the debate and Gore's debate preparation set him up for it:

Bush delivered the one-liner with an affable style that stood in sharp juxtaposition to Gore's non-verbal dismissiveness of Bush's arguments (and, by extension, of his intellect). The line was unfair but Gore handed it to him, by attending to the facts and figures rather than to the *stories* Bush had been telling the public about Gore.

(Westen, 2007)

So, according to Westen (2007), George W. Bush emerged from the exchange as a nice guy with a sense of humor and Gore as an unfeeling policy wonk. With that single line about inventing the calculator, Gore's character was called into question and with it the value of his data, all of it reducible to "fuzzy math."

The larger problem of Democratic campaign rhetoric of 2000 candidate Al Gore and 2004 candidate John Kerry (who were both defeated by Republican George W. Bush) was that it had been based on an *expected utility* model of rational choice, said Westen (2007). The Democrats spent their time adding up the expected costs and benefits (or pros and cons) of alternative options and weighing in their probabilities, but that simply was not how voters made their decisions. While these Democrats placed their stock in "the marketplace of ideas," the Republicans had "a near monopoly in the marketplace of emotions." In politics, Westen concluded, "when reason and emotion collide, emotion invariably wins" (2007).

From these pithy quotes, we can conclude that Drew Westen is an expert phrase maker, but, if he is right, what inferences should we draw about persuasion generally from his research findings and subsequent theorizing? Said Michael Shermer, "The implications of the findings reach far beyond politics. A jury assessing evidence against a defendant, a CEO evaluating information about a company or a scientist weighing data in favor of a theory will undergo the same cognitive process" (2006).

Thinking It Through

Do you see Shermer's point? How do you feel about the idea that emotions trump reason and drive decisions in the courtroom, the lab, or the Fortune 500 company?

Yet Shermer (2006) also reminds us to use our capacity for reasoned skepticism. Here are some critical questions about Westen's work that we might ask:

1   Has Westen overstated his case? Doesn't Westen himself appeal to reason in criticizing Democrats' reliance on reason? Elsewhere in his book, Westen concedes the value of a combination of reason and emotion, but this does not come through in his either–or rhetoric about reason versus emotion.

2   Might humans calculate their self-interests in a manner consistent with (rational) expectancy-value theories without being fully aware of their thought processes?

3   Could it be that things such as party loyalty, which Westen counts as "emotional" identifications, also serve as relatively rational cognitive shorthands in our fast-paced, message-dense society?

PRIMING EFFECTS

Westen's work on the non-conscious activation of emotions by the use of seemingly unobtrusive cues comports with a larger body of theory and research on **priming**. Bargh (2006) defines priming as the "non-conscious activation of knowledge structures," and later (Bargh & Huang, 2009) explains that "priming" refers to the passive, subtle, and unobtrusive activation of relevant mental representations by external, environmental stimuli, such that people are not and do not become aware of the influence exerted by those stimuli. This "non-conscious activation" can be an everyday occurrence, and also be a powerful component in persuasion.

To understand "priming," we need only to turn to a research example, where psychologists at Yale University conducted an experiment to study its effects. Through a simple priming exercise, the researchers were able to alter college students' judgments about a stranger by handing them a cup of coffee. The stranger was actually a confederate of the researchers posing as a lab assistant who asked for a hand with a cup of either hot or cold coffee after arranging to be bumped into while also holding textbooks, a clipboard, and a large sheaf of papers. Those students who held a cup of iced coffee rated a hypothetical person they later read about as being much colder, less social and more selfish than did their fellow students, who had momentarily held a cup of hot coffee. Apparently they were unaware of the manipulation (Carey, 2007).

Priming is present in all aspects of life, but it should be especially familiar to students of journalism and mass communication, where priming effects have been demonstrated by researchers making seemingly slight alterations of newspaper headlines and news reports (Dillard & Pfau, 2002). In addition to mass communication scholars, social psychologists have made advances in the study of priming, suggesting from experimental research using simultaneous brain scanning that widespread social influence of little noticed objects, and not just words, along with neurological processing, produces priming effects. Says Bargh, "Nearly all forms of social representation can be primed, it seems—activated incidentally or unobtrusively in one context, to influence what comes next without the person's awareness of this influence" (2006).

For example, research has evidenced the powerful effects of singular versus plural pronouns. Said Bargh:

> One of the more extreme examples of the "power of concepts" is the well-known study by Gardner, et al. (1999) in which priming Chinese participants with many first-person singular ("I, me") pronouns caused them subsequently to endorse more Western than Asian values (e.g., individualism over collectivism), while priming North American participants with first-person plural ("we, us") pronouns caused them to endorse more Asian than Western values. Such a simple priming manipulation is sufficient to "change" (temporarily, of course) the cultural values and orientation

of Chinese and Americans. Similarly, in a study by Chen, Lee-Chai, and Bargh (2001) the same kind of pronoun priming manipulation altered how participants used their assigned power over another participant (i.e., selfishly versus altruistically). These findings seem amazing and mysterious, but I suggest this is to some extent because we find it hard to understand how a single concept such as "I" or "we" can have such dramatic influence over our behavior in these domains, especially when there is only weak at best semantic relation between prime and dependent measure.

(Bargh, 2006)

In other studies, it was found that business students were more likely to act competitively toward one another in the presence of a briefcase on a table as opposed to objects not normally associated with a business environment (Kay, et al., 2004). And a faint whiff of citrus was all it took in another study to get research subjects to tidy up more thoroughly than subjects not exposed to the smell of the cleaning liquid (Carey, 2007). Studies of this sort are similar in some ways to research on hypnotism and subliminal suggestion, except that the objects, the odors, and so on are open to awareness; what's unconscious (or "non-conscious") are the brain processes activating congruent social perceptions and behavior as a result of exposure to these stimuli. Says Carey:

The new studies reveal a subconscious brain that is far more active, purposeful and independent than previously known. Goals, whether to eat, mate or devour an iced latte, are like neural software programs that can only be run one at a time, and the unconscious is perfectly capable of running the program it chooses.

(Carey, 2007)

The recent research on priming effects underscores Westen's findings from neurological research on seemingly non-rational cognitive processing. But is it possible that we humans have evolved in such a way as to rely on careful reasoning some of the time and non-rational cognitive shorthands, including gut feelings, at other times? We turn to that question next.

TWO SYSTEMS THEORIES

Two systems theories posit that, when it comes to persuasion, there are two components operating. One part of our decision making comes from automatic, unreflective decision making; the other from our more rational and reflective self. Let's consider two of these theories in turn.

(1) Elaboration Likelihood Model: Two Routes to Persuasion

The **elaboration likelihood model (ELM)** is an attempt to integrate a vast body of persuasion theory and research about an important insight: Persuasion is a consequence not just of external cues but also of the thoughts that the persuadee generates in response to external communications (Petty & Cacioppo, 1986, 1996). Fundamental to the ELM approach is the distinction between *central* and *peripheral* routes to persuasion.

The central route involves greater elaboration of thoughts than the peripheral route. People who process information centrally ask themselves probing questions, generate additional arguments, and possibly seek new information. Those who become persuaded after mental labor of this sort tend to be resistant to counter-arguments and to remain persuaded months afterward. Attitudes formed or changed via the central route are also more easily called to mind and are more predictive of behavior.

But not everyone has the motivation or ability to engage in central processing. Indeed, none of us engage in central processing all the time. We couldn't possibly, even if we wanted to, given the demands on our psyches of the hundreds of messages to which we are exposed every day. Peripheral processing involves the use of cognitive shorthands, sometimes called **heuristics** (Chaicken, 1987). If central processing is mindful, peripheral processing is relatively mindless—but not entirely so. Sales customers traveling the peripheral route may be taken in by an attractive salesperson, the lure of a free gift, the appeal of a celebrity figure, or the number, rather than quality, of reasons presented to them. Such persuasive effects tend to be short-lived, however.

Central and peripheral processing are not mutually exclusive; much of the time, we use them in combination. Degree of involvement is a major determinant of which route we emphasize. When we truly care about a matter—for example, when we genuinely need information and know we need it—the lure of a free gift or an attractive salesperson isn't as likely to work on us. This has been demonstrated in numerous experiments.

These experiments have revealed that the degree to which a person is involved in an issue determines how much he or she thinks about the issue. For example, if you are told that a proposal to divide your university into undergraduate and graduate campuses has a good chance of being put into effect while you are enrolled, there, you are more likely to generate pro- or anti-division arguments than if you believe that university division is a long way off (Petty & Cacioppo, 1996).

Whatever your prior predispositions, they are likely to intensify if you are led to anticipate that a message is important or will have significant consequences for you. For example, if you learn that a speaker favors adding a comprehensive exam in all majors as a condition for graduation at your university, and if, like most students, you aren't particularly excited about taking such tests, then chances are that you will rehearse counter-arguments to yourself even before you hear the speaker, and thus become further entrenched in your opposition. If you're the unusual student who believes that tests of this sort are a good idea, you're likely to think of supporting arguments and thus strengthen your support in advance of hearing the speaker. If you expect that the speaker will be advocating these pre-graduation tests for use at some other university, however, it is a good bet that your opinions will moderate, rather than intensify, in advance of the speaker's presentation (Petty & Cacioppo, 1996).

High issue involvement also leads to greater attention to quality of arguments. In the study from which the foregoing example was taken, Petty and Cacioppo (1996) exposed half the students to eight powerful arguments and half to eight relatively weak ones. An example of a strong argument was that "graduate and professional schools show a preference for undergraduates who have passed a comprehensive exam." A weak argument was that "by not administering the exam, a tradition dating back to the ancient Greeks was being violated." As predicted, involved participants paid more attention to the quality of arguments, generating favorable thoughts and persuasion for the strong arguments and counter-persuasion based on internal counter-arguing for the weak arguments.

Thinking It Through

How do we decide that an argument is "weak" or "strong"? Who gets to say? What is your definition of "weak" and "strong" argumentation?

If, as a persuader, you believe you have strong arguments, you may wish to stimulate involvement by your audience. One way to do so, of course, is to make your message personally relevant to them, but you can do so as well by such simple expedients as using second-person pronouns (e.g., "*you*") as opposed to such third-person pronouns as "*one*" or "*he*" and "*she*" (Burnkrant & Unnava, 1989).

Thinking It Through

Check out your textbooks, including this one. Do they use second-person or third-person pronoun? Are WE talking to YOU? ☺

Some people enjoy thinking about a wide range of topics, whereas others have what Cacioppo and Petty (1982) call a low *need for cognition*. For example, some people report thinking "only as hard as I have to" and say that they "like tasks that require little thought once I've learned them" (Petty, et al., 1994). These people apparently are far less affected by the quality of an argument than are people with a high need for cognition (Cacioppo, et al., 1983).

People cannot always be induced to care about what should be important to them, nor is there any guarantee that the central route to persuasion will lead to an attitude change. Other things being equal, central processors are likely to generate thoughts consistent with their initial predispositions (Petty & Cacioppo, 1996). Still, if one side of an issue has demonstrably superior arguments going for it, those arguments are most likely to influence people via the central route—hence the vital importance in our society of facilitating central processing on highly consequential matters.

(2) Nudge Theory

University of Chicago economist Richard Thaler and legal scholar Cass Sunstein are social planners with a keen sense of our foibles as human beings and a strong desire to "nudge" us into making wiser decisions. Like Westen, they see us as highly prone to make a decision by gut feeling.

"I have this gut feeling that I should
have another beer."

FIGURE 2.9   *As we all know, we often depend on gut feeling in making decisions, and often with uneven results.*

Artist: Parolini, Elmer. Caralogue Ref. epa1627.

Reprinted with permission of Cartoonstock.com.

Like Bargh, Kay, and other "priming" researchers, Thaler and Sunstein recognize the importance of stimuli in our environments that can exert seemingly non-conscious influences. Moreover, even when we attempt to calculate our self-interest, we wind up basing our choices on biases of one sort or another—not just confirmation biases, but **anchoring biases, status quo biases, optimism biases,** and other rules of thumb such as **representativeness biases** that can get us and those around us into trouble. Here are some examples:

1   Anchoring biases: Anchors are starting points for our thought processes. Asked to estimate the population of a medium-sized city like Milwaukee, Wisconsin, we tend to overestimate its size if we come from a large city like Chicago and to underestimate its size if we're from a relatively small city like Green Bay. We start with what we know, or at least think we know, and we do the same in calculating how large a donation to give to a charity or how much to spend on a birthday gift for a good friend. As you may have gathered from their book's title, authors Thaler and Sunstein (2008) believe that these decisions can be "nudged." For example, when charity solicitors ask for more, they tend to get larger donations. More about nudges shortly.

2   Status quo biases: College students tend to sit in the same seats all through a semester, even without a seating chart. It's what Thaler and Sunstein (2008) call the default option, the one requiring the least effort and the least attention. Of far greater consequence, their professors tend to stay with their initial asset allocations when they invest in a retirement savings plan, however ill-suited these allocations are to changing economic times.

3   Optimism biases: While students consistently overestimate the grades they'll receive, their professors are similarly overconfident about the student evaluations they'll receive.

    Although the divorce rate in the United States has hovered around 50% for many years, rare are the bride and groom who predict that their marriage will end in divorce. Overconfidence reigns in drunken driving, in unprotected sex, in eating habits that end in obesity, and in estimates of immunity from harm. Paradoxically, we humans abhor losses of every kind but often do nothing to prevent them and a lot to bring them about.

4   Representativeness biases: These are the rules of thumb on which we form and act upon our stereotypes. Geeks can't play college football. College football stars can't be good students. Say Thaler and Sunstein, "The idea is that when asked how likely it is that A belongs to category B, people … answer by asking themselves how similar A is to their image of B" (2008).

Sunstein Sidebar

FIGURE 2.10

www.npr.org/templates/story/story.php?storyId=104803094

Cass Sunstein, who served in President Obama's Office of Information and Regulatory Affairs, recently got the chance to put what he preaches into practice. Sunstein supported an experimental program designed to prevent teenage girls from becoming pregnant. The city of Greensboro, N.C., offered teenage girls a dollar for every day that they were not pregnant, enabling the city to cut major expenses. Sunstein is a supporter of this program because it is created around the human psychology. Did this experiment work, you wonder? Yes, it was a success: Teenage pregnancy rates dropped.

This is not to say that we always act irrationally. In fact, none of the foregoing biases are wrong all of the time. But they are wrong with sufficient frequency that we would be ill-advised to ignore them.

As with the ELM model, for Thaler and Sunstein competence and motivation are important components of the reflective system (i.e., of central processing), but that reflective system is usually slower and more painstaking, and therefore tends to be in conflict with the more impulsive sides of our nature. As the airplane shakes on encountering turbulence, System I says, "We're about to die" while System II responds, "Planes are very safe." System I says, "Barking dogs are dangerous." System II says, "Barking dogs don't usually bite."

System I thinking works fine when we have mastered a skill like tennis or golf; then "too much thinking" often gets in our way. It stands in our way when we nibble on M&Ms unthinkingly while trying to lose weight and it gets us into big trouble when we use it to make big decisions, like which car to buy or which colleges to apply to. Subsequent chapters will offer further evidence on just how mindless big decisions can be.

It is good news, though, that we are "nudge-able." Oftentimes, successful nudges require little more than an application of the old James-Winans principle: "What holds attention determines action" (Stephen & Pace, 2002; Winans, 1915). The M&Ms we've been nibbling on can be removed from the table. The celery hiding in the back of the vegetable bin can be placed on the table instead. Schools can increase consumption of healthy foods in their cafeterias simply by rearranging the display of what's available: fruit at eye level, for example, chips down below. A stunning example of how nudges can work was provided at Amsterdam International where images of large black houseflies were etched onto the base of each public urinal so as to catch and hold the users' attention, remind them of their duty to direct the flow as best they can, and in this way reduce the spillage. By one estimate, accuracy improved by 80% (Sunstein, 2008).

Nudge theory comes with an ethic of persuasion to be discussed further in later chapters. Suffice it to report here that the ethic nods in two seemingly opposite directions at once: (1) toward paternalism, with its traditional assumption that papa knows best and (2) toward libertarianism, with its assumption that people should be left as free from control or coercion by others as possible. Critics have assailed it from both directions: There can be too much nudging, and there can also be not enough. But what blogger Kip Esquire calls nudge theory's "soft paternalism" also raises the question of who is doing the nudging. Says "Kip's law," "Every advocate of central planning always—*always*—envisions himself as the central planner" (Esquire, 2008).

PERSUASION AS A LEARNING PROCESS

Overheard at the Deli Counter of a Large Supermarket

Salesperson (S): Sir, how would you like to try a sample of our newest imported cheese? It's called Sagamento.

Customer (C): Well, I'm not sure. I'm not much of a cheese eater.

S: [Noncommittally] Oh? How's that?

C: Well, you see I do like some cheese, but—

S: Mhm! [Enthusiastically]

C: But I don't like the presliced stuff, and I don't enjoy slicing it myself either.

S: [Laughing] Great! This is a spread. Do you like pimentos?

C: Yes, I do.

S: [Nods vigorously] Well, Sagamento combines pimentos and Brie. It's really delicious!

C: Sounds good, but—

S: Here, try some on this cracker. It won't cost you a penny.

C: Ummm, good! I'll take a small slice.

S: This package okay?

C: Well, all right.

This customer just underwent a learning process. The three parts of that process included (1) acquiring new information, (2) getting incentives to act, and (3) making favorable associations. This process is examined in this section.

Persuasion involves information processing and takes place in stages: (a) from conception of the message to reception; (b) from reception to acceptance or yielding; and (c) from yielding to overt action (McGuire, 1985). These stages are like a chain, and the chain is no stronger than its weakest link.

Reception alone includes *exposure* to the message (stopping by the deli counter rather than walking by), *attention* to the message (actually looking and listening), *comprehension* (understanding what the salesperson had to say), and *recall* (remembering it accurately). Ironically, those people who are best able to comprehend and recall a persuasive message (the reception stage) are least likely to yield to it (to alter their judgments). The customer at the deli counter seems to have been one such hard sell.

On the other hand, people most likely to yield to a persuasive message are least likely to process it accurately (McGuire, 1968, 1985). Intelligent, self-confident, well-educated people are competent at receiving persuasive messages but also more likely to be critical of them. Their opposite numbers tend to be more gullible but also are likely to find some persuasive messages difficult to understand and remember. Hence, people of moderate intelligence tend to be most persuasible (McGuire, 1985; Rhodes & Wood, 1992).

Persuasion and Incentives

Persuasion theorists agree that incentives are essential in getting people to act, but they often disagree about why people are motivated to act. Consider once again the purchase of Sagamento cheese at the supermarket deli. One possible explanation for the successfully concluded exchange is that the customer was "trained" to buy the cheese in a manner not unlike a pigeon in a psychological learning laboratory. The process of successively shaping appropriate customer responses by use of positive reinforcements is known as **operant conditioning** (Kincheloe & Horn, 2008; Skinner, 1953). But an alternative explanation is that the sales clerk and the customer had simply reasoned together until a rational decision to purchase the Sagamento had formed in the customer's mind.

Operant conditioning works by rewarding desired behavior and withholding rewards—perhaps even using punishments—until the desired behavior is forthcoming. But in a non-interactive situation, the persuader can only help the persuadee imagine a rosier future by adoption of the recommended action and perhaps a bleaker future unless the proposal is adopted. For example, when watching late-night television, it is not uncommon to see ads for breakfast at fast-food restaurants. We're not likely to get off the sofa and drive out at that moment, and, even if we did, the breakfast would not be available. But it will be in the morning, and the restaurant wants us to imagine starting our day without having to prepare breakfast; instead, we can enjoy their food.

FIGURE 2.11   *Late night television breakfast ads are not intended to get us immediately out of the door. Instead, they help us to imagine a brighter morning where we can have a hearty breakfast without the effort of cooking it.*
Courtesy of Getty Images.

Television and film are also used to dramatize potential rewards and punishments. Using a technique known as **vicarious modeling**, O'Connor (1972) was able to reverse the lifelong patterns of social inactivity of severely withdrawn children simply by having them view a 23-minute movie. Each scene of the movie showed a child such as themselves first watching a social activity, then joining in to everyone's enjoyment (see also Bandura, 1977; Saracho & Spodek, 2007).

As a general rule, the greater the incentive, the greater the likelihood of successful persuasion. But an exception to this rule is the principle of **insufficient justification** (Brehm, et al., 2002; Wicklund & Brehm, 1976). Here is how it works:

1   Encourage half the participants in your experiment to perform an objectionable action—perhaps role-playing a position repugnant to them or writing a counter-attitudinal essay. Be sure to provide insufficient justification for performance of the act. That is, don't pay them much, have the request come from an unattractive source, or require that a good deal of effort be spent on the task.

2   Compare the attitudes of the participants given insufficient justifications for performance of the act with those given sufficient justification—for example, those paid 10 times as much, those urged to participate by an attractive source, or those required to expend minimal effort.

The predicted outcome is counter to what we might expect, but typically is confirmed by research (Preiss & Allen, 1998). Surprisingly, counter-attitudinal action under conditions of insufficient justification for the action tends to lead people to modify their attitudes. What this means is that people work to bring their attitudes into line with their actions.

This is a reversal of the ordinary process of persuasion, where messages first alter our attitudes, and then go on to subsequently change our behavior (Brock & Green, 2005; Cooper & Scher, 1994). So what is going on here? Are people more favorably inclined toward performance of the objectionable action? Might they even come to argue on behalf of positions they initially found repugnant?

The results of these studies are fairly consistent. One possible explanation for why they turn out as they do is that people tend to infer their attitudes from their actions when they have reason to believe that their actions are not the result of external causes. Another is that acting one way and feeling another under conditions of insufficient justification is cognitively dissonant and uncomfortable; we change our attitudes to get relief from the psychological pain of that dissonance. Want to know why volunteers for the unpopular war in Vietnam reported greater satisfaction with it (especially if they had been wounded in the war) than those who had been drafted? Try explaining it by way of the principle of insufficient justification.

Persuasion by Association

In some of the earliest research on animal learning, a previously neutral stimulus was paired with a stimulus known to evoke favorable or unfavorable reactions. Then the original stimulus was removed. In this way, then, the hungry dogs in Pavlov's animal laboratory learned to salivate at the sound of a bell previously linked with food. The phenomenon, known as **classical conditioning**, has widespread applications (Staats & Staats, 1963). Classical conditioning theorists have developed principles governing the acquisition of responses to new stimuli, their transfer to new situations, their extinction, and so on. One immediate application to persuasion is the menu so enticing that we can "almost taste the food." Much as we may scoff at dogs that salivate to the sounds of bells, how different are we who salivate to words?

Indeed, humans form all types of associations to objects, some conscious, others unconscious. Inferences about people are formed in this way. For example, in Tolstoy's *Anna Karenina*, Anna's husband is unimpressed with the attorney who had been recommended to him until the lawyer, without looking up from his desk, suddenly snatches a housefly in mid-air and crushes it in his hand. Inferences of this type are often spontaneous and automatic, according to Uleman and Bargh (1989), and they are by no means confined to judgments about other people. Try comparing oranges and grapefruit on the basis of the traits of sunny versus cloudy, intimate versus distant, faster versus slower, older versus younger, more intellectual versus less intellectual.

Don't think about the task very much: Just let your mind go. Students confronted with this task frequently complain that the task is meaningless. Why should "sunny" attach to orange any more than to grapefruit? Yet overwhelming numbers of respondents report viewing the orange as sunnier, more intimate, and faster; the grapefruit as older and more intellectual (Dichter & Berger, 2002). Findings of this sort are not lost on persuaders, as the discussion in Chapter 12 on analyzing product advertising indicates.

PERSUASION AS PSYCHOLOGICAL UNBALANCING AND REBALANCING

Psychological inconsistency disturbs people, enough so that they will often go to great lengths to reduce or remove it. Numerous consistency theories have been put forward by psychologists, some referred to by that name, others labeled as *balance theories*, *dissonance theories*, or *congruity theories* (Petty & Cacioppo, 1996). **Psychological balance theories** are therefore important to the study of persuasion because imbalances create motivation for attitude change, and persuaders may be quick to exploit them, even foster them. If we can create in you a feeling of conflict, you will likely work to reduce or eliminate it. And then, if we can suggest something that will supposedly resolve the imbalance, you'll be disposed to listen and consider

FIGURE 2.12   *As this Dilbert cartoon shows, people will go to great lengths to feel psychologically balanced. Therefore, imbalance creates the motivation for attitude change, opening the door for persuasion.*

Source: http://search.dilbert.com/comic/Cognitive%20Dissonance

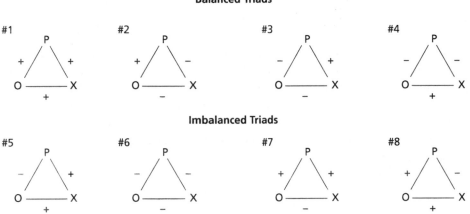

FIGURE 2.13   *Balanced and unbalanced triads.*

From *Attitudes and Persuasion: Classic and Contemporary Approaches* by Petty, R. F. and Cacioppo, J. T. Copyright © 1996 by Westview Press. Reprinted by permission of Westview Press, a member of Perseus Books, L.L.C.

it. You'll be inclined to buy our product or adopt our plan, because you'll want to do what it takes to get things back to a more even state.

One way to think about psychological inconsistency is to consider how it stems from perceived discrepancies between our attitudes toward other people, our attitudes toward objects, and the attitudes of others toward the same objects. For most of us, balanced states are preferable to imbalanced states. For example, if Wallace likes (+) pizza and Wallace likes (+) Kate, Wallace would find it psychologically consistent for Kate to like (+) pizza. But a sense of imbalance (psychological inconsistency) would be created for Wallace if Kate said she hates (−) pizza or if Kate reported liking (+) pizza but Wallace came to dislike it (−). Even discrepancies in *degree* of liking can be uncomfortable, according to some consistency theorists. For example, if Kate's favorite food was pizza and Wallace liked it only a little, this too could be discomfiting for Wallace, perhaps leading him to think less of Kate, more of pizza, or both.

A NEUROSCIENCE APPROACH TO PERSUASION

What if we could figure out what happens in the brain when someone encounters a persuasive message? A new area of research is seeking to do exactly that via the application of neuroscience principles. In particular, neuroscience researchers are using functional magnetic resonance imaging (fMRI) of the brain, applying it *while* the persuasive messages are actually being received and measuring brain activity in that moment to see the impact of the message.

Functional MRI works by detecting the changes in the brain—when a brain area is more active it consumes more oxygen, and to meet this increased demand, blood flow increases to the active area (Devlin, 2007). fMRI can therefore be used "to produce activation maps showing which parts of the brain are involved in a particular mental process" (Devlin, 2007). Using this new approach, researchers are "using imaging to examine what happens in the brain when someone hears or reads a message designed to spur them to action, whether that's to use more sunscreen, quit smoking" (Azar, 2010).

This scientific approach to studying the impact of persuasion is said to supplement and enhance traditional behavioral methods:

> Because behavioral methods can only assess one measure at a time, it has not been possible to assess the simultaneous cognitive, affective, and social processes that may occur in concert during persuasion attempts or determine the relative priority with which each contributes to effective persuasion presented.
>
> (Falk, 2010b)

To put it simply, there are limitations that come from research that depends on self-reports and surveys: memories fail, people may misunderstand and misinterpret the questions posed, etc. With a neuroscience approach, we can measure what the brain is actually doing at the moment the persuasive message is presented (Falk, 2010b). Furthermore, fMRI scans can be used in concert with traditional behavioral methods to offer even more validity to the findings.

For example, a recent study examined the impact of anti-smoking ads on smokers, and found through imaging that the rational arguments in the ads mattered more than the format of the ads, and that merely increasing ads' sensory impact probably would not improve outcomes (Wang, 2013). This has direct impact on practical planning for future ads. As the researchers note, "since sensory effects are usually more costly to produce than well thought-through arguments, our observation may be of immediate utility to producers contemplating how to allocate their budgets (Wang, 2013).

In another study, California college students were recruited to participate in an experiment where they were shown persuasive messages about the importance of using sunscreen, and on follow-up the researchers were able to establish that the students did actually use more sunscreen in the week following the experiment by surveying them. On the surface, it seemed clear that the persuasion worked. What the research demonstrated, though, was that particular areas of the brain were engaged as the persuasive slides were viewed, and that the brain's real-time response to persuasive communications complemented the self-report measures and provided additional predictive capacity (Falk, 2010a).

We only need to think for a moment to consider the potential impact of the neuroscience approach, and we can see it goes far beyond messages about smoking or sunscreen. Corporations and political campaigns, for instance, will likely become very interested in employing fMRIs as they seek to create persuasive appeals that they believe our brains cannot resist. As research advances in this area, we are truly entering a brave new world of persuasion!

SUMMARY

From its origins as a field of study, psychology has been divided between theories emphasizing similarities between humans and other animal species and theories emphasizing humans' seemingly distinctive capacity for reason. It should not be surprising, therefore, that psychological theories of persuasion should divide in similar ways. One possible explanation for the successfully concluded exchange at the supermarket deli is that the customer was conditioned to buy a package of Sagamento not unlike a pigeon in a psychological laboratory being trained to hop on one foot, then the other. But an alternative explanation is that the conversants had simply reasoned together until a rational decision to purchase the Sagamento had formed in the customer's mind. Less easy to explain in rational terms is our tendency to salivate at menus offering mouth-watering desserts.

The theorists featured in this chapter were by no means unmindful of such features of human animality as the role of emotion in persuasion, of seemingly unconscious associations, as well as of incentives for action. Westen (2007) underscores the role of non-rational factors but by his own style of argument making implicitly acknowledges the role of rationality. Priming research dramatically attests to the influence of non-rational, indeed non-conscious influences on attitudes.

Two system theories, such as Thaler and Sunstein's nudge theory (2008) and Petty and Cacioppo's ELM model (1996) credit reason with making a great deal of difference to persuadees under some conditions, but they also recognize that there are times when humans respond automatically, habitually, even unconsciously. BVA theory pictures humans as distinctive by virtue of their capacity to derive attitudes from their beliefs and values but does not exclude the roles of emotions and unreason in the formation of beliefs and values. Likewise, Fishbein and Ajzen (1975) see human action as a weighted combination of attitudes toward the behavior in question and subjective norms, the weight varying depending on how much importance is assigned in the given case to what valued others think. The product of this type of seemingly rational calculation, however, might be the decision to join a religious cult or a right-wing militia. Poorly supported group stereotypes can also influence the formation of beliefs and values, say the proponents of schema theory.

The persuadees in McGuire's (1968) theory vary between those who remain unpersuaded because they are critical of what they understand, those unlikely to be persuaded because of difficulties comprehending and recalling the message, and a middle-range group that is most persuasible because it is neither too critical to resist accepting the persuader's recommendations nor incapable of understanding them.

Again and again, reason is mixed with unreason and downright irrationality most clearly, perhaps, in theories of psychological consistency. Although the attempt to reconcile conflicting cognitions or attitudes seems rational, it can lead two friends to sever a relationship over something as trivial as the taste of pizza.

So what should the persuader make of all this? Explicit in some theories, implicit in others, are guidelines for selling an XL7 Zippo sedan, coaxing a deli customer into trying a package of Sagamento, and convincing Americans that William Clinton should have been impeached and removed from office or continued as president and been celebrated for his accomplishments.

For example, if your goal is conversion, encourage people to role-play positions counter to their existing attitudes but offer minimal incentives to try out these roles. If your goal is a fully convinced ally who will remain supportive of your position in the face of counter-arguments, appeal to the message recipient by way of the central route to persuasion. But if it's a quick sell that you're after, consider providing cognitive shorthands (these will be discussed in far more detail in Chapter 7).

These same guidelines, offered to help you achieve success when you seek to persuade someone, should also serve as warning signals to you when someone is trying to persuade you. Beware, for example, that the innocent "eyes" you give to the deli salesperson's question may land you with far more Sagamento than you really wanted. As for that sexy-looking XL7 Zippo sedan, why not? We only live once.

QUESTIONS AND PROJECTS FOR FURTHER STUDY

1   In light of your reading of this chapter, how different are humans from laboratory rats, dogs, pigeons, and so forth?

2   Share an instance from your life when you were persuaded primarily through rational choice. And then, share one where two systems theories best explained how you were persuaded to a decision.

3   How does the principle of insufficient justification represent a reversal of the ordinary process of persuasion? How might it be used to explain a soldier's reported satisfaction with service in an unpopular war? Can you think of other instances where this reversal might present itself?

4   Consider the definition of "intentions" in this chapter: They are the joint product of attitudes toward behaviors and subjective norms. Share a time in your life when you've experienced a conflict between your attitudes and subjective norms. How did you resolve it?

5   Michael Shermer offers the following comment on the research of Drew Westen: "The implications of the findings reach far beyond politics. A jury assessing evidence against a defendant, a CEO evaluating information about a company or a scientist weighing data in favor of a theory will undergo the same cognitive process." Discuss why should this be a cause for concern.

6   The best way to learn new terms is to try your hand at illustrating them with examples of your own. Try doing that with respect to the following:

   a   The relationship between beliefs, values, and attitudes.
   b   The relationship between attitudes, subjective norms, and public actions.
   c   The differences between central and peripheral processing.
   d   How the learning of an attitude (e.g., liking yogurt) might be influenced by new information, by associations, and by expected benefits.
   e   How the act of publicly expressing a commitment to a position may reinforce privately held attitudes.
   f   The differences between response reinforcement, response shaping, and response changing.
   g   How schemas influence information processing.
   h   The principle of insufficient justification.
   i   Balancing and unbalancing.

7   What is a theory? What is your theory about the relationship between logic and emotion in persuasion? How might research be used to test your theory?

EXERCISES

1   After reading this chapter, write your own statement about the role of reason and emotion in persuasion.

2   Select a controversial political or moral issue and identify the underlying beliefs, values, and attitudes on both sides of the question.

3   Select a contemporary blog that offers editorial opinion on an issue of current interest. In a group, analyze the blog through the lens of the psychological bases for persuasion that are presented in this chapter.

4   Find a journal article that incorporates one of the models or theories presented in this chapter and present its findings to the class.

5   Find a good example of social-scientific hypothesis testing or of rhetorical criticism. Recast the scientific essay in the genre of criticism or vice versa. Then, discuss what is gained or lost in each instance.

KEY TERMS

- Anchoring biases
- BVA theory
- Classical conditioning
- Confirmation biases
- Elaboration likelihood model (ELM)
- Expectancy-value theories
- Heuristics
- Insufficient justification
- Nudge theory
- Operant conditioning
- Optimism biases
- Priming
- Psychological balance theories
- Representativeness biases
- Response changing
- Response reinforcing
- Response shaping
- Status quo biases

- Subjective norms
- Theory of reasoned action
- Two systems theories
- Vicarious modeling

WEB LINKS

- Sunstein article
  www.npr.org/templates/story/story.php?storyId=104803094

- ABC article and video on nudge theory
  http://abcnews.go.com/GMA/Parenting/story?id=7594097&page=1

- Skipping class rationalizations
  http://Chainletters.net/chainletters/skipping-class-rationalizations

REFERENCES

Abelson, R. P., & Rosenberg, M. J. (1958). Symbolic psycho-logic: A model of attitudinal cognition. *Behavioral Science*, 3, 1–13.

Ajzen, I. (1991). The theory of planned behavior. *Organizational Behavior and Human Decision Processes*, 50, 179–211.

Ajzen, I., & Fishbein, M. (1980). *Understanding attitudes and predicting social behavior*. Englewood Cliffs, NJ: Prentice Hall.

Azar, B. (2010). More powerful persuasion: Today's brain-imaging research could make tomorrow's arguments even more convincing. *American Psychological Association*, 41(4), 36.

Babrow, A. S. (2001). Uncertainty, value, communication, and problematic integration. *Journal of Communication*, 51(3), 553–573.

Bandura, A. (1977). *Social learning theory*. Englewood Cliffs, NJ: Prentice Hall.

Bargh, J. A. (2006). What have we been priming all these years? On the development, mechanisms, and ecology of nonconscious social behavior. *European Journal of Social Psychology*, 36(2), 147–168.

Bargh J. A, & Huang J. Y. (2009). The selfish goal. In Moskowitz G. B., & Grant H. (eds), *The psychology of goals*. New York: Guilford, pp. 127–150.

Brehm, S. S., Kassin, S. M., & Fein, S. (2002). *Social psychology*. Boston: Houghton Mifflin.

Brock, T. C., & Green, M. C. (2005). *Persuasion: Psychological insights and perspectives*. Thousand Oaks, CA: Sage Publications.

Burnkrant, R. E., & Unnava, H. R. (1989). Self-referencing: A strategy for increasing processing of message content. *Personality and Social Psychology Bulletin*, 15, 628–638.

Cacioppo, J. T., & Petty, R. E. (1982). The need for cognition. *Journal of Personality and Social Psychology*, 42, 116–133.

Cacioppo, J. T., Petty, R. E., & Morris, K. J. (1983). Effects of need for cognition on message evaluation, recall and persuasion. *Journal of Personality and Social Psychology*, 45, 805–818.

Carey, B. (2007, July 31). Who's minding the mind? *New York Times*. Retrieved July 14, 2009, from www.nytimes.com/2007/07/31/health/psychology/31subl.html?pagewanted=1&_r=1&ref= science

Chaicken, S. (1987). The heuristic model of persuasion. In Zanna, M. P., Olson, M., & Herman, C. P. (eds), *Social influence: The Ontario Symposium* (vol. 5). Hillsdale, NJ: Lawrence Erlbaum, pp. 3–39.

Cialdini, R. B. (2009). *Influence: Science and practice* (5th ed.). Boston: Pearson.

Cooper, J., & Scher, S. J. (1994). When do our actions affect our attitudes? In Shavitt, S., & Brock, T. C. (eds), *Persuasion: Psychological insights and perspectives*. Needham Heights, MA: Allyn & Bacon.

Devlin, H. (2007). *What is functional magnetic resonance imaging (fMRI)?* Retrieved June 17, 2014, from PsychCentral: http://psychcentral.com/lib/what-is-functional-magnetic-resonance-imaging-fmri/0001056

Dichter, E., & Berger, A. A. (2002). *The strategy of desire*. Edison, NJ: Transaction Publishers.

Dillard, J. P., & Pfau, M. (2002). *The persuasion handbook: Developments in theory and practice*. Thousand Oaks, CA: Sage Publications.

Emory University (2006, January 24). *Emory study lights up the political brain*. Retrieved July 14, 2009, from http://www.emory.edu/news/Releases/Political Brain1138113163.html

Esquire, K. (2008, May 4). Kip's law sighting: Ms. Maureen Felix of West Orange, New Jersey. Message posted to http://kipesquire.powerblogs.com/kip's_law/

Falk, E. B. (2010a). Predicting persuasion-induced behavior change from the brain. *The Journal of Neuroscience, 30*(25), 8421–8424.

Falk, E. B. (2010b). The neural correlates of persuasion: A Common network across cultures and media. *Journal of Cognitive Neuroscience, 22*(11), 2447–2459.

Festinger, L. (1957). *A theory of cognitive dissonance*. Palo Alto, CA: Stanford University Press.

Fishbein, M., & Ajzen, I. (1975). *Belief, attitude, intention, and behavior*. Reading, MA: Addison-Wesley.

Gass, R., & Seiter, J. (2013). *Persuasion, social influence, and compliance gaining* (5th ed.). New York: Pearson.

Heider, F. (1958). *The psychology of interpersonal relations*. New York: John Wiley.

Iyengar, S., & McGrady, J. (2005). Mass media and political persuasion. In Brock, T., & Green, M. (eds), *Persuasion: Psychological insights and perspectives*. Thousand Oaks, CA: Sage Publications.

Kahneman, D. (2011). *Thinking, fast and slow*. New York: Farrar, Straus and Giroux.

Kay, A. C., Wheeler, S. C., Bargh, J. A., & Ross, L. (2004). The influence of mundane physical objects on situational construal and competitive behavior choice. *Organizational Behavior and Human Decision Processes, 9*(1), 83–96.

Kincheloe, J. L., & Horn, R. A. (2008). *The Praeger handbook of education and psychology*. Santa Barbara, CA: Greenwood Publishing Group.

McGee, M. (1998, August 31). Judging presidential character. *CRTNET* (listserv of the National Communication Association).

McGuire, W. (1968). Personality and susceptibility to social influence. In Borgatta, E. F., & Lambert, W. W. (eds), *Handbook of personality theory and research*. Chicago: Rand McNally.

McGuire, W. (1985). Attitudes and attitude change. In Gilbert, D., Fisk, S., & Lindzey, G. (eds), *Handbook of social psychology* (4th ed.). New York: Oxford University Press.

Miller, G. R. (1980). On being persuaded: Some basic distinctions. In Roloff, M. E., & Miller, G. R. (eds), *Persuasion: New directions in theory and research*. Beverly Hills, CA: Sage.

O'Connor, R. D. (1972). Relative efficacy of modeling, shaping, and the combined procedures for the modification of social withdrawal. *Journal of Abnormal Psychology, 79*, 327–334.

Perloff, R. M. (2003). *The dynamics of persuasion: Communication and attitudes in the 21st century*. Philadelphia: Lawrence Erlbaum Associates.

Petty, R. E., & Cacioppo, J. T. (1986). *Communication and persuasion: Central and peripheral routes to attitude change*. New York: Springer-Verlag.

Petty, R. E., & Cacioppo, J. T. (1996). *Attitudes and persuasion: Classic and contemporary approaches*. Boulder, CO: Westview. (Original work published 1981)

Petty, R. E., Cacioppo, J. T., Strathman, A. J., & Priester, J. R. (1994). To think or not to think: Exploring two routes to persuasion. In Shavitt, S., & Brock, T. C. (eds), *Persuasion: Psychological insights and perspectives*. Needham, MA: Allyn & Bacon.

Porter, J. (2013, June 13). *Jeremy Porter communications and strategy*. Retrieved June 10, 2014, from The Political Brain by Drew Westen: www.jrmyprtr.com/the-political-brain-by-drew-westen-book-review/

Preiss, R. W., & Allen, M. (1998). Performing counterattitudinal advocacy: The persuasive impact of incentives. In Allen, M., & Preiss, R. W., *Persuasion: Advances through meta-analysis*. Cresskill, NJ: Hampton.

Rhodes, N., & Wood, W. (1992). Self-esteem and intelligence affect influenceability: The mediating role of message reception. *Psychological Bulletin*, 111, 156–171.

Saracho, O. N., & Spodek, B. (2007). *Contemporary perspectives on social learning in early childhood education*. Charlotte, NC: Information Age Publishing.

Shermer, M. (2006, July). The political brain. *Scientific American*. Retrieved July 14, 2009, from www.scientificamerican.com/article.cfm?id=the-political-brain

Skinner, B. F. (1953). *Science and human behavior*. New York: Free Press.

Staats, A. W., & Staats, C. K. (1963). *Complex human behavior*. New York: Holt.

Stephen, E. G., & Pace, R. W. (2002). *Powerful leadership: How to unleash the potential in others and simplify your own life*. Upper Saddle River, NJ: FT Press.

Sunstein, C. (2008, August 27). Tricking people into doing the right thing. *Good Magazine*. Retrieved July 15, 2009, from www.good.is/post/tricking_people_into_doing_the_right_thing1/

Thaler, R. H., & Sunstein, C. R. (2008). *Nudge: Improving decisions about health, wealth, and happiness*. New Haven, CT: Yale University Press.

Uleman, J. S., & Bargh, J. A. (eds). (1989). *Unintended thought*. New York: New York University Press.

Wang, A.-L. (2013). Content matters: Neuroimaging investigation of brain and behavioral impact of televised anti-tobacco public service announcements. *The Journal of Neuroscience*, 33(17), 7420–7427.

Westen, D. (2007). *The political brain: The role of emotion in deciding the fate of the nation*. New York: PublicAffairs Publishing.

Wicklund, R. A., & Brehm, J. (1976). *Perspectives on cognitive dissonance*. Hillsdale, NJ: Lawrence Erlbaum.

Winans, J. A. (1915). *Public speaking, principles and practice*. Cambridge, MA: Harvard University Press.

CHAPTER 3

Persuasion Broadly Considered

THE GLOBALIZED RHETORICAL HYPOTHESIS

Persuasion occupies a curious place in contemporary society. Criticized by some for being too manipulative, it is assailed by others for not being manipulative enough. Some economists and political scientists minimize its importance in the overall scheme of things, believing that it is money and power that really do the talking in society. Along with such rough synonyms "rhetoric" and "propaganda," persuasion often falls short of other standards—of objectivity in science and in news reporting, for example.

Differences of opinion about the status of persuasion spill over into controversies about its scope. The question becomes this: What exactly counts as persuasion? No one doubts that paradigm cases such as when a salesperson is using rhetoric to get a customer to make a purchase is an instance of persuasion, nor do we question that advertisements are intended to persuade us. At issue is whether to limit our scope to a **restricted view** of persuasion, focused exclusively on paradigm cases such as these, or to consider a **globalized view**, which at its most extreme holds that there is no escape from rhetoric—not even in our seemingly most authentic encounters with others (Leff, 1987; Schiappa, 2001; Simons, 1990; Vitanza, 2013). Sometimes calling it "**Big Rhetoric**," the globalist view encourages us to look under the rug for evidences of non-obvious rhetorical motives, meanings, and methods. At the very least, it proposes we entertain the "hypothesis" of a rhetorical presence or dimension in all that we humans say and do (Schiappa, 2001; Simons, 1990; Vitanza, 2013). This chapter offers several core concepts and principles that entertain the **globalized rhetoric hypothesis**. This hypothesis suggests that distinctions between persuasion and "non-persuasion" tend to be overblown, and argues that there are many gray areas where persuasion is present but not explicit, and these instances are both interesting and worthy of study.

This is not to say that communication functions *only* to persuade. Instead, when considered via this globalized view, persuasion becomes a dimension of all human activity, manifested in such things as how the news is reported, in how entertainment is presented, in how "high culture" is defined, and even in what counts as the "fine arts." The globalized view of rhetoric posits that it is no accident that we tend not to notice the persuasion all around us, because habits of inattention are themselves rhetorical and culturally ingrained. Moreover, we don't notice the rhetoric in our midst because persuaders of all kinds attempt to pass themselves off as non-persuaders as a way of overcoming our defenses. That they do so is part of what makes persuasion suspect in contemporary society.

One reason we don't notice the persuasion all around us comes from a set of popular but mistaken beliefs about communication. For example, when most of us think about communication, we commonly think that each message contains a single meaning serving a single purpose. In contrast, this chapter offers a series of claims, chief among them that communication is often multi-motivated, operating on multiple levels and serving multiple functions.

Also inadequately understood are the cumulative effects of messages. When messages are repeated again and again, they can become taken for granted as "true." What happens in a society likes ours, for example, when consumers are repeatedly

---

Thinking It Through

We know a guy who is a gadget and technology junkie. Whenever a new computer, a new music system, a new cell phone, or a new gaming system is introduced and advertised, he is first in line to buy it. He spends thousands of dollars on these items, and thousands of hours programming them, transferring data, and learning how to operate these objects that he is convinced he "needs."

If you asked him, he'd tell you he is saving time and effort by staying up to date. Do you agree? How do his choices impact his daily life? And what about his finances? Most of all, how has he been persuaded to think about his place in the world?

What is your relationship with consumer goods like cell phones, clothes, shoes, or sporting equipment? How does the cumulative effect of messages impact you? Are you a thoughtful consumer of persuasive messages, or are you more prone to be susceptible to them?

bombarded with the message that their happiness depends on what they own? How are we persuaded to shape our personal lives, ones that are lived out when no one is looking, based upon the persuasive messages of a consumer society?

Of special interest here is how multiple messages and their cumulative effects shape **dominant cultural ideologies** (DCIs), the systems of beliefs and values that tend to go unquestioned in a society. Imagine, for example, how strange you would find it if someone were to question your taken-for-granted capitalistic DCI about private property by challenging the belief that the shoes you are wearing aren't your own. You'd likely respond with stunned silence, not even able to conceptualize what the comment meant. Over your lifetime, you'd been persuaded, subtly and directly, through multiple messages presented again and again, to conceive of the world in a particular fashion, and it would be very difficult to step outside of your strongly ingrained ideological framework to entertain other perspectives.

Ultimately, this chapter is about the gray areas of persuasion, those spots where persuasion is subtle and veiled. Instead of focusing on paradigm cases with black and white persuasion (like when a lawyer seeks to persuade the jury to acquit his client), it considers the aspects that are veiled, overlooked, and thereby often very powerful (like when we go to the toy store and notice how the aisles are set up to persuade

TABLE 3.1   *The Gray Areas of Persuasion*

SOME CONCEPTS	AND THEIR RELEVANCE TO THIS CHAPTER'S DISCUSSION
Communication	is defined in the *Encyclopedia of Communication Theory* as "mutually understood symbolic exchange" (Littlejohn & Foss, 2009).
Persuasion	is defined in this textbook as "human communication designed to influence the judgments and actions of others."
Restricted view of rhetoric	focuses primarily on paradigm cases of persuasion, making clear black–white distinctions between persuasion and non-persuasive communication.
Globalized view of rhetoric	argues that the distinction between persuasion and non-persuasion is overblown, suggesting that there are many gray areas where persuasion is present, but subtle and veiled.
Dominant cultural ideologies (DCIs)	are the systems of belief that tend to go unquestioned in a society. Based in culture, DCIs influence us at an individual level. Because of their unquestioned status, DCIs are of interest when considering the globalized view of rhetoric.

children about their gendered roles: Barbie dolls for girls, and trucks for boys). By way of preview, the chapter seeks to accomplish three goals. First, it will review those principles of communication upon which a discussion of the gray areas of persuasion can be built: (1) god and devil terms, and (2) five key principles of communication that are central to the topic. Second, it will discuss some of the ways in which individuals engage in the gray areas of persuasion themselves, examining such things as impression management and deception. And, third, it will apply the globalized rhetoric hypothesis, demonstrating how "big rhetoric" functions in supposedly objective areas (journalism, science, and the like) and how it works to shape ideology. The chapter concludes with a discussion of the role persuasion plays in the globalization of cultural beliefs and values, as will be evidenced in a section on "Americanization," and concludes with some brief thoughts on the ethical implications of persuasion broadly considered.

"PERSUASION" VERSUS "NON-PERSUASION"—GOD TERMS AND DEVIL TERMS

In any culture, certain symbols function as *god words* or *devil words*—symbols of approval or derision, of group identification or dis-identification (Burke, 1969a, 1969b; Weaver, 1995). This is readily apparent for such *god words* as "freedom," "democracy," and "capitalism" and for such *devil words* as "slavery," "totalitarianism," and "anarchism." Words of this kind tend to be defined, illustrated, and differentiated from their supposed opposites in ironclad ways.

Distinctions between terms tend to become rockbound and rigid, and there is no middle ground. In conventional parlance, for example, a nation is either "democratic" or "dictatorial." People decide that it cannot be neither or some of both, and the net effect of these verbal treatments is persuasive indeed. When a society strongly identifies with its *god words* and strongly "dis-identifies" with its *devil words*, its values become highly resistant to change because they are no longer even regarded as values. They become as real and as solid as the ground beneath our feet.

God terms and devil terms abound, and the reality is in the eye of the beholder. For example, the conventional wisdom holds that good friends express themselves *authentically* to us, while false friends *manipulate appearances* to persuade us and use us. Our nation exports "documentary" films abroad while our enemies distribute "propaganda" films. Our schools are said to "educate" or "acculturate," but school teachers rarely claim to "indoctrinate." Employers "orient" or "train" but never "brainwash" their employees. Poets and dramatists "express" themselves or create "art" but never purport to indulge in "mere rhetoric" or "persuasion." Situation comedies and computer games "entertain" us but do not "persuade" us. Scientists "describe," "explain," "reason," or "prove" but have little need for "persuasive appeals."

As will be argued in subsequent sections, it is not just concepts connected with government, friendship, education, work, and art that become rigidly entrenched.

Even a word like "persuasion" suffers from a similar hardening and ends up being placed solidly in the category of a devil term, standing meekly in opposition to god terms like "truth," "honesty," and "fact."

The result is that, when the words "persuasion," "propaganda," and "rhetoric" are used in references to educators, artists, scientists, and newscasters, they are frequently terms of derision. To label scientists or newscasters as "rhetorical" or as engaging in "propaganda" is to suggest that they have somehow violated principles held in high esteem by their professions. In these contexts, the terms have come to mean "deception" or "impurity," something that the language-user wishes to avoid.

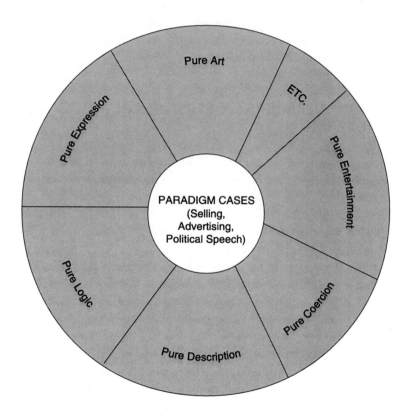

FIGURE 3.1   *Compares two views of persuasion (updated from the 1976 edition of Simons' Persuasion in Society). In a "conventional map," areas are solid or white, designating persuasion vs. non-persuasion. There is pure logic, pure expression, pure art, pure entertainment, pure description, etc. that count as "non-persuasion." And then, there are the paradigm cases of clearly identifiable persuasion, including selling, advertising, political oration, etc. In our map, all elements of the conventional map are included, but in addition, gray areas are added to show that things are not as tidy as conventional wisdom suggests.*

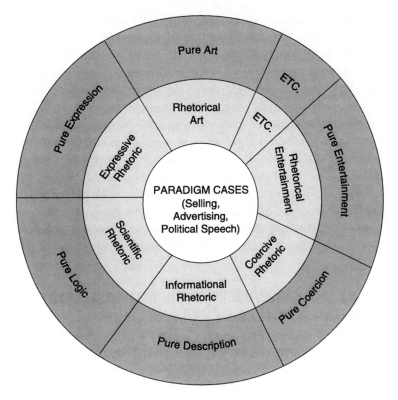

FIGURE 3.2   *Companion to Figure 3.1 (the second view of persuasion).*

In popular discourse we might say, "Her *rhetoric* stood in the way of her reason." Or, "The argument is that global warming is man-made and isn't scientific; it's liberal left *propaganda*." Or, "I wish my teacher would stick to the facts and stop trying to *persuade* us."

Only in relation to such words as "coercion," "force," and "power" does "persuasion" tend to function as a god term, and there it seems to depend on whether we are opposed to particular users of force or supportive of them. For example, we say, "I wish the demonstrators would try to persuade us rather than try to shove their program down our throats." But we also say, "I wish the President would stop talking about the economy (e.g., giving persuasive speeches) and start doing something about it (forcing change)." Generally speaking, "persuasion" is contrasted favorably with "coercion" in our culture, and we tend to associate it in relation to coercion with acts and persons we approve.

It should be clear by now that in a great many contexts "persuasion" and its near synonyms are emotionally loaded terms. There is a range of cases in which our culture regards "persuasion" neutrally or as a necessary evil, but that range is limited. Largely, the range is restricted to paradigm cases of persuasion like those cited in Chapter 1: a politician presenting a campaign speech, a trial lawyer's summation to a jury, a legislator urging passage of a bill, and so on. But even there, it should be noted, we often attach a negative attitude to the activities of such prototypical persuaders as the politician, the salesperson, the advertiser, and the public relations consultant. This may be one reason why good friends, news reporters, teachers, poets, dramatists, entertainers, scientists, etc. resist thinking of themselves as persuaders and don't want to be thought of as persuaders by others.

In contrast to such polarized thinking, a broader view of communication argues that thinking in "either–or" fashion robs us of its richness and complexity. It denies us the opportunity of glimpsing non-obvious rhetorical motives, methods, meanings, and effects in talk and symbolic action that may seem on the surface to be purely expressive, purely informative, purely aesthetic, and the like. Figures 3.1 and 3.2 present two "maps" of persuasion's domain: (1) the conventional map with a restricted view of persuasion, and (2) an expansive map with a globalized view of rhetoric. Our case for map 3.2 is developed further in the remainder of the chapter.

PREVIEW TO THE GLOBALIZED VIEW OF PERSUASION: FIVE KEY COMMUNICATION PRINCIPLES

The ability to communicate is a miracle. By way of sounds in the air, bytes on the screen, or marks on the page, we can express our love for another, share our deepest longings, display our emotions, and explain new ideas that can change the world. And, even as communication seems to us as one of the most natural of activities, there is so much happening every time we seek to share a message or communicate an idea.

The argument of this chapter builds on some rather profound yet seemingly simple communication principles; taken together, these principles provide an undergirding through which we can understand better the globalized rhetoric hypothesis. This globalized view posits that communication in general and persuasion in particular are generally more complex and sophisticated than they often appear on first glance, and, often, the most powerful persuasion is also the most subtle. In order to understand how such subtleties come into being, we need to think for a moment about the way communication functions. Our discourse is much more than a sender encoding a message that will be decoded by a receiver. In reality, it is (1) **multi-motivated**, (2) **multi-layered**, (3) **multi-dimensional**, (4) **multi-directional**, and (5) **multi-faceted**. Let us consider each of these communication principles in turn.

Principle 1 Communication Is Multi-motivated: It may operate on multiple levels and may serve multiple functions

Communication is rarely as simple as it first appears, and it can do more than one thing at once. Consider a simple example: You turn on your television news to check on the day's football scores, and you hear your local newscaster (1) "objectively" giving the report, while (2) signaling convincingly his identification with your home town football team. He's reporting, but he's also communicating that you and he are on the same side, which is a good thing for ratings and for his job security. In this instance, we see that his communication is multi-motivated: There is more going on than appears at first glance.

The same concern for combining accurate information giving with persuasion can be found in the advertisements for products we buy and in the images of ourselves that we share with others. Persuasion coexists comfortably with the transmission of data, and there is no "either–or" to separate it from non-persuasion.

Thinking It Through

Share your resume with your class, and talk about how you have managed the multi-motivated challenges you faced as you created it. You want to present yourself honestly, but you also want to persuade a potential employer to offer you an interview. How did you balance the challenge? Do your classmates and professor find your resume (1) persuasive and (2) representative of your personality and skills? Critique it together, and edit it in light of what you are learning in this class.

Other examples abound. Television docudramas combine fact and fiction in an informative, entertaining, and persuasive manner. News websites specialize in news that informs and entertains, all the while pulling in potential customers for the websites' advertisers. TV infomercials are designed to sell a product or service, but they do so in the guise of a lecture, an interview, or a product demonstration.

The same is true for academia. For example, consider textbook publishing: On the one hand, textbooks adopt a perspective. At the same time, they communicate information. And, most importantly, they work to do both simultaneously. You need only read the preface to this book and compare it with other college textbooks on "persuasion" to see this multi-motivated communication in action. Furthermore, consider college teaching. It must inform but also should be interesting, and dare we say it should even entertain? Important ethical questions might be raised about whether and under what circumstances educators should advocate (see Chapter 15), but few object to educators motivating their students. That too involves persuasion.

Principle 2 Communication Is Multi-layered: Broadly stated, "the message" includes not just what is said verbally, but also the source, medium, context, receiver, and accompanying non-verbals

In early communication models, "the message" was what was said, as transmitted by a *source* (e.g., a speaker) to a *receiver* (e.g., a listener or reader) via a *channel* or *medium* (e.g., a telephone) (Berlo, 1960). Presupposed in some models was an additional element: a *context* or *contexts*. These days we recognize that source, receiver, medium, and context can have message value in their own right and that non-verbal elements can have as much as or more influence than a message's verbal components. This holds true for communication of every kind, not just paradigm cases of persuasion.

The myth of the self-contained *message* (nearly always viewed as verbal in the early theorizing) remains useful for some purposes, as in descriptions of experiments that test for the effects of variations in message content. But the mythic content of this principle becomes self-evident once we begin to vary the other components of the transmission model while holding the verbal message constant. Consider the differences between "I love you" stated flatly or earnestly, communicated via e-mail or face-to-face, in a bar on first meeting or after 25 years of marriage. The context of the message impels and constrains the sender while providing the receiver with cues as to how the "I love you" should be interpreted. As if to underscore this point, mass communication scholar Marshall McLuhan entitled one of his books *The Medium is the Message* (McLuhan, 1967).

To be sure, not all of this has been news to persuasion scholars. It had long been known, for example, that the **ethos** of the orator—his or her personal credibility— could be no less important than the speaker's logical arguments (**logos**) and emotional appeals *(**pathos**)*, and could be the dominant factor. Almost as if he were speaking on behalf of rhetoricians, Ralph Waldo Emerson made this case when he famously proclaimed: "Who you are speaks so loudly I can't hear what you're saying." But it was the work of social psychologists that confirmed by way of experimental research the importance of perceived competence and trustworthiness while evidencing the significance of previously underestimated source factors, such as physical attractiveness. Likewise, critical studies have illustrated the importance of credibility factors outside the traditional realm of rhetoric.

For example, work in critical studies has shown that the believability of a scientific claim can be affected by the reputation of the authors, the prestige of the journal in which their work appears, the choice of language, and the number of eminent authorities they cite in support of their thesis (Latour, 1986, 1987; Sokal, 1999; Van Noorden, 2014). These too are source credibility factors. The same article on ESP would stand a greater chance of being accepted by scientists if it appeared in the *Journal of Experimental Psychology*, for example, than if it appeared in a popular magazine. Scientists may also gain credibility by the language they use. The style of scientific and academic reports is marked by the appearance of impersonal detachment and passivity, as if to convey the impression that scientific procedures and data have an "out-there" existence (Blair, et al., 1994; Gusfield, 1976; Ceccarelli, 2011).

The point here is that there is more to the message than just the words said. Context, medium, source, verbals, and non-verbals all matter, and each of the components of the transmission model can influence the meaning(s) given to the message by the receiver, who is also one of the variables. In an important sense, persuasion takes place on the message recipient's terms.

Principle 3 Communication Is Multi-dimensional: What is said can come in a variety of forms

The ancient Greeks and Romans devoted an entire division of rhetoric to *style* and another to the *delivery* of the message. Meticulous attention was given to forms of address, including figures of speech, things such as metaphor and simile (discussed in Chapter 6). They instructed orators in the arts of emphasis and de-emphasis, of abbreviation and elaboration, and of presentational styles both plain and ornate. Above all they underscored the importance of how things were said and, significantly for our purposes, many of their examples came from the arts, including poetry and drama.

Yet over time there came a hardening of the oppositions between rhetoric and the creative arts, as though oratorical eloquence, such as Lincoln's Gettysburg Address, was not aesthetic, and as though poetry and music and painting and sculpture and all the other creative arts were in no way rhetorical. "True" artists, it was said, were "above" persuasion. Their job was not to preach to us but to express their feelings aesthetically. In textbook terms, their acts of artistic creation were **consummatory**: They were ends in themselves. And in return, if we were responsive to the poet or painter or composer, we were reacting by evincing consummatory interest, but not by modifying our attitudes and behavior. The latter, which is the realm of rhetoric, was considered to be unnecessary and perhaps accidental byproducts of our experience.

FIGURE 3.3   *This sculpture, entitled* Pinocchio on a Roulette Wheel, *is created of found objects like blocks of wood and a trash can lid, and then cast in bronze and painted. It is interesting artistically in its own right, but what persuasive messages is it sending? Consider Pinocchio, whose nose grows as he tells lies, and the game of roulette, a game of chance. What multi-dimensional messages about life might sculpture James Parlin be seeking to communicate? What do we see as we look closely at the sculpture?*

Once again, though, we find ourselves drawn to the views of the ancients, sharing their opinion that it is impossible to draw hard and fast distinctions between art and rhetoric. Moreover, we are not always inclined to think less of an artist just because he or she has persuasive intent. Doing so would require, for example, that we dismiss the poetry, painting, music, and theater of protest: Picasso's *Guernica*, Springsteen's *Born in the USA*, Ibsens's *Enemy of the People*, Cameron's *Hedwig and the Angry Inch*, the satire of Jonathan Swift.

Old myths die hard, but this one seems on the verge of being laid to rest. Rhetorician Wayne Booth put the matter well many years ago:

> If all good art has no rhetorical dimension, as so many have argued, then rhetoric is left to those who will use it for the devil's purposes.... How much better it would be if we could develop an understanding of how great literature and drama does in fact work rhetorically to build and strengthen communities.
>
> (Booth, 2000)

Principle 4 Communication Is Multi-directional: Messages may have unintended effects on unintended audiences, not least of all on the message sender themselves; through communication, we also persuade ourselves

Messages are not just aimed at receivers who are "out there." In fact, they can impact us as well, in at least three ways. First, when we communicate a persuasive message to another, we often reinforce and intensify the opinion we hold; we persuade ourselves to recommit to our view. Second, we can engage in self-persuasion, using self-talk to debate positions and persuade ourselves of the best course of action. And third, we use rationalization to persuade ourselves that the course we've chosen makes sense.

First, how does it reinforce our own beliefs when we seek to persuade another? Isn't it contradictory to argue for a position to which we are not fully committed? Perhaps it's not as uncommon as it seems, as the following example will demonstrate.

It is likely that we all can remember describing to a third party a situation in which we felt we were slighted—say, for example, a situation in which we received an evaluation or a grade lower than we would have liked. If we were honest, we'd admit that a decent case could be made to justify the evaluation based on the work we'd put into the project, but, as we describe the situation to our friend, we can feel our indignation rise. As we seek to persuade our friend to accept our side of the story and to sympathize, at the same time we persuade ourselves of the rightness of our case, intensifying our own belief in our shaky cause. It is through situations such as this that we see an unintended effect of persuasion.

But it is not just in our personal lives that such reinforcing self-persuasion occurs. As Simons has argued in his rhetorical history of the period from 9/11 to the occupation of Iraq, the second Bush administration engaged in similar efforts. As it sought to persuade the American public that the war in Iraq was the appropriate policy position, it likewise persuaded itself, reinforcing the belief within the White House to stay the course. As Simons notes, the Bush administration

> increasingly fell victim to its own desperate efforts to prop up the case for war, offering, for example, overly optimistic projections for success in Iraq based on spurious statistics, denying high-level authorization for the use of torture while at the same time calling for exemptions to the Geneva Convention's strictures against torture, and [engaging in] efforts to discredit former acting ambassador to Iraq, Joseph Wilson, who had been a vociferous critic of some of the administration's earlier intelligence claims.
>
> (Simons, 2007)

The voices of the Bush administration were united as one in arguing on behalf of the war, and the efforts bolstered the team, helping them to deflect serious questions about events on the ground, torture, and intelligence, and persuading them to hold firm to their position that the war was the right course for America.

Moreover, it is not just that we reinforce our own views as we seek to persuade others. Billig (1996) has argued that we regularly persuade ourselves even when no one else is being addressed. Thinking, he says, is a form of argument and counter-argument. He notes that we learn how to think from attending to others' arguments, but he adds that we also learn from comparing the arguments we have with ourselves against our subsequent experiences (Billig, 1996).

For example, one of your authors, Jean, has an ongoing intrapersonal debate about organizing her desk. On the one hand, it takes time to go through papers, filing away the important ones and eliminating those that are unnecessary. On the other hand, to not take the time leads quickly to a disordered mess where nothing can be found. Subsequently, she has persuaded herself, most of the time, to spend the time getting organized each day, because it will provide benefits later when items can be located with ease. Right now, though, if you could see her desk as these words are being written, you'd quickly decide that she'd failed to persuade herself about the benefits of tidiness and order. Clearly, the process of intrapersonal persuasion is ongoing.

And so, we see that through interpersonal and intrapersonal communication, self-persuasion occurs. Finally, there is a third way that we persuade ourselves, and that is through Freudian defense mechanisms, most notably rationalizations. Rationalizations are the excuses and justifications we provide to ourselves after the event when we need to make judgments about the choices we've made. When we've eaten the whole container of rocky road ice cream, or avoided calling Aunt Mae for the twelfth consecutive Sunday, we need to work to persuade ourselves that our actions are not as irresponsible as we know they are. And so, we engage in rationalization: We tell ourselves that we deserve a tasty treat after a hard week, or that Aunt Mae is too busy with her bowling league on Sundays to talk to us and we don't want to intrude. We persuade ourselves that we are okay.

Self-persuasion is one of those gray areas of persuasion—fascinating to explore but not central to the purposes of this book, and so it will see little attention here. We could justify our relative inattention to self-persuasion on grounds that there isn't space enough to discuss it, but that would be a rationalization.

Principle 5 Communication Is Multi-faceted: Every utterance about substantive matters (about content) is also an interpersonal encounter that invariably projects an image of the communicator

When we communicate about a topic, at the same time we project an image of ourselves, and these image projections, in turn, "comment" on the substantive component of the message. Thus, Watzlawick, Beavin and Jackson (1967) speak of "levels" of communication. Messages at the relationship level *metacommunicate*: They communicate about communication.

Take the substantive message "Two eggs over light." A simple "please" at the end of that sentence may transform an order to a waiter into a request. Also, at the relationship level, it tells the waiter something about the customer: "See, I'm not the type of person who orders other people around."

But this is not the only thing that gets metacommunicated, because the customer also transmits relationally by way of gestures, inflections, facial expressions, timing, distance, dress, and grooming. Thus, a smile may reinforce the "please," but the customer's hurried manner may suggest that both the smile and the "please" were perfunctory. (Note in this example how communication may take place at multiple levels. Humans are forever communicating about communication, then communicating—verbally and non-verbally—about themselves.)

People cannot *not* project relational images of themselves as they communicate about substantive matters. As Paul Watzlawick famously noted, **one cannot *not* communicate** (Watzlawick, et al., 1967). Those who try to *not* present an image to others—who instead try to be natural, avoid artifice, and express their thoughts or feelings directly—often wind up communicating the image of not appearing to project an image. This is one of the many paradoxes of communication we will have to confront.

The distinction between substantive messages and image projections is important for the study of persuasion. Whether or not we are functioning as persuaders at the content level, we may still be persuading at the relationship level. In long-term relationships, as those between friends or relatives, such relational image projections are often more important than what gets said at the content level. Rarely, for example, is a dispute between romantic partners about who should make the bed in the morning only about bed-making. Images about self and other invariably get communicated, including images of power, trust, and affection.

Although substantive messages are carried largely by verbal means, messages at the relationship level are transmitted mostly by non-verbal means. These are discussed at some length in Chapter 5. Non-verbal stimuli range from clearly intentional winks to innocent-appearing blinks. But even the blinks, as we shall see, can be contrived.

APPLYING THE PRINCIPLES: GLOBALIZED RHETORIC IN PRACTICE

The foregoing communication principles provide the groundwork from which to explore some of the ways that we seek to persuade others via indirect means. In such instances, we are not engaged in obvious black and white persuasive efforts—we aren't directly setting out to advocate a position, make a sale, or change someone's mind. Nor are we presenting a speech or taking a side in a debate. Instead, we are quietly seeking to shape thinking, both our own and that of others. While not an exhaustive list, what follows examines some of the communicative devices and techniques employed in less obvious forms of persuasion: (1) **Impression Management**, (2) **Denial of Persuasive Intent**, (3) **Expression Games**, and (4) **Persuasion in the Guise of Objectivity**. Let us consider each in turn.

Technique One: Impression Management as Persuasion

Just how much of our life is occupied with concerns about the images we project is a matter of some debate. The issue is a sensitive one, particularly for those who pride themselves on their individuality or who regard manipulation of any type as intrinsically immoral (Johannesen, 1996). Nevertheless, it appears that sensitivity to how others perceive us develops early in life and leads to a rhetorical sophistication at impression management in adulthood (Dillard, et al., 2000; Rosenberg & Egbert, 2011). Psychologist Erving Goffman has linked impression management to an actor's performance in the theater, noting that we all have a sense of front stage, where the "audience" can see us, and backstage, where we are hidden away from view and able to discontinue our act (Goffman, 1959). This sense of performing front stage grows from the recognition that we communicate images of ourselves whether we want to or not; we therefore work at doing something about how we are perceived—at *promoting* an image and not just projecting one.

Yet this does not mean that most people care *only* about how others see them. Rather, their efforts at impression management may be paired with or balanced against other concerns, including some that they ordinarily view as exclusively non-rhetorical. Some of their acts may be *multi-motivated*. They may wear blue jeans, for example, because jeans are comfortable and relatively inexpensive, because they like the way they look, *and* because wearing the jeans may please or impress valued others. Similarly, they may attempt to inform or entertain or please others aesthetically *and* seek to impress them.

Sometimes, our motivations are so complex that we ourselves have great difficulty deciding which ones are primary. A former student commented in a paper

Thinking It Through

Have you ever thought about the dress code for your professors? Some dress in business attire; others come to work in jeans or worse. What impression are they communicating through their self-presentation? How does it impact the class and your learning? Do you prefer a more formal professorial style or one that is more casual? Why?

that she had "banished" makeup from her face because she did not like having to be careful of the finished product, unable to laugh, cry, or touch for fear of marring the surface. She added that she had grown ashamed of her need to fix her face and angered by the feeling that something always needed repair. But on further reflection, it occurred to her that another motive might have been operative. By not wearing makeup, she could protect her ego with the belief that, if she really wanted to, she could be a raving beauty. Not wearing makeup allowed her the security of not trying, much like the second-grader who dares not risk failure by attempting to read.

Thinking It Through

In what ways are your clothes, your dialect, your cosmetics, your manner of speaking, etc., persuasive to others or to yourself? How do you balance the various motivations you might have (i.e., feeling comfortable, displaying professionalism or attractiveness) in your daily life?

Ultimately, impression management is applied persuasion, as we seek to influence the way others perceive us. It is sometimes goal-specific: For example, it can be a means of gaining the trust we need to win over audience support for a controversial proposal. Yet much of the "imaging" we do is not designed for any particular or immediate purpose. It is more general, as we seek to persuade others to see us as we'd like to be seen. It is like putting money in the bank and trading on it when we need it. We literally bank on our images, building up an account of impressions about ourselves upon which we can depend (Rogers, 2007; Smith, 2006).

Technique Two: Denial of Persuasive Intent: "I'm Not Being Persuasive Here …"

From the recognition that we cannot *not* communicate, it is but a short step to the realization that it is often impossible *not* to function as persuaders. Persuasion is all around us. Consider, for example, a "no-frills" box of tissues. Ordinarily, boxes of tissues, like most supermarket packages, announce themselves as instances of attempted persuasion. They are attractively adorned and delicately scented. They display a brand name made famous by expensive advertising.

That is not the case with this generic package. It seeks to present a surface image of "the real" as opposed to the rhetorical. Indeed, there is something so starkly "unrhetorical" about the package that one gets the impression of extra effort expended to distance the product from its brand-name competitors by making it seem "anti-rhetorical." No name (not just the absence of a brand name) appears on the box. The lettering announcing its contents is plain black on white. We are told with rather unnecessary exactitude that its 200 2-ply tissues are 8.25 inches by 9.71 inches in size. Perhaps the packagers, while providing a reduction in price, are also trying to persuade us that the box is in some sense "virtuous" for being non-rhetorical. They would be hard-pressed, in any case, not to present a persuasive message of any type within a supermarket context.

No-frills packages are by no means the only things made to seem non-rhetorical. Persuaders often go to great lengths to persuade us that they are not persuaders, and they often succeed as persuaders by disarming us in precisely this way. "I'm not trying to advise you," says the clever parent. "I just want to ask you a question." Of course, the advice is couched as a question.

Planting a thought in a message recipient's mind can be accomplished even by declaring a rumor about an electoral candidate to be untrue—for example, a headline stating mayoral candidate "Andrew Winters *Not* Connected to Bank Embezzlement." The effects of *innuendo* in newspaper headlines have been well illustrated in studies by Wegner, Wenzlaff, Kerker and Beattie (1981) and reconsidered in computer-mediated communication by Lai and Farbrot (2014). They compared the success of headlines aimed at fictitious candidates such as Andrew Winters that took the form of questions ("Is Karen Downing Associated with a Fraudulent Charity?") with directly incriminating statements about a candidate ("Bob Talbert Linked With Mafia"). All these headlines resulted in negative perceptions of the candidate; the form that they took made little difference (Pratkanis & Aronson, 2001).

Once a thought is planted in the consciousness it can be extremely difficult to dislodge. For example, during the 2008 presidential election caps, a rumor floated suggesting that Barack Obama was a Muslim. Factcheck.org, as well as the mainstream news media, corrected the rumors, and Obama himself repeatedly discounted the falsehoods. Yet at a Republican rally only weeks before the election, a supporter of John McCain, Gayle Quinnel, went to the microphone and told the audience that "Obama is an Arab."

McCain quickly took the microphone from Quinnel and corrected her, proclaiming "No ma'am; he's a decent family man, citizen, that I just happened to have disagreements with on fundamental issues" (*Huffington Post*, 2008). But despite being corrected by McCain on national television in front of a large crowd, Quinnel retained her original opinion, as evidenced by a news interview she gave after the rally. Her candidate's words failed to persuade her, and she suggested that she planned to keep spreading the false rumor, as the transcript below shows:

Gayle Quinnell: I went to the library in Shakopee and I got lots of … three pages of information about Obama …

Adam Aigner of NBC News: So even though Senator McCain told you that he didn't feel that was true and you ought to be more respectful, you still fear that [Obama is a Muslim]?

Quinnell: I still do. Yeah. I'm not alone. I go to Burnsville, the main Republican headquarters and I do a lot of work over there. A lot of sending out mail and talking to people. And all the people agree with what I'm saying to you about Obama.

Aigner: Then do you feel there are a lot of volunteers for McCain who feel that way?

Quinnell: Yes. A lot of them. In fact I got a letter from another woman that goes over there to Burnsville and she sent me more things about Obama.

Aigner: What was on the letter?

Quinnell: Oh all kinds of bad things about him and how, I mean I have to tell you to call me. It's all bad.

Reporter: Are a lot of people getting this letter and are a lot of people believing it and is that turning a lot of votes or support for McCain?

Quinnell: Yeah I sent out 400 letters. I went to Kinkos and I got them all printed out. And I sent about 400 letters. I went in the telephone book and sent them out to people. So they can decide if they would want Obama.

(Huffington Post, 2008)

Quinnel was not alone in her beliefs. In July 2012, a Pew Research Center poll showed that 17% of registered voters polled still believed Obama was a Muslim, and that 65% of those holding that view are uncomfortable with Obama's religious stance as they understand it. Not only that, the false belief has been in place for some time: When Pew asked the same question in August 2010, 19% of polled voters said Obama was Muslim (Pew Research Center, 2012).

There is a clear reason to explain why masked persuasive intent works, and one that is well known to communication researchers—when people are forewarned that a communicator intends to persuade them, they will usually mount a psychological defense. Perhaps they'll tune out, or perhaps they'll recite counter-arguments to themselves even in advance of exposure to the communicator's message (e.g., Petty & Cacioppo, 1996). This defensive reaction is especially likely if the issue is of some importance to the persuadees or if they suspect that the communicator is up to no good—that he or she is manipulative, exploitative, and perhaps deliberately deceptive (Benoit, 1998; Fukada, 1986; Papageorgis, 1968; Petty & Cacioppo, 1977). Knowing this, persuaders often present themselves as innocent of any persuasive designs on the recipients of their messages. Rather, they try to suggest, they are just out to inform, to entertain, to ask a few questions, or perhaps to express their innermost feelings.

This happens even in television ads when, for example, a professional actor completes a commercial pitch and, with the cameras still on him, turns in obvious relief from his task to take real pleasure in consuming the product he has been advertising (Goffman, 1974). This is just one way in which the appearance of naturalness is used by advertisers in an attempt to dispel audience suspicions. Radio and TV ads have used children's voices, presumably because these seem unschooled. Street noises and other effects give the impression of interviews with unpaid respondents. False starts, filled pauses, and overlapping speech simulate actual conversation. As a general rule, we know that whatever yardsticks may be used by one person to distinguish persuasion from non-persuasion can be exploited by others to deceive their listeners or viewers about their persuasive intent, or at least to make their messages appear more authentic or more objective.

But is seeming unrehearsed a sign of non-persuasion? Sometimes it is, but often it is not. As Axelrod (2007) argues, "It is possible—and essential—to prepare for spontaneity." For example, the makers of campaign commercials often stage scenes to look unstaged, and encourage candidates to "act natural."

Consider how this might impact your life. Imagine you are at a job interview and you are asked a serious question. You respond by pausing, looking away from the interviewer, and acting as if you are in deep thought, mulling over the question and your response. Only you know what is in your mind at that moment, and you might be thinking about nothing deeper than last night's football game that you watched on television, but your goal is to persuade the interviewer that you are an intelligent and wise applicant who thinks through issues with care. Here is the question: Is looking away from the job interviewer a sign of non-persuasion? Clearly, that is not the case. Yet, by a type of perverse logic, some persuaders deliberately shift their gaze away from the job interviewer from time to time to create the appearance of being sincere, honest, and not too slick, and the wise interviewer works to sort out sincere thoughtfulness from deception. Similarly, at work and at school we have all probably encountered "yes-men" and "yes-women," those people who learn to disagree with their superiors just enough to negate the impression of being panderers while still playing up to them.

In the category of deception about persuasive intent is another, and even deeper level: deception about deception. This interesting type of interaction takes us beyond the relational level of communication to meta-meta levels (communications about relational communication and beyond). Most deceptive messages carry with them the implicit metacommunication: "This is not a deceptive message." To carry conviction, these deceptive metacommunications may require deceptive meta-metacommunications in their support. Note here that all deception is persuasion, although not all persuasion is deception.

FIGURE 3.4   *Deception about persuasive intent is often obvious to everyone but the boss!*
Artist: Myers, David. Catalogue Ref. dmy0075. Reprinted with the permission of Cartoonstock.com.

Thinking It Through

What does it mean that all deception is persuasion, although not all persuasion is deception? If you had to write an essay exam question explaining this idea, what would you say?

In situations where people are suspected of concealing or distorting information, observers heed their non-verbals rather than their apparently deliberate verbal messages. For example, if Lucy thinks her friend Tom is lying to her, she is more likely to study his face, body, or vocal cues than to listen to what he is saying. Here, the semantic content of a verbal message counts for less than its style. If she detects a furtive glance, an embarrassed hesitation, excessive blinking, or a trembling lip, Lucy may not be able to determine what Tom may be concealing, but she will assume that he is concealing something.

Embrace and Pose

FIGURE 3.5

Bill Clinton is only the second president in American history to have been impeached, and in his case, it was because he lied to a grand jury about improper sexual behavior. As might be imagined, during the period of investigation, reporters kept chasing down leads about Clinton's possible past affairs. Under a cloud of suspicion and accusation, Bill and Hillary Clinton went on vacation and "just happened" to be caught embracing on a Virgin Islands beach. Was this an assault on their privacy by an unscrupulous, paparazzi-like photographer, as the Clintons claimed? Or was this a shrewd attempt by the couple to offset bad publicity while pretending to be outraged at the press? Most newspapers bought the official White House line on the event, despite reports that the Secret Service had blocked access to the beach area from which the photo was taken but left it unprotected on the day of the kiss.

One person who voiced suspicion was Bill Kovach, then curator of the Nieman Foundation, who "wondered about whether the Clintons, as they were dancing, really believed they were alone. 'I'm skeptical how candid it was. ... I have difficulty believing that we have, in that photograph, been witness to something deep and meaningful in the relationship between the president and the first lady'" (Shogren, 1998, p. A10).

Technique Three: Deception About Persuasive Intent: Expression Games

Another gray area of communication involves expression games; these are contests over the control, and detection of control, of our expressive behaviors. As Goffman notes, in "every social situation we can find a sense in which one participant will be an observer with something to gain from assessing expressions, and another will be a subject with something to gain from manipulating this process" (Goffman, 1969). With expression games, a persuader seeks to sell a particular message via, in part, non-verbal control, while the persuadee seeks to decipher the levels of messages that are being shared and arrive at a fair judgment about the situation at hand.

Expression games can get extremely complicated, particularly in military conflicts. Rival nations may go to great lengths to stage deceptions or to conceal their detection from those who staged them. During World War II, for example, the British arranged for the Germans to discover false secrets on the corpse of a high-ranking but fictitious military officer. They constructed dummy airfields to camouflage real air war preparations and to persuade the Germans to expend effort and ammunition on false targets. Vials of chemicals were dropped behind enemy lines with instructions to German troops on how to foil their medical officers by creating the impression that they had succumbed to major diseases. When German spies were detected, they were allowed to remain in the field and generally fed innocuous or false information. Sometimes, however, they were fed true and important information as a way of persuading them and their superiors that they had not been detected.

To deceive the enemy about manipulative intent, it was often necessary to mislead the communicator of the deceptive message as well. Rather than instructing French resistance workers not to warn the Germans about Allied invasion plans, the British gave them false information, instructed them to keep it secret, and assumed that, as a matter of course, some would be captured by the Germans and would reveal the false information very credibly under torture.

Such expression games operate at a very high level, involving matters of life and death. That being said, it is not just during war time or in moments of global crisis that expression games come to the fore. At other times, they are mundane. For example, a cheating spouse may deliberately show signs of guilt or embarrassment over a relatively minor concealment, such as neglecting to mention that he shared a beer after work with a co-worker rather than coming straight home, in the hope that his wife will not investigate the more serious issue of his ongoing infidelity. In fact, expression games can even be rationalized as being in the best interest of the person being subjected to the game. For instance, your doctor can converse with you and show apparently sincere interest in your self-diagnosis about your health concerns, but then frame your problems as symptoms, that are medically manageable phenomena that the doctor has the specific expertise to treat (McLean, 2007). The key to knowing you have entered the arena of expression games is when a persuader is manipulating the communicative process for some sort of gain, and engaged in deception about persuasive intent.

Technique Four: Persuasion in the Guise of Objectivity

Impression management and deception are gray areas that are rooted in interpersonal interaction, whether they are face-to-face with our close associates or mediated contacts between ourselves and people like politicians who are seeking our votes. We shift now to another category where persuasion exists, but is veiled: persuasion in the guise of objectivity. With this, we move from interpersonal to public communication, and examine the rhetoric therein contained. Accounting statements and cost-benefit analyses, news reports, scientific articles, and reported discoveries of social problems, among other things, fall into this gray area.

Some may wish to argue that such items as those just listed are in fact forms of non-persuasion. But, employing a globalized view of persuasion, we would suggest that these messages, which are generally classified as "objective," make serious claims on the human psyche (and often for good reasons). Each purports to provide "truth" or "knowledge" of some sort, arrived at disinterestedly. Yet because the appearance of objectivity can be a powerful form of persuasion, it is wise to view claims to pure objectivity with suspicion.

News Reporting

News reports, unlike commentaries and editorials, are supposed to be devoid of persuasion; they are supposedly objective, and sometimes they approach that ideal. But journalists are aware that their choice of what news to cover and what not to cover, as well as their decisions about how to cover it, has enormous consequences (Bennett & Entman, 2000). Decisions of this kind have **priming**, **agenda-setting** and **framing** effects.

Media priming is the process in which the media attend to some issues and not others, and thereby alter the standards by which people evaluate situations (Severin & Tankard, 1997). Agenda setting involves the order of importance given in the media to issues, and the subsequent order of significance attached to the same issues by the public and politicians (McQuail, 1994). And framing (to be discussed in Chapter 6) structures our perspectives on an issue: The media focus attention on certain events and then place them within a field of meaning (Iyengar, 1991; Jamieson & Cappella, 2008; Johnson-Cartee, 2005; Kurtz, 1998; Pan & Kosicki, 1993; Price, et al., 1997). Let us examine each in order.

First, there is media priming, which influences our judgments of where to best focus our attention. For example, when Fox News's or MSNBC's reporters lead off a program with a focus on a politician's lifestyle instead of the politician's policy positions, that influences us to see the lifestyle issues as better or more relevant areas of focus than policy concerns (Jamieson & Cappella, 2008). This influences not just our evaluations: It also has an indirect effect on policy making. For example, in the ongoing controversies over national security versus the protection of civil liberties, reminders in the news of the devastation caused by the 9/11 terrorist attacks primes citizens and policy makers to focus on national security; on the other hand, stories about brave whistleblowers who share secret documents so that citizens can become informed of what their government is actually doing serve to prime us for a focus on civil liberties.

A second way "objective" news reporting can become persuasive is through *agenda setting*. In its classic formulation, agenda setting doesn't tell us what to think; instead, it tells us what to think about. Price, Tewkesbury and Powers (1997) view agenda setting as a kind of media priming that is concerned with presenting to us what is important (or unimportant) among the many issues that might come our way.

The third way supposedly objective reporting becomes rhetorical is through *framing*. The basic idea of framing is that the media focus attention on certain events and then present those events in a way that gives them meaning. Framing is unavoidable, and even taught in schools of journalism. For instance, introductory textbooks on news reporting suggest that there can be many "right" ways to present the same issue or event. A murder trial can be framed and viewed: (a) through the eyes of the victim reliving the crime; (b) through the anguish of the suspect's family; (c) through the talk in the neighborhood where the crime was committed; (d) by reading the face and questions of the jurors; (e) by capturing the drama of the dueling lawyers; (f) from the perspective of those who analyze evidence under a microscope; (g) from the carnival of media coverage.

Given that every news story is enclosed in a frame, some theorists have argued that objectivity in news reporting is virtually impossible. Storytelling of every kind requires selection. Not everything can be said about an object, and not everything can be given equal emphasis. Thus, selections deflect even as they reflect; in calling attention to some things, they prompt inattention to others (Burke, 1966).

Others object that viewing framing as merely rhetorical misses the point of journalistic framing at its most consequential—when it identifies the most relevant competing news frames in a story and then determines which of them best captures its essence (e.g., Kent, 2006; Mander, 1999) When Hong Kong was turned over to China in 1997, was this the result of a "handover" or a "takeover" (Lee, et al., 2001)? Was Serbian mistreatment of Bosnian Muslims such as to warrant the label of "genocide," or were most journalists right in framing the story as one of "shared blame" (Kent, 2006)? Was Edward Snowden, who gave American government documents to *The Guardian*, better labelled a "whistleblower," which is defined by the Associated Press as "a person who exposes wrongdoing"? Or was he really just a "leaker," which the AP defines as "a person who *simply asserts* that what he has uncovered is illegal or immoral"? (Press, 2013, italics ours). What comment does it make about the value of American privacy when most journalists and editors end up labeling him a "leaker"? (Press, 2013). Such issues are vitally important, and reporters honestly struggle to try to understand and then report what "really happened" in these cases.

Even as reporters take great effort to frame stories appropriately, the process of selection-deflection is by no means random. Institutional pressures force editors and reporters to play up the dramatic, the sensational, and to play down news that doesn't sell newspapers or ad time. What's more, candidates, campaign managers, celebrities, and other professional persuaders attempt to *spin* the news that will be reported, so as to influence, for example, reports on who "won" last night's televised campaign debate. And so, when we put it all together, it seems clear that journalism's claims of objectivity are more guise than reality.

*But then, there's always **truthiness** …*

The increased pressure to present news in ways that generate media profit has come under strong critique and has led to successful popular programs like *The Daily Show with Jon Stewart* that openly proclaim they are presenting "the fake news." Under the comic frame of tongue-in-cheek staunch objectivity, these programs offer biting social commentary of contemporary news practices. Through meta-communicative reversal upon reversal, Stewart critiques what passes for objectivity in the news, while Stephen Colbert proclaimed that "truthiness" is now the standard by which news is presented, consumed, and judged. Within a comic *frame*, they *set an agenda* of critique and *prime* us to approach corporate American journalistic practices with a critical eye. Playing on our doubts about the claims of neutrality in the news, they persuades us to consume news with care and urge us to be more analytical persuadees. Not only that, but they do so with success, as displayed by a study from the Annenberg Public Policy Center showing that, in particular, Colbert is doing a better job of teaching people about campaign finance than CNN, MSNBC, and Fox News (*Study: Stephen Colbert*, 2014).

Scientific Writing

Scientific writing, like news journalism, purports to give information rather than persuade, but the trappings of science can be used as tools of advertising and public relations (Jackall, 1995; Williams & Gajevic, 2013). Not uncommonly, for example, industries set up seemingly disinterested scientific institutes whose professed purpose is to serve the public good but whose real aim is to discredit their opponents' charges that the industry's product, whether it be cosmetics, explosives, paints, leathers, furs, or medicines, is a threat to the public good.

As the Union of Concerned Scientists reports,

Corporations that stand to lose from the results of independent scientific inquiry have gone to great lengths to manipulate and control science and scientists by:

- **Terminating and suppressing research**. Companies have controlled the dissemination of scientific information by ending or withholding results of research that they sponsor that would threaten their bottom line.
- **Intimidating or coercing scientists**. Corporations bury scientific information by harassing scientists and their institutions into silence. Scientists have been

threatened with litigation and the loss of their jobs, have had their research defunded, have been refused promotion or tenure, and have been transferred to non-research positions, leading to self-censorship and changes in research direction.

- **Manipulating study designs and research protocols.** Corporations have employed flawed methodologies in testing and research—such as by changing the questions scientists are asking—that are biased toward predetermined results.
- **Ghostwriting scientific articles.** Corporations corrupt the integrity of scientific journals by planting ghostwritten articles about their products. Rather than submitting articles directly, companies recruit scientists or contract with research organizations to publish articles that obscure the sponsors' involvement.
- **Publication bias.** Corporations selectively publish positive results while underreporting negative results. While not directly corrupting science itself, these publishing and reporting biases skew the body of evidence.

(Union of Concerned Scientists, 2012)

Of course, science at its most objective is a far cry from such crass corporate manipulation and attempted public persuasion. But to speak of the scientific report as fully objective is to ignore too much evidence to the contrary, and the tradition of writing persuasively in the sciences has a long and rich history. For example, in a series of articles, John A. Campbell (1970, 1974, 1975, 1986) showed that Charles Darwin relied on much more than simply "presenting the facts" to persuade his readers to accept his evolutionary theory.

Darwin began his work *On the Origin of Species by Means of Natural Selection* by telling the reader how, after returning from his voyage on the *Beagle*, he spent five years "patiently accumulating and reflecting on all sorts of facts" before beginning to develop his theory. This was consistent with the prevailing approach to science at the time, where it was understood that generalizations were developed only after gathering lots of data.

The problem here is that Darwin's notebooks don't match his rhetoric. In fact, they show that he began to engage in highly speculative theorizing while still on the *Beagle*. A few years after the publication of the *Origin*, in a letter to a younger scientist, Darwin recommended that one should "let theory guide your observations," but he also suggested minimizing the role of theory in publication, because too much theory leads others to doubt one's observations (Campbell, 1975). Clearly, Darwin realized that the most persuasive approach to presenting scientific work to the public didn't need to be a description of the actual processes the scientist went through in developing his or her ideas.

In the *Origin*, Darwin also made abundant use of the language of natural theology, language with which his readers would have been familiar. Natural theology relies on the complexity and design found in nature as offering scientific support for the existence of an intelligent deity. Darwin, however, cleverly turned the argument on its head.

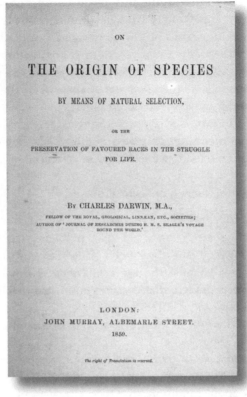

FIGURE 3.6   *Charles Darwin realized he needed to employ persuasion to help his nineteenth-century audience consider what would certainly be seen as a radical theory of the origin of life.*
www.btinternet.com/~glynhughes/squashed/darwin.jpg Reprinted with permission of Hughes Design.

Animal breeders, he noted, are very effective at producing breeds that are useful or interesting to humans; they do this through selective breeding. And natural selection, the process by which the most fit organisms of a species survive and reproduce in nature, must be infinitely more effective than that, because natural selection works continuously on characteristics that humans might not even be aware of. With this artful argument, the intelligence of the deity was subtly replaced by the power of natural selection, and not only that—the persuasive language of natural theology was turned to support Darwin's theory of evolution.

Even if we were to assume that scientific inquiry is simply a matter of fact gathering and logical inference, it would be hard to deny persuasion's role in scientific reporting. To cite a contemporary example, the AIDS researcher who prepares a scientific report for an AIDS research conference must decide how to title the report, how to frame the issues, how to write the report stylistically, how to make interpretations of the research data appear convincing, and how to deliver the report orally and visually with maximum clarity and believability. Even so seemingly straightforward a process as citing past work on the AIDS researcher's topic becomes an opportunity to impress research foundations with the importance of the work, to forge alliances with respected colleagues, and to attack rivals (Latour, 1987). Bruno Latour likens the citational stratagems of the clever researcher to the moves and counter-moves of an expert billiard player.

In sum, we have seen in this brief overview the presence of rhetoric in the way experiments are described, findings are presented, research is funded, and more. Even in science, we see the guise of objectivity.

Societal Naming of Social Problems

Another gray area of persuasion under the guise of objectivity arises around the topic of the societal naming of social problems. The question is this: Do societies discover social problems objectively, or do they construct them rhetorically? Seventy years ago, for example, the terms *child abuse, date rape*, and *sexual harassment* did not exist. Clearly, though, that does not mean that the problems designated by the terms also did not exist, right?

There are at least three schools of thought on the matter:

1   *Mundane realists* argue that problems such as child abuse are every bit as real as skin cancer or infant mortality; putting a name to them only assists in talking about conditions that have long existed.

2   *Strict constructionists* argue that language is constitutive of reality, rather than merely reflective of it. Who we are as individuals and as groups, how we understand ourselves to be joined together in time and space, and what we consider to be problems or non-problems all depend on the language we select to "create," as it were, the worlds we inhabit. A strict constructionist would say, for example, that in cultures past "infant mortality" was not labeled as a problem because it was seen rather as a routine occurrence.

3   *Contextual constructionists* argue that social problems are neither entirely discovered nor entirely fabricated. They point to widely varying statistics on alleged problems (Best, 2004, 2008) such as child abuse to show that these problems do not simply exist "out there." For example, estimates of the magnitude of child abuse in the United States have ranged from the minuscule to the all-inclusive, depending on how the term was defined. At the same time, contextual constructionists reject the "anti-realism" of their strict constructionist colleagues. Child abuse may be a social construction, they concede, but the problem would not have been categorized, named, quantified, and the like, had there not been a basis in fact for multiple injuries to children, documented by pediatric radiologists and shown by investigators to be the work of parents or

parent substitutes. Like strict constructionists, contextual constructionists assign persuasion a significant role in explaining what estimates of the nature and magnitude of a social problem any given society takes to be real. Still, they believe that some estimates are better than others (Best, 1989; Hacking, 1991; Miller & Holstein, 1993).

We do not seek to tell you where you should come down on these three schools of thought, but we do note that all three agree that social problems come to be recognized as such only after we have *named* them. Prior to being named, these problems likely existed in the world, but they were not seen as "social problems" until we identified them as such and persuaded others to agree with our identification. Once they have been named, categorized, ranked, and identified, they are transformed.

HOW MULTIPLE MESSAGES SHAPE IDEOLOGIES

As this chapter has attempted to demonstrate, defining the boundaries of persuasion's domain is not as easy a task as many might think. There are gray areas, things that sometimes are persuasive and other times are not. And then, there are cases where persuasion may seem pronounced on one day but muted the next. There are things that are thought to be objective, but in fact are infused with persuasive elements. To confuse things even more, we are confronted with the fact that people are complex: Their motives for communicating are varied and sometimes they do not even know how much persuasion exists in their discourse. One communicative act may stem from many motivations, operate on many levels, and have many effects via multiple forms of influence, some of them unintended. And now, returning to where this chapter began, it is worth considering how these gray areas and multiple messages create cumulative effects and shape our dominant cultural ideologies (DCIs), those systems of belief and value that generally go unquestioned.

We don't have to look to lofty tomes to consider such issues. Any given episode of a television program will do. Television shows often have unintended effects, including ideological effects. When young adults turn on the Disney Channel to view its wholesome fare, they are being persuaded to see the world in a particular fashion: perfectly manicured homes that are filled with attractive families that are always able to resolve issues by the end of the program. The children are creative, clean, and respectful; they value education, sports, and the arts. The parents are wise, attractive, and involved, and finances are never an issue as the children are always perfectly dressed in the latest teen fashions. Watching Disney's programming, elementary school children and their junior high siblings are persuaded to embrace Disney's capitalistic/democratic/consumeristic ideology and imitate it.

The same is true of adult contemporary television programming such as a crime drama like *CSI* or an animated comedy program like *South Park*. From programs like

FIGURE 3.7   *When young adults turn on the Disney Channel to view its wholesome fare, they are being persuaded to see the world in a particular fashion: perfect American homes that are filled with attractive teens and fun-loving families that are always able to resolve issues by the end of the program.*

CSI, we are persuaded to believe that science provides rapid speed answers, even to vicious murders. From *South Park*, we hear animated children saying the must vulgar and interesting things, and our American ideology that places high value on freedom of speech is reinforced.

If any given television or advertising segment may affect a viewer's ideology, what are the effects of a daily dose of television? The difference that multiple messages can make is well illustrated by product advertising. An ad may be both *informational* and *transformational*—that is, it tells you about a product and, if effective, makes a customer out of you (Leiss, et al., 2005). But the combined effect of multiple advertisements is truly transformational. As consumers, we generally assume that the arguments and slogans and pictures used to advocate for a product are merely means to an end. We fail to recognize that these means are being reinforced even as the product is being promoted.

Consider television ads for medicinal products such as pain relievers and nutritional supplements. An underlying and oft-repeated premise of these advertisements is this: Got a problem? Take a pill! In fact, got a problem you didn't know you had? Let us tell you about it and give you a pill for that as well. We watch the ads and hope that the pharmaceutical advertisers are not deliberately striving to turn America into a nation of pill poppers. We know that no single advertisement has that effect, but still, if we reflect for a moment, we realize that the combined effect of these multiple messages creates an attitude, an ideology, and one that impacts how we conceive of our health, our bodies, and our lives.

These messages combine with yet others—for one-stop shopping, for dinner in a box, or even education in a box—that mold and reinforce the values not just of material acquisition but of a certain type of acquisition: of purchased passivity, of being served, of life made unthinkingly, unblinkingly easy, where every problem has a quick and easy solution: All we need to do is make the purchase (Barber, 2007). A thousand or more ads for "a sexier you" (or some such slogan) sell not just the hair rinse or cologne or breath freshener but also the assumption—learned from childhood on—that sexuality needs to be purchased; what we bring to relationships on our own is not good enough.

Thinking It Through

Have you seen the many ads for earning a college degree online? Usually, they have a person in her pajamas proclaiming that she can do her course work whenever she wants to, without leaving her bedroom.

While these degrees may in fact provide excellent educations, consider another question: how does the rhetoric of "college in your pajamas" change the definition of a college degree? What do you think?

This is not to say that product advertising's version of the good life is monolithic and unchanging. Together with news and entertainment programming over the Internet or via traditional media outlets, advertising reflects currents in the culture—some of them conflicting—even as it molds and reinforces them. Some components of the culture's dominant ideology have remained in place through the years—for example, its celebration of "family values." Others have changed to reflect America's increased diversity, including a greater diversity of family lifestyles. But either way, the multiple messages work together to create, sustain, and reinforce our cultural ideology, portraying "appropriate" and "inappropriate" social relations, defining norms and conventions, providing "common sense" understandings, and articulating our central preoccupations and concerns. In so doing, they confirm, reinforce, and often help create our sense of ourselves and our place in the world (Fiske, 1987). Together with other mass media of communication, they are remaking the world itself.

PERSUASION AND IDEOLOGY: AMERICANIZATION

When we think about what it means to be "American," what images comes to mind? Likely, American *things* enter our thoughts: July 4 celebrations, the Statue of Liberty, hamburgers, a favorite professional football team, denim jeans, pick-up trucks, rock music, and the like. But also, *ideas* that Americans value also arise: democracy, individualism, "freedom," the Christian religion, capitalism, and more. This raises some questions: What are "American values"? Are these values superior to other nations' values? Who gets included, and who gets excluded when we consider American values? What does it mean to be "American"? And how were we taught, or should we say *persuaded*, to learn, accept, and internalize these values? Important questions all.

British Prime Minister David Cameron wrote an editorial recently where he worked to engage these questions from his nation's perspective. His felt the need to do so because of England's "Trojan Horse Controversy," where six Birmingham schools were placed under "special measures" after concerns were raised about how the schools had been taken over and "Islamised" by Muslim hardliners (Gilligan, 2014). Reported issues involved forced gender segregation with girls put at the back of the class, an Arabic teacher leading nine- and 10-year-old children in anti-Christian chanting, curriculum restricted to "comply with a conservative Islamic teaching", the end of Christmas parties and celebrations, and more (Gilligan, 2014). The affected schools are populated primarily with devout Muslim families, mostly emigrants from Pakistan, which further complicated the issues. Cameron decided he needed to speak out on the issue, and set out to define what it means to be British, and why British values matter.

Cameron began by providing his list of British (and Western) *values*: "a belief in freedom, tolerance of others, accepting personal and social responsibility, respecting and upholding the rule of law—are the things we should try to live by every day." He then went on to link these values to British *things*, as he proclaimed that for him, "they're as British as the Union flag, as football, as fish and chips." Finally, he spoke of how these values would be promoted in England, proclaiming that "it isn't enough simply to respect these values in schools—we're saying that teachers should actively promote them. They're not optional; they're the core of what it is to live in Britain" (Cameron, 2014).

Responses to Cameron varied, some supportive, some opposed, as might be expected when a national leader proclaims a once-and-for-all definition of what a person must believe to be considered a member of that nation. For those who agreed with the Prime Minister, there was a sense of relief that someone had finally spoken out and said what needed to be said, political correctness be damned. Those in opposition presented strong objections to being labeled as "other" than British because they did not share Cameron's definition of national identity; they saw British-ness as a much broader and inclusive category than Cameron's words implied.

What especially rankled his opponents was that built into Cameron's presentation was a sense of "either/or", where people were fully British by his standards, or were something other. Most distressing was that the "otherness" too often implied a different ethnicity, skin color, or religion. British Muslim, Myriam Francois-Cerrah, argued that

> Cameron's op-ed is a clear means of expressing the dominance of white, secular liberal Britons, and articulating the commensurate respect of that supremacy from those deemed subordinate, in this case, minorities and specifically Muslims from some of the most impoverished areas in the country.
>
> (2014)

For Francious-Cerrah, Prime Minister David Cameron came off as clearly insensitive to value differences.

As we can see by considering the challenges presented by the Trojan Horse Controversy, we are undergoing an ideological revolution of immense proportions (e.g., Barber, 1996; Nye, 2004; Combs & Nimmo, 1993; Friedman, 2007; Lakoff, 1997). In the United States and much of the rest of the world, traditional cultural and moral values espoused by the white Protestant majority are being called into question. Meanwhile, the world has engaged in a celebration of consumerism, of materialism, and of what some critics lament as unbridled narcissism (Barber, 2007). This revolution in lifestyles and values has a distinctively American flavor, creating imitations and adaptations of American popular culture in Tokyo and London, Shanghai and Buenos Aires, Moscow and Tel Aviv.

Labeled "supercapitalism" (Reich, 2007), an element of American "soft power" (Nye, 2004), "McWorld" (Barber, 1996), a "clash of civilizations" (Huntington, 1996), or simply "Americanization," the new consumeristic and interconnected global economy has provided both positive and negative consequences as it has shifted power away from workers and onto consumers and investors. It has also created pockets of backlash as people seek to preserve their cultural values and identities: the case of the Trojan Horse Controversy presents clearly a backlash to Western values as a British Muslim community seeks to inculcate the values it believes are important into its schoolchildren.

Therefore, non-Western communities and Westerners alike recognize and worry about the serious negative social consequences of Americanization: "These include widening inequality as most gains from economic growth go to the very top, reduced job security, instability of or loss of community, environmental degradation, violation of human rights abroad, and a plethora of products and services pandering to our basest desires" (Reich, 2007). American capitalist ideology clearly has a downside, and there are good counter-arguments to challenge it. Arguably, America is way behind China, Japan and others when it comes to students' academic rankings, falling behind cultures that place a premium value on education, harmony, and cooperation. Ignoring these values and bowing instead to the currently dominant

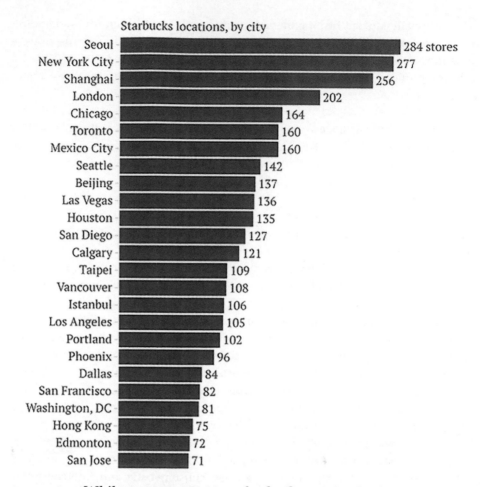

Starbucks locations, by city

City	Stores
Seoul	284 stores
New York City	277
Shanghai	256
London	202
Chicago	164
Toronto	160
Mexico City	160
Seattle	142
Beijing	137
Las Vegas	136
Houston	135
San Diego	127
Calgary	121
Taipei	109
Vancouver	108
Istanbul	106
Los Angeles	105
Portland	102
Phoenix	96
Dallas	84
San Francisco	82
Washington, DC	81
Hong Kong	75
Edmonton	72
San Jose	71

FIGURE 3.8   *While we expect to never be far from a Starbucks when visiting Seattle, we should also notice that a 2014 report shows that six of the top ten cities for Starbucks are outside the United States.*

Source: http://chicago.cbslocal.
com/2014/05/28/a-starbucks-on-every-street-corner-in-downtown-chicago-its-pretty-close/

American entertainment media with its outlaw culture, its ridicule of study and self-discipline, and its tendency toward unrestrained narcissism weakens us all.

That being said, American corporate and capitalistic ideology is powerfully persuasive, and what has been said thus far about multiple messages having unintended (or only partially intended) ideological effects goes a long way toward explaining the Americanization of the world's cultures. Mattel's Barbie doll, which in 2013 continued to hold first place as the number one toy for girls according to the National Retail Federation, is but one of a number of internationally marketed and merchandized symbols of America that participate in the making of Americanization.

A recent special issue of the *New York Times Magazine* showed Pepsi drinkers in New Delhi; the Nike insignia over a store in Beijing; the Lucky Strikes logo in Yangon, Myanmar (Burma); the familiar symbols of Burger King in Germany and of IBM in Ho Chi Minh City, Vietnam; and signs for Marlboro in Tripoli, Libya, and for Texas Fried Chicken in Cairo. McWorld is a little girl clutching her very own Barbie doll in that Burger King in Germany or Texas Fried Chicken in Cairo, and consuming not just the products to be had but also their functions as symbols of things and lifestyles American.

What the world thinks it wants, what it fantasizes it wants, is increasingly influenced by Hollywood versions of the good life. In recent surveys of top-grossing films, considering worldwide grosses, every one of the 100 top-grossing movies of all time were American (*All Time Box Office*, 2014).

Americanization is MTV, CNN, the NBA play-offs, the NFL SuperBowl, and *Big Bang Theory*, *Grey's Anatomy*, and *American Idol* in syndication—just to mention some of the TV fare that reaches across the globe. It is the names and logos and trademarks of Nike, Marlboro, Levi, Apple, Microsoft, Coca-Cola, KFC, and a hundred other familiar brands—together constituting a new international language. It is theme parks such as Euro-Disney, located just kilometers away from what used to be the cultural capital of Europe. Americanization is American-style malls featuring American products: These, says Barber, have become theme parks in their own right

FIGURE 3.9 *Evidence of McWorld can be found globally, and a great example of the trend is the entry of McDonald's restaurant.*

Source: http://image.minyanville.com/assets/dailyfeed/uploadimage/070611/mcd_china_1309983541.jpg

(2007). Above all, Americanization is the combined effects of these component parts on the hearts and minds of the world's citizens, particularly its young people. These effects, suggests Barber (2007), are synergistic.

Synergy in persuasion is most clearly illustrated by mammoth "infotainment" corporations such as Disney seeing to it that all their component parts—Disney Studios, Disney theme parks, Disney stores, the Disney Channel, ABC television, ESPN, and A&E—are coordinated to produce maximum profits for such blockbuster hits as *Lion King*, the movie; *Lion King*, the video; and *Lion King*, the Broadway play.

But synergy is also at work at a broader, ideological level in the combined effects of American films, food chains, sitcoms, and the rest inviting the world to buy American, think American, and fantasize American. Most obviously, that ideology is one of consumerism, with its attendant cry of "gimme, gimme, gimme" (Barber, 2007). Along with consumerism has come a devaluation of class consciousness; there are no workers in an Americanized world, only consumers. But this is not all. Hollywood and Madison Avenue also shape values of secularism, passivity, vicariousness, and an accelerated pace of life. American television and movies celebrate youth, disdain authority, flirt with violence, and are bathed in sex. It is little wonder that traditional cultures, such as some members of Britain's Muslim population, find such worldviews threatening.

But, you might be wondering, why is there this extended discussion of Americanization in a textbook on persuasion? The answer is simple: clearly, Americanization's persuasive force shapes us all. It affects what we buy, how we work, how we live, and even what we think we need. It is an ideological formation of great persuasive force, not just for Americans but for humans across the globe. When we consider the synergistic persuasion of our supercapitalistic Americanized world, one thing seems certain: The clearly intentional, single-track, effects-limited messages that come to mind when speaking of paradigm cases of persuasion are not the only influences, nor necessarily the most significant influences, on the world's judgments and actions.

SUMMARY

The purpose of this chapter has been to use the globalized rhetoric hypothesis to expand what might be called the "conventional view" of persuasion. This conventional view is the one that confines "persuasion" to paradigm cases: it is only about political speeches, product advertisements, sales pitches, public relations, newspaper editorials, and the like. Further, the conventional view tends to draw black and white divisions between what is "persuasion" and what is not. By that definition, this textbook is not persuasive; to quote the very old television show *Dragnet*, it is "just the facts and nothing but the facts."

But as the globalized rhetorical hypothesis suggests, there are instances of communication where the intent to persuade is not so clear-cut or where persuasive intent is commingled with other motives for communicating; those who adopt the rhetorical hypothesis are generally convinced that, when it comes to persuasion, there is a lot of "gray area" mixed in with the black and white.

Therefore, even though the "gray area" cases explored in this chapter fall outside what might be called the "core" of persuasion, they are still crucially important. Appreciating their influence on society requires a perspective on any given communicative act as multi-motivated and multi-leveled. What's more, communication often has persuasive effects beyond those that were clearly intended. Moreover, in some contexts, persuasion is simply unavoidable.

Table 3.1 charts these gray areas, identifying four that have been the focus of the chapter. What constitutes the gray areas of persuasion are those that are masked as—or mixed with—information giving, scientific demonstration, entertainment, and seemingly authentic, spontaneous expression.

A caveat here is needed, though: not all guises are deliberate disguises, intended to deceive and manipulate. The professions of science and journalism make legitimate claims on our attention, even as we may find evidence of persuasion rather than "pure" logic or "pure" description. Entertainment does not cease to amuse us or interest us just because it also persuades us. The generic box of tissues that attracts us by its "realness" still contains objects that we can really use. The blue jeans that promote an image of unadorned authenticity also cover the lower half of the body— comfortably, durably, and relatively inexpensively.

Although Part II of this book focuses on those core paradigm cases of persuasion, the perspective on communication introduced in this chapter will help you to identify those non-obvious instances of persuasion that often apply to persuasion's core as well. Moreover, the principles presented here build upon those articulated in Chapter 2 and establish the groundwork for you as you are introduced in Chapter 4 to the coactive approach to persuasion.

1   Human beings project images of themselves as they communicate about substantive matters.

2   Communicators are not entirely in control of the effects they produce.

3   Messages make connections between things—between, say, the car being advertised and the life of luxury with which it is linked. As the ad sells the car, it also reinforces desire for a life of luxury.

4   Message recipients are co-creators of meaning. In so doing, they often self-persuade in ways unintended by communicators.

5   Generally, the message is mostly thought of as what is said by the communicator, whether verbally or non-verbally. But broadly speaking, the message is anything to which the message recipient attends and assigns meaning. It may include the context of the message, not just the text; it will probably include the source of the message, not just what is said.

Taken together, these principles should help us better understand a number of things: How, for example, product advertising promotes ideologies, not just products; how what we take to be reality is in part rhetorically constructed; and how news of Tiger Woods's latest contract helps sell both Wheaties and Tiger Woods.

QUESTIONS AND PROJECTS FOR FURTHER STUDY

1   Do you actively seek to promote an image of yourself to others, or do you merely project one? What is the image you seek to cultivate?

2   How do you address your professors? How do they address you? What's being metacommunicated about power, respect, and liking by these interactions?

3   Consider the case of Gayle Quinnell, the woman who expressed her concerns about Barack Obama at a rally for John McCain. Even after being presented with contrary evidence from her chosen candidate, Quinnell still said that she was going to work to share information that even McCain said was false. Why could McCain not persuade her?

4   Is there a dominant, widely shared ideology in this country, or are there many competing ideologies with no single dominant ideology? How would you describe your own ideology?

5   What is objectivity? As a communicator, is it possible to be fully objective? Discuss in relation to news, textbooks, tax statements, scientific reports, and so forth.

6   Keep a journal for one week and look for instances of gray areas of persuasion that you encounter.

7   What is your reaction to the notions of Americanization and supercapitalism? Is the Americanization of cultures around the world a good or bad thing?

8   What connections, if any, can be drawn between the concept of "truthiness" and Barber's description of "McWorld"?

EXERCISES

1   Interview a senior citizen about a controversial contemporary cultural issue (such as gays in the military, evolution versus creationism, abortion, corporate bailouts, etc.) and, based on their stated responses, develop a description of their DCIs. Then, compare them with your own.

2   Present your resume to the class and have it evaluated by your peers and professor, discussing how successfully you have performed impression management.

3   Applying the globalized rhetoric hypothesis, do a careful rhetorical critique of Chapter 3, with a focus on uncovering and analyzing the DCIs presented.

4   Find a journal article that incorporates one of the models or theories presented in this chapter and present its findings to the class.

5   Persuasion is everywhere—i.e., YouTube, sitcoms, and even on TV when they raise the volume when commercials come on. Get into groups and come up with an unusual and unnecessary product to endorse to the class. (Be creative—act out a commercial, draw an ad on paper, etc.) The product should be something that ordinarily people would not buy, such as rough toilet paper or garlic-flavored gum.

6   Find a YouTube clip of a "regular" non-celebrity person who is engaging in some form of rationalization. Present it to the class and analyze it, and don't forget to focus on the fact that people often don't even realize they are engaging in rationalization as they are doing it.

KEY TERMS

- Big Rhetoric
- Communication is
  - multi-motivated
  - multi-layered
  - multi-dimensional
  - multi-directional
  - multi-faceted
- Consummatory
- Denial of persuasive intent
- Dominant cultural ideologies (DCIs)
- Ethos, pathos, logos
- Expression games
- Globalized rhetoric hypothesis
- Globalized view (of persuasion)
- God words, devil words
- Impression management
- One cannot *not* communicate
- Persuasion in the guise of objectivity
- Priming, agenda setting and framing
- Restricted view (of persuasion)
- *The Medium is the Message*
- Truthiness

REFERENCES

All Time Box Office—Worldwide Grosses. (2014, June 13). (IMBd.com, Producer) Retrieved June 13, 2014, from Box Office Mojo: http://boxofficemojo.com/alltime/world/

Axelrod, A. (2007). *Getting your way every day: Mastering the lost art of pure persuasion.* New York: AMACOM.

Barber, B. (1996). *Jihad vs. McWorld: How globalism and tribalism are reshaping the world.* New York: Ballantine.

Barber, B. (2007). *Consumed: How markets corrupt children, infantilize adults, and swallow citizens whole.* New York: Norton.

Bennett. W. L., & Entman, R. M. (eds). (2000). *Mediated politics: Communication in the future of democracy.* New York: Cambridge University Press.

Benoit, W. L. (1998). Forewarning and persuasion. In Allen, M., & Preiss, R. A. (eds), *Persuasion through meta-analysis.* Cresskill, NJ: Hampton.

Berlo, D. (1960). *The process of communication: An introduction to theory and practice.* New York: Holt, Rinehart and Winston.

Best, J. (1989). *Images of issues.* New York: Aldine de Gruyter.

Best, J. (2004). *More damned lies and statistics: How numbers confuse public issues.* Berkeley: University of California Press.

Best, J. (2008). *Star-spotting: A field guide to identifying dubious data.* Berkeley: University of California Press.

Billig, M. (1996). *Arguing and thinking: A rhetorical approach to social psychology* (2nd ed.). Cambridge: University of Cambridge Press.

Blair, C., Brown, J., & Baxter, L. (1994) Disciplining the feminine. *Quarterly Journal of Speech* 80, 383–409.

Booth, W. (2000). The scope of rhetoric today. In Berger, A. (ed.), *Media and communication research methods: An introduction to qualitative and quantitative approaches.* Thousand Oaks, CA: Sage Publications, p. 52.

Burke, K. (1966). *Language as symbolic action.* Berkeley: University of California Press.

Burke, K. (1969a). *A grammar of motives.* Berkeley: University of California Press.

Burke, K. (1969b). *A rhetoric of motives.* Berkeley: University of California Press.

Cameron, D. (2014, June 14). *British values aren't optional, they're vital. That's why I will promote them in EVERY school: As row rages over 'Trojan Horse' takeover of our classrooms, the Prime Minister delivers this uncompromising pledge …* Retrieved June 22, 2014, from *Daily Mail Online*: www.dailymail.co.uk/debate/article-2658171/DAVID-CAMERON-British-values-arent-optional-theyre-vital-Thats-I-promote-EVERY-school-As-row-rages-Trojan-Horse-takeover-classrooms-Prime-Minister-delivers-uncompromising-pledge.html

Campbell, J. A. (1970). Darwin and the origin of species: The rhetorical ancestry of an idea. *Speech Monographs,* 37, 1–14.

Campbell, J. A. (1974). Nature, religion and emotional response: A reconsideration of Darwin's affective decline. *Victorian Studies,* 18(2), 159–174.

Campbell, J. A. (1975). The polemical Mr. Darwin. *Quarterly Journal of Speech,* 61, 375–390.

Campbell, J. A. (1986). Scientific revolution culture: The case of Darwin's origin. *Quarterly Journal of Speech,* 72, 351–376

Ceccarelli, L. (2011, Summer). Manufactured scientific controversy: Science, rhetoric, and public debate. *Rhetoric & Public Affairs,* 14(2), 195–228. Retrieved January 17, 2015.

Combs, J. E., & Nimmo, D. (1993). *The new propaganda.* New York: Longman.

Dillard, C., Browning, L. D., Sitkin, S. B., & Sutcliffe, K. M. (2000). Impression management and the use of procedures at the Ritz-Carlton: Moral standards and dramaturgical discipline. *Communication Studies,* 51, 404–414.

Fiske, J. (1987). *Television culture.* New York: Methuen.

Francois-Cerrah, M. (2014, June 18). *What are Cameron's 'British values'?: The discourse on British Values smacks of new-imperialism in a post-colonial world.* Retrieved June 21, 2014, from aljazeera.com:

http://www.aljazeera.com/indepth/opinion/2014/06/what-are-cameron-british-values-201461810827740835.htlm

Friedman, T. (2007). *The world is flat 3.0: A brief history of the twenty-first century*. New York: Picador.

Fukada, H. (1986). Psychological processes mediating the persuasion inhibiting effects of forewarning in fear arousing communications. *Psychological Reports*, 58, 87–90.

Gilligan, A. (2014, June 15). *Trojan horse: How we revealed the truth behind the plot: The Birmingham schools scandal has been exposed - but the problem is far from over*. Retrieved June 22, 2014, from *The Telegraph*: http://www.telegraph.co.uk/education/educationnews/10899804/Trojan-Horse-how-we-revealed-the-truth-behind-the-plot.html

Goffman, E. (1959). *The presentation of self in everyday life*. New York: Anchor (reprint Penguin Books, 1990).

Goffman, E. (1969). *Strategic interaction*. Chicago: University of Chicago Press.

Goffman, E. (1974). *Frame analysis*. New York: Harper & Row.

Gusfield, J. (1976). The literary rhetoric of science. *American Sociologist*, 41, 11–33.

Hacking, I. (1991). The making and molding of child abuse. *Critical Inquiry*, 17, 275–288.

Huffington Post (2008, October 10). McCain responds to "Arab" epithet at rally: "Obama a decent family man." Retrieved July 11, 2009, from www.huffingtonpost.com/the-uptake/mccain-responds-to-arab-a_b_133820.html

Huntington, S. (1996). *The clash of civilizations*. New York: Penguin

Iyengar, S. (1991). *Is anyone responsible? How television frames political issues*. Chicago: University of Chicago Press.

Jackall, R. (1995). The magic lantern: The world of public relations. In Jackall, R. (ed.), *Propaganda*. New York: New York University Press, pp. 351–399.

Jamieson, K., & Cappella, J. N. (2008). *Echo chamber: Rush Limbaugh and the Conservative media establishment*. New York: Oxford University Press.

Johannesen, R. L. (1996). *Ethics in human communication* (4th ed.). Prospect Heights, IL: Waveland.

Johnson-Cartee, K. S. (2005). *News Narratives and News Framing*. Lanham, MD: Rowman & Littlefield.

Kent, G. (2006). *Framing war and genocide: British policy and news media reaction to the war in Bosnia*. Cresskill, NJ: Hampton Press.

Kurtz, H. (1998). *Spin cycle: How the White House and the media manipulate the news*. New York: Touchstone Press.

Lai, L., & Farbrot, A. (2014) What makes you click? The effect of question headlines on readership in computer-mediated communication, *Social Influence*, 9(4), 289–299, doi:10.1080/15534510.2013.847859

Lakoff, G. (1997). *Moral politics: What conservatives know that liberals don't*. Chicago: University of Chicago Press.

Latour, B. (1986). *Laboratory life*. Princeton: Princeton University Press.

Latour, B. (1987). *Science in action*. Cambridge, MA: Harvard University Press.

Lee, C.-C., Pan, Z., Chan, J. M., & So, C. Y. K. (2001). Through the eyes of U.S. media: Banging the democracy drum in Hong Kong. *Journal of Communication*, 51, 345–65.

Leff, M. C. (1987). Modern sophistic and the unity of rhetoric. In Nelson, J., Megill, A., & McCloskey, D. (eds), *The rhetoric of the human sciences: Language and argument in scholarship and public affairs*. Madison: University of Wisconsin Press, pp. 19–37.

Leiss, W., Kline, S., & Jhally, S. (2005). *Social communication in advertising: Persons, products, and images of well-being* (3rd ed.). New York: Routledge.

Littlejohn, S., & Foss, S. (2009). *Encyclopedia of communication theory*. Thousand Oaks, CA: Sage Publications.

Mander, M. S. (1999). *Framing friction: Media and social conflict*. Urbana: University of Illinois Press.

McLean, P. D. (2007). *The art of the network: Strategic interaction and patronage in renaissance Florence*. Durham, NC: Duke University Press.

McLuhan, M. (1967). *The medium is the message: An inventory of effects*. New York: Bantam.

McQuail, D. (1994). *Mass communication theory: An introduction*. London: Sage Publications.

Miller, G., & Holstein, J. A. (eds). (1993). *Constructionist controversies: Issues in social problems theory*. New York: Aldine de Gruyter.

Noorden, R. Van (2014, February 24). *Publishers withdraw more than 120 gibberish papers*. Retrieved June 17, 2014, from *Nature*: www.nature.com/news/publishers-withdraw-more-than-120-gibberish-papers-1.14763

Nye, J. (2004). *Soft power: The means to success in world politics*. New York: Public Affairs/Perseus Books Group.

Pan, Z., & Kosicki, G. M. (1993). Framing analysis: An approach to news discourse. *Political Communication*, 10, 55–75.

Papageorgis, D. (1968). Warning and persuasion. *Psychological Bulletin*, 70, 271–282.

Petty, R. E., & Cacioppo, J. T. (1977). Forewarning, cognitive responding, and resistance to persuasion. *Journal of Personality and Social Psychology*, 35, 645–655.

Petty, R. E., & Cacioppo, J. T. (1996). *Attitudes and persuasion: Classic and contemporary approaches*. Boulder, CO: Westview. (Original work published 1981)

Pew Research Center (2012, July 26). Little voter discomfort with Romney's Mormon religion. Retrieved June 17, 2014, from www.pewforum.org/2012/07/26/2012-romney-mormonism-obamas-religion/

Pratkanis, A., & Aronson, E. (2001). *Age of propaganda: The everyday use and abuse of persuasion*. New York: Henry Holt and Company.

Press, E. (2013, August 3). *Whistleblower, leaker, traitor, spy*. Retrieved June 13, 2014, from *The New York Review of Books*: www.nybooks.com/blogs/nyrblog/2013/aug/05/whistleblower-leaker-traitor-spy/

Price, V., Tewksbury, D., & Powers, E. (1997). Switching trains of thought: The impact of news frames on readers' cognitive responses. *Communication Research*, 24, 481–506.

Reich, Robert B. (2007). *Supercapitalism: The transformation of business, democracy, and everyday life*. New York: Knopf.

Rogers, W. (2007). *Persuasion: Messages, receivers, and contexts*. Lanham, MD: Rowman & Littlefield Publishers.

Rosenberg, J. and Egbert, N. (2011). Online impression management: Personality traits and concerns for secondary goals as predictors of self-presentation tactics on Facebook. *Journal of Computer-Mediated Communication*, 17, 1–18. doi: 10.1111/j.1083-6101.2011.01560.x

Schiappa, E. (2001). Second thoughts on the critiques of big rhetoric. *Philosophy and Rhetoric*, 34, 260–274.

Severin, W. J., & Tankard, J. W. (1997). *Communications theories: Origins, methods, and uses in the mass media*. New York: Longman Publishers.

Shogren, E. (1998, January 6). Candid Clinton photos hit, hailed. *Los Angeles Times*. Retrieved January 19, 2017, from http://articles.latimes.com/1998/jan/06/news/mn-5394

Simons, H. W. (1990). *The rhetorical turn*. Chicago: University of Chicago Press.

Simons, H. W. (1993). The rhetoric of the scientific research report: "Drug-pushing" in a medical journal article. In Roberts, R. H., & Good, J. M. M. (eds), *The recovery of rhetoric: Persuasive discourse and disciplinarity in the human sciences*. Charlottesville: University Press of Virginia, pp. 148–163.

Simons, H. W. (2007). Rhetoric's role in context, beginning with 9/11. *Rhetoric & Public Affairs*, 10, 183–194.

Smith, G. (2006). *Erving Goffman*. New York: Routledge.

Sokal, A. (1999). *Fashionable nonsense: Postmodern intellectuals' abuse of science*. New York: Picador.

Study: Stephen Colbert's late show teaches viewers more than Fox, CNN And MSNBC. (2014, June 13). Retrieved June 13, 2014, from Design and Trend: www.designntrend.com/articles/14887/20140603/study-stephen-colberts-late-show-teaches-viewers-more-fox-cnn-msnbc.htm

Union of Concerned Scientists. (2012). *Heads they win, tails we lose: How corporations corrupt science at the public's expense.* Cambridge: Union of Concerned Scientists. Retrieved June 13, 2014, from http://electromagnetichealth.org/electromagnetic-health-blog/usc-report/

Vitanza, V. (2013, March 22). Vitanza's big rhetoric and "some more" (J. Butts, interviewer). Retrieved June 17, 2014, from http://alex-reid.net/2013/03/vitanzas-big-rhetoric-and-some-more.html

Watzlawick, P., Beavin, J. H., & Jackson, D. D. (1967). *Pragmatics of human communication.* New York: Norton.

Weaver, R. (1995) *The ethics of rhetoric.* Mahwah, NY: Lawrence Erlbaum.

Wegner, D. M., Wenzalaff, R., Kerker, R. M., & Beattie, A. E. (1981). Can media questions become public answers? *Journal of Personality and Social Psychology, 40,* 822–832.

Williams, A., & Gajevic, S. (2012, August 1). SELLING SCIENCE?: Source struggles, public relations, and UK press coverage of animal-human hybrid embryos. *Journalism Studies,* 14(4), 507–522. doi: 10.1080/1461670X.2012.718576

PART II

The Coactive Approach

CHAPTER 4

Coactive Persuasion

- Using Receiver-Oriented Approaches
- Being Situation Sensitive
- Combining Similarity and Credibility
- Building on Acceptable Premises
- Appearing Reasonable and Providing Psychological Support
- Using Communication Resources
- Summary
- Questions and Projects for Further Study
- Key Terms
- References

When Senator Barack Obama was considering a run for the presidency, conservative black writer Shelby Steele predicted that he'd lose (Steele, 2007). Steele said that Obama was too much like Oprah, a conciliator who was too eager to concede his opponent's strong points and too willing to play down his own. Implicitly, said Steele, people like Oprah Winfrey and Barack Obama had cut a deal with white America: we'll forgive you your past transgressions against black people; in return, you'll accept us as people like yourselves and agree that our commonalities far exceed our differences in skin color. Steele greatly admired Winfrey and Obama for this approach, but argued that such conciliation was too tame for the rough and tumble of electoral politics and twenty-first-century governing.

Future historians will decide the bigger questions about Barack Obama's presidential effectiveness and his rank in the measures of presidential greatness. That being said, on the issue of a 2008 presidential victory, Steele was wrong. Obama didn't lose, and that was the result of many factors, not least of which was the meltdown of the economy and the weakness of his opponent, John McCain's campaign. But a third reason *for* his victory and his re-election four years later would prove to be the very thing Steele said would *doom* it: his unifying and non-aggressive style.

Obama rhetorical style displays a "yes-but" approach, one that demonstrates agreement and understanding first, and then seek reciprocal treatment second. This was no more present than when, as a new president, he addressed the Arab world during a 2009 speech in Egypt. In this speech he reminded his audience that "the Jewish people were persecuted for centuries, and anti-Semitism in Europe culminated in an unprecedented Holocaust," and went on to add it is also

> undeniable that the Palestinian people—Muslims and Christians—have suffered in pursuit of a homeland. For more than sixty years they have endured the pain of dislocation. Many wait in refugee camps in the West Bank, Gaza, and neighboring lands for a life of peace and security that they have never been able to lead.
>
> (Obama, 2009)

With these words, Obama defined the situation and asserted that, like the Jews, the Palestinians, too, were victims who suffered. "Yes," the American president seemed to say, "there are legitimate arguments for Arab anger." He then, literally, added the "but", completing the "yes-but formulation:

> *But* if we see this conflict only from one side or the other, then we will be blind to the truth: the only resolution is for the aspirations of both sides to be met through two states, where Israelis and Palestinians each live in peace and security.
>
> (Obama, 2009)

"Yes-but" is one of a number of stratagems used by coactive persuaders in seeking to *bridge differences* with their audiences so as to secure preferred outcomes. *Coactive persuasion* is an umbrella term for the ways that persuaders work to move toward persuadees psychologically so that they will be moved, in turn, to accept the persuaders' position or proposal for action. This book's conception of it derives primarily from Aristotle's *Rhetoric* (Rapp, 2002), from Kenneth Burke's writings on *identification* (e.g., A *Rhetoric of Motives* (1950/1969b), from social-psychological theory and research (e.g., Allen & Preiss, 1998; Brock & Green, 2005), and from reports by practitioners in fields as diverse as politics and psychotherapy.

Defining the Terms

Coactive persuasion is an umbrella term for the ways that persuaders work toward persuadees psychologically so that they will be moved, in turn, to accept the persuaders' position or proposal for action.

Just what form coactive persuasion takes depends on the situation, and it can be employed in mass media situations or interpersonal ones. If interpersonal, the forms employed depend on whether persons A and B are locked in a conflict of interests or merely have a difference of opinion. When employed in mass media, the form coactive persuasion takes depends on whether the objective is to convince one's co-conversationalist or to persuade a third party (such as the voters in a political

FIGURE 4.1 *President Obama employed a "yes-but" approach, one that demonstrated agreement and understanding first, and then sought reciprocal treatment second, when as a new president, he addressed the Arab world during a 2009 speech in Egypt.*

contest). In a staged confrontation, as when two presidential candidates are facing each other in a television debate, coactive persuasion may be highly combative toward the adversary even as it appeals coactively to the target television audience. Thus, although coactive persuasion is essentially "friendly" persuasion, it is not without its weaponry.

Taken together, the components of the coactive approach (listed in Box 4.1) constitute a logic of "rhetorical proof," as opposed to the logics expected from scientists or mathematicians. Above all, the coactive approach involves adaptation, finding in audiences and situations the grounds on which appeals are presented and arguments addressed.

This difference in logics was illustrated by the 1993 refusal of Congress to provide funding for an expensive but highly promising vehicle for research in physics known as the supercollider. Physicists dubbed the funding refusal by Congress as "the revenge of the 'C' students." Many years later "there is still consternation among the scientific community" over the decision to cut off funding for the proposed "Superconducting Super Collider near Dallas, and it is seen as a decision that continues to have consequences for the nation's scientific competitiveness" (*Space Daily*, 2008). This situation is exacerbated by the Swiss having unveiled its own powerful particle accelerator, with some scientists saying that the United States now finds itself in the "minor leagues" of particle physics (*Space Daily*, 2008). Yet, said communication scholar John Angus Campbell (1996), if we recognize this as an instance of failed persuasion, we might ask who really deserved the middling grade. "Were the 'C' students the legislators who failed to grasp the national interest in physics, or were they the physicists who failed to adapt their arguments to a popular forum?" (Campbell, 1996). The physicists' job was to close the gap between their belief in the merits of building a supercollider and what Congress saw as the public interest. They needed to work harder to find language that could resonate with members of Congress, and they failed to do so.

Sometimes even attempts at reinforcing existing shared beliefs can involve gaps in understanding. For example, a political campaign manager, perceiving a gap between the current level of activity by campaign volunteers and the amount needed to win at the polls, may attempt to reinforce the volunteers' commitments to the cause. How persuaders can best bridge the psychological divide is the subject of this chapter and the focus of Part II of the book. This section of the book has direct implications for persuadees as well. The principles and techniques of coactive persuasion introduced here are also employed by persuasion professionals in the mass media—where ordinary citizens like us are far more likely to function as persuadees.

Box 4.1 Components of Coactive Persuasion

Coactive persuasion:

- is receiver-oriented, taking place largely, although not entirely, on the message recipients' terms;

- is situation sensitive, recognizing that receivers (e.g., audiences, persuadees) respond differently to persuasive messages in different situations;

- combines images of similarity between persuader and persuadee while promoting images of the persuader's unique expertise and trustworthiness;

- addresses controversial matters by appeals to **premises** the audience can accept;

- moves audiences from premises to desired actions or conclusions by both appearing reasonable and providing psychological support;

- makes full use of the resources of human communication.

USING RECEIVER-ORIENTED APPROACHES

Coactive persuasion recognizes that receivers of messages are by no means cut from the same cloth. As an extension of this principle, it underscores the need to provide "different strokes for different folks." For example, consider an instance where the Department of Communication at a large university sought to have its course in public speaking made mandatory for all undergraduates. To appeal to the College of Business, it noted the practical benefits. To colleagues in Education, it characterized public speaking as especially relevant for teachers and their students. The Department recognized, however, that these appeals would cut little ice in its own College of Liberal Arts, which prided itself on maintaining traditional academic values in the face of pressures for practicality and relevance. Accordingly, the chair of the Communication Department circulated to his colleagues in Liberal Arts a long and scholarly memo on the humanistic rhetorical tradition that characterized public speaking training as a venerable practice that began with the preparation of citizen-orators in ancient Greece and Rome. They were duly impressed.

This important principle can be illustrated with another example, this one from psychotherapy. One of the hardest things for patients to do, report Watzlawick, Weakland and Fisch (1974), is to display to the therapist the symptoms they are so eager to control. Here is how Watzlawick, Weakland and Fisch use the principle of "different strokes for different folks" in working to overcome their patients' resistance:

To the engineer or computer man we may explain the reason for this behavior prescription in terms of a change from negative to positive feedback mechanisms. To a client associating his problem with low self-esteem, we may concede that he is evidently in need of self-punishment and that this is an excellent way of fulfilling this need. To somebody involved in Eastern thought we may recall the seeming absurdity of Zen koans. With the patient who comes and signals, "Here I am—now you take care of me," we shall probably take an authoritarian stand and give him no explanation whatsoever ("Doctor's orders!"). With somebody who seems a poor prospect for any form of cooperation, we shall have to preface the prescription itself with the remark that there exists a simple but somewhat odd way out of his problem, but that we are almost certain that he's not the kind of person who can utilize this solution.

(Watzlawick, et al., 1974)

Coactive persuasion, then, is *receiver-oriented* rather than *topic-oriented*. This distinction may become clearer by contrasting the preceding receiver-oriented examples with one that is topic-oriented. When computers were first coming on the market, the sales manager of the computer division of a large electronics firm lamented,

I can't understand why my company isn't selling computers as effectively as IBM. We have the best computers in the world. What's more, I've written out a sales spiel for my people that's dynamite. All they have to do is memorize it and say it smoothly. Our products should do the rest.

When this sales manager was asked to compare his company's approach to IBM and suggest how IBM achieved its success, he said,

Oh well, you see IBM uses a different type of salesperson than we do. Our sales staff is all former engineers; what we care about is our products, and our people know them inside and out. IBM hires these "personality types" who sit down with the customers and get real chatty with them. The fact is they spend more time listening to the customers yak about their problems than on selling their products. It's a waste of time to me, but I have to admit that it works.

What the sales manager failed to realize, of course, is that by "wasting time" listening to the customers' problems, IBM's salespeople were accomplishing a great deal. Besides showing interest in the customer as a human being—a factor of no small consequence in itself—they were learning firsthand how to tailor their messages to achieve their intended effects. IBM's approach might be characterized as receiver-oriented. The approach contrasts quite favorably with the topic-oriented approach of IBM's competitor. The differences in the two approaches are summarized in Table 4.1.

TABLE 4.1 *Comparison between Topic-oriented and Receiver-oriented Approaches*

TOPIC-ORIENTED APPROACH	RECEIVER-ORIENTED APPROACH
Assumes that all receivers are alike	Assumes that all receivers are unique, or, at the least, that some differences make a difference
Decides for receivers what they need, want, know, value, etc.	Learns from receivers, if possible, what they need, want, know, value, etc.
Selects specific persuasive goals for any one occasion on the basis of persuader's own timetable	Selects specific persuasive goals for any occasion on the basis of the receivers' readiness to be persuaded
Communicates at receivers by means of a "canned" presentation	Communicates with receivers by adapting the message on the basis of a mutual interchange if at all possible
Promotes solutions on the basis of their supposed intrinsic merits	Promotes solutions on the basis of their capacity to resolve or reduce the receivers' special problems

BEING SITUATION SENSITIVE

Situations vary. What persuades in the boardroom may fail miserably in the bedroom. What works at an outdoor rally before a partisan crowd will surely seem out of place in a televised interview. The clowning that might be appropriate at a fraternity party would be highly inappropriate at a funeral.

One situational variable is the force of the emotional commitment involved. It is important to distinguish between differences of opinion and conflicts of interest. It is one thing for strangers on a train to disagree about whether abortion is murder; it is quite another for a husband and his pregnant wife to have the same disagreement. Not much is at stake in the first instance, whereas in the second example, the controversy might well end up in a divorce court.

Another situational variable is time. Compare the difference, for example, between a 50-minute college lecture and a 30-second television sound bite. Professors like us, who are in the habit of delivering long-winded lectures, often discover the pitfalls of condensing what we have to say for television news. Having time to think likewise makes an enormous difference in the quality of the receiver's message-processing ability (Petty & Cacioppo, 1996; Erwin, 2001). Faced with message overload and pressing deadlines for decision making, even the most discriminating message recipient is likely to rely on cognitive shorthands.

A third factor to consider in analyzing situations is audience expectations. Recall that situations often impel and constrain communicators in predictable ways, thus giving rise to such rhetorical genres as the eulogy and the commencement address.

Coactive persuaders need to learn what is expected and perhaps even required of them in situations of a given type. Then, having drawn on guidelines for dealing with that type of situation, they must develop a sense of what makes the situation they confront unique. Some situations are easy to deal with: for example, it is easy to bestow praise at a retirement dinner for an executive who served the company well. Other situations challenge the rhetorical skills of even the most talented improvisers.

One such situation is when a public figure is caught in wrongdoing and seeks to persuade the public to forgive, understand, and move on. This seems to happen regularly in politics, where politicians from New York to California and every place in between have been caught engaged in inappropriate sexual conduct. It likewise happens in popular culture, especially in the age of cell phones, where celebrities like golfer Tiger Woods are caught texting about extramarital sex, married politician Anthony Weiner is outed for sending sexual photos of himself to women he met online, or singer Chris Brown is caught abusing his romantic partner, the singer Rihanna. The most profound example of such a situation over the last few decades, though, was the one created by the actions of President Bill Clinton.

Consider former President Bill Clinton's rhetorical situation on August 17, 1998 when he made a public apology on television and admitted that he had, since January of that year, misled the public about his affair with White House intern Monica Lewinsky (Simons, 2000).

In theory, political apologists have numerous options at their disposal:

1 If the case against is unproved and likely to stay unproved, they can deny.

2 If the case against is unproved and likely to stay unproved, they can differentiate between the acts *committed on their watch* versus the acts for which they are *personally* to blame. They can reinforce this move by pledging corrective action.

3 If they can point to notable achievements in the past and the potential for more in the future, they can brag about the good job they are doing.

4 If the case against is weak or the credibility of the attackers is suspect, they can attack the attackers.

5 If the significance of the wrongdoing is open to question, they can minimize it.

6 If the facts of the case are in dispute, they can admit only what they have to when it comes to wrongdoing, personal culpability, significance, or relevance.

7 If the argument against them appears credible, they can justify their questionable behavior as contributing to the worthy ends they accomplished or attempted to accomplish.

8   If it won't unduly tarnish their reputation and the ability to do their job, they can differentiate between the impulsive or momentarily distracted self (who committed the wrongdoing) and the normally trustworthy, competent "real" self.

9   If there is no way to deflect responsibility, they can express contrition, but only in proportion to the perceived significance and relevance of the personal wrongdoing, and combine expressions of remorse with corrective action or pledges of corrective action.

10 If the argument is likely to appear credible, they can appeal for closure/termination of the case in the interests of getting on with more important affairs of state.

The foregoing list, offering up tactics for use when the rhetorical form of *apologia* is required, seems straightforward enough; the average persuader could simply select the most appropriate items from the list above and proceed to apologize. But situations often change, plots often thicken and rhetorical problems often deepen, and such was the case in this instance. In this case, President Clinton hoped or assumed that his affair with Monica Lewinsky would remain unproved, so he denied it, bragged about his accomplishments, and argued that he needed to "get back to work for the American people." But then, subsequent to his denials, came incontrovertible evidence, with DNA traces linking Clinton to Lewinsky on Monica's dress.

This new, unseemly, odd, and unprecedented situation presented a list of challenges and questions. What should President Clinton have said when the cover-up he staged and attempted to keep hidden was exposed to public view? Did the new situation effectively undermine his earlier claims that his alleged wrongdoing was strictly a private matter, and thus irrelevant, to the conduct of his office? If so, should he have held fast to his insistence on a right of privacy or shifted to another rhetorical tack? Moreover, Clinton's denials and attempted cover-up were linked by the media to previous patterns of evasion and were thus seen by some as indelibly ingrained in his character. Should he then have pleaded for mercy?

Add to this another situational constraint: Clinton's apparent defects of character—including, perhaps, an "addiction" to illicit sex and to risk more generally—are not readily forgiven in American society. If he had offered these as excuses, might they have further tarnished his reputation and ability to govern? What then? What if the legal appeals and objections devised by his attorneys to spare him from further embarrassment were repeatedly turned down by the courts? This happened.

What could Clinton possibly have said, once he finally admitted to some degree of wrongdoing after prolonged denials and delays? What if his expressions of contrition in leaked grand jury testimony were not believed? Should he have exploited the vulnerability of his attackers to attack, at the risk of undermining the apparent sincerity of his expressed remorse?

YOUNG BILL CLINTON

FIGURE 4.2   *President Bill Clinton was able to save his presidency through his artful understanding of how Americans saw his personal situation.*
Artist: Berklin, Phillp. Catalogue Ref. pbe0081. Reprinted with permission of Cartoonstock.com.

What if complete candor at the point of exposure could have placed him in severe legal jeopardy, while a legalistic defense risked alienating him from the citizenry? This question is not merely hypothetical—the dilemma was quite real. What happens if, in light of the circumstances, Clinton's pleas for closure, for getting on with the nation's business, are seen by many as transparently self-serving? What happens if those who are on his side or who are at least reluctant to remove him from office are themselves divided as to what sort of apologia would satisfy them? What should be done then?

From such hypothetical problems—quite real in Clinton's case—dilemmas are created, and it becomes the persuader's central task to grapple with them successfully. Chapter 10 will present a critical assessment of Clinton's handling of this difficult rhetorical situation in his apologia of August 17, 1998.

For our purposes at this point, though, our discussion of President Clinton's peccadillo demonstrates how the situation forcefully impacts the ways in which a persuader proceeds. The emotional commitment of the audience, the timing of events, and the public's expectations concerning what would be a fitting response all were factors as the President sought to craft a persuasive message that would work. A color-by-the-numbers response would have surely failed in this case; what was required was a creative response that was situation specific.

COMBINING SIMILARITY AND CREDIBILITY

Coactive persuaders move toward the audience psychologically by establishing relational bonds. Verbally but also non-verbally, they express caring and concern for the audience as individuals, demonstrate respect for their feelings and ideas, and perhaps display affection as well. Coactive lecturers, for example, may deliberately breach the rules for a platform speech by stepping out from behind the podium to address the audience directly, perhaps interrupting the formal presentation to engage members of the audience in conversation. Even in a formal presentation, the coactive persuader will give the impression of communicating *with* the audience rather than communicating *at* them.

Especially important to audiences is evidence of membership group similarities. The persuader may move toward the persuadees psychologically by emphasizing similarities in background, experience, and group affiliation and also by displaying evidences of commonality through dialect, dress, and mannerisms. These signs of commonality not only enhance the persuader's attractiveness to the audience but also serve indirectly to express shared beliefs, values, and attitudes.

It is little wonder, then, that advertisers often feature testimonials by "plain folks." In 30-second spots, the advocate of a brand-name detergent is often portrayed as the neighbor next door. In longer infomercials, the advertiser may feature a variety of role models, each representative of a different demographic group or culture type. And long before the comedian Jeff Foxworthy sought co-identification with us by listing the ways in which each of us "might be a redneck," the former governor of Louisiana, Huey Long, launched his extraordinary political career during the Depression of the 1930s by use of the *plain folks device*. In the classic film *All the King's Men* (1950/1986), Long (given the name Willie Stark in the movie) stood before a group of downtrodden farmers at a local carnival and said,

> You're all a bunch of hicks! That's right.
> Hicks! You're hicks and I'm a hick
> and us hicks are gonna run the state legislature.

Such rhetoric is powerful; it works to suggest that the persuader and the persuadees share much in common. It causes us to stop and listen, most of all because we trust people who think like we do.

Evidence of interpersonal similarity is clearly essential for the coactive persuader, but so, too, is it important on most occasions for persuaders to appear *different* from their audiences. We want to take direction and advice from people who are more expert, better informed, and more reliable than we are, because if persuaders know no more than we do on a matter, why would we need to listen to them? The general point is that although interpersonal similarity almost always results in *attraction* toward the persuader as a person, it doesn't always yield *credibility*. Attraction is generally important on issues of value and taste, whereas dissimilar but more expert sources tend to be more effective on important questions of belief (McGuire, 1985; Bohner & Wanke, 2002). If, for example, you were looking around for a new brand of coffee, chances are that you would be more influenced by the judgments of friends than by experts. But on other matters, you would likely seek expertise; you would ordinarily trust experts on medical matters, or on a question of the law. The "ideal" communicator, ultimately, is often one who seems both similar enough and different enough to appear overall as a *super-representative* of the audience. This is as true for

FIGURE 4.3 *An example of a super-representative persuader is Bruce Springsteen, who presents himself as a member of the working class, even as he has won multiple Grammy awards, an Oscar, and two Golden Globe awards for his creative musical work. Here, he appears with then-Democratic presidential nominee U.S. Sen. Barack Obama (D-IL) during a campaign rally in the rust-belt city of Cleveland, Ohio, on November 2, 2008 in Cleveland, Ohio. It is surely no accident that Cleveland is the home of the Rock and Roll Hall of Fame, which adds to the forces of Springsteen's status with his audience.*
Artist: Joe Raedel: Getty Images of North America.

ordinary friends and acquaintances that we count as *opinion leaders* as it is for celebrity figures such as leading politicians and media stars.

Thinking It Through

An interesting exercise is to think about the persons whose opinions you value most. How are they similar to you? How are they different?

But how do we recognize credibility? The major determinants of a persuader's credibility are perceived expertise and trustworthiness. This includes such qualities as perceived intelligence, honesty and dependability, maturity and good judgment. Other important credibility factors are power and dynamism. Power is the extent to which the speaker is perceived by the audience as willing and able to use rewards and punishments. Dynamism includes verve, passion, enthusiasm, and the like. Hart & Daughton (2004) argue that persuasion is always, to some extent, credibility driven. "Persuasion," they say, "comes to us embodied. Most people cannot separate the substance of a message from its author. This is especially true in spoken persuasion where the speaker's attitudes, voice, and personal appearance interact constantly with what the speaker says" (Hart & Daughton, 2004).

Personal credibility is especially important when what's being said arouses an audience's suspicions. When the claims seem harder to accept on first glance, the communicator's *ethos* can help us to overcome our doubts about the message. As a corollary of this important principle, Woodward and Denton (2014) suggest that strong content can overcome doubts about a speaker's personal credibility.

Heath & Heath (2007) distinguish further between a speaker's credibility and the message's *internal credibility*. To have credibility, a message needs to have details that hang together and are memorable. In one study (Shedler & Manis, 1986) Heath and Heath are able to show how irrelevant details gain credibility and made a substantial difference. University of Michigan researchers ran a simulated trial where two sets of subjects playing jurors were given a fictitious script of a trial to read regarding a Mrs. Johnson and her fitness as a mother. The two scripts had the same arguments, and the only difference was the level of detail. In one group, the eight arguments in favor were given vivid details, and the arguments against were not. For the other group it was the opposite. For instance, a vivid example in her favor reported that "Mrs. Johnson sees to it that her child washes and brushes his teeth before bedtime."

The additional details were purposely irrelevant to the argument, but six out of ten of the jurors hearing the vivid version of the favorable arguments judged the mother to be suitable, whereas only four out of ten of the jurors who heard the opposite version came to that conclusion (Shedler & Manis, 1986). The details boosted the credibility of the argument, even though they should not have mattered. The reasoning, said Heath and Heath, was as follows:

"If I can mentally see the Darth Vader toothbrush, it's easier to picture the boy diligently brushing his teeth in his bedroom, thus reinforcing that Mrs. Johnson is a good mother." The detail reinforced the internal credibility of the message."

(Heath & Heath, 2007)

BUILDING ON ACCEPTABLE PREMISES

The distinctive character of coactive persuasion is nowhere more manifest than in conflict situations or where there are sharp differences of opinion between people.

Picture a persuader, Ann, and a persuadee, Bill, who differ about issue X. In the face of their disagreement, a number of options are available for settling their differences. One approach is that of the **objectivist**. Operating from what she perceives as greater knowledge or wisdom on the matter, Ann may elect to tell Bill what is best for him. Parents, and sometimes teachers as well, do that—not always with great success. Or Ann may attempt to "demonstrate" the cold logic why her way of thinking is the only way. This is the **sage on the stage** method. For the thoroughgoing objectivist, hard fact and cold logic are, and ought to be, the sole arbiters of disputes, and everyone ought to reason as the objectivist does.

A second way to approach differences of opinion is that of the **privatist**, who merely asserts his or her feelings on the matter at hand, offering no reasons, no appeals, and no support for the views of any type. If Bill remains unconvinced of the merits of Ann's views, that's okay. If Bill shifts position, so much the better, but Ann does nothing to bring that shift about. Privatism stems from a deep-seated antipathy toward persuasion. To the privatist, all persuasion is immoral manipulation.

Should Bill remain unmoved by declarations of truth, cold logic, or personal feelings, Ann may be tempted to move against Bill combatively by vilifying, ridiculing, or threatening Bill. These **combative** modes of influence often prompt message recipients to become increasingly antagonistic, or perhaps to withdraw from further discussion.

The coactive persuader tends to prefer the carrot (inducements) to the stick (coercion) in conflict situations and prefers, where possible, to rely exclusively on talk to reduce or resolve differences. It is not, however, talk of a merely uncalculated, expressive nature. Coactive persuaders reason with their audiences. They offer arguments in support of their more controversial claims and evidence in support of their arguments. In these respects, the methods of the coactive persuader are not unlike those of the objectivist. The coactive persuader, however, is less concerned with showing that he or she is right—with winning arguments—than with *winning belief.* This requires arguments that begin from general premises that the audience can accept.

A *premise* is a hook on which to hang an argument. Depending on the context of the discussion, it may be a definition, a value assumption, or a general observation.

The coactive persuader operates on the principle that, once we get people to agree with a premise, we have them halfway to agreeing with the conclusion as well. For example, an organization specializing in securing adoptions of difficult placements manages to get the cooperation of a pro-choice advocate and a pro-life advocate who had once been friends but who had long since stopped speaking to one another. It accomplishes this seemingly remarkable feat by identifying a premise shared to both: Neither views abortion as the preferred option for poor, unmarried pregnant women, if indeed a viable alternative can be found. Both the pro-choice and pro-life activists agree that increasing the opportunities for adoption is consistent with their otherwise opposed philosophies. By asserting and then appealing to this shared premise, the adoption agency persuades both activists to offer their support.

In many situations, it may be necessary to make the case for the reasonableness of a premise. Thus, for example, you may oppose awarding formal recognition to a new African regime on the grounds that it is ruthlessly tyrannical. But someone may be able to convince you that our government and most other governments typically extend formal recognition to regimes that violate the rights of their citizens. Once you grant the premise that recognition does not necessarily mean moral approval, the persuader is then in a much better position to convince you that our government should recognize the African regime:

> (Major premise) To recognize a government isn't necessarily to signal approval of it but rather to acknowledge that it exercises control over its people.
> (Minor premise) The new African regime surely is in control of its people.
> (Conclusion) Therefore, the United States should recognize the new African regime.

In building from acceptable premises, persuaders generally start from premises that they themselves accept, and they then make a point of emphasizing those points of agreement that they share with their audience. Ultimately, in addition to providing hooks on which to hang arguments, these **common-ground appeals** make the persuader appear more trustworthy and more attractive.

Through emphasizing such relational similarities, persuaders create *identification* with the audience. We need to remember, too, that whenever we selectively name something (e.g., if we say that persuasion is a "tool"), we identify ourselves as someone who sees the world through a particular lens; if we engage in "naming" with an eye toward persuasion, we can induce our audience to share our view and see them come to feel a second sense of identification with us. We can combine these two forms of identification, as when our selective naming also expresses the affiliations and attitudes we have in common with our audience. Kenneth Burke provides a tongue-in-cheek illustration of this in his poem *He was a Sincere, Etc.* We'll consider the poem in detail in Chapter 15, but a short clip here will exemplify well the present point about identification:

He was a sincere but friendly Presbyterian—and so
If he was talking to a Presbyterian,
He was for Presbyterianism
If he was talking to a Lutheran,
He was for Protestantism
If he was talking to a Catholic,
He was for Christianity
If he was talking to a Jew,
He was for God …

(Burke, 1968)

Box 4.2 *Us vs. Them*

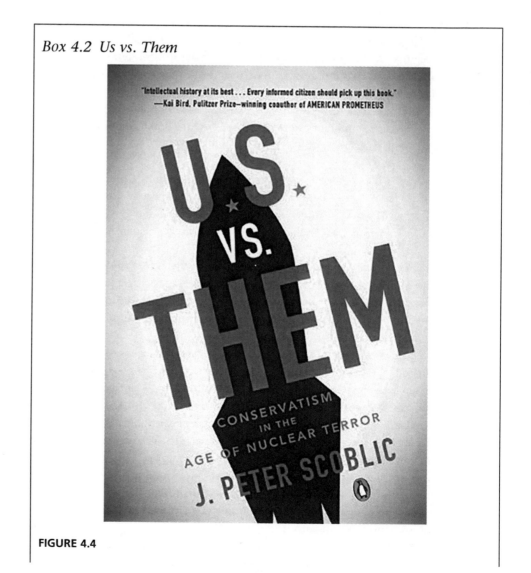

FIGURE 4.4

Peter Scoblic's *Us Versus Them* provides an interesting example of a persuader using selective naming to create identification with his readers as he seeks to persuade them of the correctness of his thesis. In the book, he rails against what he defines as American conservatism's "us versus them" and "good versus evil" thinking in foreign affairs, suggesting that much of the danger in the world has evolved from this mentality. Grounding the conservative view (as he defines it) in a historical context, he traces it to the nation's beginnings, when the colonists were "in fact surrounded by enemies—Native Americans on one side, European imperialists on the other—a condition that bred a sense of moral and nationalistic exceptionalism" (Kaplan, 2008; Scoblic, 2008).

Scoblic's case is for nuclear disarmament with the former Soviet bloc and with America's traditional allies; we will stand down together for a safer world. But does this *quid pro quo* principle apply equally to America's current enemies or perceived threats—to North Korea, for example, or to Iran's nuclear program? No, he says. It's only "natural" to protect one's own. These terrorist threats ("them") must be made to disarm first, and completely. Then the rest of "us" can proceed with arms reductions. So much for the ambiguities of "us" and "them" (Scoblic, 2008).

Typically, the coactive persuader moves from agreement to disagreement on highly sensitive controversial issues, or at least delays direct confrontation until agreed-on issues have been identified. Two variants of this bridge-building process are the **yes-yes technique** and the **yes-but technique**. In both cases, little or no hint of any disagreement with the audience is expressed until after a whole string of assertions is communicated about which agreement is sure. The object is to establish a habit of assent, to get receivers nodding "Yes," "That's right," and "You said it" either aloud or to themselves. Once this is done, the audience will presumably be receptive to more controversial assertions.

Using the *yes-yes* approach, the persuader lays the groundwork for the case by identifying a number of acceptable principles or criteria by which the case will later be supported. Thus, the vacuum cleaner sales rep might say:

> If you're like most of the people I meet, you also want a vacuum cleaner that really cleans, one that picks up the ashes and the threads and the crumbs that hide in the corners. I'd guess too that in these tough times you don't feel like getting stuck with big bills.... Well, okay, I know just what you mean.... Here's our new kind of vacuum cleaner, and it fits your specifications exactly.

Using the *yes-but* approach, persuaders begin by noting those arguments of the message recipient with which they can agree, and then, having shown how fair-minded they are, they offer a series of "buts" that constitute the heart of their case.

An example of the yes-but technique introduces this chapter, and it is the hallmark style of President Obama.

Box 4.3 *The Yes-But Technique Applied: Getting One's Voice Heard in Local Politics*

We often think government doesn't listen, but we can make a difference if we try. Imagine that you live in a small town, one with crumbling sidewalks and budget deficits. Yet, you know that the town has a sidewalk ordinance: Each citizen is responsible for maintaining his or her sidewalk, and, if they don't do it, the city can intervene, install a new sidewalk, and bill them for it. Yet, the law is rarely enforced. In an effort to change that, you might use the *yes-but* technique with an elected city official, and say something like this:

I understand that the city is facing real financial hardships right now … you've got that balloon pension payment coming due, and money from the state is being reduced. It must be really difficult to find ways to maintain our infrastructure, and I'm sure you're worried about delayed maintenance. On top of that, when money gets tight and the town isn't maintained, it is less likely to attract new residents or new businesses, creating this vicious cycle … and that just makes things even worse! It's no fun being in city government right now … I can see what you're going through, and I feel your pain!

Yes, all that's true, *but* you know what else? We do have a law in town about sidewalk maintenance, and it's not being enforced. And until we do that, our town will keep looking shabbier and shabbier. Sidewalks are crumbling and weeds are growing out of them; it is only a matter of time until someone stumbles and ends up getting hurt, and then we risk having the city get sued. It's time to make folks fix up their sidewalks—it will make our town look a lot better and it will make our walkways safe so that our seniors and disabled folks don't fall. And, we need to do it to make sure people maintain their respect for the laws of our community.

You say you don't have the staff to enforce the existing law? *Yes*, I hear you—that's a problem. *But* I work at a college, and I know that you could have unpaid interns working in city hall to do these inspections and helping with lots of other tasks, too! It would be a great opportunity for them to learn about how government really works. Most of all, though, isn't this your job? I want to vote for you in November and I want to be able to urge my friends to do the same, and I know I can count on you to get to work on this so that I can give you my full support on Election Day.

Although coactive persuasion generally builds on areas of agreement between persuader and persuadee, it need not do so to be successful. What counts from a purely practical standpoint is that the persuadee finds the arguments attractive, not that the persuader be enamored of them. Suppose that Rachel is an agnostic, and her friend Rashid is fervently religious. Although it might enhance Rachel's credibility if she were able to share Rashid's religious convictions, Rachel need not be a believer herself to convince Rashid of the disadvantages to believers of mandating prayer in schools. Rachel can make the case from the believer's perspective, pointing out, for example, the many occasions in history when religious groups have benefited from separation of church and state.

Similarly, a college professor may not care whether students get As or Cs in her courses; she may even decry their obsession with grades and be concerned only with whether they learn what she has to teach them. But knowing that grades are a major concern of most students, the professor may nevertheless appeal to their desire for good grades as a way of inducing them to keep up with the readings in the course. In these, as in other examples, coactive persuaders may move toward the message recipient to the point of offering reasons for belief or action that are not their own, and that they even find personally distasteful, but that they expect the receiver will find compelling.

The approaches of the college professor, and of Rachel in the previous example, are known as **reasoning from the perspective of the other**. How ethical is the approach? Is it dishonest to advance reasons for belief or action that one does not personally find appealing? Reason giving of this sort is surely one explanation as to why mere mention of the word persuasion often elicits negative feelings. The persuader may take a coldly calculating approach to the task, much like the ancient Roman poet Ovid in his playful advice to would-be Casanovas:

> On deceiving in the name of friendship; feigning just enough drunkenness to be winsome; on astute use of praise and promises; inducement value of belief in the gods; deceiving deceivers; the utility of tears; the need to guard against the risk that entreaties may merely feed the woman's vanity; inducement value of pallor, which is the proper color of love; advisability of shift in methods, as she who resisted the well-bred may yield to the crude, ways to subdue by yielding; the controlled use of compliments; become a habit with her; enjoy others too, but in stealth, and deny if you are found out; give each of her faults the name of the good quality most like it.
>
> (Quoted in Burke, 1969b)

APPEARING REASONABLE AND PROVIDING PSYCHOLOGICAL SUPPORT

American culture tends to separate fact from value, reason from emotion, and to decide that only questions of fact and logic can be addressed rationally. This commonsense perspective remains, even as research into emotions continues to complicate this position and advance our understanding. Heath and Heath go so far as to count "emotion" as one of the six necessary components for getting ideas to stick in our minds. Emotion, for them, provides a hook to cause us to attend to a message so that it does not become immediately lost in the constant garble of messages that confront us (Heath & Heath, 2007).

Correspondingly, there is a tendency to denigrate all appeals to emotion and all expressions of emotion as in some sense irrational. This may be one reason that people who are scientifically minded often object to the use of dramatic narratives; they tug at the heartstrings, sometimes eliciting emotional responses in place of coolheaded analysis. Although persuaders ought not to allow emotion to stand in place of reason or to overwhelm reason, they are entitled to provide their audiences with a feeling for problems and not just a dry accounting of them.

In light of this debate between coolheaded rationality and emotional sophistry, consider the following example. Microsoft CEO Bill Gates, a man who certainly appreciates rationality and science, recently demonstrated the power of emotional appeals during his talk at TED (Technology, Entertainment, and Design) in 2009. He released a jar full of mosquitoes into the meeting to mingle with his elite audience of technology titans, Hollywood stars, and politicians. "Malaria is spread by mosquitoes," Gates said while opening a jar on stage. "I brought some. Here, I'll let them roam around. There is no reason only poor people should be infected" (*Fox News*, 2009).

FIGURE 4.5   *Microsoft CEO Bill Gates demonstrated the power of emotional appeals during a TED talk. As he released harmless mosquitoes into a room filled with the rich and famous, he said, "Malaria is spread by mosquitoes. I brought some. Here, I'll let them roam around. There is no reason only poor people should be infected."*
Source: TED

With that act, Gates engaged the emotions of his audience and communicated some serious facts about malaria. We can also be fairly certain that his action prepared his audience to listen more seriously to his discussion about this global problem. It was a profoundly powerful statement, one that was fundamentally rational and fundamentally persuasive (and no, the mosquitoes he released were not carriers of malaria) (*Fox News*, 2009).

As suggested in Chapter 2, audiences often need incentives to act. In Rank's (1982) colloquial terms, they need to be convinced that proposals for action will help them either "get a good" (acquisition), "keep a good" (protection), "get rid of a bad" (relief), or "avoid a bad" (prevention). In the case of Bill Gates, the release of the mosquitoes served all four of Rank's functions: His audience became quickly persuaded that, working together, they could *get* the good result of working toward the elimination of malaria, thereby *keeping* their own good health, and *getting rid* of the suffering caused by the disease, and *avoiding* the spread of the disease to where it would infect even more of the world's humanity.

It has already been a number of decades since the field of psychology spawned what is now regarded as "classical" theories of persuasion, ideas that have stood the test of time (Erwin, 2001; Petty & Cacioppo, 1996). These provided the springboard for much of the theorizing reviewed in Chapter 2 on how to appeal to audience needs and desires while at the same time not appearing unreasonable. It is from those theories that emerge some guidelines for the coactive persuader.

Coactive persuaders should do the following:

1   Attempt where possible to link their position or proposal with beliefs and values already held by the audience. They should remind the audience of beliefs and values consistent with their position, while challenging undesired beliefs and schemas with new information. Likewise, they should attempt to elevate the importance of shared values while challenging or minimizing the importance of undesired values.

2   When urging action on a proposal, convince their audience not just that the proposal is a good one, but also that it has the support of people the audience most admires. But if the audience's subjective norms are likely to work against adoption of the proposal, they should urge self-reliance rather than dependence on what others think.

3   Simplify the message for those who would otherwise have difficulty understanding it. At the same time, they should anticipate and respond to possible objections from those who are more informed, more confident, better educated, or more intelligent. Similarly, they should encourage issue involvement and provide strong arguments for people whose opinions will matter in the long run, and help them resist counter-arguments. They should help those unable or unwilling to engage in detailed attention to find the cognitive shorthands necessary to make short-term commitments.

4   Exploit the potential benefits of interactive situations by reinforcing desired responses to questions while withholding reinforcements for undesired responses.

5   Exploit the tendency of persuadees to form conscious as well as unconscious associations among people and ideas. And, they should dress and act in such a way that audiences will form favorable inferences about their competence, trustworthiness, and attractiveness. Likewise, they should polish their ideas into language that audiences will find attractive.

6   When confronting persuadees who are opposed to their position, encourage role-playing of the desired behavior, but under conditions of minimal justification for performance of the act. Similarly, they should encourage those sympathetic to their views to act on them, even in modest ways, because this will provide reinforcement.

USING COMMUNICATION RESOURCES

Coactive persuasion at its best makes artful use of the various ways in which messages may be framed (see Chapter 6) and delivered (see Chapter 9). The persuader's message includes not just what is said but how it is said, both verbally and non-verbally. Every utterance is the end product of a set of conscious or unconscious decisions, from among a huge array of possible choices, which constitute what Burke (1969a) has called the **resources of ambiguity** in language. Burke's phrase is a way of suggesting that there are multiple ways to label something: categorize it; define it; illustrate it; or compare it; contrast it; contextualize it. For example, at the annual company holiday party, a co-worker whispers to you in anger that the boss "has been hitting on half the people in the office." If you want to *intensify* your co-worker's rage, you'd agree that yes, the boss is a pig or a roach or a worm or simply an animal. If you want to *downplay* the matter, you'd assure your co-worker that your boss is just an old goat.

Language choices may involve far more than mere labeling. Responding to another animal label—the charge that he and some of his colleagues in the House of Representatives had been behaving like "ostriches" in refusing to see the wisdom of President Ronald Reagan's policy toward Nicaragua—Representative Barney Frank responded with an ancient rhetorical technique known as **peritrope** (a table-turning). According to Representative Frank, the member of Congress who had heaped insult on the ostrich, not to mention on his colleagues, was sadly deficient in his ornithological knowledge. The ostrich, Frank said, was a great survivor, capable when riled of delivering a lethal kick. With its large eyes and keen vision the ostrich was ever alert. And, contrary to myth, the ostrich does not stick its head in the sand. "So there you have it," concluded Frank. "The ostrich is a rugged, wily, and frugal bird. Indeed, in a scrap between an ostrich and a Member of Congress, I would bet on the ostrich" (Jamieson, 1998).

Communication is not confined to words alone. The surroundings in which the message is delivered make a difference, and persuaders are sometimes able to select and arrange them. In keeping with the notion of moving toward the persuadee psychologically, the coactive persuader tends to prefer close physical settings over more distant ones. It is better to lecture in a room with too few chairs than too many. And it is better to air disagreements over a drink or a meal than in an atmosphere that announces itself as "strictly business." It is better to be seated next to the other than in a position directly opposite the other.

The persuader's choice of *medium* can make a difference as well. A medium is a carrier of messages, a means through which messages may be expressed. Broadly speaking, the medium may be oral or written, verbal or non-verbal, direct or indirect, but within these general categories, communicators may select from among a wide variety of message forms. An advertiser may choose among newspapers, magazines, word of mouth, television, Internet, and more. An executive may elect to convey the same message by telephone, memo, e-mail, bulletin board, platform speech, blog, conference, Twitter, loudspeaker, informal conversation, or company newspaper. The modern protester and activist may be credited with having invented any number of message forms: teach-ins, sit-ins, rock festivals, festivals of life, performance art, guerrilla theater, and, today, social networking sites like Twitter and Facebook.

Strictly speaking, a medium is nothing but a message carrier. The various media differ, however, not just in their technical capabilities but also in the feelings generated toward them. For example, face-to-face communication is generally perceived as warmer and more personal than indirect forms of communication. As anyone knows who tries summarizing the experience of having just seen an engaging film to a friend, a medium is also a source of information in its own right. Each medium has its own range of expressive potential. Each has a *grammar* based on the medium's unique production capacities. Grammar variables in photography, for example, include camera angle, selection of focus, depth of focus, shot framing from close-up to long-shot, and focal length of the lens. Television, film, and digital technologies add to photography such variables as dissolves, fades, cutting speed, zooms, tilts, pans, and changes in focus, as well as objective or subjective perspective (Meyrowitz, 1991).

And then, today, we are living in the midst of a revolution when it comes to media, an era where we are exploring new grammars and managing our encounters more than ever before.

Thinking It Through

Interview someone older and discover their attitudes about new technology. For example, ask them about how they feel about the tendency to be constantly connected. Do they see their cell phone as essential or as a bother? Ask them about the changes they've seen in their lifetime, and how they feel about them. Then, compare their responses to your own taken-for-granted notions about media.

On the one hand, we use media to avoid or limit our contacts: We send an e-mail to the person in the next room rather than walk down the hall, or deliberately make a phone call when the person will not be available because we'd rather just leave a brief message than talk. We check our caller ID before we answer the phone, and sometimes we just let the call go to voicemail. On the other hand, today's media keep us connected virtually and globally; we are always on call. Most of us would be uncomfortable without our cell phone, and we spend a great deal of time checking in, reporting on our progress through the grocery store or the traffic jam; we live today in a world where we are never alone and never offline. We create web pages and post them. We text, learning the codes, shorthands, and norms of that medium. We Twitter, learning to truncate our lives into 140 characters. And we Facebook, "friending" strangers and sharing our status without restraint.

Thinking It Through

Do you have a page on Facebook? What is on it? How much do you share? What is appropriate to upload, and what should stay off the page?

Who do you connect with as virtual friends? Will you "friend" anyone, or are you selective? Have you "friended" your parents and professors? And if you have, does that color what you say and do on the site?

Do you ever think about who is looking at the virtual life you display and the traces you are leaving behind? What are the benefits and dangers of these media? And how do you think it has affected you as a living human being to exist in a time where you are virtually always connected and always visible?

In the midst of all the changes, though, we are still drawn to human connection. When we visit the county fair or the home show, we stop and watch the live demonstration where the salesman demonstrates the latest gadget to aid us in chopping, slicing, and dicing. When a new politician who displays oratorical excellence comes onto the national scene, we are drawn in and delighted. When a member of the clergy shares a religious message with force and power, we take it in. When we propose to our beloved, we craft the message and deliver it face-to-face. Media do affect us; they bring new possibilities and new challenges to our lives. But, when all is said and done, we still, ultimately, want to be in the living presence of our fellow humans.

SUMMARY

Coactive persuasion is a method of bridging differences, of moving toward persuadees psychologically in the hope that they will be moved in turn to accept the persuader's position or proposal. It consists, essentially, of six components:

1   Being receiver-oriented rather than topic-oriented—communicating on the message recipient's terms.

2   Being situationally sensitive and seeking to match our message to the requirements and expectations the situation presents.

3   Combining expressions of interpersonal similarity with solid displays of ethos, including expertise, knowledge of subject, trustworthiness, and the like; responding to the persuadee's desire to be addressed by a credible, and not just a likable, source.

4   Building from shared premises but also, if necessary, reasoning from the perspective of the other.

5   Moving audiences to the desired conclusion or action by both appearing reasonable and providing psychological support.

6   Using fully the resources of human communication.

Coactive persuasion functions somewhat differently in conflict and non-conflict situations. More will be said about persuasion in conflict situations in Part III, where it will be suggested that the object is not always to persuade the antagonist. Sometimes, the coactive persuader behaves competitively or even combatively with his or her antagonist to win support from third parties. This is typically the case in political campaigns and in struggles on behalf of a cause by social movements.

Ultimately, coactive persuasion involves being fully committed to the process of persuasion, and it requires that we take risks. Rather than delivering canned speeches, we talk with our audience, thinking about their needs, wants, desires, and psychological state. We think about the situation, and adjust our discourse so that it fits comfortably into it. We select the best media, or, when we are constrained, we work within those media constraints effectively. And we think about our own goals and desires, not compromising or selling out our values or our intellect. We are engaged, active, and alive, as is our audience. And in that meeting of the minds, we reach a level of identification wherein mutual and human interaction really takes place.

QUESTIONS AND PROJECTS FOR FURTHER STUDY

1   Illustrate how the idea of *bridging differences* can be brought to bear on receivers who already agree with you.

2   Is it possible to "move toward" someone psychologically if your initial positions on a controversial issue are miles apart?

3   How might the principle of "different strokes for different folks" be applied to a situation in your own life?

4   Illustrate the differences between winning an argument and winning belief.

5   Have you ever had to defend yourself against charges of wrongdoing? Describe the situation, including the problems of persuasion you confronted. How did you handle the situation?

6   Think about recent candidates for high office. Which one of them best combined similarity and credibility? Which one was least successful at this?

7   Illustrate the differences between the yes-yes approach and the yes-but approach with examples of your own choosing.

8   Illustrate reasoning from the perspective of the other with examples of your own.

9   When is it appropriate to use emotional appeals? When is it not?

10 As a way of appreciating further what coactive persuasion entails, try composing two versions of an e-mail to someone with whom you disagree on a matter of concern to both of you.

   i   Version 1 should exhibit the style of the objectivist. In this form of the letter, you should state your position, provide the best reasons you can find to support that position, and undermine your opponent's arguments. Prove that you are "right."

   ii   Version 2 should exhibit a coactive style. Rather than lecturing at your reader, reason with him or her. Try organizing your letter as follows:
        a   State the issue under consideration.
        b   State the reader's position as clearly and as fairly as you can. Show that you understand the opposing position.
        c   Indicate areas of agreement, including contexts in which the reader could be "right."
        d   Identify areas of doubt or disagreement, while at the same time affirming your respect for the other. Don't at any point antagonize the other.
        e   Suggest consideration of your ideas. Promote them with premises the reader is likely to find attractive. Perhaps point out ways in which your respective ideas are complementary, each supplying what the other lacks.

KEY TERMS

- Apologia
- Approaches to differences:
  - coactive
  - combative
  - objectivist
  - privatist
- Coactive persuasion
- Common-ground appeals
- Internal credibility
- Peritrope

- Plain folks device
- Premises
- Reasoning from the perspective of the other
- Resources of ambiguity
- Sage on the stage
- Super-representative
- Yes-but technique
- Yes-yes technique

REFERENCES

Allen, M., & Preiss, R. W. (1998). *Persuasion: Advances through meta-analysis*. Cresskill, NJ: Hampton.

Bohner, G., & Wanke, M. (2002). *Attitudes and attitude change*. Philadelphia: Psychology Press.

Brock, T. C., & Green, M. C. (2005). *Persuasion: Psychological insights and perspectives*. Thousand Oaks, CA: Sage Publications.

Burke, K. (1968). *Collected poems 1915–1917*. Berkeley: University of California Press.

Burke, K. (1969a). *Grammar of motives*. Berkeley: University of California Press. (Original work published 1945)

Burke, K. (1969b). *A rhetoric of motives*. Berkeley: University of California Press. (Original work published 1950)

Campbell, J. A. (1996). Oratory, democracy, and the classroom. In Soder, R. (ed.), *Democracy, education, and the school*. San Francisco: Jossey-Bass, pp. 211–243.

Erwin, P. (2001). *Attitudes and persuasion*. Philadelphia: Psychology Press.

Fox News (2009, February 5). Bill Gates unleashes swarm of mosquitoes on crowd. Retrieved July 7, 2009, from www.foxnews.com/story/0,2933,488348,00.html

Hart, R., & Daughton, S. M. (2004). *Modern rhetorical criticism* (3rd ed.). Boston: Allyn & Bacon.

Heath, C., & Heath D. (2007). *Made to stick: Why some ideas survive and others die*. New York: Random House.

Jamieson, K. H. (1998, March). *Civility in the House of Representatives: An update no. 20*. Retrieved October 25, 2010, from www.annenbergpublicpolicy center.org/Downloads/Political_Communication/105thCongressCivil/REP20.PDF

Kaplan, F. (2008, April 27). Changing world, unchanging worldview: A critical look at the roots of George W. Bush's foreign policy. *Washington Post*. Retrieved July 7, 2009, from www.washingtonpost.com/wp-dyn/content/article/2008/04/24/AR2008042402896.html

McGuire, W. J. (1985). Attitudes and attitude change. In Lindzey, G., & Aronson, E. (eds), *Handbook of social psychology* (3rd ed., vol. 2). New York: Random House, pp. 233–346.

Meyrowitz, J. (1991). The questionable reality of media. In Brockman, J. (ed.), *Ways of knowing: The reality club*. New York: Prentice Hall.

Obama, B. (2009, June 4). Obama Egypt speech. Retrieved July 5, 2009, from www.huffington post.com/2009/06/04/obama-egypt-speech-video_n_211216.html

Petty, R. E., & Cacioppo, J. T. (1996). *Attitudes and persuasion: Classic and contemporary approaches*.

Boulder, CO: Westview. (Original work published 1981)

Rank, H. (1982). *Questions you can ask about advertising.* Park Forest, IL: Counter-Propaganda Press.

Rapp, C. (2002). Aristotle's rhetoric. In Zalta, E. N. (ed.), *The Stanford encyclopedia of philosophy.* Retrieved July 5, 2009, from http://plato.stanford.edu/entries/aristotle-rhetoric/.

Scoblic, J. P. (2008). *Us versus them: How a half century of conservatism has undermined America's security.* New York: Viking Press.

Shedler, J., & Manis, M. (1986). Can the availability heuristic explain vividness effects? *Journal of Personality and Social Psychology,* 51, 26–36.

Simons, H. W. (2000). A dilemma-centered analysis of William Clinton's August 17th apologia: Implications for theory and method. *Quarterly Journal of Speech,* 86, 438–453.

Space Daily (2008, May 25). Swiss supercollider puts U.S. on sidelines. Retrieved July 5, 2009, from www.spacedaily.com/reports/Swiss_super collider_puts_US_on_sidelines_999.html

Steele, S. (2007). *A bound man: Why we are excited about Obama and why he can't win.* New York: Free Press.

Watzlawick, P., Weakland, J., & Fisch, R. (1974). *Change: Principles of problem formation and problem resolution.* New York: Norton.

Woodward, G., & Denton, R. (2014). *Persuasion and influence in American Life* (7th ed.). Long Grove, IL: Waveland.

CHAPTER 5

Resources of Communication

- Resources of Language
- The Basic Tools
- Non-Verbal Resources
- Visual and Audiovisual Resources
- Resources of the New Media
- Summary
- Questions and Projects for Further Study
- Exercises
- Key Terms
- References

Today, it would seem strange to see smokers lighting up in restaurants, in office buildings, and on airplanes. That, though, was not the case just a few decades ago, when smoking in public spaces was seen as the norm. During that time, a debate raged between smokers, who felt they had the "right" to engage in the legal activity of smoking, and non-smokers, who felt they should not be subjected to dangerous secondhand smoke.

The tobacco industry responded with a campaign of its own. Prohibited from advertising on radio and television, it turned to the print media. One such ad, by the R. J. Reynolds Tobacco Company, was apparently designed to defuse or neutralize the attitudes of non-smokers hostile to the cigarette industry while providing emotional support to smokers for what was already becoming a socially undesirable habit (Figure 5.1).

In the full page ad, the tobacco company typified the concerns of the smoker and the non-smoker, using two columns of text to present an imagined dialogue. Both columns contained the identical number of lines and narrative forms, and each assertion stood as a counterpoint to its opponent's. Non-smokers said things such as "We're uncomfortable.... To us, the smoke from your cigarettes can be anything from a minor nuisance.... Because you can invade our privacy without even trying. Often without noticing." Smokers responded with, "We're on the spot.... Smoking is something we consider to be a very personal choice, yet it's become a

[Available from *Time*, February 20, 1984; pp 64–65]

A message from those who don't to those who do.

We're uncomfortable.

To us, the smoke from your cigarettes can be anything from a minor nuisance to a real annoyance.

We're frustrated.

Even though we've chosen not to smoke, we're exposed to second-hand smoke anyway.

We feel a little powerless.

Because you can invade our privacy without even trying. Often without noticing.

And sometimes when we speak up and let you know how we feel, you react as though we were the bad guys.

We're not fanatics. We're not out to deprive you of something you enjoy. We don't want to be your enemies.

We just wish you'd be more considerate and responsible about how, when, and where you smoke.

We know you've got rights and feelings. We just want you to respect our rights and feelings, as well.

A message from those who do to those who don't.

We're on the spot.

Smoking is something we consider to be a very personal choice, yet it's become a public issue.

We're confused.

Smoking is something that gives us enjoyment, but it gives you offense.

We feel singled out.

We're doing something perfectly legal, yet we're often segregated, discriminated, even legislated against.

Total strangers feel free to abuse us verbally in public without warning.

We're not criminals. We don't mean to bother or offend you. And we don't like confrontations with you.

We're just doing something we enjoy, and trying to understand your concerns.

We know you've got rights and feelings. We just want you to respect our rights and feelings, as well.

Brought to you in the interest of common courtesy by
R. J. Reynolds Tobacco Company

FIGURE 5.1

very public issue.... We're doing something perfectly legal, yet we're often segregated, discriminated against, and even legislated against." The dialogue went on and ended with each side making the exact same final point: "We know you've got rights and feelings. We just want you to respect our rights and feelings as well." The ad's conclusion thereby suggested that some level of "understanding" has been reached in the controversy. (The imagery from the ad is available on the web page that accompanies this textbook.)

Reynolds's key language strategy was **typification**. The company typified smokers and non-smokers by, in effect, putting words in their mouths and excluding other, more damning, words. In playing down the negatives while playing up the positives, Reynolds was doing with language what persuaders since time immemorial have done. They typified the two sides by presenting the smoking argument as a small difference of opinion. Imagine what would have happened if the ad had presented the disagreement more stridently, with the non-smokers had been represented as saying, "We're hopping mad. To us, the smoke from your cigarettes can be anything from a minor irritant to a real threat." Imagine that their message had gone on to mention the health dangers they attributed to secondhand smoke, not just their exposure to it. The message communicated would have been transformed.

By the same token, in the ad, why are the smokers "on the spot"? Why is smoking for them a "choice" (not to mention a "very personal choice"), rather than an addiction? Surely a comparable ad by the American Cancer Society would have put things in different ways.

As in this example, then, language offers resources for critical analysis that can also be used by persuaders to suit their own ends (Burke, 1969). This chapter identifies verbal stratagems for winning belief as well as tactics persuaders can employ for purposes of **compliance gaining**. It also catalogs the persuaders' non-verbal resources and briefly surveys media resources, including the rhetorical potential of new media. Persuaders need always to keep in mind that these means of persuasion will fall short of their mark, and may even backfire, unless they are well adapted to ends, audiences, and situations.

RESOURCES OF LANGUAGE

"Language," said Kenneth Burke, "does our thinking for us" (Burke, 1973). What could he have possibly meant? Normally we assume the opposite—that we're using language in our thinking and communication—and this is true: We do indeed do that. But what Burke intended by his pithy remark was that we think in terminologies that are not exclusively our own. As children, for example, we learn to distinguish between "patriotism" and "disloyalty," as though these terms were unambiguous. This is but a small part of a political socialization process that nation-states use to "teach" their dominant versions of right and wrong. Over time the unambiguous meanings of terms such as these tend to become *reified*; that is, they come to be treated as mundane realities rather than as **social constructions**. In that capacity, said Burke, they serve as **terministic screens**, deflecting attention from other possible views.

In challenging our normal understandings of the language–thought–reality relationship, Burke was not alone. Over the course of his career, postmodern theorist Michel Foucault argued that words don't *represent* things; rather, they are the "violence" that we humans do to things. He argued that such notions as madness, deviance, and criminality arise in "discourses" that normalize and naturalize, obscuring as they do the role that power has played in their formation and in the process shaping our "subjectivities."

For example, Foucault's work examined how we make sense of the situation when confronted with people whose behaviors are deviant. Are they "fools" to be placed on a "ship of fools"? Are they suffering from "madness," or are they "hysterical"? Or are they "mentally ill"? All of these conceptions have existed and our definitions have changed over time. Perhaps even more important, the dominant conception at any historical moment determines how we understand both those who are deviant and ourselves (who, presumably, are "normal"). What's more, the dominant conception gets translated into the actual choices we make about how to deal with those we've labeled. If we decide someone is "mentally ill," for example, we might seek to treat the illness. On the other hand, if we label him "mad," we might lock him away.

Foucault therefore believed that the "discourses" we create are vitally important. Postmodern critic Jacques Derrida took it even further, suggesting provocatively that language is all: There is "nothing outside the text" (1976). He agreed that every text has a context, but he asked us to remember that the context is also a text. This is true as well for the objects that surround us and the actions we take. Derrida argued that language-like activities such as saluting the flag can be "read" as though they were texts. Fredric Jameson spoke of a "prison-house of language" which we "inhabit" (1972).

These critics all suggest that language permits and indeed enables creative expression. It is interesting to note, though, that the novelty of these theorists' claims in effect undermines the claims themselves. We can apply their critiques to their own writings, looking to see how *they* create "texts" and employ "discourse" to shape reality. But thanks to their work, we gain more tools for analyzing and understanding the interactions between language and our world. The more tools we have in our toolbox of communication, the more inventive we can be as persuaders and as critics in our use of language. In what follows we hope to add to your verbal toolboxes both terms and distinctions that can make you more effective at both tasks.

Let's begin with a comparative example. Recall from Chapter 1 the analysis of the course catalog description for COM 390R as evidence of how the style of a persuasive message can prompt suspicion, even incredulity:

Catalog Description

COM 390R Seminar in Contemporary Rhetorical Criticism. *May be repeated for credit when topics vary. Semester topics have included dramatistic criticism, content analysis, and methodologies for movement studies. Prerequisite: Upper-Division Standing.*

The absence of verbs and adjectives, the failure to define terms, and the seemingly bureaucratic character of the language create the impression that the authors of this class description were not particularly interested in encouraging enrolment in the course.

Compare that catalog description with the ad for the online and for-profit University of Phoenix (see Figure 5.2).

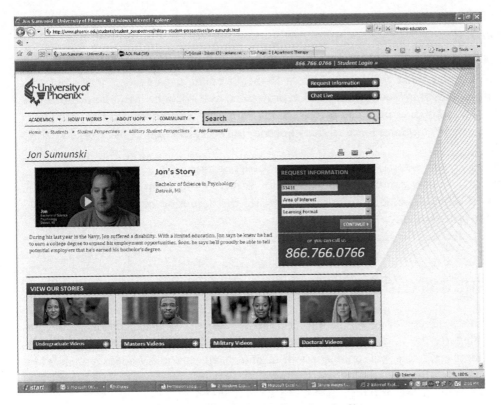

FIGURE 5.2 *Advertisement for Phoenix University Online.*
www.phoenix.edu/

Whoever crafted this University of Phoenix ad has acquired a number of conventional tools for pulling the Internet reader in, but the ad as a whole displays creativity particularly in the way it targets audiences who do not traditionally think of themselves as college students: spouses, mothers, fathers, grandparents, and people with full-time jobs. If they were confronted with the COM 390R course description, these people might feel discomfort as they struggled to decipher the code contained therein. They would notice that the COM 390R ad does not welcome, invite, or encourage them to join the class, and, in fact, hints at just the opposite—the course description seems to say that, if students wish to join the class, they will have to do the work required to fit in. But the University of Phoenix ad does just the opposite: It reaches out to invite students into the classroom, telling them the school will work to make sure they will be welcomed and successful in their studies. Ultimately, it exemplifies the concepts this chapter will introduce, displaying a sophisticated use of the resources of language to connect with its audience.

Thinking It Through

Notice the ways in which the University of Phoenix seeks to normalize a new definition and understanding of what counts as a "university." It is a for-profit online organization that employs mostly working professionals as instructors, rather than professors. Its curriculum is standardized, and its instructors teach the material as provided by the school. Formerly, such an enterprise would be labeled as something like a "correspondence school," but the University of Phoenix has worked hard to resist such labels.

Considering Burke, Foucault, and Derrida, think about these questions: What is a university? Does the University of Phoenix fit your definition? Why do you think it is so important to this school to be seen as a "university"? What is gained or lost as we normalize the definition of "the university" to include online and for-profit schools?

THE BASIC TOOLS

The basic tools of verbal communication are names (i.e., labels), classifications (i.e., categorizations), definitions, descriptions, comparisons, and contrasts. With these linguistic devices we can magnify or minimize, elevate or degrade, sharpen or blur, link or divide, simplify or complexify, conceal or reveal, contextualize or decontextualize, and make good, bad, or indifferent.

For instance, it is a commonplace to talk about contrast through the labels *black* and *white*. "It's as clear as black and white," we might say, wanting to show the distinctions we are presenting are obvious. *Black* and *white* are also used sometimes as shortcuts for classification, as when we go to the movies and the cowboys with black hats are the bad guys, whereas those in white hats are the heroes; when Darth Vader enters the scene, his appearance cues us as to how to think about him.

Given our tendencies to use these two colors to communicate so many things, it is not surprising that African Americans decided they needed to comment on and also reclaim the language of color in a positive way. In the latter part of the twentieth century, scholars began to critique the negative connotations associated with the term "black" and civil rights activists proclaimed that "Black is beautiful." This conversation is ongoing and profound, and highlights the points we are making here about the ways in which language functions to create, shape, and sustain our world.

Kenneth Burke provides us with useful tools for thinking about these issues and arguments, providing a model through which we can begin to get a handle on the history of the discussion of race in America. It begins with an understanding that we use language in a way that causes *black* and *white* to stand in solid contrast with each other, and from there takes up the issue of "equality." Implied here are linguistic issues: Once they are contrasted, can the contrasted people or things ever be equal? And if so, how?

All systems of belief, Burke says, answer to the questions: *What equals what, what opposes what, what leads to what, what follows what, what stands above (or below) what, and again, what's good, bad, or indifferent?* (1973). If we apply these questions to the history of the intersections of race and language in America, we can begin to glimpse how language functions to create, shape, and sustain systems of belief.

From their inception, ideas of race have carried with them ideas of superiority and inferiority, where white skin was presumed superior. These ideas have been bolstered by claims to authority, including scientific and religious authority. In 1776 when the American colonists' Declaration of Independence was crafted, few propertied males considered blacks as their *equals*, but neither did they include property-less males and women in asserting that "all men are created equal." Applying Burke's questions, we see that, at the founding of our nation, black did not *equal* white and white *stood above* black in the minds of most white citizens.

What then would it take to end slavery in America? Abolitionists invoked God in support of their views, but white supremacists found biblical justification as well for continuing slavery. Most agreed that the Bible *stood above* human opinion, but the Bible could be understood in opposing ways. The issue became which hierarchy of beliefs and values was correct, and the North and South fought over these questions (among others) during America's civil war. And, while the North won the war and thereby abolished slavery, the issue of *"what equals what"* still remained an unsettled question.

Similar questions concerning equality were raised a century later and answered in similar ways. Segregationists aligned behind banners of white supremacy and States' Rights, claiming divine and constitutional justifications for their positions. They feared that desegregation would destroy the South as they knew it, and they were right about that. As Burke might put it, the segregationists argued that blacks *stood below* them; that using the language of *equality* (and thereby making equality a reality) would lead to outcomes they felt they could not abide. Proponents of desegregation, such as Martin Luther King, Jr., likewise claimed biblical and legal authority for their claims to equal treatment under the law, and, when state or local law forbade their demonstrations or repudiated their claims, they appealed to "higher law." In Burke's terms, they argued that God's morality and the values of the nation's founding *stood above* the traditional views of the segregationists. This time, the proponents of equality triumphed.

The point of this example is not to provide a comprehensive explanation concerning the issues of race in America; that would be far beyond the scope and topic of this book. But this brief example demonstrates a point: "Equality" is a complex idea. The history of civil rights in America has been a chronicle of a noble fight to transform the definition of this term into one that includes all humanity. The quest has involved guns and suffering, but it has also involved words. And, as the words have come to be defined in new and better ways, the belief systems of the nation have changed and grown.

FIGURE 5.3

http://www.natcom.org/uploadedImages/More_Scholarly_Resources/Virtual_Bookshelf/Crable%20Burke.jpg

Try it Yourself: Applying Kenneth Burke's Kitbag

- What equals what?

- What opposes what?

- What leads to what?

- What follows what?

- What stands above (or below) what?

- What's good, bad, or indifferent? (Burke, 1973)

Suppose that, in a panel discussion of alternatives to teenage children having children, the question comes down to whether condoms should be distributed free to all high school students. You're probably familiar with the various positions and arguments on this longstanding controversy. How might Burke's tools be used to sort out the arguments?

Here's a hint to get you started: You might begin with the commonplace position that contraception is preferable to abortion. Abortion equals murder of a real or at least potential human life, goes one version of this argument. Moreover, sanctioning murder of a child would lead to immoral conduct and disrespect for life.

Keep going. Consider issues such as whether a "potential human life" equals a "real human being." Etc. What are the other positions and their arguments?

"The Illocutionary Force of Language"

The philosopher John L. Austin recognized that language can be used, in certain circumstances, to perform actions (*How to Do Things With Words*, 2004). He termed this the **illocutionary force of language**. Austin's view is now often referred to as **speech act theory** (see John Searle, *Speech Acts: An Essay in the Philosophy of Language*, Cambridge University Press, 1969).

The *illocutionary* force of an utterance is distinguished from the act of *locution*, which is simply making meaningful utterances. So, for example, when I say "It's raining right now," I haven't *done* anything beyond making a statement about the weather. However, if I say "I promise to be home by 10 PM tonight," I *have* done something: I've made a promise.

Of course, the illocutionary force of an utterance will depend on the context in which it is made. So if *I* say "I sentence you to 10 years in prison," I haven't really done anything, but if a *judge* says it in a court of law after a jury has pronounced a defendant guilty, the judge has done something significant.

Can you think of utterances that have illocutionary force and describe the circumstances in which they have that force?

Intensify/Downplay

As we see in the R. J. Reynolds ad, language is most often used to play up the positives and play down the negatives. And you need look no further than a recent General Motors (GM) ad campaign to see how such practices are employed in innovative ways.

In the midst of a serious economic recession, and after accepting a taxpayer-funded bailout, GM declared bankruptcy in mid-2009. It quickly reorganized, placed its bad assets into a separate unit, and came out of bankruptcy only 40 days later. But the impact of the filing was powerful as people grappled with the reality that a gigantic American corporation had fallen. GM had to decide what it would say, and committed to spend between $40 million and $50 million per month while under Chapter 11 on its "reinvention" advertising campaign (Vranica, 2009). The primary television ad from the campaign featured scenes of Detroit and America and displayed images of American can-do spirit. With a rock guitar strumming in the background, viewers saw images of American auto workers, boxer Muhammad Ali, the American moon landing, workers raising a building together, and moments from sports when teams were either near defeat or on the edge of comeback.

In the ad, the male voiceover said the following:

Let's be completely honest.
No company wants to go through this.
But we are not witnessing the end of the American car.
We are witnessing the rebirth of the American car.
General Motors needs to start over in order to get stronger.
There was a time when 8 different brands made sense.

Not anymore.

There was a time when our cost structure could compete worldwide.

Not anymore.

Reinvention is the only way we can fix this. And fix it we will.

[DRUMS KICK IN]

So here's what the new GM is going to be.

Fewer stronger brands. Fewer stronger models.

Greater efficiencies. Better fuel economy and new technologies.

Leaner. Greener. Faster. Smarter.

This is not about going out of business.

This is about getting down to business.

Because the only chapter we are focused on is chapter one.

(Fine, 2009a)

FIGURE 5.4 *GM's "reinvention" advertising campaign featured the iconic statue in tribute to Detroit boxer Joe Lewis, known also as "The Fist," which can be found in Detroit's Hart Plaza. The statue represents Lewis's punch inside and outside the ring. The fist memorializes the fact that Lewis held the world heavyweight title longer than anyone in history, and also symbolizes Lewis's fight against racial injustice.*
http://renardberrysr.com/sitebuilder/images/detroit_fist-600×453.jpg.

What does the ad downplay? The list is long. It doesn't mention the bailout made by American citizens to the tune of $50+ billion. It doesn't mention bankruptcy, hiding that fact behind the vague pronoun "this." It doesn't mention that its CEO was booted from his post by no less than the President of the United States, primarily because the company failed under his watch and he was unable to deliver a reasonable plan to lead the company forward. It doesn't mention its seemingly out-of-touch executives who flew in their private jets to ask for a taxpayer bailout. And it doesn't mention that GM had been appearing to ignore its own decline for years, even as companies like Toyota passed it by.

At the same time, the company intensifies its American roots, and even conflates itself with America. It appeals to nationalism and cloaks itself in American "pull yourself up by your bootstrap" mythology. It intensifies its displays of working-class people, sports, gleaming steel and gritty hard work. And it offers up the words and imagery of rebirth. In the ad, GM becomes Rocky Balboa—down but not out. Of course, not alluded to is the fact that Rocky never really existed.

In the midst of this, though, the ad is fascinating because it does allude to the problems the company was facing. But even in so doing, the ad intensifies what it believes to be another winning message: "We've learned our lesson." It plays up a "confessional" tone—it is almost as if "GM" were personified as a guest seated on the couch on Oprah Winfrey's television show. The ad downplays any hint at apology, but intensifies repentance. It promises, in word, song, and image, that from this day forward the company will do better.

Taken all together, the message has force. It intensifies an American myth of this sort: We are Americans; we stick together and protect what is part of our nation. We believe in renewal, and second chances, especially when the sinner is a member of our tribe, one who confesses and repents. And most of all, we never give up on ourselves or on each other. Therefore, we won't give up on GM.

The research on the impact of the ad campaign suggests that the message had the power to shape and change opinion. Data provided by Zeta Interactive, based on an algorithm scan of much of what is online, noted that the campaign strategy seemed to pay off, as GM buzz rose to "73% positive and 27% negative in 2 weeks, compared with being only 59% positive in the month leading up to the campaign launch—a 14% positive buzz increase" (Fine, 2009b).

Hugh Rank's Six Components of Intensify/Downplay

The National Council of Teachers of English has long been involved in efforts to help students analyze persuasive discourse. One of the more influential scholars working with the Council was Hugh Rank, a member of the council's Committee on Public Doublespeak, who identified **repetition, association, and composition** as key components of intensifying, and **omission, diversion, and confusion** as key components of downplaying. His analytic scheme is further illustrated below.

QUESTIONS YOU CAN ASK ABOUT ADVERTISING

Based on Hugh Rank's intensify/downplay pattern, a simple framework to analyze complex communication

Ads INTENSIFY the "good" by means of *repetition, association, composition*

Repetition

How often have you seen the ad? On TV? In print? Do you *recognize* the brand name? trademark? logo? company? package? What key words or images repeated within ad? Any repetition patterns *(alliteration, anaphora, rhyme)* used? Any slogan? Can you hum or sing the musical theme or jingle? How long has this ad been running? How old were you when you first heard it?

Association

What "good things" *already* loved or desired by the intended audience are associated with the product? Any links with *basic needs* (food, activity, sex, security)? With an appeal *to save or gain money*? With desire for *certitude or outside approval* (from religion, science or the "best," "most," or "average" people)? With desire for a sense of *space* (neighborhood, nation, nature)? With desire for *love and belonging* (intimacy, family, groups)? With other "growth needs" or desires (esteem, play, generosity, curiosity, creativity, success)? Any "bad things"—things *already hated or feared*, as in a "scare-and-sell" ad? Are *problems* presented, with products as *solutions*? Are the speakers (models, endorsers) *authority figures*: people you respect, admire? Or are they *friend figures*: people you'd like as friends, identify with, or would like to be?

Composition

Look for the basic pattern of "the pitch": (1) HI (2) TRUST ME (3) YOU NEED (4) HURRY (5) BUY. What are the attention-getting (HI) words, images, devices? What are the confidence-building (TRUST ME) techniques: words, images, smiles, endorsers, and/or names? Is the main desire-stimulation (YOU NEED) appeal focused on *our benefit-seeking* to get, or to keep a "good"; or to avoid, or to get rid of a "bad"? Are you the target audience? If not, who is? Are you part of an unintended audience? What context: when and where did the ads appear? Are *product claims* made for: superiority, quantity, beauty, efficiency, scarcity, novelty, stability, reliability, simplicity, utility, rapidity, or safety? Are any *"added values" suggested or implied* by using any favorable associations (*see above*)? Is there any urgency-stressing (HURRY) by words, sounds, movement, pace? Or is a "soft sell" conditioning for later purchase? Are there specific response-triggering words (BUY): to buy, to do, to call? Or is it conditioning (image building or public relations) to make us "feel good" about the company, to get favorable public opinion on its side (against government regulations, laws, taxes)? Persuaders seek some kind of response!

   In a wider context of an implied narrative, ads often *suggest* a larger story, script, storyline, or narrative featuring *"You"* with a role in a wider social context. A role implies a belief (*a basic worldview, a lifestyle—as caretaker? as hedonist?*), a purpose (*meaning, goal, direction*) and a plan (*a process, a way, a script, steps to be taken*) to get there, using certain behaviors (*specific things to buy, do, wear, drive*), and certain rules (*a social code of conduct*) to be followed. Are these explicitly stated? Or, more commonly, are they suggested or implied by the context—the presenters, background scene, activities—within the ad?

Ads DOWNPLAY the "bad" by means of *omission, diversion, confusion*

Omission

What "bad" aspects, disadvantages, drawbacks, hazards, have been omitted from the ad? Are there some unspoken assumptions? An unsaid story? Are some things implied or suggested, but not explicitly stated? Are there concealed problems concerning the maker, the materials, the design, the use, or the purpose of the product? Are there any unwanted or harmful side effects: *unsafe, unhealthy, uneconomical, inefficient, unneeded?* Does any "disclosure law" exist (*or is needed*) requiring public warning about a concealed hazard? In the ad, what gets less time, less attention, smaller print? (*Most ads are true, but incomplete.*)

Diversion

What benefits (e.g., low cost, high speed) get high priority in the ad's claim and promises? Are these your priorities? Significant, important to you? Is there any *"bait-and-switch"*? (Ad stresses low cost, but the actual seller switches buyer's priority to high quality.) Does ad divert focus from key issues, important things (*e.g., nutrition, health, safety*)? Does ad focus on side-issues, unmeaningful trivia (*common in parity products*)? Does ad divert attention from your other choices, other options, such as: *buy something else, use less, use less often, rent, borrow, share, do without?* (Ads need not show other choices, but you should know them.)

Confusion

Are the words clear or ambiguous? Specific or vague? Are *claims and promises* absolute, or are there qualifying words (*"may help" "some"*)? Is the claim measurable? Or is it vague "puffery"? (*laws permit most "seller's talk" of such general praise and subjective opinions.*) Are the words common, understandable familiar? Uncommon? **Jargon**? Any parts difficult to "translate" or explain to others? Are analogies clear? Are comparisons within the same *kind*? Are examples *related? Typical? Adequate? Enough examples?* Any contradictions? Inconsistencies? Errors? Are there *frequent* changes, variations, revisions (in size, price, options, extras, contents, packaging)? Too complex: too much, too many? Disorganized? Incoherent? Unsorted? Any confusing statistics? Numbers? Small Print? Paperwork? Do you know exact costs? Benefits? Risks?

Tactics for Intensifying

Repetition

One way to intensify good or bad points about a person, a product, or an idea is to repeat them again and again. People are comfortable with what is familiar, which is one reason why all cultures have chants and rituals based on the principle of repetition. The most common example of repetition in persuasion is the use of slogans and jingles in advertising. Some advertisers keep the same slogans for years. For example, we are all familiar with "M&Ms melt in your mouth, not in your hand." Notice the alliteration of the letter *m*. Another example is "Jaguar: Don't dream it. Drive it."

Association

Another tactic of persuaders is to intensify by linking a person, idea, or product to something already either loved/desired by or hated/feared by the intended audience. Advertisements often play on our most basic desires, such as security, love and belonging, esteem, relaxation, and self-improvement. Many of the words that persuaders associate themselves with are **glittering generalities**: words that seek to make us approve or accept without examining the evidence. Most often, the associations are indirect, but they can also be direct, as when a political candidate declares that he or she is for "faith, freedom, and family." Candidates for public office have a list of "positive, governing words" that they use when speaking about themselves and their policies. Notice here just some of the words beginning with the letter *c: candid, caring, challenging, change, children, citizen, commitment, common sense, compete, confident, control, courage,* and *crusade.* Barack Obama opened his campaign for the Democratic presidential nomination with one of those words, using the slogan "Change you can believe in."

In addition to the use of association to intensify the persuader's good points, association can also be used to play on the audience's fears or hatreds (intensifying the other's bad). An ad for home insurance, for example, may show a picture of a house ravaged by a fire, followed by directions for how to obtain insurance. An old public service announcement shows an image of eggs frying in a pan, followed by the warning, "This is your brain on drugs." In politics, association is often accomplished by *name calling*—linking a person or idea to a negative symbol. The persuader hopes that the receiver will reject the person or idea on the basis of the negative symbol, rather than by examining the evidence. For example, those who oppose budget cuts may refer to fiscally conservative politicians as "stingy," thus creating a negative association, although the same person could equally be referred to as "thrifty" by supporters. Similarly, candidates have a list of negative words and phrases that they use when speaking about their opponents. Some of these are *betray, coercion, collapse, corruption, crisis, decay, destroy, endanger, failure, greed, hypocrisy, incompetent, insecure, liberal, permissive attitude, shallow, sick, traitors,* and *unionized.*

Thinking It Through

Conservative Republican Leader Newt Gingrich understood the power of words many years ago. Go to www.informationclearinghouse.info/article4443.htm and read his famous 1995 GOPAC list of words that Republicans should use to get their message across. How many of those words are still being used by politicians today in much the same way?

Composition

The arrangement of words in a print advertisement and the organization of ideas in a speech are examples of composition. Reynolds positioned itself as somehow "above the battle" between smokers and non-smokers by its symmetrical counter-balancing of the two messages and by the ad's simple black-and-white design. It reinforced the image of neutrality by its tag line: "Brought to you in the interest of common courtesy." Some print advertisers combine repetition with association in compositions that link brand names with little more than verbal reminders, such as Dos Equis's "Stay thirsty, my friends." Other print ads are thick with technical details, not because the average reader is ever going to read them but because they suggest know-how and instill customer confidence.

Tactics for Downplaying

Omission

One downplaying tactic involves omitting information about the bad points about a person, product, or idea. This is sometimes called *cardstacking*—selecting only information that supports the persuader's point of view. All communication involves some omission because not everything can be said about an object. But omission can also be used to deliberately hide or conceal information. Some other common cases of omission involve telling a half-truth and quoting someone out of context. Unfortunately, these tactics have become part of the thrust and parry of political commercials. For example, a George W. Bush ad in the heat of the heavily contested South Carolina primary in 2000 boasted that "while Washington politicians deadlocked, I *delivered* a patients' bill of rights" (cited in Jamieson, 2000). But according to Jamieson, even though it did pass in Texas, Bush was far from enthusiastic about signing it into law.

Meanwhile, Bush's principal campaign opponent in the primaries, Senator John McCain, declared in South Carolina that he had forsworn the use of attack advertising and would henceforward run a purely positive campaign. He challenged his opponent to do the same. But in a subsequent televised debate, Bush pulled from his pocket an attack flyer from McCain's campaign (Jamieson, 2000).

Advertisers often omit drawbacks, hazards, or disadvantages, leaving out things such as the high cost of a product. They may also omit mention of concealed problems. For example, "fat free" cookies or ice cream often are filled with sugar and have almost as many calories as the regular brands. Ads for alcohol, coffee, or laxatives never say, "This is an addictive drug." Until required by law, cigarette companies never told consumers that cigarettes were linked to lung cancer. Finally, one well-known baby food manufacturer (naturally) chose not to mention in its ads that apricots and pears from concentrate have little nutritional value.

Diversion

Diversion consists of downplaying by shifting attention away from another's good points or one's own bad points or away from key issues by intensifying side issues. During election campaigns, candidates are often accused of diversion by concentrating on abstract concepts such as "family values," rather than concrete issues such as changing Medicare benefits. Another type of diversion used frequently in political arenas is the **ad hominem argument**, whereby the person, rather than the idea, is attacked. For example, someone might argue:

> I can't see why we should listen to the governor's proposal concerning the need for a tax increase to keep college tuition affordable. After all, he has spent the last 20 years in state government, getting his paycheck from taxpayers; he is hardly an unbiased source.

Confusion

Yet another tactic for downplaying one's own weaknesses or the other's strengths is to make things so chaotic and complex that people give up trying to understand. This can be done by use of intentionally faulty logic, euphemisms, jargon, or anything that blurs clarity or understanding. A general name for this is **doublespeak**: language intentionally used to mislead. According to William Lutz (1989), four types of doublespeak are prevalent in contemporary culture: **euphemism**, **jargon**, **gobbledygook**, and **inflated language**.

1   **Euphemism** is a device used to make an unpleasant reality more acceptable. In ordinary social discourse, for example, we might say that someone "passed away" or "went to the other side," rather than died. A bathroom may be referred to as a "rest room." Used in this way, euphemisms are not problems. They become problematic, however, when they are used to deceive. For example, comedian George Carlin notes that traumatized veterans returning home from World War I were referred to as "shell-shocked," a term that accurately conveyed the horrors of war. After World War II, people began to refer to the same phenomenon as "battle fatigue," a term that was a bit more euphemistic but still conveyed the notion of combat as a source of discomfort. After the Vietnam

War, people referred to "post-traumatic stress disorder," a phrase that is almost completely disconnected from the realities of war.

2   *Jargon* is the specialized language of a trade or profession. Within a specialized group, it is often a type of verbal shorthand that allows people to communicate quickly and efficiently. When used as a downplaying tactic, however, jargon often obscures meaning and makes simple things seem complex. Examples of jargon include referring to smelling as "organoleptic analysis," glass as "fused silicate," and a thermometer as a "fever computer." Legal language is full of such jargon: If you lose your property through theft, it is called "involuntary conversion." In advertising, we often see jargon in ads for drugs, automobiles, and equipment such as cameras and computers.

Academia is also a good source of jargon. A controversy erupted when a physicist (Sokal, 1996) wrote a nonsensical article, "Transgressing the boundaries: Toward a transformative hermeneutics of quantum gravity." The author pretended to use quantum theory to "prove" that reality is socially constructed, and his article was accepted by a leading journal in the field of literary criticism and published as genuine. His intention was to point out the prevalence of jargon in academia, and he succeeded all too well.

3   *Gobbledygook* or *bureaucratese* is similar to jargon, except that gobbledygook occurs when a persuader attempts to overload the audience with long, complex sentences that sound impressive but actually don't make any sense. Sokal's quantum theory article demonstrates the use of gobbledygook:

> In quantum gravity, as we shall see, the space-time manifold ceases to exist as an objective physical reality; geometry becomes relational and contextual; and the foundational conceptual categories of prior science—among them, existence itself—become problematized and relativized.
>
> (1996).

4   *Inflated language* is designed to make the ordinary and mundane seem important or things that are simple seem quite complicated. Sometimes, this is merely funny, as when a manicurist is called a "nail technician" or an elevator operator is called a "vertical transport captain." It becomes controversial, however, when used in military "technospeak," where death is "collateral damage," destroying cities is a "countervalue attack," the MX missile is a "damage limitation weapon," and a night-time invasion is a "predawn vertical insertion." The effect of such language is not only to create confusion but to mask the reality behind the words.

Compliance-Gaining Tactics

Compliance-gaining tactics are those used to effect changes in overt behavior, not just in beliefs, values, or attitudes. Compliance gaining is most often associated with interpersonal encounters: a salesperson closing a deal after lengthy talks with a client, a physician convincing a sick patient to take the prescribed medication, a son or daughter getting parental permission to use the family car for the evening.

Compliance gaining isn't always a matter of persuasion. Force or the threat of force can coerce compliance. Large sums of money or promises of same can induce people to work long hours, endure unpleasant working conditions, and even risk their lives. But these "power" strategies need persuasion to make them palatable; without it, coercion and material inducements produce only grudging compliance.

What, then, are the resources for compliance gaining available to the persuader? Researchers generally conclude that there exist two conversational constraints when dealing with compliance gaining in European-American culture: *social appropriateness* and *efficiency*. *Appropriateness* refers to whether a message is nice, civil, pleasant, proper, or courteous (Wilson, 2002). *Efficiency* refers to whether a message is direct, immediate, and relevant (Wilson, 2002). The point here is that when we are seeking to gain compliance, a pleasant request will generally work better than a nasty order; a direct message will work better than hinting or beating around the bush.

Researchers have found that the relative success of various compliance-gaining tactics also depends on situational factors. What works with intimates may not work with strangers. What works for physicians may not work for their patients (Boster, 1990). Ensuing chapters compare the use of compliance-gaining stratagems in a number of settings. For now, this chapter merely identifies verbal resources for persuasion-based compliance gaining. It provides a partial list, along with examples. This is taken from an article that has done much to advance our understanding of compliance-gaining possibilities (Kellermann & Cole, 1994).

A Sampling of Compliance-Gaining Methods

1 *Altercasting (negative):* Try to get others to comply by pointing out that *only a bad person would not do what is wanted.* That is, try to gain their compliance by noting that only a person with negative qualities would not comply.

2 *Altercasting (positive):* Try to get others to comply by pointing out that a *good person would do* what is wanted. That is, try to gain their compliance by noting that any person with positive qualities would comply.

3 *Altruism:* Try to get others to comply by asking them to *give you a hand* out of the goodness of their heart. That is, try to gain their compliance by asking them to be altruistic and just do it for you.

4   *Audience-use:* Try to get others to comply by having a group of other people present when you make your request. That is, try to gain their compliance by *asking them in front of other people* as a way to back up your request.

5   *Self-feeling (negative):* Try to get others to comply by stating that not doing so will result in an automatic decrease in self-worth. That is, try to gain their compliance by pointing out that *they will feel worse about themselves* if they do not do what you want.

6   *Self-feeling (positive):* Try to get others to comply by stating that doing so will result in an automatic increase in their self-worth. That is, try to gain their compliance by pointing out that they will feel better about themselves if they do what you want.

7   *Suggest:* Try to get others to comply by offering suggestions about what it is you want them to do. That is, try to gain their compliance by subtly proposing an idea that indirectly points out and describes what it is you want them to do.

8   *Surveillance:* Try to get others to comply by indicating your awareness and observation of what they do. That is, try to gain their compliance by referring to your general vigilance, surveillance, scrutiny, and/or monitoring of their behavior.

9   *Third party:* Try to get others to comply by having someone else ask them for you. That is, try to gain their compliance by getting someone else to intervene and do it for you.

10   *This is the way things are:* Try to get others to comply by telling them they have to because that is just the way things are. That is, try to gain their compliance by referring to rules, procedures, policies, or customs that require them to comply.

11   *Value Appeal:* Try to get others to comply because of important values that compel action in this instance. That is, try to gain their compliance by pointing to central and joint beliefs that should guide what they do.

12   *Why not?* Try to get others to comply by making them justify why they should not. That is, try to gain their compliance by pointing out there are no real grounds for not doing so.

Source: From "Classifying compliance gaining messages: Taxonomic disorder and strategic confusion," by K. Kellermann and C. Cole (1994) in *Communication Theory*, 4, pp. 3–60. Copyright © Oxford University Press. Used with permission.

NON-VERBAL RESOURCES

Meghan McCain took to the national stage as a campaigner and blogger during her father Republican John McCain's 2008 race for the presidency. Since his defeat, she has become a self-appointed and articulate spokeswoman on behalf of a centrist and youthful Republican perspective, traveling the nation to advocate that the Republican Party must shift away from the conservative right if it wishes to regain its national prominence.

In her quest to put a new "face" on the party, McCain posed (clothed) and talked about her sex life in the April 2012 *Playboy* magazine (O'Connor 2012). She has been willing to make appearances on all sorts of television programs, presenting herself verbally and non-verbally as being very different from the average stereotypical conservative Republican. She gave a speech to the Log Cabin Republicans (an organization for gay Republicans) in April of 2009 where she said:

> I am concerned about the environment. I love to wear black. I think government is best when it stays out of people's lives and business as much as possible. I love punk rock. I believe in a strong national defense. I have a tattoo. I believe government should always be efficient and accountable. I have lots of gay friends. And yes, I am a Republican.
>
> (Thornhill, 2009)

She famously took on right-wing pundit Laura Ingraham on *The View*, responding to Ingraham's insult about McCain's weight by proclaiming that Ingraham could "Kiss my fat ass!" (*Huffington Post*, 2009). Perhaps her biggest media challenge, though, was when she appeared on the liberal talk show *Real Time with Bill Maher*. The talk show, a live HBO telecast, was hosted by Maher and made up of a panel of three guests, including liberal CNN pundit Paul Begala. McCain was brought out late in the program and seated next to Maher, away from but facing the panel of three guests.

The discussion quickly put McCain on the defensive. She noted that she felt nervous, and at one point said that she was likely the only Republican at the table. The live studio audience was liberal-leaning and harsh. But McCain noted that, if the Republican Party ever hoped to regain its status, people like her would need to come on such programs as Maher's and engage the debate.

The interview became especially tense at one point when McCain said that she felt that the Obama administration "has to stop completely blaming everything on its predecessor." When Maher asked McCain if she really thought this was what Obama was doing, McCain said, "I do to a degree."

Begala immediately shook his head and said, "Not to enough of a degree, I'm sorry not nearly enough." He then began to explain how President Reagan blamed Jimmy Carter for years, to which McCain responded blithely, "You know I wasn't born yet so I wouldn't know." Begala fired back, "I wasn't born during the French Revolution but I know about it" (Sabloff, 2009).

FIGURE 5.5   *Meghan McCain as guest on Real Time with Bill Maher.*
http://cdn.videogum.com/img/thumbnails/posts/maheraww_210x.jpg

Commentary on McCain's appearance on the show varied from critical to supportive. As Amanda Hess noted, McCain was "clearly no match for a televised debate with Paul Begala—few people are. Begala made a living ridiculing Republicans on CNN" (2009). Hess continued:

> Somehow, watching a 48-year-old analyst verbally beat up on a 24-year-old blogger doesn't excite me as much as media reports have indicated it should. The whole clip makes me a bit ill, actually: the insane shrieking from the audience; Maher moving to physically shield McCain, as if she needs the host's protection.
>
> (2009)

Whether Begala was fair in his remarks or not is beyond the scope of this discussion and we'll leave it to each reader to draw his or her own conclusions. For our purposes, though, Hess's commentary is informative. The non-verbal communication she observed on the program made her terribly uncomfortable. This media moment is an instructive instance of the complexities of non-verbal communication.

Consider Meghan McCain's approach to advocacy in general, and how non-verbally rich it is. Her presentation and her arguments are primarily non-verbal. She presents herself physically as the anti-Republican stereotype. She dresses in hip fashion and sports a tattoo. She agrees to do an interview, and to include photos, in *Playboy*. She uses vulgarities when they suit her purpose, and she does it on national television. She seeks to demonstrate, through her style of non-verbal presentation, that the Republican Party is a good political home for people like her.

On the Maher show, she noted that what mattered most about her appearance there was her physical presence in that space, proclaiming that Republicans like her need to go on liberal television programs. But then, when the verbal communication become difficult, she literally withdrew physically, causing the normally cynical Bill Maher to soften his voice, touch her arm, try to draw her back to the table, and literally protect her from harm.

McCain gets credit for her efforts; she is featuring non-verbal communication in her efforts at persuasion. We know little about what she says and thinks about matters of domestic and foreign policy; instead, we know about her: her look, her style, her attitudes. And, it is to such non-verbal practices that we now turn our attention.

Channels of Expression

Experts on non-verbal communication have identified a number of channels of expression, each capable of influencing receivers in myriad ways.

Vocalics involve the auditory channel, including rate, volume, pitch, voice quality, and articulation. Also known as *paralanguage* and *paralinguistics*, vocalics focus on the way that vocal cues play a significant role in projecting images of self. Furthermore, vocalics come into play in metacommunicating relational messages, informing and advising us about how speakers intend their substantive messages to be understood. Consider, for instance, this message: "Of course I love you; I married you, didn't I?" The vocalics determine the greater part of how the message will be received. If it is said with a lilting, joyful, and warm voice, it communicates one message. On the other hand, if it is delivered with a bored, distracted, or angry voice, it communicates something entirely different.

We can and do often control our vocalics for effect. But it is worth remembering that communicating the right inflections isn't always easy. Much of what persuaders say non-verbally is outside their conscious control.

Kinesics, the visual channel, includes posture, gestures, fidgeting, and other body movements, as well as eye behavior and facial expressions. Birdwhistell (1970) has estimated that the face is capable of producing 25,000 different expressions. Ekman and Friesen (1975) claim to have discovered eight positions for the eyes alone. Smiling and direct eye contact are generally found to increase attractiveness and perceptions of trustworthiness, but message recipients are also often wary of contrived expressions.

Still, this has not stopped some persuaders from using a technique known as *mirroring*. As its name implies, mirroring involves matching the looks or behavior of the person you are trying to influence. Lexis, a former student, discovered at a sales training seminar that it could be taken to wild extremes:

Fresh out of college, a lump of educated clay, I entered the world-famous Techno executive sales training program. The first words out of the instructor's mouth were: "The key to your success at Techno is the principle that people buy from people they like." I sat in my chair very nonplussed by this comment as we spent virtually the remainder of the day talking about how to make your customer like you.

One component of "similarity" Techno called the "chameleon technique," meaning, do exactly what your customer does. Imitate body posture, speech volume, visual cues, etc. In training, we put this theory into practice by role-playing: leaning forward when the customer leaned forward, lowering or raising our voices in accordance with the customer's volume, etc. I can vividly remember my first sales call, hearing my mother's faint, gentle commands to sit up straight and cross my legs while my customer, a toy manufacturer, lounged and swiveled in his chair. I glanced nervously at my manager, normally a very erect dude, but he too was slouched in his seat giving me the visual cue to do the same. Within a few months this "mirror and matching" became second nature—customer in relaxed posture, me in relaxed posture.

The whole "similarity" principle, we like people who are similar to us, was delivered at Techno via the "15-second rule." Within the first 15 seconds in the customer's office, it was critical to uncover one or two key things about the person: weekend sailor, a kid the same age as your pre-schooler, animal lover, etc.

Once this information was gathered, it was then used to begin the rapport building or "similarity" creating process. Typical customer meetings began with a 10- to 15-minute discussion of last night's game, next month's fishing trip, or where your kid was applying to college.

One particular example was instructive. Robert, the same upright sales manager in my "chameleon" example, had 20/20 vision. One day, while on a sales call with a spectacled customer, Robert reached into his pocket and pulled out a pair of glasses. When the meeting was over, on the way to the car, I asked Robert when he found out he needed glasses. He said, "I don't, but lots of my clients wear them so I bought a pair." I looked at him, perplexed. "But Robert, if you don't need them, doesn't wearing them make you feel dizzy?" He replied, "They aren't real. They're just frames with glass; they're fakes."

Proxemics is the study of how space and spatial relationships communicate. It includes things like eye contact, how close you get to another, or even (in conjunction with the use of space) how loud or soft your voice becomes (Rogers, 2007).

Many years ago, anthropologist Edward T. Hall distinguished among zones or territories of communication, noting that virtually everything that a person "is and does is associated with space" (Hall, 1968). It is no small matter that his findings from so long ago still resonate; it was he who first identified the ways we manage space and distance. Hall noted that distances between people can be grouped, ranging from about 18 inches (*intimate* distance) to 25 feet or more (*public* distance). Between these extremes are *personal* distance (18 inches to two feet) and *social* distance (four to 12 feet).

Cultures vary, though, in zones of comfort. For example, Latin Americans tend to be comfortable at closer distances than do persons reared in Northern European cultures, according to Hall. Still, all cultures seem to place taboos on excessive closeness by strangers and excessive distance by intimates. Persuaders violate them at their peril when they communicate interpersonally, but our culture permits all manner of visual displays of intimate distance, as in magazine advertising.

Proxemics also covers spatial positioning, as in who sits where around a table. Diplomatic negotiations between rival nations have been known to stall interminably over the size and shape and seating arrangements of the negotiating table. Pellegrini (1971) discovered that people seated at the head of the table tended to be regarded as more persuasive, more talkative, more dominant, and more self-confident.

The meaning of proxemics is generally connected with things like: (1) power, (2) level of involvement with others, and (3) positive or negative sentiment (Rogers, 2007). We can often see this played out when we visit professional offices; if you go to the office of your college president, for example, you will likely see a large office with a large wooden desk. The desk will likely provide a solid barrier between you and the president, and the chair sizes will vary so that the president's desk chair is higher and larger than the one on which you sit. This configuration communicates the authority of the office, and also communicates that there exists little involvement between you and the president. Without saying a word, the proxemics speaks loudly, and you, as visitor in the space, respond appropriately with deference and respect.

Thinking It Through

Spend a week observing offices and desks. Notice your professors: Do they set their desk as a barrier between you and them, or do they have the desk positioned so that they turn away from it to chat with you?

Notice the administrative assistants on campus: do they have desks, or are their "desks" more like tables?

Notice yourself and your friends: What sort of desk do you have?

What do these artifacts communicate? How do people set up their space to either shield themselves from others or share closer space with them? Why do some people have barrier-like desks, while others have desks that offer little protection and privacy?

Haptics refers to the tactile channel of communication, the arena of touch. Hornick (1992) has demonstrated the rhetorical benefits of touch. Bookstore customers touched on the arm tended to shop longer and buy more; supermarket customers who had been touched were more likely to taste and purchase food samples; restaurant customers tipped servers better if they had been touched by them.

But touch can be discomfiting, both for the touchee and the toucher. A former student, Carol Mickey, tested the effects of touch and closeness in her role as head waitress at a busy downtown restaurant that catered to men. For several weeks, Mickey and the waitresses who worked under her supervision alternated between their normal, businesslike way of approaching male customers and a more intimate style that included increased eye contact (the servers looked at the customers as they ordered, then wrote the orders down on their pads), greater physical proximity (the servers rubbed shoulders with customers as they pointed out specials), and greater individuation (the servers wore name tags). When the more intimate style of service was adopted, tipping increased as much as 20% to 30%. But, although Mickey and her team enjoyed the money, they could not sustain the requisite level of closeness. Some felt guilty, others embarrassed at intruding themselves in these ways.

Chronemics is the study of how time communicates. As with space and touch, cultures assign meanings to being fast or slow, early, late, or on time. These are among the variables of chronemics. Americans as a whole tend to value being promptly on time, and also moving generally at a more rapid pace than most cultures. But, even with that being said, chronemics varies depending on what part of the United States one is visiting.

Dealing with appointment times is an issue of chronemics, and it communicates. If you know someone who is always late, you likely consider that person rude. Yet those with power have more latitude; if you have an appointment with your college dean, you'll likely be on time, but you won't be surprised if the dean is not. And we all likely have known someone who uses time almost passive-aggressively, keeping us waiting so as to demonstrate some level of power over us.

Ultimately, it seems that the old joke of the psychoanalyst was actually not so funny: if arrived early for therapy, you were anxious; if you arrived late, you were angry; if you arrived precisely on time, you were clearly compulsive. No matter what you did, you couldn't win!

In sum, deciphering non-verbal communications is seldom reducible to formula, despite what the psychoanalyst in our joke would have patients believe. Often, it is not clear what a wink or a blink (or other non-verbal behavior) means in a given context; also, contexts themselves may be no less complex than the non-verbal "texts" we are trying to interpret. Moreover, even when we think we've discerned "the meaning" (recall the discussion of multiple meanings in Chapter 3), we often have difficulty finding the words to describe it. You know that your good friends who are in a romantic relationship are going through a rough patch. You observe Jared reaching over to tenderly rub Pat's back. Is this a sign of love, or is Jared pretending? What could we possibly learn about the context to decipher this situation with confidence? Mightn't the answer we finally arrive at admit of both possibilities, but in a way that is difficult, if not impossible, to verbalize?

Minimally speaking, non-verbal communications seem to be capable of having six effects (Harris, 2002; Hickson & Stacks, 1985):

1   Repetition: Nodding while saying "yes."

2   Contradiction: Coldly, perhaps sarcastically, saying to an intimate, "Je t'adore."

3   Accentuation: *"No way!"* as opposed to "no way." If you try stressing a different word in this sentence each time as you repeat this question, you'll see how accentuation works: "When was the last time you saw Paris?"

4 Complement: Laughing while saying "That's funny."

5 Substitution: Nodding agreement instead of verbalizing it.

6 Regulation: Fidgeting, putting books away, and so forth as your professor drones on after class was supposed to end.

But this list of effects is indeed minimal and does not capture the range of meanings in something as apparently simple as the rubbing of Pat's back. After all, messages (non-verbals included) may be multi-motivated and multi-leveled, much communication is implicit rather than explicit, and receivers co-participate in the making of meaning. Lists such as this also do not capture the "both–ands" of experience. Does a bikini reveal or conceal? Or, does it do both?

VISUAL AND AUDIOVISUAL RESOURCES

On his way to a charity ball, Senator Jones is photographed walking down a hotel corridor with a priest on one arm and a gorgeous model on the other. This presents the photo editor of a newspaper with an interesting question. Should the photograph be used as is to accompany the newspaper's story on the charity ball? Why not? The senator, after all, is Catholic *and*, at the time of the photograph, had something of a reputation as a philanderer. Photographing the senator between the priest and the model is therefore appropriate. On the other hand, the newspaper could dramatically *reframe* the senator's visit to the charity ball by cropping the photograph. Depending on its politics, it could cut out the priest and leave the model, or cut out the model and leave the priest, or perhaps downplay the senator's presence altogether by selecting instead a photograph of the charity host and hostess dancing together.

As this example makes clear, language is not alone in being able to link or divide, elevate or downgrade, play up or play down. Indeed, the six linguistic components of intensifying/downplaying identified by Rank (1976) have their visual and audiovisual counterparts. The newspaper, for example, could have played up the senator's promenade to the charity ball by placing its photo of him on the front page. Alternatively, it could have buried the photo on the society page.

Another aspect of visual persuasion is the way a scene creates a backdrop for persuasive messages. For example, in ads for diapers, you can expect to see a neat and tidy home in the background. Ads for cognac usually take place against a background of sophistication and elegance. Ever since Ronald Reagan mastered the art of visual presentation in 1984, political candidates have been careful to be photographed against visually compelling backdrops to air on the evening news.

It is far more compelling to see a candidate surrounded by American flags than it is to see a candidate speaking inside a warehouse to an audience that is half asleep.

Other aspects of visual and audiovisual persuasion appear in film, television, and video presentations; these call into consideration the use of camera angle,

FIGURE 5.6   *American politicians, such as NJ Governor Chris Christie, almost always sport "flag pins" on their lapels and also surround themselves with American flags in public speaking situations.*

editing, lighting, sound, and music. Generally speaking, high-angle shots give the impression of a character's vulnerability, whereas low-angle shots make a character look powerful. Wide-angle shots of a crowd cheering its leader can arouse intense emotion from a film or television audience. Fast cuts convey dynamism and action, whereas slow dissolves indicate softness (these operate much like the use of straight lines versus curves in pictorial design). Lighting, too, can be soft or harsh, meant to convey dreamlike sentimentality or documentary realism.

Advertising exploits the grammar of the visual and audiovisual every bit as effectively as feature-length films do. A 30-second spot for Diehard batteries appears on television in October and rehearses for viewers the memory of a winter snowstorm. The familiar sounds are heard of an engine that wants to turn over but cannot. The camera zooms to a high-angle close-up of the driver whose look of utter frustration says it all. We know what it means: we need to get a new Diehard battery now, before winter comes and we end up stuck without transportation.

Miller argues that scenes such as these work through common narrative codes that we have internalized (2003). The appeal of things like the Diehard commercial resides in our "narrative literacy" (Miller, 2003). We have the feeling of having been there before, and our brains also lock away fantasy scripts in memory that clever advertisers can evoke. We know that Jeep Cherokees can't climb rugged cliffs, just as we know that drinking Corona beer won't put us on a beach in Mexico—but we also know how to suspend disbelief for the sake of a vicarious adventure. What we generally aren't aware of at the moment is how the conventions of the visual and audiovisual are working their magic on us.

RESOURCES OF THE NEW MEDIA

In its efforts to "hear from" as many people as possible, the board of an affluent, fast-growing suburban school district decided to post its controversial proposal for student school transfers on the Internet and invite responses. It succeeded beyond expectations, garnering 2,000 hits on its website and about 500 comments. It also avoided the usual raucous meetings on school transfers, where, in the past, angry parents had registered long-winded objections in person. This time, the process was orderly, and many people expressed satisfaction with the amended plan. Yet even its supporters expressed regret that the board had essentially made up its mind on the basis of e-mail commentary in advance of any face-to-face engagement. Moreover, at the one meeting it did hold, speakers were limited to two minutes each. Summaries of e-mail responses were provided by the board, but what was missing was the *feeling-tone* of the objections. If surveying by way of the Internet became routinized, people wondered, what would happen to the old sense of community?

Today we talk not just of "new" media such as the Internet but also of a *convergence* of the resources of telecommunication, made possible by greatly expanded bandwidths. Already, we see online advertising exploding, and the Internet has revolutionized political campaigning, ushering in something that could become much more akin to direct democracy than representative government. The Internet has already established itself as having a role in redistributing power across the globe, as it opens up pathways to information that a decade ago could only have been imagined.

Some, though, fear that the politics of tomorrow will be little changed by the Internet. Once corporate barons and dictatorial governments figure out how to get a handle on the technology, they will control it, limit it, and use it for their purposes. Already, we have seen instances of censorship of the Internet, and it is worrying to see a company like Google seek to appease the Chinese government by "setting up a new site—Google.cn—which will censor itself to satisfy the authorities in Beijing" (*BBC News*, 2006; Richburg, 2010). Google claims it has taken this action because it would be more damaging to pull out of China altogether (*BBC News*, 2006; Richburg, 2010), and that concern is real. But at the same time, it is distressing to see the Internet controlled in such a fashion.

To be sure, the Internet opens up possibilities for persuaders that did not exist a decade or two ago. By its nature, the technology increases the speed with which persuadees can be reached and enables persuaders both to learn more about their target audiences and to target each market segment with greater precision (see

Chapter 12). Increasingly, then, political campaigners, advertisers, and movement leaders can custom-tailor their messages.

Persuadees, for their part, can order up messages, including persuasive messages, by way of the Internet. The Internet enables users to order up the portions of newspapers they wish to read online and view television on their schedule. Specialized news and opinion services, along with blogs, are now well established to service specialized readerships. Search engines exist to scan the various universes of information available on any given topic, and are becoming more sophisticated every day. The much vaunted freedom afforded by the Internet, however, usually requires exposure to advertisements that Internet browsers don't want to see. From the advertiser's perspective, of course, this is a decided plus: it provides them with the chance to reach a nearly captive audience (Shapiro, 1999).

The Internet also permits considerable interactivity. In chat rooms and on social networking sites, participants can function as persuaders one moment, persuadees the next. We can chat online at the poker table with real people as we play global Texas Hold 'Em. And now, with simulation games like Second Life, we can create completely new personas for ourselves that will interact in real time with other created beings.

It is no longer difficult to imagine cyberspace in the imminent world of complete technological convergence. Convergence could greatly increase the choices available to consumers, while at the same time rendering choice making relatively simple. In a broadband world, says columnist Andrew Sullivan (2000):

> Even the distinctions among telephone wires, cables, and satellites will be erased. There will be one cultural-economic tube, and you'll be at the end of it—eagerly clutching your credit card that can make telephone calls, get cash out of ATMs, and earn you frequent-flier miles.

SUMMARY

One way of thinking about persuasion is as an art of the sayable. Many things can be said pro or con about a person, an idea, or a proposal for action; moreover, the things to be said can be said in many ways. By their choice of labels, descriptions, comparisons, definitions, and so forth, persuaders can make a difference in the way things are perceived and evaluated. They can, for example, minimize or maximize, reveal or conceal, sharpen or blur, link or divide, and make something seem good, bad, or somewhere in between.

The persuader, then, has many choices, and this chapter's exploration of language resources focused on tactics for intensifying and downplaying while also providing illustrations of persuasive compliance-gaining techniques. Getting people to comply—that is, to act as you wish they would act—is not always a matter of persuasion. The power of monetary incentives and coercive pressures is sometimes an adequate substitute for persuasion, but, unless accompanied by persuasive arguments and appeals, it generally produces only grudging compliance.

Besides being an art of the sayable, persuasion is an art of the non-verbal: of gestures and inflections, settings and physical arrangements, timing and touch. The non-verbal can reinforce the verbal or nullify what's been said, in effect contradicting it. As with language, this chapter explored the resources of the non-verbal.

Brief consideration was given as well to the resources of the visual and audiovisual. The example of the senator photographed between the model and the priest reminds us that the visual, too, can intensify or downplay, especially in these days of digital imaging whereby, with no difficulty at all, reality is created in the editing room.

What, then, of the new media and of the emerging convergence of telecommunications transmission systems? There seems little question but that persuaders are now able to custom-tailor messages to ever narrower audience segments and with incredible speed. Message recipients now have greater freedom to select messages, except those they are forced to see and hear as a condition for signing on with transmission providers. There is also greater opportunity for interactivity. Just what effects these changes will have on the private sector, or on the way global business is conducted, remains a matter of considerable dispute at this point. The question is not whether product advertising, political campaigning, and other such paradigmatic forms of persuasion will be transformed, but the extent of that transformation.

QUESTIONS AND PROJECTS FOR FURTHER STUDY

1   Think of the ways you use the resources of verbal and non-verbal persuasion in the course of a day. What do you routinely play up and play down?

2   Think of an incident when you had to choose your words carefully. How did you use language to conceal or reveal, magnify or minimize, elevate or degrade, sharpen or blur, link or divide, simplify or complexify, or make good, bad or indifferent? What functions were performed by labels, definitions, and descriptions; by contrasts and comparisons; and by the way things were contextualized or decontextualized? How would you say things differently if you had a chance to choose your words again?

3   Repeat the same exercise, but this time focus on the non-verbal elements in a difficult rhetorical situation. How many did you deliberately choose?

4   Is it possible to know whether someone is genuinely in love or merely acting the part? How can you know? How can you know that you know? Are non-verbals as easily decipherable as verbal expressions? Can we see through them more

readily? What features of the context need attention to decipher the non-verbal text?

5   Provide your own examples of non-verbal communication's six meaningful effects.

6   Illustrate how the six verbal components of intensifying and downplaying, identified by Rank, have their visual and audiovisual counterparts.

7   What changes has the Internet produced in the choices available to persuaders and persuadees? What changes has it made in your life? What will persuasion be like with increased telecommunications convergence?

EXERCISES

1   Select a controversial political or moral issue and analyze it using Kenneth Burke's toolkit, applying each of Burke's six questions to the situation.

2   Select a contemporary blog that offers editorial opinion on an issue of current interest. In a group, analyze the blog through the lens of Rank's model that is presented in this chapter.

3   Find a communication journal article that incorporates the work of Burke, Foucault, or Derrida, and present its findings to the class.

KEY TERMS

- Ad hominem argument
- Cardstacking
- Chronemics
- Compliance gaining
- Doublespeak
- Euphemism
- Glittering generalities
- Gobbledygook
- Haptics
- Illocutionary force of language
- Inflated language
- Jargon
- Kinesics
- Omission, diversion, and confusion
- Proxemics
- Repetition, association, and composition
- Social constructions
- Speech act theory
- Terministic screens
- Typification
- Vocalics

REFERENCES

Austin, J.L. "How to do things with words." *Literary Theory: An Anthology*. Ed. Julie Rivkin and Michael Ryan. Malden, MA: Blackwell Publishing, 2004. Print.

BBC News (2006, January 25). Google censors itself for China. Retrieved July 13, 2009, from http://news.bbc.co.uk/1/hi/technology/4645596.stm.

Birdwhistell, R. L. (1970). *Kinesics and context.* Philadelphia: University of Pennsylvania Press.

Boster, F. J. (1990). An examination of the state of compliance-gaining message research. In Dillard, J. (ed.), *Seeking compliance: The production of interpersonal influence messages*. Scottsdale, AZ: Gorsuch Scarisbrick, pp. 7–17.

Burke, K. (1969). *A rhetoric of motives.* Berkeley: University of California Press. (Original work published 1950)

Burke, K. (1973). *The philosophy of literary form: Studies in symbolic action* (3rd ed.). Berkeley: University of California Press.

Derrida, J. (1976). *Of grammatology* (G. Spivak, trans.). Baltimore: Johns Hopkins University Press.

Ekman, P., & Friesen, W. V. (1975). *Unmasking the face.* Englewood Cliffs, NJ: Prentice Hall.

Fine, J. (2009a, June 3). GM's puzzling new "reinvention" TV ad. *Business Week*. Retrieved July 12, 2009, from www.businessweek.com/innovate/FineOnMedia/archives/2009/06/gms_puzzling_ne.html

Fine, J. (2009b, June 18). Is GM's "reinvention" ad campaign working? Study says: maybe! *Business Week*. Retrieved July 12, 2009, from www.businessweek.com/innovate/FineOnMedia/archives/2009/06/is_gms_reinvent.html

Hall, E. T. (1968). Proxemics. *Current Anthropology*, 9(2/3), 83.

Harris, T. (2002). *Applied organizational communication.* Mahwah, NJ: Lawrence Erlbaum.

Hess, A. (2009). Meghan McCain schooled, spanked, murdered: Political debate or snuff porn? *Washington City Paper*. Retrieved July 13, 2009, from www.washingtoncitypaper.com/blogs/sexist/2009/06/24/meghan-mccain-schooled/

Hickson, M. L., & Stacks, D. W. (1985). *NVC: Nonverbal communication.* Dubuque, IA: William C. Brown.

Hornick, J. (1992). Tactile stimulation and consumer response. *Journal of Consumer Research*, 19, 449–458.

Huffington Post (2009, March 16). Meghan McCain on "The view": Kiss my fat ass!" Retrieved July 13, 2009, from www.huffingtonpost.com/2009/03/16/meghan-mccain-on-the-view_n_175319.html

Jameson, F. (1972). *The prison-house of language: A critical account of structuralism and Russian formalism.* Princeton: Princeton University Press.

Jamieson, K. H. (2000). *Everything you think you know about politics—and why you're wrong.* New York: Basic Books.

Kellermann, K., & Cole, C. (1994). Classifying compliance gaining messages: Taxonomic disorder and strategic confusion. *Communication Theory*, 4, 3–60.

Lutz, W. (ed.) (1989). *Beyond 1984: Doublespeak in a post-Orwellian age.* Urbana, IL: National Council of Teachers of English.

Miller, T. (2003). *Television.* New York: Routledge.

O'Connor, M. (2012, April 15). *Meghan McCain poses for Playboy: 'I'm strictly dickly".* Retrieved June 27, 2014, from Gawker: http://gawker.com/5893652/meghan-mccain-poses-for-playboy-im-strictly-dickly

Pellegrini, R. J. (1971). Some effects of seating position on social perception. *Psychological Reports*, 28, 887–893.

Rank, H. (1976). *Intensify/downplay.* Urbana, IL: National Council of Teachers of English.

Richburg, K. B. (2010, July 10). *Google compromise pays off with renewal of license in China.* Retrieved June 27, 2014, from The Washington Post: www.washingtonpost.com/wp-dyn/content/article/2010/07/09/AR2010070902137.html

Rogers, W. (2007). *Persuasion: Messages, receivers, and contexts*. Lanham, MD: Rowman & Littlefield.

Sabloff, N. (2009, June 20). Paul Begala schools Meghan McCain. *Huffington Post*. Retrieved July 13, 2009, from www.huffingtonpost.com/2009/06/20/paul-begala-schools-megha_n_218469.html

Searle, John. (1969). *Speech acts: An essay in the philosophy of language*. Cambridge: Cambridge University Press.

Shapiro, A. (1999). *The control revolution*. New York: Public Affairs.

Sokal, A. D. (1996). Transgressing the boundaries: Toward a transformative hermeneutics of quantum gravity. *Social Text, 4*, 217–252.

Sullivan, A. (2000, June 11). Dot.communist manifesto. *New York Times Magazine*, 30–32.

Thornhill, S. (2009, May 23). Meghan McCain: A chip off the maverick block. *Associated Content News*. Retrieved July 13, 2009, from www.associatedcontent.com/article/1776808/meghan_mccain_.html

Vranica, S. (2009, June 22). GM will hold ad budget steady. *Wall Street Journal*. Retrieved July 12, 2009, from http://online.wsj.com/article/SB124562414399735483.html

Wilson, S. (2002). *Seeking and resisting compliance: What people say and what they do when trying to influence others*. Thousand Oaks, CA: Sage Publications.

CHAPTER 6

Framing and Reframing

WHAT ARE FRAMES?

Matt wants to connect the nine dots shown in Figure 6.1 by four straight lines without lifting his pen or pencil from the paper. (The solution to the problem appears in Figure 6.2, but do not peek until you too have worked on the problem for at least two minutes.)

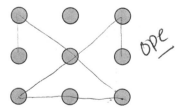

FIGURE 6.1 *The goal: Connect the nine dots with by four straight lines without lifting his pen or pencil from the paper.*
Public domain

At first, like nearly everyone who comes across this problem for the first time, Matt assumes that the nine dots comprise a rectangle and that he can't go outside the box formed by the dots. But this self-imposed rule dooms all attempts to solve the problem. It is only when he questions the assumption that he must stay within a set of invisible boundaries, and recognizes that the task allows greater freedom than he'd initially assumed, that he can step outside the frame of his own making and deal with the problem effectively (Figure 6.2).

This lesson has enormous implications for persuasion. As in the example below, framing sometimes suggests going outside of the box. At other times, it suggests changing the box altogether, as when, for example, the mainstream media agreed to call individuals who came to the USA without proper documentation "undocumented immigrants" and to avoid using terminology like "illegal aliens." The reasons for the change are rooted in journalistic accuracy and respect. First, calling someone an "illegal alien" is legally inaccurate. Being in the USA without proper documents is a civil offense, not a criminal one, a fact that is underscored by Supreme Court Justice Anthony Kennedy, who wrote in response to Arizona's controversial immigration law that "as a general rule, it is not a crime for a movable alien to remain in the United States" (Vargas, 2012). "Think of it this way: In what other contexts do we call someone is illegal? If someone is driving a car at 14, we say 'underage driver,' not 'illegal driver'" (Vargas, 2012). Second, the terminology "illegal alien" is dehumanizing, calling to mind the dictionary definition of alien: "unfamiliar, and disturbing and distasteful" (Head, 2014). Consequently, using the term "undocumented immigrants" more accurately describes the situation, and does so without demeaning the individuals so labeled. The change makes sense for journalism, but that is not all. Reframes of this sort encourage audiences to think in new ways.

Attempts at reframing often meet with resistance, even when they can be helpful to people. As psychotherapists Watzlawick, Weakland, and Fisch (1974) point out, it is not simply the perspective people have on particular issues that gets in the way of finding solutions to problems; often, it is their more general tendency to regard any and all categories as fixed and proper:

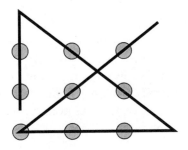

FIGURE 6.2   *There are various solutions to the puzzle, but they all require us to think "outside of the box."*
Public domain

Once an object is categorized as the member of a given class, it is extremely difficult to see it as belonging also to another class. This class membership of an object is called its "reality"; thus anybody who sees it as the member of another class must be mad or bad. Moreover, from this simplistic assumption there follows another, equally simplistic one, namely that to stick to this view of reality is not only sane, but also "honest," "authentic," and what not. "I cannot play games" is the usual retort of people who are playing the game of not playing a game, when confronted with the possibility of seeing an alternative class membership.

(Watzlawick, et al., 1974)

When frames do become a reality for people, they can become every bit as constraining as a prison and every bit as emancipating as a liberating army.

METAPHORS AS FRAMES, FRAMES AS METAPHORS

A frame is one among a number of possible ways of seeing something, and a reframing is a way of seeing it differently; in effect changing its meaning. A common denominator in all these cases is perspective taking. Here we draw examples from several fields to identify types of frames, illustrate how framing works, and suggest what makes some frames (and reframes) more persuasive than others. In the process you'll be introduced to several frame theorists and researchers.

Metaphors as Frames

Frames typically derive their power from one or more metaphors. Like its close cousin the simile, a metaphor is a comparison of sorts, a way of seeing one thing in terms of something else (Burke, 1969). Metaphors are non-literal comparisons, however, and for that reason they tend to be more powerful than simile expressions. In the hands of a creator of metaphors, for example, "love" is not "*like* a red, red rose": it *becomes* a red, red rose. Some metaphors serve only to add force or drama or life to a description (screaming headlines, yellow journalism), but others serve also as framing devices by which to direct or redirect thought on a matter.

For each of us, there exist areas where metaphors work to frame how we experience life, involving things such as government, politics, corporations, and the law. What is perhaps most interesting about the frames in these areas is how taken-for-granted they are. We generally don't even notice them, and they thereby often exercise persuasive power over us without our noticing it has happened. It is to such situations we now turn our attention.

FIGURE 6.3   *As Kenneth Burke reminds us, a metaphor is a way of seeing one thing in terms of something else.*
Reprinted with permission of offthemark.com

Example 1 Why presidents go to war

Think for a moment about the way American presidents talk about "war" and you'll realize that President Obama did something quite rare when he authorized his administration's drug czar to reject the nation's longstanding "war on drugs" metaphor, recommending instead that America's illegal drug problems be viewed primarily from a public health perspective (Fields, 2009). Soon after being confirmed to head the White House Office of National Drug Control Policy, drug czar Gil Kerlikowske traced out the negative implications of the war metaphor and offered that as a justification for the new frame: "Regardless of how you try to explain to people it's a 'war on drugs' or a 'war on a product,' people see a war as a war on them. We're not at war with people in this country" (Fields, 2009). Going forward, he said, the drug problem in America would be managed through a "complete public health model for dealing with addiction" (Fields, 2009). In Obama's 2015 budget, 43 cents out of every dollar in his $25.4 billion plan for dealing with drugs in American would be earmarked for prevention and treatment (Novack, 2014). In addition, political discussion concerning the option of offering clemency to drug criminals who are languishing in prison over long-past drug offenses is now under consideration (Bazelon, 2014). With these actions, the Obama administration has worked to change the frame about illegal drugs in America; henceforth, instead of battling an enemy, our leaders would be offering treatment. Consider the consequences of this reframe: In place of militaristic imagery, the United States Executive Branch would use the language of healing and restoration of "sick" individuals. This was a dramatic shift in focus, with real-world policy implications.

Despite Obama's rejection of the frame in the case of illegal drugs, the metaphorical war frame has long been a favorite of presidents. Consider the many uses that previous presidents made of the "this means war" metaphor. President Lyndon Johnson declared a *War on Poverty*. Ford pledged an all-out *War on Inflation*. President Carter insisted that the energy problem presented us with *"the moral equivalent of war."* And President George W. Bush declared a *War on Terror*. As Lakoff and Johnson observed, the war metaphor is not simply an emotionally loaded term; it also structures thought and directed action, generating a network of entailments. There is an "enemy," a "threat to national security," which requires "setting targets," "reorganizing priorities," "establishing a new chain of command," "plotting a new strategy," "gathering intelligence," "marshaling forces," "imposing sanctions," "calling for sacrifices," and on and on (1980). The war metaphor highlights certain realities and hides others. It is not merely a way of viewing reality; it constitutes a license for policy change and political or economic action. The very acceptance of the metaphor provides grounds for certain inferences: There is an external, foreign, hostile enemy; the situation will require high priority status; the populace will have to make sacrifices; and if we do not meet the threat, we will not survive.

It is important to remember, though, that it is not the only metaphor available. There are always multiple ways to present an unclear situation. Yet, the war metaphor prevails often, probably because it is so useful to presidents. After all, when a nation is at war, its citizens are all called to its defense. Not only that, they are more inclined to follow their leaders and they are hesitant to criticize them. In a "time of war," loyalty to country matters, and that sense of rallying around the flag can be very valuable to a president who seeks to accomplish his or her agenda.

Example 2 Party politics

Republican pollster Frank Luntz, who specializes in Republican "message development," is well known in conservative circles for his research-tested framing metaphors (Luntz, 2007). Luntz was responsible for much of Newt Gingrich's 1994 "Contract for America," and more recently he has guided conservatives on the strategic use of such terms as "war on terror" instead of "war in Iraq," "climate change" instead of "global warming", and "government takeover of health care" instead of the "Affordable Care Act" (Luntz, 2002, 2004, 2007; Adair, 2010). He argues persuasively for the power of framing and backs up his claims with focus group data and analysis of voting patterns, demonstrating that political framing can influence elections.

According to linguist Geoffrey Nunberg, though, Luntz's list of policy metaphors is only the smallest part of the picture. Luntz's work pales in comparison, Nunberg argues, with the Republicans' success in transforming the word "liberalism." In just the past few decades, says Nunberg, Republicans have remade the framework under which we traditionally understood liberalism (i.e., the New Deal, workers' rights through unionism, and equality for everyone) and reframed it as an elite lifestyle (2006). Stanley Fish describes that, in Nunberg's book:

> A succession of lively chapters explains how the Republicans turned "government into a term of abuse"; torpedoed affirmative action by introducing and promoting reverse discrimination; made "liberal" into a word of accusation; redefined the middle class so it encompassed everyone from the proprietor of a corner grocery to the president of the United States (all standing in alliance against the effete mob of latte-drinking, Volvo-driving Eastern seaboard snobs); invented a cultural divide that masks the economic divide between the haves and have-nots; narrowed Franklin Roosevelt's four freedoms into the freedom of corporations to do what they like; drove a wedge between "patriotic" and "liberal," so that one cannot be said to be both; and, in general, "radically reconfigured the political landscape" in ways that even liberals themselves accede to because the right's language is now the default language for everyone.
>
> (2006)

Nunberg's argument is that conservative success is far more deeply rooted than being a matter of simple word choice. The way in which Americans understand their social condition has been transformed as a substantial and serious reframing of central concepts. He writes that "resentments that have their roots in economic inequality" have been transformed into debates about values,

> making programs that chiefly benefit the wealthy sound like they're aimed at benefiting the middle class, turning *government* into a term of abuse, and making reservations about the direction of American foreign policy sound like signs of weakness of purpose or questionable loyalty.
>
> (Nunberg, 2006)

This change is so profound that even those on the left "can't help using language that embodies the worldview of the right." So, for example, if the word "values" turns up in a political conversation, "it will be understood without reflection to refer to a specific set of stances—pro-family, pro-American, pro-merit, pro-religion, anti-special-interests, anti-quotas, anti-abortion, anti-gay-marriage, anti-assisted-suicide" (Fish, 2006).

Nunberg offers up a convincing thesis about framing and politics. Even in an era of Democratic ascendancy, Nunberg suggests, the term "liberal" remains transformed. Not only that, "liberals" themselves have to cope daily with that transformation, as they adjust to the newly agreed-upon framework. On this they get little help from the mainstream news media:

> Wherever you look, the liberal label is almost exclusively reserved for middle-class whites. Phrases like *working-class liberals, Hispanic liberals* and *black liberals* are virtually nonexistent, though *conservative* is used to describe members of all those groups.... It's as if you can't count as a liberal unless you can afford the lifestyle.
>
> (Nunberg, 2006)

Example 3   Corporate sloganeering

Anyone choosing a framing metaphor must decide what will be intensified and what will be downplayed. Consider the following slogan for the ad agency Spiro and Associates, "the low cholesterol ad agency." In small print, the ad agency boasts, "no fat," "low cholesterol," "no gimmicks," no "drawn-out, formal presentations." The style of the ad reinforces this boast. It is spare, unadorned, and black and white. It "speaks" to its readers in a clipped, informal, decidedly conversational tone.

To appreciate better the low-cholesterol frame, consider a couple of framing alternatives. Might Spiro and Associates do better as the "no frills" agency? But that suggests a reduction in quality as well as in price. What if its competitors, those who prefer dining to dieting, find a different gustatory image more appealing: "the filet mignon of ad agencies" that "sells the steak, not just the sizzle"? But in these days of widespread health concerns, the low-cholesterol appeal is likely to have more takers. Besides, the "filet mignon" frame would *downplay* what the Spiro and Associates agency wants to *highlight*—that is, because of its "no fat" approach, it is able to undercut its competitors in price.

Example 4   Courtroom oratory

The artful use of a metaphor is an important mark of the polished speech or essay. Sometimes, not often, the right one comes to mind. Wayne Booth (1978) provided this particularly good example of reframing by metaphor in a jury trial:

> A lawyer friend of mine was hired to defend a large Southern utility against a suit by a small one, and he thought he was doing fine. All of the law seemed to be on his side, and he felt that he had presented his case well. Then the lawyer for the small utility said, speaking to the jury, almost as if incidentally to his legal case: So now see what it is. They got us where they want us. They holding us up with one hand, their good sharp fishing knife in the other hand, and they sayin' "You sit still, little catfish, we're just going to gut ya'."
>
> (Booth, 1978)

In this example, a contest between relative equals is transformed into a saga of David versus Goliath. Moreover, the speaker not only manages to link himself with his audience in opposition to the lawyer for the larger utility but also redirects attention from the substantive issues toward the personalities involved. Every last detail of this seemingly casual remark, from its Southernisms and "down home" grammatical style to the choice of a catfish (as opposed, say, to a carp), supports the frame the lawyer is trying to create. Imagine, says Booth, that the speaker had tried to frame the picture of victimization using a different metaphor:

> *The big utilities just expect us to stand around helplessly while they sap our vital forces.*
>
>   or
>
> *And so the big utility is trying to disembowel the company I represent, right before our very eyes.*

  Clearly, the catfish motif is rhetorically superior.

(Booth, 1978)

Sometimes "Frames" Can Go Bad!

Every year, English teachers from across the United States submit their collections of actual analogies and metaphors found in high school essays. Here is a sample:

1   Her face was a perfect oval, a circle that had its two sides gently compressed by a Thigh Master.

2   His thoughts tumbled in his head, making and breaking alliances, underpants in a dryer without Cling Free.

3   He spoke about love with the wisdom that can only come from experience. He was the guy who went blind because he looked at a solar eclipse without one of those boxes with a pinhole in it and now goes around the country speaking at high schools about the dangers of looking at a solar eclipse without one of those boxes with a pinhole in it.

4   She grew on him. She was a colony of E. coli, and he was room temperature Canadian beef.

5   She had a deep, throaty, genuine laugh—that sound a dog makes just before it throws up.

6   He was as tall as a six-foot, three-inch tree.

7   McBride fell 12 stories, hitting the pavement—a Hefty bag filled with vegetable soup.

8   John and Mary had never met. They were two hummingbirds who had also never met.

9   He fell for her hard. His heart was a mob informant, and she was the East River.

10   Even in his last years, Granddad had a mind of a steel trap, only one that had been left out so long, it had rusted shut.

11 The plan was as simple as my brother-in-law Phil. But unlike Phil, this plan just might work.

12 The young fighter had a hungry look, the kind you get from not eating for a while.

13 He was a lame duck. Not the metaphorical lame duck, either, but a real duck that was actually lame, maybe from stepping on a land mine or something.

14 The ballerina rose gracefully en Pointe and extended one slender leg behind her, a dog at a fire hydrant.

15 He was deeply in love. When she spoke, he thought he heard bells, as if she were a garbage truck backing up.

"Frames" as Metaphors

Paradoxically, just as metaphors are frames, so the term *frame*, when applied to language, is itself metaphorical. The metaphor of a linguistic frame is at least partially visual, conjuring up images of the way the subject in a photo is "framed" (a president photographed in his office with the American flag behind him versus that same president in a photo with his family), frames in a motion picture (e.g., a battle between cowboys and Indians, first seen from the perspective of the cowboys, then from the perspective of the Indians), building frames (verbal "constructions") and picture frames (e.g., gilt edged versus unadorned). Just as there are frames around pictures, so may there be talk about frames as frames of frames; recall the discussion of levels of communication in Chapter 3.

Frames do not come in a "one size fits all" container, though. Different types of frames do different work. In any prolonged dispute, we should be able to identify a variety of types of framing/reframing.

One category of frames is an *argument frame*. For example, when the pessimist and the optimist argue about whether the glass is half full or half empty, they are debating one reality, but seeing it differently. Or, when the American ambassador to the United Nations says that France's threat of a veto has made the United Nations "irrelevant," the French ambassador says "*Au contraire,*" arguing instead that France's veto threat has helped to make the U.N. "relevant" for the first time in many years.

A *perceptual frame* presents the same reality, but different perspectives. This category of framing is persuasive in that it broadens the scope of the discourse; encouraging participants to think about things in new and different ways. We need to "step outside the box" to solve the nine-dot problem. The dots on the page do not change. One must see them differently, expanding one's imagination beyond the imaginary enclosures the dots suggest, to solve the problem.

FIGURE 6.4 *A casual family photograph of a famous politician like Barack Obama provides a "frame" for us to think about the politician in a particular manner, usually as a "person just like us."*

An *issue frame* takes an ambiguous situation and applies a frame to define it. Often, framers using this style of discourse begin by saying *"The issue is …"*, hinting that what follows will be objective reality. This category of framing is persuasive in that it limits the scope of the discourse; it prescribes what can be said.

A final category of frame is the *meta frame*. This category of framing transforms the way a message is understood. The catfish metaphor presented earlier, as used by the attorney for the small company, exemplifies this configuration, as does the Clarence Thomas case study that will come later in the chapter.

Entman's Definition of Framing

There is clearly a good deal of ambiguity surrounding the notions of framing and reframing, and some writers have therefore attempted to rein the terms in. To frame, suggests Entman (1993), is to *select some aspects of a perceived reality and make them more salient in a communicative text, in such a way as to promote a particular problem, definition, causal interpretation, moral evaluation, and/or treatment recommendation* for the item described.

Thinking It Through

Metaphorical thinking is prevalent all throughout language, even when it seeks to be "fact based." Prove it to yourself: Go through this chapter and identify places where metaphors are used, such as here "to rein in."

Note how this definition fits the examples provided thus far. Indeed, the war metaphor diagnoses, evaluates, and prescribes (Entman, 1993; Gamson, 1992; Lakoff, 2006). The catfish metaphor shifts our attention from the *substantive* frame and presents instead a *metacommunicational* frame, one that makes salient the *relationship* between the two utility companies, suggesting a negative moral evaluation of the larger one.

Entman (1993) adds that frames reside in four locations in a communicative process, which may or may not coincide. These are (1) the communicator, (2) the text, (3) the receiver, and (4) the culture.

Communicators make conscious or unconscious framing judgments in deciding what to say, guided by frames (often called schemata) that organize their belief systems. The *text* contains frames, which are manifested by the presence or absence of certain key words, stock phrases, stereotyped images, sources of information, and sentences. These textual elements work together to provide clusters of facts or judgments that reinforce the messages. The frames that guide the *receiver's* thinking and conclusion may or may not reflect the frames in the text and the framing intention of the communicator. The *culture* is the stock of commonly invoked frames. In fact, culture might even be *defined* as the empirically demonstrable set of common frames exhibited in the discourse and thinking of most people in a social grouping.

CULTURAL FRAMES AND VERBAL REPERTOIRES

This last notion—of cultural frames—is particularly interesting. On many a social or political issue, the culture seems to supply competing aphorisms. Should the college art student take a risk and go on a date with that attractive classmate who's just transferred into the university? Perhaps yes. After all, "nothing ventured, nothing gained," "love is all you need," and "the early bird catches the worm." On the other hand, "love hurts," "look before you leap," "the grass is greener on the other side," and "love is like war; easy to begin but very hard to stop."

These are just a sampling of the seemingly opposed framing expressions that pass for the common sense of Western culture. They are seemingly opposed because as Billig (1987) has observed, the aphorisms don't directly contradict one another when taken literally. Moreover, they are typically invoked selectively, as needed, to make a point or craft an image, and they are persuasive. In this respect, they are like the lines of argument that the ancient Greek and Roman rhetoricians taught would-be orators and that law schools still teach prospective lawyers today. For example, the lawyers wishing to prove that the defendant could have murdered his wife in the time he had available could turn to Aristotle's *Rhetoric* (Cooper, 1932) for lines of argument—called topoi—that can be used in establishing possibility. At the same time, Aristotle's *Rhetoric* would also provide ways to establish impossibility—for example, that the defendant's alibi was ironclad.

People hold in their heads not just seemingly opposed aphorisms and lines of argument but entire *repertoires* of verbal response that they invoke, depending on what they take to be the relevant frame in a given situation. Americans are willing to support "preventing Medicare from going bankrupt by reducing the annual rate of increase in Medicare funding." But they are strongly opposed to "cutting back on Medicare spending." Or, they support a "culture of life" while also supporting "the death penalty."

Americans are able to shift repertoires, especially when competing cultural myths about what it means to be an American are called into play. As reflected in decades-long controversies about taxes, affirmative action, and universal health care, Americans tend to shift between the two dominant cultural frames of "self-reliance" and "equality." Let a politician emphasize either frame, and people tend to nod their support for it, at least until they hear another politician evoking the competing frame. The frames are not easily reconciled; thus, public opinion tends to be divided on such issues as welfare and affirmative action, with many people registering ambivalence and with pronounced shifts in expressed attitudes depending on how questions are worded or to whom they are talking or listening (Edelman, 1971;

Gamson & Modigliani, 1989). When efforts are made to reconcile the two frames, confusion frequently results. For example, most Americans favor the consideration of race in providing opportunities for blacks to compensate them for past mistreatment (here emphasizing the frame of equality). They want their governing institutions to be color-blind, however, in allocating rewards (here emphasizing the frame of self-reliance). But admission to college or graduate school is both an opportunity and a reward (Gamson & Modigliani, 1989). What do they do then?

Faced with challenges to their positions, proponents and opponents of affirmative action (or welfare, or government-subsidized health insurance) engage in *spin control.* Correspondingly, they reframe incoming information or opposing arguments in an effort to make them fit with their positions. Supporters of affirmative action insist that they are not opposed to self-reliance; they simply want to "help minorities help themselves." Opponents of affirmative action declare that they are not opposed to equality, but the equality that is most truly "American," they insist, is "equality of opportunity." Similarly, although opponents of affirmative action castigate it as "preferential treatment," supporters call it "compensatory treatment." Each group, meanwhile, invokes rival sayings, mottos, slogans, and catchphrases that have been woven throughout centuries into the fabric of the culture (Billig, 1987). "God helps those who help themselves," says the champion of self-reliance. "Love thy neighbor as thyself," says the egalitarian. And so the battle of competing frames goes on.

Thinking It Through

Americans generally cling to and value the notion of self-reliance. We are considered responsible adults when we can "make it on our own." At the same time, Americans often have help along the way: Mortgage interest on our houses reduces our taxes, public school is "free" for students because it is paid for through our taxes, student loans are often subsidized by the government, and public universities are able to provide more affordable tuition than private schools because they receive tax dollars from the citizens of the states in which they are located.

How do you frame the debate between self-reliance and equality? Do you recognize how the taxes paid by others benefit you, or do you see your life as one where you are on your own?

What are the origins of the frames you use to decide about issues, and what are the ramifications of the frames you choose? How do they impact your actions and reactions?

Linguist George Lakoff has done extensive work in this area, arguing that Americans metaphorically conceive of politics and policy through the framework of the "family," with two frames competing for attention: the **strict father frame** and the **nurturant parent frame**. The "strict father" frame emphasizes discipline and self-sufficiency, where the "nurturant parent" frame focuses on fairness and cooperation (Lakoff 1996, 2004, 2006; Lakoff & Wehling, 2012). The frames are not easily reconciled, and, when activated, they can shift public opinion on such issues as taxes and universal health care, with many persons registering ambivalence and with pronounced shifts in expressed attitudes depending on how questions are worded or to whom they are talking or listening (Edelman, 1971; Gamson & Modigliani, 1989).

George Lakoff on Metaphors, Framing, and Politics

Over the past twenty-five years, one of the most interesting researchers on the persuasive power of framing and metaphors is George Lakoff, who developed a detailed analysis comparing and extending two competing frames. He notes that most of us are "bi-conceptual," in that we engage both frames and apply them to particular parts of our lives. For example, a professor may use the strict father model with her students, expecting them to be responsible and disciplined when it comes to their school work, and at the same time use a nurturant parent model at home with her children. Lakoff notes that when politicians activate a particular frame in a voter's mind and connect it with themselves, they increase greatly the chances of earning that citizen's vote.

Look at the table below and, notice how the frames stand in direct contrast to each other. Which column is closer to your worldview?

TABLE 6.1 *Lakoff's Model Comparing Frames*

STRICT FATHER MODEL	NURTURANT PARENT MODEL
The world is a dangerous place—there is evil in the world.	The world is a gift; there are dangers, but we can work to make it better.
The world is competitive, with winners and losers.	The world is by nature cooperative, and that is often unrecognized.
Children are born bad. Our responsibility when it comes to our children is to teach them self-discipline and obedience.	Children are born good. Our responsibility when it comes to our children is to nurture and protect them.
It is moral to pursue your self-interest—when you do well, you are helping improve the world.	It is moral to pursue fairness—when all have the chance to do well, the world is just.
A good person—a moral person—is one who is disciplined enough to be obedient, to learn what is right, to do what is right, and to pursue self-interest to prosper and become self-reliant.	A good person—a moral person—is one who is honest, who fights for fairness, and who fights against discrimination and greed.
The opponent is considered a "do-gooder," one who is trying to help someone else rather than working on self-reliance. The do-gooder stands in the way of creating self-reliant individuals.	The opponent is one who places his or her self-interest above all else, who does not recognize the inter-connectedness of our world.

Framing the news

News reporters may frame projections of the future as rosy or dour by the sources they cite. Like persuaders generally, they invite consideration of some facts and not others through their use of *issue frames*.

"*At issue*" (or "*the issue*") said the advocate at the decision point for invading Iraq, "is whether we can risk delay given the strong likelihood that Saddam Hussein possesses weapons of mass destruction." "*At issue*" said the opponent of invasion "is whether we can risk going into Iraq when the evidence on WMDs is weak and when we have no plan for getting out of Iraq once we go in."

Reporting from an African nation on the suffering of a tribal group at the hands of the government, a reporter rejects talk of random killings and says matter-of-factly, "*the issue* is nothing less than genocide." Through such framing, the reporter limits how we think and talk about the issue at hand.

Even as reporters strive to be "objective," the news comes to us encased in a frame, and the frame influences what we conclude about the story. For example, imagine that the United States is anticipating an outbreak of a disease that will kill 600 people. The government is planning a program to reduce the casualties and the media wants to report on the story. Researchers have found that the way the information gets framed influences whether viewers will support the government's proposal or not.

Consider these two statements:

1   "If Program A is adopted, 200 people will be saved."

2   "If Program B is adopted, there is a one-third probability that 600 people will be saved and a two-thirds probability that no people will be saved."

In fact, the statements are saying the same thing but framed differently. And when these options were tested on research subjects, 72% supported option A whereas only 28% supported option B. When a situation is framed in terms of potential gains (200 saved), it seems that people don't want to gamble.

But now, look at these two statements:

1   "If Program A is adopted, 400 people will die."

2   "If Program B is adopted, there is a one-third probability that nobody will die and a two-thirds probability that 600 people will die."

In this scenario, the research outcome was reversed: 22% preferred option A, and 78% preferred option B. When a situation is framed in terms of potential losses (400 die), people are more persuaded to take risks (Tversky & Kahneman, 2004).

The point here is that, in an instance like this, there is no deliberate bias and no shading of the facts. Yet, research demonstrates that the frame that is selected matters, and influences greatly how we take in the story and are persuaded to respond to it.

Iyengar suggests that news reports can be classified (based on form of presentation) as either episodic or thematic (1991). An **episodic news frame** takes "the form of a case study or event-oriented report and depicts public issues in terms of concrete instances" (Iyengar, 1991). The **thematic news frame** of the same event "places public issues in some more general or abstract context" (Iyengar, 1991). Thematic stories include things like reports on changes in governmental welfare expenditures or stories about the backlog in the criminal justice process. Conversely, episodic stories cover things like the bombing of an airliner or a story about an attempted murder:

> The essential difference between episodic and thematic framing is that episodic framing depicts concrete events that illustrate issues, while thematic framing presents collective or general evidence. Visually, episodic reports make "good pictures," while thematic reports feature talking heads.
>
> (Iyengar, 1991)

Most news is episodic, laments Iyengar; the framing focus is on shorter and visually oriented stories, which limits the information. And then, compounding the problem, says Bennett, is the fact that newsrooms have changed; because of governmental deregulation and the rise of huge media conglomerates, there is less investigative journalism, more infotainment, more soft features, and more of a play-it-safe mentality that affects the ways in which the news gets framed:

> As a result, there is more debate on the air and in print about the lyrics in teen music, the language of shock jocks, or an exposed breast during the Super Bowl halftime show than about how to improve the quality of democratic news environment.
>
> (Bennett, 2007)

Such framing trends are worrisome to scholars like Bennett, who claims that the "American press is in crisis" (Bennett, 2007). We agree—the frame matters. It is troubling when framing patterns tend more toward the episodic coverage of stories and fewer stories are framed to provide analysis, context, and detail. And it is distressing when the drive for profits causes media outlets to frame the hard news as just more infotainment. The problems for journalism are vast right now, and beyond the scope of our brief analysis of how framing is present in the news. That being said, we can add this point to the discussion: Frames are a fact. To serve the public ethically, news editors and reporters should consider with care which frames they use, understanding that their choices impact the lives of the public they are called to serve.

RESEARCH ON FRAMES AND REFRAMES

The difference that a frame (or reframe) can make in persuading people to change their behaviors has been amply demonstrated by social psychologists (e.g., Kahneman & Tversky, 1984). A few examples of research findings are reviewed below.

Example 1

A   This beef is 75% lean.

B   This beef is 25% fat.

In this study, focusing on positive product attributes produced more favorable ratings (Levin & Gaeth, 1988). But consider the following:

Example 2

A   Women who do breast self-examinations have an increased chance of finding a tumor in the early, more treatable stage of the disease.

B   Women who do not do breast self-examinations have a decreased chance of finding a tumor in the early, more treatable stage of the disease.

Here, the negatively worded message produced greater compliance with recommendations for breast self-examinations (Meyerowitz & Chaiken, 1987). Negatively framed messages appear to be more persuasive when detailed processing is called for.

Example 3

In studying how leading questions can influence eyewitness testimony in the courtroom, Loftus and Palmer (1974) showed participants a film depicting a multi-car accident. After the film, participants were asked one of two leading questions:

A   About how fast were the cars going when they *smashed* into each other?

B   About how fast were the cars going when they *hit* each other?

Participants presented with wording A not only estimated that the cars were going faster but also were more likely to report having seen broken glass at the accident scene, although none was shown (Loftus & Palmer, 1974).

METACOMMUNICATIVE FRAMES

As discussed in Chapter 3, metacommunication is communication *about* communication. Two types of metacommunication are (1) *reflexive* and (2) *responsive*.

(1) Reflexive Metacommunication

Reflexive messages interpret, classify, or in other ways comment on one's own messages. Much of this is done non-verbally (see Chapter 3). But consider the following response by then-President Richard Nixon when a reporter asked why he held press conferences irregularly: "It's not that I'm afraid to do it. I have to determine the best way of communicating, and also, *and this will sound self-serving, and is intended to be,* I have to use the press conference" [italics added] (Cohen, 1988). The reporter supplied the substantive frame: Why do you hold press conferences irregularly? Nixon merely stayed in frame when he answered that question directly. But he went "meta" to himself when he said "and this will sound self-serving," and he went "meta-meta" when he said, "and is intended to be."

Reflexive metacommunication at the beginning of a speech or essay can be highly persuasive because it "frames" the message to come in the way that the speaker wants it to be heard. The persuader generally classifies the message, indicating the purpose or purposes of the communication, previews the upcoming substantive message, and metacommunicates explicitly as well as implicitly about themselves in relation to the audience. The strategic character of these framing opportunities is revealed by comparing what is said with what could have been said.

For example, Congressman Fudge has returned to his home district to address an audience of business leaders and to consult privately with a few of them regarding what they want from him. He also wants to seek their general support for his legislative priorities. His subject is a national sales tax, which many in his audience oppose but which he is inclined to support. Fudge decides he won't get into an open confrontation with the many sales tax opponents in his audience. Instead, he introduces his speech as a "discussion of options for raising federal revenues to support needed programs."

Rather than stating overtly that he wants the audience's support for the tax, he says that he intends to "inform" them of recent research by his staff on "revenue enhancement." Rather than organizing his speech around the benefits of a national sales tax and the costs of not creating one, he declares that he first wants to "explore" alternatives with them. All these are framing maneuvers that Fudge uses in talking about his own subsequent talk, and they work to set the boundaries for what fits into the discussion and what does not.

Thinking It Through

Think about a time in your life when you used reflexive metacommunication persuasively. It might have been in a conversation with a family member, or with an employer, or with a romantic partner, where you began the encounter by explaining what you intended to discuss and why. In what ways did that discursive choice act to guide what could be said, and, maybe more importantly, what could NOT be discussed?

(2) Responsive Metacommunication

Responsive metacommunication is the frame-altering reply to what others have said in interactive situations. Note the following responses to the question "Have you got the time?"

1   "If you've got the money, honey, I've got the time." Or

2   "Your English is improving." Or

3   "What is time, anyway?"

The central point of these examples is that responsive metacommunication transforms (and sometimes breaks) the frame. Usually, there is an expectation that we will directly reply to questions in a given situation. If instead we choose to step back from a question in order to question the questioner's motives, tone, premises, right to ask certain questions, or right to ask any questions at all, then we will have "gone meta" (and broken the frame of direct address). Going meta also occurs when we comment favorably on a question or on the questioner's mode of delivery.

Moreover, communicators may comment not only on something that's just been said but also on larger segments of an interaction ("This conversation is getting out of hand"), on the interaction as a whole ("I didn't know this was to be a cross-examination"), or, for that matter, on multiple interactions involving different groups of interactants ("Why do you Americans always seem to privilege your own cultural premises?"). All these are instances of metamoves that can be highly persuasive because they shift the discussion to entirely different areas.

REFRAMING IN POLITICAL CONFRONTATIONS: "GOING META"

Today, Clarence Thomas is known mostly as a reliably conservative justice on the U.S. Supreme Court. But, his path to the court was not a smooth one. During the intensely watched Senate Judiciary Committee hearings in 1991, he confronted allegations of sexual harassment from Professor Anita Hill, his former employee.

FIGURE 6.5 *Clarence Thomas, testifying at his 1991 confirmation hearings for the Supreme Court, where he answered the accusations of Anita Hill.*
Courtesy of Getty Images

Although the nomination hearings occurred over two decades ago, they are still intensely studied by scholars in many disciplines, and the issues they raised are as relevant as today's news.

During the hearings, which were televised and widely viewed, Anita Hill brought forward her charges against Thomas in a distinctive communicative style. She engaged consistently in activities that might be characterized as direct exchange— that is, she concentrated on doing what was expected of her at the hearings, according to all the explicit rules of communication and implicit "taken-for-granteds" (Hopper, 1981) for that situation. Asked a question, she answered it directly. Challenged by a follow-up to her response, she attempted to meet the challenge directly. What she did not do was "go meta."

By contrast, in his opening statement, Thomas sought to place the hearings themselves in question: "This is not American. This is Kafkaesque. It has got to stop." Then he let his questioners know which questions he would answer and which questions he considered out of bounds. "I am here specifically to respond to allegations of sex harassment in the workplace.... I will not allow this committee or anyone else to probe into my private life." In his second statement, Thomas found new ways to castigate the hearings: a "circus," a "national disgrace," a "high-tech lynching." Then he proceeded to inform the committee that he had chosen not to listen to Anita Hill's testimony: "No I didn't: I've heard enough lies." Admonished by Democratic Senator Howell Heflin for not listening to the testimony and thus denying himself a chance to refute it, Thomas challenged Heflin's premise: "Senator, I am incapable of proving the negative." Only after Thomas had engineered a reframing of the committee hearings did he deign to respond directly to questions, and even then he maintained non-verbally the persona of the beleaguered victim (*New York Times*, 1991; Thomas, 1991).

When Judge Thomas cast himself as the victim of a "high-tech lynching," he reframed the hearings in two important respects. First, by the act of "stepping outside the circle" of question and reply, he broke from the frame of business as usual. Second, by his lynching metaphor, he placed a particular stamp on that business, a particular way of seeing it. The effect of Thomas's metamoves was to displace attention from his own guilt or innocence to that of the Judiciary Committee. Now it was the Democratic majority's turn to shift in their seats as Senator Heflin sought in vain to regain control of the situation. Arguably, the Democrats could have so bolstered Anita Hill's case against Clarence Thomas during the hearings that Thomas's later repudiation of the process would have seemed shrill, unfair, self-serving, and hypocritical. Perhaps someone among the members of the Democratic majority could have "gone meta" to Thomas's metamoves, effectively calling them into question. Surely, Thomas and his Republican handlers had to know that "going meta" in such a confrontational way was a risky undertaking.

But the Thomas forces also knew that the Democratic majority's legitimacy had been significantly eroded in the regular hearings on Judge Thomas's nomination, during the negotiations leading up to the Hill–Thomas hearings, and at the Hill–Thomas hearings themselves. Having observed, for example, the Democrats' failure to come to Anita Hill's aid in the face of withering questioning by then-Republican Senator Arlen Specter, they concluded that they could attack with impunity (Nelson, 1991).

This is not to say that Thomas's success was foreordained. On the face of it, after all, the metaphor of a high-tech lynching hardly suited a congressional hearing peopled by supporters and not just opponents, at which the principal accuser of a conservative appellate judge was another African American. But Thomas managed rhetorically to deflect attention from the questionable logic of the metaphor, providing what television critic Walter Goodman (1991) saw as having all the earmarks of a theatrical performance. Said Goodman, "He was innocent and hurt, indignant and outraged. His frequent references to family and his language—'a living hell'—seemed to have been influenced by television melodrama" (1991).

Judge Thomas's undoing of the Democratic majority at the hearing by way of biting commentaries on his situation provides vivid illustration of the power of metamoves. In keeping with the notion of levels of communication, these are a way of going "one up" in the situation by arrogating to oneself the role of interpreter—hence, the frequent references here to going meta. But going meta requires a rhetorical balancing act, pivoting on the high wire of perceived legitimacy. There were reasons, after all, why Anita Hill did not go meta. Her almost exclusive reliance on direct exchange promoted an image of demure self-confidence, of politeness and a sense of propriety, of consideration for her interlocutors' interests and not just her own, and of someone who had nothing to hide. Thus, meta-goers must skillfully balance the potential gains of enhancing their reputations, shaping agendas, and influencing judgments against the dangers of appearing unjustifiably intrusive, disruptive, contentious, or evasive. Meta-goers in confrontational situations must also weigh into the balance their relative legitimacy against that of their opponents.

"Having" legitimacy is rhetorically akin to holding the chips necessary to call or raise in a poker game. In each case, it is a matter of rights or entitlements. But calculations of legitimacy are by no means as easy as chip counting. Ultimately, legitimacy is performative, a matter not simply of what one has but of what one can do to shape audience perceptions of what one has. Legitimacy, then, is also subject to frame altering.

Legitimacy is also contextual. Were Judge Thomas sitting on his own bench, there would be little question of his right to deflect questions by commenting on them. Were he a teacher responding to a student or a therapist responding to a patient, he might be granted the right to provide not just any interpretation but the "authoritative" interpretation in that situation. But what are the rights of a Supreme Court nominee at a Judiciary Committee hearing on charges of sexual harassment? The waters were uncharted. Surely, a complex mix of counteracting factors entered into the public's determination of Thomas's rights, as they typically do in all political confrontations.

REFRAMING IN PSYCHOTHERAPY

When people come into psychotherapy, it is often because the meanings and interpretations they have given to the events in their lives haven't worked to remedy their problems and may indeed have contributed to them. Much of what falls under the rubric of reframing in psychotherapy involves helping people create new meanings and new ways of making sense of their experiences that might lead to new possibilities for adaptive action. Clinical psychologist Paul Wachtel (1993) provides the example of Bret, whose wife experienced considerable anxiety at parties with people she didn't know. When Bret's wife reluctantly agreed to attend these parties, she stayed so close to him that Bret would inevitably berate her for her excessive "clinginess." Bret was troubled by his attitude toward his wife, however, whom he loved and enjoyed being with when they were together by themselves. Wachtel chose to reframe Bret's report by responding, "Your wife seems to feel most relaxed when she's alone with you" (1993). Said Wachtel:

> It is interesting to note that the comment simply restated what Bret had been describing, but from the opposite vantage point. One could equally describe Bret's wife as *less* comfortable with strangers, or as *more* comfortable alone with him. But although the two ways of framing the facts were logical equivalents, they were not at

all equivalent psychologically. The second vantage point highlighted a different meaning to the behavior and had different implications for their relationship. Moreover, by interrupting the pattern of bickering that had developed between them about this issue, the reframing created space for a different equilibrium to develop and for them to renegotiate how they would deal with their differing experiences of social occasions.

(1993)

Just as it is impossible to *not* metacommunicate when an individual is joined in time and space with others, so it is impossible to *not* supply a frame. A central issue for psychotherapists is whether to provide an objectivist or coactive frame in registering interpretations of the patient's reported problems.

Consider the familiar case of two persons locked in a vicious cycle of reproach and recrimination. Partner A withdraws from the relationship because of feeling trapped by Partner B's possessiveness. But Partner B clings because of the feeling that Partner A is slipping away. Conceivably, the therapist could declare objectively that each is contributing to the problem and suggest steps that they could take to rectify it. But matters are seldom that simple. The couple may be invested in their own "objective" analyses of the source of the problem and in their anger toward the other. Neither may be consciously aware of their own role in contributing to the problem. One or both may become defensive on being questioned about it, fearing, perhaps, that they will be judged as mad or bad. They may resist change in the relationship because, bad as it is, it has its satisfying moments and may be preferable to some untried alternative.

The **objectivist approach to psychotherapy** assumes that there is one best description of the patient's problems and one best explanation for their causes. The job of the therapist is to help the patient overcome defenses to face up to the deep, dark, disturbing truths denied to consciousness by the patient's self-deceiving nature. By this account, knowledge of the repressed "real" self is an essential step toward cure. Insofar as patients resist self-discovery, they must also be confronted with their resistance. Never mind that this frequently sets up an adversarial relationship between therapist and patient.

An extreme example of the objectivist approach is found in a case report by classic psychoanalyst Otto Kernberg (Wile, 1984). It involved a conflict between Kernberg and a female patient who had gotten increasingly angry at Kernberg for telling her that she was masochistic, defensive, and infantile and that she wanted to have intercourse with her father as well as with him. According to Wile, "Although this may be everyday common sense talk to psychoanalysts, such statements may seem strange and accusatory to many others" (1984).

The **coactive approach to psychotherapy** rejects objectivism in favor of a view of the therapist as one who helps the patient construct a *version* of the truth, one that will be more productive for the patient than the perspective that helps perpetuate and perhaps aggravate the patient's problems. This pragmatic orientation assumes that there is no single truth about problems and their causes but rather multiple truths or perspectives. This perspective on truth itself licenses the therapist to use language flexibly, strategically, and coactively, whether in questioning the patient or in offering interpretations of what the patient presents. Here, as in ordinary persuasive discourse, attention must be paid not just to the substantive message but to the attitudes toward the patient expressed in the therapist's metacommunications. Of crucial importance are verbal framings (and non-verbal accompaniments) that elicit cooperation, enhance self-esteem, and lead to conflict-resolving, fear-reducing, or skill-enhancing action.

Wachtel has done an admirable job of illustrating the differences in objectivist versus coactive approaches. Instead of phrasing interpretations in forms such as "You are trying to hide ...," "You are denying ...," and "You're really very ...." Wachtel urges "framing comments whose meta-message conveys permission for the patient to reappropriate previously warded-off feelings" (1993). Here are some examples:

> *You seem rather harsh with yourself when you sense any hint of sexual feeling.* [Instead of "You avoid acknowledging sexual feelings."]
>
> *You seem to expect something terrible to happen to you if you have any wish to be taken care of.* [Instead of "You're defending against feelings of dependency."]
>
> *I have the sense that you're angry at your mother but think it's awful of you to feel that.* [Instead of "You're a lot angrier at your mother than you realize."]

In these examples, the therapist moves toward the patient psychologically by opening a permissive space for mutual exploration of the patient's problems. A coactive persuader, rather than an objectivist, is at work here.

Putting Frame Analysis Methods to Work: A Review and an Extended Example

Recall from Chapter 1 that methodologies for rhetorical criticism must be adapted to the task at hand. Goals of critical analysis vary, as do the objects of analysis. We've seen in this chapter that frames and reframes come in several varieties and serve many purposes. In this concluding section we urge you to review the chapter's many examples with an eye to the varied purposes of the persuader and to the different analytic tools that can usefully be employed by the message analyst. Use this review to fashion critical assessments of your own. Here are some examples:

- The Obama administration's reframing of illegal drug use in America as a *medical* problem, no longer to be viewed from the frame of *war*. Critical analysis often requires teasing out the implications of a shift in metaphors. Our analysis derives from Lakoff and Johnson's (1980) excellent work on the *entailments* of the war metaphor, as applied, for example, to earlier "wars" on poverty and inflation. We suggest you try your own hand at analyzing another commonplace conceptual metaphor: that of arguments as wars. How many examples can you find of everyday expressions (e.g., the "overpowering argument," "defeated by an argument") in which arguments are seen as wars? Suppose arguments between people were "reframed" as cooperative as "a dance," for example? What would be the new entailments? How would the reframing shift our perspectives on argument?

- In rhetorical critic Wayne Booth's example, the lawyer for the small utility company uses a down-home grammatical style and "Southernisms" to cast the small utility company as David and the larger utility as Goliath. Featured by Booth is a catfish metaphor, but the metaphor is embedded in a narrative of victimage. "You sit still, little catfish, we're just going to gut ya'" (Booth, 1978). In this as in nearly all instances of good frame analysis, metaphors are important, but so too are their accompanying details, including, in this case, the attorney's folksy style of presentation. As Gamson has argued, frames are part of a *package* that may include slogans, stock phrases, stereotyped images, sources of information, and examples (1998). Booth also convinces us of the power of the catfish metaphor by contrasting it with lesser metaphors.

- Judge Clarence Thomas's put-down of the Senate Judiciary Committee's hearing on his nomination (calling it a "high-tech lynching") involves a very different *context* than in the "catfish" example, but shares with it the sense of Thomas as victim, as "David fighting Goliath." As with the previous examples, the critic is obligated to take apart the metaphor (why "high-tech" lynching?) but also to provide context sufficient to enable us to appreciate its likely effectiveness. Why was Thomas able to pull off so audacious a "meta-move" as a challenge to the very legitimacy of the Senate committee hearing his case?

- Assessing frames (or reframes) in light of goals, contexts, style, and metaphorical entailments are features of the foregoing examples. But different methodological tools are needed in identifying cultural frames as in Billig's claim that cultures supply seemingly competing aphorisms: "Look before you leap" versus "Nothing ventured, nothing gained" are among his examples (Billig, 1987). Here the analyst can no longer focus in depth on a single message but must turn to broad samplings of discourse to nail down a claim.

- The same thing is true of broad generalizations such as Lakoff's on the competing family metaphors used by Americans in rendering political judgments or Nunberg's on the appropriation by Republicans of the meanings of commonplace terms such as "liberals" and "values." Nunberg has made good use of search engines such as Google's to compare frequencies of "liberal elite" versus "business elite" in everyday parlance about elitism—this statistical evidence shows how liberalism has been so thoroughly reframed as an elite lifestyle that it has even eclipsed popular references to business elites. You might do similar search engine comparisons using other pairs of terms.

Our final, extended example, employing a tradition of rhetorical criticism ("metaphor criticism"), should cut closer to your direct experience. Let's say you are trying to sort out your understanding of college life: What metaphors come to mind? There are many possibilities: college is a family, a community, a home. But then, it is also a circus, a prison where you are counting down the days until your sentence is up, or a job. College could be the mall—you pay your money and purchase classes. Or, college could be like a mental hospital, where you say what they want you to say so that you can get out. Or perhaps you see college as a conversation, one where you interact with others and share interesting thoughts.

Once you've created your list of metaphors, you need to analyze them to see what kinds of frames exist. For example, the metaphor of college as a mall might lead to a frame of a transactional business relationship—you've paid your money, you do what you need to, and you get a degree. That frame can lead to you saying things like "I paid for this class. If I can read the book, take the tests, and pass, I shouldn't be forced to attend class." Or, the metaphor of college as a conversation might lead to a frame of communal lifelong learning. With that frame, you find yourself on the Internet looking up more about subjects that have been introduced in class, and when you are socializing with friends, you find the topics of discussion often gravitate toward subjects that are being discussed in your courses. With that frame, school work is not something to be completed as quickly and with as little effort as possible. Instead, it is closely connected with your intrapersonal and interpersonal life.

After you've established the frames, the next step is to analyze them. Are there frames that stand in direct opposition to each other, as did George Lakoff's frames for politics and the family? Are there frames that are companions, ones that can coexist easily? (i.e., college as a family; college as a home). Do the frames offer positive or negative perspectives on the situation? And, do the frames compete to explain the same reality? Is there conflict with the frames where they are competing to see which one will prevail? (Think, "the glass is half full," "the glass is half empty" here.) Or, are the frames working to explain something that is ambiguous? Are they seeking to define the situation? (Think, "the issue is …" here.)

Once you've completed this analysis, you can begin to put it all together and draw conclusions. Oftentimes, you will likely find that there are competing frames and that is the source of the issue: Your parents see your college as a party, whereas you see it as a home; you see your college as the mall, but your professor views it as your job.

After you've completed this analysis, you'll likely have many sheets of paper. What's next? Conclude your work by creating a summary of your findings, forming a thesis sentence and then backing it up with your evidence: "I have come to see my life through the frame of an independent adult who can exist on her own, which metaphorically plays out in my feeling that college is my home." And naturally:

Mom and Dad are struggling with that. They love me and don't want me to grow up, and they are adopting the metaphor of "college is a party" as the explanation for why I am spending less time with them in our family home.

When you've completed your analysis, it is up to you how to proceed. You can put it in the drawer and feel comforted with having sorted out something. Or, you can use it as a device to metacommunicate in a non-threatening way about the situation. By sharing your analysis, you can not only inform yourself, but you can enlighten the others in your life as well.

The Steps for Using Metaphor Criticism to Analyze Frames

1   Get a detailed description of your "text."

2   Make a list of all the metaphors in the text.

3   Analyze the metaphors to find the frames.

4   Analyze the frames, looking for:
    a   opposite frames;
    b   companion frames;
    c   positive versus negative frames;
    d   same reality frames;
    e   frames of definition.

5   Draw conclusions: What follows from the frame for you and others involved?

6   Create a thesis: one sentence that sets down your findings.

7   Support your thesis with details from your analysis.

SUMMARY

The terms *framing* and *reframing* are ambiguous yet useful nonetheless. Cultures supply frames (e.g., the power of positive thinking and the need to avoid wishful thinking), people select them (being in an optimistic or pessimistic frame of mind), and texts contain them ("Think positive," "Be realistic"). In all these cases, the organizing of a perceived reality is taking place. The persuader who urges positive thinking is connecting life's dots in a particular way. The dots may include ideas about causation ("Where there's a will, there's a way"), about problems ("You're too picky"), and solutions ("Always look on the bright side of life"). As Entman (1993) maintains, frames may also suggest moral evaluations ("It's unfair of you to put down my hopes and aspirations"). As addressed to a person who is routinely pessimistic, the recommendation to "chill out" is a reframe, a proposal to restructure life's dots, or, to use a different metaphor, to think outside the boxes of pessimism and despair. As in these examples, not only are "framing" and "reframing" metaphors, but also reframing is often accomplished by the use of metaphor.

Cultures typically offer competing frames on a controversial topic—justice versus mercy as applied to capital punishment, for example. This is a source of ambivalence or indecision for many people. Persuaders, then, have an opportunity to tilt audience opinion in one direction or the other—toward the rough justice of capital punishment or toward the tender mercy of limited incarceration.

So what difference does a frame make? It has been well documented in framing research that respondents will often prefer one framing alternative to another by wide margins, although only the language has been altered, not the actual meanings or consequences. Most impressive, perhaps, is research showing that eyewitnesses to an accident can be persuaded to conjure up memories of broken glass in a video of an accident simply by being asked, via a leading question, about the cars "smashing" into each other, rather than "hitting" each other.

Frames (and reframes) may be *substantive* or *metacommunicative*. In the latter category are two subtypes: reflexive metacommunications and responsive metacommunications. Reflexive metacommunications figure importantly in the introductions to speeches or essays where, in effect, persuaders strategically frame the substantive messages they will later be presenting.

Responsive metacommunications are of particular significance in interactive situations. Here, a communicator may "go meta" to a prior communication or to the message context, rather than staying within its frame. The notion of going meta suggests communicating not just *about* but also *above* (at a higher level), and, indeed, metamoves in political confrontations are typically a form of one-upmanship.

In psychotherapy, therapists can often defuse unnecessary anxiety in patients by offering coactive reframes rather than objectivist reframes. Instead of phrasing interpretations in forms such as "You are trying to hide ...," "You are denying ...," and "You're really very ...," Wachtel (1993) urges framing comments whose metamessage conveys permission for the patient to face up to previously warded-off feelings; for example, "You seem to expect something terrible to happen to you if you have any wish to be taken care of" (instead of "You're defending against feelings of dependency").

This chapter has shown that frames are persuasive, ubiquitous, and fascinating. And, through the application of a step-by-step method of analysis, we can gain a greater understanding of how they work in our lives. With such understanding, we will be more forceful persuaders and critical analysts of the persuasion that is directed toward us.

QUESTIONS AND PROJECTS FOR FURTHER STUDY

1 Most people are unable to solve the nine-dot problem. Then, after it is explained to them, they say, "Of course! Why didn't I think of it?" How would you account for their difficulty?

2 Think about the differences between playing by the rules and playing with the rules. What examples do you come up with? Is one of these alternatives always better than the other? If not, what should be the meta-rule about rule playing?

3 Provide examples of your own of metaphors and similes. Can you think of any generative metaphors?

4 Upon reading about Lakoff's nurturant parent and strict father models, with which did you most relate? Do you know someone who adopts the opposite model? How, if at all, do Lakoff's frames increase your understanding of yourself and others?

5 Try reframing what initially seemed like a hopelessly difficult problem.

6 Provide examples of the difference between reflexive and responsive metacommunication.

7 What is "going meta"? Provide examples of your own choosing of successful metamoves.

8 Think about a political figure of interest and develop a description of how that person has been framed. What can be said about the way we understand Barack Obama or Donald J. Trump based on framing? What about Hillary Clinton or Sarah Palin?

9 Have you ever been the "victim" of framing? What happened? How did you resolve the situation?

EXERCISES

1 Do a Google search of either George Lakoff or Frank Luntz and find a representative article, or visit your campus library and check out one of their many books. Apply the steps for analyzing frames provided in this chapter, analyzing your subject, and present your findings to the class.

2 Do an Internet search and find a video of the Clarence Thomas confirmation hearings. Watch selections from the testimony of Anita Hill and then do the same for Clarence Thomas. Who is more persuasive, and why?

3   As a class project, make a CD of music and songs that work together to frame an issue of interest in a particular way. Try to find varying genres of music, but find songs that all fit the same frame.

4   Interview as many members of your family as possible (and separately) about their views and perceptions of you. See if thematic frames arise to categorize your personality, abilities, and place in the family (i.e., your relatives tell you that you have always the *hard worker*, be it in sports, in school, or in the home). How did that frame come into existence? What metaphors are included in the framing? How does the frame make you feel about yourself? Do you agree with it? How has it affected you? What have you done to reinforce the frame, or to overcome it? What would it take to change the frame, assuming you wished to do so?

KEY TERMS

- Coactive approach to psychotherapy
- Episodic news frame
- Frame
- Nurturant parent frame
- Objectivist approach to psychotherapy

- Reflexive metacommunication
- Responsive metacommunication
- Strict father frame
- Thematic news frame
- Topoi

REFERENCES

Adair, B. (2010, December 16). *PolitiFact's Lie of the Year: 'A government takeover of health care'*. Retrieved June 28, 2014, from Politifact.com: www.politifact.com/truth-o-meter/article/2010/dec/16/lie-year-government-takeover-health-care/

Bazelon, E. (2014, April 25). *Power of the Pardon: Obama may finally use his. But can mass clemency fix a broken criminal justice system?* Retrieved June 28, 2014, from Slate.com: www.slate.com/articles/news_and_politics/jurisprudence/2014/04/mass_pardon_obama_may_grant_clemency_to_thousands_of_drug_offenders_that.html

Bennett, W. (2007). *When the press fails: Political power and the news media from Iraq to Katrina*. Chicago: University of Chicago Press.

Billig, M. (1987). *Arguing and thinking: A rhetorical approach to social psychology*. Cambridge: Cambridge University Press.

Booth, W. (1978). Afterthoughts on metaphor: Ten literal "theses." *Critical Inquiry*, 5, 175–188.

Burke, K. (1969). Four master tropes. In Burke, K. (ed.), *A grammar of motives*. Berkeley: University of California Press. (Original work published 1945)

Cohen, N. (1988, September 8). Meta-musings. *New Republic*, 7–8.

Cooper, L. (1932). *The rhetoric of Aristotle: An expanded translation with supplementary examples*. New York: D. Appleton Century.

Edelman, M. (1971). *Politics as symbolic action*. Chicago: Markham.

Entman, R. M. (1993). Framing: Toward clarification of a fractured paradigm. *Journal of Communication, 43,* 51–58.

Fields, G. (2009, May 14). White House czar calls for end to "war on drugs." *Wall Street Journal.* Retrieved July 14, 2009, from http://wsj.com/article/SB124 225891527617397.html

Fish, S. (2006, July 16). They write the songs. *New York Times.* Retrieved July 14, 2009, from www.nytimes. com/2006/07/16/books/review/16fish.html

Gamson, W. (1992). *Talking politics.* New York: Cambridge University Press.

Gamson, W., & Modigliani, A. (1989). Media discourse and public opinion on nuclear power: A constructionist approach. *American Journal of Sociology, 95,* 1–37.

Goodman, W. (1991, October 13). Thomas' testimony: Not the usual Saturday morning fare. *New York Times,* A30.

Head, T. (2014). *Illegal immigrants or undocumented immigrants?* Retrieved June 28, 2014, from About. com Civil Liberties: http://civilliberty.about.com/ od/immigrantsrights/qt/illegal_undoc.htm

Hopper, R. (1981). The taken-for-granted. *Human Communication Research, 7,* 195–211.

Iyengar, S. (1991). *How television frames political issues.* Chicago: University of Chicago Press.

Kahneman, D., & Tversky, A. (1984). Choices, values, and frames. *American Psychologist, 39,* 341–350.

Lakoff, G. (1996). *Moral politics: What Conservatives know that Liberals don't* (2nd ed. [2002] *Moral politics: How Liberals and Conservatives think.*) Chicago: University of Chicago Press.

Lakoff, G. (2004). *Don't think of an elephant: Know your values and frame the debate.* Vermont: Chelsea Green Publishing.

Lakoff, G. (2006). *Whose freedom? The battle over America's most important idea.* New York: Farrar, Straus, and Giroux.

Lakoff, G., & Johnson, M. (1980). *Metaphors we live by.* Chicago: University of Chicago Press.

Lakoff. G., & Wehling, E. (2012). *The little blue book: The essential guide to thinking and talking democratic.* New York: Simon and Schuster.

Levin, I. P., & Gaeth, G. J. (1988). How consumers are affected by the frame of attribute information before and after consuming the product. *Journal of Consumer Research, 15,* 374–378.

Loftus, E. E., & Palmer, J. C. (1974). Reconstruction of automobile destruction: An example of the interaction between language and memory. *Journal of Verbal Learning and Verbal Behavior, 13,* 585–589.

Luntz, F. (2002). The environment: A cleaner, safer, healthier America. Memo to Republican politicians. Retrieved November 11, 2010, from www.guardian. co.uk/environment/2003/mar/04/usnews. climatechange

Luntz, F. (2004). *The best and worst language of 2004: Key debate phrases.* Luntz Research Companies report.

Luntz, F. (2007). *Words that work: It's not what you say, it's what people hear.* New York: Hyperion.

Meyerowitz, B. E., & Chaiken, S. (1987). The effects of message framing on breast self-examination attitudes, intentions, and behavior. *Journal of Personality and Social Psychology, 52,* 500–510.

Nelson, J. (1991, October 15). Democrats give little aid to Hill. *Philadelphia Inquirer,* A6.

New York Times (1991, October 13). Excerpts from Senate hearings on the Thomas nomination, A30.

Novack, S. (2014, March 24). *Here's how Obama plans to spend $25 billion on the war on drugs.* Retrieved June 28, 2014, from National Journal: www. nationaljournal.com/health-care/here-s-how-obama-plans-to-spend-25-billion-on-the-war-on-drugs-20140325

Nunberg, G. (2006). *Talking right: How conservatives turned liberalism into a tax-raising, latte-drinking, sushi-eating, Volvo-driving, New York Times-reading, body-piercing, Hollywood-loving, left-wing freak show.* Cambridge, MA: Public Affairs Publishing.

Thomas, C. (1991, October 12). My name has been harmed. *New York Times,* A10.

Tversky, A., & Kahneman, D. (2004). The framing of decision and the psychology of choice. In Balota, D., & March, E. (eds), *Cognitive psychology: Key readings*. New York: Psychology Press, pp. 621–630.

Vargas, J. A. (2012, September 21). *Immigration debate: The problem with the word illegal*. Retrieved June 28, 2014, from Time.com: http://ideas.time.com/2012/09/21/immigration-debate-the-problem-with-the-word-illegal/

Wachtel, P. L. (1993). *Therapeutic communication*. New York: Guilford.

Watzlawick, P., Weakland, J., & Fisch, R. (1974). *Change: Principles of problem formation and problem resolution*. New York: Norton.

Wile, D. B. (1984). Kohut, Kernberg and accusatory interpretations: Do we have to harm clients to help them? *Psychotherapy*, 21, 353–364.

CHAPTER 7

Cognitive Shorthands

- **Cialdini's Seven Principles**
- **Is Cialdini onto Something? A Critical Assessment**
- **The Highly Persuadable Persuadee**
- **Summary**
- **Questions and Projects for Further Study**
- **Exercises**
- **Key Terms**
- **References**

> I can admit it freely now. All my life I've been a patsy. For as long as I can recall, I've been an easy mark for the pitches of peddlers, fund raisers, and operators of one sort or another. True, only some of these people have had dishonorable motives. The others—representatives of certain charitable agencies, for instance—have had the best of intentions. No matter. With personally disquieting frequency, I have always found myself in possession of unwanted magazine subscriptions or tickets to the sanitation workers' ball.

So confides Robert B. Cialdini (2009), a leading social psychologist, in the introduction to his highly influential book on social influence. Readers of Cialdini's book discover that Cialdini is not alone; we too are among the easily persuaded. Cialdini has compiled some powerful techniques of persuasion, but he offers two contrasting explanations for their power. One is that humans are like mother turkeys—we are programmed to respond automatically to specific triggering stimuli. "Click" goes the triggering stimulus, he writes, and "whirr" goes the fixed-action response. This explanation assumes that there isn't much we can do about our "gullibilities."

The other explanation is that we are like fliers who have put our planes on automatic pilot at precisely those times when we need to be in direct control. Maybe the problem is with the automatic pilot device. Maybe the problem is with the information it is getting or with our failure to get a second opinion. But the important thing is that we can do something about the problem. We can disengage our automatic pilots and engage in thoughtful, rather than mindless, message processing.

This chapter will critically examine these seemingly opposed frames and other problems as well. It is designed in part to illustrate how critical methods can be brought to bear on textbook persuasion, including the rhetoric in textbooks such as this one that are about persuasion. In the process, it will pave the way for Chapter 8 on reasoning and evidence. First, however, the chapter will survey Cialdini's compilation of influence techniques. Following upon its examination of Cialdini's text, the chapter will survey other work on cognitive shorthands, including case studies of human persuadability. It will conclude then with tips on what you can do when you take over from your own automatic pilots.

CIALDINI'S SEVEN PRINCIPLES

Cialdini (2009) organizes his collection of influence techniques around seven principles: (1) **contrast**, (2) **reciprocity**, (3) **consistency**, (4) **social proof**, (5) **authority**, (6) **liking**, and (7) **scarcity**. These cognitive shorthands, he argues, are especially needed when we haven't the inclination or wherewithal to engage in more mindful message processing.

For example, a visitor from a foreign country decides to stop in her American hotel's bar for a beer. She knows nothing about American beers, and the question of which beer to choose isn't terribly important to her. The bartender seems like a competent and friendly sort of person, so she asks him for a recommendation. Rather than indicating his personal preference, he tells her that Budweiser is the most popular beer in America. On the basis of the *cognitive shorthand* that "popular = good," she decides to order a Budweiser. Besides, she assumes, an authoritative, likable source wouldn't lead her astray. In this instance, we see Cialdini's principles in action. Let's examine them more carefully.

Contrast

Contrast has to do with the sequencing of message stimuli. Just as a moderately heavy object may seem heavy after you have lifted a light one, or relatively light after you have lifted a heavy one, so the order of occurrence of social stimuli can make a difference in how you perceive them. Even our own romantic partners may seem less attractive after we view exceptionally attractive models in magazines (Cialdini, 2009; Li, et al., 2007). So, too, may photos of a possible blind date seem relatively unattractive after we see good-looking actors or actresses on our favorite television programs.

On the basis of this same "psycho-logic," clothing sales personnel are instructed to attempt to sell an expensive suit first and then offer a comparatively inexpensive item, rather than the other way around. Even a moderately priced sweater may seem affordable by comparison. Were the salesperson to sell the sweater first, the cost of the suit might well seem exorbitant (Cialdini, 2009). Similarly, real estate brokers

FIGURE 7.1 *The fascinating case of singer Susan Boyle exemplifies well Cialdini's principle of "contrast." Stepping onto the stage to perform on Britain's Got Talent, Boyle was presented as an unmanicured spinster who lived with her cat. The judges and the audience presumed she would perform poorly. But then, she began to sign "I Dreamed a Dream," a showstopper from Les Miserables, and brought down the house. Her singing was lovely, to be sure, but it was the fact that her performance was such a contrast to what was expected that turned her into a global YouTube sensation.*

sometimes take customers through undesirable setup properties, called decoys, before showing them the ones they truly intend to promote. Car dealers try to sell optional extras to the customer after the price of the car itself has been agreed to. They know that the cost of each option will seem minuscule relative to the cost of the car the customer has already agreed to buy.

Reciprocity

Persuaders can exploit our inclination to repay in kind what others have done for us. When a charitable organization sends us a donation request and includes in the envelope unrequested address labels, we are more likely to send back a donation to their cause. And what about selling raffle tickets? Cialdini (2009) reports on a suggestive experiment by Regan (1971) in which a confederate—that is, an accomplice of the experimenter—increased raffle sales to those research participants for whom he had earlier provided the unsolicited gift of a soft drink. Department stores exploit this principle by providing free samples of selected items. The Amway Corporation likewise gave potential customers an entire kit of trial items in a hand-delivered package called the "bug." The salesperson emphasized that the customers might try the trial items "for 24, 48, or 72 hours, at no cost or obligation," but the salesperson knew that precisely this pitch was likely to incur a felt obligation by the customers to buy at least some of what they had been tempted to try.

In this, as in so many exploitations of the reciprocity principle, the persuader provides something that costs relatively nothing. The expense to the real estate broker of the "gift" of a ballpoint pen is miniscule, but it can help influence the customer to purchase the house. The job applicant's "gift" of a compliment to the job interviewer costs nothing, but it is given because it might land the job. The restaurant waiter's "gift" of a warning to the party of eight that the appetizer they are about to order "isn't very good this evening" costs the waiter nothing, but it leads to increased income, because, thanks to the advice, the grateful diners trust the waiter, follow his suggestion to order a more expensive wine, and provide a larger tip in gratitude for the advice (Cialdini, 2009). These cases of gifting are far removed from "primitive" gift cultures where giving has intrinsic value and where goods and services are given without an explicit agreement for immediate or future rewards; instead, they exemplify market economies where everything is a commodity and where society operates through an explicit exchange of goods or services for money or reward (Hyde, 2007).

"Vincent the Waiter"

Robert Cialdini writes of his experience observing the slyly sincere waiter, Vincent, who used reciprocity to increase his income. Vincent had various methods for appealing to customers, but with parties of 8 to 12 people, his approach was to seemingly argue against his own interest. Cialdini writes:

> His technique was veined with genius. When it was time for the first person, normally a woman, to order, he went into his act. No matter what she elected, Vincent reacted identically: His brow furrowed, his hand hovered above his order pad, and after looking quickly over his shoulder for the manager, he leaned conspiratorially toward the table to report for all to hear "I'm afraid that is not as good tonight as it normally is. Might I recommend instead the ___ or the ___?" At this point, Vincent suggested a pair of menu items that were slightly less expensive than the dish the patron had selected initially.
>
> With this single maneuver, Vincent engaged several important principles of influence. First, even those who did not take his suggestions felt that Vincent had done them a favor by offering valuable information to help them order. Everyone felt grateful and consequently, the rule for reciprocity would work in his favor when it came time for them to decide on his gratuity. Besides hiking the percentage of his tip, Vincent's maneuver also placed him in a favorable position to increase the size of the party's

FIGURE 7.2

order.... Moreover—and here is where seeming to argue against his own interests comes in—it proved him to be a trustworthy informant because he recommended dishes that were slightly less expensive than the one originally ordered.

To all appearances, he was at once knowledgeable and honest, a combination that gave him great credibility. Vincent was quick to exploit the advantage of this credible image. When the party had finished giving their food orders, he would say, "Very well, and would you like me to suggest or select wine to go with your meals?" As I watched the scene repeated almost nightly, there was a notable consistency to the customers' reaction—smiles, nods, and for the most part, general assent.... Looking pleased, Vincent, who did know his vintages, would respond with some excellent (and costly) choices. He was similarly persuasive when it came time for dessert decisions.

By combining the factors of reciprocity and credible authority into a single, elegant maneuver, Vincent was able to inflate substantially both the percentage of his tip and the base charge on which it was figured.

(Cialdini, 2009)

A variant of the reciprocity principle is the rejection-then-retreat approach, sometimes known as the **door-in-the-face (DITF) technique**. This approach involves making an extreme request of a potential donor, favor giver, or authority figure. Then, having placed the persuadee in a position where she or he is likely to turn you down, you come through with a comparatively more reasonable request. The approach clearly has echoes of the contrast principle as well.

For example, a boy scout approaches a stranger with a request to buy some 10-dollar tickets to a boy scout-sponsored circus. The customer refuses, but feels guilty for turning the youngster down. The boy scout suggests an alternative: "If you don't want to buy any tickets, how about buying some of our big chocolate bars? They're only a dollar each." A variation on this theme is the old student joke: A female college student calls her parents to tell them that she is dropping out of school to go on the road with her Carney boyfriend. She explains that this is for the best, given that she is pregnant with his baby; she doesn't plan to get married, she says, because she's not sure she loves the father, but she does love the circus. After her parents respond with tears and shock, she comes clean. She tells them, "Everything I just said was a lie. There is no boyfriend, I'm not pregnant, and I'm not leaving school. I did earn a 'D' in English this semester, though, and I wanted to let you know!"

Consistency

A key principle, consistency, is the impulse to bring our beliefs, values, and attitudes into line with what we have already done or decided. *"Once we make a choice or take a stand, we will encounter personal and interpersonal pressures to behave consistently with that commitment"* (Cialdini, 2009; italics in original). For example, gamblers at a racetrack express greater confidence in their decisions after they have actually laid down their bets (Cialdini, 2009). Contestants who bother to write "in 25 words or less" why they like Bozo Corn Chips are apt to increase their regard for the chips as a result. Voters who put the signs of a particular politician in their yards are almost certain to vote for that candidate. Our impulse to consistency increases with our voluntary, overt commitment, with our publicly expressed decisions, and with the actions we have already taken.

Like the contrast and reciprocity principles, consistency is a useful cognitive shorthand much of the time. Certainly there is value in appearing consistent; we are called fickle if we change our minds too often. We are thought to be strong-minded when we hold the line. And, as any of us who have stayed too long in a bad relationship can attest, unthinking consistency can help us cope; it can substitute for difficult and sometimes painful thought. "Sealed within the fortress walls of rigid consistency," says Cialdini, "we can be impervious to the sieges of reason" (2009).

Cialdini offers numerous examples of rigid consistency. For example, he writes of a group of recruits to Transcendental Meditation, a self-help organization, who were challenged to have doubts about the organization after another visitor effectively demolished the leader's presentation at the first meeting of the group. But rather than allowing these doubts to overcome their earlier decision to join, many of the recruits decided to pay up at their first opportunity. One of the recruits explained that he hadn't intended to put down any money that evening, but he really wanted to believe that TM could help him achieve his goals. He said that when he heard the visitor's powerful critique, he knew he had better give the organization money immediately because, if he didn't, he would go home, start thinking about the critique, and never join up (Cialdini, 2009).

Thinking It Through

Cialdini was not the first to consider the psychological desire for consistency. Cognitive Dissonance Theory, first suggested by Leon Festinger in 1962, posits that, when we experience psychological tension, we will seek to adjust our judgments to bring the situations we face into harmony.

For example, we may want to "buy American" and support American workers. Furthermore, we may resist the notion of buying products that were made in sweatshops. But, when we visit our campus bookstore, we find the clothing is all imported from third-world countries. In that situation, dissonance results, and we will work to bring the situation into harmony. We might decide to make the purchase, concluding that we are in fact supporting the poorest families by purchasing the items, and that in fact sweatshops do provide desperately needed jobs. We might decide that "school spirit" is vastly over-rated and that we didn't really want the items we were considering. We may buy American-made t-shirts and decorate them ourselves with our school's logo. And so on.

The point, though, is that we will think it through and find ways to create feelings of psychological balance and to eliminate dissonance.

A tactic of persuasion is to create dissonance and then offer a remedy for it.

Watch television for an evening and you'll see what we mean. Take note of the ads. Make a list of how often you see examples of cognitive dissonance introduced, only to have consumer products offered as remedies to reduce or eliminate that dissonance.

Consistency can build on small commitments. For instance, during the Korean War, the Chinese effectively indoctrinated some American prisoners at their "training sessions" by first having them admit publicly that "the United States is not perfect." Then the prisoner might be asked to prepare a list of problems in the United States. Later, he might be asked to read his list to other prisoners. Each step in the indoctrination process seemed harmless enough on its own, but, together, these voluntary, public commitments became powerful sources of self-persuasion (Cialdini, 2009; Schein, 1961).

A counterpart to the door-in-the-face technique is the **foot-in-the-door (FITD) technique**. Here the persuader secures a modest commitment as a prelude to a far bigger one. Freedman and Fraser (1966) are credited with one of the most impressive demonstrations of this phenomenon. A researcher, posing as a volunteer campaigner, went door to door in a residential California neighborhood pleading with homeowners to accept placement on their front lawns of a rather large, public service billboard with the words "Drive Carefully" scrawled clumsily on it. Nearly all in one experimental group refused. But another group had been visited two weeks earlier by a different volunteer worker and had been asked to display a little three-inch square sign saying "Be a Safe Driver." This group complied with the subsequent request by a margin of three to one. Obviously, the second group sought to maintain psychological consistency; they had agreed to post a sign about "driving" and to refuse the second sign would seem akin to a refusal of the sign's content. Ultimately, their desire to maintain a consistent position turned out to be persuasive indeed.

Social Proof

Canned laughter on television sitcoms, tip jars in bars that are "salted" with a couple of dollars in advance of the arrival of customers, salted collection boxes in church, "everybody's doing it" appeals in ads, and product testimonials by satisfied customers—these are among the many examples Cialdini (2009) provides of *social proof*. "This principle states that we determine what is correct by finding out what other people think is correct" (Lun, et al., 2007, as cited in Cialdini, 2009).

Such imitation can be useful, and looking to others for guidance about what actions are appropriate works quite well normally (Cialdini, 2009). But social proof also can be misleading, such as when drivers fail to go to the aid of an accident victim on the highway because no one else seems to be stopping and when, as actually happened, 38 residents of a Queens, New York, neighborhood watched a killer stalk and stab Catherine Genovese to death without so much as calling the police. Again, one possible explanation for the inaction: Nobody else seemed to be going to the woman's aid. In one experiment, a college student appearing to have an epileptic seizure received help nearly all the time when a single bystander was present but only 31% of the time when five bystanders were present (Cialdini, 2009; Latané & Darley, 1968). The assumption that individuals make that "because nobody is concerned, nothing is wrong" is appropriately called pluralistic ignorance.

Imitation can also work for the social good, such as when children in a nursery school learned to overcome their fears of dogs after seeing one youngster playing happily with a dog for just 20 minutes a day (Bandura, 1973). In another experiment, film clips showing children successfully interacting with their dogs had a similar fear-reducing effect. Bandura calls this behavioral modeling. Consistent with the principle of social proof, it seems to be most effective when there is more than one model to imitate.

A striking example of social proof was the mass suicide at Jonestown, Guyana, at which nearly all of the 910 people who died did so in a seemingly orderly, voluntary way.

No doubt one reason for their conformity was the charismatic power of the group's spiritual leader, the Reverend Jim Jones, who had urged his followers to drink a strawberry-flavored poison. But as Cialdini (2009) underscores, this incredible event could not have occurred had the group been subjected to normal social

FIGURE 7.3   *A striking example of social proof was the 1978 mass suicide at Jonestown, Guyana, in which nearly all of the 910 members of Reverend Jim Jones' "People's Temple" committed suicide in a seemingly orderly, voluntary way.*
Photo Courtesy of Getty Images

influences. A year earlier, however, the group had moved from San Francisco to the hostile environs of a jungle clearing in Guyana, far removed from any social influences but their own. In these circumstances, they could be led to choose social proof over survival.

Liking

Cialdini's (2009) first example of the principle of liking is the Tupperware party, featuring not only the salesperson as persuader but also, and perhaps more important, the hostess who has invited all her good friends to attend. Similarity and familiarity tend to increase liking, and liking, as we noted in Chapter 4, is especially influential when it is perceived as mutual. The house party has all these ingredients.

Ultimately, we go to house parties of all sorts not because we need the products, but because we feel loyalty to our friends. The products are often more expensive than comparable store brands and they are not items we'd generally place on our weekly shopping lists. What's more, even when we've purchased more than we need of a product, we're likely to keep going to the house parties when good friends invite us. That is the persuasive power of the principle of "liking."

Compliments enhance liking, and, says Cialdini, "We tend as a rule to believe praise and to like those who provide it" (2009). There are limits, of course, but Cialdini tells of Joe Gerard, the world's "greatest car salesman," who each year sent out holiday cards to 13,000 former customers with nothing else printed on them but his name and the words "I like you." His customers liked getting them.

The Tupperware party does not just depend upon friendship, though—it also builds on several of Cialdini's preceding principles. Everyone receives a gift from the Tupperware salesperson, not just those who compete successfully at party games. Thus the impulse of reciprocity is at work. All partygoers are also urged to speak publicly about the virtues of the Tupperware items they already own. This creates pressures toward new purchases for the sake of consistency and serves as a kind of "self-sell" (Pratkanis & Aronson, 2001). But most of all, each new purchase at the party is also a kind of social proof to the others present.

JESUS CHRIST AND HIS DISCIPLES AT THE LAST TUPPERWARE PARTY

FIGURE 7.4 *Edwin Decker's biting satire takes its cue from the principle of "liking." The disciples agree to buy Tupperware because it is Jesus who offers it to them. It is only Judas, the betrayer, who challenges Jesus rationally about the products.*

Then Jesus did pass the Tupperware to his disciples, and said

"This ... is my product line. It will keep the blood of the everlasting covenant fresh for weeks."

Jesus then showed them the deluxe set.

He opened his arms wide, and said

"Perhaps I can interest you in the hamburger press and freezer set?

The hamburger press and freezer set makes a great Christmas gift."

And the disciples passed it around to each other.

And Paul said, "Write me down for a set, Jesus."

And John said, "Me too."

And Peter said, "I'll take two, one for my sister and one for my brother."

And Judas testified, "But, Jesus, doth not Ziploc bags serve the same function as Tupperware and yet is much cheaper?"

(Reprinted with permission of Edwin Decker.)

Authority

Expressed liking and authority can be powerful motivators. Cialdini (2009) offers the example of the "rectal earache" (Cohen & Davis, 1981). A physician orders ear drops for the right ear of a patient. But rather than writing out the words "right ear," the doctor writes "place in R ear." Obediently, the duty nurse places the prescribed number of drops in the patient's anus. As Cialdini commented:

> Obviously, rectal treatment of an earache made no sense, but neither the patient nor the nurse questioned it. The important lesson of this story is that in many situations in which a legitimate authority has spoken, what would otherwise make sense is irrelevant.
>
> (2009)

What happened in this case is that the participants considered only the authoritative status of the doctor, and did not evaluate the situation in its entirety.

Like coercion and material inducements, authority in and of itself is not persuasion. But individuals taken in by the mere trappings of authority are persuaded, and Cialdini (2009) provides some outstanding examples.

Actors who play authorities on TV shows aren't the same authorities in real life. Yet there is carryover. For example, the actor Robert Young, who played the role of Marcus Welby, M.D., in a long-running television drama, was perceived as a highly authoritative figure in commercials counseling against caffeine and for decaffeinated Sanka coffee (Cialdini, 2009). And, more recently, MasterCard initiated a program where women could chat online with authorities about how, as mothers, they could prepare their homes for the holidays. The "expert" mothers providing the counsel were Florence Henderson and Jane Kaczmarek, whose credentials came only from their acting roles as TV moms in *The Brady Bunch* and *Malcolm in the Middle* (Cialdini, 2009).

In another example, a researcher posing as a doctor was able to get 95% of regular duty nurses to comply with a phoned request to administer 20 milligrams of Astrogen to a specific ward patient. But phoned-in prescriptions were contrary to hospital policy, and Astrogen was not an authorized drug on the ward stock list. Moreover, the dosage prescribed was dangerously excessive and obviously so. Fortunately, the nurses were stopped from actually administering the drug by an observer who explained to them the nature of the experiment (Cialdini, 2009).

Clothes, as well as titles, can make the non-authority into an apparent authority. In one simple experiment, the same 31-year-old man jaywalked half the time in a freshly pressed business suit and half the time in a work shirt and trousers. He was followed by pedestrians against the traffic light three and a half times as often when wearing the suit (Cialdini, 2009).

Scarcity

"On sale for a limited time only." "Hurry, only two left in stock." Cialdini defines the scarcity principle as follows: *"opportunities seem more valuable to us when they are less available"* (2009; italics in original). Or, as he puts it even more succinctly: "Less is Best and Loss is Worst" (2009).

For example, two customers are observed by a salesperson to be interested in a certain appliance item:

> I see you're interested in this model here, and I can understand why; it's a great machine at a great price. But, unfortunately, I sold it to another couple not more than 20 minutes ago. And, if I'm not mistaken, it was the last one we had.
>
> The customers register dismay. Couldn't the salesperson check to be sure, one of them asks. "Well, that is possible, and I'd be willing to check," says the salesperson. "But do I understand that this is the model you want, and if I can get it for you at this price, you'll take it?" Once the scarce item has been magically "found," the principle of consistency takes over. Having committed themselves to the purchase, many customers actually buy it.
>
> (Cialdini, 2009)

Seemingly scarce items appear even more valuable if consumers believe there is competition for them. Thus, there may be a mad scramble when an item is placed on sale; Filene's Basement, for example, has for over 60 years held its annual "Running of the Brides," where on the morning of the sale "the doors open at 8am, brides and their helpers rush to the racks, grab wedding gowns and immediately start trying them on" (Filene's Basement, n.d.). Apparently, when the crowd is let loose, it takes less than 60 seconds for the racks to be stripped bare. Evidently the women just grab

FIGURE 7.5 *The annual Filene's Basement "Running of the Brides."*

as many dresses as they can, go off in a corner, strip down and start trying them on. Then the brides start bartering with each other for dresses until they find the perfect gown (Filene's Basement, n.d.).

It is not just potential brides who respond to scarcity appeals, though. A prospective buyer may show renewed interest in a house when told by the realtor that "a physician and his wife moving into town" are likely bidders on the property (Cialdini, 2009). Young people may find a dance club more attractive when customers are kept waiting in line outside although there may be space inside. Parents may drive many miles and search many websites to find the scarce Tickle Me Elmo or Doc McStuffins dolls that the children want for Christmas (Consolewii, 2008).

Like authority, it is *perceived* scarcity, not *real* scarcity, that counts. Perceived scarcity is relative to what we have known or expect to know. Not surprisingly, the chocolate chip cookie in a jar with but two cookies is rated more attractive as a consumer item than the same cookie in a jar with nine other cookies. More interesting, when one group of research participants discovered that the number of cookies in a jar had been reduced from ten to two, the cookies just made "scarce" were rated more positively than when there were only two cookies in the jar all along (Cialdini, 2009). At the end of the day, it seems safe to conclude that we generally seem to want what we think we can't have, and we will work to get it. Not only that, but we will convince ourselves that we need an item, or that the item is better than its competitors, when we think it is in short supply.

Consequently, the principle of scarcity, like the other principles listed here, serve as shortcuts, or perhaps short-circuits, to thinking. They make life easier at times, and they are rooted in folk wisdom and "common sense," but they also make us vulnerable to unscrupulous persuaders. Too often, these principles fail to serve us well—they shut down our abilities for critical analysis. We would be best served to use caution when we find ourselves in the arenas in which they most commonly present themselves.

IS CIALDINI ONTO SOMETHING? A CRITICAL ASSESSMENT

We have offered high praise for Cialdini's work and considered it at length, while also promising a critique. We offer the critique because (1) it is needed if one hopes to have a full understanding of all the ramifications of Cialdini's extensive and important contributions to our understanding of how persuasion functions, and (2) it provides the opportunity to display in action the work of rhetorical critics. The study of "persuasion" is not just about how persuaders practice their art, but also includes analysis of persuasive practices. And that being said, it is worth noting that some of the most interesting rhetorical criticism analyzes artifacts like textbooks, legal briefs, and business reports that claim to present "the facts" in an objective fashion. To put it another way: It is easy to do rhetorical criticism of television advertising, where persuasion is obvious and expected. It is more challenging, and often more important, to do rhetorical criticism of artifacts where persuasion is veiled. It is to that task we now turn our attention.

Our critique of Cialdini begins with this simple claim: He is not only an expert *on* persuasion but also an expert *at* persuasion. We see that in his opening confessional. Rather than speaking of others (his readers?) as the gullible ones, he names himself.

Recall the lines: "I can admit it freely now. All my life I've been a patsy." The rhetorical technique of including himself among the foolish is called *humble irony* (Burke, 1961). Its effect is to disarm the reader, creating the impression of a warm and caring individual who shares the readers' vulnerabilities. It's as if Cialdini were testifying at something akin to an Alcoholics Anonymous meeting. Call it "Patsies Anonymous." His introduction seeks to cause us to identify with him, and it uses his *principle of liking* to reduce our defenses.

His work also obscures important differences in the phenomena he groups together, overlooking tensions or inconsistencies between principles, and ignores important contingencies. Furthermore, he downplays the fact that the task of the persuader is far more complex than he would have us believe. Most important, despite having made this observation himself, he sometimes overlooks the fact that persuadees can learn to say "no" to persuaders. No lower-order animal can make that statement. This is a key point, for it stands in contrast with Cialdini's "Mother Turkey" metaphor, but provides the basis for his metaphor of the "Automatic Pilot."

Issue 1 Obscured Differences

Of Cialdini's list of principles, the one causing the biggest problem on this account is his *principle of consistency*. He treats it as an impulse to bring our beliefs, values, or attitudes into line with our commitments, especially our expressed, public commitments. Fishbein and Ajzen (1975) group this type of reasoning under the heading of **evaluative consistency**. If we've bet on a horse to win, we want to believe that it will win. If we value our lives, we want to believe that we will be immortal. Cialdini provides a perfect example of evaluative consistency in the case of the recruits to Transcendental Meditation: they preferred to put up their money rather than be overcome by doubts; they wanted to believe TM would work, and so they paid their fees even as they admitted that the evidence against TM seemed somewhat convincing. Examples such as this one make us seem silly and irrational indeed.

What Cialdini overlooks and obscures is that there exists a sister concept in the consideration of how we humans seek to maintain consistency in our thinking and living. Another broad class of consistencies that is the essence of good reasoning and the enemy of blind, evaluative consistency is called **probabilistic consistency** (Fishbein & Ajzen, 1975; Hale, et al., 2002). We see it, for example, when we reason correctly from premises to conclusions, from facts to empirical generalizations, and from beliefs and values to attitudes. Fishbein and Ajzen provide an example to demonstrate the difference between these two forms of consistency through a discussion of Nikita Khrushchev, who served as president of the Soviet Union at the same time that John F. Kennedy was president of the United States.

It was the height of the Cold War, where the USSR and the USA came close to nuclear conflict during the Cuban Missile Crisis. Americans generally viewed the USSR as an enemy and held President Khrushchev in disdain. But, Americans did not all share the same reasons for their conclusions, even if they reached similar ones. To make this point, and to display the difference between evaluative and probabilistic consistencies, Fishbein and Ajzen presented the following illustration:

> A more interesting example is given by a person's inferential belief that "Khrushchev was immature." In terms of *evaluative consistency* this inference would be made by an individual who disliked Khrushchev as well as immaturity; in terms of *probabilistic consistency*, this inference could be a function of the belief that Khrushchev took off his shoe and banged in on the table in the United Nations and the belief that people who behave in this way are immature.
>
> (Fishbein & Ajzen, 1975; italics added)

Their point is clear: Even when two people arrive at the same conclusion ("Khrushchev is immature"), their path to that conclusion cannot be assumed to be similar. In this case, the first person arrives at a conclusion that is consistent with his beliefs, attitudes, and values; the second arrives at a conclusion that is consistent with his good reasoning. Cialdini's problem is that he combines these two forms of consistency, highlights the former, and neglects the latter.

Issue 2 Contradictory Tensions Between Principles

Each of Cialdini's principles seems to stand nicely on its own, and sometimes they combine powerfully, as in the Tupperware example—but not always. Recall the research on behavioral modeling in which young children's fears of dogs were overcome by what Cialdini called *social proof*. In the two research studies cited, successful persuasion resulted from a child viewing other children playing with dogs. Invariably, though, the most persuasive appeal does not always come from a peer. It can come from other of Cialdini's categories, for example, as when a teacher uses her *authority* to persuade a child to view a situation differently; such persuasion is common when important questions of fact are in dispute and the teacher is seen to have the expertise.

As we can see, there exists a tension, and maybe even a contradiction, between these categories: Are we persuaded by our peers, our equals, those we admire, and those who are most like us? Or are those who are most different from us the strongest persuaders? Consideration of this tension is important, especially when one seeks to create a template for how persuasion functions, but Cialdini's work does not take it into account. The fact is, though, that sometimes interaction with peers, our feelings of affinity for them, and *social proof* will carry the day for persuasion, and at other times interaction with superiors, our feelings of respect, and *authority* will be more persuasive.

A key point, underscored in Chapter 1, is that any given approach to persuasion is rarely superior to a comparable alternative in all circumstances. Instead, we need multiple research studies before we can make generalizations that state the conditions under which one approach is likely to be superior to its alternatives. All other things being equal, for example, a person who is more similar to us and presumably more likable should be more persuasive than a dissimilar and presumably more expert person when facts are not at issue. But the reverse would likely be the case, for example, as when we are uncertain of the best way to treat a newly acquired medical problem or confront a serious legal issue. At that point, we call upon a doctor or a lawyer (Norman, 1976). Situations and circumstances matter. Cialdini agrees:

> All the weapons of influence discussed in this book work better under some conditions rather than in others. If we are to defend ourselves against any one weapon it is vital that we know its optimal working conditions in order to recognize when we are most vulnerable to its influence.
>
> (Cialdini, 2009)

Considered in this context, however, two persuasive devices discussed by Cialdini present particular problems: the door-in-the-face (DITF) technique (discussed under the heading of *reciprocity*) and the foot-in-the-door (FITD) technique (discussed under the heading of *consistency*). As O'Keefe (2002) points out, "The door-in-the-face strategy turns the foot-in-the-door strategy on its head." In effect, if we want to sell you something, the DITF approach says that we should offer a more expensive item first and then sell you something cheaper. Yet, the FITD approach says we should offer an item that costs less and use that approach to sell you something that costs more. But we can't do both, and we are left to wonder how to resolve this seeming paradox. Cialdini presents both as principles of persuasion; he does not compare them, he does not mention the apparent contradiction, nor does he tell us under what conditions one is likely to be more effective than another. Others have, though; for example, it has been established that a delay between an initial and a subsequent request seems to markedly lessen the effects of DITF but not FITD (O'Keefe, 2002), but no one yet can say why this is the case. A recent quantitative study directly comparing DITF and FITD found that the DITF technique affected purchasing intentions, while FITD did not (Baas, 2012). Ultimately, research findings suggest a greater level of complexity when it comes to such matters, and dealing with the contradictory tensions among his principles would be an area where Cialdini could provide a more refined analysis.

Issue 3 Unidentified Contingencies

One of Cialdini's favorite stories takes place at a jewelry store near an Indian reservation in Arizona. It seems that the proprietor was having immense difficulty selling a certain allotment of turquoise jewelry to her tourist clients. Exasperated, she scribbled a note to her head saleswoman before leaving town, "Everything in the display case, price ½." When she returned, she discovered that everything had been sold—and at twice the price, rather than half the price. The head saleswoman had misread her scribbled note, marking up all the items by a factor of two.

Why had the customers purchased the marked-up jewelry? Cialdini explains as follows:

> The customers, mostly well-to-do vacationers with little knowledge of turquoise, were using a standard principle—a stereotype—to guide their buying: "expensive = good." Thus, the vacationers, who wanted "good" jewelry, saw the turquoise pieces as decidedly more valuable and desirable when nothing about them was enhanced but the price. Price alone had become a trigger feature for quality; and a dramatic increase in price alone had led to a dramatic increase in sales among the quality-hungry buyers. Click, whirr!
>
> (Cialdini, 2009)

The first thing to notice about this example is the contingencies of persuasion that Cialdini identifies. By his account, these weren't just any message recipients—they were well-to-do vacationers. Furthermore, this wasn't any product—it was difficult-to-assess Indian turquoise. Presumably, then, based on Cialdini's description of the situation, the trigger "expensive = good" would not necessarily apply to other customers buying other items. Presumably, too, there was no Indian jewelry store nearby at which to do comparison shopping, because, if there had been, the well-to-do shoppers would have likely noticed that the prices at the shop seemed out of line.

But more to the point, is a shopper's tendency to think "expensive = good" really analogous to a mother turkey's instinctual reaction of caring when she hears the "cheep-cheep" of a turkey chick? Probably not, but this is the comparison Cialdini makes.

A question that creates doubts about Cialdini's analogy comes easily to mind: Does he think that even these well-to-do vacationers would have applied the same click-whirr principle had the items been marked up by a factor of 20, rather than 2? Even among consumers brought up to believe that "you get what you pay for," there is a countervailing impulse to avoid getting ripped off. The key observation here is made by Michael Billig (1995, 1996), who maintains that consumers tend to position their decisions between opposing frames such as "you get what you pay for" and "value for the money." Ultimately, then, there is more to this example than meets the eye, and, before we decide what caused individuals to respond, we have to do everything we can to incorporate all of the contingencies in the decision-making process.

Issue 4 Mother Turkeys versus Automatic Pilots

Cialdini's First Frame: The Mother Turkey

The devices Cialdini (2009) identifies are powerful. They work because we rely on cognitive shorthands, which are fallible. One question, however, is whether we gullible persuadees are incapable of resistance or are capable of doing something about our naïveté. Cialdini's "Mother Turkey" metaphor may be the wrong one—others could easily be substituted—but it is a metaphor he employs as he presents human beings as essentially and irremediably reflexive animals, responsive as persuadees to specific triggering cues in precisely the same way that the turkey responds to specific triggering cues.

Consider the case of the mother turkey. Turkey mothers are good mothers—loving, watchful, and protective. They spend much of their time tending, warming, cleaning, and huddling the young beneath them. But there is something odd about their method. Virtually all of this mothering is triggered by one thing: the "cheep-cheep" sound of young turkey chicks. Other identifying features of the chicks, such as their smell, touch, or appearance, seem to play minor roles in the mothering process. If a chick makes the "cheep-cheep" noise, its mother will care for it; if not, the mother will ignore or sometimes kill it (Cialdini, 2009).

Cialdini's (2009) Mother Turkey may be a bit too rigid for some tastes, but the worst is yet to come. Cialdini cites a study by an animal behaviorist, appropriately named M. W. Fox, of a mother turkey's reactions to a stuffed polecat:

> For a mother turkey, a polecat is a natural enemy whose approach is to be greeted with squawking, pecking, clawing rage. Indeed, the experimenters found that even a stuffed model of a polecat, when drawn by a string toward a mother turkey, received an immediate and furious attack. When, however, the same stuffed replica carried inside it a small recorder that played the "cheep-cheep" sound of baby turkeys, the mother not only accepted the oncoming polecat but gathered it underneath her. When the machine was turned off, the polecat model again drew a vicious attack.
>
> (Cialdini, 2009)

Now, the turkey seems not only rigid but downright stupid. Indeed, Cialdini (2009) likens the female turkey to an automaton whose maternal instincts are under the control of that single sound. This sort of thing is not unique to the turkey, he adds. Mechanical patterns of action such as these can involve intricate sequences of behavior, such as entire courtship or mating rituals. A fundamental characteristic of these patterns is that the behaviors that compose them occur in virtually the same fashion and in the same order every time. It is almost as if the patterns were recorded on tapes within the animals. When the situation calls for courtship, the courtship tape gets played; when the situation calls for mothering, the maternal behavior tape gets played. *Click* and the appropriate tape is activated; *whirr* and out rolls the standard sequence of behaviors.

Thus far, Cialdini (2009) has been talking only about lower-order animals. Now comes the crucial linking argument to humans:

> Before we enjoy too smugly the ease with which lower animals can be tricked by trigger features into reacting in ways wholly inappropriate to the situation, we might realize … that we too have our preprogrammed tapes; and, although they usually work to our advantage, the trigger features that activate them can be used to dupe us into playing them at the wrong times.
>
> (Cialdini, 2009)

Still, Cialdini's "Mother Turkey" hypothesis is not completely convincing. At best it applies to automatic, unconscious processes and to peripheral processing of the sort described in Petty and Cacioppo's (1996) ELM model and in Thaler and Sunstein's (2008) nudge theory (see Chapter 2). What it does not do is account for resistance to persuasion.

But Turkeys Cannot Say "No"

Cialdini (2009) emphasizes at various points how we can choose to say "no" to compliance seekers who would subvert our cognitive shorthands. His advice is instructive but would appear to run counter to his "Mother Turkey" hypothesis. For example, if we have determined that a compliance professional's gift or concession was a tactic rather than a genuine favor, "we need only react to it accordingly to be free of its influence" (Cialdini, 2009). If we realize "in the pit of our stomachs" that we have been trapped into complying with a request that we have no wish to perform, we can turn tables on the influence-seekers, explaining to them exactly how we think they've been manipulating us (Cialdini, 2009). If we "feel in our hearts" that we've been foolishly consistent, then we can learn to trust those feelings and stop being foolish (Cialdini, 2009). If we have reason to suspect that social evidence has been purposely falsified, as in the case of canned laughter tracks on a TV comedy, we can make conscious decisions not to be influenced by it.

Sounds simple, doesn't it? Indeed, if our stomachs, our hearts, and our reason have all been working for us, how turkey-like could our responses have been in the first place?

Cialdini's Second Frame: The Faulty Automatic Pilot

Midway through his book, Cialdini (2009) provides a perfect example of reframing one's argument. Without abandoning his "Mother Turkey" metaphor, he interposes another metaphor, that of the flier running on faulty automatic pilot. This device, he says, does some wonderful work. "With it we can cruise confidently through a myriad of decisions without personally having to investigate the detailed pros and cons of each" (Cialdini, 2009). But there are occasional problems with automatic pilots:

> These problems appear whenever the flight information locked into the control mechanism is wrong. In these instances, we will be taken off course. Depending upon the size of the error, the consequences can be severe. But, because the automatic pilot … is more often an ally than an enemy, we can't be expected to want simply to disconnect it. Thus we are faced with a classic problem: how to make use of a piece of equipment that simultaneously benefits and imperils our welfare.
>
> Fortunately, there is a way out of the dilemma. Because the disadvantages of automatic pilots arise principally when incorrect data have been put into the control system, our best defense against these disadvantages is to recognize when the data are in error. If we can become sensitive to situations where the automatic pilot is working with inaccurate information, we can disengage the mechanism and grasp the controls when we need to.
>
> (Cialdini, 2009)

With his faulty automatic pilot, Cialdini appears to have found a more appropriate metaphor for human complexity. This is not to say that we humans are entirely distinctive animals by virtue of our capacity to reason, but there are major differences between the mother turkey and the automatic pilot. Both operate automatically, but the automatic pilot operates only insofar as we choose, while the mother turkey has no choice in the matter. We control the automatic pilot even as we allow the automatic pilot to control the movement of our airplane. Moreover, automatic pilots have sophisticated sensing and error-correcting devices; they are not likely to confuse an airstrip with a shiny roof. Just in case, we can check our automatic pilots against our manual controls. We can look out the windows of our mental cockpits to see if we're taking an intellectual nosedive. Unlike the mother turkey, we can generally bring multiple sensing and error-correcting devices to bear on a given situation. We can read and interpret these multiple cues, rather than merely reacting to them reflexively. We can, for example, let belief consistency serve as a corrective to evaluative consistency and have tests of the expertise and trustworthiness of authority figures serve as a corrective to the mere trappings of authority.

Is Cialdini onto Us? Our Critical Assessment of Our Critical Assessment

After thinking about our critique of Cialdini's "Mother Turkey" frame, we wondered what he might say by way of reply. And, being good debaters, we are prepared to argue the opposition's case. We imagine him saying something like the following:

> It's true that humans have error-correcting capacities, but one has only to look at Chapter 2 in this textbook for evidence in humans of non-conscious, unthinking, involuntary, automatic influence. Recall the research you cited in that chapter about priming without awareness; I cite additional examples in my own book. You cite brain-scan research by Westen and his associates, showing how emotion-centered regions of the "primitive" brain are activated defensively by voters as an unconscious way of protecting prejudices. It should no longer surprise us that we behave in some respects like so-called "lower-order animals"; after all, we share considerable DNA not just with primates but with the common fruit fly. You write with a certain "patsies-are-us" fondness for the hungry restaurant customer who is classically conditioned to salivate like Pavlov's dogs by nothing more than the "mouth-watering" dessert menu. You envision another scenario at the deli counter where a customer is conditioned to buy a package of Sagamento cheese not unlike a pigeon in a psychological laboratory being trained to hop on one foot, then the other. So why not admit that you are just as susceptible to such influences?
>
> What's more, you cite Thaler and Sunstein on our many "biases" and the ELM model on unthinking peripheral processing. Why assume that all this is correctable by self-monitoring? You clearly prefer the "Automatic Pilot" metaphor to the "Mother Turkey" metaphor, and who wouldn't, given that it massages our very fragile egos? But haven't you yourself provided enough evidence to suggest that we can't dispense with "Mother Turkey" or some other such humbling metaphor? "Mother Turkey" isn't a rival metaphor to "Automatic Pilot." Rather, it expresses another side to human behavior—the reflexive "blink-like" side rather than the controlled "wink-like" side.
>
> One day, perhaps, these two "systems" of cognitive processing will be encompassed by one overarching theory. Until then I'll be content to risk the criticism of inconsistency by use of both metaphors.

And the Debater's Trophy Goes to ...

You, our readers, must decide which side in this imagined debate is more persuasive. We can tell you what we think: Cialdini's research contributes a great deal to our understanding of persuasion, and we find his work academically solid and highly accessible. Yet, we also argue that he is making a persuasive case. He is using rhetoric to present to us his views about how rhetoric functions. And we find his rhetoric to be just as worthy of analysis as he finds that of the jewelry salesperson, the Tupperware lady, and the transcendental recruiter that he offered up for examination.

The fact that his writing is persuasive is neither unique nor surprising. In fact, there's a whole area of study, *rhetoric of science*, where scholars study artifacts that contain data that are presented as "facts." Often hiding in these "fact-based" papers, lab reports, and statistics is evidence of rhetorical intent. Likewise, as we noted earlier, researchers in the field of *critical studies* seek to find the less obvious (and thereby more powerful?) persuasion that is present in everything from our college course descriptions to our favorite songs. Finding and analyzing this hidden rhetoric, which is often tucked away in places where we don't expect it to be, is both fascinating and important. It is where some of the most significant work on the humanistic side of persuasion studies is taking place today.

THE HIGHLY PERSUADABLE PERSUADEE

Nothing that has been said by way of criticism of the "Mother Turkey" metaphor negates Cialdini's central point about the widespread use of cognitive shorthands. To paraphrase Abraham Lincoln, you can persuade nearly all the people some of the time, and you can persuade some of them nearly all the time.

Some people apparently have great difficulty defending against the seductive appeals of professional persuaders. Children, people who are old, recent immigrants, and persons with little education or low intelligence are especially vulnerable to advertising messages (Schudson, 1984). People with low self-esteem and low to moderate intelligence tend to be relatively easy marks for these messages, particularly if the messages are kept simple enough for them to understand (McGuire, 1985; Stiff, 1994). Insecurities about social status make some persuadees highly receptive to snob appeals for upscale brand names, particularly if these appeals are coupled with reminders of social shame (Messaris, 1997; O'Keefe, 2002). The highly intelligent are just as prone to "bias blind spots" as the rest of us, in that they can evaluate others, but they cannot see the errors in their own thinking. Even worse, because of their high intelligence, the highly intelligent may be prone to inflated self-confidence, which makes them even more vulnerable to persuasion (Lehrer, 2012; West, et al., 2012). None of this would seem unusual to professor of Psychology and Nobel Laureate Daniel Kahneman, who writes in *Thinking, Fast and Slow* that his research has done little to improve his own mental performance: "My intuitive thinking is just as prone to overconfidence, extreme predictions, and the planning fallacy as it was before I made a study of these issues" (2012). As discussed in Chapter 2, an inability to process complex messages thoughtfully leads many people to engage in peripheral processing.

Thus, it is easy to say that "others" have difficulties when it comes to persuasion. But what about "us"? Are *we* able to rise above the non-thinking situations that Cialdini speaks about? In fact, the answer is almost certainly "no." The tendency toward peripheral processing, including reliance on cognitive shorthands, is impossible to avoid in today's fast-paced, message-dense society. All of us rely on cognitive shorthands when the stakes are low, and many of us do so when the stakes are high. High motivation increases message scrutiny (Booth-Butterfield & Welbourne, 2002) and, on the whole, more competent message processors are better able to separate fact from fancy, but motivation to get things right is no guarantee that we will get them right.

Moreover, the tools of sound reasoning and good judgment often elude otherwise competent message processors when they need them the most. What Thaler and Sunstein (2008) call the **optimism bias** may help to account for what in Chapter 1 we referred to as the **"not me" phenomenon**, which is our predisposition to see others as highly persuadable but not ourselves. It also helps account for things like accidents caused by drunken driving, because we imagine that even as others are not in any shape to drive, we are different. We believe that we are the ones who can make it home.

When biases of this kind are unchecked by central processing—that is, when we are flying unselfconsciously on automatic pilot—the risks to ourselves and others increase dramatically. But that's not all. Our impressions of others, whether favorable or unfavorable, are now known to form in a matter of seconds, and they are automatically primed by cues consistent with our stereotypes (Gladwell, 2005; Thaler & Sunstein, 2008). Susceptibility to persuasion is also driven by social influences of the sort that Cialdini describes. The following case studies vividly illustrate how prone to error and bad judgment smart, well-intentioned, highly motivated message processors can be.

Case Study 1 How Doctors Using Shortcuts Puts Your Health at Risk

We begin with a case that displays that intellect and training do not inoculate people from using cognitive shorthands in ways that can short-circuit good decision making. In fact, as we will see, in those moments when we are under the most pressure, we have an increased likelihood of persuading ourselves of the validity of faulty answers and solutions because of the stressors in our midst. For most of us, this is inconvenient. But for physicians, this can be a matter of life and death.

Jerome Groopman, a doctor who teaches at Harvard Medical School, is the author of *Your Medical Mind: How to Decide What Is Right for You* (2012) and *How Doctors Think* (2007). Both books, but especially the latter, is "a mixture of methodological theorizing, personal history (Groopman, with his endearingly gimpy wrists and painfully fused spine, has suffered much at the hands of his colleagues), and entertaining stories of misdiagnoses and miraculous saves" (Anderson, 2007). In *How Doctors Think*, and in the *New Yorker* article that accompanies it, Groopman tells the story of an experimental psychologist turned physician named Pat Croskerry. As a medical student in the 1980s, Croskerry was struck by the relative inattention given by the profession to cognitive processing in clinical diagnoses and decision making. Said Groopman, "Croskerry's instructors rarely bothered to describe the mental logic they relied on to make a correct diagnosis and avoid mistakes" (2007).

In 1990, Croskerry headed up the emergency department at Dartmouth General Hospital, where he was surprised by the number of errors made by doctors under his supervision. He kept lists of the errors, trying to group them into categories, and, in the mid-1990s, he began to publish articles in medical journals on flawed decision making, drawing on his background in cognitive psychology to explain the errors. Said Groopman, "By calling physicians' attention to common mistakes in medical judgment, he has helped to promote an emerging field in medicine: the study of how doctors think" (2007).

Research from the 1980s and 1990s had suggested that medical errors occurred about 15% of the time, but Croskerry suspected that the error rate was much higher. The good news was that the sources of error were readily identifiable and preventable. They were errors in the use of **heuristics** (which are also known as "rules of thumb," educated guesses, intuitive judgments or common sense). In effect, they were errors brought about by the faulty use of cognitive shorthands. Said Groopman:

> Doctors typically begin to diagnose patients the moment they meet them. Even before they conduct an examination, they are interpreting a patient's appearance: his complexion, the tilt of his head, the movements of his eyes and mouth, the way he sits or stands up, the sound of his breathing. Doctors' theories about what is wrong continue to evolve as they listen to the patient's heart, or press on his liver. But research shows that most physicians already have in mind two or three possible diagnoses within minutes of meeting a patient, and that they tend to develop their hunches from very incomplete information.
>
> Heuristics are indispensable in medicine; physicians, particularly in emergency rooms, must often make quick judgments about how to treat a patient, on the basis of a few, potentially serious symptoms. A doctor is trained to assume, for example, that a patient suffering from a high fever and sharp pain in the lower right side of the abdomen could be suffering from appendicitis; he immediately sends the patient for X-rays and contacts the surgeon on call. But, just as heuristics can help doctors save lives, they can also lead them to make grave errors.
>
> (Groopman, 2007)

As we can see by Groopman's depiction, physicians are influenced greatly by their first impressions, and we all know that first impressions are often incorrect. What's more, if we recall Thaler and Sunstein's (2008) list of "biases" from Chapter 2, we see here that Groopman's description of the way physicians make medical diagnoses can suffer from **representativeness errors**. Doctors assume that new cases are likely to fit a known pattern, and they are thereby unprepared for the atypical. This is especially true when, as with a flu epidemic, the next patient complaining of similar symptoms as previous patients seen the same day is automatically assumed to have the same disease.

Now add the influences of Cialdini's principles of *liking* and *evaluative consistency* (2009) and the plot thickens even more. Doctors who like their patients may wish to spare them from arduous tests of uncertain value—but at the risk of missing out on crucial diagnostic information (Groopman, 2007). And doctors, being human, are prone to Thaler and Sunstein's *optimism bias* (2008). They tend to make decisions based on what they wish were true and then, like the racetrack bettors described by Cialdini, they often compound that error by rationalizing it for the sake of *consistency*.

Yet another source of error stems from what Groopman describes as the "availability" heuristic: the tendency to make judgments based on the ease with which relevant examples come to mind (2007). But recall from Chapter 2 that what comes to mind may be primed by even the most irrelevant influences such as the faint smell of citrus in the room or a briefcase on a table.

Ultimately, what this case demonstrates is that even highly trained and intelligent professionals depend too often on cognitive shorthands. Even physicians, who know their decisions will impact directly the life of their patient, can become trapped in the click and whirr of autopilot responses (Cialdini, 2009). Or, as Groopman puts it, when "people are confronted with uncertainty—the situation of every doctor attempting to diagnose a patient—they are susceptible to unconscious emotions and personal biases, and are more likely to make cognitive errors" (2007).

Groopman concludes that medical training needs to recognize that "how doctors think can affect their success as much as how much they know, or how much experience they have" (2007) and furthermore, that we, as patients, must become active participants, indeed negotiators, in decisions about our health care (Groopman & Hartzband, 2011; Levitin, 2011).

Case Study 2 How Financial Advertisers Using Shortcuts Puts Your Money at Risk

We have first considered the case of how cognitive shorthands can impact our health. Now let us see how they impact our wallets. As of this writing, the world economy is struggling to regain its footing after a harsh and global recession that seemingly came upon us overnight in 2008. Employment, manufacturing, housing markets, governments, pension funds, and banking have all been severely affected, and experts in many fields are working to understand the causes, scope, and long-term impact of this global economic retraction. In this climate, it seems even more important that people keep an eye on their investments and seek sound advice about how to manage their scarce resources.

Investing in the twenty-first century has become a complex enterprise, one where most people depend upon the advice of professionals. One typical place where such advice can be found is in popular financial media. Magazines, television channels, and newspapers provide specialized sites that offer financial advice, and these sites also include ads. Such ads have one goal: they seek to persuade us to invest with the firms the ads represent. And, as Mullainthan and Schleiffer (2005) demonstrate, the ads use cognitive shorthands to bolster their claims and get our business.

Mullainthan and Schleiffer examined ads from 1994 to 2003 in the financial magazines *Money* and *Business Week*, covering a period that coincided with the birth, growth, and explosion of the technology and Internet bubble that ended circa 2000. These magazines typically cater to educated, upscale investors for whom, presumably, relevant, reliable information in investment advertising would be much in demand. What these investors typically got, however, was less than useful; the ads typically counseled prudence before the bubble when aggressive investing would have paid off, encouraged investment at the height of the bubble when they should have counseled protection of assets, and appealed to anxieties about stock price declines after the bubble burst when investors should have been encouraged to buy. They did so, moreover, by way of appeal to the cognitive shorthands of *authority* and *social proof* with little in the way of relevant factual information.

Merrill Lynch's advertising from the period is illustrative. Before the bubble, when the sound advice would have called for aggressive investing, Merrill featured two ads, called: "A Tradition of Trust" and "The Difference is Merrill Lynch." The first, showing a grandfather and grandson fishing, talked about how to protect one's assets and slowly accumulate wealth through patience, consistency, and skill—just as in fishing. The second ad played again on the fishing analogy, featuring grandpa and grandson on the virtues of saving.

In 1999, as the Internet bubble was about to burst, when caution should have been advised, a Merrill Lynch "Human Achievement" ad showed a 12-year-old girl carrying a skateboard and wearing a helmet. The skateboard suggested adventure, the helmet suggested protection. This ad, said Mullainthan and Schleiffer (2005), offered a much hipper and more modern image than in the previous ads, but one that combined the frames of caution and risk in the slogan, "Protected Growth Investments." And then, by 2000–2001, just when Internet stocks were at their peak, Merrill Lynch substituted the theme of "opportunity" for "protection." One ad, entitled "Be Bullish" showed a bull wired to a semi-conductor board, hinting here at the gains to be made by getting on board the new wired world of Internet investing.

After the market declined, which would normally be seen as a good time to invest because stock prices were reduced, Merrill went back to the theme of protection with an "Ask Merrill" ad that counseled trust in its expertise. A page-sized question mark suggested the need for answers in the face of insecurity and uncertainty. Finally, ironically, Merrill returned back to protection and intergenerational fishing in a new "Total Merrill" campaign.

Mullainthan and Schleiffer (2005) concluded that ads during the period belied a "traditional" model of persuasion that is based on fact and reason, and instead supported a "behavioral" model of persuasion where the object was not to change beliefs, but to play on pre-existing beliefs, linking them by a "web of associations" to promoted products and ideas.

Among those pre-existing beliefs, of course, is that we should rely on the cognitive shorthand of *authority* and simply trust Merrill Lynch. "Thank you, Merrill," we should say to ourselves, as we and countless other sagacious investors parted with yet another hard-earned dollar based on Merrill's advice. Given that we were trusting in authority, we should never mind that Merrill Lynch changed its tune at just the wrong times and in precisely the wrong directions. And then, once we'd invested with the firm, Merrill would count on another of our cognitive shorthands, *consistency*, to rationalize the commitments we have made to invest with the brokerage house.

Case Study 3 How Crooks Using Shortcuts Steal from People Both Gullible and Wise

Practically everyone in the investment world knows the name Bernard L. Madoff. On March 12, 2009, Madoff pled guilty to 11 felonies and admitted to operating the largest investor fraud ever committed by an individual. He founded the Wall Street firm Bernard L. Madoff Investment Securities LLC in 1960, and was its chairman until his arrest. On December 10, 2008, Madoff told his sons that the asset management arm of his firm was a giant Ponzi scheme—or "one big lie"—that bilked $50 billion from investors of all types. He is now serving a 150-year sentence in a federal prison in Butner, North Carolina.

Relatively few people know the name John G. Bennett, Jr. By comparison to Madoff's Ponzi scheme, the plan Bennett hatched for getting investors to part with their money was small: millions in some cases, but not tens and hundreds of millions, went to Bennett's Foundation for New Era Philanthropy. Ultimately, while it does not match that of Bernie Madoff's in size, Bennett's thievery is considered the worst *charity* scandal in American history (Raspopow, 2014). Hundreds of venture capitalists, officers and directors of charitable institutions, and prominent civic leaders entrusted large sums of money, falling prey to "a phony, primitive get-rich scheme" that promised a six months' return of two dollars for every dollar they entrusted to the foundation (Arenson, 1995, p. E4). Bennett claimed that he'd found a group of generous secret donors who would match charitable donations. And, despite how flimsy and unlikely the pitch sounds in retrospect, donors piled on board (Raspopow, 2014).

Madoff was a brilliant con-artist; Bennett's phony get-rich scheme was relatively primitive. Yet the similarities abound. Both stories vividly illustrate how even the rhetorically sophisticated can be prompted to fly dangerously on automatic pilot.

Seven explanations for their gullibility repeatedly came up in interviews with those taken in by both men.

1   *Persuasive skills.* Madoff was described as a master marketer who used an understated approach:

> He never overplayed his hand. At a club where social climbing is common but mocked, the Madoffs were modest, never ostentatious, unassuming people. Bernie never obviously hustled anyone. He let them come begging to him, and he knew they were rich.
>
> (Biggs, 2009)

Likewise, Bennett was known as a "supreme salesman."

2   *Credibility.* Madoff was a prominent philanthropist and a pillar on Wall Street whom nearly everyone looked up to for his exceptional savvy. One investor remarked, "The returns were just amazing and we trusted this guy for decades— if you wanted to take money out, you always got your check in a few days. That's why we were all so stunned" (*Fox News*, 2009). Bennett was said by his friends to be a man of great decency, a born-again Christian who had spent his adult life helping others (Dobrin, et al., 1995).

3   *Connections.* Madoff and Bennett exploited their connections to charitable institutions, civic organizations, and friends in high political places. Madoff had close ties to the "so-called 'Jewish circuit' of well-heeled Jews he met at country clubs on Long Island and in Palm Beach" (Lambiet, 2008). Bennett's religious ties were to born-again Christians. The slick brochure put out by his Foundation for New Era Philanthropy bore the logo of a farmer sowing seeds under a glorious sun and the logo: "Sowing the seed God gives us today cultivates excellence tomorrow." A *Newsweek* article identified Madoff's scheme as "an affinity Ponzi" (Biggs, 2009).

4   *Endorsements.* Respondents in both cases testified to the importance of endorsements from intermediaries who had the trust of the financial, religious, and civic communities who invested with Madoff and Bennett. Madoff fostered a veneer of exclusivity and created an A-list of investors that became his most powerful marketing tool. From New York and Florida to Minnesota and Texas, the money manager became

> an insider's choice among well-heeled investors seeking steady returns. By hiring unofficial agents, tapping into elite country clubs and creating "invitation only" policies for investors, he recruited a steady stream of new clients. During golf-course and cocktail-party banter, Mr. Madoff's name frequently surfaced as a money manager who could consistently deliver high returns. Older Jewish investors called Mr. Madoff "the Jewish bond."
>
> (Frank, et al., 2008)

The *New York Times* account in the Bennett case echoed Cialdini; the donors were busy people; as such, they looked for shortcuts. What better way than to turn to their friends for advice? (Arenson, 1995)

5   *Investor Commitments.* Investing was filled with continued doubt, especially when returns on investments seemed too good to be true; hence, one way of relieving the dissonance was to suppress the doubt. As one Bennett investor put it, "By the time you get your hook in your mouth, you're saying, 'Hey, another $100,000? Sure!' " (Dobrin, et al., 1995). Some Madoff investors were wary of removing their money from his fund, in case they could not get back in later:

> Barbara Fox, president of a Manhattan estate agency business, said she "literally begged" him to take her money but he refused. Others who were not so lucky include Mort Zuckerman, owner of *The New York Daily News*, and Steven Spielberg, the film director, whose charity the Wunderkinder Foundation was a Madoff client.
>
> (Dovkants, 2008)

6   *Scarcity, Snob Appeal.* Madoff's fund was considered exclusive, giving the appearance of a "velvet rope" (Henriques, 2008). Likewise, not every non-profit was deemed eligible to invest with New Era, its documents said. To get in, a non-profit had to meet rigorous criteria. It had to be willing to invest at least $50,000. It had to be screened and sponsored. It had to be one of the select few.

7   *Mystery.* Madoff generally refused to meet directly with investors, which gave him an "Oz" aura and increased the allure of the investment (Appelbaum, Hilzenrath, & Paley, 2008). Bennett's document promised that investments would be matched in 6 months by a network of esteemed, extremely wealthy givers who insisted on remaining anonymous. Some givers assumed that they knew who these behind-the-scenes backers were. It turned out that they did not exist.

As discussed in Chapter 6, our culture provides alternate "sense-making" frames for alternative positions on a great many issues. As Chapter 7 notes, we depend on cognitive shortcuts to manage our days, and sometimes these shortcuts really are short-circuits to bad decisions that cause us to be vulnerable to unethical persuaders. When applied to investing, various frames and shortcuts provide rationalizations and rationales for seizing new opportunities, for following the crowd, for timing the market, for investing in "sure winners." As finance has gone global and become ever more complex, it is little wonder that even the wise and the wealthy are sucked in by "get-rich" schemes.

SUMMARY

The alternative to mindful processing, according to Cialdini, involves reliance on a variety of external cues and automatic, information-processing mechanisms, including the none-too-reliable filter of evaluative consistency. Cialdini organizes these mental shorthands under seven principles: contrast, reciprocity, consistency, social proof, liking, authority, and scarcity.

These frequently operate in tandem, as in the example of the Tupperware party. To take another example, suppose that your neighbors take exception to your habitually parking your car in front of their house. You could, of course, try reasoning with them: you prefer to park in front of your house, but your housemates always seem to get there first. This argument metacommunicates caring, which should at least make you appear more *likable* to your neighbors, even if it isn't entirely convincing. Perhaps, too, you could elicit from your neighbors an expression of sympathy for your plight, and you could then exploit their self-professed caring by appealing to the principle of *consistency*. Also, you could, without being asked, shovel the snow off their sidewalk—that would incur a *reciprocal* obligation. You could inform them that there's nothing illegal about what you've been doing—you have it on the highest *authority*. You could point out that the practice of parking in front of other people's houses is common on your street—thus invoking the principle of *social proof*. You could, if worst came to worst, try the rejection-then-retreat approach. You are thinking about buying a motorcycle and keeping it in front of their house along with the car. Would they object? Yes? Well, all right then, you'll stick with the car. By *contrast*, this smaller violation may actually appear reasonable.

Cialdini's seven principles are by no means original to him. But this chapter has focused on his compilation of them for several reasons. First, because of his rich and varied examples from the field, Cialdini shows that these mental shorthands are used by real people in everyday situations, and not just in contrived experiments. Second, Cialdini is an uncommonly adept persuader in addition to being expert on persuasion; his writings are examined as an example of textbook rhetoric.

But most important, Cialdini provides dramatic illustration of the difference a frame makes. Are we humans really as unreflective as mother turkeys? If so, then we might as well resign ourselves to our gullibilities. Or, are we human beings better described as "turner-oners" and "turner-offers" of our automatic pilots? If this is the case, we then have real reason to hope. Cialdini gives us both metaphors but never reconciles them. We've imagined Cialdini as saying in response that we can't reconcile them either.

Reluctantly we concede that he's got a good case. The case studies we've presented illustrate how vulnerable smart, well-educated persuadees can be to Cialdini's "weapons of influence" and to their own error-prone heuristics. Recent research on priming should help us better understand why physicians so often misdiagnose, why purchasers of expensive technological gadgets succumb to the liking heuristic, and why experienced investors fall for the trappings of authority.

Let these case studies, then, serve as a reminder to all of us to check out our automatic pilots on a regular basis and to rely, as surgeons and airline pilots now do, not just on our own error-prone judgments but on checks by others of those judgments. Like the physicians described by Groopman, the more we learn about how we think, the more our judgments are likely to improve. Awareness of our foibles is not automatically self-correcting but it helps. Although we cannot and should not abandon our mental shorthands, we can learn to process messages more critically when it is truly important for us to do so. By the same token, persuaders cannot always count on winning over audiences by appeal to cognitive shorthands. In some circumstances, they must truly reason with audiences, and, when they do, the quality of their arguments often makes a difference.

QUESTIONS AND PROJECTS FOR FURTHER STUDY

1   This chapter has argued that Cialdini uses techniques of persuasion in the very process of writing about persuasion. Can the same be said of the writing in this book? If so, where and how?

2   What did you think of the critique of Cialdini's "Mother Turkey" hypothesis? What might you say in Cialdini's defense?

3   How have you been influenced by the seven principles Cialdini discusses? Think about jobs you've had, relationships you've been in, or shopping you've done, and summarize your reflections.

4   Have you worked as a restaurant server? If so, what do you think of the techniques of the restaurant waiter? Discuss his approach in class.

5   Which of Cialdini's categories of shorthand do you employ the most often in your life?

6   Discuss the issue of "optimism bias" and the "not me" phenomenon. Why is it that we think we are exempt from persuasion?

7   The chapter presents case studies of important situations where cognitive shorthands can affect thinking. Can you think of others?

EXERCISES

1   Do a Google search of Robert Cialdini, seeing where and how his work has been both received and applied. Present your findings to the class.

2   Interview three people who make their living as persuasion professionals. Ask them to reveal their tricks of the trade that "work every time." Then, mention

the principles identified by Cialdini in this chapter and see if they ring true to the people you interview. Summarize the results of your interview survey in a brief report.

3   Try your hand at doing a critique of a chapter in this textbook, using as your model our critique of Cialdini. Look especially for internal contradictions, finding where the rhetoric raised more questions than it answers.

4   Download, read, and present to class a "rhetoric of science" research paper. How does it differ, if at all, from other efforts at rhetorical criticism where persuasion is obvious and readily accepted?

5   Observe yourself for a day or two and notice when you have imposed one of Cialdini's seven principles in your efforts to persuade someone. Did your attempt work, or did it fail, and why?

KEY TERMS

- Authority
- Consistency
- Contrast
- Door-in-the-face (DITF) technique
- Evaluative consistency
- Foot-in-the-door (FITD) technique
- Heuristics
- Liking
- "Not me" phenomenon
- Optimism Bias
- Probabilistic Consistency
- Reciprocity
- Representativeness errors
- Scarcity
- Social proof

REFERENCES

Anderson, S. (2007, March 18). The talking cure. *New York Magazine*. Retrieved June 24, 2009, from http://nymag.com/arts/books/reviews/29427/

Appelbaum, B., Hilzenrath, D. S., & Paley, A. R. (2008, December 13). All just one big lie. Bernard Madoff was a Wall Street whiz with a golden reputation. Investors, including Jewish charities, entrusted him with billions. It's gone. *Washington Post*, p. D01. Retrieved June 25, 2009, from www. washingtonpost.com/wp-dyn/content/ article/2008/12/12/AR2008121203970.html?nav= email page

Arenson, K. W. (1995, May 21). Embarrassing the rich. *New York Times*, p. E4.

Baas, R. (2012). *The effect of the foot-in-the-door and the door-in-the-face technique on purchase intention and attitude in a commercial setting and the moderating effect of persuasion knowledge*. Amsterdam: Universiteit van Amsterdam. Retrieved August 10, 2014, from www.google.com/url?sa=t&rct=j&q= &esrc=s&source=web&cd=5&cad=rja&uact= 8&ved=0CE8QFjAE&url=http%3A%2F%2Fdare. uva.nl%2Fdocument%2F448569&ei=tXLzU5P2PK qIjAKYhIGoBQ&usg=AFQjCNH1F2A2eu5qoPfbE3 0ec-5wZZ9DdQ&sig2=UiSKcWXRv5xjaGdmJqZo- g&bvm=bv.73231344,d.cGE

Bandura, A. (1973). *Aggression: A social learning analysis*. Englewood Cliffs, NJ: Prentice Hall.

Biggs, B. (2009, January 3). The affinity Ponzi scheme. *Newsweek*. Retrieved June 25, 2009, from www. newsweek.com/id/177679

Billig, M. (1995). *Banal nationalism*. Thousand Oaks, CA: Sage Publications.

Billig, M. (1996). *Arguing and thinking* (2nd ed.). Cambridge, UK: Cambridge University Press.

Booth-Butterfield, S., & Welborne, J. (2002). The elaboration likelihood model: Its impact on persuasion theory and research. In Dillard, J. P., & Pfau, M. (eds), *The persuasion handbook: Developments in theory and practice*. Thousand Oaks, CA: Sage Publications, pp. 155–173.

Burke, K. (1961). *Attitudes toward history*. Boston: Beacon. (Original work published 1937)

Cialdini, R. B. (2009). *Influence: Science and practice* (5th ed.). Boston: Pearson.

Cohen, M., & Davis, N. (1981). *Medication errors: Causes and prevention*. Philadelphia: G. F. Stickley Co. (cited in Cialdini, 2009).

Consolewii (2008). Top deals on Wii Fit for Christmas. *Article alley*. Retrieved June 23, 2009, from www. articlealley.com/article_693569_32.html

Dobrin, P., Sataline, S., & Ferrick, T., Jr. (1995, May 21). New Era played on dire need for cash, and nonprofits swallowed their doubts. *Philadelphia Inquirer*, pp. A1, A18.

Dovkants, K. (2008, December 16). Revealed: Magic Madoff's family "piggy bank" in the heart of Mayfair. *The London Evening Standard*. Retrieved June 25, 2009, from www.thisislondon.co.uk/ standard/article-23602414-details/Revealed:+ Magic+Madoff%E2%80%99s+family+%E2%80% 98piggy+bank%E2%80%99+in+the+heart+of+ Mayfair/article.do

Festinger, L. (1962). *A theory of cognitive dissonance*. California: Stanford University Press.

Filene's Basement (n.d.). Running of the brides. Retrieved November 11, 2010, from www. filenesbasement.com/running-of-the-brides/

Fishbein, M., & Ajzen, I. (1975). *Belief, attitude, intention, and behavior*. Reading, MA: Addison-Wesley.

Fox News (2009, March 10). Bernard Madoff will plead guilty to 11 charges in financial fraud case, faces 150 years in prison. Retrieved March 10, 2009, from www.foxnews.com/story/0,2933,508304,00. html

Frank, R., Lattman, P., Searcey, D., & Lucchettifund, A. (2008, December 13). Fraud hits big names. *Wall Street Journal*. Retrieved June 25, 2009, from http:// online.wsj.com/article/SB122914169719104017. html?mod=djemalertNEWS

Freedman, J. L., & Fraser, S. C. (1966). Compliance without pressure: The foot-in-the-door technique. *Journal of Personality and Social Psychology*, 4, 195–203.

Gladwell, M. (2005). *Blink*. New York: Little, Brown, & Company.

Groopman, J. (2007, January 29). How doctors think. *The New Yorker*. Retrieved June 24, 2009, from www.newyorker.com/reporting/2007/01/29/070129fa_fact_groopman

Groopman, J., & Hartzband, P. (2011). *Your medical mind: How to decide what is right for you*. New York: Penguin Press.

Henriques, D. (2008, December 20). Madoff scheme kept rippling outward. *New York Times*. Retrieved June 25, 2009, from www.nytimes.com/2008/12/20/business/20madoff.html?_r=1&em=&pagewanted=print

Hale, J. L., Householder, B., & Greene, K. (2002). The theory of reasoned action. *The persuasion handbook*. Thousand Oaks, CA: Sage Publications.

Hyde, L. (2007). *The gift: 25th anniversary edition*. New York: Vintage.

Kahneman, D. (2012). *Thinking, fast and slow*. London: Penguin Books Ltd.

Lambiet, J. (2008, December 12). Bernie Madoff's arrest sent tremors into Palm Beach. *Palm Beach Daily News*. Retrieved June 25, 2009, from www.palmbeachdailynews.com/news/content/news/2008/12/12/ponzi1212.ht

Latané, B., & Darley, J. M. (1968). *The unresponsive bystander: Why doesn't he help?* New York: Appleton-Century-Crofts.

Lehrer, J. (2012, June 12). *Why smart people are stupid*. Retrieved August 19, 2014, from *The New Yorker*: www.newyorker.com/tech/frontal-cortex/why-smart-people-are-stupid

Levitin, D. J. (2011, October 7). How patients think, and how they should. *The New York Times*. Retrieved August 19, 2014, from www.nytimes.com/2011/10/09/books/review/your-medical-mind-by-jerome-groopman-and-pamela-hartzband-book-review.html?pagewanted=all

Li, W., Moallem, I., Paller, K. A., & Gottfried, J. A. (2007). Subliminal smells can guide social preferences. *Psychological Science*, 18, 1044–1049.

McGuire, W. J. (1985). Attitudes and attitude change. In Lindzey, G., & Aronson, E. (eds), *Handbook of social psychology* (3rd ed., vol. 2). New York: Random House, pp. 233–346.

Messaris, P. (1997). *Visual persuasion*. Thousand Oaks, CA: Sage Publications.

Mullainthan, S., & Schleiffer, A. (2005). *Persuasion in finance*. Retrieved June 25, 2009, from http://icf.som.yale.edu/pdf/behavconf05papers/Shleifer.pdf

Norman, R. (1976). When what is said is important: A comparison of expert and attractive sources. *Journal of Experimental Social Psychology*, 12, 294–300.

O'Keefe, D. J. (2002). *Persuasion: Theory and research* (2nd ed.). Thousand Oaks, CA: Sage Publications.

Petty, R. E., & Cacioppo, J. T. (1996). *Attitudes and persuasion: Classic and contemporary approaches*. Boulder, CO: Westview. (Original work published 1981)

Pratkanis, A., & Aronson, E. (2001). *Age of propaganda: The everyday use and abuse of persuasion*. New York: Henry Holt.

Raspopow, C. (2014, March 2). *The three worst charity scandals*. Retrieved August 19, 2014, from www.therichest.com/business/companies-business/the-three-worst-ngo-scandals/?view=all

Regan, R. T. (1971). Effects of a favor and liking on compliance. *Journal of Experimental Social Psychology*, 7, 627–639.

Schein, E. (1961). *Coercive persuasion*. New York: Norton.

Schudson, M. (1984). *Advertising: The dubious persuasion*. New York: Basic Books.

Stiff, J. B. (1994). *Persuasive communication*. New York: Guilford.

Thaler, R., & Sunstein, C. R. (2008). *Nudge: Improving decisions about health, wealth, and happiness*. New Haven, CT: Yale University Press.

West, R.F., Meserve, R.J., & Stanovich, K.E. (2012, September). Cognitive sophistication does not attenuate the bias blind spot. *Journal of Personality and Social Psychology*, 506–519, doi:10.1037/a0028857

CHAPTER 8

Reasoning and Evidence

- Propositions of Policy, Fact, and Value
- Changing, Repairing, or Retaining a Policy: The Stock Issues Revisited
- Types of Evidence as Resources of Argumentation
- Fallacies Reconsidered
- The Case of Gulf War Syndrome
- Summary
- Note
- Questions and Projects for Further Study
- Exercises
- Key Terms
- Web Links
- References

Gun owner Lee Bird cares about his second amendment rights, and he thinks it's important that he has the right to carry his gun where and when he wants. A resident of Arizona, Bird says that the contemporary push to remove restrictions from carrying weapons into public places has "made his trusty .38 caliber Smith and Wesson Special revolver as much a part of his life as brushing his teeth" (Hwang & Murphy, 2014). Arizona's loosening of gun laws is a recent change, and it is worth recognizing that prior to 2010, the state "heavily restricted who could own a handgun or banned the concealed carry of handguns altogether" (Hwang & Murphy, 2014). That is no longer the case, and presently, Arizona is one of seven states that does not require gun owners to get a permit to carry a concealed weapon (Hwang & Murphy, 2014). Given that, Bird now takes his gun with him wherever he goes.

Changes in current laws concerning firearms and the reactions on both sides of the issue demonstrate that the American debate about gun rights and gun control, one that has been especially heated and adversarial for the last 40 years, continues to rage. Some of the new discussion, certainly, is linked to recent mass shootings, with a particular focus on the 2012 shooting at Sandy Hook Elementary School where a sole gunman shot and killed 20 children and six teachers with an arsenal of firearms. The Sandy Hook shooting and the reactions afterward led to the creation in 2014 of former New York mayor Michael Bloomberg's gun control group, *Everytown for Gun Safety*, to which he pledged $50 million of his own fortune in an effort to minimize the influence of the pro-gun National Rifle Association (Caldwell, et al., 2014). On the other side of the issue, the NRA has seen increases in membership and donations since Sandy Hook, and in the days immediately following the shooting, saw a surge of about 8,000 new members a day (Howerton, 2012).

> A resurgence of the gun control movement is challenging the status quo, while groups to the right of the NRA are also growing. Nonprofit organizations on each side are battling like they haven't in years, all trying to shape the country's politics and win over the American people.
>
> (McDaniel, et al., 2014)

These battles are not new, and pioneers in the contemporary fight for stricter gun control include two unlikely individuals, Jim Brady and his wife, Sarah Brady. In 1981, Jim Brady was serving as White House Press Secretary under President Ronald Regan when he was shot and seriously wounded by John Hinckley, Reagan's would-be assassin. His injuries left Brady confined to a wheelchair and with slurred speech (Simon, 2011). These event in 1981 led Brady to advocate for stricter gun control for the rest of his life. It is a testament to his tenacity that his death, in 2014, was ultimately ruled a homicide resulting from the gunshot wound he suffered three decades earlier (Hermann & Ruane, 2014).

The advocacy of Sarah and Jim Brady, which still goes on today through the Brady Campaign to Prevent Gun Violence, led to the passage into law in 1993 of the Brady Bill, a law that required background checks before someone could buy a gun (which are now standard practice and instant) and a ban on assault weapons (which has now lapsed) (Aborn, 2009). Passage of the Brady Bill took a dozen years of advocacy, during which time supporters of stricter gun regulation had to overcome strong resistance from the NRA. Sarah Brady served as a spokesperson for the gun control movement until her death in 2015, and, in 1986, wrote an article describing their ordeal:

> On the morning of January 2, 1981, my husband Jim Brady received a call from President-elect Reagan, asking him to be his press secretary. It was a dream come true for Jim—the culmination of many years of hard work in politics.
>
> The next two and one-half months whizzed by. There was the excitement of the inaugural, Jim's nightly appearances on network news, the flurry of parties following his long hours at the White House. We never expected it to end so abruptly.
>
> On the morning of March 30, 1981, as Jim was about to leave for work, he decided to go upstairs and wake our 2-year-old son, Scott. It was to be the last time he would climb those stairs to Scott's bedroom. At 2:30 that afternoon, Jim was shot through the head by John Hinckley. Jim nearly died. The President and two of his security men also were seriously wounded.

> Five years later, I still wonder how the John Hinckleys of the world can go into a store, buy a handgun—no questions asked—and shoot people because they hear voices or have strange visions.

(Brady, 1986)

Sarah Brady's story contains the rudiments of an argument—about the insanity of allowing the John Hinckleys of the world to purchase handguns—backed up by a piece of evidence, the Hinckley case itself. By strict standards of logic, however, this story is insignificant, because it is about an isolated case, an "*n* of 1," as they say in statistics texts. Clearly, Sarah Brady would need a lot more evidence before she could make her case convincing.

This chapter connects the principles of reasoning and evidence to the larger tasks of preparing a persuasive case (in the role of a persuader) and of evaluating a persuasive case (in the role of a message recipient). These tasks require balancing the standards of sound reasoning and credible evidence against the realization that persuasion typically takes place under conditions that are less than ideal for reflective argumentative exchange (van Eemeren, et al., 1993). These conditions include those in which committed, sometimes passionate communicators, operating under time constraints, must adapt their arguments to audiences with limited information on topics that are likely to arouse audience passions and prejudices as well. Accordingly, like Sarah Brady, persuaders cannot always be expected to win belief by logic alone.

Since the tragic events that transformed her life, Sarah Brady has headed up the Brady Center to Prevent Gun Violence and the Brady Campaign. The website describes the organization as follows:

> The Brady Campaign works to pass and enforce sensible federal and state gun laws, regulations, and public policies through grassroots activism, electing public officials who support common sense gun laws, and increasing public awareness of gun violence. Through our Million Mom March and Brady Chapters, we work locally to educate people about the dangers of guns, honor victims of gun violence, and pass sensible gun laws, believing that all Americans, especially children, have the right to live free from the threat of gun violence.
>
> The Brady Center works to reform the gun industry by enacting and enforcing sensible regulations to reduce gun violence, including regulations governing the gun industry. In addition, we represent victims of gun violence in the courts. We educate the public about gun violence through litigation, grassroots mobilization, and outreach to affected communities.

(Brady Campaign, n.d.)

Sarah Brady has dedicated all of her time and energy to her quest "to enact and enforce sensible gun laws" (Brady Campaign, n.d.). Her dedication has been tenacious, and her 1986 article, which recounts the story she has told countless times over the years since, packs a wallop. Its narrative details—of the parties, of the network news appearances, of Jim Brady's impulsive farewell to his son on the morning before he was shot—are not logically essential to her case for gun regulation, but they give the reader a *feeling* for what the shooting of her husband meant in lived experience. The opening to Sarah Brady's article also contributes greatly to her *ethos;* it literally *authorizes* her to speak as someone who has experienced the tragic consequences of unregulated handgun ownership firsthand. Brady couples this story with another, about a visit to Centralia, Illinois, Jim's hometown:

> A friend invited Scott, then 6 years old, and me for a ride in his pickup truck. We got in. Scott picked up what looked like a toy pistol and pointed it toward himself. I said, "Scott, don't ever point a gun at anyone, even if it's only a toy." Then, to my horror, I realized it was no toy. It was a fully-loaded handgun that our friend kept on the seat of his truck for "safety" reasons. I wondered how many other careless adults left handguns lying around for children to pick up. My mind went back to the day Jim was shot, then to the day one of my best friends was murdered—with a handgun—by her enraged boyfriend. I decided I had to do more than think about handgun violence—I had to do something to try to stop it.
>
> (Brady, 1986)

The tales about the loaded gun and about the killing of one of Sarah Brady's best friends were almost as powerful as the story about Jim Brady. If anything, they establish Sarah Brady as more similar to her readers and less remote from them than does the Jim Brady story. Together, the vignettes about her life give Sarah the image of being a *super-representative* of her audience. Lest there be any doubt about her credibility, she adds that she is a Republican and a conservative—not some wild-eyed liberal who wants to ban or confiscate guns and further restrict use of hunting rifles. Sarah Brady takes pains to emphasize that she is not in that camp:

> What I am for is finding a way to keep handguns out of the wrong hands—the hands of the mentally incompetent; small children; drunks, drug users and criminals; and the person who, on the spur of the moment, decides that he wants to purchase a handgun to "settle" an argument.
>
> (1986)

She also employs *enthymematic* arguments in her article. An **enthymeme** invites the reader to supply and endorse premises that are missing from the argument but left implicit. It is a truncated argument that rests on a premise or premises it assumes its audience will accept. Virtually all persuasive discourse is enthymematic, as Aristotle observed long ago.

Most conspicuous in the opening story is the premise that the near killing of the president's press secretary (let alone, of the president) is a bad thing. But numerous other premises are embedded in the narrative that derives from our culture. Indeed, Sarah Brady's story recounts back to us our own traditional image of the American

Thinking It Through

To understand enthymemes, we must begin with syllogisms.

Syllogisms are forms of reasoning that begin with a major premise, add a minor premise, and arrive at a conclusion. The most famous one states:

Major premise: All men are mortal.
Minor premise: Socrates is a man.
Conclusion: Socrates is mortal.

Enthymemes suppress one or more of the parts of the syllogism, leaving it for the audience to fill in themselves. They are effective persuasively, because the audience does the work to, in effect, persuade itself.

If you think about it, you will see that many advertisements contain enthymemes. The lonely college guy pops open a beer, for instance, and suddenly a party ensues. The conclusion: "Opening up some beer is the cure for loneliness." Based on that, viewers are left to fill in the premises.

Can you think of other examples? Think about recent ads you've seen, and try your hand at deciphering the enthymemes.

dream: of Jim Brady's deserved rise to the top on the basis of hard work; of the call from Mr. Big; of glamorous parties mixed with more hard work; of little Scott fast asleep in an upstairs bedroom; of Mrs. Brady standing up for her beliefs.

Despite the combined power of the stories Sarah Brady tells, they are still only about three cases and they offer little insight about what gun regulation would actually accomplish. General claims, such as those made by Sarah Brady for gun regulation, are most likely to be believed when they are bolstered by a variety of arguments. It is to these issues we now turn.

PROPOSITIONS OF POLICY, FACT, AND VALUE

Propositions are debatable assertions, of which three types are generally recognized: policy, fact, and value.

Policy, Fact, Value—An Overview

Proposition of policy: Debatable assertions about what should or should not be done.

Proposition of fact: Debatable assertions about what is true or false.

Proposition of value: Debatable assertions about what is good or bad, moral or immoral.

Sarah Brady's proposal for gun regulation is an example of what argumentation theorists call a *proposition of policy*—a controversial recommendation for action of some sort, to be taken in the future. As with any proposition of policy, certain recurring questions, called **stock issues**, are logically relevant to the decision on gun regulation:

1   Is there a *need* for a change—that is, is there a problem or deficiency of some type in the present way of thinking or of doing things? Persuaders often identify several problems with the current system, rather than focusing on any one of them. Thus, Brady could have dealt separately with the problems of gun availability to drunks, drug users, and criminals, in addition to children and the mentally incompetent.

2   Is the proposed policy *workable?* In theory, at least, would it remedy the problem or deficiency? Does the plan meet the need?

3   Is the proposed policy *practical?* Are the means (money, enforcement machinery, etc.) available for bringing about the change?

4   Is the proposed policy reasonably *free from greater evils*, or is the cure worse than the disease?

5   Is the proposed solution the *best available* solution?

In the limited space that she has available, Brady chooses to focus on the need for a change, on workability, and especially on the issue of greater evils. This last issue is crucial because as she points out in her article, the gun lobby, led by the NRA, had been arguing that "there is no middle ground on handguns in America." Note how Brady turns the gun lobby's arguments against them:

> The gun lobby uses scare tactics to play on the fears of women, attempting to make them believe that any gun control laws will make them defenseless. The NRA, for example, produced a brochure to "educate" women on the effectiveness of handguns for self-defense. Black with spatters of red blood, the brochure's cover read: "Tell them what rape is. Be graphic. Be disgusting. Be obscene. Make them sick. If they throw up, then they have the tiniest idea of what it is!"
>
> Women, understandably, feel vulnerable to acts of violence, and the gun lobby takes advantage of these fears in an attempt to increase sales and expand the handgun market.
>
> (1986)

In addition to putting forth a variety of arguments, the persuader should—if time and space permit—use a variety of evidence. For example, statistics are a nice complement to extended narratives. Statistics from 2009 show that Brady's analysis from 1986 has changed little concerning gun violence (Illinois Council Against

Handgun Violence, 2010), and in her article Brady attempts to show that a handgun kept for self-defense is more likely to hurt or kill a family member than an intruder:

> Data collected by Handgun Control, Inc., a pro-control lobbying group, shows that 1,200 people are killed in handgun accidents each year—as compared to 200 intruders who are killed by handguns kept for self-defense. And my son's experience with a loaded "toy gun" is repeated hundreds of times each year. On the average, one child a day is killed in a handgun accident—most because they found a loaded handgun carelessly left lying around the house. In addition, according to the Centers for Disease Control, approximately 52% of the 15–24-year-old females committing suicide in 1980 used handguns. That represents a sizeable increase from the approximately 32% who shot themselves to death in 1970.

(1986)

Although these data on the dangers of handgun-related accidental deaths and suicides are impressive, they are by no means the last word on the subject. Nor is Brady's take on the NRA pamphlet the only take. Nor, for that matter, is her handling of the other stock issues for a policy proposition irrefutable. The NRA can make a good case that Brady goes too far and that legal restrictions affect only the law-abiding, while others think that the Brady Bill didn't go far enough. At last report, there were more than 70 million gun owners in the United States, with about 45 million owning handguns, according to the NRA-Institute for Legislative Action. When fully in force, the Brady Bill created only a modest reduction in gun-related deaths. Thus, on a great many issues, including gun control, there may be no demonstrable best solution.

This is another way of saying what was said earlier: persuasion deals in matters of judgment, rather than certainty. Under the circumstances, it makes little sense to speak of the persuader as proving a case beyond the shadow of a doubt. What constitutes "proof" varies from situation to situation and from audience to audience. Similarly, it makes little sense to think of persuasive arguments as definitive or compelling, or as weapons with which to demolish an adversary.

This, however, is not an invitation to impulsive or random decision making or to perpetual indecision. Indeed, for the persuader, careful inquiry should precede impassioned advocacy. Before we promote ideas to others, we should ask ourselves whether the position we are about to endorse is one we truly believe. We need to check our basic assumptions and ask ourselves whether we have been treating assumptions as facts, ignoring counter-arguments, or perhaps trusting too much in the opinions of others without thinking things through ourselves. The process of inquiry may lead us to abandon our initially held convictions, or it may strengthen them. It should lead in either case to a more sophisticated sense of the issues at hand and to a position reflecting the topic's complexities. Once persuadees become satisfied that our position, although not without flaws, is the "least worst" among the alternatives available, they should find us credible and come to support our view.

On the other side of the situation, as message recipients, we should practice what might be called an art of mistrust. We should question the persuader's premises, either verbally or to ourselves. Furthermore, we should question the links the persuader makes between premises and conclusions and between evidence and generalization. We should examine the persuader's choice and treatment of language, and claims to authority or expertise. But having practiced the art of mistrust, we shouldn't be afraid to commit to the persuader's position once he or she has earned our assent.

The Brady proposal, as noted, was a proposition of policy. Such propositions suggest that a message recipient should (or should not) engage in some action or be in favor of (or opposed to) some action. Policy propositions may be quite general ("The government should do more to stop global warming") or quite specific ("City Council should pass Bill 239765 to further regulate industrial waste disposal"); positive ("Buy American") or negative ("Let's not let patriotism determine purchases"); important ("Please marry me") or relatively unimportant ("Let's serve duck, not chicken"); and explicit ("Don't go to school at Old Ivy U.") or implicit ("Do you really want to go to a snob-ridden school?").

A proposition is debatable in the sense that there is room for argument about it. *Argument* involves staking out and supporting a claim that is not already known or agreed on. On the one hand, as Brockriede suggests, argument involves the region of uncertainty: "If certainty existed, people need not engage in what I am defining as argument" (1990). On the other hand, says Brockriede, "An arguer must perceive some rationale that establishes that the claim leaped to is worthy of at least being entertained" (1990). A claim, then, is not truly debatable unless some rationale exists for its support.

CHANGING, REPAIRING, OR RETAINING A POLICY: THE STOCK ISSUES REVISITED

Stock issues (recurring questions), discussed briefly in connection with the Brady example, could be defined as "systematized common sense." In this section, we will turn our attention in closer detail to five stock issues around which persuaders are logically obligated to advance arguments: *need, workability, practicality, freedom from greater evils,* and *superiority relative to other possible solutions.*

First, let's consider the stock issue of need. Generally speaking, people assume the desirability of existing policies, practices, systems, and the like *unless the need for a change has been demonstrated.* Car owners do not change their cars unless they perceive something wrong with the old car. Physicians do not operate unless they perceive something defective about one of the systems (e.g., respiratory, circulatory) that keep the patient going. In the same way, most people would not endorse basic changes in welfare laws unless they believed there was something seriously wrong with those laws. Existing policies are presumed "innocent" until proved "guilty."

The second commonsense assumption is that the solution would fit the need or problem. This is the stock issue of *workability*. Rather than buying a new car when the old one gets a flat tire, a car owner is more likely to repair or replace the flat tire. Rather than operating, physicians prescribe medication to heal a minor respiratory problem. Rather than getting rid of welfare policies on grounds that they are inefficiently administered, lawmakers are likely to prefer keeping the policies but getting rid of the inefficiencies. In the jargon of argumentation theory, persons may opt for *repair* of a policy or system or thing rather than outright *change*.

This being said, a proposed policy or solution should not, if possible, fall short of the need; it must address the third stock issue of *practicality*. If an old car is wrecked beyond repair, its owner will feel compelled to get a new one. If medication will not suffice, the physician may decide to operate. If inefficient administration is inherent in the present welfare policy—that is, if, whenever and wherever it is administered, problems of inefficiency seem to recur—lawmakers may feel obliged to support a new policy.

The last commonsense assumption is that, compared with other possible policies, the proposed policy must offer the most advantages and the fewest disadvantages; it must address the fourth stock issue of *freedom from greater evils* and the fifth stock issue of *having superiority relative to other possible solutions*. A brand-new Lexus might handily satisfy a driver's needs, but its costs may render it impractical. An operation might be successful but create new and dangerous problems for the patient. A new welfare policy might be desirable, but it may not be superior to other possible plans being considered.

Often, when the need for a change is conceded or when persuaders are reasonably assured that their audiences share their goals, an entire presentation or written article may be structured around *comparative advantages*. The persuader's obligations are met by showing that the proposed plan (a) is an improvement on the present system and (b) can be favorably compared with other alternatives.

This conversation between two college room-mates, Lucas and George, focuses on the first task:

Lucas: I think it is time to move off-campus. I hate living in the dorms and I hate eating cafeteria food. In general, I hate living on campus. So many freshmen; so much noise.

George: Yes, but living on campus has many benefits. If we move into an apartment, who will cook our meals? Who will clean the bathroom? Who will we socialize with? It seems to me that what we are doing now is the best alternative.

Lucas: You're wrong. Look at it this way—if we move off campus, we will save a lot of money. In fact, I figure that our housing cost will drop by about a third. Besides, the freedom to come and go without worrying about dorm rules and regulations far outweigh any reason to stay in the dorms. Besides, I like the idea of just having time to stay away from campus and relax.

George: Well, I hadn't thought of it like that. I especially hadn't thought about the cost savings, and I expect that between you and me we can cook better than the cafeteria. Let's move!

(Warnick & Inch, 1994)

If, as a persuader, you believe that an existing policy or system should be *retained* more or less as is, your first obligation is to refute objections to the present way of doing things. George does this (but then falls for Lucas's argument). Proponents of change, like prosecutors in a law court, have the burden of demonstrating that something is seriously wrong with the system or policy. This is called the **burden of proof**. You, as a defender of the status quo, have a lesser obligation, called the **burden of refutation**. You may choose to go on the offensive, however, showing how the system being attacked by others actually does its job quite well. You also may argue that the changes being proposed by others would not solve existing problems nearly as well, or that proposals for change would introduce new and greater evils. Insofar as you make positive assertions ("The existing welfare system is doing just fine") rather than merely challenging the claims made by proponents for change or major repair ("Where's their evidence that the current welfare system is inherently inefficient?"), you, too, take on a burden of proof.

Although there is a commonsense logic to the assumptions behind stock issues for a proposition of policy, the way people apply these assumptions often reveals their irrationality. In the first place, the conditions labeled as problems or non-problems are often branded as such on highly questionable grounds. For instance, as a result of the auto manufacturers' careful indoctrination programs, a current automobile can constitute "a problem" simply by being three years old. In the absence of substantive information for choosing among headache pills, mouthwashes, or premium beers, the advertiser may promote a product, and consumers may buy it, on the basis of snob appeal, color preference, or because it's "lighter."

Furthermore, it is not uncommon that the solutions we concoct for remedying a problem turn out to be inappropriate or worse. One common difficulty is balancing *workability* and *practicality*. What is most workable in theory may be least doable in practice. Often, we are faced with the choice of seeking to eliminate the causes of a problem or trying to contain its ill effects. That choice is difficult enough, but it is often compounded by the rhetoric of such debates. Consider, for instance, the debates about global warming and climate change. Effects-oriented advocates label cause-oriented reformers as dreamers or utopians and label themselves as pragmatists; cause-oriented reformers respond that trying to control symptoms or effects of a problem is a bit like putting a Band-Aid® on a gushing wound or using a pain reliever to get rid of an infection.

Thinking It Through

Find an editorial about global warming and analyze it in light of stock issues. Especially, too, look for whether it focuses on remedies that are effects-oriented or cause-oriented. Finally, look at how the editorial paints its opponents. Do the arguments against the opposition resemble the description presented here?

In the midst of it all, though, we must remember that actions aimed at managing the effects of a problem are often more practical and more workable in the long run. Often (although not always), it is fruitless to try to eliminate causes. They are obscure, they are hopelessly entwined, or there are simply too many of them. Moreover, getting at a bad effect need not be a mere Band-Aid. Hunger, unemployment, lack of education, and so on are all parts of a system. When you change the effects in one part of the system, you may change other parts as well. With enough food in their stomachs, poor people may be more prone to look for jobs and be better prepared to succeed once they are hired. These are among the system-wide changes that can occur by getting at particular effects.

Proposals for change not only may be ineffective but also may make a problem worse. Psychotherapists Watzlawick, Weakland and Fisch (1974) have even suggested that it is not the initial difficulties people experience that get them into real trouble; rather, it is the solutions they devise to remove these difficulties. For example, fearing that you might be at a loss for words if you dare to do a classroom presentation from notes, you commit all of your remarks to memory, but then go blank at the time of the presentation and thus are truly at a loss for words. Concerned that your romantic partner has been behaving flirtatiously at parties, you react with jealous rage, thus increasing the probability that your partner will seek solace in the arms of another. Here, once again, effects are looping back on their causes, but this time in negative ways.

And what about when we are the ones who are being persuaded? Although the focus here has been on what the policy advocate should do, the message recipient has much to think about as well. Stock issues take different forms, depending on whether a persuader advocates change, repair, or retention of a policy. As the message recipient, you should be alert to some of the pitfalls in reasoning and evidence when policy advocates address problems or move from considerations of need to their proposed solutions. Did the policy advocates cover all the stock issues or perhaps treat one or more of them superficially? Did the communicators meet their burden of proof or, in the case of persuaders who advocate for the retention of a policy, their burden of refutation? Consider as well the relation between the alleged need for a change and the claims made for the workability of the proposed policy: They should mesh. Has the appropriate balance been struck between the dream of workability and the realities of practicality? Has a convincing case been made that, on balance, the advantages of this plan outweigh its disadvantages? Of the various plans currently under consideration, does the plan advocated have the most advantages? Having directed your critical antennae to the presentation or essay, also remember that there is only so much that the communicator can do given the constraints of time or space.

Recall that propositions of any type are debatable; there must be room for argument. Accordingly, propositions of fact are not in themselves established facts. Rather, they are *belief* claims for which factual evidence is needed.

Beliefs are the building blocks of attitudes. At bedrock are claims of the "How do I know?" variety:

- My intuition tells me it's so.

- My senses tell me it's true.

- My tipster rarely fails me.

- The authority quoted in the article I read is very knowledgeable.

- The majority is usually right.

- Because I said it, it must be so.

Propositions of fact are topics of consideration in their own right. Warnick and Inch divide them into three types:

1 **Causal claims**
   Capital punishment deters crime.
   Smoking marijuana harms your health.
   Violence on television affects children's behavior.

2 **Predictive claims**
   A staffed space mission will reach Mars by 2020.
   Our economy is headed for a massive depression.
   A severe shortage of teachers will occur by the year 2025.

3 **Historical claims**
   The Shroud of Turin was worn by Jesus in the tomb.
   The author of *On the Sublime* was not Longinus.
   Lee Harvey Oswald was the sole assassin of John F. Kennedy. (1994)

For example, when discussing the policy proposition that capital punishment should be made legal (or illegal, depending on the state), people generally debate whether capital punishment deters crime. The same is true of value claims such as the assertion that capital punishment is immoral. These are *subpropositions* or *sub-subpropositions* of the broader policy claim. Table 8.1 should help make this last point clearer by illustrating the structure of Sarah Brady's case.

TABLE 8.1   *Structure of Sarah Brady's Case in Support of the Brady Bill*

PROPOSITION: THE BRADY BILL SHOULD BE SUPPORTED

1 Handguns need to be kept out of the wrong hands (subproposition).
   a This includes persons who are mentally incompetent (sub-subproposition).
   b This includes the criminal element (sub-subproposition).
   c Not doing so would be unjust (sub-subproposition).
   d Not doing so would continue to incur great costs to society (sub-subproposition).

2 The Brady Bill helps keep handguns out of the wrong hands (subproposition).
   a Its provision of a national safety check helps identify persons know to be mentally incompetent (sub-subproposition).
   b Its provisions of a waiting period and a national safety check deters criminals from purchasing guns (sub-subproposition).

3 The Brady Bill will not interfere with the legitimate interests of ordinary citizens (subproposition).
   a It will not further curtail hunters (sub-subproposition).
   b It will not prevent ordinary citizens from owning handguns (sub-subproposition).

Most, but not all, of the supporting claims in Table 8.1 are factual. But consider such value terms as "unjust," "the wrong hands," and "legitimate interests." Terms such as these signal the possibility that disputants may become embroiled in a battle over definitions. What do "unjust," "the wrong hands," and "legitimate interests" mean? Controversies over propositions of fact can be just as intense, but there is greater likelihood of agreement on the meaning of key terms. Here are some contrasting examples of propositions of fact and value.

Propositions of Fact

1   Cutbacks in the welfare program have helped widen the gap between the rich and the poor.

2   Mandatory seat belts have reduced traffic fatalities by 20%.

3   The People's Republic of China is not really a communist state any longer.

4   Censorship of literature only increases its sales.

5   On the average, the top hitters in baseball get paid more than the top pitchers.

Propositions of Value

1   Widening the gap between the rich and the poor is immoral.

2   Mandating seat belt use is more ethical than merely advising people to wear them.

3   It's better to try and then fail than never to make the attempt.

4   It's not the government's job to regulate morals.

5   Basketball is more fun to watch than baseball.

Although values tend to be resistant to change, they are not impossible to change. Through the years, for example, Americans have become more open to ethnic and racial diversity, more accepting of gay and lesbian rights, and more tolerant of religious differences. At the same time, they have become more insistent on marketplace freedoms and less accepting of government regulations. But these changes have taken a good deal of time.

More realistically, on any one occasion, it may be possible to see value controversies in a new light, perhaps reframing the issues, perhaps downplaying objectionable values while highlighting values consistent with a proposed policy. For most of us, the basic values that we hold dear exist in a precarious state of balance. We want freedom but also order, spontaneity but also control, property rights but also human rights, stability but also change, what is equitable but also what is profitable. Thus, for example, opponents of gun control may believe that the right to bear arms is inviolable while at the same time valuing the safety and sanctity of human lives. These conflicts within ourselves can provide an opening for persuaders. In fact, supporters of the Brady Bill could (and did) argue that they opposed gun-related violence but not gun ownership. More recently, in Philadelphia, proponents and opponents of gun control came together on behalf of an experimental program to reduce gun-related violence.

TYPES OF EVIDENCE AS RESOURCES OF ARGUMENTATION

The believability of factual claims rests on evidence and on inferences drawn from that evidence. Evidence can also be brought to bear on value issues. Meredith, for example, favors locking up cocaine users for possession of even small quantities of the drug. She argues that drug use is immoral, and, when pressed on the matter, she explains that no person has a right to inflict harm on self or others. Kristina counters with questions about the consequences of Meredith's position. How is cocaine dangerous, she asks, and for whom? For the user, perhaps, but what evidence is there that others are directly affected? If we lock up cocaine users for harming only themselves, does this set a dangerous precedent? If, on the other hand, we were to decriminalize use of the drug, would this bring its users out into the open, making them more likely to go for treatment? Are there studies, she asks, that might address this question, or at least experts who can render informed opinions?

Evidence can take the form of stories (narratives), statistics, or testimony. The Sarah Brady (1986) article provides ample illustration of the power of extended narratives. The stories she tells wrap evidence and reasoning together in a way that both paints a vivid picture and drives home the intended conclusion. But stories of this sort take a lot of time (or space), and they cover a limited number of cases. Hence, persuaders sometimes combine extended narratives with a series of specific examples as well as statistical generalizations.

Specific examples contain the bare bones of a story: the who, what, when, where, how, and possibly the why, but without the detail: "In 1981, my husband was shot by a crazed gunman who'd been allowed by the government to have a gun—no questions asked." "When my son was 6 years old, he nearly killed himself playing with a loaded handgun that had been left on the seat of a pickup truck in which we'd been riding." Abbreviated stories of this sort give the persuader ample opportunity to exhibit the range and variety of cases covered by the factual claim. Even then, critical audiences might ask: Are the alleged facts true? Are they relevant and representative, and are there enough of them to warrant the generalization?

These same questions may be asked about statistics. The great virtue of statistics is that they quickly cover the territory marked out by the claim. But statistics may also lead to faulty inferences, as when the sampling is unrepresentative, when the statistical unit is inappropriate, or when a comparison is made between non-comparable data.

Suppose, for example, that the data gathered by Handgun Control, Inc., on the number of people in the United States killed in handgun accidents each year had been drawn from a few atypical states and then extrapolated to the others. Or consider the possibility that the organization's category of "intruders killed by handguns kept for self-defense" had excluded anyone previously known to the handgun user, including would-be rapists or other assailants who just happened to be acquaintances or family members. Should only strangers be counted in the statistical unit known as "intruders"?

Evidence can also include first-person accounts, testimony by witnesses, secondhand reports, such as those provided by journalists or historians, and finally testimony by authorities. These, too, can help substantiate a factual claim but can also be misleading. First-person accounts are often self-serving, whereas witnesses—as to an auto accident—are often inaccurate. Secondhand reports are only as trustworthy as the firsthand reports on which they're based.

War coverage provides an outstanding example of problems in gathering evidence first- and secondhand. In the early years of the war in Iraq, seasoned reporters returned from visits to that troubled nation with glowing accounts of the progress of American forces. Usually, however, they got their firsthand information through controlled exposure to the war as embedded reporters; the military controlled what the reporters saw and where they went. Or, they relied for their information on what government officials told them. They ended up reporting breathlessly about the dramatic rescue of Private Jessica Lynch, only to learn from Lynch herself that the event had not occurred as advertised, and they reported as fact government-sponsored misinformation concerning the death of Pat Tillman.

Despite the potential unreliability of first-person accounts, testimony by witnesses, and secondhand accounts, these can also be invaluable in substantiating a factual claim, and the claim can be bolstered as well by appeal to authority. For example, Sarah Brady's case would be much more impressive if she had cited an expert on handgun use, preferably a lifelong member of the NRA, who conceded, on the basis of his or her own studies, that passage of the Brady Bill was likely to reduce gun crime by a substantial amount each year.

As with all other forms of evidence, message recipients have reason to be suspicious of authority; some arguments from authority are fallacious. Still, few have the resources to check matters out firsthand. Indeed, most of what people call "fact" is accepted on the authority of someone (e.g., teachers) or something (e.g., newspapers). (Science is in itself a major source of authority these days.) Even if most of our factual knowledge were based on direct observation, we could still benefit from the judgments of authorities on how to interpret those facts.

The characteristics we tend to value in authorities cited by persuaders are much like the characteristics we value in the persuaders themselves. Are they competent? Are they trustworthy? Do they exercise good judgment? Are they in a position to render informed judgments in the matter at hand? These virtues are all the more important when we have reason to be suspicious of the persuader's own credibility. A case in point was the David Letterman on-air discussion of his inappropriate sexual affairs with staffers and the attempt to blackmail him.

Talk show host David Letterman stunned his audience on October 2, 2009 when he delivered a 9-minute monologue where he explained that he'd been the victim of blackmail, and that the blackmailer was using factual data about Letterman's private sexual history to attempt to extort millions of dollars from the celebrity. The monologue is memorable for many things, not least Letterman's honest admission of the "creepy things" he'd done. But the most credible evidence for Letterman's argument that he was a victim (and not a victimizer) came by way of his citing powerful authorities:

So then we call an operation called the Special Prosecution Bureau, which is a division of the Manhattan District Attorney's Office. We call down there, and we say, can we run a couple of things by you guys? (laughter) So we took the stuff down there and they said, whoa, hello, this is blackmail. (laughter/applause) So they said, what you want to do is get another meeting with this guy and find out if he's serious, because, you know, we all have a bad day, and stuff like this (laughter) can slip through the cracks, you've inadvertently blackmailed someone. (laughter)

So they have the second meeting, and the question was posed: "Are you aware, that this is serious, this could be a crime."

And [the alleged blackmailer responds] "No, no, I'm fine with that. And oh, by the way, not only am I writing a screenplay. I'm writing a book."

So I thought, well, that's nice. You have a companion piece. You have the film, and you have the book. What do you, read the book first, then go to the film? Do you watch the film then you read the book? Do you take the book and read along at the film? (laughter) It's all coming up roses for me now. (laughter) Because, remember, this guy knows creepy stuff about me. So they had the second meeting and he was reassured that everything was just fine. And then a third meeting is arranged ...

So this morning I did something I've never done in my life. And it was a combination of just unusual and scary—this whole thing has been quite scary—I had to go downtown to testify before the grand jury. And I had to tell them how I was disturbed by this, I was worried for myself, I was worried for my family, I felt menaced by this. And I had to tell them all of the creepy things that I have done, that were going to be (laughter). Now why is that funny? That's, I mean. (laughter/applause) So the idea is that if they believe, in fact, a crime has been committed, then they issue a warrant, and that's exactly what happened. And a little bit after noon today, the guy was arrested. (applause/cheers)

Now of course, we get to, what was it? What was all the creepy stuff (laughter) that he was gonna put into the screenplay and the movie? And the creepy stuff was, that I have had sex with women who work for me on this show. Now. My response to that is, yes I have. (laughter/applause) I have had sex with women who work on this show (more applause).

(Comic's Comic, 2009)

What is interesting here is that, in recounting his tale, Letterman selected and cited credible authorities to first make the case that he was simply and purely a victim; it was no less than the Special Prosecution Bureau of the Manhattan District Attorney's Office he cited to define the situation on his behalf. And then, once the situation was defined through the authoritative lens, Letterman confessed to his audience what he had done, and, based on the audience's reaction, found himself forgiven and applauded for sexual harassment.

Whatever views one holds of David Letterman, it must be admitted that he knew how to select and cite credible authorities.

FALLACIES RECONSIDERED

A fallacious argument is one that fails to stand up to careful scrutiny. At first blush, it appears convincing, perhaps even compelling, and that is what makes it persuasive. But, upon examination, cracks begin to appear. For example, Tom appears to have undermined John's position on capital punishment, but John responds that Tom has misrepresented his arguments, presenting them in weakened form so that they could more easily be knocked down. This type of misrepresentation is called the *straw man* fallacy. The straw man, says John, is one of Tom's imagining. John's real case has gone unrefuted.

Tom responds, perhaps, with charges of his own. John is claiming to have been misrepresented only because his case is truly weak. John is guilty of having illogically reduced complex matters to an either–or, known as a *false dichotomy*. Or John resorts to name calling rather than addressing Tom's arguments—the *ad hominem* fallacy. Or Tom compares two unlikes as if they were sufficiently alike to be treated as analogous—the *false analogy*. Or John draws faulty inferences about causation. A *common causal* fallacy involves treating one among many causal factors as the sole cause. Another causal fallacy, known as *post hoc*, involves assuming that, because something preceded an event, it must be its cause. Defective arguments of this type are called *false cause* **fallacies**.

Textbooks on logic and on argumentation (e.g., Walton, 1992) list many categories of fallacies—too many to be identified and discussed in this book. The important thing is to get a sense of when to accept an argument and when to reject it; labels are less important. Yet it isn't always easy to decide whether an argument is sound or fallacious. Often, fallacy claims are *arguable*, that is, subject to legitimate dispute. Each side in the dispute may argue about what features of the context are most relevant, about what the communicator intended, or about how the message was received. These factors can be important, as illustrated in the following examples.

- False dichotomy? Some complex issues are usefully clarified by reducing them to two sides or to two alternatives. Mayoral candidate Chris says, "I know there are five candidates running for mayor, and of course you don't have to vote at all. But let's face it: This race is going to be won by the Democrat or the Republican, and your vote could make a difference."

- Post hoc? "When Clinton became president," says his Democratic supporter, "the economy was in the dumps. And then, under him, in just a few years it was completely revived. Clearly, Clinton was good for the economy." "Post hoc fallacy!" cries the critic of Clinton. "Clinton may have just been lucky to be in the right position at the right time." But the Clinton supporter has a comeback: "Luck, nothing. You've forgotten that the tax package he pushed through Congress in 1993 was what got the economy on track."

- Inappropriate ad hominem? When Councilwoman White's character is attacked, she cries foul, insisting that her critics stick to the issues. "You are the issue," one of them replies. "After all, the question is whether you should be re-elected."

- False analogy? "This is no time to remove Governor Green from office," says his supporter. "After all, you don't switch quarterbacks when the quarterback you've got is taking the team down the field." "Politics isn't football," says the critic. "Besides, you do change quarterbacks if the team's been heading down the field the wrong way. That's what's wrong with our state. Governor Green has moved it backward rather than forward."

As these examples illustrate, arguments should rarely be rejected at the first suspicion of a fallacy. They are best played out in the give-and-take of argumentative exchange. Sometimes, the real culprit turns out to be the one making the initial charge of fallacy. The fallacy accusation can be like the proverbial hammer, a new tool in danger of being overused and misapplied. Those of us who write about argument are not immune. For example, in a textbook on argumentation, author Don Trent Jacobs (1994) accused Rush Limbaugh of being unfair to astrophysicist Carl Sagan. Sagan, Limbaugh claimed, commented on matters about which he had little expertise, such as global warming and nuclear winter. But Jacobs's criticism of Limbaugh's critique was also suspect. He argued that, because astrophysics covers "everything that lies beyond the dominant influence of the earth," Sagan could be considered an authority on subjects relating to global climate (Jacobs, 1994). But this is akin to saying that a urologist is an expert on the big toe. After all, a urologist is a medical doctor, and the field of medicine deals with every part of the human body. For all we know, the late Carl Sagan may have been an expert on global warming and nuclear winter, but the reasoning behind Jacobs's fallacy accusation is itself fallacious.

The point thus far has been that fallacy charges are often arguable, best played out through argumentative exchange, and sometimes fallacious in their own right. Yet the concept of fallacy would have no meaning if all arguments were fallacious. This is seen most clearly in the case of well-argued disputes. Just because two people disagree does not mean that at least one of them must be committing a fallacy. Here is an example of a well-argued disagreement:

In ancient Judea, so the story goes, the Jewish elders were challenged in their opposition to idolatry by some unnamed, but presumably Roman, idol worshippers. A Roman asks the first question: "Why, if God so opposes idolatry, doesn't he destroy all the idols?" The elders ponder this tough question but then reply, "God would certainly do just that, if the idolators only worshipped useless objects. But the idolators also worship necessary objects like the sun, moon, stars, and planets. Destroying these would put an end to God's whole creation. Shall He then make an end of His world because of fools?" The Romans are not satisfied. They counter the argument with one of their own: "If God does not want to destroy the world, then let Him destroy only the useless idols." But this clever retort does not satisfy the Jewish elders. They answer with one of their own: "If God destroyed your useless idols, but kept the moon, sun, stars, and planets, you would say these are the true deities because they had been untouched by the destruction of the idols."

(Billig, 1996)

Are there ever times when an argument can be shown to be clearly fallacious? Our answer to that is an emphatic *yes*. Sometimes, a communicator commits an obvious error in reasoning. "You say that he's not in Reno? And of course we both know that Reno is in Nevada. Well, I guess that proves he's definitely not in Nevada." Or take another type of error: "If he's in Reno, he must be in Nevada. He's in Nevada. Therefore, he must be in Reno."

These errors are fairly straightforward. But sometimes a fallacious argument goes undetected for years, even centuries. Masses of people coalesce in support of the idea. As it gains supporters, it becomes more difficult to undermine. The argument itself may have more than a surface plausibility. Religious cults are often accused of errors of this type, but none of us are immune to them. Consider this story about a false cause fallacy, one that nearly everyone in the media was ready to believe at one point. It is the story of Gulf War Syndrome.

THE CASE OF GULF WAR SYNDROME

http://www.freedomsphoenix.com/Uploads/Graphics/172-0406151230.jpg
Courtesy of Associated Press.

Some of the most moving evidence heard in recent times concerned the real possibility that American soldiers serving in the 1990–1991 Persian Gulf War against Saddam Hussein had been exposed to a toxic chemical that had caused thousands of them to experience a baffling set of war-related symptoms. A health survey found a majority of vets reporting that they had delayed having children, fearing that the babies would be born deformed. Vets also feared passing on their illness to loved ones. But the principal victims appeared to be the veterans themselves. As recounted on PBS's *Frontline* (1998), veterans who had been healthy going into the war independently reported having problems with concentration, fatigue, nausea, and an inability to focus. These seemingly independent accounts were made all the more believable by visual evidence of the sorry state of those testifying, and the testimony was confirmed by eyewitnesses. So credible were the accounts that Congress was persuaded to hold a hearing on the complaints. Said Representative Bernard Sanders, (I), of Vermont, on *Frontline*: "There is no question in my mind—none, zero—that tens and tens of thousands of our soldiers are suffering from a wide range of illnesses, which I believe are attributable to their service in the Gulf" (*Frontline*, 1998).

In addition to Congress, the news media—including respected programs such as *Nightline* and *60 Minutes*—lavished considerable attention on Gulf War Syndrome. There was no shortage of plausible explanations for the alleged problem, some of them coming from respected news sources. *Dateline* speculated that radioactive debris from the uranium shell casings used to pierce Iraqi tanks might be the cause of Gulf War Syndrome. *60 Minutes* wondered if side effects from PB, a drug given to protect against the nerve gas soman, might be the cause of Gulf War Syndrome. It had, after all, been given to large numbers of troops. Several news sources speculated that chemical weapons might be to blame. Said the *Frontline* narrator, "Since the war, the DoD [Department of Defense] had repeatedly denied that U.S. troops had been exposed to chemical agents. But many vets were skeptical of these denials because during the war hundreds of chemical alarms had gone off."

Was there, then, a Gulf War Syndrome? One reason why some people practiced an art of mistrust and remained suspicious was that the facts and proffered explanations did not add up to create a single coherent narrative. In the case of Gulf War Syndrome, there were apparently too many disparate, unrelated symptoms and too many plausible explanations. Not always is science in a position to resolve controversies; nor, as argued in Chapter 3, is scientific reporting purely objective. Still, scientific analysis would be needed to resolve the controversy about Gulf War Syndrome. And as we will see, even the science presented conflicting conclusions.

To lead its initial medical investigation of Gulf War Syndrome in 1995, the Pentagon appointed Dr. Stephen Joseph, a seasoned public health physician who had worked in New York at the height of the AIDS epidemic. Working with the Veterans Administration, Joseph invited Gulf War veterans who reported feeling ill to register and undertake a full exam. Panels of scientists were asked to review everything known about any toxin that vets might have been exposed to in the Gulf. Millions were spent on a series of epidemiological studies to see whether reports of veterans' hospitalizations and deaths occurred at a higher rate than normal. On the basis of all these investigations, Dr. Joseph concluded that there was no unique Gulf War Syndrome that could be traced to chemical weapons exposure during the Gulf War (1997). He explained the situation in this way:

We found that in looking at 20,000 people in detail very very carefully from a medical point of view, we found that there was no single unifying hypothesis that could explain the symptoms of large numbers of people. There was no magic bullet. There was no mystery illness. There was no Gulf War illness. What there was was several groups of people in this 20,000 patient sample. The largest group were people who had illnesses that were readily understood by our current diagnostic framework. In some cases they were illnesses that people would have had whether they went to the Gulf or not. In some cases they were illnesses or injuries that were a result of being in the Gulf. If you have a chronic arthritis of the hip from an injury that you got jumping off the mechanized vehicle, that's related to your service in the Gulf very directly.

(Joseph, 1997)

Joseph's findings did not settle the matter, though, and some even called his report a cover-up. The debate raged on, with much being at stake. If in fact veterans had contracted serious medical conditions because of their service, they deserved care and compensation for that service. Conversely, if Gulf War Syndrome was a mythical condition, really nothing more than the result of the normal distribution of assorted ailments spread over the large numbers of troops who had served in the war, the responsibility of the military to these veterans was a different matter. Could Joseph be right in his findings, in spite of the extensive anecdotal evidence provided by the tens of thousands of Gulf War veterans? And was it not reasonable to question the Pentagon's motives here, given that a finding that the disease was real would likely mean billions of dollars in health care for affected veterans? And most of all, what if Joseph was just sincerely mistaken? What would that mean for veterans who were afflicted with an illness contracted while serving in a war, who were then being told, essentially, that is was "all in their heads"?

In response to the continuing controversy, a panel of scientific experts and veterans was brought together to serve on the congressionally mandated Research Advisory Committee on Gulf War Veterans' Illnesses. And finally, in December, 2008, the committee released a 452-page report that stated that "scientific evidence leaves no question that Gulf War illness is a real condition with real causes and serious consequences for affected veterans" (Silverleib, 2008). The report said that Gulf War Syndrome is a condition now identified as the likely consequence of exposure to toxic chemicals, including pesticides and a drug administered to protect troops against nerve gas. The report identifies two Gulf War "neurotoxic" exposures that "are causally associated with Gulf War illness." The first is the ingestion of pyridostigmine bromide (PB) pills, given to protect troops from effects of nerve agents. The second is exposure to dangerous pesticides used during the conflict (Silverleib, 2008).

According to the report, Gulf War illness turned out to be a "complex of multiple concurrent symptoms" that "typically includes persistent memory and concentration problems, chronic headaches, widespread pain, gastrointestinal problems, and other chronic abnormalities" (Silverleib, 2008). Particularly impressive was the report's systematic examination and subsequent refutation of each of the theories offered to explain away Gulf War Syndrome. The illness was identified as the consequence of multiple "biological alterations" affecting the brain and nervous system. Ultimately, the report concluded, while it is sometimes difficult to issue a specific diagnosis of the disease, it is no longer difficult to identify a cause.

The story of Gulf War Syndrome ultimately stands not just as testimony to the potential pitfalls in causal reasoning but also to the persuasive power of statistics and authoritative opinion—all of them forms of evidence that can assist audiences in making sound judgments but that in this case may have at least initially led them astray. In this case, though, a more appropriate conclusion eventually ensued. Finally, in 2013, a hearing was held before the Subcommittee on Oversight and Investigations of the Committee on Veterans' Affairs, U.S. House of Representatives. The issue before the Committee concerned diagnosis and treatment of Gulf War illness, not its existence. It took two decades, and during that time, many veterans struggled as they dealt with the illness in their personal lives as the policy dispute raged. In the end, though, American veterans with Gulf War illness were vindicated.

Pulling It together: A Glossary of Terms and Concepts

Enthymeme: A form of speech that invites the reader to supply and endorse premises that are missing from the argument but left implicit. It is a truncated argument that rests on a premise or premises it assumes its audience will accept. Virtually all persuasive discourse is enthymematic.

Proposition of policy: Debatable assertions about what should or should not be done, that make recommendations for action of some sort, to be taken in the future. With any proposition of policy, certain recurring questions, called *stock issues*, are logically relevant.

Proposition of fact: Debatable assertions that are not in themselves established facts. They are belief claims about what is true or false, for which factual evidence is needed. More often than not, factual claims serve in subordinate roles to propositions of policy.

Proposition of value: Debatable assertions that assert beliefs about what is good or bad, moral or immoral.

Stock issues: Recurring questions that persuaders are logically obligated to consider if they wish to advance a proposition of policy. Stock issues include: *need, workability, practicality, freedom from greater evils*, and *superiority relative to other possible solutions*.

Burden of proof: Proponents of change have the burden of demonstrating that something is seriously wrong with the system or policy. This is called the *burden of proof*.

Burden of refutation: In contrast to proponents of change who have the *burden of proof*, defenders of the status quo have a lesser obligation, called the *burden of refutation*. They only have to respond to the arguments put forth by the proponents of change.

Causal claims: In reference to proposition of fact, one of the three types of claims (causal, predictive, and historical). A causal claim seeks to establish cause–effect links. An example: Capital punishment deters crime.

Predictive claims: In reference to proposition of fact, one of the three types of claims (causal, predictive, and historical). A predictive claim seeks to establish what will come into being in the future. An example: A severe shortage of teachers will occur by the year 2020.

Historical claims: In reference to proposition of fact, one of the three types of claims (causal, predictive, and historical). A historical claim seeks to establish what has happened in the past. An example: Lee Harvey Oswald was the sole assassin of John F. Kennedy.

Fallacies: Arguments that fail to stand up to careful scrutiny. At first blush, fallacies appear convincing, perhaps even compelling, and that is what makes them persuasive. But, upon examination, cracks begin to appear.

SUMMARY

Persuasion typically takes place under conditions that are less than ideal for reflective argumentative exchange. Under the circumstances, persuaders cannot be expected to win belief by logic alone. Arresting narratives, for example, go beyond logic in providing a feeling for a problem, but this doesn't mean they are illogical. Nor is it antithetical to logic for persuaders to provide evidences of their own credibility on a topic. As Aristotle emphasized in his treatise on rhetoric, *logos, pathos,* and *ethos* can go hand in hand.

When persuaders reason, they typically do so by use of truncated arguments called *enthymemes* that call on their audiences to supply and endorse implicit premises. In support of a position on a complex issue, they are well advised to offer a variety of supporting arguments and evidence.

No amount of argument and evidence is likely to provide the last word on complex issues. But this does not mean that the persuaders ought to be haphazard in investigating a topic and coming to a conclusion about it, or that they are unwarranted in defending what—after investigation—they consider the best, most sensible position on the matter. To put it more positively: persuaders should practice thoroughgoing inquiry *and* advocacy. When in the role of message consumer, persuadees should listen (or read) critically but also be willing to commit to the persuader's position after questioning it.

Much of this chapter has been given over to a discussion of types of propositions and the arguments and evidence necessary to support them. Propositions are debatable assertions, of which three types are generally recognized: policy, fact, and value.

Propositions of policy urge support for or opposition to a proposed action or decision. As the discussion in connection with the Sarah Brady article indicated, policy advocates are logically obligated to advance arguments on five stock issues: need, workability, practicality, freedom from greater evils, and superiority relative to other possible solutions. Sometimes, one or more of these issues will be bypassed under the impress of time or of limited space; sometimes the persuader will treat a stock issue enthymematically, assuming audiences will agree there is not much reason to discuss it. Not uncommonly, the focus shifts from issue of need to questions of comparative advantage or to the question of which proposed solution best meets some delimited set of goals or criteria.

Advocates of change from the status quo are generally assumed to have a burden of proof, whereas those advocating retention of the present system have only a burden of refutation—unless they choose to make positive claims for the system or against proposals for change, in which case they, too, take on burdens of proof. Between the alternatives of advocating full-scale change or retention of a policy, policy proponents may urge that the current system be repaired to one degree or another—each increment of repair incurring an increased burden of proof.

Propositions of fact urge acceptance (or rejection) of a belief claim that something is true or probable. The belief claim may be causal, predictive, or historical. Often, belief claims are themselves supports for propositions of policy or value. They can be thought of as subpropositions (or sub-subpropositions, etc.).

Value propositions arise in controversies about morality, taste, propriety, and the like, or, as so often happens, when two persons share the same values but prioritize them differently. The difference between propositions of fact and value often hinges on whether persuader and audience agree on the meaning of key terms in the proposition. The guilt or innocence of a murder defendant is generally considered to be an issue of fact, for example, but the propriety of the defendant's attorneys in their handling of the case is generally seen as a question of value. Three methods of dealing with value controversies were identified: (1) examining consequences, (2) attaching a disputed value to higher-order values, and (3) appealing to shared assumptions. These often go hand in hand.

A fallacious argument is one that fails to stand up to careful scrutiny. Some arguments are clearly fallacious. But arguments should rarely be rejected at the first whiff of trouble. Often, the charge of fallacy can be successfully defended against and turned back on the accuser. Among the most common of fallacies is the fallacy of having falsely labeled an opponent's argument fallacious.

QUESTIONS AND PROJECTS FOR FURTHER STUDY

1   Do you believe that it's reasonable that existing ways of doing things should be assumed to be preferable to proposals for change? What might be said for reversing the burden of proof in the case of policy propositions?

2   Why is it sometimes better to get at the effects of a problem, rather than its causes? Can you provide examples of when the reverse is true?

3   Why, as part of an analysis of a problem, is it often a good idea to investigate what was done in the past to remedy the problem? Can history also lead us astray?

4   Can you think of value conflicts between people where efforts at persuasion are bound to be fruitless? Can you think of any that could prove fruitful?

5   Generate five examples each of a proposition of policy, fact, and value.

6   Provide five examples of your own of clear-cut fallacies, and five examples that you think could be reasonably argued either way.

EXERCISES

1   Do an Internet search on "fallacies" and develop a list of the most unusual ones you can find. Create a PowerPoint presentation that includes appropriate photos and imagery to illustrate the fallacies, making it comedic if you can, and present your list to the class.

2   Either in person, via an Internet site, or by viewing an infomercial on television, watch a sales presentation and pitch. List the propositions of fact, value, and policy that are presented. Identify any fallacies you see and hear. Write up a research report as a class project.

3   Listen with care to your favorite professor's classroom presentations for one week, and keep a journal based on the information about argumentation presented in this chapter. List the propositions of fact, value, and policy you hear. Critique them, and also evaluate your own reactions. Try to establish why this professor is in fact your favorite.

4   Consider an important governmental policy proposal that is currently in the news, either for domestic or foreign policy. Research the situation, establishing the propositions, subpropositions, and sub-subpropositions, charting them out in a fashion similar to Table 8.1 on p. 262.

KEY TERMS

- Burden of proof
- Burden of refutation
- Causal claims
- Enthymeme
- Fallacies
- Historical claims

- Predictive claims
- Proposition of fact
- Proposition of policy
- Proposition of value
- Stock issues

WEB LINKS

Brady Campaign to Prevent Gun Violence
www.bradycampaign.org/jim-and-sarah-brady
NRA-Institute for Legislative Action
www.nraila.org

REFERENCES

Aborn, R. (2009, June 26). Guns in church and the myth of the NRA. *The Huffington Post.* Retrieved July 17, 2009. from www.huffington post.com/richard-aborn/guns-in-church-and-the-my_ b_ 221 584.html

Billig, M. (1996). *Arguing and thinking* (2nd ed.). Cambridge, UK: Cambridge University Press.

Brady Campaign (n.d.). *Mission statement.* Retrieved November 12, 2009, from www.brady campaign. org/about/

Brady, S. K. (1986, May). Handguns must be kept away from the John Hinckleys of the world. *Glamour,* 84, 96–97.

Brockriede, W. (1990). Where is argument? In Trapp, R., & Schuetz, J. (eds), *Perspectives on argumentation: Essays in honor of Wayne Brockriede.* Prospect Heights, IL: Waveland.

Caldwell, L., Bohn, K., and Payne, E. (2014, April 16). *Bloomberg to spend $50 million to challenge NRA on gun safety.* Retrieved August 22, 2014, from CNN U.S.: www.cnn.com/2014/04/15/us/bloomberg-gun-safety-initiative/

Comic's Comic (2009, October 2) Full transcript: David Letterman's on-air statement about his affairs and the $2 million attempt to blackmail him. Retrieved October 21, 2009, from http://the comicscomic. typepad.com/thecomicscomic/2009/10/full-transcript-david-lettermans-onair-statement-about-his-affairs-and-the-2-million-attempt-to-blac.html

Frontline (1998, January 20). Last battle of the Gulf War. New York and Washington, DC: PBS. Retrieved November 11, 2010, from www.pbs.org/wgbh/pages/frontline/shows/syndrome/etc/script. html

Hermann, P., & Ruane, M. (2014, August 8). *Medical examiner rules James Brady's death a homicide.* Retrieved September 1, 2014, from *The Washington Post*:www.washingtonpost.com/local/crime/james-bradys-death-ruled-homicide-by-dc-medical-examiner/2014/08/08/686de224-1f41-11e4-82f9-2cd6fa8da5c4_story.html?wpisrc=al_national

Howerton, J. (2012, December 19). *NRA sees huge spike in membership after Sandy Hook massacre; Numbers said to "dwarf past trends".* Retrieved August 22, 2014, from *The Blaze*: www.theblaze.com/stories/2012/12/19/nra-sees-huge-spike-in-membership-after-sandy-hook-massacre-numbers-said-to-dwarf-past-trends/

Hwang, K., & Murphy, K. (2014, August 16). *Across the nation, guns can be carried into more public places*. Retrieved August 22, 2014, from Gun Wars—News21: http://gunwars.news21.com/2014/across-the-nation-guns-can-be-carried-into-more-public-places/

Illinois Council Against Handgun Violence (2010). *The facts about firearm violence*. Retrieved July 17, 2009, from www.ichv.org/facts-about-gun-violence/general-facts-about-gun-violence/

Jacobs, D. T. (1994). *The bum's rush*. Boise, ID: Legendary Publishing.

Joseph, S. (1997). The last battle of the Gulf War [interview transcript]. Retrieved July 17, 2009, from www.pbs.org/wgbh/pages/frontline/shows/syndrome/interviews/joseph1.html

McDaniel, J., Griner, A., and Krebs, N. (2014, August 18). *Fast-growing national gun control and gun rights advocacy groups escalate activism*. Retrieved August 22, 2014, from ABC7News Denver: www.thedenverchannel.com/decodedc/fast-growing-more-aggressive-national-gun-control-and-gun-rights-advocacy-groups-escalate-activism

Silverleib, A. (2008, December 9). Gulf War illness is real, new federal report says. *CNN Health*. Retrieved July 17, 2009, from www.cnn.com/2008/HEALTH/11/17/gulf.war.illness.study/

Simon, S. (2011, March 26). *Jim Brady, 30 years later*. Retrieved September 1, 2014, from NPR: www.npr.org/2011/03/26/134878570/jim-brady-30-years-later

van Eemeren, F. H., Grootendorst, R., Jackson, S., & Jacobs, S. (1993). *Reconstructing argumentative discourse*. Tuscaloosa: University of Alabama Press.

Veterans Affairs (2013). *Gulf War: What kind of care are veterans receiving 20 years later?* U.S. House of Representatives, One Hundred Thirteenth Congress, First Session, Wednesday, March 13, 2013. Subcommittee on Oversight and Investigations of the Committee on Veterans' Affairs. Washington, DC: U.S. House of Representatives. Retrieved September 11, 2014, from www.bing.com/search?q=gulf+war%3A+what+kind+of+care+are+veterans+receiving+20+years+later%3F+form=EDGEAR&qs=PF&cvid=4fdba136dc5f4a80931f4a5510b26604&pq=gulf+war%3A+what+kind+of+care+are+veterans+receiving+20+years+later%3F#

Walton, D. (1992). *Plausible argument in everyday conversation*. Albany: State University of New York Press.

Warnick, B., & Inch, E. S. (1994). *Critical thinking and communication* (2nd ed.). New York: Macmillan.

Watzlawick, P., Weakland, J., & Fisch, R. (1974). *Change: Principles of problem formation and problem resolution*. New York: Norton.

PART III

Context for Persuasion

CHAPTER 9

Going Public: Delivering a Presentation That Persuades

- **The Genuinely Committed Persuader**
- **Strategic Planning: A 3-Step Process**
- **Making Ideas Stick**
- **Organizing Persuasive Presentations**
- **Summary**
- **Questions and Projects for Further Study**
- **Exercises**
- **Key Terms**
- **References**

Frederick Douglass, born in 1818 to a slave and her master, escaped from a Southern prison-house of bondage to become one of the great orators and essayists for racial equality of the nineteenth century. His early life is testimony to the potential of humankind to triumph over adversity. His adult life is testimony to the power of public persuasion.

Douglass committed the crime, punishable by death at the time, of secretly teaching himself to read and write while a slave. The fugitive-orator came to the attention of abolitionist leader Henry Lloyd Garrison, who reported in the preface to Douglass's (2004) autobiography that he was spellbound by Douglass's oratory on first hearing him at an anti-slavery convention in Nantucket, Massachusetts, in 1841:

> I shall never forget his first speech at the convention—the extraordinary emotion it excited in my own mind—the powerful impression it created upon a crowded auditorium, completely taken by surprise—the applause which followed from the beginning to the end of his felicitous remarks.
>
> He came forward to the platform with a hesitancy and embarrassment, necessarily the attendants of a sensitive mind in such a novel position. After apologizing for his ignorance, and reminding the audience that slavery was a poor school for the human intellect and heart, he proceeded to narrate some of the facts in his own history as a

FIGURE 9.1 *Frederick Douglass.*
Public domain

slave, and in the course of his speech gave utterance to many noble thoughts and thrilling reflections. As soon as he had taken his seat, filled with hope and admiration, I rose, and declared that Patrick Henry, of revolutionary fame, never made a speech more eloquent in the cause of liberty, than the one we had just listened to from the lips of that hunted fugitive. So I believed at the time—so I believe now.

(Garrison, 2004)

"Going public" is that moment when the private self goes public in support of a position or proposal. For audiences, it is often the moment they are called to a decision. For speakers such as Douglass, it is generally the moment when a commitment to exercise leadership has been made.

The focus of this chapter is on the one-shot presentation or message. This stands in contrast with organized persuasive campaigns, which contain sustained attempts to influence groups or masses of people through a series of messages. Campaigns—political, product advertising, and issue-oriented—are covered in the rest of Part III. This chapter looks primarily at what the individual communicator must do to win over audiences.

THE GENUINELY COMMITTED PERSUADER

Going public is scary for most people. When surveys are conducted, public speaking always ranks at or near the top of our collective "fears," scoring higher on such lists than the fear of death. This fact led the comedian Jerry Seinfeld to note years ago that, if we are at a funeral, most of us would prefer to be in the casket rather than delivering the eulogy.

While Seinfeld is exaggerating for comic effect, there is some truth in what he says. Yet our fears can be reduced, especially if we are willing to do the necessary work of gathering research materials, coming to an informed judgment on the topic at hand, preparing the message, rehearsing our presentation, and then risking ourselves in genuine expressions of commitment. Authentic, knowledgeable expression makes for the most moving and memorable persuasive presentation. Even when a communicator is a hired gun who is paid to persuade on behalf of a client or employer, he or she does best when there is belief in what is being promoted. It also helps overcome the debilitating fears of public address.

STRATEGIC PLANNING: A 3-STEP PROCESS

Persuasion tends to work best when we are genuinely committed, and that requires strategic planning and skillful presentation. The following scheme for strategic planning pulls together much of what has been said thus far in this book about how to persuade. Two fictitious case studies, one of a speech-planning effort, the other of planning for delivery of a radio editorial, are used to illustrate each of the three steps of strategy formulation.

Step 1 Goals, Audience, Situation

Before we can persuade, we must first evaluate where we are and where we wish to go. We must think about who makes up our audience, and what matters to them. This is what Daniel Pink calls "attunement" (2012). We must also do a bit of analysis to figure out how our beliefs and values will color the ways in which we approach the task before us. This involves thinking about a number of issues:

1   What's the rhetorical exigency, if any, that confronts us?

2   What is our goal? What outcome do we wish to see?

3   What are the chief constraints we will be facing?

4   What's expected, and perhaps required, of us in this situation?

5   What do we know, believe, and value? How will that influence our presentation?

6   What does our audience know, believe, and value? How will that influence the presentation?

These are primary questions that persuaders need to address, and, depending on the situation, there may be others as well. For example, if your presentation is part of a larger effort at persuasion, say a community-wide campaign, you will need to think about how it can best serve that larger cause. Are there, for example, key opinion leaders in the audience who can be recruited to energize others in the community? If, as often happens, the audience is divided on the issues being addressed, you may need to develop different strategies for different audience segments. Perhaps you will need to target some of them for primary attention while striving not to antagonize others.

A number of the questions just listed address goals in relationship to the audience and the situation. It is often the case in persuasive situations that presenters want to energize their audiences to take action in behalf of their cause, but sometimes there are constraints and expectations that may affect such direct advocacy. For example, the audience may be hearing of the situation for the very first time and, therefore, will not be ready to make public commitments without more time and information. Or, perhaps the situation is such that it does not permit active recruiting. In those cases, one needs to adjust objectives accordingly, deciding on the more attainable goal of giving the audience a better appreciation of the problem and convincing audience members that the proposed solution is worthy of further consideration.

These are substantive goals. Relational goals are also important. When you've finished your presentation, what impression do you want to leave with the audience of who you are as a person? Furthermore, what will you communicate to them about how you feel about them? Such relational issues matter because, after all, you may want or need to come back. In addition, if you've managed the relational issues well, it will be more likely that you'll be able to capitalize on their initial favorable impression in your subsequent efforts at persuasion. Ultimately, you must think about what sort of reputation you create for yourself through your presentation.

But how can we determine what the audience is like? What can be learned about the situation? The answers to these questions vary with the extent of the persuader's ambitions. Running a national or even a community-wide campaign typically involves scientific polling. Campaign planners also attempt to learn more about audience attitudes and situational expectations by gathering together selected individuals for intense questioning. For the simpler situations we are most likely to encounter, two approaches can guide us: informal **demographic analysis** and informal **ethnographic inquiry**.

First, we can draw inferences about the audience from demographic information, which includes such things as sex, age, and socioeconomic status. Some obvious issues present themselves: an older audience will likely be less informed about trends that are influencing 20-somethings; a young audience will not have the personal history with events from generations past. President Reagan will be a strong memory for some; for others, he is a historical figure. Thus, when politicians make the persuasive appeal that we need to return to the policies of Ronald Reagan, demographics impact what that means to the various audiences who hear it. Such demographic observation is both obvious and important—we need to consider how people will *understand* information based on their personal histories. But there is an even more interesting issue that is less obvious; it is the matter of how demographics translate into the ways in which people *process* information.

FIGURE 9.2 *Demographic analysis will cause a speaker to realize that older audiences have a personal memory of the presidency of Ronald Reagan while younger audiences will see him as a historical figure, and a successful persuasive presentation must adjust accordingly.*

For example, older, well-educated audiences are generally more open to complex verbal arguments, whereas younger audiences who have spent their lives exposed to daily diets of television and little else will probably be more drawn to visual displays (Hamlin, 1998). In addition, audiences grow and change over their lifetimes, and individuals have their own "marketplace metacognition" and "social intelligence" that informs them (Wright, 2002). With advances in technology, such habits of the mind are becoming even more entrenched, so much so that researcher Marc Prensky makes the distinction between **digital natives** and **digital immigrants** (2005/2006). In explaining what this means for teaching, he notes that:

> Our students are no longer "little versions of us," as they may have been in the past. In fact, they are *so* different from us that we can no longer use either our 20th century knowledge or our training as a guide to what is best for them educationally.
>
> I've coined the term *digital native* to refer to today's students (2001). They are native speakers of technology, fluent in the digital language of computers, video games, and the Internet. I refer to those of us who were not born into the digital world as *digital immigrants*. We have adopted many aspects of the technology, but just like those who learn another language later in life, we retain an "accent" because we still have one foot in the past. We will read a manual, for example, to understand a program before we think to let the program teach itself. Our accent from the predigital world often makes it difficult for us to effectively communicate with our students.
>
> (Prensky, 2005/2006)

Prensky's point is that demographics impact profoundly the very ways in which we process information. Those who are older will have an "Internet accent," always translating through their first language, the "language of print." Those who are younger are native speakers of digital code, assuming they come from an economic class and situation where technology is readily available to them. And if we wish to persuade, we must attend to these demographic particulars, evaluating the demographics of our audience and also the ways in which those demographics affect the way that people think.

Once we have established the demographic situation, we should then conduct an informal ethnographic and situational analysis, especially if we are confronting an audience that is demographically dissimilar to us. We can do this by talking with audience members or persons similar to them, learning from them what their attitudes are concerning the position or action we'll be defending. If we suspect they will be opposed to our cause, we need to find out if they are generally hostile or if their attitude is one of mild disagreement. Conversely, if they generally support us, we will want to know if they are presently undecided or already in strong agreement with us. It's an obvious point, but one worth repeating: The attitude of the audience toward the topic always should shape the way in which a persuasive presentation is created.

But in addition to their attitudes, we should attempt to glean what beliefs and values our audience holds to support those attitudes, including their perceptions of us. We need to try to determine as well what they know (or think they know) about the topic, and whether and why they care about it. One way to do this is to use the "what would your friends say" approach: "What do you think your friends and family might say about single payer health insurance as a policy for the United States?" The benefit of this approach is that we are more likely to get honest information, because the person we are asking speaks in general terms and does not feel pressure to self-disclose a personal opinion that might be poorly received.

After getting a sense of the attitudes, values, and beliefs held by the audience, it is also useful to find out as much as we can about the situation as a whole. If we've been invited to give a speech, for example, we should find out how large the audience will be, and what the physical setting will be like. Other situational questions arise as well: Who will do the introductions? How much time will be allotted? Will there be questions afterward? What form will the questions take? Should we expect the questions to be hostile or friendly? Who is likely to ask them and how far-reaching will they be? What will we be expected to know or admit we don't know in the question and answer period?

The goal of this informal ethnography is to find out what it will take to convince our audience to support our stance, and perhaps even energize them to work on behalf of our cause. Given that, as we do our analysis, we should be guided by empathy—we want to come to understand as fully as possible the attitudes, beliefs, and values of those who will be listening to or reading our message. On what common ground can we build? What arguments and evidence will our audience likely find believable? What appeals (to reason and emotion) can we offer that will make them feel that they have a personal stake in the outcome of this controversy? And so on.

What follows are two case studies that take up the issues that have been presented here and trace them through as demonstrations of single-shot persuasive presentations. As we describe what is involved in each of our three steps, we will also apply the information to these hypothetical cases. Let us begin here with an application of Step 1: Goals, Audience, Situation.

Example 1 Richmond, Virginia, Tobacco Marketing Speech

In 2009, President Obama signed a law that places greater regulation on tobacco in the United States, with the particular goal of reducing the tobacco companies' abilities to market cigarettes to American youth. Emily's class in *Persuasion* at the University of Richmond has decided to build on that effort and launch a community-wide campaign to get corporate executives of tobacco companies in the Richmond area to agree to voluntary restraints on marketing to young people in other countries around the globe. As part of that campaign, she has wrangled an invitation to address members of the Richmond Teachers Association (RTA) at their annual conference.

She has 10 minutes to make a presentation plus 10 minutes for questions and answers.

She learns from the president of the RTA that its members are generally undecided about the proposal for voluntary restraints. Many people in Richmond depend on the tobacco companies for employment, and although these public and private schoolteachers care deeply about young people, they tend not to think much about the effects of tobacco on young people outside the United States. Still, virtually everyone in Richmond is aware that the marketing of tobacco products has become highly controversial.

This is the rhetorical situation that Emily is confronting. On top of that, Emily is a total stranger to her audience and can claim few credentials other than her status as a junior majoring in communication at the University of Richmond. She is younger than her audience; she is a digital native while they are digital immigrants. Emily decides that the best approach would involve urging support for the campaign but not enjoining the audience to commit to active participation in its behalf.

Example 2 *Teenage Pregnancy Radio Editorial*

The campus radio station at Big City University airs 1-minute guest editorials at 5:59 each weekday evening by just about anyone connected with the university who is willing to propose a topic, stay within decency guidelines, and come to the studio to record it. Few people listen to WBCU; its broadcast range doesn't extend much beyond the campus. Still, Maggie, who is a student at BCU, is eager to speak in behalf of a cause about which she is passionate: free condom distribution to high school students. As a 21-year-old single mother of a 2-year-old boy, she can speak from experience about teenage pregnancy. That being said, Maggie does wonder what this mostly college-age audience will think of her proposal to provide free condoms to Big City high school students beginning in the ninth grade. From her conversations with students, it appears that her peers are divided between those sympathetic to her cause and those who are indifferent and ill informed. Both groups of students seem to perk up when she tells them about her own personal experience. She decides to combine *response reinforcing* for the former group with *response shaping* for the latter.

Maggie realizes that, as far as demographics are concerned, she has much in common with her audience, which is mostly made up of students. Her audience has come of age in an era of readily available birth control, co-ed dorms, and sexual liberty, with all the good and ill that follows from that. They also agree that it is very important to prevent teen pregnancy, because they themselves are students who believe in the value of higher education and understand how an unplanned pregnancy can transform a young person's future. Generally, Maggie believes her audience will not be hostile to her message, especially if she humanizes it with her own story.

Step 2 Initial Strategizing

Once the goals, audience, and situation have been analyzed, we move on to Step 2: Initial Strategizing, where presentation planning actually begins. It seems obvious, but, before we begin, it is important to note that the first step always precedes the second, and also that Step 1 always needs to be completed, even when time is short. The most brilliant presentation founders without a clear objective. The best persuader will fail if he or she provides a presentation that annoys, insults, or disregards the values, beliefs, and attitudes of the audience. And, the presentation must be appropriate to the situation. That being said, once those tasks are accomplished, the presentation planning moves to the next stage, and there are three issues to consider.

1   What are the chief obstacles that I will have to confront? How can I overcome them?

2   What resources can I bring to this situation? How can I best deploy them? What opportunities for persuasion are available? How can I best exploit them?

3   How should I actually prepare my presentation?

The first two questions in this list, focusing on potential problems and on assets and opportunities, should lead us to some sound decisions on overall strategy. Decisions on the particulars of self-presentation are covered in question 3.

In doing this initial strategizing, we should consider the presentation in relation to the principles of coactive persuasion that were presented in Chapter 4. We need to think, for example, about ways to overcome skepticism or outright disagreement by building on shared premises and shared experiences. We might think about how we can exploit personal attractiveness and credibility or perhaps how we will work to overcome audience doubts about competence and trustworthiness. We should evaluate what we know or can learn about our topic that might help to overcome audience apathy and perhaps move audience members to action. And we should think about how we might best arrange our materials so that our presentation is enthusiastically received and easily remembered. We can think about what we can do non-verbally to augment the verbal message. And we should think about the physical and social setting for our presentation: What can we do to overcome such problems as noisy air conditioning or to exploit such opportunities as are provided by friendly questioning from the floor? A major resource is the message itself. If we've done the necessary research, it will show. If we've exercised good judgment, it will show. If we've organized well, it will show.

In this stage, we can also think about the non-verbal resources at our command. We each have a voice and a body that can work for us or against us. A poised beginning—not too fast, not too slow—can communicate confidence. Gestures and facial expressions can complement the verbal message, perhaps adding emphasis or metacommunicating feelings that are impossible to express verbally. A presenter's voice can be like a musical instrument, able in a nuanced way to express irony, amusement, interest, detachment, conviction, ambivalence—perhaps sequentially or even simultaneously. The actor inside of each of us can assume the role of teacher, sermonizer, editorialist, or advertiser. Ultimately, we can use non-verbals to enjoin the audience to think with us as we puzzle out a problem with them: "Let's do this together," our voice and body can be saying. Or, if we use non-verbal communication ineffectively, we can end up metacommunicating panic, disinterest, condescension, self-loathing, or any of a number of feelings and attitudes that will speak so loudly that our audience won't be able to hear what we are saying. Whatever else we do, we should seek to use non-verbal communication to create the impression that we are comfortable, and that we are talking with our audience, rather than at them.

Example 1 Richmond, Virginia, Tobacco Marketing Speech

Having determined that she will be permitted 10 minutes of presentation time plus 10 minutes for questions and answers to convince members of the RTA to support her group's campaign, Emily takes stock of the resources she has available to win them over, and the outlines of a strategy begin to form in her mind. This speech will need evidence—plenty of it—of harm from tobacco marketing geared toward young people. But before she presents that evidence, she will need to build rapport with the audience, establishing herself as a friend, rather than an enemy. She will also need to build common ground on her central premise that, although the good of the tobacco companies and of the Richmond economy is important, serious and widespread harm to children anywhere in the world is an overriding concern.

This is not an easy premise to sell, she realizes. She decides to begin with evidence of harm to children and then document the worldwide aspects of the problem. Her research show that:

- Between 80,000 and 100,000 children worldwide start smoking every day. Fifty percent of children who begin smoking in adolescent years continue to smoke for an average of 15 to 20 years.
- Half of long-term smokers will die from tobacco. Every cigarette smoked cuts at least five minutes of life on average—about the time taken to smoke it.
- About 15 billion cigarettes are sold daily—or 10 million every minute.
- Smoking is on the rise in the developing world but falling in developed nations. The tobacco industry has marketed accordingly; it knows that it needs to market aggressively to developing nations.
- A survey from a few years ago found that nearly 80% of American advertising executives from top agencies believed cigarette advertising *does* make smoking more appealing or socially acceptable to children.

And so on. Emily decides to use these data in a PowerPoint presentation. As to the matter of building rapport, she will note that her family has lived in Richmond for four generations. Her mother is a retired schoolteacher who introduced Emily to the RTA's president, Dorothy Foxworth. Concerning the fact that tobacco is Richmond's bread-and-butter industry, Emily notes that, like everyone else in this town, she was raised with the conviction that tobacco could do no wrong.

Having established her bona fides, Emily figures she can get down to business. She decides to use the *"yes-but" approach. Yes*, Philip Morris's welfare is important. Many of us have friends and family who've worked for the company. *But* we can't ignore the effects of tobacco marketing on children. (With this, she will launch into her PowerPoint.)

Emily decides to conclude with a brief appeal for voluntary restraints on tobacco marketing overseas. She has arranged to have a friend in the audience ask the first question, one that Emily herself has written. She intends to leave nothing to chance!

In response to the question about voluntary restraints, she will argue from the perspective of the **method of residues**. The tobacco companies, she will say, have three choices.

1   They can hope the U.S. government, and the governments of other nations, will do nothing. That's unlikely, especially given recent legislation to severely limit tobacco sales to children in the United States. There is a trend already in place, and it is likely to continue.

2   They can wait for government to impose restraints. If it does, the restraints are likely to be harsh.

3   They can curtail their overseas marketing to children voluntarily. This is the third and remaining option (the "residue"). Voluntary curtailment can give a much-needed public relations boost to the industry while weakening the movement for government-imposed restraints.

As for the rest of the question and answer period, Emily anticipates the questions and rehearses her answers as best she can. At no point does she write out or memorize those answers; she wants to stay fresh and alive during this portion of her presentation.

Example 2 Teenage Pregnancy Guest Editorial

Maggie thought initially that her guest editorial was going to be easy. On reflection, though, she realizes that she has much too much to say. Moreover, she has concluded that trying to squeeze everything in by talking quickly is precisely the wrong way to go. Furthermore, she realizes that her presentation is constrained because it will have no visuals. She cannot depend on PowerPoint, facial expressions, gesture, appearance, and the like to help her communicate her message. She can use only sound.

She decides on a sixfold strategy:

1   Use a loud and prolonged sound—something similar to the beep of the emergency radio control system—to get attention. Then follow with a startling

statistic. "Hi, I'm Maggie Friendly. During the time of the sound that you just heard, X number of children were born to single teenage mothers." (Maggie plans to compute the exact number on average from yearly statistics.)

2   Paint a vivid picture of the problems of teenage pregnancy for child and parent. (Time limit: 20 seconds.)

3   Make an example of herself. "I know because I've been there. I thought I was in love and now I'm a single mom. My son, Jason, and I are lucky because I've got my parents to help me in so many ways as I care for my son. But many teens and their children are not so lucky."

4   State her position. "Let's face it, teens are having sex. They're not going to stop just because some teacher lectures them not to."

5   Accent the positive. (This is a framing decision. Maggie could have stayed negative.) "But you know, the teenage birthrate is going down. One big reason is that high schools around the country are giving out condoms to their students as early as the ninth grade."

6   Design a conclusion especially for listeners already on her side: "Help support Big City Planned Parenthood in their efforts to get free condoms distributed in our high schools. Call 555–5111 for further information."

Maggie writes out her editorial word for word, records it until she likes the way it sounds, sees that its timing is about right, brings the recording to the radio station, gets an okay, then heads for the computer to edit it down to what will be aired.

Step 3 Test-Marketing and Revision

Creating a persuasive presentation is different from constructing an informative one; it is always more challenging and often more interesting. In persuasive presentations, we must do all of the things that are required when sharing information, but then we must *add* advocacy; in persuasive presentations, we must take a side and encourage our audience to share our perspective. Because of that, testing out the message is crucial. When test-marketing a presentation, two questions arise:

1   Now that I've prepared the presentation, what do the sorts of people I want to persuade think of it? Have I created the "right" message after all?

2   Assuming that there are problems (or missed opportunities) in my initial strategizing, how can I best revise my plans?

Sometimes in our haste to complete our presentation, we might want to see this step as unnecessary. Lots of people, including many professional persuaders, sometimes initially think it is. But they ignore it at their peril.

People like Republican Communication Consultant Frank Luntz, for example, conduct constant and rigorous research to devise messages that are persuasive. His 2009 28-page report chronicling his test-marketing of language tells Republicans precisely which words to use to persuade Americans to accept their perspectives about health care. He demonstrates, for example, a test-marketed Republican message, calling it "Words that work":

As a matter of *principle*, Republicans are firmly committed to providing genuine *access* to *affordable*, *quality* healthcare for every American. The time has come to create a *balanced*, *common sense approach* that will *guarantee* that Americans can receive the care they *deserve* and protect the *sacred doctor-patient relationship*. We will oppose any *politician-run system* that *denies you the treatments* you need, when you need them.

(Luntz, 2009, italics in original)

And then, he contrasts that message with an inferior one that a Republican might use, one that focuses on America in decline, categorizing it "Words that do not work":

There's another thing that *Americans should be concerned* about if we are going to have government run healthcare: 75% of all the innovations in healthcare in the world *come out of this country*. There's a reason for that. It's because even though *we don't have a good market*, the market we still have generates entrepreneurship, invention, advancement, and excellence in terms of new ideas and new cures and new treatments in healthcare. *That will go away* under government run healthcare, and with it tons of jobs.

(Luntz, 2009, italics in original)

In the report that accompanies these examples, Luntz documents in detail why he has identified the terms as he has, backing up his assertions with solid data from his focus groups, linguistic research, and test-marketing of persuasive messages. He is nationally known for such research, and his impact in shaping discussions on important policy issues in the United States is pronounced. A recent study found that Luntz's framing of health care came to permeate the media, where his recommended terminology was consistently employed instead of more neutral terms on Fox News, and also made up "a significant percentage" of the terms used on CNN, MSNBC and on the nightly news broadcasts on ABC, CBS and NBC (Strupp & Willis, 2013). Ultimately, he teaches us that test-marketing and revision are crucial components of persuasion. Like Luntz, we too can (and should) test-market and revise our persuasive messages with care so that they reach their intended targets.

Thinking It Through

When you read Luntz's positive example of persuasive discourse, did you find it convincing? Why or why not?

Take it one step further. Now that you've been introduced to Luntz's work, do a bit of content analysis. Spend some time listening to Republican spokespersons and measure how often they use the exact words and phrases he recommends. Turn on your favorite news channel, or check out the web pages and blogs of conservative spokespersons to see for yourself the impact Frank Luntz has had in the creation of conservative persuasive political discourse.

Example 1 Richmond, Virginia, Tobacco Marketing Speech

In preparation for her speech to the RTA, Emily has lost nearly every friend she's ever had in the process of anticipating questions from the audience and testing out possible responses, practicing out loud and fine-tuning her ability to think on her feet. They think that her PowerPoint presentation will be effective, but they recommend including more information on the nature and effects of marketing by U.S. tobacco companies overseas. They also suggest that she prepare a handout of websites that reinforce her case, and bring copies to pass out to the people in attendance. Emily takes their advice.

Example 2 Teenage Pregnancy Radio Editorial

On arriving at the studio, Maggie learns from the station manager that he likes everything except her personal testimonial. There's nothing wrong with the words, he says, but her tone suggests that she's not too sorry she got pregnant. After all, her family is helping her out.

Maggie thinks more about this, and realizes that is not her message at all. Memories come back to her of the pain of rejection by her lover, of the embarrassment at telling her mom that she was pregnant, of the loneliness she felt on having to stay home every day with her newborn, of the joy she felt at seeing her baby smile for the first time. When she has finished thinking things through, she goes back into the studio. She is now ready to tell the world what she really means about single motherhood.

In summary, a persuasive presentation, at its most basic, revolves around establishing clear goals, finding ways to communicate those goals to unique audiences, testing and retesting in an effort to ensure that the audience hears the message as intended and responds as hoped, and then, finally, sharing the message with boldness and commitment. The 3-step approach presented here provides a way to organize oneself and begin. The focus throughout the process is on the audience, and whether the goal is to post a single comment on a blog, deliver a formal presentation, create an editorial, or even propose marriage, this approach will provide the system by which we can increase our rate of persuasive success.

MAKING IDEAS STICK

Have you ever wondered why some ads seem to run forever, while others disappear only days after they've been introduced? Heath and Heath take on these issues, and many more, in their book *Made to Stick*, where they consider the issue of **stickiness**— that is, the art of making ideas unforgettable. Their book offers useful research concerning communication, and it is to their model that we now turn.

Sticky messages of all kinds gain their adhesive ability from six traits. Ideas that stick are 1) simple, 2) unexpected, 3) concrete, 4) credible, 5) emotional, and 6) include stories. (Note that this very list exemplifies its point: it spells "success" [almost] and thereby makes it easier to remember.) Let's consider each point in turn, with an eye toward creating persuasive single-shot messages.

1. Sticky Ideas Have *Simplicity*

Simplicity involves getting to the "essential core of our ideas" (Heath & Heath, 2007a). The effect of simplicity is forced prioritization, because we have to eliminate much and keep only what matters. It leads us to be "masters of exclusion" (Heath & Heath, 2007a). The goal is to find the *core* message and assert it with as much *compactness* as we can. For example, consider the Golden Rule: Do unto others as you would have them do unto you. It is the ultimate model of simplicity, a one-sentence statement so profound that we spend a lifetime learning to follow it (Heath & Heath, 2007a).

Compactness alone, though, isn't enough. "The earth is flat" is compact, but untrue. The goal here does not involve speaking in sound bites; rather, it is to "create ideas that are both simple *and* profound" (Heath & Heath, 2007a).

For example, consider the pomelo. A non-sticky way to describe it is that a pomelo is the largest of the citrus fruits. The rind is very thick but soft and easy to peel away. The resulting fruit has a light yellow to coral pink flesh and can vary from juicy to slightly dry and from seductively spicy-sweet to tangy and tart.

The description above may be accurate, but it fails to stick, and you can prove it to yourself if you try to repeat what you've just read. How can we make the message stick? We can try this simple and compact description: "A pomelo is basically a super-sized grapefruit with a very thick and soft rind" (Heath & Heath, 2007a). If you notice how much more easily that message is retained, you will begin to understand how ideas can be made to stick.

FIGURE 9.3   *How can you explain a "pomelo" and make the idea stick?*

2. Sticky Ideas Are *Unexpected*

How do we get a person's attention and how do we keep it? We do it when we "violate people's expectations" (Heath & Heath, 2007a). We can employ surprise, but surprise alone is fleeting and only a small component of the issue. For an idea to stick, it needs to do more than just surprise a person; it also must generate interest and curiosity (Heath & Heath, 2007a). When we introduce the unexpected, it makes people want to find answers and resolve the questions of why they were surprised.

One way to achieve this goal is to communicate the message in a way that breaks the audience's "guessing machines" and then helps them redefine what is before them. For example, customer service at Nordstrom's confounds customers' expectations in fascinating ways, and thereby communicates the idea that they are not the typical department store:

- A Nordie irons a new shirt for a customer who needed it for a meeting that afternoon.

- A Nordie cheerfully gift wraps products a customer bought at Macy's.

- A Nordie warms customers' cars in winter while they finish shopping.

- A Nordie refunds money for a set of tire chains even though Nordstrom's doesn't sell tire chains.

Such behaviors communicate a positive message in an unexpected way; they dislodge preconceived ideas and cause people to think anew. Furthermore, these behaviors ripple out as the stories of the unexpected encounters are recounted; they work to create the sticky idea that Nordstrom's offers unparalled service (Heath & Heath, 2007a). This unexpected arousal of curiosity focuses our attention and causes the questions to stick. A witty instance of this is the book, *Why Do Men Have Nipples?* (Leyner & Goldberg, 2005). Speaking about the title, Heath and Heath explain:

> That's a solid question. Chances are, you don't have an immediate answer. And yet you weren't frothing with curiosity about the man-nipple-problem until the book title called attention to the gap in your knowledge. You know something: Men have nipples. You don't know something: Why. That's a gap .... And the gap creates the itch.
>
> (Heath & Heath, 2007b)

3. Sticky Ideas Are *Concrete*

We make our ideas clear by explaining them "in terms of human actions, in terms of sensory information" (Heath & Heath, 2007a). Sticky ideas contain concrete images— "ice-filled bathtubs, apples with razors"—that stand in contrast with things such as "mission statements, synergies, strategies, visions," which are "often so ambiguous to the point of being meaningless" (Heath & Heath, 2007a).

A forceful example involves the classic experiment undertaken by a 1968 teacher in an effort to teach her students about prejudice. Martin Luther King, Jr. had just been murdered and the nation was in shock. Realizing that discrimination could not really be explained to third graders, Iowa teacher Jane Elliot sought to make prejudice tangible.

She divided the class into brown- and blue-eyed groups, and told the blue-eyed children that they were superior and smarter. Blue-eyed students got rewards and extra recess, while brown-eyed students had to wear special collars and sit in the back. The result was astounding, because very quickly friendships dissolved and the children became nasty, vicious, and discriminatory. Through her exercise, the idea of prejudice became concrete for the students, and still resonates with us today.

4. Sticky Ideas Are *Credible*

In order for an idea to stick, it must be believed. "Sticky ideas have to carry their own credentials. We need a way to help people test our ideas for themselves—a 'try before you buy' philosophy for the world of ideas" (Heath & Heath, 2007a). Heath and Heath offer a number of ways to create the kind of credibility that will cause ideas to stick, including such things as the creation of internal credibility, the use of vivid details, the judicious use of statistics, and the establishment of testable credentials.

They also note that sometimes we are lucky enough to have that one example which is enough to establish credibility in a given domain. They call this the **Sinatra test**, borrowing lyrics from the song *New York, New York* to make the point: "If I can make it there, I'll make it anywhere." As they note, if you have catered a White House function, you can cater anywhere. You've gained credibility from that sole instance that will carry you forward (Heath & Heath, 2007a).

Too often, say Heath and Heath, when we are trying to build a case for something, we "instinctively grasp for hard numbers. But in many cases this is exactly the wrong approach" (2007a). A better way to build credibility for an idea is to use the **human-scale principle**, which brings statistics to life by contextualizing them in terms that are more human, more everyday.

For example, consider this list of hard statistics from a poll of 23,000 employees:

- Only 37% said they have a clear understanding of what their organization is trying to achieve and why.

- Only one in five is enthusiastic about their team's and their organization's goals.

- Only one in five said they had a clear "line of sight" between their tasks and their team's and organization's goals.

- Only 15% felt that their organization fully enables them to execute key goals.

- Only 20% fully trusted the organization they work for.

(Heath & Heath, 2007a).

To find a way to make these statistics credible in order to persuade a group that a problem exists, and to make the idea stick, there exists the need to translate these statistics and humanize them. So, instead of listing the statistics, we might argue the following:

If, say, a soccer team had these same scores, only 4 of the 11 players on the field would know which goal is theirs. Only 2 of the 11 would care. Only 2 of the 11 would know what position they play and know exactly what they are supposed to do. And all but 2 players would, in some way, be competing against their own team members rather than the opponent.

(Heath & Heath, 2007a)

As this example demonstrates, using the *human-scale principle* provides information with credibility that goes beyond mere statistics, and causes it thereby to stick.

5. Sticky Ideas Are *Emotional*

Another prerequisite for creating messages that stick is the need to appeal to emotions. We need to get people to care about our ideas. The following case study, in which participants are persuaded to donate money to charity, exemplifies clearly the power of emotional appeals:

Save the Children

Consider this statement: "If I look at the mass, I will never act. If I look at the one, I will." Researchers at Carnegie Mellon University tested this ideal, wanting to see how people would respond to making a charitable donation to an abstract cause versus a single person. In effect, they were measuring the power of emotion as a factor in persuasion.

Participants were offered $5 to complete a survey, and they received an envelope to donate to Save the Children as well. Individuals whose survey included a reading of specific statistics donated $1.14, but individuals who read about a specific individual child donated $2.38, over twice as much. Clearly, the emotional appeal had an impact on causing the persuasive message to stick.

6. Sticky Ideas Include *Stories*

The final component to creating ideas that stick is the use of stories. "The right kind of story is, effectively, a simulation. Stories are like flight simulators for the brain" (Heath & Heath, 2007a). Ultimately, stories get people to act on their beliefs.

Stories are effective teaching tools that contain wisdom; they show how context can mislead people to make the wrong decisions and illustrate causal relationships that people hadn't recognized before. Not only that, they highlight the unexpected and showcase the resourceful ways in which people have solved problems (Heath & Heath, 2007a). Given that, they make ideas stick (Heath & Heath, 2007a).

One particularly effective type of story is the **springboard story**, which is a narrative that tells people about the possibilities before them. For example, consider the case of Jared, whose inspirational weight loss story helped to sell Subway sandwiches all across the nation. Jared, a junior in college, weighed 425 lbs and doctors told him he would be lucky if he lived past age 35. During spring break he went on a Subway diet, where he ate subs three times a day. After three months he'd dropped 100 lbs, and Subway realized they had a great story to tell. With Jared as spokesperson, a supremely successful advertising campaign was born.

In conclusion, in *Made to Stick,* Heath and Heath offer the argument that there are six elements necessary if we wish to create ideas that will overwhelm what they call the **curse of knowledge**. The problem, as they present it, is that "once we know something, we find it hard to imagine what it was like not to know it. Our knowledge has cursed us" (Heath & Heath, 2007a). Because of *the curse of knowledge*, we find it difficult to "share our knowledge with others, because we can't readily re-create our listener's state of mind" (Heath & Heath, 2007a). With the six principles presented here, we have a checklist to aid us as we take our ideas and transform them, and create messages that will be heard and remembered by those we encounter.

ORGANIZING PERSUASIVE PRESENTATIONS

Some readers of this text have had extensive training in public speaking. Some are skilled in making professional presentations. And others are coming to the topic for the first time. No matter what our experience, though, we can all benefit from considering an overview about how to construct and deliver professional one-shot persuasive presentations. It is to that topic that we now turn our attention.

Think back to Emily's presentation, discussed earlier as a case study in this chapter. Because message recipients process information in stages, audience members for Emily's presentation would be unlikely to act on her proposal unless they evaluated it favorably. But they would not evaluate it favorably unless they understood it. And, to understand it, they needed to attend to it. But they may not expose themselves to her message if they suspected they wouldn't benefit from it.

This *Attention–Comprehension–Evaluation–Action model* is simple, but it has its drawbacks. For one thing, evaluation begins from the moment of attention and includes assessments of the presenter as well as what the presenter has to say. Attention doesn't stop with comprehension. A vague or ambiguous message may, under some circumstances, yield a more favorable evaluation than a clear one. Much depends on the audience and the situation.

All this has implications for organizing messages. For example, as the next section describes, the tasks of getting attention and orienting receivers belong primarily to the beginning of the presentation, but these tasks must also be carried out throughout. And, as this chapter later notes, sometimes it is advantageous not to reveal all about purpose or position in the opening, even though as a general rule we should. Consider what follows, then, provisionally.

Introduction

Whether presented orally or displayed via PowerPoint slides, the introduction to a presentation is the place to *get the attention of receivers* and then *orient them to the message*. It is the place to create a favorable first impression. Indeed, building rapport with the audience and projecting just the right image to the audience must accompany everything else a presenter does.

Although the introduction is presented first, the final draft should not be prepared until the body and conclusion of the message are firmly established. Persuaders tend to make conclusions too long and introductions too short. They are anxious to delve into the meat of their presentations, and, once into it, they have difficulty wrapping it up succinctly.

Getting Attention

Audiences heed selectively the messages they see and hear. Countering these tendencies often requires careful planning and great ingenuity, especially at an event such as a large outdoor rally. Even with a captive audience, and even when the situation is conducive to careful listening, presenters may have to fight their way past apathy and competing stimuli. Consider the job of a visiting speaker at a campus academic conference. At first, the listeners make physical adjustments: They put their books under their chairs, remove their sweaters, and shift to get comfortable in their seats. Next come social adjustments, which may go on for several minutes. They chat with those around them ("Hi Josh, Hi Luisa. Guess who I saw at the cafeteria this morning?"). In the midst of all this, the guest lecturer is all but forgotten on the stage.

If the presenter simply begins with "Today I'm going to talk about ...", he or she risks being ignored by an audience that has not yet made the transition from everyday life to the presenter's message. To overcome this and pull the audience in, the presenter opens with an *attention-getter*: a humorous anecdote, brief quotation, startling statistic, thought-provoking question, pithy reference to the audience or the occasion, or factual illustration. This helps the audience make the transition from inattention to focused listening, and generates interest in the topic that is to come.

Orienting the Audience

"First I tell 'em what I'm gonna tell 'em. Then I tell 'em. Then I tell 'em what I told 'em." Such is an anonymous country preacher's formula for successful sermons. But why follow the example of this minister? Why not simply "tell 'em"? Although persuaders may sometimes wish to postpone revealing purpose and position or to mask logic behind a veil of ambiguity, at least some understanding of a message is almost always a prerequisite to acceptance of a proposition.

Whether via PowerPoint or from the pulpit, presenters need to begin to orient their audiences by stating the thesis—that one central idea that sums up what the entire presentation is about. The thesis determines what the main points will be, what types of material the speaker will select to support the main points, and how the presenter will introduce and conclude the message. Listeners need a clear notion of what will be discussed and why. Rather than saying, "I think something should be done to change divorce laws," Lionel might say, "I'm here to ask for your support for a proposal to abolish the two-year separation requirement for obtaining a no-fault divorce in the Commonwealth of Pennsylvania."

But it is not enough to simply state the thesis. Whatever the structure of the body of a persuasive presentation or essay, it is always useful to preview it in the introduction. Thus, Lionel might indicate that he will first discuss flaws in the present divorce system, then their causes, and then their solutions. Or he might preview only the first section of the body of the message, identifying the three or four inherent problems with the present divorce laws and the order in which they will be discussed. He will focus on key receivers so that they can grasp the main ideas and their logical relationships.

In a longer and more complex treatment of a subject, the speaker should prepare the audience thoroughly for what is to come. Still, he will need to be strategic in deciding how to prepare them. He may have to indicate what he will not be talking about. In a speech advocating full no-fault divorce, for example, Lionel could say, "Now I'm not here to promote divorce. What I'll be asking you to support is the plan proposed by former divorce lawyer Herbert Sherbert of the Commonwealth of Pennsylvania."

Lionel might also want to define key terms. What exactly is no-fault divorce? On almost any controversial issue, there are bound to be key terms that need defining. The most familiar form of definition is the dictionary definition. It names something, puts it into a category, and then separates it from members of that category. No-fault divorce might be defined as "a system of divorce that allows dissolution of a marriage, without findings of wrongdoing by either party." In and of themselves, however, dictionary definitions tend to be too abstract. Often, it is helpful to supplement them with examples and perhaps with further explanation. Definitions should ordinarily be acceptable to the audience, but the speaker may need to take time to defend his definition. Perhaps Lionel could cite an authority in its support or ask his audience to accept the definition for purposes of discussion (like a ground rule in baseball or football) without necessarily endorsing it fully.

In a 10-minute presentation, a persuader might need to introduce historical or other background material before beginning the body of the message. How many states have no-fault divorce at present? How did the idea originate? What other states include separation requirements, and how long are they? These are just some of the factual questions that might be discussed briefly in the introduction.

Chances are that the body of a presentation or essay favoring passage of unrestricted no-fault divorce legislation will begin with an indictment of the present system: its manifest evils and the reasons that it must be replaced, rather than simply repaired. Such an indictment assumes that there is something wrong with the system in principle, that the alleged problems stem from the nature of the system, rather than from particular practices associated with it. But what is "the system"? What are its underlying principles? Often, the basic principles of the system are not at all obvious. An indictment of the present divorce laws might well be preceded by analyses and explanations of their underlying principles—their inherent assumption, for example, that every marital break-up should be tempered by lengthy separation rules before a divorce is granted.

Body

After stating the thesis, the next step is to establish main points—the reasons that justify the thesis. These may be organized around the stock issues discussed in Chapter 8. Or Lionel could simply say, "I support unrestricted no-fault divorce for the following five reasons." In the body of the speech, the persuader may also raise and refute counter-arguments (more on this later in the chapter).

Main points should usually be simple, declarative sentences that contain *one* memorably stated idea. Lionel won't say:

> True unrestricted no-fault divorce, by eliminating the requirement of blame on either party and the possible sense of embarrassment one of them might have at having wronged the other and providing rapid resolution, is preferable to the existing system that chains partners in unhappy marriages for years before allowing them to move on with their lives. That, in any event, is my first reason for advocating it.

Instead, Lionel might say, "Why am I for unrestricted no-fault divorce? Reason 1: No government-required chains should bind divorcing partners together."

A useful mnemonic device for remembering how to organize discussion of a main point is **NESC: Name it. Explain it. Support it. Conclude it.** Having stated the main point (naming), you may well need to clarify it (explaining) and to provide evidence and arguments in its defense (supporting). When supporting our point, though, we must remember the importance of holding the audience's attention. We can make supporting materials more interesting and memorable by rounding off statistics, paraphrasing long or dull quotations, interspersing seriousness with humor, and using vivid analogies or comparisons. And then, once we have nailed down our main point, it often helps to restate it (concluding). Whether by returning to the outline overview in a PowerPoint slide, or by saying the point aloud, it is wise to re-orient the audience and keep providing them with a "map" so that they can chart the progression of the message.

A coactive, conversational style, one that communicates with the audience rather than at them, is important. Part and parcel of that style is the transformation of dry, abstract statistics into terms that audiences can understand on a personal level. Rather than saying that "51.5% of married people in the Commonwealth of Pennsylvania terminate their marriages by way of divorce," Lionel might say, "More than half of all marriages in Pennsylvania end in divorce." Better still:

> You probably know at least two couples planning to tie the knot in the next year. Well, if past is prophet, Becky and Sam may hang in there, but don't count on Tanya and Tim. More than half of all Pennsylvania marriages end in divorce.

In planning a presentation, we need to pay attention to our word choices and find ways to make our language robust. Even the language of normally dull "orienting" materials can be livened up. For example, longish presentations with four or five points typically need transitional statements to remind audiences of where the presentation has been and alert them to where it is heading. But instead of saying, "Now that I have established that the elimination of separation requirements saves time, I want at this juncture to discuss how unrestricted no-fault divorce can save money as well," Lionel might say, "We've seen that unrestricted no-fault divorce saves time. But does it save money?" Connectives such as these invite curiosity. Should Lionel then say, "It is my second contention that unrestricted no-fault divorce does in fact provide significant cost savings"? Probably not. Instead he might say, "I think it does. Lots of money. And that's my next point."

Conclusion

The rule of thumb for presentations is to wrap things up quickly—perhaps in one third the time required for the introduction. But that depends on whether the persuader's goal is to convince the audience and stop at that or is an attempt to activate them. A 10-minute presentation to simply convince the audience to agree might close with a vivid restatement of the thesis and a summary of the main points. Lionel might say, "And so in conclusion, I repeat: The people of Pennsylvania need unrestricted no-fault divorce for these reasons: ..." But should he wish to activate his audience, he will probably need to tell them how to act (who, what, when, where, and how), and he may need to pound home the need for urgency:

> You can make a difference by calling or e-mailing State Senator Getwirthy, chair of the Senate committee that oversees divorce laws. But you'd better act now because countervailing forces are out there in the Commonwealth that would like to make divorce laws even *more* restrictive. Here's how you can contact Getwirthy.... Let him know that you give a damn.

Finally, if time permits, the presenter should probably try to solicit overt pledges of support, preferably from respected audience members. Lionel might, for instance, even ask the audience to consider ways of making a difference on this issue. Suggestions on how to act will probably have more influence coming from them.

What has been presented in this section is an overview of the basics that are needed to create presentations of all sorts; it is included here because the ability to organize a persuasive presentation is a crucial communication skill. Effective presentations require more than a list of bullet points on a group of PowerPoint slides. Instead, successful persuasive presentations organize and present messages coherently so that audiences can weigh them and come to agreement.

Resources for the Persuader

Use the following as reminders of principles covered earlier in the book. Make use of the principles as needed. Refer to earlier chapters for elaboration of the principles. Keep in mind that this is but a partial list.

Theoretically Derived Resources

1 From Aristotelian Theory: Combine (a) Ethos (perceived competence and trustworthiness of the speaker), (b) Pathos (the motivational/emotional appeals you can offer your audience), and (c) Logos (the perceived logic of your case).

2 From BVA Theory: Influence attitudes by directing thought about audience beliefs and values: (a) Make positive beliefs and values appear more salient while downplaying the importance or relevance of beliefs and values harmful to your cause, (b) strengthen some beliefs and values and weaken others, and (c) add advantages or positives to those your audience has already thought of.

3 From the Theory of Reasoned Action: (a) Convince audiences that valued others would have them act as you have recommended they act, or (b) play down the importance of what valued others think.

4 From the Elaboration of Likelihood Model (ELM): (a) Encourage central processing (for more powerful, longer-lasting effects) by increasing audience ability and motivation to think long and hard about the issues, while helping them along with sound arguments and good evidence, favorable to your cause; and/or (b) encourage peripheral processing favorable to your cause by such triggers of relatively mindless acceptance as expressions of liking for your audience, appearing personally attractive, and naming celebrities who have endorsed your position or proposal.

5 From Learning Theories: (a) Assist audiences in information processing, from reception to yielding, being mindful of the need to overcome resistance at the yielding stage by the better educated, more confident, and more intelligent members of your audience, while facilitating comprehension among their opposite numbers. (b) Present incentives to your audience by projecting rewards from adoption of the recommended action and penalties from inaction or from choosing the wrong course of action. (c) Link your proposal with all manner of favorable associations (both conscious and unconscious) while linking what you oppose with unfavorable associations.

6 From the Coactive Model of Persuasion: (a) Use "different strokes for different folks." (b) Combine evidences of interpersonal similarity with an emphasis on those differences that make you appear more expert, better informed, and more reliable. (c) Build on premises acceptable to your audience, rather than proceeding expressively, or combatively, or as an objectivist. If necessary, make a case for the reasonableness of your premises. Build from common ground, possibly using a yes-yes or yes-but approach, or reason from the perspective of the other.

Framing and "Languaging" Resources

1 Selectivity: Think of choice of labels, definitions, descriptions, comparisons, contrasts, contextualizations, and so on as weapons in your arsenal of persuasion. Be strategically selective.

2 Intensify/Downplay: (a) Intensify through repetition, association, and composition. (b) Downplay through omission, diversion, and confusion. Choose framing metaphors with a view toward their intensifying and downplaying functions.

3 Creative Reframing: Be prepared to think unconventionally and to assist your audience in dissolving or resolving problems by going "outside the nine dots." One way to go outside the dots is by use of generative metaphors.

4 Cultural Frames and Verbal Repertoires: (a) Remember that our culture's notions of common sense contain seemingly opposing frames that you can exploit to advantage. (b) Practice spin control by selecting from among the range of possibilities those sayings, those lines of argument, and those word choices that work best for you.

5 Introductory Frames: Take special care with the frames you will use to talk about the type of talk you are about to give. Are you here to "inform" the audience, to "explore" some ideas with them, to "sell" them on an idea, or to "advise" or "counsel" them? Remember that audience resistance can sometimes be overcome by persuading in the guise of non-persuasion.

6 Going Meta: Frame the context for the issues you are discussing as well as the opposition to your point of view by way of metamoves that make prior communications the subject of your communications. For example, consider commenting on the assignment your instructor has given you. (But also review Chapter 6 on the risks of going meta.)

Argumentative Resources

1 Stock Issues: Consider organizing the body of your speech around stock issues. If it's a proposition of policy you're dealing with, decide first whether you want to change, repair, or retain the policy. This will determine your approach to the stock issues, including your burdens of proof and refutation.

2 Evidence: Use the different forms of evidence—stories, statistics, brief examples, testimony—in combination.

3 Storytelling: Tell stories that pack an emotional wallop while at the same time helping to build your case. Provide details that invite audiences to supply premises of their own, favorable to your case.

4 Statistics and Examples: Be prepared to show that the factual claims are accurate, that they are relevant and representative, and that there are sufficient statistical data (or examples) to warrant the generalization.

5 Testimony: Provide testimony, especially from perceived authorities and from eyewitnesses. If necessary, make a case for the credibility of your sources.

6 Cognitive Shorthands: Don't neglect those in your audience who will be looking for logical shortcuts. For example, be prepared to use social proof (e.g., opinion poll evidence) in support of your case, and leave audiences with a sense that your position or proposal is psychologically consistent with the beliefs and values they hold dear.

SUMMARY

Sometimes, a presentation must be put through multiple drafts until it comes as close as possible to meeting the multiple demands that are placed on it. But for most of us, most of the time, what is needed is the freshness and spontaneity that comes from preparing well, revising as needed, but then not writing out the presentation or memorizing it, but instead deliberately altering its wording during rehearsal so that we are best prepared to communicate with audience members, rather than at them.

Persuasive presentations should combine genuine commitment with the necessary craft skills. Preparation requires strategic adaptation of goals and materials to audience and situation. For this, we recommend our 3-step process for analysis and urge presenters to review the many resources identified here for exploiting strategic opportunities and overcoming obstacles. Message preparation can benefit from bringing psychological principles to bear on the case at hand. It can exploit framing and "languaging" strategies. The arguments presented should provide audiences with both psychological satisfaction and compelling logic.

Preparation begins by deciding on a general topic, gathering materials, coming to judgment, and formulating substantive and relational goals for the audience as a whole and perhaps for different audience segments. The next step is to organize the message, being sure to make provision in the introduction for building rapport with the audience, gaining members' attention, and orienting them as needed to topic, thesis, background information, and the like. The body of the message should build around main points that are clearly tied to the thesis, with each point named, explained, supported, and concluded (NESC). The conclusion should be brief if the only purpose is to sway opinion, longer to mobilize the audience for action.

Presentations should ordinarily be explicit and up-front about their thesis, but there are times for building logically to a conclusion, rather than stating it at the outset. Generally, too, the message should both advance the speaker's side while refuting the opposition's, but there are times to concede what cannot be denied (yes-but) or, in the interest of time, to dwell only on one's own case. The more extreme the position in relation to the audience, the more credible the speaker (or possibly the speaker's sources of testimony) needs to be. Alternatively, the speaker should probably advance a more moderate position that falls within the audience's latitude of neutrality if confronted with an audience that is highly ego involved in the topic. When fear appeals are used, they should be combined with specific, doable recommendations for action and assurances that the action recommended will overcome or at least reduce the problem.

These generalizations about message design and the principles here identified for adapting to different types of audiences offer up overarching approaches to the topics, but come with the caveat that audiences are made up of living, breathing humans. They are varied and unpredictable. And so, while general approaches provide a starting place for thinking about these issues, flexibility and creativity are needed in the application of these generalizations. In sum, we suggest that presenters consult the advice, use it where they can, and break the rules when they must.

QUESTIONS AND PROJECTS FOR FURTHER STUDY

1   How can you best combine expressing genuine commitments together with the skills of message preparation and self-presentation? In your experience, which resources discussed in this book are most useful for exploiting the opportunities and overcoming the obstacles persuaders confront? Is it possible, in your opinion, to strategize, organize, and still appear authentic?

2   In your view, which type of audience is hardest to adapt to: a hostile or highly critical audience, an indifferent and uninformed audience, a conflicted audience, a sympathetic audience, or an audience containing a mix of all these audience segments?

3   Consider blogs in light of the discussion in this chapter. Which, if any, of the ideas discussed here are integrated into to blogosphere?

4   Watch the 1968 powerful video recounting Jane Elliot's exercise with her students. Was her approach to persuasion ethical? Evaluate and discuss it.

5   Think about the many classroom speeches and lectures you have heard in your college career. Who stands out and why? Evaluate the excellent instructors in light of what you've learned in this chapter.

EXERCISES

1   Try practicing a presentation aloud without deliberately altering your wording. Do you experience a tendency to over-memorize? On the other hand, have you experienced the benefits of talking a speech through conversationally with a friend, perhaps relying only on a minimal outline? Do a 6-minute, but professional, persuasive presentation for your class using an outline with no more than 10 words or phrases, plus the quotations or complex statistics that you might find necessary to type out verbatim and then read to your audience.

2   Try experimenting with different message designs, for example, an explicit up-front statement of thesis versus a message that builds logically to a conclusion, or a one-sided message versus a both-sided message that is either refutational or non-refutational. Test-market these alternative designs with people similar to those you will ultimately attempt to persuade.

3   Plan and execute a 60-second guest radio editorial for a fictitious radio station on Main Campus. Submit a recording plus a two- to three-page strategic plan. Be sure to include the test-marketing stage.

4   Look more deeply into the persuasive practices of historical figures. Read the speeches and learn about Frederick Douglass. Using the PowerPoint tips in the chapter, create an effective presentation wherein you make the case for how and why a historical figure exemplified excellence in persuasion.

5   Spend one hour viewing or listening to a nationally known political partisan commentator (like Bill O'Reilly or Rachel Maddow) who holds a view very different from your own. Evaluate the persuasive message considering the text's discussion of adapting to audiences. Write a report and make a brief presentation to your class, integrating the advice provided in this chapter concerning excellence in presentations.

KEY TERMS

- Curse of knowledge
- Demographic analysis
- Digital immigrant
- Digital native
- Ethnographic inquiry
- Human-scale principle

- Method of residues
- NESC
- Pre-persuasion
- Sinatra test
- Springboard story
- Stickiness

REFERENCES

Douglass, F. (2004). *Narrative of the life of Frederick Douglass: An American slave*. Whitefish, MT: Kessinger Publishing. (Original work published 1845)

Garrison, W. L. (2004). Preface. In Douglass, F., *Narrative of the life of Frederick Douglass: An American slave*. Whitefish, MT: Kessinger Publishing. (Original work published 1845)

Hamlin, S. (1998). *What makes juries listen today?* Little Falls, NJ: Glasser LegalWorks.

Heath, C., & Heath, D. (2007a). *Made to stick: Why some ideas survive and others die*. New York: Random House.

Heath, C., & Heath, D. (2007b, February 20). Right-handed cats and the gap theory of curiosity. *PowellsBooks.Blog*. Retrieved June 29, 2009, from www.powells.com/blog/?p=1854

Leyner, M., & Goldberg, B. (2005). *Why do men have nipples? Hundreds of questions you'd only ask a doctor after your third Martini*. New York: Three Rivers Press.

Luntz, F. (2009). The language of healthcare 2009. Retrieved June 29, 2009, from http://wonkroom. thinkprogress.org/wp-content/uploads/2009/05/ frank-luntz-the-language-of-healthcare–20091.pdf

Pink, D. (2012). *To sell is human*. New York: Riverhead Books.

Prensky, M. (2005/2006). Listen to the natives. *Educational Leadership*, 63(4). Retrieved June 28, 2009, from www.ascd.org/authors/ed_lead/el2005 12_prensky.html

Strupp, J., & Willis, O. (2013, October 7). *Study confirms Fox used GOP-friendly language to try to stop health care reform*. Retrieved November 18, 2014, from Mediamatters for America: http://mediamatters. org/blog/2013/10/07/study-confirms-fox-used-gop-friendly-language-t/196319

Wright, P. (2002). Marketplace metacognition and social intelligence. *Journal of Consumer Research*, 677–682.

CHAPTER 10

Persuasive Campaigns

- **Campaign Stages and Components**
- **Types of Campaigns**
- **Public Relations Campaigns**
- **Indoctrination Campaigns**
- **Summary**
- **Questions and Projects for Further Study**
- **Exercises**
- **Key Terms**
- **References**

On January 1, 2014, Brittany Maynard was told that she had terminal cancer. Not only that, but her cancer was particularly vicious, and after initial treatment, she was told in April that she had stage four brain cancer and just six months to live. She was just 29 and recently married, and now she was facing a future where she would endure terrible pain, seizures, and loss of her mental abilities. After researching her situation, she decided against chemotherapy and radiation, and with her husband and parents, left her home in California to relocate in Oregon, a state that allowed terminally ill patients to end their lives legally with the assistance of a physician and under careful conditions. Maynard had decided that she wished to have the option of ending her life on her own terms, at a time that made sense for her family and for her. She created a list of things she wished to do, including trips to Canada, British Columbia, and the Grand Canyon, and set her death date for November 1.

Maynard also resolved to make her story public and to advocate for a cause that had suddenly become central in her life: the Death with Dignity movement. At the time of her diagnosis, only five states permitted physician-assisted death for terminal patients, and Maynard believed the option should be open to all. She was angry this was not the reality in the United States and that she had to move to a neighboring state to exercise the right; furthermore, she understood that most terminally ill people would not have the flexibility and the finances to do what she was doing. She aligned with the most prominent organization working on this issues, *Compassion and Choices*, a non-profit that works to improve patient rights and choices for the terminally ill, and beginning October 6, she launched an online video campaign where she "became a champion for expanding death-with-dignity laws nationwide" (Miller, 2014). In effect, she started her own campaign to fight for this cause.

The issue was polarizing, as Maynard knew it would be; she knew she would face criticism. Many argued on religious ground that only God can end a life, and that "suicide" is always against God's plan. Often these views came from those facing similar situations. Examples abound, but long-term quadriplegic and devout evangelical Christian Joni Eareckson Tada exemplifies the religious view well as she proclaimed:

> If I could spend a few moments with Brittany before she swallows that prescription she has already filled, I would tell her how I have felt the love of Jesus strengthen and comfort me through my own cancer, chronic pain and quadriplegia.
>
> (Tada, 2014)

Others feared that *Compassion and Choices* was taking advantage of Maynard to advance their own goals. Wesley J. Smith articulated this view as he argued that "assisted suicide movement leaders are *always on the lookout for attractive cases to further their cause*, and clearly believe they have one in Maynard" (2014).

Maynard faced the criticisms with grace and poise, answered the objections, and kept the focus on telling her story. She proclaimed that she was not committing suicide, resisting from the start that framing of the issue. In her mind, it was cancer was killing her. She loved life and did not want to die. Therefore, it made no sense to label her choice as "suicide." When it came to religious objections, she noted that others, who did not even know her, could not impose their belief systems onto her life. She noted again and again that she had done her research and was making a carefully and fully informed decision. No one was forcing her, and no one was controlling her.

She quickly found that she had a national platform from which to advocate, as in the weeks after its release, more than 9 million people viewed the video of her describing her illness and talking about her recent wedding, how much she will miss her beloved dogs, and all of the things she wanted to do before she died, and she set her death date for November 1 (Sanburn, 2014). Mainstream print and broadcast outlets found her a compelling spokesperson, and rushed to share her story. It also didn't hurt that Maynard was young, beautiful, intelligent, and well-spoken. Her personal biography was compelling, and she was presented as a person who had led a life of global adventure and mission, and now she was going to face death as she had lived her life: head on.

On November 1, 2014, Maynard ended in her Oregon home, surrounded by her loved ones, and the impact of her campaign continued on after her death. In December, 2014 she was named as one of *People* magazine's 25 most intriguing people of 2014 for her role as "The Crusader" in the death-with-dignity movement. In the two months after her campaign began, 20 newspapers in 11 states endorsed death with dignity and lawmakers in 16 states pledged to introduce bills (*Brittany Maynard Named*, 2014). In addition, Brittany left behind *TheBrittanyFund.org* to continue her work, and Compassion and Choices continues her advocacy moving forward.

The Maynard-led effort to advance death with dignity is a model of campaign effectiveness. The single speech or other one-shot communication described in Chapter 9 is important, but seldom does it achieve a significant, enduring impact on its own. That job is left to persuasive campaigns—organized, sustained attempts at influencing groups or masses of people through a series of messages. Campaigns take many forms—political campaigns (discussed in Chapter 11), product advertising campaigns (Chapter 12), and various issue-oriented campaigns (Chapters 10 and 14). This chapter discusses other campaign types, presents a model of campaigning as a multi-stage, multi-message process, and then explores in more detail two particular types of campaigns: **public relations campaigns** and **indoctrination campaigns**.

CAMPAIGN STAGES AND COMPONENTS

Campaigns proceed developmentally, through stages, each stage building on the last, yet each exhibiting a life of its own. The following outline of stages and their respective components is intended to be quite general, so as to encompass a wide variety of campaign types. As indicated by Figure 10.1, the stages in our model do not terminate as each "next" stage begins; planning, for example, is a continuous process throughout any campaign.

A Planning

Campaigns first arise from a sense that interests (e.g., a corporation's profits) or values (e.g., a people's safety or survival) held dear by an organization must be protected or advanced. But to succeed, a campaign must have specific goals. The goal might be to elicit specific behaviors, earning, for example, enough votes to win election as club president, or enough raffle sales to enable the college orchestra to make an overseas trip, or enough support from local townspeople to get city council approval for a bicycle-only lane on Main Street. Or the goal might be more abstract, as when a campaign is less concerned with specific behavioral payoffs than with influencing beliefs and values.

Goal Setting

The audience and situation are central components in the formulation of goals. For example, a fundraising campaign on behalf of a community orchestra should not be so aggressive that it garners the orchestra an overseas trip at the price of reduced attendance at local concerts. Other concerns arise as well in goal formulation. For

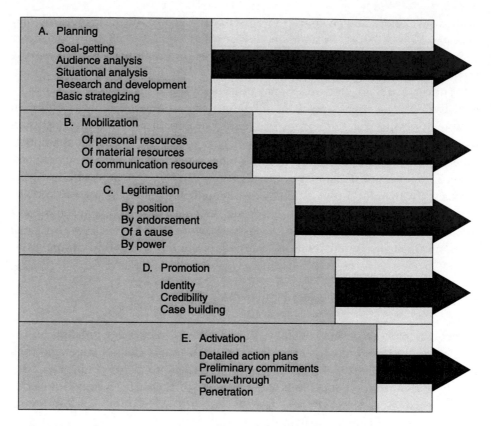

FIGURE 10.1   *Campaign stages and components model (CSCM).*
Reprinted with permission of Herbert W. Simons from Persuasion: Understanding, Practice, and Analysis

instance, will those who volunteer for this fundraising effort feel good about themselves when it's been completed? Will they have made friends rather than lost them, honored their consciences rather than betrayed them? Can people commit to the cause without feeling utterly consumed by it? The organization, for example, would not want to sell raffle tickets to raise money if events involving gambling would compromise the ethics of its members.

Situations are seldom ideal for the fulfillment of campaign goals. Given that, it is always a good idea to formulate primary goals at several levels, including (a) what the campaign would ideally like to achieve, (b) what it expects to achieve, and (c) what would be the bare minimum that would still make the campaign worthwhile. Such analysis is crucially important and can save much time and frustration later, because there are times when a large-scale information campaign is of questionable value when measured against the time, effort, and money expended to conduct it. For example, it has proven far more effective—and cheaper—to simply mandate installation of air bags in automobiles rather than to construct a campaign to educate and convince consumers that air bags are an option they should purchase for their automobiles.

An example of flexible goal setting involves efforts by the Temple Issues Forum (TIF) to place issues of higher education higher on the agenda in Philadelphia city politics. TIF's official mission was to promote public debate and discussion at Temple University on issues of potential interest to the university community. Its main purpose was to stimulate civic and intellectual engagement by students, not to influence city politics. But having run a televised mayoral forum at Temple on the topic of "Higher education and the city," TIF's planning group identified a number of issues that fairly begged to be addressed through the long term and not just by way of a one-time-only mayoral forum. These included issues of marketing the city as a world-class center for higher education and of encouraging its college and university graduates to remain in the city and perhaps start businesses in the area. It included as well issues of urban education: how better to prepare urban high school graduates to do college-level work.

TIF's planning group toyed with the possibility of promoting action on all these fronts, and it even talked with a foundation representative about organizing a consortium of colleges and universities in the Philadelphia area to be called "Greater Collegiate Philadelphia." But group members knew that this goal was remote, although the other goals were difficult to realize but not completely beyond the group's capacity to make a difference. Minimally speaking, TIF's planning group was confident it could succeed at its agenda-setting goal, and it anticipated that everyone, including TIF itself, would benefit from the mayoral forum. So, in keeping with the principles of goal seeking, TIF had short- and long-term goals, as well as optimal, realistic, and minimal goals.

TIF's planning group began with faculty and administrators inexperienced at urban affairs, but it expanded to include urban specialists. Still, its top leadership was inexpert at managing the more ambitious aspects of its campaign plan. They therefore sought out consultants, including city representatives who had been working on some of these issues for quite some time.

Formulating a Basic Strategy

Although campaign strategies must frequently be revised in light of new developments, it is nevertheless possible at the outset to formulate global strategies. A basic, coactive rule of basic strategizing is that to get what you want you must help those you're trying to influence get what they want.

Some campaigns persuade indirectly. Safe sex and pro-social sexual attitudes have been promoted indirectly on social media beamed at teenagers that mixes nine parts entertainment with one part serious instruction. Use of designated drivers after parties has been promoted via planted dialogue in television sitcoms. Consumer goods are promoted in entertainment programming via product placement, as are corporate images—all for a price. Some corporate public relations efforts proceed by way of low-visibility campaigns—a news report favorable to the company planted in one news outlet, an editorial planted in another.

Basic strategizing often involves selecting an appropriate frame for the appropriate time and situation. Affirmative action, for example, sells poorly as "preference" but well under the rubric of "fairness." Some health maintenance campaigns do well stressing the benefits associated with performing healthy behaviors; others do well stressing the costs associated with not doing so. Abortion can be framed as murder or as a woman's choice, but advocates of legalized abortion have found it increasingly difficult to frame their arguments for reproductive choice as being grounded in protection of the mother's life. The days of illegal and dangerous back-alley abortions have faded from public memory, making the "choice" frame less powerful than it once was.

Reform-minded groups often combine persuasion with coercion (e.g., threats) and material inducements (e.g., promises of benefits) in campaigning for social change. Campaigns for environmental protection, tobacco regulation, consumer protection, and auto safety requirements have combined agitation with litigation. Even when change advocates have lost in the courts, the publicity given their court challenges has succeeded in whipping up public fervor, especially when children were shown to be among the primary victims.

Normative influence can also alter behavior and might find its way into a campaign. For example, social ostracism is increasingly being used in place of imprisonment in campaigns to rid inner-city communities of drug dealers. Humiliation rather than incarceration is also becoming the strategy of choice in curbing pornography in cyberspace and child abuse. Confronted with a shoplifter, a California judge ordered the guilty individual to wear a T-shirt that said in bold letters: "I Am a Thief."

Some reformers believe that it may be possible to devise campaigns to effect sweeping changes in social norms, for example, by making it unpopular for teenagers to use drugs, keep guns, practice unsafe sex, and smoke tobacco. A California public ad campaign targeted to African Americans showed a black child with a faded-out image of a smoking woman in the background. The ad read, "He has his daddy's eyes and his momma's lungs. Secondhand smoke kills." The implications of this ad are (a) "Smoking kills," and (b) "We must protect our children" (*Working to Inspire Social Change*, 2014).

In devising basic strategies, as in formulating campaign goals, planners need to be alert to the possibilities of unintended, undesired effects. A health education program encouraging weight control may exacerbate problems of anorexia and bulimia, and can also lead to "fat shaming." Public service advertisements such as the one depicting black smokers as inattentive parents may, by their use of negative presentations, may create unhelpful racial stereotypes.

Social activists need also to balance what they perceive to be the good of the community against threats to the assumed beneficiary's autonomy. What could be better, asks the social engineer, than to find ways to substantially reduce self-destructive teenage practices by using peer pressure to get young people to conform to positive norms or face rejection? Certainly this is preferable to incarceration on the one hand or no influence on the other. Yet libertarians have long echoed John Stuart Mill's conclusion that normative control represents "a social tyranny more formidable than many kinds of political oppression, since, though not usually upheld by such extreme penalties, it leaves fewer means of escape, penetrating more deeply into the details of life, and enslaving the soul itself" (1859).

The strategies identified in this section can be ordered on a continuum from most controlling to least controlling. In their classic work, Zaltman and Duncan (1977) identify *power* strategies as the most controlling. Examples include legal mandates, brute force, threats, and control over financial resources. Next comes *persuasion*, as in commercial advertising and campaign speeches. These strategies, so necessary in motivating individuals and in overcoming their resistance, are nevertheless considered manipulative by Zaltman and Duncan, and more repressive than their third category, which they call *normative-reeducative*. Campaigns described as "public information" fall solidly within this category, especially when the issue in question is how best to solve an acknowledged problem (e.g., drunk driving) and the presentation is relatively unbiased. Finally, Zaltman and Duncan list *facilitation*, a strategy by which foundations and government agencies seek to promote the arts or aid communities by providing them with additional resources, "no strings attached." This strategy assumes that the beneficiary is capable of rationally committing those resources to useful ends.

Choosing less controlling strategies can be problematic. A small-scale, short-term, media-only information campaign directed at a widespread, longstanding, systemic social problem is bound to fail. Are drug addicts "freer" for not having given up their self-destructive habits because some well-meaning health officials believed that ineffectual public information campaigns were ethically more preferable than more potent but more controlling power and persuasion strategies? Who gets to decide which aid beneficiaries are so rational that they can be offered resources with no restrictions attached? If a community leader pockets the money rather than using it to assist the community, was the resource strategy truly freedom enhancing or freedom restricting?

B Mobilization

Mobilization consists of locating, acquiring, developing, and exploiting the material and human resources necessary to run the campaign. What management experts refer to as the research and development function of business organizations has its counterpart in persuasive campaigns. It involves the gathering of arguments and evidence to be used in building persuasive messages, as well as the development of know-how for implementation. The failure to take these necessary steps is common among amateur campaigners. One well-intentioned student attempted to launch a campaign to require bicycle safety education in public schools. Intuitively, he decided that the best way to get action was to testify at a meeting of the city school board. Unfortunately, he had not yet come up with a plan for such a program, discovered how and where decisions of this type are made in the school system, sought to determine whether any groups might have been interested in aiding his campaign, or even developed documented proof of the existence of a problem. He ended up seriously embarrassing himself and undercutting his campaign before it had gotten off the ground.

A clever group can work toward fulfilling several campaign requirements simultaneously. At a metropolitan university, several students sought to organize a consumer action group. The leaders recognized that they would need student support to build and maintain the organization and advance its goals and they sought an approach that would help legitimize the group and promote its values at the same time. A mini-campaign was launched for a campus referendum on whether the campus bookstore should sell goods such as college logo sweatshirts that had been produced in foreign sweatshops. The vote was in favor of not using sweatshop-produced products, and the group went next to the administration with a strongly worded request that the bookstore's policies be adjusted to support fair-trade products—or find itself in the embarrassing situation of opposing an organization that had widespread student support. Not surprisingly, the administration proved anxious to please.

Other resources may include access to channels of influence and to the mass media, as well as basic information and know-how needed to communicate effectively. A student body leader used her acquaintance with the mayor's daughter as a way of gaining access to the mayor, who proved to be a valuable supporter. Another used the business contacts he'd made during his internship to find high-level support, advice, and assistance. Commercial organizations have long purchased market analyses, mailing lists, media expertise, and media time. Indeed, television advertising alone can easily take up 70% or more of a political campaign budget.

C Legitimation

Legitimacy is something conferred by others. Implicitly or explicitly, they grant the right to be heard and be taken seriously and perhaps even the right to issue binding directives. If a campaign organization lacks legitimacy at the outset, its leadership needs to be anointed with legitimacy—if only for purposes of the campaign—by those who already possess it. Hence, the importance of what Bettinghaus and Cody call "checking in with the power base" (1994). This may include not only those in official positions of power but also informal opinion leaders:

> The role of the legitimizer is a peculiar one. He is seldom active in the early stages of a social-action campaign. He does not make speeches in favor of the proposal. He does not write letters to the newspaper, and he frequently will ask that his name not be associated with the new idea. He may not want to give a formal approval to a new

proposal. But he can effectively block the adoption of a new idea by saying, "No!" If he simply agrees that a proposal is a desirable one he may well clear the way for future operations by the change agent and eventual adoption of the proposal.

(Bettinghaus & Cody, 1994)

The more popular one's cause, the easier it is to acquire authority and to gain endorsements from power brokers. Those seeking minor reforms may well be granted the blessings of key legitimizers. But those seeking more widespread changes are likely to threaten the institution or community's interests in preserving the status quo; they can therefore expect to be threatened by opponents of change. Still, the change-minded group may use coactive persuasion to establish its legitimacy by representing its cause as one that any virtuous individual must endorse. Programs may be defended in the name of God or the Founding Fathers or the Constitution or the legitimizers' pocketbook interests. Here the promotion of a cause and the legitimacy of its campaign are joined.

D Promotion

Once a campaign has taken effective steps to plan, mobilize resources, and secure legitimacy, it is in a powerful position to promote itself before a wider audience. Effective promotion, in turn, should open doors that may have previously been closed to personnel, material, and communication resources, as well as endorsements by key influencers. The ideal persuasive campaign has continuity from beginning to end of the promotion process. An advertising campaign may first leak information about an exciting new product via social media, seeking to make the message go viral as an interesting rumor. Then, the official product rollout will take place, a public event attended by celebrities and regular folk, where the product will be formally introduced and hyped. In conjunction with the public rollout, simultaneous blanket advertising will appear in traditional print and broadcast media outlets. Then, users will begin weighing in on social media with positive reviews of the product, which will add to its dominance in the marketplace. After the new product has become established, later campaigns may tone down the original appeal to novelty and focusing instead on features that have been added. These updates, presented in a campaign that is similar to the first product launch, will create "buzz" and make the updated version of the product a "must have."

Four elements are key to promotion for campaigns. As already noted in this chapter, a campaign must have (1) effective planning that creates a winning case, and (2) legitimacy via continued support from key decision makers. In addition, and detailed below, successful advocacy requires that the campaign creates, promotes, and sustains (3) identity and (4) credibility.

Identity

Political candidates are nowhere without name recognition. Commercial advertisements do better getting negative attention than no attention. Worthy charities must somehow stand out from others making a claim on the public's generosity. So it is that campaign managers work assiduously at formulating memorable slogans, devising labels and catchy jingles, and finding clever ways to build repetition of the same campaign themes.

Effective identification symbols are those that serve members of the campaign organization (giving them an identity), as well as the larger public. Some groups choose identification symbols mostly to promote in-group solidarity. These may include special songs, handshakes, flags, ceremonies, uniforms, and speech patterns. Others seek to export their symbols to the greater public. For example, the original pink ribbon campaign of the Susan G. Komen Foundation was in support of those who had survived breast cancer, but the ribbon and the color pink have now evolved into widespread symbols in support of research for breast cancer. Now, every October, during Breast Cancer Awareness Month, it is "pink and balloons, women smiling in sneakers walking and walking, companies slapping breast cancer logos onto every bit of merchandise under the sun" (Doucette, 2014). The identification of pink items with breast cancer awareness has been so successful that there is now a counter-campaign that offers commentary on the wisdom of the pink ribbons, where critics worry that not enough money is actually going into breast cancer research.

FIGURE 10.2 *Some see the pink ribbon as evidence of successful campaign penetration; others see it as evidence that the fight against breast cancer has been diffused and resist what they call "pinkwashing." In that, we see a persuasive advocacy campaign being challenged by a new campaign which critiques its practices.*

The concern is not with the ribbons, but with the corporations who have seen marketing opportunities. Called "pinkwashing," the critique focuses on "a company or organization that claims to care about breast cancer by promoting a pink ribbon product, but at the same time produces, manufactures and/or sells products that are linked to the disease" (*Before You Buy Pink*, n.d.). In addition, critics worry that the "pervasiveness of the pink ribbon campaign leads many people to believe that the fight against breast cancer is progressing, when in truth it's barely begun" (Lerner, 2010). This critique shows the original campaign's success and shortcomings, as critics condemn how successfully the pink ribbon has come to be identified with breast cancer awareness. In addition, it is interesting to note that the use of the terminology "pinkwashing" has created a counter-identity by which the new persuasive campaign resists the first one.

Credibility

Moving beyond the creation of a favorable and memorable identity, the campaign leadership must establish its own believability as well as the credibility of the group as a whole. The first step for leaders is to promote respect, trust, and attraction from their own followers. Here, especially, deeds, not just words, are important. Occasionally, followers will be taken in by a charismatic firebrand, but for the most part they will want concrete evidence that this individual has their interests at heart, is capable of delivering, and possesses such qualities as intelligence and expertise, honesty and dependability, and maturity and good judgment.

Establishing personal or group credibility to the satisfaction of suspicious outsiders may be considerably more difficult.

E Activation

Building a compelling case is not enough. Unless the campaigner seeks only to communicate information or to modify attitudes, it is necessary to make special provisions for the action stage.

Detailed Action Plans

Campaigns often fail because the campaign target lacks specific information on how to act. Voters must be told where to vote and how to vote. People with problems must learn how to get help. In the case of campaigns for institutional change, there are bound to be misinterpretations unless plans for action are made concrete. According to the Center for State and Local Policy, a formal action plan (1) involves central campaign members from the start, (2) identifies clear goals, (3) creates a consistent message, (4) develops a timeline, and (5) creates a plan for sharing information, including a memorable website (O'Hara, 2008). As the Center notes, a well-designed campaign not only provides a desired result, but also creates networking opportunities for the organization, promotes the cause, raises the visibility and credibility of the organization, and develops positive relationships for the future (O'Hara, 2008).

Preliminary Commitments

Professional campaigners have learned that it is wise to secure partial, preliminary commitments from people before the final action is taken. Short of obtaining cash donations, charity solicitors may work toward obtaining campaign pledges. Realtors may offer rentals of homes with options to buy. Sales organizations may allow free home trials for the price of a refundable deposit. If at all possible, the preliminary commitment should be of a public nature and should entail some effort by the individual. The attitude of the individual should be strengthened by the act of overt commitment.

Follow-Through

On Election Day, each major party mobilizes a large campaign organization for poll watching, telephoning, chauffeuring, babysitting, and so on. Advertisers seek to make buying a habit among those who have made initial commitments. Revivalist campaigns work at translating instant "conversions" into weekly church attendance.

Social activists may be granted authority and resources to put programs into operation themselves (at least on a trial basis), or they may get promises of action from an institution. In the latter case, more than one externally initiated program has failed for lack of administrative follow-through. The campaign organizations have been at least partially to blame for not maintaining the pressure. A good rule of institutions is that institutional policies are what their administrators do about them. Often, it is precious little.

In the case of programs administered initially by the campaign organization itself, there is a similar danger that once the innovation has been effectively sold, campaign activists will become lazy or indifferent or begin caring more about their reputations than about the persons they claim to be serving. At some point, the new innovation must be institutionalized, and this is another juncture fraught with potential problems. Several years ago, a group of students at an urban university helped form a voluntary organization that successfully ran a day camp for disadvantaged children. For three summers, the organization endured and even thrived on its poverty, its dearth of trained leaders, and its lack of formal ties to the university. Then, with the members' consent, the university began providing large amounts of money, facilities, and technical assistance. The support was now there, but the spirit was gone. The appropriate socioemotional adjustments for institutionalization had not been made.

Penetration

In the ideal campaign, those reached directly become persuaders themselves. Advertisers dance for joy when radio listeners begin humming aloud the jingle they have heard in the commercial. New converts to a religious group are often asked to proselytize in its behalf. Political campaigners often rely on opinion leaders to carry their television messages to others. In each case, there is penetration beyond the initial receivers to their own interpersonal networks.

The effective conclusion to a campaign for institutional change occurs not simply when the change is put into practice but when others begin hearing about it, speaking favorably about it, and even attempting to emulate it. Serving as a model for others is often a small campaign group's most important accomplishment.

Social activism finds some of its most difficult challenges in communities wedded to health-endangering traditions. Research shows that best practices for penetration have been known for decades, as theorists have identified five components of the change process: (1) identifying community leaders willing and able to bestow legitimacy on campaign messages and activities, (2) identifying leaders and organizations most effective in sustaining long-term coordinative activity, (3) generating media and other education campaign strategies geared to the community's social and cultural traditions, (4) dealing with potential conflict in the community over the campaign's goals and activities, and (5) creating long-term impact on the community's allocation of resources (Finnegan, et al., 1989). Coactive strategies of persuasion are widely used in promotion of the campaign's objectives.

6 Evaluation

Campaign assessments should take place periodically to make corrections in the path of campaigns, and, at their conclusion, to evaluate their overall effectiveness. Small-scale campaigns may be forced to rely on informal surveys and self-assessments; large, well-funded campaigns must answer to their donors whether the benefits exceeded the costs. Formal surveys and focus groups are staples of campaign evaluations, but better still is evidence of concrete achievements. Evaluation should always have an eye toward the original goals of the campaign, and can be (1) *formative* (employing pre- and post-testing), (2) *process-oriented* (examining how closely the campaign followed the original plan), (3) *summative* (assessing outcomes, usually via quantitative methods), or (4) *effectiveness-focused* (measuring attitudinal and behavioral change) (Rice & Atkins, 2013).

Concerning health campaigns, Storey (2008) has evidenced the difficulties in overcoming resistance to changes in bad habits like excessive smoking and over-eating, particularly with people disinclined to attend to proactive health messages in the media. Still, it is heartening that health education campaigns do make a difference. Snyder, Hamilton, Mitchell, Kiwanuka-Tondo, Fleming-Milici, and Proctor analyzed 48 health campaigns conducted in the United States for which evaluation data could be found in the published literature. Overall, they found that health communication campaigns using mass media achieved on average an eight percentage point change in behavior among members of the targeted population, with greater effect sizes achieved by campaigns that targeted larger audiences. The size of the effect varied by type of behavior, with seat belt use, oral health, and alcohol abuse reduction campaigns being the most successful. Greater effects were found for campaigns focused on adoption of new behaviors compared with prevention or cessation of problem behaviors (Snyder, et al., 2004).

TYPES OF CAMPAIGNS

Campaigns take many forms. Some are multimillion-dollar efforts by *Fortune 500* companies. Others are grassroots undertakings by fledgling social movements that must rely exclusively on volunteers. By use of advertising, a well-heeled product manufacturer or political candidate can control the content, placement, and timing of a message, in this way enhancing the likelihood of reaching the intended target with the intended message. Well-respected groups such as the League of Women Voters and the United Way can also count on generous dollops of free publicity. Health education campaigns typically have the weight of public opinion behind them.

But groups out of the mainstream are likely to be struggling for traditional media attention or given negative attention by the news media and rarely have sufficient resources for paid advertising (Baxter, 1981; Gitlin, 1980; Salmon, 1989; Rice & Atkins, 2013). Moreover, to successfully advance a program markedly at odds with prevailing norms is far more difficult than, say, encouraging allegiance to the flag, even when a "deviant" group has ample resources and equal media access.

Campaigns by social movements (see Chapter 14) typically lack legitimacy. Conversely, public schools have so much legitimacy that their efforts at indoctrinating young children aren't usually thought of as persuasive campaigns at all. The socialization of young children has historically involved the passing on of a tradition, uncontested and unopposed. Campaigns not labeled as such typically enjoy uncontested control over communication channels of every sort—from the family to the mass media—and tend therefore to be powerful indeed.

Convincing people to embrace a new doctrine, or ideology, or lifestyle (i.e., indoctrination) is different from selling a product or promoting a candidate or corporate image. Consider, for example, the differences between product advertising

Thinking It Through

Did your school wage a "campaign" to persuade you to become a good citizen? What do you think about the framing of elementary education in such a manner?

FIGURE 10.3 *We don't generally think of schools as places of persuasive campaigns, but the socialization of young children has historically involved the passing on of a tradition, uncontested and unopposed. Campaigns not labeled as such typically enjoy uncontested control over communication channels of every sort—from the family to the mass media—and tend therefore to be powerful indeed.*
Source: http://ww1.hdnux.com/photos/30/45/66/6446516/3/628x471.jpg

campaigns (see Chapter 12) and political campaigns (see Chapter 11). Both are generally well-organized, carefully planned activities, extending through long periods. Yet in a political campaign, said Republican consultant John Deardourff:

> All of the sales take place on the same day. The timing is important. You deliver on Election Day or it doesn't make a difference. In political advertising you are not interested in small market shares. The political advertiser can't be satisfied until he has 51% of the market. The political salesman—I hate that term—has got to find ways to communicate with all kinds of people. The commercial advertiser knows how much money he will spend. But in a political campaign you almost never know. You improvise.
>
> (Quoted in Blumenthal, 1980, p. 188)

Even sharper contrasts may be drawn between advertising campaigns and indoctrination campaigns. In the latter, there is generally no equivalent of a product to purchase or a place such as a supermarket at which to purchase it. Individuals might experiment with ideologies and lifestyles, but generally this comes at much greater cost than in trying out most commercial products. For example, imagine, if you will, the task of selling the Chinese communist leadership at the time of their decision in 1937 to join forces with their former deadly enemy, the nationalist Kuomintang, so that they could be a united front against China's Japanese invaders. One moment, the communist guerrillas are ordered to kill anyone wearing the uniform of the Kuomintang; the next moment, they had to be persuaded to take off the Red Star insignias that they had worn proudly on the shoulders of their uniforms and replace them with the emblems of their former enemy. As this example illustrates, conversions to new ways of thinking involve much greater commitments, and, of course, there are no money-back guarantees.

We now turn our attention to two sorts of persuasive campaigns, broadly considered: public relations campaigns and indoctrination campaigns.

PUBLIC RELATIONS CAMPAIGNS

Depending on which author you read, public relations campaigns are either the scourge of modern society or the source of much of its progress. Keith Butterick notes that critics of public relations argue that it is impossible to define the field because "there is nothing of substance to PR: it is all illusion, all spin and floss" (2011). Rampton and Stauber argue that the public relations industry seems sometimes to "take perverse pleasure in exploring the 'intellectual' challenge of rehabilitating clients who are appalling beyond the pale" (2001). They note that following the rape conviction of Mike Tyson and the controversial acquittal of O. J. Simpson on murder charges, the trade periodical *Public Relations Tactics* devoted its cover story and several articles to discussing how best one might manage the public relations challenges of these two men (Rampton & Stauber, 2001). And says Robert Jackall, "In the world of public relations, there is no such thing as a notion of truth; there are only stories, perspectives, or opinions" (2010).

PR proponents deny the charge of ethical indifference, pointing with pride to the code of ethics and accreditation program of the Public Relations Society of America. They insist that public relations is not "mere" rhetoric or spin; rather, "its main aim is to create understanding" (Baines, et al., 2004). It stands above and in contrast to "advertising, whose main aim is to generate awareness and sales, or propaganda, whose aim is to suggest (in the true meaning of the word) what individuals should believe" (Baines, et al., 2004). Public relations advocates argue that their clients, like defendants in a criminal trial, have a right to the best possible representation. PR critics respond that the courtroom is inherently adversarial, and that entitles each side to place its best possible case before the judge and jury. PR firms, by contrast, offer their services to one side only, and that side tends to be richer and more powerful. PR proponents deny that they operate in non-competitive environments—sometimes yes, more commonly no. Moreover, the tactics of persuasion they use in making a corporate client look good are not much different from those any one of us uses on a day-to-day basis in making ourselves look good. PR critics respond that this is just PR about PR (Jackall, 2010).

Public relations campaigns address issues with a view toward heading off problems, managing crises, sometimes going on the offensive, but in all cases attempting to make their clients look good (Newsom, et al., 1989; Jackall, 2010). Looking good can in turn translate into increased sales, new clients, stock popularity, political access, respect within the industry, and much more.

Two types of PR efforts are singled out for attention here: **corporate issue advocacy** and **crisis management campaigns**.

Corporate Issue Advocacy

Many organizations take public stands on controversial issues: Industry lobbies, social movements, opinion magazines, professional organizations such as the American Medical Association, political action committees, and political parties are among them. Until relatively recently, large corporations were reluctant to get into the fray lest, in pleasing some consumers, they offended others. But over the last 40 years, times have changed, and corporate America, led by the Mobil Corporation (now merged with Exxon), has led the way. We turn now to an analysis of a classic public relations campaign.

Upon viewing this campaign, the first thing we notice is how timely it seems. The print ad analyzed below, with very little adjustment, could run today. The buzz words and the issues remain much the same as they were when the ad first appeared. Stereotypes used are completely recognizable. In light of the global changes the world has seen since this campaign's genesis, it is fascinating to see how the rhetorical maneuvers used still resonate.

Mobil's issue advocacy campaign began in 1970. It placed editorial ads, known as **advertorials**, in major newspapers, magazines, and service club magazines. From time to time, it also sought access to the television airwaves. This proved difficult in the 1970s because of network restrictions and federal regulations, but Mobil managed nonetheless to piece together the equivalent of its own network for an award-winning ad series called "Fables for Now." The network consisted of independent outlets and network affiliates from which Mobil purchased 30 minutes of airtime for high-class entertainment programming comparable with its *Masterpiece Theater* series on PBS. Into this aristocratic fictional environment Mobil placed its semi-fictional "Fables"—all cleverly mounted "lessons for now" performed by leading arts companies. These ads, it was assumed, would reap image benefits for Mobil even if its arguments weren't convincing. But Mobil's arguments were convincing, in part because they were framed in a disarming entertainment context.

Less effective—and pulled off the air—was an ad series commingling Mobil editorializing with the appearance of television news reporting. Many viewers objected to these ads as deceptive even as they were pulled in by "fables" editorializing in the guise of entertainment.

Still, the most enduring of Mobil's advocacy campaigns has been its print advertorial series. Like other large corporations, Mobil focused on environmental issues, public health and safety, and what it took to be excessive taxation and regulation by government (Smith & Heath, 1990; Sterling, 2009). Mobil's Herb Schmertz believed corporate America had a story to tell, one that might reach the intellectual establishment with correctives to what he and his colleagues at Mobil took to be anti-business editorializing and reporting by the mainstream press. The need for the petrochemical industry to tell its side of the story seemed especially pressing at the time. Mobil and the other big oil companies had been accused during the 1970s of creating artificial oil shortages, exerting monopoly control of oil resources, reaping windfall profits, polluting air and water, colluding with oil-producing nations, bribing politicians in other lands, making illegal campaign contributions, and withholding information. But Mobil was also at this time riding the winds of change toward political conservatism in America, a trend manifested in part by shifts among some leading liberals toward the conservative camp. There was already a movement in Washington toward lower corporate taxes and deregulation—a movement, by the way, that Mobil executives claimed to have helped propel by Mobil's advertorials.

Any analysis of individual campaign messages is often enhanced by placing them within their larger campaign contexts. The advertorial reproduced in Figure 10.4 appeared early in Mobil's efforts to answer industry critics while attempting to win support for its pro-business philosophy. Before pronouncing judgment on this message, we must consider where Mobil was coming from and where it was heading. A clue to its image management objectives is to be found in the title: "Liberals, *logical* allies of business." Mobil is surrounding itself here with the aura of objectivity. The key rhetorical strategy in the Mobil ad is one of divide and conquer. Although liberals are typically identified with one another by way of a single cultural stereotype, they are here divided into two types, the better to vilify the "unthinking" liberals, while permitting Mobil the opportunity to woo "thinking" liberals. Grouped in a "favorable" cluster of terms, along with business (including Mobil), rationality, help for the needy, and democracy are thinking liberals. Grouped in the "unfavorable" cluster, along with pro-government, anti-business attitudes, are reflexive, knee-jerk, unthinking liberals. The latter group is also identified with help for the needy and democracy, but its members' inability to realize these values places them at odds with themselves.

Recall from Chapter 5 how language choices may be used to elevate or degrade. Then consider how Mobil framed business and government in this ad. Business is represented in paragraph 6 as a company's "management," while government is represented by city hall and by "government bureaucrats." Imagine, by contrast, if government had been represented by a popular governmental building ("When the White House calls …"), while business had been represented as "corporate bureaucrats."

Business and the rational mind

Liberals, logical allies of business • The snobbery factor • A plea for independent thinking

We cannot, for the life of us, understand why so many liberals in this country are so hostile to private business, when in our opinion they should be working with business to achieve what should be their basic objectives.

Liberals have been among the prime movers in the enactment of much of this country's social legislation—Aid to Dependent Children, Social Security, housing for the poor and the elderly, school lunches, and other programs. All of these programs have to be financed by revenues derived mainly from taxes on individual and corporate income.

The greater these incomes—which is to say, the more prosperous American business is—the greater the tax revenues. When incomes drop, as in a recession, so do tax revenues. Social programs then have to be reduced accordingly or supported by deficit financing, which over any extended period means inflation. For the poor and for people living on fixed incomes, inflation is the cruelest tyranny of all.

It therefore would seem to us that in all logic liberals should be as pro-business as they are pro-social progress. And we believe many more of them would be if it were not so fashionable intellectually to be part of the "trendy left." Too many of them respond unthinkingly to social and academic pressures rather than engaging in clear, independent analysis.

Part of the problem appears to be snobbery, pure and simple. To many of what might be called the professional liberals, business—indeed, our whole industrial society—is impossibly vulgar. To some it is esthetically offensive. And because business can prosper only by serving the masses of people, some consider it unbearably plebeian.

Yet one of the continuing threads in the mainstream of liberal thought has long been a dedication to the democratic process and to the right of the masses of people to make their voice heard—and heard effectively. If people stop buying a company's goods or services on any large scale—or just make a credible threat to stop—that company's management tends to listen, and listen attentively. But if you think government is anywhere near as responsive, just recall your last encounter with your City Hall, or your maddening correspondence with a government agency.

Government can become so pervasive that it becomes virtually impossible for the citizenry to turn it around and change its course; indeed, ours may already have become so. But it's doubtful that business could ever get so big or so unresponsive, because it is subject to reaction in the marketplace and to public opinion generally, and to legislation that can curb an entire industry overnight.

What should be a tip-off to any thinking liberal is that an anti-business posture, complete with the cliches that too often substitute for thinking, is mandatory in many liberal circles and is not to be subjected to rigorous intellectual examination. It is a knee-jerk reaction, arising largely from conditions that ceased to exist many years ago and to some that never existed at all.

Lionel Trilling wrote: "It has for some time seemed to me that a criticism which has at heart the interest of liberalism might find its most useful work not in confirming liberalism in its sense of self-righteousness but rather in putting under some degree of pressure the liberal ideas and assumptions of the times." (*The Liberal Imagination: Essays on Literature and Society*, Charles Scribner's Sons, 1976.)

We find puzzling the extent to which liberals often seem impelled to weaken the economic structure on which not just social progress, but indeed our national livelihood depends. To them we suggest the following, oversimplified but nevertheless pointing up the heart of the matter:

Without adequate profits, no businesses.

Without businesses, no jobs.

Without jobs, no social programs.

Mobil

FIGURE 10.4 *An example of a Mobil advertorial.*

© 1979 Mobil Oil Corporation

Note also Mobil's use of *caricature*. To caricature someone is to exaggerate or distort their distinctive features, usually for comic effect. Often, a complex figure is made into a recognizable stock character from literature or the arts. The "professional liberal" is consistently caricatured in the Mobil ad as an unthinking fool and is likened in paragraph 5 to another stock character in our culture, the haughty dowager type who scoffs condescendingly at anything new or different. Who but such a snob would use such phrases as "impossibly vulgar," "aesthetically offensive," and "unbearably plebeian"? Mobil achieves something of a rhetorical coup by these language choices. Government, conventionally viewed as on the side of the people, is now to be seen as distant and uncaring, whereas government's liberal supporters emerge as false friends of ordinary folk.

Who, asks Mobil in subsequent paragraphs, is truly responsive to the people? Not those foolish, snobbish, anti-business liberals, and certainly not those government bureaucrats. No, it is business that cares; indeed, it is business that is truly democratic. By Mobil's rational way of thinking, democracy *is* responsive customer service. Missing from Mobil's argument is the full sense of democracy, not just customer service but government "of the people, by the people and for the people." Still, Mobil's brief for business is a powerful one, and, in helping make that case, it helped itself.

Thinking It Through

Compare Mobil's print ad, analyzed here, with a current public relations advocacy ad by an energy company. How has their message changed? What remains the same? What do you make of the fact that so little has seemed to change in this discussion?

Crisis Management Campaigns

We turn now to another classic public relations situation, one related to a case we have featured throughout this book. When President Bill Clinton's affair with Monica Lewinsky had become clear beyond the point of possible evasion or outright denial, he and his team of public relations experts faced a crisis—indeed, the greatest presidential crisis since Nixon and Watergate. Virtually all public relations professionals face emergencies of one type or another—unexpected events or circumstances that demand urgent action. Some emergencies result in temporary disruptions but little long-term damage. Others immediately threaten the life of the organization or escalate into crises. Either way, a comprehensive crisis management campaign is necessary. In an age of instant telecommunications, public thirst for scandal, and competition among the media for news that sells, any disaster—an oil spill, a train wreck, an industrial explosion—is apt to become a public relations crisis. So, too, may allegations of wrongdoing require crisis management campaigns: a product recall combined with charges of negligence, complaints of inappropriate business practices, rumors of corruption in political office, or complaints in the Clinton case of abuse of office and of a subsequent cover-up.

In the early stages of a crisis, facts are in doubt, rumors abound, and all opinions are equally valid. The news goes through cycles: first there are reports, then expert analyses, then call-in shows and in-depth investigations. As the story gathers legs, interest builds. Blame is likely to be assigned along with demands for corrective action.

Into this firestorm the crisis management team must step—quickly yet carefully. Any mistakes they make early in the crisis management campaign may come back to haunt the organization, as happened when Clinton and his lawyers stonewalled at first, then sought, for several months, to shift blame and then distract the public from the Lewinsky affair while playing "gotcha" with inquiring reporters.

As in the Lewinsky case, public relations professionals must be in constant contact with key decision makers, and they in turn are almost always unwise to rely on their own counsel. Even as suspicion drives out trust within the organization, lines of internal communication must be kept open and a facade of optimism and togetherness presented to the general public. To whatever extent possible, the crisis management team should line up support from authority figures outside the organization, looking especially for sympathetic media coverage.

However competent the public relations team, it must expect that its damage control efforts will be less than fully successful. Even routine rhetorical situations are dilemma-laden, and crisis management is especially problematic. As organizational crises deepen, enemies pounce, competitors look to exploit weaknesses, and erstwhile friends crawl into the woodwork or go public with their disappointments. In pressure cooker environments, people make mistakes, and that adds to the crisis management team's rhetorical dilemmas. Yet some organizations weather these problems, whereas others fold.

Chapter 2 used the Clinton–Lewinsky scandal to illustrate the psychological principles of persuasion. Chapter 4 presented guidelines-in-theory for the political apologia but also illustrated why Clinton's unique rhetorical situation on August 17, 1998, made those guidelines difficult to apply. These sections of Chapters 2 and 4 provide the context for the dilemma-centered analysis that follows.

The dilemmas Clinton confronted in his speech to the American people on August 17 were not entirely unique. They included ethical dilemmas (e.g., truth-telling versus evasiveness of a sort that might enable him to continue doing his job as president); conflicting role requirements (the temptation to attack, the need to express contrition); the need to balance the conflicting logics of law, politics, and psychology; and the problem of needing to appeal to multiple and conflicting audiences. An analysis of three excerpts from Clinton's apologia will illustrate how rhetorical dilemmas can be successfully managed in times of crisis.

Excerpt 1 Opening Comments

Good evening. This afternoon in this room, from this chair, I testified before the Office of Independent Counsel and the grand jury. I answered their questions truthfully, including questions about my private life, questions no American citizen would ever want to answer.

Still, I must take complete responsibility for all my actions, both public and private. And that is why I am speaking to you tonight.

President Clinton spoke carefully here, attempting to make each word just right. Yet David Maraniss (1998), his biographer, found these opening paragraphs self-contradictory, their key terms, such as "truthfully," "private life," and "complete responsibility," vague or ambiguous. Maraniss probably has Clinton about right in his readings of these opening comments. Maraniss might have added that in taking "complete responsibility for all my actions" without specifying *what* actions, if any, he was apologizing for, Clinton was again being misleading and perhaps hypocritical. The question remains, however, whether the opening remarks worked for or against Clinton's interests. No doubt many Clinton haters saw through the duplicities and now hated Clinton all the more. But for the mass of Americans who disapproved of Clinton's transgressions but who approved of his job performance, the opening chords of supplication mixed with gritty determination, of paradoxically untruthful truthfulness and irresponsible responsibility, might well have been the right chords.

Excerpt 2 The "Confession"

As you know, in a deposition in January, I was asked questions about my relationship with Monica Lewinsky. While my answers were legally accurate, I did not volunteer information. Indeed, I did have a relationship with Miss Lewinsky that was not appropriate. In fact, it was wrong. It constituted a critical lapse in judgment and a personal failure on my part for which I am solely and completely responsible. But I told the grand jury today and I say to you now that at no time did I ask anyone to lie, to hide or destroy evidence or to take any other unlawful action. I know that my public comments and my silence about this matter gave a false impression. I misled people, including even my wife. I deeply regret that.

The chief criticism of the August 17 speech is that Clinton appeared insufficiently contrite. Politicians, pundits, and the general public repeatedly expressed anger, or at least regret, at Clinton's failure "to say I'm sorry to the American people." Some journalists remarked on the gap between Beltway opinion and public opinion, but *The New York Times*, in an editorial on August 19, 1998, bolstered its charge of "betrayal and embarrassment" towards the president, especially because Gallup poll data indicated that 58% of those surveyed believed Clinton should have made an outright apology. Clinton's insincerity, it was argued, came through in the flatness of his tone and the anger on his face but also in his words. Why did he call it a "critical lapse" in judgment when the affair had been longstanding? Why did he say he "misled people" rather than just admit that he "repeatedly lied"? Why the passive note: "gave a false impression"? Why didn't he admit that he "deliberately deceived"?

Clinton's confession does seem rather hollow. One critic defended the choice of words "because Presidents ought not grovel" (McGee, 1998). "'It was wrong' should be as good as 'I am sorry' in the apology department, and a lot preferable in the Presidential dignity department" (McGee, 1998). But Clinton could have appeared more repentant without groveling, and on subsequent occasions he expressed more remorse for his wrongdoing. To account for Clinton's persistent unwillingness to acknowledge fully the dimensions and depth of his wrongdoing will require examining further the dilemmas he faced.

Excerpt 3 The Attack

I can only tell you I was motivated by many factors. First, ... by a desire to protect myself from the embarrassment of my own conduct. I was also very concerned about protecting my family. The fact that these questions were being asked in a politically inspired lawsuit, which has since been dismissed, was a consideration, too.

In addition, I had real and serious concerns about an independent counsel investigation that began with private business dealings 20 years ago, dealings I might add about which an independent federal agency found no evidence of any wrongdoing by me or my wife over 2 years ago. The independent counsel investigation moved on to my staff and friends, then into my private life. And now the investigation itself is under investigation. This has gone on too long, cost too much and hurt too many innocent people.

The appearance of insufficient remorse was reinforced by Clinton's retreat to legalisms in this excerpt and by his continued attack on the Starr investigation. Yet Clinton's insistence (in the previous excerpt) on legal accuracy and on his innocence as regards suborning of perjury or other possible obstruction of justice is eminently understandable given the directions the independent counsel investigation had taken. He was facing the real possibilities that charges would be brought before the House Judiciary Committee; that he would then be impeached or be forced to resign; and that, at the least, he would be rendered more vulnerable to conviction for civil and criminal offenses once he left office.

Had Clinton the luxury of dealing only with those among his hearers who were raised permissively, a confession of addiction to sex or to risk might have been in order, complete with a tear-filled narrative about the difficulties he and his mother faced at the hands of an abusive husband and stepfather. But although millions of Americans seek treatment for addictions, they tend not to vote for politicians who confess to needing psychological treatment, especially not for addictions. As Francis X. Clines put it: "For many veterans of the political wars, the merest hint of any psychological flaw is the ultimate taboo for a candidate and especially for the man occupying the patriarchal office of the presidency" (1998).

Were this a purely political or moral crisis, Clinton could have confessed more forthrightly to the dimensions and depth of his wrongdoing while reminding Americans by word and by deed of the good that he had done. Republicans such as Orrin Hatch who were eager to get on with the nation's business had pleaded with the president to come clean and express complete remorse in return for some measure of forgiveness from them. But in this context (and in the subsequent impeachment inquiry in the House and trial by the Senate), the offer had something of the quality of a double bind. Clinton would truly be damned if he did and damned if he didn't.

Instead, Clinton opted for vagueness, ambiguity, and equivocation. Days later, the news media carried stories of Clinton's political advisers complaining of having been "dissed" by Clinton in the preparation of the speech and dismayed by the president's continued legal hairsplitting. Yet the legal team's prevailing logic ultimately proved correct: Clinton could eventually earn the forgiveness of most Americans, but the independent counsel, the Republican-dominated House and Senate, and the courts would prove more demanding.

As for Clinton's decision to press ahead with yet another attack on Kenneth Starr, this, too, was criticized by Clinton's political advisers and by the media. Psychologically, if not logically, it seemed inconsistent with his earlier expressions of remorse.

Arguably, then, the attack on Starr with its reminder of monies wasted on five years of fruitless investigations into the Clintons' affairs should have been omitted from the speech. Perhaps it was time to leave that job to supporters, as has frequently been done in the past.

But another approach suggests itself, one exemplified by retired Senator Dale Bumpers's (1999) memorable oration during the Senate impeachment trial. Conceding horrible wrongdoing by Clinton, of a sort that his good friend would never be able to live down, Bumpers was able in the same speech to deplore the excesses of the independent counsel's investigation. "The president suffered a terrible moral lapse," said Bumpers. His conduct was "indefensible, outrageous, unforgivable, shameless." But the president was also a victim of a "relentless, unending investigation" that had brought financial ruin to completely innocent associates of the Clintons as well. Like Bumpers, Clinton could have turned the either–or of contrition versus attack into an acceptable both–and, but to do so he needed to find words and visible expressions of remorse far more powerful than those he employed.

Thus did Clinton and his crisis management team attempt to handle the president's rhetorical dilemmas. In the rest of the speech, Clinton sought to win sympathy by continuing to insist that this was a private matter, of no business to anyone except his wife, their daughter, and "our God." He also sought closure on the matter. It is time, he said "to move on."

What "grade" should be given Clinton's effort at crisis management? Did Clinton do as well as could be expected given his difficult rhetorical situation? Were his remarks appropriate not only to the immediate situation but to the challenges that lay ahead?

Judged solely on the basis of Clinton's resourcefulness in addressing the dilemmas he confronted, Clinton earns for his August 17 apologia a B+. This is probably a much higher grade than most experts and politicians would have given him (Simons, 2000). In retrospect, we know that the roughly two-thirds of Americans who opposed a protracted investigation by the independent counsel into the president's sex life held steady in objecting to a long investigation by the House Judiciary Committee, to impeachment of Clinton by the House, and to a full-scale trial in the Senate (Kolbert, 1999). These were probably the same Americans who would have been predisposed toward closure on August 17, with perhaps a reprimand from the Congress as a precondition for ritual termination of the case. Numbered among them were longstanding supporters of Clinton, but they probably also included Americans who had become tired of the whole affair, others who found the sex talk embarrassing or bad for their children to hear, and still others of varying political persuasions who never believed that the affair and subsequent cover-up were the big deal that the independent counsel's office had made of it and who saw Starr and the religious right as the greater threat to America's well-being.

One final comment concerns the difference a frame makes in the management of dilemmas. Kathleen Jamieson (personal communication, October 1998) suggested that Clinton should have not just apologized but instead defined the terms of his possible redemption. Needed was a pledge of corrective action consistent with Clinton's high approval rating as president. Said Jamieson, Clinton should have said (in words to this effect): "I let you down, and for that I'm deeply sorry. That's why I intend to spend the rest of my term as president making it up to you."

That sounds exactly right.

INDOCTRINATION CAMPAIGNS

Indoctrination campaigns are called many things. Some are called "informational" or "educational," others get called "propaganda." Some are accused of employing "**mind control**," and others are suspected of engaging in "**subliminal persuasion**." Some are considered "cults," whereas others are seen as mainstream organizations. The difference is often one of who gets to define what is socially acceptable and what is self serving, biased, and of dubious value to society (Ellul, 1965; Hogan & Olsen, 1989; Jowett & O'Donnell, 2006; Sproule, 1997; Perloff, 2014). Is a high school social studies unit on the virtues of patriotism "education" or "propaganda"? What if the unit celebrates the doctrine of "my country right or wrong?" Is it then education or propaganda? Suppose, on the other hand, that the unit celebrates America's constitutionally protected rights to free speech, extending even to flag burning? Is that education or propaganda? Suppose that by some odd turn of events, it is not *our* patriotism being celebrated in a social studies course but that of our enemy's? In the business of labeling, it seems to matter little who the "we" and the "they" are; all nations "educate" self-servingly in relation to their supposed enemies, and powerful nations get to make their labels stick (Alinsky, 1971).

Significantly, for most people, the social studies unit on patriotism will not ordinarily be thought of as campaigning of any type. Nor will the preachments in celebration of authority by parents, religious leaders, government, or the Cub Scouts. All have a role in indoctrinating—or some might say "socializing" or "acculturating"—children and "re-socializing" those previously indoctrinated. A traditional function of socialization has been to promote hierarchical identification—the parent, the teacher, the minister, the Almighty, the Founding Fathers, the current leaders—forming in unformed minds a seamless web of perceived beneficence. This brings benefits to all authority figures while simultaneously adjusting those indoctrinated to the social order. Learning that "our" leaders are trustworthy is a part of the process of socially constructing reality, discussed in Chapter 3. It is not by accident that George Washington's portrait is a fixture in American elementary school classrooms.

Against the backdrop of early socialization come efforts by some groups to "re-indoctrinate" or "re-socialize." Some of these groups are called "revolutionary"; others are called "religious cults"; still others are branded as "reactionary" or as "just plain wacko," but nearly all of them have been said by their critics to involve some such phenomenon as "mind control," "thought control," or **brainwashing.**" In the remainder of this section we'll consider the varying sorts of indoctrination campaigns and ask what's "really" involved in mind control, whether the techniques of influence said to "brainwash" others (e.g., members of today's "spiritual cults," American POWs during the Korean War) are different in kind or degree from those used by mainstream groups, and whether thoughts can be controlled subliminally. Most of all we'll seek to add clarity to a debate where labels like "brainwashing" have themselves functioned as weapons of influence.

Possibilities for "Mind Control"

"Mind control: Psychological reality or mindless rhetoric?" So asked Philip Zimbardo (2002), a past president of the American Psychological Association, in an article urging his colleagues to revisit some of psychology's most highly contentious issues. If "mind control" conjures up images for you of extreme forms of influence—from Nazi propaganda to "brainwashing" by cult leaders such as the People's Temple Jim Jones—then you're in Professor Zimbardo's ball park. It was Jones in Guyana who managed to convince 900 cult members, all U.S. citizens, to commit suicide or murder friends and family. Arguably, mind control can be a good thing, or so we are sometimes told; search the Internet, for example, and you will find many sponsored sites that promise weight loss, confidence building, relief from insomnia, and much more. Or end your cigarette addiction in one session with a skilled hypnotherapist. These, if they work, are relatively benign forms of influence; but those that Zimbardo has in mind are far more sinister:

> A basic value of the profession of psychology is promoting human freedom of responsible action, based on awareness of available behavioral options, and supporting an individual's right to exercise them. Whatever we mean by "mind control" stands in opposition to this positive value orientation.
>
> (2002)

He goes on to define mind control as:

the process by which individual or collective freedom of choice and action is compromised by agents or agencies that modify or distort perception, motivation, affect, cognition and/or behavioral outcomes. A body of social science evidence shows that when systematically practiced by state-sanctioned police, military or destructive cults, mind control can induce false confessions, create converts who willingly torture or kill "invented enemies," and engage indoctrinated members to work tirelessly, give up their money—and even their lives—for "the cause."

(Zimbardo, 2002)

Professor Zimbardo (2002) maintains that at the very heart of the controversy over the existence of mind control is a bias toward believing in the power of people to resist the power of situational forces, a belief in individual will power and faith to overcome all evil adversity. It is exemplified in Jesus' modeling resistance against the temptations of Satan, and not demonstrated in the vulnerability of Adam and Eve to the serpent's deception.

More recently, examples abound that challenge this person-power misattribution. From the 1930s on, there are many historical instances of state power dominating individual beliefs and values. In Stalin's Moscow show trials, his adversaries publicly confessed to their treasons. Catholic Cardinal Mindszenty similarly gave false confessions favoring his communist captors. During the Korean War, American airmen confessed to engaging in germ warfare after intense indoctrination sessions. The Chinese Thought Reform Program achieved massive societal conversions to new beliefs.

In his *The Skeptic's Dictionary*, Robert Todd Carroll (2003) defines "mind control" (and its synonyms) as "the successful control of the thoughts and actions of another without his or her consent." Says Carroll, the term generally implies "that the victim has given up some basic political, social, or religious beliefs and attitudes, and has been made to accept contrasting ideas." On this, he and Zimbardo appear to agree. Carroll proposes that we:

eliminate as examples of mind control those activities where a person freely chooses to engage in the behavior. Controlling one's thoughts and actions, whether by self-discipline or with the help of others, is an interesting and important topic, but it is not the same as brainwashing or programming people without their consent.

(2003)

He adds:

Using fear or force to manipulate or coerce people into doing what you want them to do should not be considered to be mind control. Inquisitions do not succeed in capturing the minds of their victims. As soon as the threat of punishment is lifted, the extorted beliefs vanish. You do not control the mind of someone who will escape from you the moment you turn your back.

To render a woman helpless by drugs so you can rape her is not mind control. Using a frequency generator to give people headaches or to disorient them is not the same as controlling them. You do not have control over a person's thoughts or actions just because you can do what you want to them or render them incapable of doing as they will. An essential component of mind control is that it involves *controlling* another person, not just putting them out of control or doing things to them over which they have no control.

(Carroll, 2003)

Thinking It Through

We've offered a number of definitions of "mind control" in this section. How would you define it, and why?

Mind Control Controversies

Cialdini (2009) and Pratkanis and Aronson (2001) have argued that the "respectable" groups with which we normally affiliate, such as fraternities and religious organizations, use similar forms of influence to those employed by religious cults— not as extreme, say, as those used to "brainwash" American POWs, but different only in degree.

It might surprise you to learn that Zimbardo fundamentally agrees. Mind control, he maintains, is neither magical nor mystical, but a process that involves a set of basic social psychological principles:

Conformity, compliance, persuasion, dissonance, reactance, guilt and fear arousal, modeling and identification are some of the staple social influence ingredients well studied in psychological experiments and field studies. In some combinations, they create a powerful crucible of extreme mental and behavioral manipulation when synthesized with several other real-world factors, such as charismatic, authoritarian leaders, dominant ideologies, social isolation, physical debilitation, induced phobias, and extreme threats or promised rewards that are typically deceptively orchestrated, over an extended time period in settings where they are applied intensively.

(Zimbardo, 2002)

A semester's worth of terms is wrapped together in this single paragraph, but we have made reference to most of the terms before, particularly in Chapters 2 and 7. Zimbardo seems to be suggesting that what appear to be differences in degree can become differences in kind when powerful techniques of influence are combined together in a campaign of indoctrination over an extended period of time.

A frequently cited example of mind control, made popular by the 1962 cult classic film, *The Manchurian Candidate*, was the alleged "brainwashing" of American prisoners by their Chinese captors during the Korean War. What techniques of influence were used on the prisoners? Was this truly a case of persuasive control so powerful that it was impossible to resist? It is to those questions we now turn our attention.

"Brainwashing"

Common to efforts at re-socialization, says clinical psychologist Patrick Pentony (1981), brainwashing involves the undermining of a belief system or ideology. C. H. Schein (1961) provided a vivid account of how this was done, based on interviews with former prisoners.

Schein (1961) labeled the process of undermining belief systems as *demolition* and identified three components of this *unfreezing* stage: (1) invalidation, (2) induction of guilt-anxiety, and (3) the provision of psychological safety. In the attempted re-socialization of American prisoners during the Korean War, this invalidation involved a gradual chipping away of basic beliefs under highly controlled conditions: sleep, social contact, exercise, and the like were made contingent on "progress" at giving up long-held convictions.

In the Korean War case, there was quite a bit of coercion present to aid persuaders in their efforts. That "luxury" is not afforded to persuaders in less constricted environments, such as when a college student goes to a meeting of a religious group "just to see what it's all about." In such cases, the need still exists for a three-stage unfreezing process, but the way in which those stages are performed is necessarily transformed. Persuaders cannot easily withhold basic human needs, and so they adopt other methods to accomplish their aims.

In situations such as religious conversion meetings for students, persuaders will focus on the guiding ideology of the individual in their efforts to recruit him or her, seeking to provide *psychological safety* first in preparation for the *invalidation* process that will follow. In addition to starting the recruitment process with a focus on the student's present beliefs and providing a supposed zone of safety, the persuaders will also hone in on any tension or *guilt* that already exists. They will emphasize the positive aspects of the conversion experience and point to the group itself as remedy for those tensions. At the same time, they will ensure that potential converts are engaging in behaviors and social interactions within the group, and this new social network in turn will contribute to a change in cognition for the convert (Richardson, 2014). As Richardson notes, this form of outreach is effective because, in fact, "conversion usually is deciding to agree with your best friend" (2014). This overall approach will aid the efforts of the religious group because, as we know, research shows that the most susceptible targets for religious conversion are idealistic people who are seeking to accomplish personal change and/or are experiencing enduring, acutely felt tensions, especially those who, during a crisis or turning point in their lives, tend to see the world from a religious perspective (Lofland, 1977; Richardson, 2014).

In conversion situations, persuaders know that it is difficult to create true and sustained changes in the strongly held beliefs and tradition of recruits. However troubled we are by apparent contradictions and inadequacies of the ideologies we hold dear, we are much more likely to attempt to patch them up than to give them up. Thus, the persuader seeking to convert us must tread lightly in challenging our beliefs, lest we ignore these challenges or reject them outright and end up dismissing the persuader as well. Therefore, persuaders must move slowly and gently, and they must be careful not to openly dismiss our core beliefs if they wish to succeed in recruiting us. Zimbardo, Ebbesen, and Maslach (1977) describe this process of quiet invalidation in their example of the recruiting efforts by the Unification Church of Sun Myung Moon: "Nonacceptable responses elicit an immediate uniform reaction from all members of the group; they are saddened, never angered, by deviant acts or thoughts. The consequence is the arousal of guilt for upsetting them by your disagreement" (Zimbardo, et al., 1977).

When the targets' belief systems have been invalidated, they are ripe for the acquisition of a new structure of beliefs. This takes place during what Schein (1961) refers to as the *transitional* stage. By this time, resistance is largely gone, and the targets are anxious to replace the logics that have failed them. This process involves (a) new definitions of terms, (b) broadened or altered perceptions, and (c) new standards of evaluation and judgment.

A *refreezing* stage completes the re-socialization process, according to Schein (1961). Here the props that supported the old belief system—self-confidence, group support, and belief consistency—are restored to be made serviceable for the new. When the refreezing effort is successful, the new belief structure is incorporated into the larger personality pattern and into the individual's way of relating to others. Efforts are made at this stage to discourage backsliding and to encourage active, overt commitment to the new way of thinking. Converts are often urged to engage in activities that will advertise and simultaneously reinforce their newly acquired beliefs. It is not uncommon to see new converts to a religious faith being encouraged to make their profession of faith public, to tell others, or even to go out and evangelize.

Thinking It Through

Think of a group of this sort to which you belong, or of which you have personal knowledge. How closely, if at all, do their recruiting practices follow the model that has been offered here? Trace this out step by step, comparing the group's practices with the stages we've listed, and see what you discover.

Cults and Cult-Like Groups

The introduction to this section suggests that fraternities and religious organizations "use similar forms of influence to those employed by religious cults—not as extreme, say, as those used to 'brainwash' American POWs, but different only in degree." But can we compare the re-socialization efforts of groups outside the mainstream with those of more mainstream organizations? Do the military, the Scouts, the campus fraternity or sorority at pledge time, a church on summer retreat, and self-help organizations such as Alcoholics Anonymous engage in re-socialization efforts such as those described earlier? Pratkanis and Aronson (2001) maintain that all such groups are cult-like to one degree or another. Perhaps they don't deprive members of food and sleep or force them to give up their belongings and identity, as the Reverend Jim Jones reportedly did in Jonestown, Guyana, before ordering his followers to give up their lives. Maybe individuals aren't "love-bombed" at a church retreat in the same way that the Moonie leaders bestowed hugs and kisses on new recruits rather than heaping scorn on those who hadn't "gotten it yet." Still, these groups seem to share with religious cults some or all of the following characteristics:

- *Closed System of Thought.* In cult situations, providing recruits with a new version of reality while eliminating all other sources of information is commonplace. Ideological isolation can happen through imposed censorship or, even more powerfully, through induced self-censorship where the re-socialized recruit will develop a closed system of thinking into which new or competing information can be filtered and fitted. New language and new jargon are endlessly repeated (e.g., "Krishna consciousness," "Victory in Jesus") to make fiction sound like fact (Pratkanis & Aronson, 2001). One result of this, for example, will be that efforts to separate the recruit from the cult or cult-like group will end up being dismissed as the work of the devil. Another result is that recruits will be less inclined to critical thinking and more inclined to follow the instructions of the group: Orders from on high to lie or steal for the group are more likely to be assimilated into the newly acquired belief system.

- *Us–Them Mentality.* Pratkanis and Aronson (2001) speak of the creation of a *granfalloon*. The recruits are the chosen; others are the unredeemed. Having been chosen imposes a responsibility on recruits to embrace the group and break from the "other" world. Initiation into the group may involve ritual sacrifices, for example, surrender of material possessions or submission to a hazing, physical scarring, or other baptism of fire. With pride in "us" often comes hatred of "them": perhaps parents, or greedy capitalists, or all non-believers.

- *Escalating Commitment.* Having persuaded recruits to become converts to the group and its closed system of thinking, leaders of the cult or cult-like group may make increased demands, requiring more sacrifice, more labor, more expressions of affection for the leader, and more attachment to the group as signs of continued commitment. Recall from Chapter 2 the principle of insufficient justification. If recruits can be convinced that their sacrifices are voluntary, this brings psychological pressure on them to "purify" their thinking: They need to keep working to eliminate all doubts—all dissonance— about the worthiness of the group and its mission.

- *Hero Worship.* The group's leader is special, perhaps mythically so. Stories may be circulated within the cult or cult-like group about exceptional deeds and powers—leaders may even proclaim themselves to have a direct pipeline to the Almighty. This is the original meaning of *charisma.* Only the group's leader can offer divine guidance—or, even more stunning—only the group's leader *is* God.

- *Proselytizing the Unredeemed.* Whether the group's ideology is religious or secular, its members are sent out to do missionary work—to convert the unconverted. As they attempt to persuade others, they further persuade themselves—another manifestation of the principle of insufficient justification.

- *Disruption of Counter-arguing.* Recruits are not given time to think for themselves. When they are not at distractedly scheduled events such as morning prayers, afternoon lectures, and evening songfests, they may be kept constantly in the company of group enthusiasts—even during trips to the bathroom. Once on board, the group members will be kept busy doing proselytizing or performing assigned chores. Should (perish the thought) group members begin thinking for themselves, their doubts or disagreements may be explained away as the work of a satanic force.

- *Vision of a Better World.* For Heaven's Gate, another group that succumbed to mass suicide, it was the opportunity to shed "their earthly containers." For members of L. Ron Hubbard's Church of Scientology, it is the chance to achieve a state of "clear" in this world. This is the great prize: a glorious life after death or a heaven on earth, made possible by attachment to the group and adherence to its teachings. The prize becomes all the more attractive in contrast to the misery of the unclear, the unsaved—those fated for an afterlife of fire and brimstone or of a hell on earth.

The list is a useful guide to deciphering the persuasive tendencies of the groups with which we align ourselves. Clearly, we can see how elements included here are part of college Greek life, American religious communities, self-help groups, and even activist groups fighting for change. The word "cult" truly is a loaded term; it is filled with all sorts of negative connotations. Given that, it is interesting to consider that there likely are some cult-like tendencies all around us, and, not only that, we are susceptible to their persuasive power.

Extreme Suggestibility and "Recovered Memory"

Like so much in the media, accounts of extreme influence in campaigns of indoctrination tend to be exaggerated. Yet by no means all these stories are fanciful. Psychologists Anthony Pratkanis and Elliot Aronson (2001) offer up the tale of police officer Paul Ingram and his two daughters as a bone-chilling lesson in the power of indoctrination to destroy a family and wreck an innocent life.

In 1988, Ingram, at age 43, was a pillar of his community: chief civil deputy of the sheriff's department in Olympia, Washington, active in politics and a respected member of his church. On November 28 of that year, he was arrested for sexual molestation of his daughters. Ericka at the time was 22 years of age, Julie was 18. A series of investigations by a pastor, a clinical psychologist, and two police detectives prompted Ingram to confess that he was guilty. According to his own confession, devout evangelical Christian Ingram and his wife Sandy had been abusing their daughters for 17 years. Ingram acknowledged being the leader of a satanic cult engaged in ritual killings of infants and animals on the family's farm. He confessed that he had impregnated one of his daughters, and then forced her to submit to an abortion. He added that his home served as headquarters for a group of pedophiles who would get drunk and routinely rape Julie.

Said Pratkanis and Aronson:

> What makes this story even more remarkable is that there is no evidence that what Ingram admitted to ever occurred and much evidence that, at the very least, parts of it never could have happened. For example, after massive police investigations, including large-scale excavations of Ingram's farm, no physical evidence of murdered infants and animals was ever found. Despite an extensive search, the doctor who allegedly performed the abortion was never located. The Ingram family doctor found no physical evidence of abuse when he examined the daughters.... Court-ordered examinations failed to find scars on the bodies of Ericka and Julie—scars that they claimed were the results of repeated satanic tortures. Ericka still publicly claims that she carries these scars and had denounced the sheriff's office for refusing to arrest 30 doctors, lawyers, and judges whom she identified as part of the satanic conspiracy and whom she claims continue to murder innocent babies. Other than Ingram's confession, there is no evidence to corroborate the allegations of sexual abuse made by Ericka and Julie.
>
> (2001)

What prompted Ingram's daughters to charge him and his wife with sexual molestation, and why did he confess? In a nutshell, the daughters and their father proved highly suggestible: the former in response to therapists and religious counselors who had encouraged them to see themselves as victims; the father, already guilt-ridden, out of a conviction that those around him who acted as though the accusations were true couldn't all be wrong. Ironically, the most compelling evidence of Paul Ingram's innocence was itself the product of suggestion. It came from a demonstration performed by Berkeley social psychologist Richard Ofshe, an expert on cults who had been called in by prosecutors for advice on how to investigate the case.

From the start, Ofshe was suspicious of the case against Paul Ingram. He decided to test his suspicions by determining whether Ingram would accept as true an entirely fabricated incident. Was it not true, he was asked, that he had forced his son and daughter to have sex in his presence? Ofshe instructed Ingram to try to recall the scene. The next day he did, providing a detailed account of how he had ordered his children to undress and commanded Ericka to kneel and have oral sex with his son while he watched (Pratkanis & Aronson, 2001).

Paul Ingram was given a 21-year sentence for a crime most experts agree was never committed, and ended up in jail. He came to believe in his innocence, though, fought to exonerate himself, and was finally released from prison in 2003.

The point in light of our topic here of *indoctrination campaigns* is profound. This case demonstrates how innocent people can be coerced, cajoled, and arm-twisted into confessing to even incredible crimes. Not unlike in the Salem witchcraft confessions (Johnson, 1994), in Ingram's case the allegations were supported by the clergy (along with assorted psychotherapists), and the publicity brought much desired attention to those individuals. Furthermore, under the influence of the experts (e.g., clergy in Salem, psychotherapists in the Ingram case), and the general community, the allegations grew and more people were accused. In both cases, the influence of therapists, coupled with group support and encouragement, resulted in even more elaborate allegations. And finally, both ended in great suffering for the accused.

The "Subliminal Persuasion" Controversy

If you Google, you'll likely find all manner of ads for self-help sites that promise to deliver increased "mind power" subliminally. Wikipedia, that source for folk wisdom and more, devotes space to the topic, and defines a subliminal message as one that is:

> embedded in another medium, designed to pass below the normal limits of the human mind's perception. These messages are unrecognizable by the conscious mind, but in certain situations can affect the subconscious mind and can negatively or positively influence subsequent later thoughts, behaviors, actions, attitudes, belief systems and value systems. The term *subliminal* means "beneath a limen" (sensory threshold). This is from the Latin words *sub*, meaning under, and *limen*, meaning threshold.
>
> (Retrieved July 15, 2009)

It's part of folk culture to believe that people can learn subliminally, but also that they can be manipulated subliminally—convinced to do what they might otherwise choose not to do. Popular belief in the power of subliminal advertising stemmed from James Vicary's 1957 research experiment conducted at a drive-in movie theater. Movie screens project 26 frames per second. Vicary flashed one-frame images of Coca-Cola® and popcorn too quickly to be perceived by the naked eye. Yet Vicary reported that Coca-Cola sales increased 18% and popcorn sales 57.8%. When Vicary repeated his study under controlled conditions, however, the results did not bear out his original research (Weir, 1984).

Despite Vicary's failed attempts at proving it exists, there are still theorists who have continued to advance the theory of subliminal persuasion. Most well known is Wilson Bryan Key (1973, 1976, 1980), author of *Subliminal Seduction* and other books filled with dire warnings about the pervasiveness of hidden messages in advertising. He presents examples of the word "sex" embedded in the ice cubes of an ad for Gilbey's Gin or baked into Ritz crackers. He argues that these ads trigger subconscious emotional responses, so that people remember the ad and product when they are in the marketplace. Although he cites numerous studies to support his claims, most of them had no control or comparison groups, nor was he ever able to show that subliminal techniques made people behave in ways that they would not ordinarily do. Ultimately, Wilson Bryan Key does not cite a single case of an advertiser admitting to using subliminal tactics. Pratkanis and Aronson note:

> Finding that 62% of the subjects feel sexual, romantic, or satisfied when they see a gin ad with the word *sex* embedded in the ice cubes tells us nothing about the effectiveness of the *sex* implant. What would happen if the word *sex* was removed from the cubes? Perhaps 62% of the subjects would still feel sexy, romantic, or satisfied. Perhaps more, perhaps fewer would feel this way. Without such a comparison, we do not know.
>
> (2001)

Pratkanis and Aronson suggest that people's beliefs and expectations play a strong role in the "effect" of subliminal persuasion. In a 1958 study conducted by the Canadian Broadcasting network, the words *phone now* flashed on screen 352 times during a popular Sunday evening program. Telephone use did not increase, and 500 respondents who tried to guess the message failed. Yet people reported feeling hungry or thirsty, probably because they thought the message was aimed at getting them to eat or drink (2001). This also explains the current popularity of self-help tapes, on which subliminal messages meant to build self-esteem or to aid in memory retention are embedded beneath soft music or the soothing sounds of the ocean. In another study, participants were given tapes that they thought were meant to build self-esteem, but which really contained messages concerning memory retention. Although tests five weeks later revealed no change in self-esteem, they were convinced that their self-esteem had improved—even though the subliminal messages were about memory retention (Greenwald, et al., 1991).

Many social psychologists have concluded that subliminal persuasion is a myth. Pratkanis was co-author of a study (Greenwald, et al., 1991) that demonstrated, they claimed, that subliminal tapes have no therapeutic value. He calls belief in subliminal persuasion pseudoscience—made convincing by the allure of a phantom—a distant, much desired, seemingly realistic but ultimately unavailable goal. Most pseudosciences, he says, are based on belief in a distant or phantom goal:

> The trick, of course, is to get the new seeker to believe that the phantom is possible. Often the mere mention of the delights of a phantom will be enough to dazzle the new pseudoscience recruit. After all, who wouldn't want a better sex life, better health, and peace of mind, all from a $14.95 subliminal tape?"
>
> (Pratkanis, 1995)

In Pratkanis's view, the subliminal persuasion "myth" is emblematic of how pseudo-sciences are sold. The rhetoric of pseudoscience, he claims, is much like the rhetoric of cult leaders, relying on manufactured credibility, vivid appeals, inducements to rationalize one's premature commitments, pre-persuasion (e.g., defining what is at issue as though it is the only issue), establishing granfalloons, and alibis for promises gone unfulfilled. For example, he says that subliminal-tape companies even use product differentiation to respond to negative subliminal-tape studies. The claim: "Our tapes have a special technique that makes them superior to other tapes that have been used in studies that failed to show the therapeutic value of subliminal tapes" (Pratkanis, 1995).

In light of this subliminal controversy, readers here should know that the two authors of this book (Herb and Jean) have engaged in a fairly heated debate. Until we neared completion of this book, we had been fully convinced that Pratkanis was right. Now though, we're not so sure.

In the previous edition of *Persuasion in Society*, Herb had concluded that advertisements presented subliminally probably have no effect while ads whose subtle, barely noticed enticements to buy are among the most powerful. He quoted Mark Crispin Miller for support:

> We are accustomed to think of these subtleties in quasi-Pavlovian terms, as hidden stimuli that "turn us on" without our knowing it: nipples airbrushed into sunsets, lewd words traced into some ice cubes, etc. But this conception of the way ads work and of the way we apprehend them, is much too crude. They function, not mechanically, but poetically, through metaphor, association, repetition, and other devices that suggest a variety of possible meanings. The viewer, therefore, does not just watch once and start salivating, but senses gradually, half-consciously, the commercial's welter of related messages.
>
> And just as the viewer needn't recognize these subtleties in order to take them in, so, perhaps, the advertisers themselves may not know their every implication, any more than a poet or filmmaker is fully aware of all that his work implies.
>
> (Miller, 1981)

We would still be convinced that subliminal persuasion is pseudoscience were it not for Herb's chance encounter with some very respectable science by Ran Hassin (Ferguson & Hassin, 2007; Hassin, et al., 2007, 2009) and other priming researchers. Could Hassin and his colleagues have discovered the psychological equivalent of a black swan?

Hassin and his associates were interested not in how "movie popcorn" sales could be increased, but in something far more important: the molding and modifying of **implicit nationalism** (Hassin, et al., 2009). What follows is their description of their research project:

> In this paper we review recent advances in the examination of implicit nationalism. In the first set of experiments we survey, the Palestinian, Israeli, Italian, and Russian flags were primed (or not, in the control conditions) and their effects on political thought and behavior were tested. In the second set the American or the Israeli flag was primed (or not) and prejudice toward African Americans or Palestinians (respectively) was examined.
>
> The results of all experiments suggest that the **implicit activation** of national cues has far-reaching implications on political thought and behavior as well as on attitudes toward minorities. Under the assumption that the image of national flags is associated in memory with national ideologies, these results suggest that national ideologies can be implicitly pursued in a way that significantly affects our thoughts and behaviors.
>
> (Hassin, et al., 2009)

Now, let's translate this is into more common English. What do Hassin, Ferguson, Kardosh, Porter, Carter, and Dudareva mean by "implicit nationalism" and by its "implicit activation"?

As to the first question, nationalism is an ideology, a system of ideas that unites a group of people around its guiding beliefs and values, while dividing them from others. It causes them to see the others as "outsiders," "aliens," "foreigners," and the like. *Implicit* nationalism is based on subtle things in the environment, such as a national flag hanging from the entrance to a building, that demonstrate the nationalism that exists. Such things have the potential to bring to mind—or, in the jargon of cognitive sciences, to *prime* or *activate*—our national ideology. We see our flag and our ideological feelings of connection to our country are brought to mind.

Michael Billig's fascinating work (1995) on banal nationalism is one example of this conception:

> Billig explicitly endorses the idea that this activation may occur nonconsciously and that people are largely unaware of the downstream effects of this activation on their behaviors, thoughts, and emotions. This view makes perfect sense when considered from the perspective of the cognitive sciences.
>
> (Hassin, et al., 2009)

As for nationalism's "implicit activation," this is where subliminal influence enters the equation. It involves things like the possibility of socialization or re-socialization campaigns that incrementally shape our beliefs about who "we" are. When Americans celebrate July 4 in the United States, for example, with flags, parades, ceremonies, and fireworks, feelings of patriotism and nationalism will likely arise within most of them. No one has to say directly: "You must feel patriotically about the United States." The message is implicit in the images, and it is activated within the individuals.

Implicit activation needn't be entirely subliminal. Recall from Chapter 2 the priming research in which the faint smell of citrus or the presence of a briefcase (versus flowers) could make a difference in our attitudes and behavior. But, and here is the key point, persuasive stimuli *can* be subliminal, or at least that's what Hassin's data show.

In Hassin's pioneering study, participants were shown subliminal images of the Israeli flag. This subliminal exposure was presented to both right-leaning and left-leaning Israeli Jews, and was controlled in the experimental laboratory. The question of the participants' awareness (or unawareness) of the flag stimulus was checked and rechecked:

> Participants in all experiments came to our Q4 laboratory and were told that they would take part in an experiment in which sentences will appear in different locations on the screen, preceded by cues that mark the location of their appearance. The "practice phase," in which participants were to "practice responding to the cues" allowed us to prime images of the Israeli flag.
>
> Participants were asked to indicate, by pressing a key, whether each "cue" appeared in the upper or lower part of the screen. Unbeknown to them, each "cue" was immediately preceded by an image of the flag (or that of a control stimulus) that was presented for no more than 16 ms. Using technical jargon, the stimuli that participants were able to consciously perceive served as *masks*. They prevented participants from consciously perceiving the *prime*, the image of the flag (or that of the control stimulus).
>
> After completing this first experiment, participants went on to do a second experiment in which they were asked to answer questions that appeared either in the lower or the upper part of the screen. Prior to every question a flag (or a control stimulus) was once again flashed for up to 16 ms (followed by a mask).
>
> To verify that this exposure to the image of the flag was indeed subliminal, we ran a separate experiment in which participants were explicitly asked to indicate whether they saw a flag or a control stimulus just before each mask. The results were clear. Participants' performance did not significantly deviate from chance, indicating that they could not discriminate between flag and control trials. We conclude, then, that our flag-priming manipulation was subliminal.
>
> (Hassin, et al., 2009)

Hassin's method, and variations thereof, has been used in studies of implicit nationalism on three continents. His Israeli study found that subliminal exposure to their national flag had a moderating effect on right- and left-leaning Israeli Jews, bringing the two groups closer together ideologically. The point: subliminal images worked to shift and change the political ideological attitudes of both conservatives and liberals in the study.

In other studies, Hassin has examined the impact of subliminal exposure to various national flags to see how it might affect attitudes toward minorities (Hassin, et al., 2007).

And so, your authors now tentatively conclude that subliminal stimulation seems clearly, at least in these studies, to have been persuasive as a socializing or re-socializing tool (e.g., Butz, et al., 2007; Ferguson & Hassin, 2007; Ferguson, et al., 2009; Kay & Jost, 2003). While still believing that most swans are white, and most claims of "subliminal advertising" is questionable at best, we now conclude that Hassin may in fact have presented us with the equivalent of a black swan.

A Closing Story

For as long as the villagers of Diabougou, Senegal, could remember, it had been custom for the young girls of the community to submit to the extremely painful and often dangerous process of female circumcision. Each year during the rainy season, the ritual circumciser of Diabougou would use a razor blade to remove the clitoris, and sometimes the inner and outer vaginal lips, of 200 children. The process was not unique to Senegal; indeed, according to the World Health Organization (*Female genital mutilation,* 2014), about 125 million African and Middle Eastern women are circumcised, and thousands die as a result. Thus, it is all the more remarkable that one educational campaign was able to turn public opinion around in much of Senegal. Beginning in July 1997, scores of Senegalese communities declared an end to female circumcision and began pressing other villages to join them.

By Walt's (1998) account, the conversion process began in 1975 when an American exchange student named Molly Melching came to Senegal and launched an intensive literacy and skills training program under the auspices of UNICEF and later through her NGO, "Tostan" (meaning "breakthrough" in the native language). Melching intended to change health practices in Senegal, but she first took pains to find out what arguments and appeals would work with the villagers. "We never spoke about sexuality," she said (Walt, 1998). Indeed, the education programs waited several months before broaching the subject of health, let alone the highly sensitive topic of clitoral removal. Other well-intentioned outsiders had wanted to make a political issue of genital mutilation, declaring it a barbaric act, but this, in Melching's view, would be counterproductive.

Key to Melching's campaign was altering the attitudes and norms of the villagers. The latter would prove especially resistant to change. Melching's expertise and obvious dedication to the Senegalese gave her enormous credibility. She used it to recruit villagers similar in most respects to the people she was seeking to influence. With these opinion leaders, she focused repeatedly on the dangers of female circumcision to the health of the children, and this proved to be the winning argument. Still, there was considerable resistance, especially among the men of the communities. But when they voiced objection to breaking with tradition, Melching's recruits were ready with normative arguments the men could understand. Said one, "When the drumbeat changes, the dance has to change, too" (Walt, 1998).

Today, Melching reports that 7000 communities across eight African countries have "publicly declared their abandonment of female genital cutting (FGC) and child/forced marriage" following their direct or indirect engagement in Tostan's Community Empowerment Program and that the organization anticipates a Senegalese national-level public declaration against these practices in 2015 (*Promoting Health and Positive Practices*, 2014).

SUMMARY

A persuasive campaign is an organized, sustained attempt at influencing groups or organizations through a series of messages. Some campaigns are product-oriented, others image-oriented, and still others issue-oriented. In the last category are campaigns aimed at eliciting specific behaviors, and others aimed at hearts and minds.

This chapter presented a general introduction to campaign planning by way of a model that covered goal setting, research and development, basic strategy, mobilization, legitimacy, promotion, and activation. Having read this section, you should be in a better position to analyze persuasive campaigns and to plan and administer small-scale campaigns of your own.

The field of public relations occasions bitter debate between proponents and opponents. At its most benign, public relations is information giving—for example, a news release announcing a corporation's appointment of a new CEO. But public relations is also sophisticated issue advocacy, and sometimes it involves no-holds-barred crisis management. By way of illustration, the chapter offered analyses of a Mobil advertisement and of President Clinton's August 17, 1998, apologia.

One broad category of campaigns gets labeled "education" by friends and "propaganda" by enemies. It involves efforts at socializing unformed minds and, more controversially, re-socialization of a sort practiced by organizations bent on converting people to new lifestyles and ideologies. Socialization campaigns typically indoctrinate under some benign label such as education or entertainment, whereas re-socialization campaigns are often alleged to involve brainwashing or thought control. There are important differences between the methods of influence used by fringe groups such as religious cults and those of culturally approved groups such as mainstream denominations, but there are also similarities. This chapter has attended to both.

QUESTIONS AND PROJECTS FOR FURTHER STUDY

1   Why do persuasive campaigns tend to be so much more influential than one-shot speeches or essays?

2   Why is goal setting a never-ending part of the campaign process?

3   How, if at all, do you distinguish between education and propaganda? In your view, is all persuasion propaganda? Be sure to test your view against difficult cases. Would you say that Molly Melching propagandized, for example?

4   Given the evidence against James Vicary and Wilson Brian Key's claims about American advertising and subliminal persuasion, why is it that the topic continues to intrigue and fascinate us? Why do we want to believe that there are hidden messages in American ads?

5   Consider corporate issue advocacy campaigns of late for such things as "clean coal" or oil exploration in America. Do you believe these campaigns sway public opinion? And if not, why do corporations spend so much money on them?

6   How has the Internet changed social movement campaigns? Do you think campaigns are achieving their goals, especially in light of the cost of implementing and sustaining them?

7   Define the word "cult." Then, define "indoctrination." Why do you think it is so difficult to arrive at one agreed-upon definition for these terms?

8   More than any previous chapter, this one raised profoundly disturbing questions of ethics.

   a   What would you do if you knew that your efforts at reducing infant mortality in an impoverished community would lead to malnutrition and civil strife among its inhabitants?

   b   Would you have been willing to use deliberate ambiguity in ghostwriting President Clinton's August 17 apologia? How about outright deception?

   c   Would you approve of instilling healthy nutritional habits in teenagers through campaigns that deliberately attempt persuasion in the guise of information giving or entertainment? Would you attempt to shame people into good health, even in the face of John Stuart Mill's critique of normative controls?

   d   In light of your answer to the foregoing question, would you bestow a prize or criticism on Molly Melching for her efforts in Senegal?

9   How would you evaluate the ethics of the Mobil advertorial and of Clinton's speech?

EXERCISES

1   Design a campaign that you or your group can reasonably hope to accomplish in a month or less. Be sure to go over the components discussed in this chapter, considering audience and situation in goal setting and opportunities as well as obstacles in basic strategizing. Then, if there is time, try to implement your plan.

2   Find a grassroots organization in your community that is engaged in a persuasive campaign. It could be a religious organization seeking to recruit new members, a political campaign, a social service organization that is seeking to raise funds or recruit volunteers, etc. Attend meetings and gather data, and write up a report analyzing the campaign's potential for success based on the presentation in this chapter. If you decide the data will help them, share them with the organization.

3   Conduct research concerning the issue of subliminal persuasion, looking at both scholarly and popular sources, and create a presentation for class presenting your conclusions about whether it truly exists or not.

4   Do an Internet search on Paul Ingram and recovered memory, writing a short paper on the topic.

KEY TERMS

- Advertorials
- Brainwashing
- Corporate issue advocacy
- Crisis management campaigns
- Implicit activation

- Implicit nationalism
- Indoctrination campaigns
- Mind control
- Public relations campaigns
- Subliminal persuasion

REFERENCES

Alinsky, S. (1971). *Rules for radicals*. New York: Random House.

Baines, P., Egan, J., & Jefkins, F. (2004). *Public relations: Contemporary issues and techniques*. Burlington, MA: Elsevier Butterworth-Heinemann.

Baxter, W. L. (1981). The news release: An idea whose time is gone? *Public Relations Review*, 7, 27–31.

Before you buy pink. (n.d.). Retrieved January 6, 2015, from Think Before You Pink.org; Breast Cancer Action: http://thinkbeforeyoupink.org/before-you-buy/

Bettinghaus, E. P., & Cody, M. J. (1994). *Persuasive communication*. New York: Wadsworth.

Billig, M. (1995) *Banal nationalism*. London: Sage Publications.

Blumenthal, S. (1980). *The permanent campaign*. Boston: Beacon.

Brittany Maynard named one of PEOPLE's 25 most intriguing people. (2014, December 12). Retrieved January 9, 2015, from Pr Newswire: www.prnewswire.com/news-releases/brittany-maynard-named-one-of-peoples-25-most-intriguing-people-300009075.html

Bumpers, D. (1999). Retired Senator Bumpers's speech [Transcript]. Retrieved July 16, 2009, from www. cnn/stories/1999/01/21/transcripts/bumpers/html

Butterick, K. (2011). *Introducing public relations: Theory and practice*. Thousand Oaks, CA: Sage.

Butz, D. A., Plant, E. A., & Doerr, C. E. (2007). Liberty and justice for all? Implications of exposure to the U.S. flag for intergroup relations. *Personality and Social Psychology Bulletin*, 33, 396.

Carroll, R. T. (2003). *The skeptic's dictionary: A collection of strange beliefs, amusing deceptions, and dangerous delusions*. Hoboken, NJ: Wiley Press.

Cialdini, R. (2009). *Influence: Science and practice* (5th ed.). Boston: Pearson.

Clines, F. X. (1998, September 30). The therapy question: Does Clinton need to turn to ministers or a psychotherapist, too? *New York Times*, p. A22.

Doucette, D. (2014, October 16). *The face of breast cancer*. Retrieved January 6, 2015, from *Huffington Post*: www.huffingtonpost.com/deborah-doucette/the-face-of-breast-cancer_b_5997528.html

Ellul, J. (1965). *Propaganda*. New York: Knopf.

Female genital mutilation—Fact Sheet No. 241. (2014, February). (World Health Organization, Producer) Retrieved January 7, 2015, from World Health Organization: www.who.int/mediacentre/factsheets/fs241/en/

Ferguson, M. J., & Hassin, R. R. (2007). On the automatic association between America and aggression for news watchers. *Personality and Social Psychology Bulletin*, 33, 1632–1647.

Ferguson, M. J., Carter, T. J., & Hassin, R. R. (2009). On the automaticity of nationalist ideology: The case of the USA. In Jost, J., Kay, A., & Thorisdottir, H. (eds), *Social and psychological bases of ideology and system justification*. New York: Oxford University Press.

Finnegan, J. R., Jr., Bracht, N., & Viswanath, K. (1989). Community power and leadership analysis in lifestyle campaigns. In Salmon, C. T. (ed.), *Information campaigns: Balancing social values and social change*. Newbury Park, CA: Sage Publications.

Gitlin, T. (1980). *The whole world is watching: Mass media in the making and unmaking of the new left*. Berkeley: University of California Press.

Greenwald, A. G., Spangenberg, E. R., Pratkanis, A. R., & Eskenazi, J. (1991). Double-blind tests of subliminal self-help audio tapes. *Psychological Science*, 2, 119–122.

Hassin, R. R., Ferguson, M. J., Shidlovsky, D., & Gross, T. (2007). Waved by invisible flags: The effects of subliminal exposure to flags on political thought and behavior. *Proceedings of the National Academy of Sciences*, 104, 19757–19761.

Hassin, R. R., Ferguson, M. J., Kardosh, R., Porter, S. C., Carter, T. J., & Dudareva, V. (2009). Précis of implicit nationalism, *Annals of the New York Academy of Sciences*, 1167, 135–145.

Hogan, J. M., & Olsen, D. (1989). The rhetoric of "nuclear" education. In Smith III, T. (ed.), *Propaganda: A pluralistic perspective*. New York: Praeger, pp. 165–180.

Jackall, R. (2010). *Moral mazes: The world of corporate managers*. Oxford: Oxford University Press.

Johnson, R. C. (1994). Parallels between recollections of repressed childhood sex abuse, kidnappings by space aliens, and the Salem witch hunts. *Institute for Psychological Therapies*. Retrieved July 16, 2009, from www.ipt-forensics.com/journal/volume6/j6_1_4.htm

Jowett, G. S., & O'Donnell, V. (2006). *Propaganda and persuasion* (4th ed.). Thousand Oaks, CA: Sage Publications.

Kay, A. C., & Jost, J. T. (2003). Complementary justice: Effects of "poor but happy" and "poor but honest" stereotype exemplars on system justification and implicit activation of the justice motive. *Journal of Personality and Social Psychology*, 85, 823–837.

Key, W. B. (1973). *Subliminal seduction*. New York: New American Library.

Key, W. B. (1976). *Media sexploitation*. New York: Signet.

Key, W. B. (1980). *The clam-plate orgy: And other subliminal techniques for manipulating your behavior*. Upper Saddle River, NJ: Prentice Hall.

Kolbert, K. (1999, January 25). Those poll-defying Republicans. *New Yorker*, 74, 25.

Lerner, B. H. (2010, October 11). *Pink ribbon fatigue.* Retrieved January 7, 2015, from *The New York Times*: http://well.blogs.nytimes.com/2010/10/11/pink-ribbon-fatigue/?_r=0

Lofland, J. (1977). *Doomsday cult.* New York: Irvington.

Maraniss, D. (1998). *The Clinton enigma.* New York: Simon & Schuster.

McGee, M. (1998, August 19). A rhetorical criticism of Clinton's speech. *CRTNET.* Retrieved November 13, 2010, from http://lists.psu.edu/cgi-bin/wa?A2=ind9808&L=CRTNET&P=R8194&D=0&H=0&O=T&T=0

Mill, J. S. (1859). On liberty. In Robson, J. M. (ed.), *Collected works of John Stuart Mill* (vol. 18). Ontario, Canada: University of Toronto Press.

Miller, M. C. (1981, September 16). Massa come home. *New Republic*, 185, 29–32.

Miller, S. (2014, November 4). *Brittany Maynard: A life, a legacy.* doi:07347456

Newsom, D., Scott, A., & Turk, J. (1989). *This is PR: The realities of public relations* (4th ed.). Belmont, CA: Wadsworth.

New York Times (1998, August 19). Betrayal and embarrassment [Editorial], p. A30.

O'Hara, E. (2008). *Planning an advocacy campaign* (Center for State and Local Policy). Retrieved January 7, 2015, from Maine Development Foundation: www.mdf.org/files/NTHPAdvocacy.pdf/275/

Pentony, P. (1981). *Models of influence in psychotherapy.* New York: Free Press.

Perloff, R. M. (2014). *The dynamics of persuasion: Communication and attitudes in the 21st century* (5th ed.). New York: Routledge.

Pratkanis, A. (1995). How to sell a pseudoscience. *Skeptical Inquirer*, 19, 19–25.

Pratkanis, A., & Aronson, E. (2001). *Age of propaganda: The everyday use and abuse of persuasion.* New York: Henry Holt.

Promoting Health and Positive Practices. (2014). Retrieved January 8, 2015, from Tostan: Dignity for All: http://tostan.org/area-of-impact/health

Rampton, S., & Stauber, J. (2001). *Trust us, we're experts: How industry manipulates science and gambles with your future.* New York: Tarcher.

Rice, R. E., & Atkins, C. K. (2013). *Public communication campaigns* (4th ed.). Thousand Oaks, CA: Sage.

Richardson, J. T. (2014). Conversion and brainwashing: Controversies and contrasts. In Chryssides, G. D. (ed.), *The Bloomsbury companion to new religious movements.* London: Bloomsbury Academic, pp. 89–102.

Salmon, C. T. (ed.). (1989). *Information campaigns: Balancing social values and social change.* Newbury Park, CA: Sage Publications.

Sanburn, J. (2014, November 3). Brittany Maynard could revive stalled 'Death With Dignity' movement. *Time.com.* (Ebscohost, compiler), doi:99206525.

Schein, C. H. (1961). *Coercive persuasion: A sociopsychological analysis of the "brainwashing" of American civilian prisoners of the Chinese Communists.* New York: Norton.

Simons, H. W. (1994). *Persuasion: understanding, practice, and analysis.* New York: McGraw-Hill.

Simons, H. W. (2000). A dilemma-centered analysis of William Clinton's August 17th apologia: Implications for theory and method. *Quarterly Journal of Speech*, 86, 438–453.

Smith, G., & Heath, R. (1990). Moral appeals in Mobil's op-ed campaign. *Public Relations Review*, 16, 48–54.

Smith, W. J. (2014, October 9). *Brittany Maynard: The vultures circle.* Retrieved January 9, 2015, from The National Review: www.nationalreview.com/human-exceptionalism/390006/brittany-maynard-vultures-circle-wesley-j-smith

Snyder, L. B., Hamilton, M. A., Mitchell, E. W., Kiwanuka-Tondo, J., Fleming-Milici, F., & Proctor, D. (2004). A meta-analysis of the effect of mediated health communication campaigns on behavior change in the United States. *Journal of Health Communication*, 9, 71–96.

Sproule, J. M. (1997). *Propaganda and democracy: The American experience of media and mass persuasion.* New York: Cambridge University Press.

Sterling, C. H. (2009). *Encyclopedia of journalism.* Thousand Oaks, CA: Sage.

Storey, J. D. (2008). Development communication campaigns. In Donsbach, W. (ed.), *The international encyclopedia of communication.* Oxford: Blackwell.

Tada, J. E. (2014, October 14). *Joni Eareckson Tada to Brittany Maynard: God alone chooses the day you die, not you.* Retrieved January 9, 2015, from ReligiousNews.Com: www.religionnews.com/2014/10/15/brittany-maynards-choice-die-personal-private/

Walt, V. (1998, June 23). Female circumcision: A village issue. *International Herald Tribune,* 11.

Weir, W. (1984, October 15). Another look at subliminal "facts." *Advertising Age,* p. 46.

Working to inspire social change. (2014). Retrieved December 17, 2014, from TobaccoFreeCA: www.tobaccofreeca.com/ads/about/

Zaltman, G., & Duncan, R. (1977). *Strategies for planned change.* New York: John Wiley.

Zimbardo, P. G. (2002). Mind control: Psychological reality or mindless rhetoric? *Monitor on Psychology,* 33(10), 5.

Zimbardo, P. G., Ebbesen, E. B., & Maslach, C. (1977). *Influencing attitudes and changing behavior* (rev. ed.). Reading, MA: Addison-Wesley.

CHAPTER 11

Staging Political Campaigns

The twenty-first century has provided many changes in political campaign persuasion. In just the last few years, campaigns have evolved to where they now incorporate interactive candidate web pages that are used to build volunteer bases and raise funds. When it comes to political reporting, blogging and tweeting in real time by traditional journalists and everyday citizens alike is superseding traditional news reporting, with the Internet providing unfiltered and unedited information that is often recorded as it happens. Most people now have cell phones with still and video cameras, serving to keep politicians honest, but also keeping them constantly on their guard for fear of unscripted remarks that might ruin their careers. Finally, the Internet itself is a repository of political artifacts at our fingertips: Thanks to Google, Wikipedia, YouTube and more, we have access to almost any document, image, or film, and we have it almost instantly.

Despite all the changes, many things about the rhetoric of campaigning remain consistent. For better or worse, today's campaign attack ads are similar in style to those in years past, distorting opponents' photos so that they will be grainy, appear unflattering, or resemble police mug shots. They have a recognizable "code" that incorporates emotions of despair, coldness, deviousness, distance, gloominess, and national shame (Berger, 2007). The verbal and visual grammar is fairly standard:

They contrast the most unattractive pictures they can find of their opponent with the most appealing photos of their own candidate, they Quote Mine, they scare you into thinking that if their opponent is elected they'll, literally, send your world straight to Hell and personally hand it over to Satan himself.

(*Attack of the Political Ad*, n.d.)

These traditional styles of campaigning have been on full display during recent campaign seasons, as candidates engaged in verbal and pictorial political combat, much of it negative. And, as Richardson points out, that's probably as it should be: "Why shouldn't candidates stress their opponents' failings? History tells us this is as American as apple pie" (2008).

A recent change in American law, the 2010 Supreme Court's decision on *Citizens United v. Federal Election Commission*, has created the opportunity for even harsher political campaign persuasion than we had seen earlier. Thanks to the Court's decision, now unions, corporations, and associations can spend unlimited amounts of money to influence elections, provided that they don't coordinate their efforts with a candidate (Mayersohn, 2014). While it is worth remembering that outside groups had existed before, this recent court ruling has changed just about everything. Formerly, groups were limited in the ways that they could spend money, there were limits on contributions, there were limits on how close to Election Day ads could run, and there were disclosure rules so that we knew from where the money came. All of that changed with the Court's ruling, as the United States entered an era of "Super PACs" with political activity by tax-exempt "dark money" organizations that don't have to disclose their donors (*Citizens United*, n.d.). What that means is that giant corporations that might formerly have feared consumer backlash for their political involvement can now use their general treasuries to funnel cash into promoting candidates who support their interests without fear of having their identities revealed, and that is exactly what is happening. Super PACS added $600 million in the 2012 election cycle (Mayersohn, 2014). And thanks to *Citizens United*, that cash can be used for all sorts of expenditures, including "political advertisements that expressly call for the election or defeat of a candidate, and electioneering communications immediately before an election" (Krumholtz, 2013).

Taken together, the tradition of negative political advertising coupled with a new influx of cash from outside groups, is transformative. Now, it is commonplace to see ads not just from candidates and political parties, but also from special interests of all sorts, and these ads can run right up until Election Day. Candidates cannot "coordinate" with Super PACS, which provides opportunity for them to deny responsibility for ads that are run on their behalf. Therefore, it is now common to see the most edgy negative ads coming from outside groups, and to hear the candidates proclaim that it is all out of their control.

The Internet and social media has also created new ways of campaigning, changing the ways voters receive and engage with political ads. Harsh ads attacking a political opponent show up on political web pages or in e-mails that are directed at targeted audiences who are already supporters of the candidate who is sending them, while softer ads that are deemed more appropriate for general public consumption appear on television, especially during the local evening news. The hope, of course, is that the dedicated folks at home will take those harsh ads and share them on places like Facebook, thereby giving candidates free media. Consequently, Facebook becomes a place of political public display, as people share posts in a manner akin to how they formerly put political signs in their yards. When we put a sign in our yard, or share a message on Facebook, we are letting those who know us see that we have a strong political orientation, and personal public endorsement can be persuasive indeed. That being said, the posts on Facebook are not uncommonly much more derogatory than a yard sign, and most of us can recall blocking a "friend" for her unkind and ubiquitous political posts.

All of this serves to remind us, to quote Finley Peter Dunne, that "politics ain't beanbag." It is a contest, and the stakes are high. And, for all the changes and technological advances, it still all comes down to a simple proposition: to win an election, a candidate must get 50% of the vote plus one. Campaigns, while sometimes annoying, are still important, and, once we pick up on the strategizing behind political campaigns, we see that they are endlessly fascinating and immensely instructive about the art of persuasion.

Way back in 1924, Calvin Coolidge's brain trust produced a silent film for movie house distribution showing "Silent Cal," as he was called, to be a man of great energy and vigor. The hyping of our modern political candidates has not changed much since those days, but it has become a good deal more sophisticated. The George W. Bush years provided a textbook's worth of lessons in how to capture the ideological right and steal the opponent's thunder through two elections. And in fact it was the Republican political experts—advising first Nixon, then Reagan, and then both Bushes—who first fashioned today's technologies for fine-tuning the electorate, targeting swing voters with market-tested, custom-tailored appeals, and, above all, raising the enormous sums of money necessary to run extravagant media campaigns. The campaigns of Bill Clinton and, even more effectively, Barack Obama, built on those Republican strategies, and today both major American political parties are experts in using every available means of persuasion to advocate for their candidates. No industry—not the soap makers nor the beer brewers nor the car manufacturers—spends as much for mass persuasion on an annualized basis in the United States as do the organizations that seek to get their candidates elected to high office. Not only that, American political campaign practices are now being imitated worldwide, complete with sound bites, photo opportunities, quick responses, nightly tracking polls, focus groups, opposition research, and devastating attack ads (Nagourney, 1999; Plasser, 2002; Hallin & Mancini, 2004; Lara, 2009).

These accoutrements of the "new politics" are overlaid on the old in the United States. The new politics is never ending; no sooner has an election been won (or lost) than the next election's hopefuls begin plotting strategy, lining up supporters, and putting on fundraisers. First-term presidents may govern more or less independently, but they always need people near them who'll answer the question, "How will this affect the chances for re-election?" The pollsters and the media consultants are seldom far from the Oval Office.

The "old" politics is confined to a period marked out as "election season," a time and a place for the type of persuasion called "campaigning." It's often marked visually by flags, balloons, decorations done in patriotic colors, posters, bumper stickers, perky music, and campaign slogans—"America must get moving again!" Election season is a special time and place separate from political business as usual. It is a time for assessing where we've been as a political people, where we are, and where we think we ought to be going—a break in the usual debates over ways and means, war and peace. Sometimes, as in the days of Lincoln and Douglas, it involves long speeches in stuffy auditoriums or long harangues at outdoor rallies, but increasingly it is marked by sound bite politics and the visual politics of YouTube, political posts on Twitter, television ads, and photo ops.

This chapter examines political campaign persuasion, both old and new, as visual spectacle and verbal argument. In particular, it will take note of the strategies and tactics of contemporary presidential campaigns, some of them so Machiavellian as to place the interests of the campaigner in competition with those of the society as a whole.

PERSUASION IN FOUR STAGES: PRESIDENTIAL CAMPAIGNING

Political campaigning in this country has become an extended operation, even for local and county offices. Presidential campaigning, in particular, proceeds actively for years, and over the life of a campaign different approaches are used. Trent and Friedenberg (2011) have provided a template for presidential campaigns and have argued that four stages exist: (1) the pre-primary period (**surfacing**); (2) the primary period (**winnowing**); (3) the nominating conventions (**legitimating**); and (4) the general election period (**contesting**). Each stage requires specialized forms of persuasion, and it is to those stages that we now turn our focus.

(1) Pre-Primary Period (Surfacing)

In a perfect world, the ideal presidential candidate is someone who would make an ideal president—a statesman or stateswoman who is able to transcend politics in the nation and engage the world's challenges. But to become president, one must be a politician in the narrow sense, able first to win the party's nomination and then also be the superior competitor in the general election. Few among the nation's leaders possess all these attributes, and those who do may choose not to run.

The prospect of having to solicit enormous sums of money deters some potential candidates; in 2016, Hillary Clinton raised over $1 billion, while Donald Trump's campaign spending was closer to $500 million; Barack Obama raised $745 million for his 2008 campaign and $715 million in his 2012 presidential campaign, whereas his 2008 Republican opponent John McCain raised $367 million and his 2012 Republican opponent Mitt Romney raised $446 million (Krumholtz, 2008; Kuhnhenn & Drinkard, 2008; Vargas, 2008; Krumholtz, 2013). Given that, it is common that candidates who run are often fabulously rich or well connected. To be taken seriously, the candidate will need organization, endorsements from influential party members, and name recognition. Of course, some individuals declare themselves as candidates not expecting to win, but because they want the chance to exercise influence and insert a particular perspective into the campaign. In 2012, we saw this with the candidacies of people like Congressman Ron Paul, Pizza Barron Herman Cain, and Congresswoman Michele Bachmann. And some run for office because they realize their ambitions for the future require that they enter what they know in advance will be a losing battle; they run to gain the name recognition to set themselves up for future races.

"Serious" contenders—those with a real chance at their party's nomination—must be recognized as such. First, they must persuade party members, news organizations, and a critical mass of citizens to think of them as a contender. They

FIGURE 11.1   *2016 presented a particularly testing pre-primary period for Republicans who wanted to challenge likely nominee Hillary Clinton. The Republican Primary race was wide open, and many entered, making the surfacing phase more difficult for individual candidates. Here is a photo of the Republican field of candidates, taken during a debate. You can imagine how difficult it would be to stand out on such a crowded stage.*
© AP/John Minchillo

must announce their intention to run and be outfitted and positioned for the journey ahead. Experienced organizers need to be recruited in every state to get the candidate's name on the ballot and to build a campaign infrastructure. The news outlets must be persuaded to quote the candidates and label them as genuine contenders so that the general public will come to see them as such. And enough citizens must be persuaded to come to believe in them so that they get a significant percentage of positive responses on polls asking the question, "If the presidential election were held today, for whom would you vote?"

Early money, and plenty of it, plays a crucial role in winning media attention, earning the respect of party regulars, and garnering additional funding from organizations and individuals that literally invest in politicians, hoping to get access and more. This is important, because year after year the best-funded candidates win. For example, *United Republic* reported that in the 2012, "the candidate with more money won the race 91 percent of the time" (VandenDolder, 2014), and *Open Secrets* reports that in 2014, "the candidate who spent the most prevailed 94.2% of the time" (Choma, 2014). This need to persuade donors to contribute raises important questions about the ethics of today's political campaigns, for, if candidates are pre-selected by wealthy campaign contributors, is the electoral process truly democratic?

In sum, gaining name recognition, building a campaign organization, and raising money are the central components of the surfacing period, which can be lengthy and last more than a year. Given that, the surfacing period presents a unique set of persuasive tasks for candidates. First, they must persuade the public of their fitness for office and that they are serious contenders. Second, they must display that they understand the political game by engaging in expected political rituals such as announcing their candidacy. Finally, they must raise money and work to establish relationships with media figures to set themselves apart from their competitors.

(2) Primary Election Period (Winnowing)

To win their party's presidential nomination, a candidate needs a majority of the convention delegates behind them. Because most delegates are elected in state presidential **primaries** and a number of primaries are scheduled early in the year, the early months of the primary season are pivotal, especially the **Super Tuesday** contests, in which a large number of states (including states with the most delegates) have primary elections on the same day.

The voting populations in primaries are different from those in general elections, and this presents interesting rhetorical challenges. Relatively few people vote in primaries, and those who do tend to be party loyalists (except in the few states that permit persons not registered with a party to vote in that party's primary). Not only are primary voters loyalists, but they tend to be ideologically committed: more conservative than the typical Republican in Republican primaries, more liberal than the typical Democrat in Democratic primaries.

Thinking It Through

Do you vote in the primaries? Do you know others who do? In your experience, do primary voters fit the model presented here?

Sometimes, a candidate runs unopposed or enjoys an early lock on the party's nomination, but most candidates are not so fortunate. Instead, they must court the ideological extremes of their party, in the process striking chords that might prove to be sources of embarrassment in the general election. And not only must competitors for their party's nomination play to its ideological extremes, but they must also adapt their campaigns to state and regional interests, recognizing that styles differ from state to state as well. New Jersey dwellers tend to expect a confrontational style of politics that is anathema in Minnesota. New Hampshirites expect candidates to address them face-to-face, whereas California requires a campaign built around heavy television advertising in the state's costly media markets. Even when running just a statewide race, such regional differences can be pronounced, Political strategist James Carville famously described Pennsylvania as "Pittsburgh and Philadelphia, with Alabama in between" (Davin, 2010) Therefore, local experience becomes crucial, because candidates must run multiple mini-campaigns simultaneously in different states.

Primaries serve most of all as places where candidates can test out their persuasive messages and get feedback from the voters. If they are wise, candidates analyze their primary performances and adjust their messages as they go, seeing the primary season as a valuable time of "spring training" that helps them get into shape for the general election. For example, in April 2008, Barack Obama made what many considered a major error when, at a private San Francisco fundraiser, he said the following:

> You go into these small towns in Pennsylvania and, like a lot of small towns in the Midwest, the jobs have been gone now for 25 years and nothing's replaced them. And it's not surprising, then, they get bitter, they cling to guns or religion or antipathy to people who aren't like them or anti-immigrant sentiment or anti-trade sentiment as a way to explain their frustrations.

> (Zorn, 2008)

Now, these comments, in and of themselves, are blunt and unguarded but not unreasonable judgments about a particular sub-set of the electorate. In fact, one of your authors (Jean) lives in the Pennsylvania area Barack Obama is describing, and she would suggest that his description is mostly accurate. But the context, timing, and location surrounding the remarks created problems. Obama made the remarks only weeks before the Pennsylvania primary. He made them to liberal, wealthy California patrons, which made the remarks sound doubly condescending. He believed he was speaking in a private setting and forgot about the possibilities of modern media, not considering that his comments might have been recorded.

FIGURE 11.2 *After making condescending remarks about the people of Pennsylvania, Barack Obama worked to repair his verbal blunder by going bowling with Pennsylvania Senator Bob Casey. In his quest to show he was a regular guy, he bowled a 37, thereby possibly reinforcing the critique that he was an elitist who did not understand working-class Rust-Belt voters.*

Not surprisingly, Obama's opponents pounced. Hillary Clinton proclaimed that she "was taken aback by the demeaning remarks Senator Obama made about people in small-town America" and that his remarks were "elitist" and "out of touch." And John McCain's spokesperson called them "nothing short of breathtaking" (Tapper, 2008). A day or two later, Obama recast his remarks, demonstrating that he'd learned from his error and needed to adjust his message:

> I said, well look, they're frustrated and for good reason. Because for the last 25 years they've seen jobs shipped overseas. They've seen their economies collapse. They have lost their jobs. They have lost their pensions. They have lost their healthcare ... And of course they're bitter. Of course they're frustrated. You would be too.
>
> (Tapper, 2008)

He adjusted his discourse into language that would resonate with rural rust-belt voters, working to frame the situation from their perspective. And then, to show he'd really gotten the message, he went bowling with Pennsylvania Senator Bob Casey in Altoona (Powell, 2008).

Obama's bowling excursion, though, where he rolled a 37, in many ways reinforced the very elitist concerns he was seeking to overcome. At one point Obama told fellow bowlers that his economic plan is better than his bowling. "It has to be," one man in the next lane called out in reply (Powell, 2008). Obama took the ribbing in good spirit and showed humility, and that helped a bit. But in fact, it wasn't until he played pick-up basketball, shot pool, and discussed college football that he really regained some credibility as an "average American." And as for the sub-set of the population who did live in rural small rust-belt towns—those who were concerned about their guns and valued their religion—he never won them over. Most of them just saw Obama's remarks as reinforcement for what they already believed about him: that he was an elite Chicago politician who didn't understand their way of life. On Pennsylvania primary day, they simply voted for Hillary Clinton or John McCain.

Consequently, the persuasive tasks for candidates during the primary period involve appealing to the more extreme and dedicated members of their party while also adjusting their messages to appeal to voters who have differing concerns depending on the part of the country in which they live. The process invariably results in *winnowing*, as candidates drop out and the contest tightens; the goal is to be the last candidate standing. Finally, the primary period presents delicate persuasive requirements because it is a fight in the family: Candidates need to remember that they are campaigning against members of their own party, and that their primary opponent might be the person who ends up being the nominee. So, during the primary, candidates must persuade voters that they are "best" while simultaneously not supplying negative attacks that the opposing party can use in the general election.

(3) Convention Period (Legitimating)

Once the primary elections are over and the choices have been winnowed down to a single winning candidate, the political party conventions formalize the party's presidential ticket and its platform—the positions it expects the candidates to run on. With presidential primaries stealing all the suspense of who the eventual nominee will be, the major television networks no longer provide gavel-to-gavel coverage, as they had in the good old days when party conventions provided much more drama and excitement. Still, the conventions have important functions to perform.

Well-orchestrated conventions can give a candidate a 10- to 15-point bump in the polls, and small wonder. Millions of voters watch, who, up until then, might not otherwise have paid much attention to the candidates. They do so, moreover, under conditions close to ideal for displaying adulation by the faithful, celebrity endorsements, a closing of ranks among party factions, and, most importantly, the presidential candidate on film and then live, presenting a nomination acceptance speech that has been carefully crafted and market tested for maximum impact on the undecided voter. The convention experience is designed to energize the party faithful and prepare them for the upcoming struggle, but the audience that matters most is outside the arena.

Convention planners work particularly hard to present a spectacular television event that will lead to voters committing early to their party's candidate—this at a time when increasing numbers of voters are postponing their decisions until October. The planners hope that a sizable proportion of those watching will find some issue or aspect of the candidate compelling. Does the platform statement on abortion convince some single-issue voters to go with one side or the other? Did the candidate's biography film capture qualities in the candidate that some viewers will find well-nigh irresistible?

The centerpiece of the convention is the nomination ritual. It begins with a film about the candidate, reviewing his or her life and accomplishments. This campaign film personalizes the candidate while at the same time demonstrating the candidate's extraordinary leadership qualities. It provides contexts for understanding and assessing the candidate as someone larger-than-life, so that, when the acceptance speech is given, it seems as if the delegates are applauding not just the person who won the primaries but a full-fledged political visionary.

On the final night of the convention, the candidate delivers a speech where he or she accepts the nomination of the party, which is rhetorically positioned to be the final and grandest moment of the event. The speech, delivered to the faithful, is frequently interrupted by applause to create a sense of political interaction: The candidate's statements are answered with positive public endorsements. It is crafted to contain memorable lines and striking imagery that can later be chopped up into 10-, 20-, and 30-second ads for broadcast in the fall. The event ends with a demonstration of party unity as friend and foe alike gather to congratulate the candidate before the candidate goes off to do head-to-head battle with the opponent from the other party.

(4) General Election Period (Contesting)

Traditionally, the conventions conclude in late summer and the general election campaign begins on Labor Day of the election year, although today serious campaigning is already well under way before then. But, by the time the general election period arrives, many uncertainties have been settled: The candidates have been winnowed down to the final contestants and the parties have legitimized their selections. From Labor Day until Election Day, the persuasive task is to garner more votes than one's opponent.

Voters decide on a candidate for a number of reasons, not all of them directly related to the campaigns being waged. For example, party identification (i.e., voting for the party rather than the candidate), while somewhat less prevalent today, remains important; generally, about one-half of all voters end up voting a **straight ticket** for one of the two major political parties. Minority parties and third-party candidates have an especially difficult time gaining traction in the American system, and this is no accident; there is a "history and array of laws, regulations, subsidies, and programs that benefit the major parties and discourage even the possibility of a challenge to the Democrat-Republican duopoly" (Bennett, 2009). So, party identification, with a solid institutional bias toward the major parties, is a relevant factor in how citizens cast their ballots.

Furthermore, the principle of social proof is operative with some Americans as they vote for candidates who are ahead in the polls, and it is in this area that the news media play a role. Jamieson's (1992) study of network coverage revealed a disturbing pattern: the candidate ahead in the polls tended to be accepted at face value in reports on day-to-day campaigning, while the candidate(s) behind in the polls was more likely to be second-guessed as having said or done something for effect and not from sincere belief. The news media strive to remain evenhanded and, in recent years, have engaged in greater public self-scrutiny (Kurtz, 1993) with organizations like FactCheck.org and Snopes.com keeping watch on the details offered by journalists. That being said, the issues and events journalists choose to cover and the way they cover them remain influential (Campbell, 2008; Cappella & Jamieson, 1997; Meyer, 2002; Tuman, 2008; D'Alessio, 2012).

Given the power of other factors in swaying voters, what, then, is the influence exerted by the candidates themselves? Is their persuasive influence during the general election period minimal unless the race is close, when it may be the decisive factor— sufficient to turn the tide or to mobilize the active support of those already inclined in their direction? Or are they highly influential, able to win converts from among substantial percentages of the electorate? This controversy continues to engage researchers on political campaigns (Campbell, 2008; Cappella & Jamieson, 1997; Perloff, 1998; Tuman, 2008, Pfetsch & Esser, 2012).

There seems to be little question that a candidate's campaign performance can be decisive in close races and can contribute to the large margin of victory in landslide elections. An example of this took place in the 2008 presidential race between John

McCain and Barack Obama. Over a mid-September weekend, the scope of American (and global) economic distress came into sharp relief, and the nation was confronted with what would become the greatest economic crisis since the Great Depression. The following Monday at a morning rally, John McCain responded to the weekend's events and struggled to find a consistent message. In the face of the weekend's Wall Street meltdown, he first said that "the fundamentals of our economy are strong" and then abruptly shifted to say that the fundamentals are "at great risk" (Barnes & Shear, 2008).

In response, Barack Obama blasted the Republican for being "disturbingly out of touch" with the reality that everyday Americans face:

> He just doesn't get what's happening between the mountain in Sedona where he lives and the corridors of Washington where he works.... Why else would he say, today, of all days—just a few hours ago—that the fundamentals of the economy are strong? Senator—what economy are you talking about?
>
> (Barnes & Shear, 2008)

With McCain's utterance of just one sentence, it seemed that the shape and tenor of the campaign shifted, and it was never to shift back. Later that day, McCain tried to do repair work. He explained that his words referred to "the American worker and their innovation, their entrepreneurship, the small business, those are the fundamentals of America, and I think they're strong" (Barnes & Shear, 2008). But later in the same speech, he talked about the country's current financial "crisis" and repeatedly said he was concerned about the fundamentals of the economy (Barnes & Shear, 2008). Ultimately, despite his efforts at repair, his original sentence took on the tenor of a mantra for his opponents and for comedians. It remained a powerful condemnation of McCain throughout the rest of the campaign.

McCain's rhetoric in response to the meltdown transformed and damaged that perception. During September he presented himself as at best unclear about the nation's domestic situation and at worst erratic in dealing with it. Obama's charge that he was "out of touch" stuck; it presented McCain as a wealthy elite and also called to mind McCain's age; he suddenly looked older and came to be openly mocked by people like Jon Stewart on *The Daily Show*, who played a clip of McCain in a presidential debate that portrayed him as a doddering old man wandering around looking for his dog.

What's more, his decision to suspend his campaign and skip the debate looked to some as cowardice and avoidance behavior. It came as two new national polls showed McCain "slipping in the head-to-head match up against Barack Obama due in large part to voters' inclination to trust the Illinois senator to solve the financial problems of the country" (Cillizza, 2008). Cowardice was a negative attribute one would never before have attached to John McCain, but it seemed to some voters a reasonable conclusion in light of the situation. And finally, the decision to suspend campaigning made McCain appear strategically unwise. It boxed him in to a double-bind: to avoid the debate raised the question of cowardice. Yet, to reverse course and attend it would make him "look the fool": Having stated that fixing the economy was the most important issue, he stood to lose face by looking less sincere if he participated. He would also look as if he'd decided the Obama camp was correct in their assessment of the situation in Washington (Relative, 2008).

Through the example of the events of September 2008, we see that the actions of candidates matter. John McCain ended up offering weak justifications for why he felt he could re-engage the campaign once he realized his challenge to Obama had failed and he did attend the debate. But, most observers, if pressed, would say that it was that two-week period in September that sealed his fate, putting Barack Obama firmly into the lead for the rest of the campaign and putting him in the White House.

As this case demonstrates, Obama was able to capitalize on McCain's blunders. This is not surprising, because research suggests that campaigns are better able to shape and reinforce responses than to change them outright. (But then again, this seems to be true of persuasion generally.)

Ultimately, in the general election phase, three types of campaign-related factors weigh on voter decisions: (1) candidates' positions on issues, (2) their perceived "habits of mind" (Jamieson, 1992), and (3) perceived attractiveness.

1 Positions on Issues

Throughout the campaign, candidates provide reasons why voters should elect them and not their opponents, but it is usually not until the general election period that most voters focus in. For some voters, hot-button issues such as social security, gun control, taxes, abortion, and foreign policy (including wars) are reasons enough to secure commitments from some voting blocks—for example "soccer moms," "NASCAR dads," blue-collar workers, peace activists, and senior citizens. Occasionally, though, candidates introduce issues that had not been on anyone's radar screen. For example, in 1960, John F. Kennedy accused then Vice President Nixon of partial responsibility for what he alleged was the nation's missile gap with the Soviet Union. The charge was false, but it effectively stole Nixon's thunder as a champion of military preparedness. Likewise the Massachusetts program of furloughing prisoners became an issue in 1988 after the Republicans introduced it in highly effective attack advertisements (to be featured later in the chapter). In any given election year, some issues are on virtually everyone's radar screen, and these, especially, require candidates to align themselves with swing voters.

2 Habits of Mind

Voters form general perceptions of candidates' trustworthiness and competence and perceptions, as well as more specific habits of mind, such as whether a candidate is genuinely a good listener, is able to make tough decisions, is disorganized, unintelligent, or badly informed. These perceptions are less the result of what candidates say about themselves than of what they exhibit under fire in general election debates, campaign events, and press conferences. Of course, advertising plays a role as well—both the candidate's and that of the opponent. Opposition research provides the basis for many an attack ad or comparison ad that contrasts one candidate's shining qualities to the other's objectionable qualities. Habits of mind are important—as important as candidate's positions on issues—and, during the general election period, candidates need to persuade voters to perceive them favorably. The winning candidate may not live up to campaign promises once in office, but it is unlikely that the candidate's habits of mind will change.

3 Attractiveness and Appearance

Candidates who appear likable, who appear to like the public (recall Cialdini, 2009, on cognitive shortcuts), and who seem physically more attractive have a decided edge over their less attractive counterparts. Are these factors the most relevant to a president's capacity to govern? Probably not, but they weigh heavily on many voters' decisions. Bill Clinton out-charmed George H. W. Bush (1992) and Bob Dole (1996), and Republicans counted on George W. Bush to do the same to Al Gore and John Kerry when they filled his campaign coffers to the brim in 2000 and 2004. In 2008, when Barack Obama appeared on *The View* and claimed that his distant cousin Brad Pitt got the better-looking side of the gene pool, journalist Barbara Walters declared, "We thought you were very sexy looking" (*Huffington Post*, 2008). In 2012, some experts saw Mitt Romney as more classically handsome than Barack Obama, but noted that Romney was perceived as cold and stiff; the contest was between "a warm, charming candidate" with an difficult record to defend running against "a statically handsome, competent candidate" who came across on television as "unavailable emotionally," and voters chose to go with warmth (Napoleon, n.d.). As Napoleon explains, just as with his predecessor Bill Clinton, Obama's win over Romney demonstrates that warm, charming candidates encourage some voters to overlook or excuse shortcomings in their performance.

Thinking It Through

Analyze a presidential race from the recent past in light of the three elements presented here. How did the candidates' stands on issues, habits of the mind, and attractiveness factor into the decisions that voters made?

The election of Barack Obama introduced another element to the discussion about the appearance of the candidate—he was the first African American to be the presidential nominee of a major party. Much discussed during his first campaign was the "Bradley Effect," an idea rooted in the 1982 California Governor's race, which suggested that, while people would tell pollsters that race didn't matter to their voting patterns, they would in fact consider it as they voted, thereby skewing the polls positively for black candidates. In fact, though, the reverse also turned out to be true. Barack Obama's race, for some voters, was the positive determining factor in their vote.

On the day after Obama was first elected in 2008, Anne Applebaum hypothesized about why his race might have benefited him. It was not just that black people voted in solidarity for him, she argued, but it was something much greater—Obama's appearance communicated that the American mythos was still true.

> Americans, white and black, liberal and conservative, are brought up to believe that their country is different, special, the "greatest nation on earth," a "city on a hill." We are all taught that our system is just, our laws are fair, our Constitution is something to be proud of. Lately, though, this self-image has taken a battering. We are fighting two wars, neither with remarkable success. We have just experienced a cataclysmic financial crisis. We are about to enter a recession. We are unloved around the world, and we know it. Electing our first black president won't by itself solve any of these problems, but [it] makes us feel good about ourselves.
>
> (Applebaum, 2008)

Applebaum's point is that Obama's physical appearance helped him win the election because it was restorative of our battered self-identificatory belief system. It reinforced that Americans are in fact who they think they are.

> Maybe it's superficial, and surely it won't last. But I am convinced that it explains a lot, both about the election result and about this weirdly euphoric aftermath. That desire to feel, once again, like "the greatest nation on earth" explains why my friend J. the Republican cried when she watched Obama's acceptance speech, even though she didn't vote for him; why people stood in those long lines to vote, all across the country; why I woke my children on Wednesday morning by singing "God Bless America."
>
> (Applebaum, 2008)

In the end, it came down to this: all Americans are told, as children, that "anyone can grow up to be president of the United States." Because we elected a black president we could now, however briefly, once again feel certain that it's true (Applebaum, 2008).

Ultimately, voters' choices are more complicated than they may first appear. We vote based on facts, values, impressions, beliefs, and attitudes, and during the contesting period candidates adjust their campaign message to appeal to as many of us as they can. In the general election phase of the campaign, we no longer hear the strident and partisan references that were evident (and expected by party loyalists) during the primary period. The rhetorical task becomes one of creating positive impressions across as wide a spectrum as possible, thereby increasing the likelihood of earning over 50% of the total number of votes.

It is not just the candidate's persona that comes into focus during the general election period, but also the candidate's platform. Rhetorically, candidates have to convince voters that they have the "right" stances on concrete issues, appealing to voters both rationally and emotively. Therefore, policy speeches are often given at strategically selected spots: perhaps a labor and jobs speech in Detroit, a farm program speech in Des Moines, a social security speech in Miami or Phoenix, or an urban recovery program speech in Los Angeles or New York. The background is as much of an incentive to believe the candidate as are the words; what's more, the carefully selected site gives the news media a "good shoot," which means the speech more likely will get media coverage.

Press conferences are regularly called, whether or not the candidates are present, and news releases are offered even if the candidates are campaigning elsewhere; web pages share the day's stories. Some candidates attempt to control press coverage by releasing statements on different subjects on different days, but, overall, the "issue-of-the-day" strategy has not worked spectacularly through time (Covington, et al., 1994; Meyer, 2002). Further, candidates work to vary their appearances, showing up on entertainment shows and releasing family photos in the quest to communicate that they are "regular" people who have habits of mind that can be trusted. In all this, the candidates' staff works to coordinate a consistent message and get them positive "free" (unpaid) coverage that is in sync with their purchased advertising messages.

Joint appearances between candidates, most often in the form of debates, are among the most dramatic persuasive events of the general election period. Having the candidates go head-to-head can pull more than 60 million viewers to their TV sets, making such debates mega-events by American broadcasting standards.

FIGURE 11.3 *Barack Obama goes shopping for books with his daughters, and pays for the books himself, thereby demonstrating that he is a "regular" person just like us.*

Candidates work doubly hard on these occasions to avoid mistakes and also to look "presidential," working to have facts at their fingertips and valuative visions crafted in metaphors and verbal images. During debates, they live by one rule: "If you haven't said it before, don't say it during the debate." Given that, debates can seem overly scripted, but, despite their limitations, they can provide a glimpse of the way candidates think and also how they deal with the unknown.

In sum, the general election period is the time when candidates shift their focus. During the first three campaign periods (surfacing, winnowing, and legitimating), candidates are mostly involved in mobilizing voters in their own party. In the contesting phase of the campaign, they must reach out to a general population that is unpredictable, one that considers many factors as it casts its votes. Through debates, advertisements, and widespread media appearances, they present their message to fickle voters and contrast themselves with their opponents, hoping to connect sufficiently with enough people to win on Election Day.

In considering political persuasion through the lens of differing campaign phases, we see that campaigns require not just diverse persuasive tactics, but also timed strategy. To be successful, the candidate not only has to use the right rhetorical approach, but also has to use it at the right time; an approach that might work well in the primary phase of a campaign might likely backfire closer to the general election. Most of all, strong candidates know that elections are not sprints—they are marathons. The right race needs to be run overall if one wishes to cross the finish line as the victor.

MACHIAVELLIANISM IN POLITICAL CAMPAIGNS: A GUIDE TO GETTING ELECTED TO HIGH OFFICE

The term **Machiavellianism** derives from Niccolo Machiavelli (1469–1527), author of *The Prince* (1977), a renowned guide to political strategy and power. Today, the term refers to communication strategies that appear to be serving audience members but rather are tools to maximize the gains of the person using them. They're the tools of persons who believe that winning is all. They're embedded in slogans in the advertisements of campaign media experts and consultants: "You can't govern if you don't win," and "When you win, nothing hurts. But you don't have to suffer to win" (ads in *Campaigns & Elections*, a trade magazine for political operatives).

This chapter has described the sorts of persuasive messages that permeate campaigns. But how candidates execute those messages—whether they manipulate their own positions, doctor those of their opponents, or deceive voters with impunity—is another matter. As you read these rules, be aware that the strategies here identified are not necessarily those that we or other political communication scholars personally endorse. The rules typically serve candidates, but the degree to which they serve society is another matter. Think about the ethics of persuasion as you read through the following suggestions for making it in American politics.

General Strategies

1   Run a permanent campaign. Whenever you face a political decision, at election time or not, ask yourself, "Will this help or harm my re-election campaign?"

2   Practice political cybernetics. Reflect voters' opinions back directly in what you say and propose. Use focus groups to try out themes and one-liners.

3   Romance the voter. Celebrate what they already believe, and never try to change them too much. Practice eating tacos with Mexican Americans, spaghetti with Italian Americans, and a little goulash in the Hungarian part of town.

4   Appear as a super-representative of the people you are seeking to influence. Be as much like your constituents as you can be, but always sprinkle your talks with quotations from Plato or Lincoln or Bono to appear more elevated than they are.

5   Subordinate issues to imagistic considerations. Use issues and talk about issues to position yourself strategically in relationship to your opponents. Consider where you stand relative to how that stand will contribute to the public's perception of your competence, your character, your good intentions, and your personal attractiveness. Remember that the ultimate campaign issue is who should get elected.

6   Forty percent will vote for you. Forty percent will vote for your opponent. This is the fact of the matter, no matter what you or your opponent does over the course of the campaign. Elections are decided by the 20% in the middle of the electorate. Don't spend time trying to convert your opponents and don't spend time with your supporters. Get to that undecided 20%.

Fundraising

1   Raise as much as you can, however you can, as early as you can. Use money to raise money, for example, by buying some direct mail mailing lists.

2   Let it be known that you will listen to funding sources for a stiff price, but only on certain matters and in discreet ways. First, work from sources consistent with your values and issue positions. Avoid obviously tainted money. Try to avoid "late" money because it almost always comes with strings attached.

3   Get around the limitations on contributions by organizing political action committees, by accepting non-monetary in-kind campaign contributions and low-interest loans, and by funneling so-called soft money contributions through your party and through PACs. Since the *Citizens United* decision in 2010, unlimited contributions can be used legally in almost unlimited ways via Super PACs, and campaign managers have been finding in the law endless creative ways to advance a candidate's campaign.

4   Deplore the reliance of contemporary election campaigns on fat-cat contributions even as you seek them out.

Physical Appearance

1   Look the part. Remember that smart phone cameras are a fact of life and you can be the subject of a photograph or video at any time. Select your attire with care: You don't want to look "richer" or "poorer" than the average voter you meet— you want them to identify with you and picture you representing them in office. Males: cut the beards, trim the eyebrows, and go for some hair replacement when needed. Females: appear businesslike with a touch of the feminine, and never carry a purse—keep yourself unencumbered so that you can shake the hands of voters.

2   Dress the part. Men should spend most of their days in conservative suits and sportswear, long-sleeved shirts, and dark shoes. Women somehow have to avoid looking either soft and demure or tough and aggressive. But they can take comfort in knowing that many women before them have moved "beyond the double bind" (Jamieson, 1995).

3   Work on your photographic poses. Look serious but friendly; tilt your head for dynamic angles; avoid looking straight into the camera. Wear a winning smile, and be photographed in gracious conversation with both beloved old politicians (legitimacy) and eager voters from various demographic groups (bandwagon appeal).

Choosing Arguments and Appeals

1   Pick a memorable slogan. Kennedy's "New Frontier," Johnson's "Great Society," Nixon's "Peace With Honor," Reagan's "A New Beginning," and Obama's "Change You Can Believe In"—these were easily remembered and could be used by voters to recall other themes. Watch out for troublesome ones, as was this one from 1988: Robert Dole's "What's the difference?", which could be interpreted either as a way to define his special features or as a type of political cynicism. Presidential candidate Barry Goldwater's 1964 campaign slogan should serve as a warning to us all. His slogan was a good one: "In your heart, you know he's right." But in the hands of his opponents the response to it became "But in your guts you know he's nuts." Is it any surprise that Goldwater lost?

2   Stand for patriotism, free-market economics, family values, destruction of the drug cartel, and other non-controversial positions. Never forget to attack government waste, even while protecting the defense contracts and the pork for your own state and area.

3   Always appear upbeat about the future. Bill Clinton won in 1992 by reminding us: "Don't Stop Thinking About Tomorrow." Even the gloomiest statistics can be pitched as "the darkness before the dawn." Barack Obama's "HOPE" or Bill Clinton's 1996 trips on the train he called "The 21st-Century Express" can be adapted effectively for use by any candidate.

4   Be ready to "go negative." Do your polling and opposition research so that you know your opponent's softest points. Particularly if you get behind in the opinion polls, take your best shots. Keep using negative ads until you've drawn even or until you seem to be losing ground again. Unless you're woefully behind, you should withdraw them before the last two weeks of the campaign so that you can finish on the "high ground." Then you can also attack your opponent's attack advertising.

5   Take courageous stands on controversial issues as long as the majority or plurality of the voters take the same stand or can be convinced to take the same stand. You may have to be careful about gun control, given the money that the National Rifle Association has distributed to campaigns, and waffling on the abortion issue is wise if you're pro-choice, given that the anti-abortion supporters seem more likely to vote on the basis of this issue than their in-the-majority, pro-choice counterparts. But otherwise, take to heart the political adage, "Follow me; I'm right behind you."

Media Politics

1   Adapt your campaign to the more than 80% of the voters who say that they get their political news exclusively from television and the Internet, including YouTube, Google searches, blogs, Facebook, television news, television advertising, and (increasingly these days) media entertainment. Create a web page and keep it up to date. Develop and use e-mail lists of supporters, keeping them in the loop about the campaign. Don't ignore social networking sites like Facebook or free media sites like YouTube.

2   Plan on new ways of getting media exposure nearly every day. Television news and blogs cater to the here and now, the ever present today, so you'll need something new or different—an issue position, an attack, an announcement about your campaign—available daily, preferably in the morning so that it can be up and running throughout the day.

3   Work on strategies for controlling the news information broadcast about you. Try the issue-of-the-day strategy to see if it will work; work for short sound bites, cuing your supporters to cheer loudly, so that the broadcast piece will show off both you and the adoring masses. Gather a crowd and hold them back with a rope; then, as you make your entrance, drop the rope and have them mob you— it makes for a great evening news picture.

4   Pick the right backgrounds for yourself. Announce your agricultural policy from Greenfield, Iowa (Jesse Jackson, 1988); offer your social reform plank in an East L.A. low-income neighborhood (George Bush, 1992); call for environmental reform from the Snake River in Idaho (Robert Kennedy, 1968); go on a fact-finding trip to South America to show your understanding of foreign policy (Richard Nixon, 1959); remind voters you're the incumbent by speaking from the White House Rose Garden (Bill Clinton, 1996); appear outside an auto factory if you're courting the labor vote (Gore, 2000). If your health is questioned, be shown on a horse whenever possible, as did Ronald Reagan during his presidency. And if you are Barack Obama, announce your historical campaign, which will destroy racial barriers from the land of Abraham Lincoln in Springfield, Illinois.

5   Control your media exposure as much as possible. The one-on-one interview program, with ground rules, is preferable to an open press conference, in that you can lead the discussion where you'd like it to go rather than dealing with a gaggle of reporters and their often snarky questions. Talk shows—especially the morning shows, or shows like *Oprah Winfrey* and *The View*—are easier to control than news programs. Live television is generally a better choice for media exposure in that it has the advantage that your words won't be cropped and edited as might happen with a recorded interview.

6   Practice, practice, practice. All but memorize answers to questions about the news of the day, your main issues, your opponent's policies and pronouncements, and the state of politics in America. Construct pieces of talk that include some facts, some well-phrased judgments about them, a proposal for study or action, and references to particular constituencies affected by the issue; these are *opinion molecules*—"a fact, a feeling, and a following" (Abelson, 1959).

Advertising

1   Remember that Americans now get more political information from candidate-controlled sources than from media-controlled sources (Jamieson, 2000). In part, this depends on striking ads and web pages that enthrall a voter; in part, it depends on your ads being interesting enough to be considered news. For the last quarter century, many print, radio, and television outlets do regular analyses of ads—commentaries, "truth boxes," and the like—so make sure your ads are pre-released to be used in these venues; that way you get a free broadcast.

2   Pictures can be worth a thousand words. As noted in Chapter 5, visual depictions can work to set ideas or propositions in people's minds. Do you want to attack your opponent's ethnic background? Don't say it—show it. Find pictures making your opponent look silly and yourself look grand. (See the Republican's "Dukakis Tank" ad shown later in this chapter.)

3   Always be technically accurate even if your implications are misleading. Condemn your opponent for missing the House's final vote on the Railroad Retirement Act renewal, as Roger Jepsen (Iowa) did when taking on Tom Harkin (Iowa) in their 1984 senatorial contest; never mind that the bill was unopposed in its second reading, so of course it would pass unanimously on its third and final reading, with or without any particular Congress member's vote.

4   Timing is everything. Begin with image ads where you introduce yourself to voters on your terms. Move into some easy issue ads; go negative if you're behind, or stay on the high road as long as you're not losing ground. Better still, do comparative advertising: contrasting your upright stand on an issue with your opponent's bad judgment (Jamieson, 1992). Be prepared to respond quickly once you're attacked. Finish with visionary ads and patriotic music; Barack Obama's final ads, including his half-hour network media buy, are exemplars.

5   If you know you're going to be hit on an issue, do *inoculation ads*. These are ads that attempt to undermine anticipated attacks before they happen, perhaps by way of forewarnings of the opponent's scurrilous plans. Knowing he would be attacked for his lack of military experience, Bill Clinton did strong pro-defense ads and delivered a speech to the national convention of the American Legion. George Bush (the elder) put out ads on his social reform measures before he was attacked for his veto of a major day care bill. Al Gore moved his Campaign 2000 headquarters from Washington, DC, to Nashville, Tennessee, so he couldn't be accused of being "inside the Beltway."

Endorsements

1   Know that low-involvement voters will judge you on such peripheral factors as the company you keep. Be pictured with veteran leaders, media personalities, and musical icons.

2   Construct endorsement teams. Get some economists to say your tax reform proposals are solid; some retired generals to comment on your ideas on first-strike needs; and some environmentalist groups to endorse your "Save the Chickadee" campaign.

3   Travel across the demographic map. Be photographed with teenagers, health club members, social activists, African Americans, Latinos, Asian Americans, new immigrants, retired persons, and so forth. Concentrate on the 50-year-olds and up, because they've got the best voting records.

Speech Making

1   Polish a set speech. You need at least one such speech frame, with your principal vision for America and your slogans in its outline, yet one flexible enough that you can substitute in various issues depending on where you're speaking. Clinton was able to make almost any issue "a bridge to the 21st century" in the fall of 1996. George W. Bush could do the same as a "compassionate conservative" in 2000, as could Barack Obama with "Change you can believe in" and "Yes we can."

2   Practice your oratorical skills for the stump and conversational skills for radio and television. Old-fashioned political oratory—us–them contrasts, appeals to patriotism, three-part lists ("life, liberty, and the pursuit of happiness"), and quotations from Abraham Lincoln—plays well at rallies. Intimate talk, with emotion-laden stories, pauses, and a soft face, plays well on television. Partisanship is better in the open air than under the lights (Atkinson, 1984).

3   Make the audience part of your message. A good speech gets an enthusiastic response, and that enthusiastic response is important to reporters and to radio and television audiences hearing it rebroadcast.

Campaign Debates

1   Never refuse outright an invitation to debate. If you're the incumbent or far ahead in the polls, however, you don't need to take the risk of a debate. Find ways to stall and avoid, complaining about timing, the format, your opponent's unwillingness to negotiate, the lack of neutral sponsors, and disagreements about the number and location of debates.

2   Treat a debate like a press conference. Concentrate on points that you want to make, rather than on any serious give-and-take on issues. One of John McCain's problems in the 2008 debates was that he kept trying to correct past misperceptions rather than thinking of his answers as little political essays that could sculpt an image of him and demonstrate his political savvy. This approach led voters to see him as disengaged, angry, and old, and likely contributed to his defeat.

3   Hold to your strengths; cover up your weaknesses. If you run into a difficult question on foreign policy, don't tackle it with inaccurate information. Retreat to your statement on general principles, perhaps with "Now I'm not going to turn this into a foreign policy seminar. Let me instead set out the principles that I believe should govern all our relations with foreign countries."

4   Treat questioners warmly. Most members of the press are well enough known to be worth having as personal friends, so create that impression. Call them by name; thank them for their efforts on behalf of the American people.

5   Choreograph the end of the debate. Memorize your final statement. Make sure that you're gracious to your opponent. Have your family rush the stage to hug you. Have your spin doctors—members of your staff or supporters who are good at positively interpreting what you said and negatively interpreting your opponent's remarks—ready to go backstage.

As the Machiavellian guide demonstrates, persuasion is woven throughout all facets of running for office. As we conclude this chapter's discussion of political campaigns, we hope that we've demonstrated that there are two ways (at least) of thinking about campaigns. For persuasion scholars, campaigns are fascinating sites of study. In analyzing them after the fact, we can learn a great deal about how persuasion actually functions. And for political consultants and candidates, running great campaigns is an art. Campaigns involve creativity, planning, and hard work. They are exciting and unpredictable, happening in real time. They are meant to be waged and won. In the midst of considering these two sides of campaigning, though, we need to remember that both the art and the analysis are important. Not only that, they interact: the academic study of campaigns informs the art of campaigning, and vice versa. Most of all, political campaigns truly are persuasion in action.

CAMPAIGN DECISIONS THAT MATTER: FIVE CASE STUDIES

If two opposing candidates follow the Machiavellian rules for getting elected to office, why is it that one wins and the other loses? Political analysts have examined presidential elections and identified a number of determinants of electoral success or failure besides campaign acumen. Sometimes, a first-term president is lucky enough to have inherited a strong domestic situation from the previous president and to ride its waves for four more years. Sometimes, party identification is so strong that it compensates for a candidate's weak campaign. Still, campaign strategizing *can* make an enormous difference (Jamieson, 2000), and what follows are five presidential campaign decisions that mattered. These case studies illustrate the art of political campaigning—not just its science. In addition, as with so much else that has been discussed in this chapter, they also raise questions of ethics.

Case 1 George H. W. Bush's Media Campaign

Background

In 1988, Republican presidential candidate George Bush trailed his opponent, Democratic Michael Dukakis, by 17 points after that summer's party conventions.

Dukakis was not a charismatic leader, but he came out of Massachusetts with a reputation as a competent and compassionate governor. Vice President Bush, on the other hand, had been tarred by the Iran-Contra scandal in President Ronald Reagan's second term of office, and Bush seemed wooden in comparison with Reagan. Still, Bush had inherited a brain's trust of some of Reagan's slickest political operatives, and in late summer they decided to put their expertise to work in the form of negative ads that pictured Dukakis as soft on defense and hypocritical about environmental protection.

But their strongest potential attack weapon was information revealing that Dukakis had been governor when **Willie Horton**, a black convicted murderer, had been released from prison under the terms of the state furlough program. After his release, Horton had kidnapped a white couple, brutally assaulting the man and repeatedly raping his girlfriend in the man's presence. Worse yet, Dukakis had failed to apologize to the couple for the tragic events that had occurred under his watch.

The Willie Horton case presented the Bush campaign with opportunities but also with something of a dilemma. Linking Dukakis with Horton could play well to supporters of capital punishment (Dukakis was opposed to it) and especially to whites who associated violent crime with young blacks such as Willie Horton. But a direct attack on Dukakis for furloughing Willie Horton might seem too blatantly racist. Besides, the Massachusetts furlough law had been signed by Dukakis's predecessor, a Republican.

(a)   (b)

FIGURE 11.4   *An ad directly linking Dukakis and Horton had been prepared by an officially independent group called the National Security Political Action Committee, which linked Dukakis and Horton without making the Bush campaign appear blatantly racist.*

(a) © AP Images (b) Created by Americans for Bush, National Security PAC

Fortunately for the Bush camp, an ad directly linking Dukakis and Horton had been prepared by an officially independent group called the National Security Political Action Committee. After the Willie Horton ad had been broadcast, all Bush's campaign operatives needed to do was to produce a second ad and tar Dukakis with a broader brush, one linking him with furloughs for convicted murderers and, even more generally, with being soft on crime.

Decision: The Furlough Ad

The furlough ad is considered by many to be a masterpiece of attack advertising. Its visual track opens with a slow-motion pan of a prison tower set against two mountains. The next visual, of a lone prison guard patrolling stealthily with a rifle, plays further on the viewers' pre-existent fears. These fears are reinforced by the metallic drone of an electronic synthesizer in the background. Then comes a revolving gate scene, the prisoners—silent, depersonalized, heads bowed—shown exiting the prison to the grating and rhythmic sounds of their own shuffle, as the narrator warns about the consequences of electing the permissive governor of Massachusetts as president. The ad works through the visual and auditory associations that viewers make: stark and shadowy, black-and-white depictions of the prison and revolving gate, and the menacing sounds and sights of prisoners being permitted to leave those gates to kidnap, mutilate, and rape. In addition, the ad offers startling statistics. As the narrator intones, "The Dukakis furlough program gave weekend furloughs to first-degree murderers," subtitles announce that "268 escaped" and "many are still at large."

FIGURE 11.5 *Still from the "Revolving Door" ad, created by the Bush campaign.*
Created by Roger Ailes of Ailes Communications, Inc.

By all accounts, the furlough ad worked well for Bush in 1988. It was a major contributor to his subsequent 30-point turnaround in the polls. Yet questions persist about the ethics of the advertisement. Because the narration and the subtitles appeared together, viewers may have been invited to make the false inference that the 268 who "escaped" were murderers. In reality, only four were murderers, and all were eventually caught and returned. Moreover, Dukakis himself did not decide who got furloughs, and prisoners who overstayed their furloughs by only four hours were counted as "escapees." A discerning viewer, operating by way of Petty and Cacioppo's (1996) central route to persuasion, might have asked, "Just how unusual is the Massachusetts furlough program? Do other states have similar programs? What is the success rate of such programs? How many prisoners were furloughed in Massachusetts without serious incident?" But most viewers did not have the motivation or the wherewithal to view the ad critically. Moreover, the Dukakis camp was extremely slow in responding to the ad, and the news media tended to focus on strategy rather than content in their reporting of the 1988 contest—on the furlough ad's impact, say, rather than on its accuracy (Jamieson, 1992).

Case 2 Bill Clinton and "A Place Called Hope"

Background

Bill Clinton articulated several themes through Campaign 1992. He began by presenting himself as a political technocrat, someone who knew how to use government to solve people's problems. During the late primaries, he spent more

FIGURE 11.6   *The Clinton and Gore couples.*

time on the "change" issue, with much talk about turning America around. He also used time and space to try to rid himself of negative attacks on his morality—his sexual life and marriage, his financial dealings in Arkansas, and his apparent penchant for changing his mind. By the time the summer Democratic convention rolled around, Clinton and his staff knew that he needed to make a major statement on political morality. How could he do that without sounding defensive or preachy?

Decision: *A Place Called Hope*

The Clinton campaign team opted for a mythic, biographical film. The last night of the Democratic convention, the chair of the meeting, then Texas Governor Ann Richards, assured the delegates that they did not have a "cardboard candidate" but a "real man" with a "story to tell." The film, *A Place Called Hope*, told that story. It was a personal story about a public man. Although the moral of the story never was articulated in so many words, it was suggested by implication again and again: *Bill Clinton's private virtues will become his public virtues when he's president of the United States.*

FIGURE 11.7 *Bill Clinton at Boy's Nation in Washington, DC, where he shook hands with John F. Kennedy.*
© AP Images

The role of *myth* is central to campaign persuasion (Osborn, 1986). Myth must be understood broadly here to include falsehood. Richard Nixon used myth in trying to construct his hometown of Whittier, California, as a value-rich environment (Black, 1970). Ronald Reagan did the same for Dixon, Illinois, and Bill Clinton, for Hope, Arkansas. But the concept of myth also refers to our understanding of life as a whole, our place in the universe, our past-present-future; understood in this way, myth becomes what Ernest Bormann (1972) calls a *rhetorical vision*, that is, our ways of seeing social life and using that way of seeing as an orientation to the world.

A Place Called Hope offered a vision of the future, but it was mostly concerned with creating a mythic past. The film was divided into four episodes. The first episode shows that Clinton came from a special place, like a true hero. Even the name—Hope, Arkansas—foretold of Clinton's greatness in this story, as did the grandparents who raised him while his mother was in school; they knew education was the way out of poverty and that segregation was wrong.

The heart of the film, however, is Episode 2, offering stories of Bill's youth. Mythic markers—signs that he was predestined to greatness—appear regularly in this segment: (a) he was born the day after his mother saw a film called *Tomorrow Is Forever*; (b) even as a youth, he confronted his drunken stepfather and protected his mother from him; (c) as a little boy, he said to his mother that "if Arkansas will let me, one day I'm going to get us off the bottom"; and (d) when he was sent to Boy's Nation in Washington, DC, he shook hands with John F. Kennedy, who seemingly anointed him as a successor.

Each of those experiences displays virtues—a vision for tomorrow, strength and protectiveness, political ambition, and achievement—that could become the grounds for his public values.

Similarly, Episode 3 has stories from Clinton's adult life. Viewers see him meeting Hillary Clinton and learn why she married him; his impulsiveness is illustrated in a story about his marriage proposal; his daughter shows us his supportive and compassionate side.

Personal knowledge of Bill Clinton is added in Episode 4 with a couple of stories from the campaign. A *60 Minutes* program during which he and Hillary talked about their marriage is reviewed through the eyes of their daughter, Chelsea, and then he is shown saying in a speech that "the hits I've taken in this campaign are nothing compared to the hits that the people of this state and this country are taking every day." The film finishes with Bill reminiscing about his youth, with home movies of a swimming hole, a small-town parade, and Chelsea doing ballet. His final line is, "I still believe in a place called Hope."

In an era when the issues—economics, health care, crime—are beyond the understanding and control of the average citizen, voters often put their faith in right-minded individuals who, they hope, act in their best interests when wrestling with those issues. **Characterological persuasion**—persuasive appeals built around "trust me" stories about the persuader's virtues—has become popular in American politics. *A Place Called Hope* is powerful as a story of Bill Clinton's virtues—virtues that the 43% of the electorate who voted for him hoped would become his public values, his measures for guiding the country.

Case 3 George W. Bush and the Swift Boat Veterans for Truth

Background

In 2000, the American presidential election ended virtually tied. Vice President Al Gore garnered more of the total popular vote overall in the nation, but the United

FIGURE 11.8   *Candidates George W. Bush and John Kerry during the 2004 campaign.*

States Supreme Court intervened and ruled that George W. Bush had prevailed in the electoral college vote count and declared him the winner. Subsequently, Bush came into office under a cloud, but only nine months later, terrorists attacked the nation, killing nearly 3,000 Americans, bringing down the World Trade Center, crashing a plane in Pennsylvania, and damaging the Pentagon. Then, in 2003, President Bush took the nation to war against Iraq under the guise that Iraq had weapons of mass destruction that could fall into the hands of the very people who had attacked the country, and, not only that, Iraq was under the boot of an evil dictator, Saddam Hussein, who deserved to be deposed so that his people could be "free."

As the campaign of 2004 got under way, it was becoming clear that the weapons of mass destruction in Iraq did not exist, causing one of the justifications for the war to unravel. Some thought that the war had been engaged under false pretenses, and went so far as to accuse President Bush of lying to the nation. Others believed that even without the discovery of the weapons, the war to depose Hussein was a worthy effort in that it freed the people of Iraq.

In 2004, therefore, the country entered the election season strongly divided; many felt that George W. Bush was not legitimately elected to the presidency, while many others credited him with bringing America through a crisis of epic proportions and keeping us safe. Some felt he had lied to the nation about the war; others believed the war was necessary and worthwhile even if mistakes were made about Iraqi weapons of mass destruction. This sense of division and unease existed as the nation was actively engaged in a war and still feeling the effects of the 9/11 attacks.

The Democrats nominated Senator John F. Kerry of Massachusetts as their candidate to challenge George W. Bush. They believed that Kerry, a decorated Vietnam war veteran, would be perceived as a forceful and experienced leader in a time of war and danger. Not only that, Kerry's military record presented a strong and positive contrast to George W. Bush, who had avoided service in Vietnam by securing a spot in the Texas National Guard under questionable circumstances. At the Democratic Convention on July 29, 2004, Kerry highlighted his military service, accepting the nomination with the following words:

> I'm John Kerry, and I'm reporting for duty. We are here tonight because we love our country. We're proud of what America is and what it can become. My fellow Americans, we're here tonight united in one purpose: to make America stronger at home and respected in the world.
>
> (*Washington Post*, 2004)

It was clear that Kerry was going to use the campaign to contrast his military credentials with those of the president, suggesting that he was the tested war hero who could handle a bungled and misguided war effort in Iraq.

Decision: Rhetorical Reversal—John Kerry's Strength Is Really a Weakness

On first glance, it appeared that Kerry had created a legitimate campaign issue. He had enlisted in the Navy, served with honor in Vietnam, and been awarded medals for courageous service. During the same time period, George W. Bush had earned a spotty military record at best, and many of his military records were simply unavailable. Kerry came home and protested the war, which rankled some, but generally his service and his years of Senate foreign policy experience appeared to trump that of George W. Bush.

Supporters of George Bush entered the fray through the creation of the Swift Boat Veterans for Truth, an independent 527 group (a tax-exempt organization, not connected directly to a candidate, that is created primarily to influence elections) that raised money, ran ads, and published a book that challenged Kerry's Vietnam service. This group characterized itself as non-partisan, but, according to released campaign information, more than half of the group's reported contributions came from just three sources, all prominent Texas Republican donors: Houston builder Bob J. Perry, a longtime supporter of George W. Bush, donated $4.45 million, Harold Simmons's company, Contran, donated $3 million, and T. Boone Pickens, Jr. donated $2 million (Krumholtz, 2008). And while their charges against Kerry were investigated and found to be untrue, they had an impact.

Kerry had earned numerous service awards, and the Swift Boat Veterans for Truth called into question whether he honestly deserved them. In fact, Kerry had worked to build a campaign on *ethos*, suggesting that he was the authentic leader while George Bush was a pretender. The Swift Boat Veterans for Truth launched a direct attack on Kerry's presentation of his biography, and thereby sought to undermine the *ethos* he had worked to present. They challenged his Vietnam account, focusing on small details and arguing that he was inconsistent—Kerry had claimed for example, to be in one war location on Christmas Eve, and the Swift Boat Veterans claimed he was somewhere else. Further, they challenged the severity of his injuries, and hinted that he didn't deserve his medals. In effect, they succeeded in *reframing* what Kerry wished to present as his strongest attribute, his *ethos*, reversing it not minimally but completely. In effect, they proclaimed Kerry not a war hero, but a traitor and a liar who was not fit to lead the nation.

At the same time that the Swift Boat Veterans were attacking Kerry's war record, journalists were calling into question Bush's military record, and his supporters came to his aid by *going meta*. They attacked the reporters, challenging the way Bush's records had been obtained and the truthfulness of those who came forward to speak out on Bush's service. They were able to completely change the subject, taking the focus away from Bush's actual record of service and directing it toward supposed reporter misconduct.

The result was that Bush's campaign was able to shift the national discussion to topics that were of great political advantage to him. Even as reporters debunked the Swift Boat Veterans, they were still talking about them, and Kerry's *ethos* as American war hero became tainted. Furthermore, through *going meta*, the Bush campaign was able to create a situation where Bush's military experience never became an issue for serious national discussion during the campaign.

The Kerry campaign's response did not help the situation—it was slow in coming and weak when it finally arrived. Ultimately, the questions about his military service that the Swift Boat Veterans raised remained until Election Day. When coupled with Bush's appeals to fear of future attack, they worked to tip the balance in George W. Bush's favor.

Case 4 Reverend Wright and "A More Perfect Union" Speech

Background

Barack Obama was an unlikely person to ultimately become the president of the United States. Born of an African (Kenyan) father and a white mother from Kansas, Obama did not come from wealth or privilege. He rose to national attention after delivering a stunning keynote address at the Democratic National Convention in 2004; also that year, he won a U.S. senate seat from Illinois, achieving an easy victory after the Republican candidate withdrew due to sexual impropriety. When he made his surprising announcement that he would seek the presidency, he was respected but untested and somewhat unknown. And so, investigations into his life in Chicago began.

Obama was a member of Trinity United Church of Christ, and had come to the Christian faith under the guidance of the church's pastor, Reverend Jeremiah Wright. The church was (and is) part of a liberal mainline American Protestant denomination,

FIGURE 11.9 *Barack Obama presenting his speech on race.*
© AP Images

and Wright was the church's flamboyant preacher and controversial figure who spoke a message of empowerment to his mostly African-American congregation of 7,500. Wright's preaching fit the style of the black churches in America: It was boisterous, lively, and provocative.

Taped clips from sermons delivered by Reverend Wright surfaced and were posted to YouTube. Soon, media scrutiny brought the sermons to the attention of the general public, and some of Wright's remarks were found to be controversial. As reported on MSNBC at the time, a videotape of one sermon captures Wright using a harsh racial epithet to argue that Hillary Clinton could not understand the struggles of African Americans:

> Barack knows what it means, living in a country and a culture that is controlled by rich white people. Hillary can never know that. Hillary ain't never been called a [N-word]!

In another sermon, delivered five days after the 9/11 attacks, Wright seemed to imply that the United States had brought the terrorist violence on itself:

> We bombed Hiroshima, we bombed Nagasaki, and we nuked far more than the thousands in New York, and we never batted an eye.... We have supported state terrorism against the Palestinians and black South Africans, and now we are indignant because the stuff we have done overseas is brought right back in our own front yards.

In a later sermon, Wright revisits the theme, declaring: "No, no, no, not God bless America—God damn America!" (Johnson, 2008).

The media in general, and the right-wing media in particular, highlighted the comments of Reverend Wright and challenged Obama to explain how he could be a member for decades in a church where sermons included such rhetoric. After attempting to deflect and avoid the issue, Obama realized he had a problem and made the decision to deal with the matter in a major speech, delivered in Philadelphia on March 18, 2008.

Decision: Reframing the Discussion of Race into "A More Perfect Union"

Barack Obama was confronted with a unique rhetorical challenge. He was the first truly viable African-American candidate for the presidency, and yet he was determined not to run as a "black" candidate. Rhetorically, his race became something difficult to discuss—it was obvious, but to speak of it ran the risk of accusations of racism. Not only that, there existed in America pockets of voters who held racist beliefs and were resistant to the election of a black person to the highest office in the land. But in America in 2008, it was improper to speak openly of such things; in March 2008, great uncertainty existed about how many voters would truly cast their ballots for a black man.

Opponents of Obama, particularly in the right-wing media, featured Reverend Wright and his inflammatory remarks with gusto. They walked a narrow line, suggesting that they were not discussing racial issues, but instead were talking about Obama's judgment for choosing to belong to a church where such seeming anti-American sentiments were expressed by the pastor. But, as any careful observer could see, Wright's primary critique was of white America and white privilege; therefore, a critique of Wright highlighted racial issues. Not only that, it highlighted Wright's anger with the injustices he perceived in America. He came across as an angry black man, and the object of his anger was white America.

And so, Obama's critics launched a multi-pronged attack via Reverend Wright. First, they called Obama's patriotism into question through *guilt by association*—if Wright criticized America, did not Obama share his views? Second, they challenged his judgment for remaining in the church. Third, they hinted at his veracity, especially when Obama suggested that he'd not been in church to hear the sermons in question. And fourth, through Reverend Wright, they reminded voters of the racial tensions that still existed in the country; if in fact Obama belonged to a black church where the pastor was a harsh critic of white America, what might that mean to the future of the country if Obama were to be elected?

In Obama's speech, entitled "A More Perfect Union," his primary persuasive tactic was one of *going meta* to *reframe* the controversy. Rather than discussing Reverend Wright's remarks and responding directly to his critics, Obama raised the discussion to a higher meta-level and chose instead to talk about race in America. He adopted the role of wise lecturer and thinker, and presented a persona that stood in stark contrast to his shrill critics on the right. And then, Obama sought to *create identification* with Americans; he *presented himself metaphorically as an embodied representation* of the diversity of the nation.

Obama opened the speech with an appeal to historical common ground by arguing that the framers had a radical vision for "America's improbable experiment in democracy," one that required a recognition that, out of many people, we are one nation—"that we may have different stories, but we hold common hopes; that we may not look the same and we may not have come from the same place, but we all want to move in the same direction."

Obama went on to explain that he understood this diversity clearly because it is "seared into [his bi-racial] genetic makeup." But, he continued, what happens too often is that this country gets sidetracked by what divides it. He suggested by implication that various campaigners had resorted to racist rhetoric and noted that Reverend Wright had done this, too. His comments:

> were not only wrong but divisive, divisive at a time when we need unity; racially charged at a time when we need to come together to solve a set of monumental problems—that are neither black or white or Latino or Asian, but rather problems that confront us all.

Obama then explained that he had not "disowned" Wright because Wright is part of him. Wright's comments might be unacceptable, but he is a good man who has worked hard for his community and inspired many. He framed Wright's remarks as being connected to old age: Wright had come of age when "segregation was still the law of the land and opportunity was systematically constricted," and, because of that fact of his life and age, Wright's divisive opinions were understandable, even while they were not excusable.

Obama's next move was perhaps the most interesting rhetorically. After having identified with Reverend Wright and the black community, and showing respect for his elder even as he disagreed with him, he then duplicated the process and identified himself with the white community, suggesting that the frustrations of whites and African Americans are not dissimilar. He implied a comparison between the newly retired Reverend Wright and his elderly white grandmother, noting that he could see the tendency toward a divisive spirit in her, the woman who had "sacrificed again and again" for him, but who was "a woman who once confessed her fear of black men who passed by her on the street, and who on more than one occasion has uttered racial or ethnic stereotypes that made [Obama] cringe." In fact, Reverend Wright and Obama's grandmother shared the same racial concerns, albeit from opposite sides, and Obama was one with them both. He was everyman; he understood and literally embodied the struggles of us all, along with understanding the values on which the nation had been founded.

He explained that the persistence of our difficulties, felt by both blacks and whites, demonstrates that "we've never really worked through" the complexities of race, that race is "a part of our union that we have yet to perfect." African Americans have not been made fully equal partners in the American dream, but many poor whites have been left out as well. Because of that, we are confronted in this election season with a "choice" between (only!) two alternatives:

> We can accept a politics that breeds division, and conflict, and cynicism.... We can play Reverend Wright's sermons on every channel, every day and talk about them from now until the election, and make the only question in this campaign whether or not the American people think that I somehow believe or sympathize with his most offensive words.
>
> We can do that. But if we do, I can tell you that in the next election, we'll be talking about some other distraction. And then another one. And then another one. And nothing will change.
>
> That is one option. Or, at this moment, in this election, we can come together and say, "Not this time." [Instead, we can come together and work for a better world.]

And with that speech, Barack Obama confronted his adversaries and diminished them. He *reframed* the discussion so that it was no longer about the remarks of a preacher; instead, it was about all for which we believed we stood. Appealing to our shared values, he closed his address with the profound suggestion that his candidacy represented the very things upon which the nation had been founded, and to "choose" a politics that does not embrace his campaign was to diminish the nation. No matter what our race, we could *identify* with Obama, because he contains us all. In the great story that was America, he was the synthesis and the culmination. The choice was ours, but the choice was also obvious. We should cast our vote for our higher angels and for him.

Case 5 Mitt Romney and the 47 Percent

Background

Mitt Romney appeared to be an unlikely choice for Republicans when Campaign 2012 first got under way. Although he had attempted a run in 2008, the Party had moved far to the right and the field was crowded with candidates who would likely be more attractive to the conservative loyalists who would vote in the primaries. He had been the governor of very liberal Massachusetts, which could be seen as good in that it might have cross-over appeal, but bad in that it called into question his conservative credentials. He was very wealthy, and refused to release his tax returns. And perhaps most troubling, he had switched positions on issues important to the party faithful; he had reversed his pro-choice stance on abortion and proclaimed

FIGURE 11.10   *Barack Obama and Mitt Romney at their 2012 Town Hall Meeting Debate.*

himself pro-life, and he had decided to oppose Barack Obama's health care plan after he had enacted a very similar plan when governor. All in all, voters struggled to get a handle on his habits of the mind. "As a moderate governor of Massachusetts who adopted staunch conservative positions as soon as he decided to run for president some six years ago, there were always doubts about exactly who the real Romney was" (Harnden, 2012).

The one clearly defined feature of Mitt Romney was that he was rich, but that, in itself, should not have been a problem. Voters understood that politics, especially at the presidential level, had become an arena for the rich and the well-connected. His wealth could certainly be seen as coming business acumen, showing his potential for dealing with the economic challenges the country was facing. The challenge was that Romney struggled to communicate that message, and instead, too often talked about his wealth in unhelpful ways.

> As comedian Dean Obeidallah commented on CNN, "Mitt Romney has opened a door on questions about [whether] he out of touch with his wealth. The $10,000 bet, saying I like to fire people, saying my wife drives two Cadillacs. Mitt's got to do something to connect with the average voter during these tough economic times."
>
> (Sarver Coombs, 2014)

Instead of presenting his wealth as an inspirational story for working-class voters, Romney too often spoke in ways that showed him distant from the lives of average voters. His words stood in contrast with his campaign's central message, one that framed Romney as a self-made business man who could do for the country what he had done in the corporate world. His was a campaign of competing frames and messages, and the Obama campaign capitalized on that with attack ads framing him as a cold corporate CEO who bought companies to close them down and export jobs.

On September 17, 2012, less than two months before Election Day, the very liberal periodical *Mother Jones* released a story and a secretly recorded video of Romney speaking to a small group of wealthy donors at a $50,000 a plate fundraiser, saying

> "There are 47 percent of the people who will vote for the president no matter what. All right, there are 47 percent who are with him, who are dependent upon government, who believe that they are victims, who believe the government has a responsibility to care for them, who believe that they are entitled to health care, to food, to housing, to you-name-it. That that's an entitlement. And the government should give it to them. And they will vote for this president no matter what.... These are people who pay no income tax." Romney went on: "[M]y job is not to worry about those people. I'll never convince them they should take personal responsibility and care for their lives."
>
> (Corn, *SECRET VIDEO*, 2012)

This video immediately blanketed the airwaves and the Internet, leaving Romney in a position to try to recast the words that had come out of his own mouth.

Decision: Using Mitt Romney's Words to Define Him

The issue for Romney was that he had not found a credible way to answer Obama's attacks on his wealth and his work—the frame that Obama was creating had some resonance. Furthermore, this challenge was exacerbated because Romney was a candidate who struggled to define himself in a political party where his record was not a comfortable fit; his campaign was doing a careful dance to present the candidate in multiple ways to multiple audiences. Was he a pro-life conservative? Yes, of course! But was he a northeastern politician who had implemented "Romneycare" in his state, making health care widely available to the people there? Yes, that too. Was he much richer than the average voter? Yes! But, could he identify with those voters? Well, yes! He goes tieless, strolls NASCAR pits, and even wears jeans from the Gap (West, 2011).

The Obama campaign released attack ads about the 47 percent issue, but Obama remained mostly silent as he waited for the right moment and the right place to confront Romney directly on his remarks. That moment did not come until the final minutes of the second presidential "town hall meeting" debate. After noting that Romney was a "good man who loves his family and cares about his faith" (Johnson, 2012), Obama sought to create and cement the **frame** into which Romney's ethos could reside, expressing his concern about Romney saying "behind closed doors that 47 percent of the country considered themselves victims who refuse personal responsibility," (Johnson, 2012). The stereotype with which Romney had struggled, that of the out-of-touch and uncaring CEO, was amplified because it was now coming directly out of Romney's mouth and caught on video. Obama seemed to be suggesting that thanks to the video, where Romney was comfortably speaking with his wealthy peers, we were finally seeing the real man.

After working to create a frame for Romney, Obama went on to incorporate Cialdini's persuasive shorthand of **contrast** as he set out to articulate his view of who made up the 47% as opposed to Romney's. He said:

> "[T]hink about who he was talking about," Obama said. "Folks on Social Security who have worked all their lives. Veterans who have sacrificed for this country. Students who are out there trying to hopefully advance their own dreams, but also this country's dreams. Soldiers who are overseas fighting for us right now. People who are working hard every day, paying payroll tax, gas tax, but don't make enough income."
>
> (Johnson, 2012)

In choosing that strategy, he rhetorically separated Romney from regular Americans, and he did so via a list of specific individuals, many of whom are high-frequency voters. He put faces behind Romney's classification of the 47% . They were not, as Romney seemed to think, anonymous people who "believe the government has a responsibility to care for them, who believe that they are entitled to health care, to food, [and] to housing." Instead, they were soldiers, the elderly, students, and the working class who were sacrificing every day.

Obama also dealt with Cialdini's communicative shorthand of **consistency**, understanding that many voters would struggle with the cognitive dissonance they felt as they wished to support the more conservative candidate, even as they felt very uncomfortable with this new evidence that revealed how Romney felt about them. Obama worked to present himself as an acceptable alternative and create a sense of shared identification, noting that he wanted to fight for the 47 percent, because

> [T]hat's what I've been doing for the last four years. Because if they succeed, I believe the country succeeds. When my grandfather fought in World War II and he came back and got a GI Bill that allowed him to go to college, that wasn't a handout—that was something that advanced the entire country and I want to make sure that the next generation has those same opportunities. That's why I'm asking for your vote and that's why I'm asking for another four years.
>
> (Johnson, 2012)

With those words, the debate ended, demonstrating the way in which Obama took control of the release and the timing of his commentary. When asked why Obama had not previously mentioned the 47 percent remark, one of his campaign strategists noted that

> [What's] most compelling [is] hearing it from Romney himself. We've got that on the air at a heavy dollar amount in key states. And it's sunk in. Ultimately the president's goal last night [at the town hall debate] was to speak past the pundits and directly to the undecided voter tuning in for the first time about the economic choice and his plans to restore economic security.
>
> (Corn, *Why Didn't Obama*, 2012)

Ultimately, Obama saved his remarks for the absolute final moments of the debate, thereby denying Romney the chance to make a full response.

With the 47 percent remark, Romney did real damage to his campaign, demonstrating that all communication matters and that candidates must remember that the camera is always on. In addition, the Obama campaign used the fallout from those remarks skillfully to reinforce the doubts voters already had about Romney, and applied persuasive campaign communication tactics in an artful manner. After seeing his private comments to rich donors revealed, Romney never effectively recovered, and that moment, which was just a moment among a closed group of supporters, cemented the direction of the campaign.

SUMMARY

The modern political campaign is a combination of the old and the new—of balloons and banners and hour-long orations but also of nightly polling and expensive advertising. Fine-tuning the electorate—targeting swing voters, determining what they want, devising messages tailored to those wants, testing those messages on focus groups and other sample voters before sending them out on a mass basis, surveying again to determine message effects, then using the information in devising new messages—is how the newer part of the game is played. But the game keeps changing even as the basic campaigning rules remain the same.

This chapter has focused on the methods by which many, many candidates run for the presidency and other offices. But should these methods be the measuring rods against which the morality of politicians, even the morality built into American democratic electoral politics, is to be judged? If ours is a republic of words and images, who is to protect us from the empty words and twisted images of self-serving campaigners? Active voters who work to learn about the total candidate and the total campaigner protect themselves, of course, and passive voters and nonvoters get what they deserve. But is that enough?

Probably not. The only institutions with enough resources to countermand and correct the moral errors of politicians are those of the Fourth Estate—the press. The *watchdog function* of the press is discussed in every first-year journalism class in the country, and it would be wonderful if we could go to sleep at night assured that the watchdogs were awake and alert. But the problem, of course, is that most—that is, well over half—of the money spent on political campaigns at the national level is given to the media. The money goes for advertising, for airtime to show biographical films, even for renting studio facilities and contracting news personnel who can be rented by a campaign for part of a year. So, is it in the media's best interest to blow the whistle on the candidates who are buying ads on the 10 o'clock news, purchasing the banner on the web page, or dropping full-page ads into the struggling newspaper?

In the long run, the answer is "yes." Journalists, too, depend on good government. In the short run, however, the answer is no better than "maybe." Most members of the press corps knew that the furlough ad was a piece of dirty politics, but they played it on news programs and rated it as if it were a blockbuster movie. The press corps also too often looked the other way as the Swift Boat Veterans for Truth bought and ran ads on their networks that promoted the re-election bid of President Bush through character assassination and half-truths about John Kerry. Apparently, the watchdogs aren't always ready to bite the hands that feed them.

In recent presidential campaigns, however, there have been signs of hope:

- CNN, as well as public radio and television, and various web-based watchdog groups have begun monitoring the factual claims of the candidate.

- C-Span's "Road to the White House" segments play and discuss advertisements, speeches, and news releases from campaigns, with public call-in time added for good measure.

- Many newspapers and media outlets now print "truth boxes" evaluating those same claims even as they honor the candidate's free speech rights and publish their ads.

- The Internet, for all of its excesses, provides the possibility for citizen journalists and bloggers to check the excesses of candidates and get the word out.

- The press periodically remembers that it, too, is a public servant. Just as citizens must demand higher ethical standards from candidates, so must citizens remind journalists of one of the prices of freedom of the press—the responsibility to serve the public interest.

QUESTIONS AND PROJECTS FOR FURTHER STUDY

1   If you were running a major political campaign, how would you visually represent your candidate's opponent? "Ugly, but not nauseatingly so"?

2   What if a reporter were to have found one political party more prone to misrepresenting opponents than its competitors? Should the reporter "tell it like it is"? What if the political party in question is technically accurate, but its implications are misleading? What should the reporter do then? Should the reporter remain evenhanded, providing a report that favors neither one side nor the other? Or should the reporter report the full scope of the situation? Is there any way for reporters to be objective in these situations? Is it fair to the voters when reporters withhold information in cases like these?

3   Is today's style of political campaigning serving the interests of democracy? What, if anything, would you do to reform it?

4   How would you characterize this chapter's framing of American political campaigning? Do you find it practical? Or is it cynical?

5   View the 1993 campaign film *The War Room*, a documentary that follows campaign operatives George Stephanopoulos and James Carville during the 1992 campaign of Bill Clinton. What is the most interesting persuasive strategy that Carville and Stephanopoulis employ? How are the stages of political campaigning portrayed, and how does the campaign strategy change to reflect the stages?

6   View the 2002 campaign documentary *Journeys with George* that follows the life of pool reporters covering George Bush's 2000 race for the presidency. Discuss what it is like to be a reporter in this situation. What challenges to objectivity do reporters face? In light of the information in this chapter and the information presented in the film, do you believe that reporters do a good job of covering presidential campaigns?

7   View a popular Hollywood film about politics such as Chris Rock's *Head of State*, Kevin Kline's *Dave*, or Robin Williams's *Man of the Year*. How does the Hollywood version compare with what you've learned after reading this chapter?

8   How are technology and the Internet changing campaigns? If you were to revise this chapter five years from now, what do you imagine would need to be included? Are these changes good for democracy, or are they harmful?

EXERCISES

1   Attend a local city council or school board meeting and observe the elected officials in action. Then, share your impressions of the expertise of those serving and the way the meeting was run. After attending the meeting, do you find yourself feeling more qualified to seek office? Or, do you perceive the job as beyond your skills and abilities?

2   Visit your local county election office and interview the officials working there. If so inclined, inquire as to what would be required to secure a place on the ballot for a spot in local government that interests you. Share your findings in a presentation to the class.

3   This chapter discusses recent instances where a presidential campaign's choices made a difference. Do research on another presidential candidate from the era of "the rhetorical presidency" (which began when television made it possible for presidents to go directly to the voters, roughly beginning with President John Kennedy) and find another instance of a campaign choice where applied persuasion made a difference. Create a PowerPoint presentation and share your findings.

4   Read a political biography of a national politician and examine how the presentation describes political campaigning. Prepare a directed book review with an emphasis on how persuasion played a role in the book.

5   Visit the county headquarters of a political party and talk with the party chair about the work they do on behalf of candidates. If possible, attend a meeting. Evaluate how effective the county party operation is at campaigns and persuasion.

KEY TERMS

- Characterological persuasion
- Contesting
- Legitimating
- Machiavellianism
- Primaries

- Straight Ticket
- Super Tuesday
- Surfacing
- Willie Horton
- Winnowing

REFERENCES

Abelson, H. (1959). Modes of resolution of belief dilemmas. *Journal of Conflict Resolution*, 3, 343–352.

Applebaum, A. (2008, November 5). *Obama's race was his ace in the hole*. Retrieved January 13, 2009 from www.slate.com/id/2203910/

Atkinson, M. (1984). *Our masters' voices: The language and body language of politics*. London: Methuen.

Attack of the Political Ad. (n.d.). Retrieved January 10, 2015, from TV Tropes: http://tvtropes.org/pmwiki/pmwiki.php/Main/AttackOfThePoliticalAd

Barnes, R., & Shear, M. (2008). McCain: Fundamentals of economy are "strong" but "threatened." *Washington Post*. Retrieved July 18, 2009, from http://voices.washingtonpost.com/44/2008/09/15/mccain_fundamentals_of_economy.html

Bennett, J. (2009). *Stifling political competition: How government has rigged the system to benefit Demopublicans and exclude third parties*. New York: Springer.

Berger, A. (2007). *Ads, fads, and consumer culture: Advertising's impact on American character and society* (3rd ed.). Lanham, MD: Rowman and Littlefield Publishing.

Black, E. (1970). The second persona. *Quarterly Journal of Speech*, 56, 109–119.

Bormann, E. G. (1972). Fantasy and rhetorical vision: The rhetorical criticism of social reality. *Quarterly Journal of Speech*, 58, 396–407.

Campbell, J. E. (2008). *The American campaign: U.S. presidential campaigns and the national vote*. College Station: Texas A & M University Press.

Cappella, J. N., & Jamieson, K. H. (1997). *The spiral of cynicism*. New York: Oxford University Press.

Choma, R. (2014, November 5). *Money won on Tuesday, but rules of the game changed*. Retrieved January 12, 2015, from Open Secrets.org: www.opensecrets.org/news/2014/11/money-won-on-tuesday-but-rules-of-the-game-changed/

Cialdini, R. B. (2009). *Influence: Science and practice* (5th ed.). New York: Pearson.

Cillizza, C. (2008, September 24). Behind McCain's decision to suspend his campaign. *Washington Post*. Retrieved July 18, 2009, from http://voices.washingtonpost.com/thefix/eye-on–2008/mccain-suspends-campaign.html

Citizens United v. Federal Election Commission. (n.d.). Retrieved January 10, 2015, from Open Secrets.org: www.opensecrets.org/news/reports/citizens_united.php

Corn, D. (2012, September 17). *SECRET VIDEO: Romney Tells Millionaire Donors What He REALLY Thinks of Obama Voters*. Retrieved January 14, 2015, from Mother Jones.com: www.motherjones.com/politics/2012/09/secret-video-romney-private-fundraiser

Corn, D. (2012, October 4). *Why Obama didn't mention the 47 percent video*. Retrieved January 14, 2015, from MotherJones.com: www.motherjones.com/mojo/2012/10/why-obama-didnt-mention-47-percent-denver-debate

Covington, C. R., Kroeger, K., & Richards, G. (1994). Shaping a candidate's image in the press. In Miller, A. H., & Gronbeck, B. E. (eds), *Press campaigns and American self-images*. Boulder, CO: Westview, pp. 89–108.

D'Alessio, D. (2012). *Media bias in presidential election coverage, 1948–2008: Evaluation via formal measurement.* Lanham, MD: Lexington Books.

Davin, E. L. (2010). *Crucible of freedom: Workers' democracy in the industrial heartland, 1914–1960.* Plymouth, UK: Lexington Books.

Hallin, D. C., & Mancini, P. (2004). Americanization, globalization, and secularization: Understanding the convergence of media systems and political communication. In Esser, B. F., & Pfetsch, B. (eds), *Comparing political communication: Theories, cases, and challenges.* Cambridge: Cambridge University Press, pp. 25–44.

Harnden, T. (2012, November 7). *Hindsight will view Romney as a poor candidate with no core values who looked deeply uncomfortable.* Retrieved January 14, 2015, from DailyMail.Com: www.dailymail.co.uk/news/article-2229083/US-Election-2012-analysis-Hindsight-view-Mitt-Romney-poor-candidate-says-Toby-Harnden.html

Huffington Post (2008, March 4). Obama skin tone darker in Clinton ad? Retrieved July 17, 2009, from www.huffingtonpost.com/2008/03/04/obama-skin-tone-darker-in_n_89829.html

Huffington Post (2008, March 28). Barack Obama on "The View": Barbara says, "You're very sexy!" Retrieved January 10, 2009, from www.huffingtonpost.com/2008/03/28/barack-obama-on-the-view_n_93861.html

Jamieson, K. H. (1992). *Dirty politics: Deception, distraction, and democracy.* Oxford: Oxford University Press.

Jamieson, K. H. (1995). *Beyond the double bind.* New York: Oxford University Press.

Jamieson, K. H. (2000). *Everything you think you know about politics—and why you're wrong.* New York: Basic Books.

Johnson, A. (2008). Controversial minister leaves Obama campaign. MSNBC.com. Retrieved January 15, 2009, from www.msnbc.msn.com/id/23634881/

Johnson, L. (2012, October 16). *Obama attacks Mitt Romney's '47 percent' comments in presidential debate.* Retrieved January 14, 2015, from HuffingtonPost.com:www.huffingtonpost.com/2012/10/16/obama-47-percent-debate_n_1972349.html

Krumholtz, S. (2008). Money wins presidency and 9 of 10 congressional races in priciest U.S. election ever. *Center for Responsive Politics.* Retrieved January 10, 2009, from http://opensecrets.org/news/2008/11/money-wins-white-house-and.html

Krumholz, S. (2013). Campaign cash and corruption: Honey in politics, post-Citizens United. *Social Research,* 80(4), pp. 1119–1134.

Kuhnhenn, J., & Drinkard, J. (2008, December 5). Obama raised $745 million, twice as much as McCain. *Chron.com.* Retrieved July 18, 2009, from www.chron.com/disp/story.mpl/politics/6148832.html

Kurtz, H. (1993). *Media circus.* New York: Times Books.

Lara, M. (2009). The incorporation of American-style campaign practices in Mexico: A comparative study of the 1988, 1994, and 2000 presidential campaigns. *Razón y Palabra,* 69, pp. 1–11. Retrieved January 11, 2015, from www.redalyc.org/articulo.oa?id=199520330086

Machiavelli, N. (1977). *The prince* (R. M. Adams, ed. and trans.). New York: Norton. (Original work written 1513)

Mayersohn, A. (2014, January 21). *Four years after Citizens United: The fallout.* Retrieved January 10, 2015, from Open Secrets.org: www.opensecrets.org/news/2014/01/four-years-after-citizens-united-the-fallout/

Meyer, T. (2002). *Media democracy: How the media colonize politics.* Malden, MA: Blackwell Publishing.

Nagourney, A. (1999, April 25). The Israeli war room. *New York Times Magazine,* 42–47, 61, 70.

Napoleon, A. (n.d.). *Mitt Romney, Barack Obama and the physical attractiveness factor.* Retrieved January 14, 2015, from Beautyexpert.org: http://webcache.googleusercontent.com/search?q=cache:3R5zM3cDDm0J:www.beautyexpert.org/images/Physical_attractiveness_is_more_important_than_most_of_us_realize.pdf+&cd=9&hl=en&ct=clnk&gl=us

Osborn, M. (1986). Rhetoric depiction. In Simons, H. W., & Aghazarian, A. A. (eds), *Form, genre, and the study of political discourse.* Columbia: University of South Carolina Press.

Perloff, R. (1998). *Political communication: Politics, press, and public in America*. Mahwah, NJ: Lawrence Erlbaum.

Petty, R. E., & Cacioppo, J. T. (1996). *Attitudes and persuasion: Classic and contemporary approaches*. Boulder, CO: Westview. (Original work published 1981)

Pfetsch, B., & Esser, F. (2012). Comparing political communication. In Esser, F., & Pfetsch, B. (eds), *Handbook of comparative communication research*. New York: Routledge, pp. 25–47.

Plasser, F. (2002). American campaign techniques worldwide. *Harvard International Journal of Press/Politics, 5*(4), 33–54.

Powell, M. (2008, March 30). Barack bowl. *New York Times*. Retrieved July 18, 2009, from http://thecaucus.blogs.nytimes.com/2008/03/30/barack-bowl/

Relative, S. (2008, September 25). Making no economic sense: John McCain suspends presidential campaign. AssociatedContent.com. Retrieved July 18, 2009, from www.associatedcontent.com/article/1063642/making_no_economic_sense_john_mccain.html?cat=9

Richardson, Glenn. (2008). *Pulp politics: How political advertising tells the stories of American politics* (2nd ed.). Lanham, MD: Roman & Littlefield Publishing.

Sarver Coombs, D. (2014). *Last man standing: Media, framing, and the 2012 Republican primary*. Lanham, MD: Rowman & Littlefield.

Tapper, J. (2008, April 11). Obama responds. Retrieved July 18, 2009, from http://blogs.abcnews.com/politicalpunch/2008/04/obama-respond–1.html

Trent, J. S., & Friedenberg, R. V. (2011). *Political campaign communication: Principles and practices* (7th ed.). Lanham, MD: Rowman & Littlefield Publishers.

Tuman, J. (2008). *Political communication in American campaigns*. Thousand Oaks, CA: Sage Publications.

VandenDolder, T. (2014, April 7). *Political candidates with the most money almost always win their election*. Retrieved January 12, 2015, from Dcinno.com: http://dcinno.streetwise.co/2014/04/07/political-candidates-with-more-money-win-elections-study-inforgraphic/

Vargas, J. A. (2008, November 20). Obama raised half a billion online. Retrieved July 17, 2009, from http://voices.washingtonpost.com/44/2008/11/20/obama_raised_half_a_billion_on.html

Washington Post (2004, July 29). Text of John Kerry's acceptance speech at the Democratic National Convention. Retrieved January 11, 2009, from www.washingtonpost.com/wp-dyn/articles/A25678–2004Jul29.html

West, P. (2011, March 5). *A whole new Romney for 2012 presidential run*. Retrieved January 14, 2015, from LA Times.com: http://articles.latimes.com/2011/mar/05/nation/la-na-romney-20110305

Zorn, E. (2008, April 11). The game-changing moment Hillary Clinton has been waiting for? *Chicago Tribune*. Retrieved July 18, 2009, from http://blogs.chicagotribune.com/news_columnists_ezorn/2008/04/the-game-changi.html.

CHAPTER 12

Analyzing Product Advertising

In March, 2009, Google launched a **behavioral targeting (BT)** ad program, which it calls "interest-based advertising" (Opsahl, 2009). In effect, what Google now does is follow our search patterns and provide us with ads that target those patterns. Here's how Google explains it:

Meet Mary

Mary's favorite hobby is gardening. With Google's interest-based advertising technology, Mary will see more relevant gardening ads because she visits many gardening websites.

Here's how that works:

1   When Mary visits websites that display ads provided by Google's AdSense program, Google stores a number in her browser (using a "cookie") to remember her visits. That number could look like this: 114411.

2   Because many of the websites that Mary visits are related to gardening, Google puts her number (114411) in the "gardening enthusiast" interest category.

3   As a result, Google will show more gardening ads to Mary (based on her browser) as she browses websites that use AdSense.

(Google Ads Preferences, n.d.)

Especially as described above, Google's program sounds benign and perhaps even welcome. Who wouldn't want to get ads targeted to their interests? Wouldn't the program save us time, especially when we are searching for a particular item we need to purchase? And most of all, isn't it better to have ads based on our interests instead of having to navigate endless Internet pop-up ads that block us from the information we seek?

But then, let's think again. In an ideal world, we would be informed up front about Google's system and be invited to opt in, but Google has not chosen that path. Instead, as the system exists, Google tracks all users unless they explicitly opt out of the program (assuming they even know the program exists!). That raises some questions. How do we feel about having our web searches tracked, traced, and cataloged? Isn't that an invasion of our privacy? Furthermore, who has access to our data and how securely is our information kept? What if there was a breach in security? Finally, do we really want a record of our Internet searches stored away somewhere? What if our employer, our health insurance provider, or the government were able to access these files? Could we be denied health coverage, fired from our jobs, or find ourselves under governmental investigation because we'd searched sites deemed questionable?

And then, there's more. When we are presented with the "ads" from Google that are directly targeted to our interests, is there any reason to think that the ads represent the best products available? In fact, all we can say about the ads is that some company or individual paid Google handsomely to be included in their Internet-based advertising program. Google is making a profit on these ads, and advertisers are finding that the ads are worthy of the expense.

As we can see by this example, with the advent of new Internet technologies, advertising is changing, as its techniques of persuasion become ever more sophisticated and issues of ethics become paramount. Such trends are compounded by the fact that advertising is pervasive. In 2014, global ad spending was projected to be a $603 billion business, 40.2% of which, $242 billion, were U.S. advertising expenditures. Consequently, Americans are the most advertised-to people on earth, with the average American exposed to over 14 minutes of commercials during every hour of television they watch (Flint, 2014). Prime-time commercials take up more airtime in the United States than in any other nation (Getz, 2006). We must remember, too, that television is only one medium for delivering ads; the average person is exposed to 1,700 banner ads per month (Volpe, 2013) and countless broadcast ads the precede videos online.

Ads are not just shared via television and Internet, though; they also permeate media that is perceived to be commercial-free. Companies pay film-makers exorbitant fees to have characters use their products. Films and home videos are preceded by trailers that promote other films, and many cinemas broadcast ads for products in addition to spots that promote the theater chain or the delectables available at the concession stand. Companies sponsor concerts in exchange for the prominent display of product logos. Advertising even overtakes local bars, as tavern owners welcome beer companies that sponsor special one-night events, complete with free alcohol samples and t-shirts, all provided by young women whose clothes are embroidered with the corporate logo. Sporting events are littered with advertising—in the name of the arena, around the baseball diamond, on race cars and drivers, and even glowing from the scoreboard. Books frequently contain inserts that are ads for other books, and newspapers and magazines often contain more advertisements for goods and services than they do articles. In fashion magazines, articles that offer beauty tips are often thinly disguised advertisements for products. Even the clothes we wear sport labels that advertise for designers or manufacturers.

Not only that, but ads are everywhere. Billboards, bumper stickers, signs, posters, and numerous other forms of publicity for persons, places, and products line our route as we travel to school or work. Every day we are confronted with junk mail, telemarketing calls, and Internet pop-up ads. Our cell phones abound with junk text messages. Often, we cannot even escape in our most intimate moments; a visit to a public restroom confronts us with display ads plastered on the inside door of the bathroom stall.

Advertising has even become commingled with education. College classroom bulletin boards in academic hallways are adorned with pamphlets offering vacations, credit cards, test preparation courses, careers in the military, and self-improvement guides. And even small children are not safe from the onslaught, as Channel One is beamed into public school classrooms where students are forced to watch programming and advertisements in return for the free school equipment that the company provides.

FIGURE 12.1 *A typical college bulletin board.*
Shutterstock.com © Ken Schulze

Advertisements have become so integral to the fabric of our lives that we may believe that we hardly notice them, and, therefore, we downplay their ability to influence us. "I never pay attention to ads," is our common refrain. But the billions of dollars spent by advertisers each year call into question our ability to resist, and also suggest that ads influence us. As Chapter 3 has argued, advertising doesn't just sell products; it also shapes and reinforces ideologies.

Over three decades ago, Michael Schudson called advertising's dominant ideology "capitalist realism" (1984). A few years later, Jonathan Dee went on to suggest that capitalist realism's central value is the "fetishism of commodities ... amount[ing] to an insistent portrait of the world as a garden of consumption in which any need ... can be satisfied by buying the right things" (Dee, 1999). As Arthur Asa Berger explains, even as we claim that we ignore ads, they are still at work, educating us about capitalistic consumer culture and our place in it: "It is advertising that 'teaches' us about the world of consumer goods—what is fashionable and 'hot,' or maybe even better for some people, 'cool'" (Berger, 2007). Ultimately, even the most "informative" advertisement reinforces the central ideological conviction that we are what we own.

Ads sell us images of our ideal selves and of the world in which we live. In attempting to position us as consumers and dispose us favorably toward products by linking them to our most cherished beliefs and values, ads also reinforce those beliefs and values, sometimes to our own detriment. Although we may not like to admit it, we often do believe that using certain products will make us particular types of people, bring us happiness, or offer us a social identity. Advertisements work when we "buy" the images they offer: images of who we are, what kind of life we should lead, how we should spend our time and money. Thus, all ads, even the most "objective," use psychological and cultural appeals to create and reinforce social meanings and identities for their users.

Thinking It Through

Arthur Asa Berger (2007) notes that a few years ago, he wrote an article about deodorant advertising entitled "I Stink, Therefore I Am." His thesis in the article was that "our bodies, which give off odors, confirm our existence and that deodorants which mask our bodies' odors, reflect an unconscious desire to be 'perfect,' to escape somehow from the physical aspects of our existence." Can you think of other examples of advertising that seek to fundamentally shape the way we place ourselves in culture and the world?

TABLE 12.1   *Top ten advertising categories of January–June, 2014*[1]

RANK	CATEGORY	JAN–JUNE 2014 ($ MILLIONS)	JAN–JUNE 2013 ($ MILLIONS)	% CHANGE
1	Retail	$7,178.8	$7,102.1	1.1%
2	Automotive	$7,032.3	$7,069.3	–0.5%
	– (Manufacturers)	$4,409.6	$4,271.4	3.2%
	– (Dealers)	$2,622.8	$2.797.9	–6.3%
3	Telecom	$4,757.5	$4,641.6	2.5%
4	Local Services	$4,755.9	$4,487.4	6.0%
5	Financial Services	$3,797.1	$3,780.0	0.5%
6	Food & Candy	$3,432.7	$3,243.5	5.8%
7	Personal care Pdts	$3,420.9	$3,581.4	–4.5%
8	Restaurants	$3,369.6	$3,357.4	0.4%
9	Direct Response	$3,008.1	$2,762.5	8.9%
10	Insurance	$2,916.2	$2,498.9	16.7%
	Total[2]	**$43,669.2**	**$42,524.3**	**2.7%**

Source: http://kantarmedia.us/press/us-advertising-expenditure-q2-2014

1. Figures do not include FSI or PSA activity

2. The sum of the individual categories can differ from the total shown due to rounding

BRANDED ENTERTAINMENT

Why do some television forensic scientists only use Apple computers in their research, and why does a cartoon character in a popular movie request "Snapple" when thirsty? The answer is that advertisers paid for the right to have their product featured, and this subtle form of advertising outreach is intended to influence us favorable toward the products featured. In addition to being bombarded by ads, we are also now the consumers of stealth advertising in the midst of our favorite television shows and movies. According to Ad Week, the total global spending on product placement in movies 2013 was an astonishing $1.8 billion (Beltrone, 2014).

Clearly, advertisers use product placement because it works. First, it affects our "implicit attitudes," so that when we are watching a program or a movie we like, our attitude toward a TV program or film becomes unknowingly associated with products placed in that TV program or film" (Zimmerman, 2013). In addition, product placement works by affecting our "implicit self-identification," so that when we watch a liked character use a brand, we can start to automatically identify with the brand as a way to vicariously experience that character's life (Zimmerman, 2013). Taken together, therefore, "product placements can be more powerful than we realize, making us implicitly prefer products even if we don't explicitly prefer them" (Zimmerman, 2013).

"The Colbert Report," (2012)	Wheat Thins	Stephen Colbert mercilessly made fun of sponsor Wheat Thins by reading its high-minded brand brief to viewers. Kraft decided to consider the whole thing a net plus.
"Secrets of the Mountain" and "The Jensen Project," (2010)	Walmart and Proctor & Gamble	These made-for-TV movies, which aired on NBC, were designed to draw consumers to buy P&G products at Walmart and drew pretty good audiences for their time slots.
"Modern Family" (2010)	Apple iPad	Apple and the producers swore that no money changed hands for an episode that saw geeky dad Phil obsess over getting an iPad as soon as it hit stores.
"Chuck" (2009) and "Community" (2014)	Subway	In both cases, grateful fans saw the brand's involvement (and money) as more or less saving their favorite show from cancellation.
"Up in the Air" (2009)	American Airlines	In this film, George Clooney travels from country to country firing people. His goal is to fly 10 million miles on American and get his name emblazoned on a place. The airline didn't pay for placement, but it did provide locations and branding.
"Sons of Anarchy" (2008-ongoing)	Harley Davidson	When approached about sponsoring the first episode of the FX series about outlaw bikers, Marks-Hand Richer, Harley's CMO, had a better idea: Instead of advertising, why don't the characters all ride Harleys?
"Transformers" (2007)	GM	As one Hollywood exec recently put it, "Transformers" was a two-hour commercial for GM. Chevrolet, Pontiac, Hummer, and GMC brands were essentially stars in the blockbuster, which grossed more than $700 million worldwide and spawned three sequels. GM said it didn't pay for the product integration, but it did provide director Michael Bay with two custom Camaros.
"The Office" (2006)	Staples	In a 2006 episode, Kevin goes nuts with a Staples MailMate shredder, eventually shredding lettuce into a salad. The big-box store went on to produce a Dunder Mifflin line of paper.
"The Oprah Winfrey Show" (2004)	Pontiac	Oprah shocked viewers when she gave each audience member a Pontiac G-6 to start the show's thirteenth season. Pontiac donated the vehicles and paid the sales tax.
"American Idol" (2002-2013)	AT&T	The longstanding partnership "taught American how to text" said Mitch Kanner, founder of Two Degrees Ventures.

FIGURE 12.2 *Top 10 product placements of the early twenty-first century.*
Source: Sebastian & Ives, 2014, p.18

WHAT IS ADVERTISING?

The very term "advertising" can connote many things. Included, of course, are television and magazine ads, as well as corporate activities such as sponsorships of NASCAR teams. Included, too, are community efforts: children advertise their lemonade stands, churches advertise their fundraising chicken dinners, and local newspaper ads offer for sale everything from automobiles to bug zappers. Individuals advertise: housekeepers, babysitters, contractors, and gardeners advertise their services. We can even "advertise" ourselves, creating profiles on social networking sites like Facebook or Match.com. Because of its ubiquitousness, therefore, we struggle to create a precise definition for "advertising," and we often just end up borrowing from Justice Potter Stewart's famous definition of obscenity: "I know it when I see it."

But we can be more precise than Justice Stewart and develop a working definition. The practice of advertising is generally considered a component of marketing, which can be defined as "the systematic planning, implementation and control of a mix of business activities" that are intended "for the mutually advantageous exchange or transfer of products" (Lake, 2008).

It's the part that involves getting the word out concerning your business, product, or the services you are offering. It involves the process of developing strategies such as ad placement, frequency, etc. Advertising includes the placement of an ad in such media as newspapers, direct mail, billboards, television, radio, and of course the Internet. Advertising is the largest expense of most marketing plans, with public relations following in a close second and market research not falling far behind (Lake, 2008).

Advertising, in sum, involves application of the persuasive principles presented in this book. Woodward and Denton (2009) propose that advertising has four major characteristics:

1   Advertising is a paid form of communication. The message is shared as a result of financial payment.

2   Advertising is a non-personal, presentational form of communication. Advertising is distinct from face-to-face sales presentations.

3   Advertising messages are concerned with the presentation of ideas, products, and services. All too often, we associate advertising only with products. Increasingly, advertising addresses political, social, and philosophical ideas. Because of the drastic increase in service occupations and employment, much advertising espouses the virtues of the various service industries.

4   Sponsors of advertising messages are identified. Sponsorship identification contributes to message accountability and financial responsibility.

In this schema, advertising involves an abstract but identified communicator (such as Proctor and Gamble) who is paying for the use of a communication channel (television network airtime) to reach diverse receivers (television viewers) with a persuasive message ("Buy Tide detergent").

Arens builds on this view and expands it to include the possibility of unpaid advertising, offering a definition that is wider in scope to suggest that advertising is "the structured and composed non-personal communication of information, usually paid for and usually persuasive in nature, about a product (goods, services, and ideas) by identified sponsors through various media" (Arens, 2003). This definition has much to commend it, but it is missing a central component in that it does not speak about the audience. Therefore, we define advertising as "***structured communication by identified groups, industries, or individuals, usually paid for and usually persuasive in nature, that adapts to various media to promote products, services, people, or ideas to targeted audiences.***"

This definition presents a number of advantages. First, it recognizes that advertising is rhetorical; it must consider the audience. Savvy advertisers begin by deciding whom it is they want to reach, and, only after that goal is accomplished, work to create ads to reach their *target audience* (*San Francisco Chronicle*, 2005). Second, this definition incorporates the reality of twenty-first-century advertising trends and the possibility of interpersonal advertising, recognizing that, especially in our contemporary world, individuals often advertise themselves. Using Internet sites such as Monster.com and eHarmony.com, we seek jobs and romance; what's more, we advertise ourselves on Facebook and LinkedIn, creating detailed personal profiles that present the image to the world of the "selves" we wish to share. Finally, this definition acknowledges the diversity of contemporary media and highlights that advertisers must adapt their persuasive messages to fit the limits and possibilities each medium provides. Our definition recognizes that the Internet has changed everything, highlighting that it is a transformative medium that provides the "potential for mass reach," giving "anyone the ability to reach aggregate audiences (niche or mass)" (Herman, 2008). Finally, our definition accounts for the changes in advertising practices that the Internet has wrought, and recognizes that advertising in the twenty-first century is no longer the province of Madison Avenue agencies.

THE CHANGING CHARACTER OF ADVERTISING CAMPAIGNS

Product advertising campaigns change with new technologies and with increased knowledge about consumer psychology. Today's television advertisements are more sophisticated than the ads of decades past. But so, too, are we more adept at tuning them out. Increasingly, as we use new technologies to skip past advertisements entirely (Lewis, 2000), advertisers develop more creative ways to engage our attention.

As Leiss, et al. (2005) note, commodities—the items we buy—have always served two functions: (1) they exist to satisfy our immediate needs for things such as food and shelter, and (2) they mark out our interpersonal distinctions—they demonstrate things such as our status, power, or rank in social groups. Commodities, therefore, have both material functions to satisfy our needs and symbolic or ideological functions to convey social meanings. Advertising and marketing serve, primarily, to educate and persuade us about the best products to meet those physical needs and mark out our status.

In agrarian and closely knit societies such as the United States before the industrial revolution, the advertising that existed occurred in a realm where the material and symbolic meanings of commodities were commonly understood. But the coming of the industrial society in the late nineteenth century altered the entire social context of advertising. For the first time, people were confronted with mass-produced goods that had been made by unfamiliar people in unfamiliar settings; moreover, the purposes and benefits of these goods were not always clear. As a result, advertising began working to connect commodities to culturally approved means of satisfying needs.

Throughout the twentieth century, consumption and the advertising of commodities became increasingly integral to American life. Leiss, et al. (2005) distinguish five phases in the development of consumer culture that are explored in this section: **idolatry**, **iconology**, **narcissism**, **totemism**, and **mise-en-scène**. These stages do not supplant one another; instead, new modes of advertising are added to the old, techniques that mark each stage are periodically revived and discarded in accordance with a particular product's requirements, and the advertisers adjust in their ever present need to engage the consumer.

Idolatry (1890–1910)

Advertising assumed its modern form at the end of the nineteenth century, when goods manufactured in industrial settings began to replace the locally produced and individually crafted goods of traditional societies. Factories were churning out goods at unprecedented levels, so manufacturers hired advertisers to extol the virtues of products, primarily through print media.

Using rational selling strategies, these ads provided the "reasons why" consumers should use a product, and they associated goods with practical characteristics such as utility, low price, and efficiency. Little emphasis was placed on understanding the psychology of consumers, and little time or money was spent on researching the characteristics of target audiences.

Iconology (1920–1940)

Leiss, et al. (2005) describe the early twentieth century as the initial phase of the consumer society. This era's rise in real income, discretionary spending, and leisure time meant that more time could be devoted to items that were not connected to bare necessities. Consequently, advertisers began to move beyond simply promoting products' attributes; they began to focus on what products *represented*. During this period, advertising agencies became professionalized and, through market research, learned how different target groups perceived products in relation to themselves. The focal point for advertising in this era became the person as user of a product, rather than the product itself. Advertising agencies hired psychologists who believed that effective ads evoked basic emotions.

One popular technique during this era was the consumer testimonial. Although this ploy had been used deceptively in patent medicine scams of the nineteenth century, it wasn't until this phase that the J. Walter Thompson agency began to use celebrities instead of ordinary people to endorse products.

These ads were said to work because they relied on a "spirit of emulation" that suggested that we want to copy those we deem superior in taste or knowledge or experience" (Fox, 1985). Ultimately, products were increasingly associated with qualities desired by consumers: status, glamour, reduction of anxiety, and happy families (Leiss, et al., 2005).

Narcissism (1950–1970)

In a third phase, advertising's focus shifted as emotion was brought clearly into the foreground. Leiss, et al. (2005) refer to this period as "narcissistic" because consumers were asked to consider what products could do for them as individuals. They were offered idealized images of satisfied consumers as "mirrors" with whom they might identify. Products promised to transform their users by providing personal change, satisfaction, and the ability to control other people's judgments with the assistance of a product. This development was facilitated by the arrival of television in 1948, a medium that lent itself to such symbolic appeals.

As advertisers became more consumer-oriented, motivational research and depth psychology began to assume a prominent role. Motivational researchers assumed that people were driven more by unconscious motives than by rational thought, and, to determine these motives, researchers used a variety of psychological techniques. Projective tests, lie detectors, and even hypnosis were used to determine why people were attracted to particular products. In precursors to modern focus groups, advertisers conducted "depth interviews" where consumers were asked to freely recall all the associations that a product brought to mind.

As a result of this audience research, advertisers began to shift to soft-sell advertising techniques such as fantasy, music, aesthetic imagery, and appeals to emotion that became part of a product's meaning. As noted by a researcher at the time, a product's image became "a total set of attitudes, a halo of psychological meanings, associations of feeling, and aesthetic messages over a product's physical qualities" (Martineau, 1957). Advertisers attempted to persuade consumers by reaching into their psyches and promising to fulfill some deep-seated desire or alleviate a long-held fear.

In a critique of advertising first written in the late 1950s, Vance Packard (1970) revealed the hidden needs addressed by advertisers, among them emotional security, reassurance of worth, ego gratification, creative outlets, love objects, power, and immortality. In one example, Packard explained that psychological research revealed the reason people bought freezers in the post–World War II period: It was because they felt uncertain and anxious and were nostalgic for the safety and security associated with their childhood memories of a mother who always provided love and food. Packard concluded that the "freezer represents to many the assurance that there is always food in the house, and food in the home represents security, warmth, and safety" (1970).

Totemism (1970–1990)

During the fourth period—the "totemic" phase—advertisers began to make products representative of lifestyle. Product-related images became symbols of social groups, as new computer technologies helped advertisers locate and identify the needs and desires of particular groups of consumers. Product images became totems, or badges of group membership, and ads invited consumers into a **consumption community** by emphasizing the community's attractiveness (rather than the product's desirability). Consumers were induced to adopt the sociocultural identity associated with those who use the product, and encouraged to communicate what types of people they were through their consumption patterns.

The sophisticated use of *demographic* and *psychographic* research distinguished the totemistic phase of advertising. Demographic variables explain many consumer choices; for example, they make it easy to understand why young mothers buy diapers whereas older persons do not. **Demographics** alone, however, cannot explain why some mothers may use disposable diapers and others choose cloth. **Psychographics** link psychology to demographics to help understand consumer behavior. Psychographic analysis explains the values, interests, activities, and opinions of different segments of the population.

A psychographic measurement technique developed in the totemic period that has gained acceptance among advertisers is the values, attitudes, and lifestyles survey. The original **VALS** system was created to explain changing U.S. values and lifestyles in the 1970s. In 1989, VALS was redefined in an attempt to maximize its ability to predict consumer behavior. A team of experts from SRI International, Stanford University, and the University of California, Berkeley, determined that consumers should be segmented on the basis of enduring personality traits rather than social values that change over time.

As noted on the current Strategic Business Insights (a spin-off of SRI International) website, the basic tenet of VALS is that people express their personalities through their behaviors. VALS specifically defines consumer segments on the basis of those personality traits that affect behavior in the marketplace. Rather than looking at what people do and segregating people with like activities, VALS uses psychology to segment people according to their distinct personality traits. The personality traits are the motivation—the cause. Buying behavior becomes the effect—the observable, external behavior prompted by an internal driver (VALS, n.d.).

VALS employs two kinds of surveys: the uniform "VALS questionnaire" and product/service/media questionnaires. The "VALS questionnaire," on the website, is used to identify the "VALS types" of individual consumers. The VALS framework shows the eight basic VALS types. The framework establishes three sources of personal "motivation" (ideals, achievement, and self-expression), evaluates the level of "resources" (energy, self-confidence, intellectualism, novelty seeking, innovativeness, impulsiveness, leadership, and vanity) available, and then combines them to form these eight categories:

1   *Innovators*. These consumers are on the leading edge of change, have the highest incomes, and such high self-esteem and abundant resources that they can indulge in any or all self-orientations. They are located above the rectangle (in Figure 12.3). Image is important to them as an expression of taste, independence, and character. Their consumer choices are directed toward the "finer things in life."

2   *Thinkers*. These consumers are the high-resource group of those who are motivated by ideals. They are mature, responsible, well-educated professionals. Their leisure activities center on their homes, but they are well informed about what goes on in the world and are open to new ideas and social change. They have high incomes but are practical consumers and rational decision makers.

3   *Believers*. These consumers are the low-resource group of those who are motivated by ideals. They are conservative and predictable consumers who favor American products and established brands. Their lives are centered on family, church, community, and the nation. They have modest incomes.

4   *Achievers*. These consumers are the high-resource group of those who are motivated by achievement. They are successful work-oriented people who get their satisfaction from their jobs and families. They are politically conservative and respect authority and the status quo. They favor established products and services that show off their success to their peers.

5   *Strivers*. These consumers are the low-resource group of those who are motivated by achievements. They have values very similar to achievers but fewer economic, social, and psychological resources. Style is extremely important to them as they strive to emulate people they admire.

6   *Experiencers*. These consumers are the high-resource group of those who are motivated by self-expression. They are the youngest of all the segments, with a median age of 25. They have a lot of energy, which they pour into physical exercise and social activities. They are avid consumers, spending heavily on

clothing, fast foods, music, and other youthful favorites, with particular emphasis on new products and services.

7   *Makers*. These consumers are the low-resource group of those who are motivated by self-expression. They are practical people who value self-sufficiency. They are focused on the familiar—family, work, and physical recreation—and have little interest in the broader world. As consumers, they appreciate practical and functional products.

8   *Survivors*. These consumers have the lowest incomes. They have too few resources to be included in any consumer self-orientation and are thus located below the rectangle. They are the oldest of all the segments, with a median age of 61. Within their limited means, they tend to be brand-loyal consumers.

(VALS, n.d.)

Thinking It Through

What is your reaction to VALS? Do you seek to immediately place yourself in a category? Do you read VALS like a horoscope, finding it "fits" for you?

Consider further: Notice the first world consumerist bias implicit in the system. Imagine how someone from a third-world country would try to make sense of VALS. Would it even make sense to such a person?

And what does it say about us that, even if we resist it, VALS, on first glance, can be seen to "make sense." What cultural baggage do we bring to our reading of VALS?

The "VALS questionnaire," the first type of survey, is integrated into custom surveys, the second type of survey, focused on companies' specific products, as well as into several syndicated surveys. These surveys enable analysis about the lifestyles of the VALS segments. Knowing the psychology, product and media preferences, and demographics gives marketers an in-depth understanding of the consumer communities and serves as a solid example of the marketing approach employed during the totemic phase of advertising. It focuses on psychology, both scientific and popular, and uses both to attempt to group consumers into lifestyle categories. From there, it helps advertisers to target their messages by appealing to consumers' lifestyle preferences. It advances understanding by suggesting that demographics alone is not enough to persuade, and offers the hypothesis that demographically similar "high-resource" individuals might not have a single motivation, but rather are motivated by the values of idealism, achievement, or individual satisfaction. And, it argues that the way to persuasive success is by establishing an individual's psychographic disposition and creating a message that appeals to it.

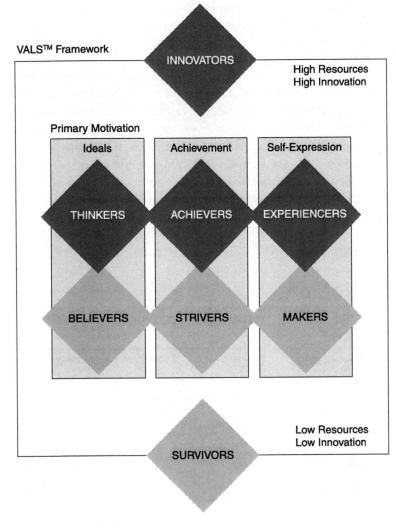

FIGURE 12.3 *The Vals Segments.*

http://www.strategicbusinessinsights.com/vals/ustypes.shtml

Mise-en-scène (1990–2000)

As consumer culture continued to proliferate and change, advertising continued to adapt. In contrast to the totemic phase, where advertisers worked to identify particular and supposedly fixed consumer lifestyles, late twentieth-century advertisers came to view contemporary life as more closely linked to the theatrical concept of *mise-en-scène*. In this phase, advertisers conceived metaphorically of consumers as theater directors who create the scenes of their lives, using products as props "in the service of a virtually unlimited set of creations and re-creations of value and shared meanings" (Leiss, et al., 2005). In sum, the thinking was that Western culture provided a level of wealth, time, and comfort that was unprecedented. The issue became one of what sort of life we might each build; life presented itself to us as a "script-writing" exercise, one in which we are in control (Leiss, et al., 2005).

But the mise-en-scène metaphor, when applied to late twentieth-century Western life, also created a problematical dilemma: "the act of scripting does not and cannot make the surrounding density of the human world disappear" (Leiss, et al., 2005). Technological advances lessened the burdens of labor and provided us with the impetus to attempt to write, produce, and direct our own lives. But, at the same time, it also highlighted the fact that there are "tens of millions, and potentially billions, of scripted lives" (Leiss, et al., 2005). By the end of the twentieth century, McLuhan's notion of the **global village** had become a reality, as we could, in real time, communicate with anyone anywhere on the planet (or even in outer space). The challenge was to create self-identity in that changed environment by placing an arrangement of elements and products into "a setting in order to achieve a unique style" (Leiss, et al., 2005).

TABLE 12.2   *Evolution of cultural frames for goods*

MEDIA FOR ADVERTISING	NEWSPAPERS/ MAGAZINES	RADIO	TELEVISION	TELEVISION	MEDIA MIX
Marketing strategy	Rational	Non-rational	Behaviorist	Segmentation	Anthropological
Advertising strategy	Utility	Product Symbols	Personification	Lifestyle	Demassifying
Period	1890–1910	1920–1940	1950–1960	1970–1980	1990–2000
Elements in ads	Product qualities; price; use	Product qualities	Product	Product	Brand image
Metaphoric-emotive themes in ads	Quality, useful, descriptive	Status, family, health; white magic; social authority	Glamour, romance, sensuality; black magic, self-transformation	Leisure, health; groups, friendship	Authenticity; spot lighting; reflexivity, diversity; transformation of objects
Cultural frames for goods	Idolatry: Products are abstracted from process of production, presented as pure use-values	Iconology: Products are embodiments of attributes, configured in social judgment	Narcissism: Products are personalized and satisfaction is judged in interpersonal terms	Totemism: Products are emblems of group-related consumption practices	Mise-en-scène: Products are props of the self-construction of changing scenes and life-scripts.

Source: From Leiss, et al., 2005. Reprinted with permission of Routledge.

In this phase, then, advertisers worked to present products, which were mass produced, as the devices through which we set ourselves apart from the group. It was an interesting paradox, to say the least, and perhaps even involved some sleight of hand, but, in the mise-en-scène phase, advertisers worked to persuade us that we could overcome our feelings of global insignificance and direct our own lives by purchasing their mass-produced goods. Their argument was this: It is through the employment of consumer goods that we demonstrate that we are unique.

The five phases of advertising presented here are useful heuristic devices to help us begin to note historical trends and also to observe the various ways that advertisers have conceived of the art of persuasion. That being said, these phases are only general typologies that overlap and often merge. Ads are rarely as singularly focused as the phases might imply, and good advertisers use all of the available means of persuasion to appeal to their audiences. This review of the historical phases of advertising, though, demonstrates that advertising has become more artful, flexible, and sophisticated as advertisers have learned more about communication, psychology, sociology, economics, and statistics. But even the most forward-thinking practitioners of the art of advertising could probably not have imagined the opportunities and challenges of the Internet era. We truly have entered a new phase, one that is much more difficult to categorize neatly.

TODAY'S PHASE: HYPERCOMMUNICATION

Imagine for a moment a woman who has lived to be 100. When she was born, women could not vote, air travel did not exist, automobiles, electricity, and radio were in their earliest stages of development, films were silent, and music was enjoyed live because that was the only way it was available. Even if she were highly imaginative and inclined toward a mind that embraced science fiction, it is unlikely that she could have ever imagined the world in which she finds herself today. As Roy Williams writes, we've entered the age of "stimuli bombardment, visual saturation, sound bites, and microscopic attention spans," where "the number of images and voices shouting for our attention has accelerated beyond critical mass" (Williams, 2006). Tocacowala assesses the results of contemporary technological realities and notes that:

> There are five major shifts that have taken place: time, place, area, speed, and power. Each creates an issue, but the combination can be a major pinpoint of pain. Time is compressed, and often victim of arbitrage. Place doesn't matter—people can blog or access content from anywhere. Area has shifted to a digital focus; content can be anything or come from anywhere. Speed of marketing, in both process and execution, is critical. And, finally, there has been an enormous power shift—people are now gods. They have the voice, the tools, and hence, the power.
>
> (As cited in Landry, et al., 2007)

The resulting effect is fragmentation of the public mind, and the era in which we find ourselves can be suitably called the era of **hypercommunication** (Williams, 2006).

Advertisers are faced today with a changed environment and a changing audience. "Eight out of ten Americans are now online, and they spend just as much time there as they do with television" (Landry, et al., 2007). Not only that, but we are becoming proficient at navigating in an online universe. As we spend hours each week scanning search engine results, web pages, and e-mail for relevant information, we gain the ability, through practice, to recognize and disregard things that are not meaningful to us (Williams, 2006). Because of that, marketing has now come to be seen as a *conversation*, and the focus "is now less about pushing messages *at* consumers and more about co-creating experiences *with* them" (Landry, et al., 2007; italics added). Consumers are seen as the new marketers, and the advertiser's message is only one input to a conversation that "consumers conduct 24/7 in digital forums, on blogs, in social networking, through YouTube, via mobile phones, and elsewhere (Landry, et al., 2007).

This is not to say that traditional advertising is extinct. We are still drawn in by creative and interesting television ads. But, over the last 20 years, more sophisticated market research tools have been developed to reach target audiences. For example, the purchase of computerized lists enables marketers to learn much more about consumers. Any time we agree to sign up for a store's "discount card," buy a product, inquire about a product, give our phone number to a cashier in a store, respond to a survey, fill in a warranty, log on to a website, or call an 800 or 900 number, our names are put on a list that can be sold to other marketers. There are lists of millionaires, persons with hypertension, gay people, heart attack survivors, compulsive gamblers, newlyweds, divorcées, and more (Tye, 1993). Today, these marketing trends are being combined with the governmental post–9/11 technology of **data mining**, also known as "big data," where our actions are even more closely tracked, often without our knowledge. Every web page's "individual views, every word typed in a search query box (also known as the 'database of consumer intentions'), every video download, and even every word in an e-mail may create one more data" (Landry, et al., 2007). Data mining works by collecting everything; then, that data is screened to see what might be useful, crucial, or important.

Market researchers now actively attempt to discern what is the most likely time for you to buy something. Called **syncographics**, this investigative tool presupposes that when consumers are anticipating an event—from a marriage or baby to a vacation or graduation—they must buy certain things. They also employ **sociographics**, used to determine how, why, and where people cluster together, as in neighborhoods, malls, online social networking sites, and entertainment centers. Researchers might identify promising neighborhoods for direct mail advertising by zip codes, survey a representative sampling of neighborhood residents, and invite some of them to form focus groups for more in-depth research on what it will take to make customers of them. The effect of all of this can be startling when we truly consider it. As Henk Campher puts it,

> They find everything about me online. They follow my digital moves. They have access to my photos, videos and even know my friends. They know the places I visit and where I buy my milk. Then they follow me. Yet I know nothing about them.
>
> (Campher, 2014)

Thinking It Through

Are you concerned that so much of your life is being tracked, cataloged, and analyzed? And if not, why not?

Have we all simply internalized a post 9/11 mindset, where we live in a world now where no information is ever truly private?

Evaluate this: Most of us do not want to live our lives as paranoid conspiracy theorists. We also rationalize our situation as one where we convince ourselves that the sheer quantity of data that is mined, coupled with the ordinariness of our lives, keeps us protected.

Yet, we agree in some fashion that it cannot be good that so much of our private information is stored away, possibly vulnerable to hackers, possibly used unfairly or inappropriately.

What, then, should our response be? How should we confront these twenty-first-century issues?

What's more, in the era of the Internet, advertisers can have real-time conversations with consumers online. They can identify and draft high "consumer influencers" as brand advocates, gather ideas to improve their products or services, and change their marketing messages and media mix instantaneously, depending on what is working or not. And they can do all of the above immediately (Landry, et al., 2007). Using *computer-generated media*, with vehicles such as blogs, podcasts, Facebook and Instagram pages, video clips, and customizable online ads, advertisers can create opportunities where the consumer "creates and distributes the brand message" (Guegan, 2007). For example, in 2014, Coca-Cola launched its global *ShareCoke* promotion, allowing people to "take the Coca-Cola script and replace it with their name on the can" (Nichols, 2014). When the campaign launched in the U.S., consumers found Coke in the grocery store labeled with the "250 most popular names among teens and millennials" (Staff, 2014). Consumers where then encouraged to "Click here to find out if [your name] made the cut", and to "personalize a virtual bottle" that could be shared on social media sites (Staff, 2014). Taking the idea one step further, Secret deodorant (shareyoursecret.com) and Greased Lightning household cleaner (filthyconfessions.com) invited website viewers to confess their secrets online (Woyke & Stead, 2006). The goal was to take the advertisements "away from old-fashioned one-way communications and closer to a rich, lively dialogue with consumers" (Guegan, 2007). Actively engaging consumers in increasingly innovative and interactive ways is important, because marketing research now shows that, "two-thirds of the touch points during the active-evaluation phase," where consumers are making their decisions about what to buy, 'involve consumer-driven activities" (Court, et al., 2009). The more engaged we become, presumably the more open we are to being persuaded to identify with and purchase the product.

As the introduction to this chapter explains, there now also exists behavioral targeting (BT), which "takes information from a user (her recent browsing patterns) and feeds back to her ads that are more relevant to her immediate needs and interests" (Smith, 2007). We only need to visit an online retailer like Amazon.com to experience BT, where once we set up an account we are welcomed to the site and greeted with recommendations for books, videos, and other goods that may hold interest for us. These recommendations are gleaned from our searches and purchases, and are often quite useful and informative. Ultimately, while it "sounds a little creepy to have ads stalk a user," (Smith, 2007), online advertising is here to stay and growing in prevalence; advertisers spent more than $1.3 billion on targeting advertising in 2011, and the figure is expect to rise to more than $2.6 billion in 2014" (Chen & Stallaert, 2014).

BT presents us with the ultimate in targeting, called **micromarketing**, and it portends to be a growing trend. Where formerly advertisers engaged in mass marketing, today they seek to provide products that are aimed to a culture that presents a "far more diverse and commercially self-indulgent society than it was in the heyday of the mass market" (Bianco, et al., 2004). "Today it is all about creating the products that are 'right for me'" says David Martin, president of Interbrand Corporation (Bianco, et al., 2004). Even a product as familiar as Tide, "which has ranked as the country's biggest-selling laundry detergent ever since Proctor and Gamble Co. took it national in 1949," has succumbed to the demand for microtargeting. It now comes in dozens of varieties: in liquid or powder, with bleach added, with diverse scents, infused with fabric softener, for high-efficiency washing machines or old-fashioned top loaders, and more. James R. Stengle, Proctor and Gamble's global marketing officer, notes that today his company's portfolio contains "not one mass-market brand, whether it's Tide or Old Spice, Crest or Pampers or Ivory. Every one of our brands is targeted" (Bianco, et al., 2004).

In an ongoing quest to suggest metaphorically that advertising is a "conversation" with the consumer, marketing in the phase of *hypercommunication* is embracing another interesting new trend: ***ethnography***. Originally an approach to anthropology, ethnography posits that people are best understood when observed in the fullest context possible; the goal is to study humans where they live, seeing how they make a living, looking at how they deal with the need for food, housing, energy, and water, observing their customs and language, and so on. Today, advertisers are beginning to employ ethnographic methods in an attempt to make the shift away from simple focus groups or in-house "behind the two-way mirror" consumer observation. Kevin Grange, a vice president for global marketing at the giant corporation Unilever, notes that his company (which markets products like Dove soap and Axe deodorant) began three years ago conducting ethnographic research. He claims the benefits are clear:

> Observing what consumers actually do, rather than what they say they do, has made a huge difference. Talking to them about things other than the product and brand offers a much deeper understanding of who they are and what motivates them.
>
> (Landry, et al., 2007)

For example, Procter & Gamble recently opened an online store, not to bring in new revenue, but to see how their customers were searching for their products (Flynn, 2014). Anheuser-Busch takes it one step further, as company-paid ethnographers now "live with a customer for a few days or stock their fridge one day and come back the next. This yields much deeper insights than only focusing on the lab environment" (Landry, et al., 2007).

In sum, today's marketers are confronted with an era of *hypercommunication*, where consumers have developed the ability to process (and reject) information rapidly, where time is compressed, where interaction takes place at any and every moment of the day, and where location is unrestrained. Responding to these changes, advertisers are now working to have ongoing virtual "conversations" with consumers, and seeking ways, through technology, to individualize advertising to the level of microtargeting. They are gathering data about us from every source available, studying our habits in our homes where possible, and working innovatively every day to find new ways to create messages that will persuade us so that we will buy their products. And while some of their contemporary practices, such as data mining, may give us pause, they are not likely to be abandoned; instead, they will likely expand. It is a brave new world in which we live, and both persuaders and persuadees are finding themselves transformed.

BREAKING WITH TRADITION IN THE PHASE OF HYPERCOMMUNICATION: ANTI-ADS

Even in changed times, we still have what we might call "traditional" advertising. Television, radio, and magazine ads are ever present, and they use diverse approaches to catch our attention. Some ads are constructed to appear to be "telling it like it is" rather than trying to persuade us. Others "go meta," appealing to consumers' assumed awareness of the distinction between advertising images and reality; they appeal to our cynical side by mocking advertising gimmicks, all the while using mockery as a gimmick in its own right. Such anti-ads have always existed, but they are a prevalent feature in the era of hypercommunication, where consumers are practiced at rapid-fire evaluation of messages and see themselves (probably correctly) as possessing finely tuned critical abilities when confronted with advertising.

Anti-ads take a variety of forms, but five styles seem to be prominent: **pseudo non-ads, code-transgressing ads, self-referential ads, self-parody ads**, and **knowing wink ads**. The categories are not discrete and there is often overlap among them, but each style works to reach contemporary consumers by distancing itself from what "traditional" advertising is imagined to be. In part, these ads appeal to us through flattery; they present themselves as complex and multi-faceted discourse and they imply that they are intended for audiences who are savvy enough to understand the multiple levels at which the discourse operates. Let us consider each in turn.

Pseudo Non-Ads

One type of anti-ad attempts to downplay or conceal that it is an advertisement by mimicking the codes and conventions associated with non-advertising forms. Through the use of supposedly candid "man on the street" interviews, for example, a corporation works to communicate its message as if it were a conversation among "regular" people. The corporations may use extemporaneous interviews with people or they may employ actors; in either event, the comments are carefully edited and organized to communicate the company's desired message.

A recent example of this trend is one engaged in by the oil companies, and especially BP In 2010, BP found itself at the center of an environmental crisis after its Deepwater Horizon drilling rig exploded, releasing more than 200 million gallons of oil into the Gulf of Mexico. This led to a public relations nightmare, one from which BP is still working to recover. One of BP's strategies was to create a campaign timed to air during the January college bowl games, especially the one between Louisiana State University and Alabama (Burdeau, 2012). These ads that suggested that the Gulf cleanup, with large investments by BP had brought the Gulf back. They featured local business people and residents, as BP even hired "chefs Emeril Lagasse and John Besh to promote Gulf seafood, it's hired two seafood trucks to hand out fish tacos and seafood-filled jambalaya to the hundreds of thousands of tourists and fans pouring into the city for the football games" (Burdeau, 2012).

> "I'm glad to report that all beaches and waters are open for everyone to enjoy!" BP representative Iris Cross says in one TV ad. "And the economy is showing progress, with many areas on the Gulf Coast having their best tourism season in years."
>
> (*BP's Commitment to America*, 2012)

This $100 million ad campaign was not without its critics (Miller, 2012). The head of the Louisiana Shrimp Association, a commercial shrimpers group, called reports about his industry "BP propaganda" as he noted that the most recent shrimp harvest had been "dismal" (Burdeau, 2012) . Area surveyor Jonathan Henderson, who has taken 200 trips to the area since the disaster, explained that every time he has visited these areas, he has found a lot of oil and that the oil on the coast is not just the tar balls. In summer 2014, he described how liquid oil still buried in the marshy soil oozed up to the surface (Abrams, 2014). Ultimately, from the perspective of environmental groups and some local residents, the damage still remains, but BP wishes that we all move on and they are intent on persuading us to do so. BP's advertising focus, labeled "greenwashing" by critics, has helped the company to repair its public relations disaster (Frick, 2014), and the use of pseudo non-ads has been central to that strategy.

Code-Transgressing Ads

Another style of anti-ads transgresses the codes by which we have learned to "read" advertising. Although traditional ads link their product with some desirable trait (beauty, innovation, etc.) and then invite consumers to identify with this idealized image, these anti-ads appeal to people who "know better" than to identify with such idealized images (Moog, 1990).

A recent clever example of this trend is an ad campaign by Post Shredded Wheat. This ad responds to the results of Western progress that have led to things like derivatives, credit-default swaps and securitized sub-prime mortgages, using contemporary woes as an opportunity to claim *non-advancement* as a selling proposition (Garfield, 2009). The ad presents fake Post spokesman, Frank Druffel, who delivers the following lines in deadpan style:

> "Has progress taken us to a better place?" he asks, as he stalks around his office. "I'd say it's taken us for a ride. Honestly, what thanks do we owe progress? We're up to our necks in landfill and down to the wire in resources and climate change is out to get us."
>
> "That's why progress plays no role inside Post Shredded Wheat. Here we put the 'no' in innovation. Post original Shredded Wheat is still just the one, simple, honest ingredient which naturally comes with vitamins, minerals and fiber. All we did was make it spoon-size. Did we go too far?"
>
> (Garfield, 2009)

This anti-ad adheres to a "code" of one of the most traditional of ad formats: a company spokesman addressing the camera directly, talking to customers from company headquarters. But, the ad is a fake send-up, and that is what makes it memorable. It works as an example of a code-transgressing anti-ad because it displays "the modern—or, actually, *post*-modern—way of doing things (Garfield, 2009). It self-consciously plays with the form, taking the tired clichés of advertising and retreading them as irony (Garfield, 2009). The fact that we immediately understand that the ad is a send-up of traditional advertising style appeals to us; it hints at our sophistication, and, if all goes well, inclines us positively toward the product. Post flatters us by trusting us to get the joke, and they hope that we remember the ad and respond by purchasing Shredded Wheat cereal.

Self-Referential Ads

Another anti-ad strategy involves absorbing the mass media's increasingly prevalent criticism of advertising by incorporating the criticisms into the ads themselves. The ads seem to twist back upon themselves like a mobius strip; as we view them, we understand that advertising agencies have created them to offer critiques of the exact practices they are engaged in at that very moment of ad creation. All this is done in order to achieve the traditional goal of getting us to buy their products. Direct TV's "Youthenize" ad presents one of the most interesting examples of this type.

The ad shows the boardroom at an imaginary cable company where a female marketing agent is showing charts and making a presentation to a group of stuffy white men about the challenges their company is facing. She explains that their company is facing a problem—thanks to new technology, Direct TV is "cleaning their clock." As they brainstorm together, one executive says what is needed is some "brand heat" and that's why he's proposing a new "tag line": *Get Youthenized!* To laughter and applause, another executive talks about how this tag line is marvelous and how the company will "Youthenize America." The scene concludes with a younger executive praising the creator of the tag line, proclaiming "I wish I was that smart!"

This ad clearly takes on corporate marketing practices and it is biting satire. It has gone viral on YouTube as a witty example of advertising, but it has also generated much discussion on blogs concerned with suicide and mental illness. And this is exactly what its creators hoped would happen. The ad has taken on a life of its own; it is an excellent example of a self-referential anti-ad.

Self-Parody Ads

Another way that contemporary corporate advertisers use anti-ads to gain attention is through *self-parody*. Whereas self-referential anti-ads focus on corporate advertising practices and offer critiques of those practices within the ads themselves, anti-ads that employ self-parody have another focus. In anti-ads using self-parody, the object of attention is the supposed spokesperson for the company who distorts the traditional role for comic effect.

William Shatner's role as "spokesman" for Priceline is perhaps the most impressive recent example of this style of advertising. His character, Priceline's "Negotiator," was killed off in 2012, only to be quickly resurrected later that year after 94% of customers surveyed told Priceline that they wanted him back (Hsu, 2012). After his resurrection, he went on to appear with his "daughter" in a 2014 Superbowl ad.

In his role as company pitchman, Shatner presents himself as a somewhat slimy but loveable character who says and does ridiculous things. In one spot, he charms a female hotel clerk into marking down a room with lines that are completely over the top: "Sometimes doing the wrong thing can feel so right," he says, placing his hand over hers on the computer's mouse. When she discounts the room by half, he purrs,

"You're so naughty" (Lentini, 2007). He is, ultimately, the complete antithesis of what a corporation might want in its spokesman. Instead of being wholesome, he's a bit creepy. He helps customers undercut the very company he is supposed to be representing. He's abrasive, pompous, and silly.

Such self-parody in advertising works because it makes use of "the peripheral rather than the central route to persuasion," explains professor of psychology Rod Martin. It is "difficult to make a compelling, logical, rational argument for these products' superiority over their rivals," so advertisers work to "evoke positive associations with the product in the minds of the viewers without encouraging them to think too much about it" (as quoted in Lentini, 2007).

In addition, the ads are persuasive because, in an era of hypercommunication, we value the creativity integrated into them. In all the clutter, they capture our attention. The reversals and switchbacks we must employ to understand the message are interesting and funny. The ads work hard to engage us; we notice, and we respond.

Knowing Wink Ads

A final category continues to be a hallmark of anti-ads, sometimes evoking gut-splitting laughter. The *knowing wink* ad communicates directly with the audience in obvious or subtle fashion, breaking the theatrical "fourth wall" for comic effect.

The "fourth wall" refers to the imaginary boundary at the front of the stage in a theater through which the audience sees the action in the world of the play. The term also applies to the boundary between any fictional setting and its audience. When this boundary is "broken" (for example, by an actor speaking to the audience directly through the camera in a television program or film), it is called "breaking the fourth wall" (Abelman, 1998).

A contemporary example of such an ad campaign is provided by the commercials for FreeCreditReport.com. These ads feature a "young slacker singing about various life problems—living in the in-laws' basement and dressing as a pirate to wait on tables in a seafood restaurant" (Clifford, 2008). In one ad the lead singer of the band of merry losers finds he can no longer afford to have a car, and downgrades to a bike; he also attends a Hollywood party, but as a waiter; and plays a character at a Renaissance fair (Clifford, 2008). These problems occur all because he had neglected to check his credit score. The ads are lighthearted and catchy, with lyrics like: "F-R-E-E, that spells FreeCreditReport.com, baby. Saw their ads on my TV, thought about going but was too lazy" (Clifford, 2008).

The ads consistently have the same cast of characters, and even sometimes refer to each other. At the Renaissance fair, careful viewers even see a return of the elderly lady who had been a customer at the seafood restaurant. The protagonist is consistently breaking the fourth wall as he sings directly into the camera to us; he sets himself apart from what is going on all around him while still performing the duties the scene requires of him. With a "knowing wink," he tells us the "real" story of his life, persuading us to stop and listen.

In sum, anti-ads in the forms of pseudo non-ads, code-transgressing ads, self-referential ads, self-parody ads, and knowing wink ads are particularly suited to our present era of hypercommunication. Grunwald suggests that these anti-ads work to persuade us through self-reference; they are heavy on faux-irreverent irony and light on substance. We become participants in an inside joke as advertisers seem to be saying: *Aren't advertisements stupid?* (Grunwald, 1993). But we are manipulated all the same. The legions of anti-ads, with their mindless jingles, faux announcers and person-on-the-street interviews, are just more examples of the devices that advertisers use to try and sell us products.

Advertising, though, which uses both traditional styles and anti-ad stylings, depends upon language. The best ad campaigns create discourse that is clever, suggestive, and memorable. Ad slogans and tag lines must communicate, but not too much. They are often artfully crafted examples of linguistic misdirection, and it is to that topic we now turn.

College Students Remember Advertising Slogans

Students surveyed at three Texas universities could correctly identify the advertising slogans for Nike, M&Ms and Taco Bell, but they may not correctly identify the significance of July 4, 1776.

Dr. Roy Busby, professor of journalism, and Leslie Carter, a student in UNT's Mayborn Graduate Institute of Journalism, asked 316 students in introductory political science and advertising classes at UNT, Texas A&M University and Southern Methodist University to identify current and older ad slogans. Names of the products were marked out in the slogans. The students also answered questions about historical events and people often covered in political science classes. Three out of four students gave more correct answers for the ad slogan questions than they did for the political science questions.

"They've been exposed to the slogans a lot more during their lives than to the political science facts," Busby said. "Obviously, repetition of a good advertising slogan still works."

At least 90% of the students correctly identified the advertising slogans for Nike ("Just do it"), M&Ms ("Melts in your mouth, not in your hands"), Taco Bell ("Yo Quiero"), Rice Krispies ("Snap, crackle, pop"), Energizer batteries ("It keeps going and going and going"), Frosted Flakes ("They're grrreat"), NBC ("Must-see TV"), the U.S. Army ("Be all that you can be") and Budweiser ("The king of beers"). Yet almost 40% of the students did not know that July 4, 1776, was the date of the signing of the Declaration of Independence. Most of those who missed the question said the Revolutionary War ended on that date. In addition, almost 40% did not write an answer to who led the Confederate forces during the Civil War. About 30% of those who answered incorrectly said it was Ulysses S. Grant, rather than Robert E. Lee.

Political science facts missed by 60–80% of the students included who was president when the Berlin Wall came down (George Bush), where the Bay of Pigs invasion occurred (Cuba), who would become president if both the president and vice president were removed from office (the Speaker of the House), the last state in the continental United States to become a state (Arizona), the president who was never elected (Gerald Ford) and what VE stands for in VE Day (Victory in Europe).

In other findings: Students frequently confused advertising slogans for different brands of beer, cars, pants and drinks. Almost every student who missed the Docker's slogan ("Nice pants") thought it was the slogan for Bugle Boy jeans ("Are those Bugle Boy jeans you're wearing?"). Students who missed the Sprite slogan ("Obey your thirst") often thought it was the Gatorade slogan ("Life's a sport. Drink it up"). Some of the older slogans for Calgon ("Calgon, take me away") and General Electric ("We bring good things to life") scored higher than slogans aimed at those in young age groups, like slogans for soft drinks and fast food restaurants.

(Excerpted from the October 23, 2000, University of North Texas News Service, https://news.unt.edu/news-releases/college-students-remember-advertising-slogans

MISDIRECTION IN THE LANGUAGE OF ADVERTISING

How do advertisers use language to persuade? Often, they use vague but suggestive language of implication rather than direct, easily verifiable claims. At other times, they protect themselves against charges of outright falsehood while still leading consumers on. It is interesting to consider the variety of forms such advertising takes.

The following are potentially deceptive claims. Although the examples used here to illustrate these claims are relatively clear-cut, if we look we will find in ads that product descriptions often fit multiple categories. Ultimately, our list of examples is not comprehensive; advertisers are endlessly creative with their discourse. But, in an era of hypercommunication, it is good for us to consider, as persuadees, how slogans, mottos, and tag lines work to create impressions about consumer products.

The "Nothing Is Better" Claim

These ads create an illusion of superiority by claiming to be "best." But the word "best" in these instances often means nothing more than "equal to." If brands are identical, they are equally good, so "best" means only that products are as good as the other products in their category.

"Bring out the Hellman's. Bring out the best." Mayonnaise contains predictable ingredients and varies little. Hellman's seeks to create the illusion of superiority with a blatantly empty slogan where it claims to be "best." But, as compared to what? And, who made the decree?

"Nothing is proven to work better or last longer than Advil. Nothing." But this doesn't mean that there aren't other pain relief products that work just as well and last just as long as Advil.

"The ultimate driving machine." BMW is a car. Here's the dictionary definition of "ultimate":

a   most remote in space or time: farthest;
b   last in a progression or series: final ("Their ultimate destination was Paris.");

c   eventual ("They hoped for ultimate success.");

d   the best or most extreme of its kind: utmost ("the ultimate sacrifice").

How does "ultimate" fit here? What evidence is there that the BMW "driving machine" is the utmost or best that there is?

The "We're Better" Claim

These ads claims superiority of some sort but do not complete the comparison. In that way, they can assert something that cannot be refuted.

"Preference—Better conditioning for better color." What does this mean?

"Cinnamon Toast Crunch—Real cinnamon and sugar in every bite." Do we really expect otherwise?

"A1 Bold Steak Sauce. It's spicier!" Spicier than what?

The "We're Unique" Claim

This type of claim says that there is nothing quite like the product being advertised. The claim to uniqueness is supposed to be interpreted as a claim to superiority.

"The one and only Cheerios," or "Lucky Charms: They're magically delicious." Why should this make us buy the product? Studies repeatedly show that there is no substantial difference between brand-name and generic cereals other than cost. The brand-name cereals are more expensive, primarily because so much of their profit goes into packaging and advertising.

Clairol: "Try new Natural Instincts. The first and only hair color with a rare blend of 3 natural ingredients, including aloe, chamomile and ginseng." Does this make the product better than its competitors? Also, why is it "rare"? Is rare necessarily better?

"Only Aquafresh Whitening has its patented whitening formula with the special ingredient Triclene." What is Triclene, and what makes it special?

The "Trivially True" Claim

This type of claim says something about the product that is true for any product in the product category. The claim is factual but presents no real advantage over the competition.

"Tidy Cat. It freshens every minute of the day." How is this (whatever it is) different from what any other kitty litter would do?

"Great Lash greatly increases the diameter of every lash." As does any mascara.

"Rolling Rock: The Natural Beer." Rolling Rock is made from grains and water, the same as any beer.

"Multi-Bran Chex: Perfect Combination of Corn, Rice, and Wheat." One would expect that all multigrain cereals could assert a similar claim.

The "Studies Show" Claim

This type of claim uses specific numbers or other intimations that its claims to superiority are based on some sort of scientific proof.

"Wonder Bread helps build strong bodies 12 ways." Even the word "helps" did not prevent the Federal Trade Commission from demanding that the ad be changed. Note how the use of the number 12 strengthens the claim. Now Wonder Bread simply claims that the bread helps build strong bodies.

"Easy-Off has 33% more cleaning power than another popular brand." Another "popular brand" often means some other type of oven cleaner sold somewhere. Also, the claim is not that Easy-Off works 33% better.

"Dimetapp: The brand recommended by doctors over 200 million times." Who's counting?

"Degree. Body-Heat Activated for an Extra Degree of Protection." This makes Degree sound like it works more scientifically than other deodorants.

The "Poetic" Claim

This claim uses feel-good words that are colorful but literally meaningless. Still, they call forth positive associations.

Olive Garden: "When you're here, you're Family." And what happens when we're away from here? And what are we when we dine at another restaurant?

Quaker Oats: "Yes, it's cold. But it warms your soul." One wonders how oatmeal can do that.

Purina Dog Chow: "All you add is love." How does one add love to dog food?

Post Blueberry Morning cereal: "A little taste of summer." What does summer taste like?

Count Chocula: "Chocolate taste so big, it's scary." What exactly is a big, scary chocolate taste?

"Gallo: because the wine remembers." Remembers what?

Clairol Herbal Essence Shampoo: "Your hair will get very, very excited!" How will this excitement manifest itself?

"Trust is Tampax Tampons." Despite the alliteration, this one defies logic.

Travelocity: "You'll never roam alone." Who is going to be always with us?

The Rhetorical Question

This technique demands a response from its audience. A question is asked, and the receiver is supposed to answer in a way that affirms the product's goodness.

"What would you do for a Klondike Bar?"

"Got a little Captain in you?"

"Got milk?"

"Bread du jour—Can't you just taste it?"

"What can Brown do for you?"

Nordic Track: "Why settle for a cheap imitation when the real thing is now so affordable?"

The Product Endorsement

A celebrity or authority appears in the ad to lend his or her qualities to the product. Sometimes, the person will actually claim to use the product. And, when the celebrity does claim to have used the product (as when celebrities talk about the Sleep Number bed they have in their home and disclose their "personal sleep number," or when they proclaim that they feed their dog Purina Dog Chow and it has reinvigorated the animal), is it likely that (1) the product has been provided to the spokesperson free of cost, and (2) the product has been put to use by the celebrity only for endorsement purposes.

Some of the better-known celebrity testimonials involve sports figures. Athletes such as Michael Jordan have appeared in commercials and endorsed products from breakfast cereal to sneakers, and Peyton Manning has endorsed everything from cars to pizza to insurance and more. These sports icons have "elevated the practice, often scoring more in endorsement and licensing dollars than from their actual sports earnings" (Creswell, 2008). Advertisers spend their money on these sports celebrities because "especially with our children," the presence of their heroes "who themselves are the embodiment of physical fitness and health, serve to very clearly 'health-wash' the products they're shilling" (Haelle, 2014).

There are agencies that work primarily to match celebrities with product endorsements, and agencies that conduct sophisticated research to aid in these efforts. For example, the *Davie Brown Index®* (DBI), which is also referred to as the *Celebrity Trust Index,* is "an independent index that quantifies and qualifies consumer perceptions of celebrities" (Miller, 2014.) The index is available only to subscribers for a fee and updated weekly, but *The New York Times* reports that the DBI tracks thousands of celebrities (Creswell, 2008). As of the end of 2014, the top five celebrities in order were Tom Hanks, Kate Middleton, Brian Williams, Morgan Freeman, and Betty White. In theory, if DBI is to be believed, these five individuals will be the most persuasive celebrity spokespersons, as we will take seriously what they have to say. It is no accident that in addition to us trusting them more than other famous people, these highly ranked celebrities would be able to draw the highest paychecks should they agree to advertisement a product.

To sum it up, advertisers seek to use language in ways that get our attention, set their products apart from the rest, and make their products memorable. And, in their quest to meet these objectives, they often end up using devices like weasel words, glittering generalities, name substitutions, and sloganeering (Rogers, 2007). As this section displays, their rhetoric is often empty and of questionable ethics; it is the very sophistry of which Plato complained. Yet, in an interesting twist, as consumers most of us give little thought to the ethical sleight of hand seen in such language, because we understand in advance that it will be mostly fake. We even go so far as to delight in the more witty attempts; we like being smart enough to be able to understand the game. The result seems to be a sort of mutual understanding between consumers and advertisers, where both work to overlook most of the misdirection in the ads. But as consumers we do this at our peril, because the ads do get into our heads and separate us from our money.

VISUAL MISDIRECTION IN PRODUCT ADVERTISING

Advertisers do not just use words. They also use pictures. And often, it is with pictures that they show visually what they would be at risk to say verbally. In the case of attack ads, discussed in Chapter 11, doctored photographs are sometimes used to malign political opponents, or images are juxtaposed, as in the furlough ad, to invite false inferences.

FIGURE 12.4 *Newsweek's unretouched cover photo of Sarah Palin.*
© Newsweek magazine.

Photojournalists may also be accused of editorializing, where, in effect, they advertise their perspective while maintaining their claims of objectivity. One interesting case occurred near the end of the 2008 presidential campaign when *Newsweek* put a photo of then Vice-Presidential candidate Sarah Palin on its cover. What was interesting in this instance is not what *Newsweek* did, but rather what it did not do: The magazine's editors presented Palin in a close-up that was so intense that part of her face was missing, but did not touch up the photo.

Supporters of Palin objected on the grounds that *Newsweek's* portrayal was a "deliberate attempt to show a very beautiful woman in a bad light," arguing (rightly) that most cover photos are "airbrushed and or touched up when someone's face is shown that close" (Baron, 2008). As Baron pointed out, one could see every flaw in Sarah Palin's face in the cover photo, and *Newsweek's* portrayal was not done by accident. Instead, Baron argued, "it was an intentional attempt to portray a 'harder' side of the soft persona America has come to know" (Baron, 2008).

Of course, others defended *Newsweek* and argued that the portrayal of Palin was lovely. But, when one compares the cover with *Newsweek's* earlier front-page portrayal of Palin during the campaign, one can see that Baron might have a point. In that photo, Palin is portrayed in a male's wrinkled blue buttoned-down shirt with a gun slung over her shoulder.

Taking the two photos together, one might agree that Palin was not presented as "soft." Of course, we could debate the effects of those photos; some will be offended by them, others will see them as portraying Palin as a strong, no-nonsense political figure. But there is one thing that is beyond debate: The photos communicated, and they suggested a persona for the candidate. They took a stance without saying a word.

Recall the photograph of the senator between the model and the priest, discussed in Chapter 5. In a cropped photo showing Senator Jones with either the priest or the beautiful model, the viewer would get the appearance of authenticity—of the real thing. This is one of the ironies of photography (and of film and video) that is only enhanced in our digital age: It can distort reality although, by virtue of its **indexicality**, it impresses us with its apparent truthfulness.

Indexicality is present, said Charles Peirce (1991), when a sign (e.g., a photo) has some physical connection to the object or event to which it refers. Examples include fingerprints, footprints, weather vanes, and thermostats. Photography is yet another example. By dint of its physical connection, it is conventionally regarded as proof that the scenes depicted in it really did occur (Messaris, 1997). Compare an ad for a laundry detergent providing before and after photographic proof of the product's cleansing powers with an ad merely asserting by way of a diagram or drawing how the chemical agents in the detergent work. The diagram might clarify, but it could not prove. The photograph, however doctored to misrepresent reality, would probably appear authentic.

Over a decade ago, Paul Messaris (1997) identified a number of ways that visuals may create false but persuasive appearances of the real in product advertising. In the years since, the technology may have become more advanced, but the practices

FIGURE 12.5   *Newsweek cover: Sarah Palin toting her rifle.*
© 2010 Judy Patrick/Alaskastock.com

remain the same. The following are among the most common ways that photography is used in ads to alter or enhance reality.

Staged to Look Real

It is a common advertising scenario: the car or truck that seems to be super-strong or indestructible. In one instance, though, the carmaker's photographic sleight of hand was challenged and came to be revealed as a strong example of visual deception. In the ad, a Volvo appeared to have survived intact after a "monster truck" ran over a row of cars, crushing them all except for the Volvo. An investigation revealed that the Volvo was strengthened by specially added steel supports and the other cars were correspondingly weakened (Messaris, 1997).

In another case, advertisers show soup being served that looks to be thick with vegetables. Not shown are the objects below the surface that push the vegetables to the top. Such food staging is common, and can even go so far as to the use of

FIGURE 12.6   *Wendy's Replica Twisted Frosty's. That's right, these are not real!*
© 2010 Oldemark LLC. Reprinted with permission.

manufactured props. The company Fake Food specializes in custom manufacturing of artificial food. It creates models to the exact needs of its customers, using real foods to create faux food models (Fake-Foods.com, n.d.).

Such "staging" is often benign. It generally works through magnifying the attributes of products or presenting them as more perfect than they could likely ever be. It persuades by deception.

Photographic Alteration

Another common form of visual deception in advertising involves photographic alteration. With twenty-first-century technology, physical appearance can be easily enhanced and transformed by use of computer imaging without leaving a trace, and there are no negatives or films to harken back to the "real" image. Says Messaris (1997), computers are routinely used to accomplish such tasks as making hair shinier and adding highlights; removing strands of hair that are falling in the wrong place; removing wrinkles, sun damage, pimples, and other skin blemishes; imparting an overall glow to the skin; whitening the whites of eyes and enlarging the pupils; reducing the size of hips and increasing the length of legs; and, of course, increasing the size of breasts.

And, as we've seen with the example of Sarah Palin, photographic touch-ups, especially of women, are now both assumed and expected.

Such visual transformation has generated a great deal of critique from feminist scholars and psychologists (among others) who link the unreal portrayals of women and girls in advertising to problems such as eating disorders, low self-esteem, sexual objectification, and unrealistic body image. And, in a fascinating response, fashion moguls are now using "non-air brushed" photography as a marketing tool. A recent issue of the French edition of *Elle* magazine portrayed photos of Eva Herzigova, Monica Bellucci, Sophie Marceau, Charlotte Rampling, and four other females without the work of makeup artists and retouchers to mask their pores, cellulite, and wrinkles (Strawn, 2009, April 13). And taking it one step further, Australian teen magazine *Dolly* recently highlighted natural photographs as well, promoting an "airbrush-free" issue where the photographs were un-retouched and labeled with a "Retouch Free Zone" stamp (Strawn, 2009, May 13).

Selection

Recall that communicators of all types have to make choices and that every selection—of a word, a photographic angle, a video sequence, and so on—is also a deflection. Understandably, product advertisers select images that will make their products look good. This can be done by shot selection, by arrangement as in a magazine ad, and by sequencing as in a television ad.

Implied Selling Propositions

Literally speaking, visuals are not a language. But an arrangement of visuals needs little in the way of verbal explanation. For example, consider an ad for an automobile. It is made up of a photo of two similar looking SUVs side by side. One is unidentified, but it has a tabby cat in its rear window. The other, a Range Rover, has a lion in the same position. The metaphor is clear: driving a Range Rover is like having a lion as a pet, which stands in stark contrast to having a metaphorical housecat for one's car (Artraj.com, n.d.).

Visuals contain no verbs or adjectives, but the familiar grammar of visual juxtaposition serves in their place to offer contrasts and analogies, causal claims and generalizations. In an ad for a laundry detergent that shows the advertised product removing a stain that a more expensive brand cannot handle, the visuals alone suggest contrast and causation. What's more, they evoke images of science—of the scientific demonstration.

The crucial element with such visual ads is that we know how to read and interpret them. The best ones present a clear metaphorical image that cannot be misunderstood, and that is why the Land Rover ad is so effective. As Jessica Sanchez notes about the ad: "Ask a man in any country which pet he'd rather own and I bet you get the same answer" (Sanchez, 2011).

FIGURE 12.7   *Implied selling propositions: Land Rover is influencing us without saying a word!*
Source: https://ameritest.wordpress.com/2011/02/24/have-ads-will-travel-tips-before-stamping-your-ads-passport/

SUMMARY

This chapter has charted changes in the connection and exchange of meanings, beginning with the idolatry phase, then moving through stages of iconology, narcissism, totemism, and mise-en-scène to today's stage of hypercommunication. Today's product advertising uses new technologies and sophisticated market research in ways we could not have imagined only a few years ago to reach changing markets, and, although some advertisers continue to rely on techniques of persuasion developed in bygone years, most are exploring new ways of getting the attention of consumers and their money. Using ethnography, data mining, behavioral targeting and more, advertisers work to learn how we think. And then they take that information and put it to use, creating ads that mock traditional conventions, simulate news reporting, and break down the fourth wall. Still others traffic in deliberate verbal and visual ambiguities, inviting consumers to project their own meanings onto the ads.

Advertisers do not tell you the good and the bad about their products; instead, they play up their good and play down their bad, while denigrating competitors' products, if they mention them at all. Broadly speaking, then, virtually all product advertising is not about truth but about persuasion, and this chapter has illustrated the myriad ways that product advertising may deceive, or at least attempt to deceive.

Product advertising can often be deceptive, but does that necessarily mean that it is dangerous? What if the viewer knows that the claims made on behalf of the expensive perfume have been exaggerated and that the model's beauty has been visually enhanced? What if that same viewer enjoys the verbal misdirection and has no problem with the digital enhancement? What if she experiences even greater pleasure from imagining herself being like this perfect woman and perhaps being seen by others as similar to the model—this by virtue of her having purchased and put on the same perfume that the model wore?

Similar questions can be asked about today's anti-ads. So what if there's a disconnection between the ad's narrative and the product being advertised? So what if another ad mocks an earlier generation's advertising conventions? So what if an ad pulls us in by getting us to laugh or prompting us to believe that it has been recorded live when it wasn't?

Product advertising has a goodly share of critics. Their list of alleged harms from particular types of advertisements is large. Beauty products promote an unattainable beauty ideal, thus causing reduced self-esteem and sometimes severe problems such as anorexia and bulimia. Women are fetishized as sexual commodities in ads of many types targeted to men. Adolescents' inclination to rebel is fueled by ads encouraging nonconformity and sometimes destructiveness. Ads for alcohol products contribute to alcoholism, ads for tobacco products cause addiction, and so on.

We believe that one way to ameliorate these negative effects of advertising is to be schooled in the art of persuasion. When you understand how the ads function, you are better able to critique (and resist) their appeal. Furthermore, society as a whole has taken steps to curb or control some of these forms of advertising—for example, there now exists a ban on cigarette advertising on television. Furthermore, the "hypodermic theory" model of persuasion has long been debunked. We are thinking beings and advertisers do not have the power to simply "inject" us with their messages—in general, consumers must assume some responsibility for their purchasing decisions. Those ads at midnight on television for fast-food burgers and pizza may tempt us to overeat, and ads with super-thin models may tempt us to diet. But, there must be a predisposition to diet to excess (or eat to excess), argue those who refuse to assign full responsibility to advertisers for food disorders. They have a point.

A more general charge, that the cumulative effects of product advertising can be dangerous, was taken up in Chapter 3. Schudson's (1984) capitalist realism captures in a phrase the commodification of consumer culture in which practically everything—including antimaterialist, anticonsumerist objects—can be bought for a price. The alleged dangers of consumerism are many: a dependence on store-bought things, rather than on ourselves; a devaluing of what enriches the society but doesn't lend itself to mass marketing; excessive materialism—you are what you own; and a narcissistic society, given over to selfish pleasures. Still, as defenders of capitalism maintain, imagine how costly the truly useful and necessary things in life would be without commercial advertising. Moreover, advertising need not appeal to the worst in us to be successful. Those who carp at commercial advertising haven't found a suitable alternative.

In a medium designed primarily to entertain, television advertising must entertain, and it is doing that better and better. But as Neil Postman (1985) warns us in a book aptly named *Amusing Ourselves to Death*, there are dangers in taking everything unseriously. Postman sees Aldous Huxley's *Brave New World* as prophetic. As Huxley saw it, "People will come to love their oppression, to adore the technologies that undo their capacities to think" (cited in Postman, 1985). It is that prophecy we must beware, and, by understanding how advertising functions, we can resist more effectively that which would seek to control us.

QUESTIONS AND PROJECTS FOR FURTHER STUDY

1   Do an inventory of products that you purchased in the last month: clothing, food items, and so on. How many did you learn about through commercials and advertising?

2   Together or in a group, do a careful self-analysis using the VALS information provided in this chapter. Then, assume the role of an advertiser and develop a plan of how you would market to someone like yourself.

3   Find examples of three ads that use traditional advertising conventions. Then find examples of anti-ads that mock those conventions, play off of them humorously, traffic in deliberate ambiguities, or blur the line between the real and the rhetorical.

4   Find examples of the various types of deceptive advertising language. In your view, are any of these potentially harmful to consumers?

5   Find examples of visual deception in advertising. Again, ask yourself whether any of these forms of deception are potentially dangerous.

6   Large retail manufacturers such as Anheuser-Busch, Procter and Gamble, Revlon, and Philip Morris provide an excellent opportunity to study advertising at work because they market different brands of the same product (e.g., beers, detergents, perfumes, and cigarettes) differently, each for a different target audience. Find examples of consumer targeting by comparing a retail manufacturer's ads for different brands of the same product type.

7   Log on to Google and investigate AdSense. Find the procedure for "opting out." How hard was it to find?

EXERCISES

1   Spend one day and keep a log of the ads you encounter through new technological formats. Notice the sidebar ads when you check your Facebook page, or the ads displayed when you use Google to find information. Jot down any text messages you receive from advertisers. Notice the ads on the websites you visit. What categories of products did you encounter? How many ads did you view? And finally, how has this exercise changed your perception of how advertisers try to influence you?

2   It's not as easy as it looks. Create an advertising slogan that is persuasive.

3   With a group, develop and write an anti-ad. Using the available technology at your disposal, produce your ad and present it to your class.

4   Go to your library and go into the "stacks," exploring the hard copies of old popular magazines from the last century. Make copies of five ads that you find interesting, ones that illustrate a concept from this chapter. Bring the ad copies to class and present them, explaining what concept they illustrate and why you find them interesting.

5   Go to a major grocery or discount store and notice the in-store advertising. Listen to the music; notice the signs and product placement; notice the labels on products. In light of this chapter, what conclusions can you draw? Create a PowerPoint presentation and present your findings.

KEY TERMS

- Advertising phases
  - Idolatry
  - Iconology
  - Narcissism
  - Totemism
  - Mise-en-scène
  - Hypercommunication
- Anti-ads
  - Pseudo non-ads
  - Code-transgressing ads
  - Self-referential ads
  - Self-parody ads
  - Knowing wink ads
- Behavioral targeting (BT)
- Consumption community
- Data mining
- Demographics
- Ethnography
- Global village
- Indexicality
- Micromarketing
- Psychographics
- Sociographics
- Syncographics
- VALS

REFERENCES

Abelman, Robert (1998). *Reaching a critical mass: A critical analysis of television entertainment.* Mahwah, NJ: Lawrence Erlbaum Associates.

Abrams, L. (2014, May 4). *The truth behind the spin: What BP doesn't want you to know about the Gulf oil spill.* Retrieved January 18, 2015, from Salon.com: www.salon.com/2014/05/04/the_truth_behind_the_spin_what_bp_doesnt_want_you_to_know_about_the_gulf_oil_spill/

Arens, W. (2003). *Contemporary advertising* (9th ed). Boston: McGraw-Hill.

Artraj.com (n.d.). Visual metaphors in advertising campaigns. Retrieved June 12, 2009, from http://www.artraj.com/blog/redpres01.htm

Baron, M. (2008). Newsweek Palin photo: Cover picture of Sarah Palin is tasteless. Retrieved November 11, 2010, from www.postchronicle.com/cgi-bin/art man/exec/view.cgi?archive= 100&num= 177468

Beltrone, G. (2014, February 24). *A by-the-numbers look at Hollywood's marketing machine.* Retrieved January 18, 2015, from Adweek.com: www.adweek.com/news/advertising-branding/numbers-look-hollywood-s-marketing-machine-155895

Berger, A. A. (2007). *Ads, fads, and consumer culture.* Lanham, MD: Rowman & Littlefield.

Bianco, A., Lowry, T., Berner, R., Arndt, M., & Grover, R. (2004, July 12). The vanishing mass market. *Business Week.* Retrieved May 29, 2009, from www.businessweek.com/magazine/content/04_28/b3891001_mz001.htm

BP's Commitment to America (2012, August 22). Retrieved January 18, 2015, from YouTube.com: www.youtube.com/watch?v=V6m-VJy8Toc

Burdeau, C. (2012, January 8). *BP ad campaign following Gulf oil spill deemed 'propaganda' by some.* (A. Press, Producer) Retrieved January 18, 2015, from HuffingtonPost.com: www.huffingtonpost.com/2012/01/08/bp-ad-campaign-gulf-oil-_n_1192600.html

Campher, H. (2014, October 8). *Data mining: The consumer becoming the consumed.* Retrieved January 18, 2015, from Huffingtonpost.com: www.huffingtonpost.com/henk-campher/data-mining-the-consumer-_b_5949580.html

Chen, J. & Stallaert, J. (2014, June). An economic analysis of online advertising using behavioral targeting. *MIS Quarterly,* 38(2), 429–459.

Clifford, S. (2008, August 5) The high cost of a "free credit report." *New York Times.* Retrieved November 11, 2010, from http://finance.yahoo.com/banking-budgeting/article/105514/The-High-Cost-of-a-'Free-Credit-Report'

Court, D., Elzinga, D., Mulder, S. & Vetvik, O. (2009, June). *The consumer decision journey.* (M. Quarterly, Producer) Retrieved January 18, 2015, from www.mckinsey.com/insights/marketing_sales/the_consumer_decision_journey

Creswell, J. (2008, June 22). Nothing sells like celebrity. *New York Times.* Retrieved June 11, 2009, from www.nytimes.com/2008/06/22/business/media/22celeb.html?pagewanted=all

Dee, J. (1999, January). But is it advertising? *Harper's,* 298, 61–72.

Fake-Foods.com (n.d.) Retrieved June 12, 2009, from www.fake-foods.com

Flint, J. (2014, May 12). TV networks load up on commercials. Retrieved January 18, 2015, from latimes.com: www.latimes.com/entertainment/envelope/cotown/la-et-ct-nielsen-advertising-study-20140510-story.html

Flynn, L. (2014, December 11). *More data, less privacy? Data mining and analytics offer challenges and tradeoffs for companies.* (Duke University, Producer) Retrieved January 18, 2015, from DukeMagazine.com: http://dukemagazine.duke.edu/article/more-data-less-privacy

Fox, S. (1985). *The mirror makers: A history of American advertising and its creators.* New York: Vintage.

Frick, W. (2014, February 5). *Study: Green advertising helped BP recover from the Deepwater Horizon spill.* (H. B. Review, Producer) Retrieved January 18, 2015, from Hbr.org: https://hbr.org/2014/02/study-green-advertising-helped-bp-recover-from-the-deepwater-horizon-spill/

Garfield, B. (2009, April 27). Room for improvement in Post's nonimprovement. *Advertising Age*. Retrieved June 12, 2009, from http://adage.com/garfield/post?article_id=136260

Getz, M. (2006, April). Drowned in advertising chatter. *Georgetown Law Journal*. Retrieved February 12, 2009, from http://findarticles.com/p/articles/mi_qa3805/is_200604/ai_n17172414/pg_1?tag=content;col1

Google Ads Preferences (n.d.). Interest-based advertising: How it works. Retrieved June 5, 2009, from www.google.com/ads/preferences/html/about.html

Grunwald, M. (1993, August 29). Metamorphosis. *Boston Globe Magazine*, 1, 13.

Guegan, P. (2007, April 23). KEEP IT SIMPLE, HONEST, FOCUSED. *Advertising Age*, 78(17), 23–23. Retrieved May 29, 2009, from http://navigator-edinboro.passhe.edu/login?url=http://search. ebscohost.com/login.aspx?direct=true&db=a9h&AN=24844395&loginpage=login.asp&site= ehost-live

Haelle, T. (2014, January 31). *Studies: Celebrity endorsements encourage unhealthy food, drinks*. Retrieved January 18, 2015, from Chicago-Bureau.org:www.chicago-bureau.org/celebrity-endorsements-encourage-unhealthy-food-drinks/

Herman, D. (2008, June 16). Advertising to audiences. *Marketing, Media, and Technology Conversations*. Retrieved June 8, 2009, from www. darrenherman.com/2008/06/16/advertising-to-audiences/

Hsu, T. (2012, August 15). *William Shatner returns from the dead as the Priceline Negotiator*. Retrieved January 18, 2015, from LATimes.com: http://articles.la times.com/2012/aug/15/business/la-fi-mo-shatner-priceline-20120815

Lake, L. (2008, May 24). Marketing vs. advertising: What's the difference? *About.com: Marketing*. Retrieved June 7, 2009, from http://marketing. about.com/b/2008/05/24/marketing-vs-advertising-whats-the-difference.htm

Landry, E., Ude, C., & Vollmer, C. (2007). HD marketing 2010: Sharpening the conversation. The team and tools you need to market in an increasingly "digitally savvy" world. *IAB*. Retrieved June 8, 2009, from www.iab.net/media/file/HDMarketing In2010newbrandFINAL.pdf

Leiss, W., Kline, S., Jhally, S., & Botterill, J. (2005). *Social communication in advertising: Persons, products, and images of well-being* (3rd ed.). New York: Routledge.

Lentini, N. (2007, March 1). Advertising: For some aging actors, self-mockery sells. *New York Times*. Retrieved June 12, 2009, from www.nytimes. com/2007/03/01/business/media/01adco.html?_r=1&scp=8&sq=lentini%20advertising &st=cse

Lewis, M. (2000, August 13). Boom box. *New York Times Magazine*, pp. 36, 38–41, 51, 65–67.

Martineau, P. (1957). *Motivation in advertising: Motives that make people buy*. New York: McGraw-Hill.

Messaris, P. (1997). *Visual persuasion: The role of images in advertising*. Thousand Oaks, CA: Sage Publications.

Miller, M. (2012, November 21). *BP plans ad campaign to help people move on*. Retrieved January 18, 2015, from BrandChannel.com: www.brandchannel. com/home/post/2012/11/21/BP-Ad-Campaign-112112.aspx

Miller, M. (2014, November 25). *Bill Cosby plunges from #3 to #2615 in Celebrity Trust Index*. Retrieved January 18, 2015, from BrandChannel.com: www. brandchannel.com/home/post/2014/11/25/141125-Bill-Cosby.aspx

Moog, C. (1990). *Are they selling her lips? Advertising and identity*. New York: William Morrow.

Nichols, J. (2014, January 14). *Coca-Cola Apologizes For 'Share A Coke' Promotion Deemed Homophobic*. Retrieved January 18, 2015, from HuffingtonPost. com: www.huffingtonpost.com/2014/01/28/coca-cola-apologizes-share-a-coke_n_4682878.html

Opsahl, K. (2009, March 11). Google begins behavioral targeting ad program. *Electronic Frontier Foundation*. Retrieved June 5, 2009, from www.eff.org/deeplinks/2009/03/google-begins-behavioral-targeting-ad-program.

Packard, V. (1970). *The hidden persuaders*. New York: Pocket.

Peirce, C. S. (1991). Indexicality. In Hoopes, J. (ed.), *Peirce on signs: Writings on semiotics by Charles Sanders Peirce*. Chapel Hill: University of North Carolina Press.

Postman, N. (1985). *Amusing ourselves to death*. New York: Viking.

Rogers, W. (2007). *Persuasion: Messages, receivers, and contexts*. Lanham, MD: Rowman & Littlefield.

Sanchez, J. (2011, February 24). *Have ads will travel? Tips before stamping your ad's passport*. (Ameritest, Producer) Retrieved January 18, 2015, from ameritest.wordpress.com: https://ameritest.wordpress.com/2011/02/24/have-ads-will-travel-tips-before-stamping-your-ads-passport/

San Francisco Chronicle (2005, August 3). Identify your target audience before crafting advertising plan. Retrieved June 8, 2009, from sfchronicle: www.sfgate.com/cgi-bin/article.cgi?file=/chronicle/archive/2005/08/03/BUGSFE1O7N1.DTL&type=business

Schudson, M. (1984). *Advertising: The uneasy persuasion*. New York: Basic Books.

Sebastian, M., & Ives, N. (2014, May 13). *Top 10 product placements of the last 10 years*. Retrieved September 25, 2016, from Ad Age: http://adage.com/article/media/top-10-product-placements-10-years/293140/

Smith, S. (2007). Behavioral targeting could change the game. *EContent*, 30(1), 22. Retrieved May 29, 2009, from www.econtentmag.com/Articles/Column/Follow-the-Money/Behavioral-Targeting-Could-Change-the-Game---18964.htm

Staff, U. (2014, Auguest 4). *Is your name on a Coke bottle?* Retrieved January 18, 2015, from Coca-ColaCompany.com: www.coca-colacompany.com/coca-cola-unbottled/is-your-name-on-a-coke-bottle-find-out-here#TCCC

Strawn, C. (2009, April 13). French Elle's no-makeup issue. *The Frisky*. Retrieved June 15, 2009, from www.thefrisky.com/post/246-french-elles-no-makeup-issue/

Strawn, C. (2009, May 13). Australian teen magazine goes retouch-free for an issue. *The Frisky*. Retrieved June 15, 2009, from www.thefrisky.com/post/246-australian-teen-magazine-goes-retouch-free-for-an-issue/

Tye, L. (1993, September 6). List makers draw a bead on many. *Boston Globe*, pp. 1, 17.

VALS (n.d.). *Strategic Business Insights*. Retrieved June 5, 2009, from www.strategicbusinessinsights.com/vals/

Volpe, M. (2013, April 29). *10 Horrifying Stats About Display Advertising*. Retrieved January 18, 2015, from hubspot.com: http://blog.hubspot.com/marketing/horrifying-display-advertising-stats

Williams, R. (2006, November 15). Advertising trends: Pushing past media overload. *Entrepreneur*. Retrieved June 7, 2009, from www.entrepreneur.com/advertising/adcolumnistroyhwilliams/article170166.html

Woodward, G., & Denton, R. (2009). *Persuasion and influence in American life*. Long Grove, IL: Waveland.

Woyke, E., & Stead, D. (2006, August 7) Feel free to embarrass yourself. *Business Week*, 14. Retrieved May 29, 2009, from www.businessweek.com/print/magazine/content/06_32/c3996008.htm?chan=mz

Zimmerman, I. (2013, March 25). *Product placement can be a lot more powerful than we realize*. Retrieved September 25, 2016, from Psychology Today: www.psychologytoday.com/blog/sold/201303/product-placement-can-be-lot-more-powerful-we-realize

CHAPTER 13

Talking through Differences: Persuasion in Social Conflicts

"Sue, is that you? Hi, it's Jake. Jake Edelman. I was wondering if you'd be willing to sell one of your demo tennis rackets—you know, the Wilson 6.2. I've been trying it out the last few weeks and I really like it. What with it being the end of the indoor tennis season, I figured you might be willing to part with it for $60."

"I can't, Jake. It would cost me $140 to replace it."

"Well, it is used, Sue, and this is its second season. How about $75?"

"Make it $80."

"It's a deal. I'll bring a check this Sunday."

In an oft-quoted passage from *A Rhetoric of Motives*, Kenneth Burke (1969) reminds us that "Rhetoric must lead us through the Scramble, the flurries and flare-ups of the Human Barnyard, the Give and Take, the wavering line of pressure and counterpressure ... the War of Nerves, the War." Burke's list is a reminder that persuasion is not always cooperative. Indeed, the situations that give rise to it are often rooted in conflict, or at least partially so, in situations both large and small. Thus, as Jake and Sue successfully talk through their differences in this chapter's opening example, they do so by bargaining for personal advantage. They arrive at a mutually acceptable solution only after haggling and compromise.

Burke adds that rhetoric does have its peaceful moments: "At times its endless competition can add up to the transcending of itself. In ways of its own it can move from the factional to the universal" (Burke, 1969). Enemies can agree to reconcile; warring parties can discover that persuasion is preferable to guns. But Burke says that the appearance of cooperation also often becomes "transformed into a partisan weapon" (Burke, 1969). This happens, for example, when a facade of friendship is used to extract favors. Burke is suggesting here that our noblest sentiments often grow out of factions and strife, but then, these same sentiments also go on to serve as partisan tools in subsequent conflicts.

If this chapter had a subtitle, it might be, "From Destructive Conflicts to Productive Dialogues." The chapter explores different types of talk in the face of differences, all involving persuasive interactions. The interactions may be private, as in the bargaining over the Wilson 6.2, or public, as in a conflict over going to war. They may consist of dialogues between friends or nasty confrontations between enemies, but all involve the give-and-take of interaction. That makes them different from prepared speeches and different again from persuasive campaigns and protest demonstrations. A good deal of planning may take place, to be sure, but, at the point of interaction, there is an element of unpredictability. All parties to the interaction must pattern planned remarks flexibly, listen carefully and critically, and adjust responses to the messages of the other. Here, too, good questions may be as persuasive as good answers.

WHAT ARE SOCIAL CONFLICTS?

A **social conflict** is a clash over at least partially incompatible interests. For several reasons, the techniques of persuasion prescribed for non-conflict situations are not always applicable to conflict situations.

First, social conflicts are not simply misunderstandings, semantic confusions, or communication breakdowns, although they sometimes begin that way. Situation comedies are rife with apparent crises between husband and wife or boss and employee in which the source of tension is an error of fact or interpretation that is easily correctable with a bit of dialogue. These might more accurately be labeled pseudo conflicts.

Second, the notion of a clash of incompatible interests presupposes something more than a disagreement, difference of opinion, or academic controversy. This point is important because people tend to minimize or wish away conflicts by treating them as if they were mere disagreements. Consider the difference between a newspaper columnist arguing that the auto workers deserve higher wages and the same argument coming from the head of the United Auto Workers in the midst of a collective bargaining session. The columnist would have been arguing a controversial position, it is true, but it is questionable whether he or she would have had anything more than an academic and passing interest in the matter. The union leader, by contrast, is quite clearly involved in a social conflict, evidenced by a clash over incompatible interests. Similarly, two people—even two intimate partners—may subscribe to divergent religious principles without necessarily being in conflict. Their interests might well become incompatible, however, if one felt morally compelled to convert the other or if, as in a marriage, both had to decide how to rear their offspring. Conflicts over principles arise whenever one party makes unacceptable claims on the other or when, in the face of divergent goals, their activities must be coordinated.

To have an interest in something, then, is to covet or value it personally, whether it is one's personal reputation, an item of scarcity such as money, or a principle such as equal pay for equal work. For two people or two groups to have incompatible interests, each must stand as an obstacle to the other. This includes business competitions and other contests for power or control, such as electoral contests. Two people may disagree on the market value of a house that is up for sale without necessarily being in conflict. But should the disputants be the seller and the potential buyer, they would indeed be in conflict. (As in the case of the tennis racket negotiations, they might well reach an amicable compromise and still have been in conflict. In any such bargaining situation, each party's relative gain over what he or she could have paid or received is the other party's relative loss.)

Third, the same people may be embroiled in a conflict on one level and in a controversy or disagreement on another level. Consider the case of two college students engaged in a graded classroom debate about Israel's relationship to the Palestinians. To the extent that either party may receive a poor grade or suffer loss of reputation from being put down by the other, they are indeed engaged in a conflict. But the conflict is not about Israel's relationship with its Arab neighbors—that remains a disagreement or difference of opinion. A conflict may sometimes involve value differences or personal animosities or competition for scarce resources, but once again, the personal interests of one party must be threatened by the other party.

It should be clear by now that appeals to reason or common ground may not be sufficient to resolve social conflicts; indeed, in such conflicts as between labor and management, buyer and seller, married partners, and Israel and the Palestinians, the combatants might well have reason to remain antagonistic. The fourth point, then, is that attitudes in conflict situations are often linked to beliefs about relative power capacities. In a classroom discussion, we often have the luxury to decide what two conflicting parties ought to do, but the realities of conflict situations generally have influence and often work against agreement on ideal solutions. In conflict situations, trust levels tend to be low, ego involvements tend to be high, and channels of communication are closed or restricted; neither side may be able to enforce its conception of an ideal outcome. Hence, "peace with honor" may be a motto attached to a truce agreement following a military stalemate, but what is considered "honorable" or "desirable" is necessarily what one can hope to get under the circumstances. What emerges most often is an implicit or explicit compromise.

COOPERATION AND COMPETITION IN MIXED-MOTIVE CONFLICTS

One of the paradoxical features of practically all social conflicts is that the adversaries are motivated simultaneously to cooperate and compete with each other. Seldom is either party served by annihilating the enemy, taking all the opponent's money, or totally incapacitating the adversary. Real-life conflicts, in this sense, are not like footraces or games of chess or poker. Instead, they contain mixed motives. To understand this fact of social conflicts is to understand why purely combative strategies of influence seldom make sense.

Consider, once again, the case of a labor-management conflict about wages. In theory, it is in the interests of labor to get as much as possible, and it is likewise in the interests of management to give as little as possible. Each, moreover, has combative weapons available (prolonged strikes, layoffs, and so on) by which to punish or cripple the enemy. Why don't they use them more often?

The obvious answer is that they have much to lose by acting combatively and much to gain through cooperation. That's not to say that cooperation is always the answer; only that it should be the default option. Winning *with* others ("win-win") is generally preferable to winning at the *expense* of others ("win-lose"), if only because in the long run the latter tends to produce "lose-lose" outcomes. Morality aside, let us examine the interests of labor and management in the potential costs and benefits exchanged by acting combatively or cooperatively.

First, purely coercive influence entails relatively high costs. For example, the union that decides to go out on strike forfeits employee paychecks during the strike period. Coactive persuasion, on the other hand, may cost little or nothing.

Second, because conflicts involve reciprocal influence, each side must calculate the repercussions of its actions in possible retaliation costs. The union may decide to go out on strike, but only at the price of incurring the wrath of the management who may strike back with even greater fury. For example, company management may hire non-union labor during the strike in an effort to break the union.

Third, the use of purely combative strategies over an issue such as wages may block the resolution of other important issues such as questions of worker health and safety. The ensuing build-up of antagonism that takes place during a labor strike or management lock-out can damage future communication and reduce trust, making what were once considered trivial questions into significant and irresolvable matters of principle once the strike has ended.

Fourth, strategies of a purely combative nature like strikes can often enrage outsiders, who then bring their own influence to bear on the situation. Some combative acts are punished by law, others are vilified by the press, and still others cause backlash reactions from the public. Teaching assistants at Yale University experienced all these problems when they tried to organize themselves into a union. Their threats to hold back reports of undergraduate student grades until the Yale administration granted them collective bargaining rights turned out to be immensely counterproductive. Not only did the administrators turn on them; so did the undergraduates (Overton, 2003).

Thus, the parties in a conflict will incur costs if they employ purely combative strategies, and benefits will more likely accompany the use of cooperative, coactive means of influence. Conflict theorists like to speak of benefits as a hypothetical benefits pie and they are fond of pointing out that the size of the pie is by no means finite. If a labor-management conflict escalates beyond control, the size of the pie ends up being reduced. But if the two sides find a way to increase productivity and profits, the size of the pie is increased. Cooperation on one issue can breed a spirit of harmony on other issues and reduce the need for offensive capabilities. Of course, if only your side behaves cooperatively, the other side can reap the benefits both of a larger pie and a larger share of the pie. Cooperation ought to be viewed as the default strategy, but not as the preferred strategy in all cases.

SYMMETRICAL VERSUS ASYMMETRICAL CONFLICTS

A conflict between persons or groups with relatively equal power to reward or punish the other is called a **symmetrical conflict**. A conflict between antagonists having unequal power is an **asymmetrical conflict**. There are, of course, degrees of asymmetry, and relative power may vary as well from one situation to another. Parents have the upper hand in most families most of the time, but children are not without their own resources, including the capacity to withhold love at precisely the moments when their parents are most in need of it. Employers tend to be "one-up" on their employees, but the imbalance is usually reduced and sometimes reversed by a variety of factors, including government regulations restricting employer prerogatives.

How we feel about conflict and how we deal with it once it arises are partly a function of our role in an organization. Within large-scale social systems such as universities and business organizations, symmetrical conflicts routinely develop. These occur between competing members of the system, as actor-actor conflicts, and as asymmetrical conflicts that take place between rank-and-file members of the system and representatives of the system as a whole, or as actor-system conflicts. For example, student organizations often engage in actor-actor competitions for new members, and they occasionally become embroiled in actor-system conflicts with university administrators about issues of student rights.

Within their spheres of authority, administrators of every type tend to be system-oriented. For these system representatives, there is an understandable preference for preventing conflict and for resolving conflicts quickly once they arise. For example, college deans try to discourage competition for funds among the departments they supervise. The deans tend to identify more with the need for order and stability in the college as a whole than with the interests of any one component of the system. Likewise, the president of the United States tends to look askance on strikes that disrupt the economy. Like the dean of a college, the president tends to be system-oriented rather than actor-oriented.

These orientations are manifested in recurring patterns of talk about conflict, that is, in genres of conflict rhetoric. Those with system orientations tend to downplay the need for conflict within their organizations; they tend to label conflicts as mere disagreements or misunderstandings. When making public statements, their emphasis is on the benefits that can accrue to all from cooperation. Of course, they tend to reserve their harshest criticisms for the "troublemakers" who initiate actor-system conflicts. From an actor orientation, on the other hand, conflict is necessary, natural, and in any case inevitable. It is not something to be prevented or wished away. From the perspectives of those who lead movements in behalf of students' rights, for example, disruptive protests may be necessary persuasive tools because they call attention to injustices.

DESTRUCTIVE VERSUS PRODUCTIVE CONFLICTS

Conflicts can be productive for both sides. But, as we've said, when the two parties each seek to win at the other's expense (win-lose), rather than working cooperatively for mutually satisfactory outcomes (win-win) the result in such cases is often a destructive, **lose-lose conflict**.

Have you ever been in a really bad relationship? Consider here not just soured relationships between lovers but also between friends, family members, housemates, or co-workers. Because these are the people with whom we are most interdependent, they are also the people with whom we are most prone to experience conflict, whether productive or destructive.

Many years ago, Morton Deutsch (1969) identified a number of recurrent patterns in destructive conflicts, and his analysis still holds true. In these lose-lose conflicts, says Deutsch, there is an increase in the size and number of principles and precedents believed to be at stake. Participants are willing to bear greater costs (both material and psychological) to "win." Each side exempts itself from norms of ethical conduct that they impose on the other. Hostility intensifies. Cooperation is driven out by suspiciousness and combativeness. There is increasing reliance on power and on tactics of threat, coercion, and deception. There is a corresponding shift away from persuasion and tactics of conciliation and rapport building. Communication becomes impoverished and unreliable. Channels are either not used or used to mislead and intimidate. Reliance is placed on espionage or on other circuitous routes for gathering information.

As a consequence, said Deutsch (1969), little confidence is placed in information provided directly from the other, and opportunities for error and selective perception are enhanced. The range of perceived alternatives is reduced. There is a reduced time perspective, a focus on the immediate. Thought is polarized, reduced to either-ors and stereotyped responses. There is greater susceptibility to fear- or hope-inspired rumors. One's own behavior is seen as more benevolent and legitimate, and there is a corresponding assumption that this "better" behavior should be more appreciated by conflict opponents. Once committed to winning at the expense of the other, there is a tendency to justify past actions and to mobilize further with each successive response by the adversary.

Thinking It Through

Try analyzing a conflict situation yourself:

Make a list of the issues Deutsch has identified here. Then, thinking back on a serious conflict you've experienced in your life, list details from your personal situation beside each item from Deutsch you've identified. How many of Deutsch's items were present in your situation? What was the tipping point that made the situation really difficult? And finally, what could you have done differently that would have reduced the number of negative items on your list?

DEALING WITH CONFLICTS PRODUCTIVELY

One reason that conflicts escalate beyond the intentions of either party is that neither knows how to cope with the resistance and hostility displayed by the other. Antagonists play the blame game. (Joe: "Everybody knows you're a liar." Chris: "Oh yeah? When did you start telling the truth?") Or they shift to a passively aggressive style of placating the other. ("Am I in the way, dear? I hate to be a pest. Have I said something or done something to offend you?") Or they engage in tactless candor. ("I've never liked you, Rasheed. Neither do most of your so-called friends") (Elgin, 1995).

Often, attempted solutions to conflicts exacerbate the problem as, for example, when we suggest to others that the conflict could easily be resolved if only they would be more reasonable. But often, when we are presented with Deutsch's characterization of the process of conflict escalation, we have had no difficulty finding examples from our own experiences when, try as we might, we could not reverse a pattern of destructive conflict. Consider this typical case.

After months of nagging her apartment mate to share equally in the performance of household chores, Chris thought she had hit on a perfect solution: a contract with Becky that would specify who would do what, when, and with what penalties for non-performance. But Chris failed to realize that the conflict had long since expanded into a fight for control over the rules of the relationship. It was no longer exclusively about sharing in the household chores. Thus, when Becky was presented with the proposal, she rejected it outright as another of Chris's efforts at imposing her way of doing things. This of course confirmed Chris's view that Becky was impossible to reason with. A wiser Chris might have put the problem to Becky: "What can we do to reach a mutually satisfactory solution?"

In conflict situations, it is all too easy to see matters solely from our own viewpoint. A former student we know complained, for example, that his impending marriage was placed in jeopardy even before it had begun. This, as he saw it, was because his fiancée constantly invoked her father's "dumb opinions" to back up her own. Little did he realize how difficult he had been making it for his fiancée to separate from her parents. His tendency to respond to her exclusively on an intellectual level was a contributing factor, because in doing so he was holding back the affection she most needed. Recognizing that individuals communicate relationally at the same time they communicate substantively was helpful for this student.

"He gets my back up." "She makes my blood boil." "That makes my hair stand on end." Expressions such as these attest to the intense visceral reactions that conflicts can generate. Yet precisely when our bodies tell us to strike back by any means, we need to be most coolheaded. Does this sound reasonable? Absolutely. But is it easy to do? No way!

What we need to do is to decide **why** to fight, **whether** to fight, **when** to fight, and **how** to fight. These are the four cardinal rules of self-management in conflict situations, according to psychologist Cynthia Shar (personal communication, 1999). The important word is *decide*. We need to take control over what our bodies are telling us by making self-aware strategic thinking in conflict situations a habit.

Decide Why to Fight

To deal with conflicts productively we must first think carefully about the situation that is motivating our desire for a fight. Is there a principle or objective worth fighting for? A wrong that clearly needs to be corrected? An obstacle that stands in the way of our legitimate interests? Thinking carefully about these matters before taking action is important. It prevents us from discovering afterward that we've been too impulsive, too carried away, or too eager to see our opponent as mad and/or bad while ignoring our own contribution to a destructive pattern of escalation. We need to be aware that our willful ignorance—denial, as psychologists often refer to it—is normal and natural but not necessarily serviceable in the long run. Before we act, we should stop and think about the long run.

Decide Whether to Fight

Even if a cause is just, it may not be in our interests to express our opposition, let alone to act on it confrontationally. We should always calculate the advantages and disadvantages if we wish to deal with conflicts productively. Is this our fight? Is it worth our commitment of time, energy, and resources? Are we prepared for the costs of expressed conflict—for its downsides? Do we have a winning strategy for achieving our ends? What would happen if we chose not to fight?

Decide When to Fight

Is this the best time to fight? Would our interests be better served by postponing overt conflict action until we've had a chance to think about it, to talk it over with valued associates, to gain pledges of support from potential allies, and perhaps to wait for the conflict to simmer down? What would be the benefits and costs of delaying action?

Decide How to Fight

Conflict avoidance is often as damaging as aggressive, self-destructive conflict behavior. Sometimes we need to fight. Sometimes coercive behavior is the only action possible. But is coercion truly necessary? Can the same ends be achieved by coactive persuasion, perhaps combined with positive inducements? Can we think of creative ways to turn a **win-lose conflict** into a **win-win conflict**? Before moving toward conflict escalation, we need to consider the alternatives.

> *Thinking It Through*
>
> Apply these four steps to the next conflict situation you encounter, and report to the class about how such application affected the situation.

Nearly always helpful in conflict situations is showing that we understand the other person's way of looking at things. Alternatively, we may need to ask for clarification from the other person as to what the problem is. Wanda, a 35-year-old graduate student, was afraid that Judy, her live-in partner, was going to leave her for a younger woman. But not even Wanda fully realized that this was what had been making her persistently angry with Judy until Judy coaxed it out of her.

When we do find ourselves being subjected to criticism, it is especially important to ask for clarification rather than become immediately defensive. Consider, for example, when we have a conflict with a boss or a supervisor. At a university, the department chair made a habit of calling each of the professors in for unscheduled private conferences, during which he made known a long list of general criticisms that he had been accumulating. Finally, George was called in. The chair mentioned that the work-study students George supervised didn't seem to be accomplishing much, and that he thought they were spending too much time on breaks. Resisting the urge to respond defensively, George instead asked for more information. He said, "Have you been unhappy with some part of my work?" The chair said he could not think of anything right then. The boss, who was really not angry or upset at George at all, mentioned a few things he'd like George to consider, which George accepted, and then they turned their attention to other matters in the department.

Recall the discussion of framing and reframing in Chapter 6. Often, the size and severity of the conflict can be reframed to make it easier to deal with. What had been labeled a racial conflict can be relabeled a conflict between two persons who happen to be of different races. "Being treated unfairly" can become "being treated unfairly on a particular occasion." An issue of principle might be reframed as a question of how best to apply a principle.

Many of the techniques for overcoming resistance and hostility were discussed in Chapter 4. Differences can be bridged coactively by reaching out to the other, emphasizing common bonds and shared experiences as well as areas of agreement on the matter in question. Humor, too, can defuse hostility.

Several years ago, a university president and a young upstart faculty member found themselves at adjacent urinals during a break in a meeting of faculty and administrators. The meeting had been extremely tense. During the meeting, the faculty member had been a constant irritant to the president, who hoped to win faculty support on a highly sensitive plan that he and his co-administrators had formulated. Many cups of coffee had been imbibed, but now, as they stood before their adjacent urinals, neither could get anything to happen. After what seemed like more than a minute had gone by with each seemingly attentive to his own task yet obviously aware of the other's presence, the two adversaries looked at each other, smiled, and then broke up in uncontrollable laughter. The second half of the meeting went far better than the first.

The techniques of coactive persuasion described in Chapter 4 and elaborated on in subsequent chapters are not unlike those recommended generally by conflict theorists to reduce defensiveness. These include (a) neutral descriptions of the situation, without an implied need for anyone to change, (b) a problem orientation—expressing a desire to work on a mutual problem without predetermined opinions, (c) empathy for the feelings and attitudes of the other, and (d) minimization of differences in skill, position, or intelligence.

More than forty years ago, Deutsch offered a beautifully artful description of productive conflict that has stood the test of time. When two or more persons get past their initial suspicions and begin to approach a conflict as their problem, noted Deutsch (1969), their talk is often lively, intense, and impassioned but at the same time creative, engaging, satisfying, and even entertaining. In productive conflicts, he observed, positions are stated directly, and there is allowance for expressions of anger as something normal and expected, even helpful. There are likely to be expressions of warm feelings as well, but care is taken to avoid premature agreement, because this only masks the underlying problem. Often, it helps to divide the conflict into parts and begin discussion of the more easily resolvable issues. Success in solving these problems breeds success with others. It also serves as a reminder of positive qualities in the other party and of common bonds. It may also lead to the realization that there is room for compromise. In breaking the conflict into parts, the two parties may even discover that their different values make trade-offs possible, each party "giving" on one issue so as to "get" on another.

"DOC" REARDON ON NEGOTIATION STRATEGIES

Kathleen Reardon's *The Skilled Negotiator* (2004) adds to what we've said so far about the art of negotiations, and her blogs for the *Huffington Post* provide a nice complement to the book. You won't find very many formulas in *The Skilled Negotiator* but you will find a great many useful principles, illustrated with examples of "how to" and "how not to." In what follows we present a digest of Reardon on (1) Versatility, (2) "Intelligence-gathering," (3) Asking Questions, (4) Negotiation Styles, (5) Framing Options, (6) Power, and (7) Negotiation Ethics.

1 Versatility

- *Don't be too giving or too selfish.* Reardon offers her own "yes-but" to our preference for mutually satisfactory outcomes. "Win-win" solutions foster good feelings and long-term good will, but the fact is that sometimes you may want to gain at the other's expense ("win-lose") or at least prevent the other from winning at your expense.

- *Don't get stuck in scripts.* Although it's generally a good thing to take charge of the negotiations by setting the agenda, framing options, and leading with strength, sometimes it makes sense to bide your time, dance around the issues, and make concessions, taking a beating on X to get Y.

- *Set goals flexibly.* Decide, she says, what matters to you most in any given situation, but avoid telegraphing it before you have heard where the other side stands and be ready to change even primary goals as new opportunities arise.

- *For every issue to be negotiated, prepare a BATNA: a "Best Alternative to a Negotiated Agreement."* The best BATNAs, she says, are carefully chosen in advance. That way you're not at a loss as to what to propose should your optimal goal prove unattainable. And that way you won't be metacommunicating a sense of frustration or failure.

- *Whatever your goals, don't be too eager for closure and don't give your cards away.* In her February 12, 2009 blog, Reardon comments on mistakes made by the Obama administration in treading too softly with the Republican opposition in Congress, letting it be known, for example, that Obama was committed to bi-partisan solutions to issues like executive pay. Her point was not that Obama should have opposed bi-partisan solutions, but rather that he gave away too much bargaining ground by committing himself to them prematurely (Reardon, 2009).

• *Anticipate obstacles to goal achievement and be ready with possible ways to overcome or ameliorate them.* Reardon cites Ifert and Roloff (1998) on potential obstacles and ways to overcome them. They are reproduced here as Table 13.1.

TABLE 13.1   *Labor management benefits pie*

OBSTACLE	DEFINITIONS AND EXAMPLES
Inadequate resources	Conveys that the skills or resources requested are poor quality: • "My sweater is dirty." • "I have only $50." • "I'm not a very good mechanic."
Possession	Indicates that he or she does not have the requested resources: • "I wasn't in class yesterday to get notes." • "I don't have the money right now." • "I left my jacket at my sister's house in Arizona."
Imposition	Indicates that granting the request would impose on prior plans: • "I'm going out tonight." • "I need to pay my other debts first." • "I'm too busy to do that."
Inappropriateness	Indicates that the request violates a rule or is socially inappropriate (also includes obstacles in which the speaker indicates that there is no need for a request): • "I think it's unfair for you to ask." • "Mind your own business." • "The music's not that loud."
Source responsibility	Indicates that it is the requester's responsibility to take care of the problem: • "You need to do it yourself." • "Do it yourself." • "That's not our problem."
No incentive	Conveys that he or she has no incentive to grant the request: • "Why should I do that?" • "There's no reason to do that." • "What's in it for me?"
Recalcitrance	He or she does not want to grant the request and provides no other reason: • "You can't borrow my car." • "I don't want to change." • "I won't do that."

OBSTACLE	DEFINITIONS AND EXAMPLES
Postpone	Does not fully comply but agrees to future compliance: • "I'll pay you back next week." • "I'll turn down the music after this song." • "I'll do it later."
State of mind	Refuses due to an emotion or mental state: • "I'm too angry to do that." • "I'm too stressed to do that." • "I'm too tired."

Source: D. F. Ifert and M. E. Roloff, "Understanding Obstacles Preventing Compliance: Conceptualization and Classification." *Communication Research*, 1998, 25, 137. Reprinted with permission of SAGE Publications.

- *Prepare a repertoire of possible responses to the moves the other party is liable to make.* Think ahead several moves, as expert chess players are wont to do. By contrast, says Reardon, amateur chess players [and negotiators] are easily led. "They react to the moves of their opponents without sufficient forethought and so are easily lured by expert communicators into abandoning their goals" (2004). Reardon provides the familiar example of an employee in search of a salary upgrade who's repeatedly thrown off track by his boss into going over his performance objectives rather than addressing the upgrade issue. Says Reardon, "Expert negotiators recognize such diversions and return the interaction to the track they desire" (2004). Here's a typical "How to" from Reardon. Jim is the employee; Bob is his boss.

Bob: "Have you gone over your performance objectives?"

Jim: "They're tattooed on my forehead. I see them in the mirror when I shave in the morning. Can I annotate a copy for you with a self-assessment we can go over?"

Bob: "It's great you can find the time to think about those things. It seems like I spend most of my time trying to keep people on deadline."

Jim: "It's a major focus with me as well. I'm all over the Foster people to get me a response on the project, and I'm breathing down Sharon's neck for those budget numbers. Is there any part of the load I can take off your back?"

Bob: "I'll think about it. In the meantime keep me updated. I don't want to be surprised."

Jim: "Sure thing. I need to get back on the phone with some people, but this weekend I'll annotate those performance objectives to help your thinking on a salary increase." (Reardon, 2004)

2 "Intelligence-Gathering"

- *In long-term endeavors, take a learning process perspective on negotiation, paying attention to the short term in service of the long term*. Reardon provides the example of Nelson Mandela who, even during his 18 years as a prisoner of South Africa's apartheid regime, was "sizing up all sides to a question and getting to know the enemy" (2004).

- *Become context-sensitive*. Rather than fixing on one negotiation strategy, take periodic readings of the changing context, and adjust your strategies accordingly. Reardon cites Karl Weick (2001) on the exemplary "sense-making" of famed fire fighter Paul Gleason who, in leading the battle against a raging forest fire, deployed many more personnel as lookouts than people to actually fight the fire. Their job was to protect the crew while at the same time charting the likely path of the fire so that it could be fought most expeditiously.

- *Become increasingly self-aware*. Learn how others see you and how they see you seeing them. (Recall these type questions as concerns in Chapter 3 about image projections at the relational level.) Do you metacommunicate confidence or insecurity, for example? Do you smile too quickly in negotiations, thus signaling a willingness to settle prematurely?

- *Find out about the other's goals, expectations, attitudes, and perceptions*. To do so, ask lots of questions.

3 Asking Questions

- *Ask open-ended questions early on*. Questions like "How do you feel about X?" or "What are you hoping to achieve today?" should be asked in the early stages of negotiations. For example, when talking with a supervisor about budget issues that might lead to staffing reductions, ask, "What are your plans for this difficult period?" to try to establish the scope and seriousness of the situation.

- *Ask conditional questions as the negotiations proceed*. These sorts of questions involve probing for specific information about proposals. Questions like "What would happen if we were to …?" and "If we proceed as you suggest, what will that mean for …?" are useful. "If we develop a three-year contract, what would be the advantages and disadvantages for you …?" provides a non-threatening way to discuss options. Conditional questions don't pin either side down. They focus on hypothetical conditions (Reardon, 2004).

- *Ask leading questions in an attempt to prompt the other party to self-persuade*. For example, "What would you do if you were in our shoes?"

encourages the other party toward empathy. "Were you as impressed as I was with the tactics used by the X Company?" and "Is there a lesson here for us?" (Reardon, 2004). Couch your opinion in a way that may cause the other to agree. Self-disclosures may also be used to encourage reciprocal disclosures.

In general, says Reardon, questions can unearth hidden assumptions, ensure that what was said is what was heard, and prompt the other negotiating party to make your points. When you enter the negotiation process prepared to be versatile in your style, open in your desire to gather information and prepared to ask the right sorts of questions at the right times, you stand a greater chance of success.

Such items as versatility and good questioning skills are things you bring to the table. But, in the midst of your personal preparation, there are other issues you must consider: *negotiation styles, framing options, power*, and *ethics* are all components of the negotiation situation, and it is to those matters we now turn.

4 Negotiation Styles

- Negotiations are likely to proceed more smoothly if you and your counterpart on the other side have compatible styles, and so wise negotiators attempt to understand both their own personal style and that of their opponents.

- Fortunately, most negotiators are comfortable with more than one style. If they're not, conflict is likely to escalate or the negotiations may simply grind to a halt.

- One way to assess and evaluate negotiation style is through application of a style inventory. Rowe and Reardon's inventory is yet another means toward intelligence-gathering (see Table 13.2).

TABLE 13.2 *Negotiation style inventory*

You **MUST answer all the questions. There are no RIGHT or WRONG ANSWERS**. The answers reflect how you see yourself, so respond with what comes first to your mind.

1 When I negotiate, I	focus on my objectives	explore workable solutions	try to understand their thinking	try to avoid arguments
2 I explain my ideas best by	being forceful	presenting my ideas logically	explaining the implication	relating my points to them
3 When I am confronted, I	react strongly to what is said	explain my position with facts	look for a common ground	give in reluctantly
4 I describe my expectations	objectively	in complete detail	enthusiastically	amicably
5 I get my best deals when I	don't make any concessions	utilize my leverage	find creative solutions	am willing to meet them halfway

6 My objective in negotiation is to	achieve my goal	convince others to accept my position	find the best solution for all	look for an acceptable solution
7 The way to win an argument is to	be self confident	be logical	have novel ideas	look for consensus
8 I prefer information that	is specific and understandable	is complete and persuasive	shows a number of options	helps to achieve rapport
9 When I'm not sure what to do, I	take direct action	search for possible solutions	rely on my intuition	seek advice from others
10 I dislike	long debates	incomplete information	highly technical material	having arguments
11 If I've been rejected, I	persist in my point of view	rethink my position	relate my ideas to theirs	try to salvage the relationship
12 If timing is important, I	press for a quick decision	rely on critical facts	propose a compromise	hope to postpone the inevitable
13 When I am questioned, I	answer emphatically	rely on data for my position	respond with a broad question	look at how it affects me
14 I prefer situations where	I am in control	I can utilize my logical ability	I can explore new opportunities	people are considerate
15 I negotiate best when	I use my experience	a technical analysis is critical	I can explore many alternatives	I am in a win-win situation
16 When I am the underdog, I	try not to show any weakness	prepare carefully	try to change the situation	match my needs with theirs
17 When one is antagonistic, I	stand my ground	reason things out carefully	attempt to rise above the situation	look for ways to reduce the tension
18 If I'm in a losing situation, I	become more determined	consider all my options	look for ways to turn it around	appeal to their sense of fairness
19 To achieve mutual gain, I	show a workable solution	clarify everyone's priorities	suggest a mutually beneficial plan	consider both sides of the issue
In negotiating, it is important to	know what each party wants	clearly identify the agenda	start by making a positive impression	recognize that each party has needs

© Alan J. Rowe and Kathleen K. Reardon 12/29/97, rev. 3/27/98 (This form may not be reproduced without written permission)

5 Framing Options

- As noted in Chapter 6, the same situation can be presented in positive, gain-oriented terms or in negative, loss-prevention terms. This is true as well of negotiation strategies. It's usually best, says Reardon, to accent the positive, although, as we saw in Chapter 6, sometimes people tend to be so loss-averse that they will miss out on net gains to protect what they have.

- Early-stage framing sets the tone for negotiations, for example, by describing the negotiation as "an opportunity for us to discover the common ground that we know exists despite surface difficulties" (Reardon, 2004). Similarly, the negotiator might propose beginning with issue X because, framing it this way: "As we both know, it is the foundation on which all the other issues rest. We could postpone the issue, and pretend that it does not exist, but that would be tantamount to mutual deception" (Reardon, 2004).

- When framing in negotiations, it is useful to employ what Erving Goffman (1967) called **focused interactions**, wherein people join together to maintain a shared focus of concern. "Disadvantage accrues," maintains Reardon, "to those who leave frames to chance, who leave them to the other side to manage, or who simply assume that the other side assumes their frame" (Reardon, 2004). Seeking focused interaction is useful, because when people share a common focus of concern, "certain types of action become required, others prohibited, and still others irrelevant" (Reardon, 2004). When negotiators suggest what should be the topic for interaction, what is most centrally at issue, and what the approach should be for discussing the issue, it can advance their agenda. It is akin to what we referred to in Chapter 9 as "pre-persuasion."

- **Reframing** has an important place in negotiations as well. Reardon provides the example of an optimistic reframe, used to counter a skeptic's pessimistic frame. The issue was whether to go in on a joint venture. The skeptic had sketched on a white board the image of a large tree hanging precariously over a cliff. Rather than erasing that image, the venture proponent went outside the box, expanding the original sketch to include deep roots. This example, which used a metaphor for frames, reshaped the discussion and provided the positive approach needed to move the negotiations forward.

6 Power

- Power is surprisingly malleable. For example, it is true that executives in the highest echelons of a company have more power than their underlings. But, respect counts for more in the long run than formal authority (Reardon, 2004). Reardon quotes a senior executive, who explains: "I've seen supervisors with authoritative power get only what they ask for .... Supervisors with respect find that people offer to do more and take on more responsibility, which in turn lightens the management load" (Reardon, 2004).

- Skilled negotiators, says Reardon, use power, but they make people feel good about being with them. They opt not to exert available power so as to crush the other party or severely limit their sense of decisional freedom. Ironically, when they *withhold* the use of power, they often end up giving the impression that they possess a great deal of power—more than they actually possess.

- Most significantly, power isn't limited to such static indicators as rank, status, intelligence, appearance, reputation or physical size. Humility and trustworthiness can be kinds of power. Connections sometimes provide power. The key, though, is that power should be exercised with thoughtful care: "Don't appear to have all the answers," suggests Reardon. "Don't appear overbearing.... Don't quibble over the small stuff.... Don't play the same hand twice.... [and] Don't let yourself get flustered" (Reardon, 2004).

7 Negotiation Ethics

- Ethics in negotiations are a sticky wicket. If we define ethics too rigidly, then few negotiators can be found who comply with all the rules of conduct. The reason for this is because negotiators exaggerate. They pretend not to be in a hurry. They ask for more than they expect to get. They seldom reveal their bottom lines (Reardon, 2004). If we ban these customary practices of negotiations, we run the risk of ethics themselves becoming irrelevant. On ethics in negotiations, Reardon is not a Platonist; in fact, she is not an ethical absolutist of any kind (Reardon, 2004).

- Despite the challenges, it is possible for opposing parties to settle *up front* on a group of contextual rules of ethical engagement for their negotiations. To a long-term negotiating counterpart, we might say, "Let's try today to continue to treat each other with the respect that has made our relationship so strong." To a new negotiating party, we might say (in language and in a presentational style with which we feel comfortable), "Let's agree right now to treat each other with dignity. Let's agree to reject the pressures to manipulate, bully, or in any way demonstrate the kind of disrespect that can only damage our short- and long-term goals." Then, assuming at least a nod of agreement, we can issue a gentle reminder should the negotiations veer off the agreed-upon track, taking care, of course, to stay on track ourselves (Reardon, 2004).

- In general, says Reardon, persuasion is ethically preferable to manipulation or coercion. "Persuasion is not something an individual does *to* another person. It is done *with* another person. It is not always pure, but it relies more on strong evidence and skillful communication than on trickery and force" (Reardon, 2004).

The Skilled Negotiator

Can you see yourself entering into negotiations with Kathleen Reardon seated across the table from you? She'd get what she wants while trying to give you what you want, all the while protecting, if she can, that most precious and most fragile of our personal properties: our egos.

But what could Reardon have possibly meant when she counseled "versatility" in deciding whether to go for "win-win" or the riskier "win-lose" strategy? What would prompt her to go all out for a win, even at the risk of an escalation-driven "lose-lose" outcome?

Elsewhere in the book, however, she stands tall in support of an ethical principle: the need to reverse a decades-long pattern in the United States of the wealthy getting richer at the expense of the poor and middle class. Why is it, she asks, that the average American's income increased only 9% over the past 20 years while the top 1% experienced a 140% increase in the same period?

She cites USC Professor Neil Gabler (2002) as arguing that the growing gap is ideologically driven. Our ideas about inequality are driven by a powerful frame: "The American Dream." Want to get rich? In America, the Land of Opportunity, you can if you try hard enough, are enterprising enough, and are patient enough. At the very least you can make it into the upper middle class. If you can't, you have no one but yourself to blame. Complaining about economic inequality does no good, the argument goes. These are among the entailments of the frame, Gabler suggests. Reardon adds that virtually all Americans have bought into the dream, along with its rejection of what conservatives have been deriding as "class warfare." She calls it a kind of national "brainwashing."

Given her stated ethical concerns, what do you think Reardon might do when she found her values being challenged? Suppose, for instance, that Reardon was involved in delicate negotiations over something seemingly unrelated to "The American Dream": whether, for example, pay increases for workers at the Beta Corporation should be adjusted to changes in the cost of living. Imagine that the negotiations were going well, until, out of the blue, her counterpart waxed eloquent about "The American Dream" and looked to her for support of the premise. What would she do? Would this prompt her to risk "win-lose"?

Probably not. But if she decided to challenge her opponent's "American Dream" frame and risk seeing a negative turn in the negotiations, you can be sure that she'd respond tactfully, authoritatively, with good evidence, and not before she'd asked her counterpart a dozen questions, in a manner that was not ego-threatening.

THE PERSUASION DIALOGUE

Many ideas about conflict, persuasion, and their intersections come to us from the most contemporary research in the field. Others are ancient but still entirely relevant to our world. Such is Plato's **Phaedrus** (1956), wherein Socrates invites fellow Athenians to consider what an ideal rhetoric might be like, as opposed to the manipulative, exploitative discourse that too often substituted for thoughtful discussion in Greek society. Some have viewed Plato's dialogues themselves as models of rhetoric; as we suggested in Chapter 1, some have observed that these conversations were stacked by Plato in favor of his mentor and were hardly free of rhetorical sleight of hand (see also Smith, 1998).

In *Phaedrus*, Socrates is sitting by a stream when he is approached by Phaedrus, an impressionable young man who has just been duped by Lysias, a well-known speechwriter whom Socrates believes tends to speak from ignorance. Having warned of the ruses of rhetoric, Socrates then proceeds to address young Phaedrus on the subject of love. As he was when he listened to Lysias, Phaedrus is easily won over, but then Socrates confesses that his own speech was insincere. Socrates' point was that persuasive effectiveness, even in a noble cause, ought not to be the standard for judging rhetoric.

What, then, are the characteristics of the ideal rhetoric? Through the centuries, that question has beguiled philosophers. Many have agreed that the ideal rhetoric is **dialogic**, not **monologic**, placing the conversants on an equal footing. But what is the nature of that rhetorical conversation? Pulling together the writings of recent philosophers, we present our own version of the **persuasion dialogue**.

Two (or more) persons get together to puzzle out an issue. They may have strong opinions on the matter, which they are free to express. Indeed, the fact of difference is expected and welcomed. Falsely minimizing differences or pretending to evenhanded objectivity is disingenuous and will not do.

The conversants see matters differently, but their object really isn't to win anything at the expense of the other. This is key. Perhaps you have been in conversations in which the demands of the subject matter literally took over. One sign of that is a willingness to consider matters afresh, without clinging to previously entrenched positions:

> "Well, Jim, I know I usually complain when America plays the role of global police officer, but Syrian President Bashar al-Assad's decision to gas his own people really bothered me. The Syrian people deserved a chance at freedom. I don't think our country could have stood by any longer and let Assad continue to oppress his people."
>
> "Funny that you say that, Wilma, because I usually favor military intervention where American interests are at stake, but when it came to intervening in Syria, I don't think we had a dog in that fight."

Persuasion dialogues may have many goals, not the least of which is the pleasures of mutual exploration of a topic and possible edification. Consensus is not a required outcome of such dialogues. Occasionally, they bring closure to an issue, but, more often, they advance its consideration by raising as many questions as they answer. What are America's interests? Who defines them, and how? What humanitarian principles justify military intervention in some cases but not in others? Often, as in this conversation, the talk spins out to related issues, without loss, it is hoped, of the initial thread.

In persuasion dialogues, positions are presented skillfully but not manipulatively. As one person speaks, the others listen carefully, trying at once to see things from the speaker's perspective while at the same time resisting the temptation to take everything that's been said at face value. Managing to combine empathic listening with critical listening isn't easy; it's part of the art of the persuasion dialogue. Competent conversationalists learn to retrieve in memory what's been said at a substantive level while also attending to what's been metacommunicated, perhaps unintentionally. Wilma might restate Jim's argument, and then ask whether she's understood him. But she might follow with an objection to his likening of the conflict between Saddam Hussein and his people to a dog fight:

> "Isn't that choice of metaphor itself a problem, Jim? Notice how it positions you as an inhumane gambler involved in a dog fight. I find that metaphor emotionally troubling; it makes it harder for me to really engage in this conversation."

Still, the persuasion dialogue remains a cooperative exchange. Perhaps the conversational partners ask questions of clarification, perhaps they raise objections, but no one seeks to dominate or to put the others down. Indeed, the opposite may happen. I put forward my case, you try to improve it, perhaps even to perfect it; I do the same for you if I can:

> "You know, Wilma, I can really see your point. Maybe we can't be global police officers, but it sure is in America's interests to promote international human rights. So, by that standard, maybe we did have military obligations in Syria."

MOVING TO DIALOGUE IN INTERPERSONAL CONFLICTS

The example just given is one of a difference of opinion, not a conflict of interests. This should not be surprising. Indeed, it is hard to imagine two or more persons in serious conflict approaching the rigorous demands of the persuasion dialogue without the help of someone—a professional mediator or facilitator, perhaps, or just a mutual friend.

The cases to be presented next illustrate the potential for assisted dialogue to help conflicting parties advance consideration of the issues dividing them. Neither case models completely the ideal of the persuasion dialogue. The first exhibits the types of resistance common to those charged with ethical wrongdoing in a conflict situation (Simons, 1995). Still, some defenses are relinquished in the company of friends, and the four participants seem genuinely, at times, to give in to the demands of the subject matter. The second case is a highly structured dialogue, made necessary, perhaps, by the polarized topic of abortion (Chasin, et al., 1996; Roth & Becker, 1992). Here the give-and-take of the persuasion dialogue is replaced initially by strategic questioning by the facilitators, designed to get pro-choice and pro-life activists to dig deeply into their psyches for possible sources of intrapersonal ambivalence and interpersonal common ground.

Case 1 A Taped Conversation About a Taped Conversation

Len, a college math professor, and Laura, a former student, had been living together off and on for six months. Laura wanted very much to get married, whereas Len was somewhat hesitant to make a lifelong commitment after such a short time together. He preferred a longer period of living together, and was not inclined to propose.

Len decided to have a serious conversation with Laura about this issue; he wanted to come to an agreement about how they would proceed with the relationship. But then, he did something odd: he secretly recorded a conversation between the two of them. He did this because he wanted everything to be "on the record." Once Laura and he came to an agreement, he wanted it to be firm. Knowing that Laura wanted to get married, and suspecting that she might reintroduce the topic and perhaps even twist his words, Len wanted to have evidence of exactly what each partner said. He wanted to be able to use the tape to remind Laura of their agreement.

On learning about the recording after the event, Laura was furious, but Len thought she was over-reacting. Their quarrel about the surreptitious recording erupted in front of Justin and Jen, Len's long-term friends who had come to know and like Laura through Len.

Justin certainly didn't want to get involved in this messy situation, and given what had occurred, he didn't want to be misquoted. And he thought Len deserved a little of his own medicine, so he suggested that the foursome's conversation about the conversation should also be recorded, but done so this time with everyone's permission.

Excerpt A

Laura: Len, what's your conclusion? Do you think it was unethical for you to do that?

Len: I was explaining … that … the only parties whom I imagined would ever hear this would be us, that it was merely a record and not a means of exposure. It was not at all meant for public consumption.

Laura: There are … there are other issues to be considered.

Len: What's the big deal?

Laura: Namely that, namely that I was deceived … and it was a conversation that required trust, and … [voice trails off].

Len: But how were you deceived?

Laura: Because I was being vulnerable and really sort of …

Len: But you would be the only one to hear it besides me.

Laura: Wait a minute. Wait! … And really reaching in and pulling out things which were very difficult for me to say because I thought and was under the impression that we were resolving something between us, things that potentially were …

Len:	We were, for all times.
Laura:	But under the circumstances you were less willing to be vulnerable and to stumble and to face up to difficult things. You knew the tape was running!
Len:	Well, you're assuming that I'm somehow …
Laura:	Your intentions were totally different than mine.
Len:	… totally natural when I'm speaking without a tape recorder, or anyone is totally natural.
Laura:	Except that it imposes another level of being unnatural when the tape is on.
Len:	If it's just the character of what we're talking about, that it makes us both unnatural; then we're equal.
Justin:	You're absolutely right.
Laura:	But when a tape is on and I don't know it, then it's more unequal.
Jen:	Right! It's knowing something that the other person doesn't know. It gives you a sense of power, or…
Justin:	Suppose you wanted to prove to Laura that she was stupid or…
Jen:	It doesn't matter if you're going to use it or not, you know, or if no one else hears it.

[Len is defensive in this portion of the conversation, because now he has friends Justin and Jen to contend with as well as Laura. Note how the process of dialogue helps not just Len but also Laura to discover why she has been so upset by his taping.]

Excerpt B

Laura:	Len, are you maintaining that this wasn't unethical?
Len:	I'm maintaining that it was …
Jen:	Borderline?
Len:	I'll tell you something. If it were done to me in similar circumstances, I would not be pissed.
Justin:	I agree with that. *You* wouldn't be.
Len:	If you did it to me; if Justin did it to me; if Jen did it to me…. If, on the other hand, someone I didn't know well did it to me, I would be very pissed and that's what's so disturbing about all of this—that you're sort of applying standards as if I'm a stranger.
Laura:	No.
Justin:	Laura wouldn't do it to you, though.
Laura:	I wouldn't do it to you.
Len:	But if you did it to me, I wouldn't mind.
Laura:	But I wouldn't do it.
Justin:	See, there are two parts to the "Do unto others as others would have done unto you." What does that mean? Well, it could mean, "Do to others what

Len: you'd find acceptable if it was done to you." Or, it could mean, "Do unto others what the other would do." And they really are two different things. Or the third, "Do unto others as you would like them to do unto you." Which is really what it means.

[Excerpt B finds Len still defending himself, this time on grounds that had Laura taped him without his knowledge, he would not be offended. This raises for all four participants the meaning and applicability of the Golden Rule: "Do unto others as you would have them do unto you." The group senses here that the principle is relevant to Len's surreptitious taping of Laura, but does it exonerate him or demonstrate his wrongdoing? The group fumbles toward some sort of understanding, but they do so together. This segment of the conversation helps them move toward closure.]

Excerpt C [After a 30-second Interlude]

Len: The other thing is, though, we each have a different borderline. We draw the lines at different points, at different angles …

Laura: That's very true, Len.

Len: And where I draw the line is not where you do it, and where you do it is not where I do it, so we're probably not going to agree on all of this.

Laura: But you got to the root of the problem, the problem of making the secret recording. You did know it was unethical and that's why you didn't tell me … that I would not have liked that. And then, you didn't respect the fact that I didn't.

Justin: That's probably true.

Len: I don't think that's true …

Laura: I think it's true.

Len: Because I wouldn't have minded being taped. I didn't have the imagination to think you would.

Laura: Then why didn't you tell me?

Justin: Because telling you would have been no good. It would have denied the opportunity to get a spontaneous, candid statement on tape.

Len: Right.

Jen: I think Justin's right. I think there are two different sets of questions.

Laura: What are the questions?

Jen: Well, whether or not it's ethical is different than whether or not, as he said, that you would be upset by it. They're two different things.

Laura: Yeah, I agree with you that he didn't think it through.

Justin: You were stupid; you weren't unethical.

Laura: No, inconsiderate, inconsiderate.

Len: [Laughs] I did not think it through, that's for sure.

Excerpt C ends inconclusively. Was Len stupid, insensitive, or downright unethical? Yet the conversation has clearly advanced consideration of this question. Laura has been wronged; even Len now understands that. But Laura now understands the reason for Len's secrecy—he did it only because he wanted to get her honest responses, and he didn't want the taping to influence what she might say. Meanwhile, Laura and Len have enjoyed the support of Len's longtime friends. All have learned something through the process of exploration.

This exemplifies a persuasion dialogue. Each partner presented his or her position with skill, but each listened to the other respondents as well. No one dominated the conversation, and no one went into the encounter seeking to "win." Instead, they worked to share perspectives and keep talking until they arrived at a new and higher level of mutual understanding.

Case 2 A Structured Conversation About Abortion

Christine and Pat grew up together and had always been friends, but now they were activists on opposite sides of the abortion issue. The last time they saw each other was outside an abortion clinic. Christine was holding up a sign saying "Abortion is murder." Pat waved a sign in Chris's face that said "Choice: A Woman's Right." Neither of them spoke.

It is hard to imagine the Christines and Pats of the world finding common ground on the abortion issue. Surely, it is among the most divisive issues facing Americans. Yet recently, a pro-life activist and a pro-choice leader tried to bring their two groups together on the basis of common interests. Through a process of dialogue, they discovered that (a) neither favored abortion as a means of birth control, (b) both preferred adoption to abortion in cases in which that option was truly available, and (c) each saw abortion as preferable to forcing a woman to have a child in a case of rape or incest. This is but one of many success stories in efforts to bridge differences between opposing interests on matters of public controversy. The Abortion Conversation Project and the Public Conversations Project have been on the leading edge of these efforts.

What type of communication is needed to get pro-choice and pro-life activists to understand and respect each other, let alone to find common ground? On divisive public issues such as abortion, attempts at direct persuasive communication between antagonists are often destructive, rather than productive (Deutsch, 1969; Roth & Becker, 1992); they virtually preclude any possibility for agreement by reinforcing us–them attitudes.

Recognizing this, a group of therapists from the Public Conversations Project decided to try a different tack (Chasin, et al., 1996; Roth & Becker, 1992). Rather than encouraging a free flow of communication between pro-choice and pro-life advocates, they set out to provide a controlled but supportive context for talk. On any given evening, four to six recruits from each side would be seated in an alternated pattern around a dinner table. A light buffet dinner was made available, during which time no one was to reveal his or her stance on abortion. Instead, they were encouraged to get acquainted informally while avoiding the issue of abortion.

After dinner, the facilitators proposed several rules for the conduct of talk about abortion. The conversants' talk would be treated confidentially. There would be no interrupting. The conversants would use respectful language (for example, using pro-choice and pro-life, rather than "anti" terms to refer to the positions of others). They would each be permitted to decline to answer any questions asked of them.

The facilitators assumed a principle that deserves considerable emphasis: If given a chance to be explored open-mindedly, people's expressed attitudes on any given controversial issue tend to soften and to exhibit signs of greater complexity, even ambivalence. This is a principle that all persuaders need to keep in mind. The converse of this principle is that, if egos are attacked, attitudes harden; psychologists call this the principle of reactivity (Brehm, 1962; Cialdini, 2009). In these sessions, conversants were encouraged to depoliticize the abortion issue and to address it instead in personal terms. They were encouraged, in effect, to function expressively, rather than persuasively. Initially, the facilitators asked all the participants the same three questions. Then the participants were invited to question each other.

The first of the facilitators' questions, asking the participants to say something about their own life experiences in relation to the issue of abortion, elicited revelations of far greater ambivalence on the topic of abortion than these activists had previously expressed publicly (or perhaps even to themselves). For example, Andrea talked of working with a pregnant teenager and her boyfriend, both from abusive backgrounds, at a church-related organization for children. As she watched the couple struggle with the issue of abortion, her own attitudes were formed. Said Andrea:

> I felt that in all fairness, I certainly had to lay out all of the alternatives that were available to them. And she said, "You know, if I have this baby, I will never have the strength to give it up for adoption, and I will sentence it to the same hell that I have lived through." ... I feel very pro-life, but I am very strongly pro-choice, because I felt like ... I could never have made that decision for that child and she did choose to abort that baby.

> (Roth & Becker, 1992)

The second question asked of everyone was "What is at the heart of the matter for you, as an individual?" One effect of asking this question was that each "camp" discovered almost as many differences in their own group as they did between groups. Linda's principal opposition to abortion was as a feminist; for Gina, it was a spiritual thing, a belief about what God intended for her to do.

Having asked the first two questions, neither of which was terribly threatening, the facilitators set the stage for their third and final question, one that invited participants to comment on dilemmas, struggles, conflicts, pockets of uncertainty, times when one value bumps up against some other value, or other murky areas within their prevailing views. Their answers suggested that even on the polarizing issue of abortion, which often generates expressions of certainty, people also experience uncertainty:

Linda: One time I was discussing this issue with a friend and said I was pro-
(pro-life)   life and he said, "Obviously you never grew up an unwanted
                   child." And he was right, they wanted me. I think of the children
                   that suffer and think to myself, would it be better if they had been
                   aborted? But then I think, they have life. But it's really hard to
                   watch children in pain and sometimes it's hard to be pro-life, but
                   at the same time, I'm so pro-life. So that's something I really
                   struggle with.

Arlene: The very idea of someone having an abortion on the basis of the
(pro-choice):   gender of the fetus just really sends me into orbit.

Carolyn: I think I could live with a political settlement which said there
(pro-life)   were some exceptions for criminal rape, incest, things like that. I
                   wouldn't be happy; I wouldn't think it was still right to kill the
                   unborn who after all was not at fault, didn't kill the rapist. But,
                   Tay-Sachs again ... if a baby's going to die a horrible death by age
                   three, you know. These are awful hard cases.

(Roth & Becker, 1992)

As Roth and Becker (1992) observe, the third question not only reveals differences within groups but also calls forth similarities in beliefs and attitudes of those on opposing sides. Furthermore, it honors each other's experience and the emotional and intellectual meanings attached to those experiences. By now, the participants "have usually dropped most or all of the demonizing stereotypes they may have brought to the meeting" (Roth & Becker, 1992), and they are ready to question and answer each other non-defensively and non-judgmentally.

As these case studies demonstrate, negotiation is possible even in the most difficult situations. Even when an issue is the closest to the heart, as people discuss their intimate relationships or profoundly ingrained values, as was the case with the participants discussing abortion, productive negotiations can take place. Participants engage in acts of mutual persuasion; they stand their ground while they listen to the other side, and they find pathways to agreement. Through the use of persuasion dialogues, seemingly impossible situations can move more closely to resolution.

SUMMARY

This chapter began with Kenneth Burke's (1969) reminder that rhetoric, the art of persuasion, is not always friendly, not always concerned with matters of a purely academic nature, and frequently occasioned by social conflicts. The chapter explored a variety of types of persuasive interaction, looking especially at how talk between antagonists could be made more productive. Although the focus of the chapter was on the sorts of everyday interpersonal conflicts that occur at work or in the home, it also examined other mixed-motive conflicts such as those involved in business negotiations. Also introduced was the persuasion dialogue, an ideal of conversational interaction more often achievable in academic controversies than in social conflicts but still worth aiming toward in conflict situations.

A social conflict was defined as a clash over at least partially incompatible interests. Conflicts are not simply misunderstandings, semantic confusions, or communication breakdowns; nor are they only disagreements, differences of opinion, or controversies—they are always something more than that. Divergent interests are at stake, interests important to one or both parties.

A focus of this chapter was on the work of Kathleen Reardon, where she provides solid guidance for ways in which we can each become a Skilled Negotiator. By focusing on (1) Versatility, (2) "Intelligence-gathering," (3) Asking Questions, (4) Negotiation Styles, (5) Framing Options, (6) Power, and (7) Ethics, we can each plan and implement approaches to reaching the best possible outcomes for the situations we face.

Ultimately, this chapter demonstrates that at the same time that antagonists are prompted to oppose each other, they also find it necessary to cooperate with each other, if only for purposes of coordinating their behavior. Hence, it recommends the use of coactive persuasion in these mixed-motive conflicts, combined with the marshaling and occasional deployment of power resources. It also offers solid recommendations concerning pathways through interpersonal negotiating. Through application of the principles presented here, we believe you will see greater persuasive success and also stronger interpersonal relationships. And that, in the end, is the primary goal as we navigate our pathway through life.

QUESTIONS AND PROJECTS FOR FURTHER STUDY

1   Do a case study of persuasion in a social conflict of your own choosing. Drawing on concepts introduced in this chapter, characterize the conflict by type, nature of participants, patterns of escalation, and possibilities for productive dialogue. How was persuasion different in this conflict than it would have been had the conflicting parties been engaged in a mere difference of opinion? Had you been one (or both) of the interactants, what would you have done differently?

2   Practice applying the techniques suggested here for turning potentially destructive conflicts into more productive ones. Do the same for conflicts that have already moved through vicious cycles of unwanted escalation. Recalling Shar's questions, decide why to fight, whether to fight, when to fight, and how to fight. Keep a journal of your efforts at dealing with interpersonal conflicts in

productive ways. Consider discussing one or more of these experiences with others in your class.

3   As president of the YRU faculty union, it's your job to protect the faculty's interests but also to serve the interests of YRU's survival at a time of state-mandated budget cuts. YRU's president has come to you with a plan to eliminate five academic departments, phasing out their majors and laying off the faculty. Drawing exclusively on our summary of Reardon on negotiations, do the following: develop a counterproposal plan that you will use in negotiating this difficult situation, considering (1) Versatility, (2) "Intelligence-gathering," (3) Asking Questions, (4) Negotiation Styles, (5) Framing Options, (6) Power, and (7) Ethics.

4   With classmates or friends, try approximating the ideal of the persuasion dialogue. Begin with a difference of opinion over values or policy, then move, if the opportunity presents itself, to the more difficult terrain of interpersonal conflict. Compare your efforts at dialogue with those of Len, Laura, Justin, and Jen.

5   On a polarizing issue such as abortion, try playing the role of the facilitator, in a manner similar to that suggested by Roth and Becker (1992).

6   The following case study, presented by novelist Lois Gould (1973), first appeared in *Ms.* magazine. On the surface, it concerns a problem of bed making. Ms. Gould's husband gets up after she does and hastily tosses the covers back on the bed—a practice she finds extremely annoying. The immediate question for Ms. Gould is how to get her husband to make the bed unlumpily. She realizes, however, that lumpily made beds are often symptomatic of the larger question of who is to have what power in the relationship. Her "rhetorical analysis" of her husband's behavior is summarized here in outline form as follows:

- My husband's habitual act is symbolic in nature.
  He is competent to make the bed unlumpily.
  - He made his own bed in the army.
  - He made his own bed in camp.
  - He taught his children to make their beds neatly.
  - Skills like these do not rust from disuse.
  - He has as much time to make unlumpy beds as I do.
  - He, as much as I, cares that the house is kept neat.
  - Only with great reluctance did he begin making the bed at all.

- The act symbolizes an interest in perpetuating power and privilege.
  Before acceding with great fanfare to my request that he make the bed at all, he offered the following arguments:
  - Who makes the bed is unimportant.
  - Making the bed would make me late for work.

- You do it faster and more efficiently.
- Why don't you hire a maid?

Once he gave in, he played the injured martyr.

If confronted over the bed's lumpiness:

- He would ask for a precise definition of a decent bed.
- He would allude to my being hung up on household sociology.
- He would suggest that I had far better things to do than carp at him over the bed, now that I didn't have to make it.

These arguments give contextual meaning to the lumpy bed. Viewed in context, the lumpy bed is a way of saying:

- I'm a very important person.
- You're not a very important person.
- I, therefore, have a right to dominate in this relationship.

What strategies of influence are most appropriate in situations such as this? Discuss this case with others and ask yourself what Gould should have done. Suppose, as she reports, she had already tried a variety of strategies, including reviewing with her husband how beds ought to be made, demonstrating with ironclad logic why her husband ought to make the bed properly, and outright pleading. What should she do next?

No doubt you have been in situations similar to this one. Write a brief description of the conflict and indicate how, in retrospect, you think you should have handled it.

KEY TERMS

- Asymmetrical conflict
- Decide:
  - how to fight
  - when to fight
  - whether to fight
  - why to fight
- Dialogic
- Focused interactions
- Lose-lose conflict
- Monologic
- Reframing
- Social conflict
- Symmetrical conflict
- Persuasion dialogue
- *Phaedrus*
- Win-lose conflict
- Win-win conflict

REFERENCES

Brehm, J. W. (1962). *A theory of psychological reactance.* New York: Academic Press.

Burke, K. (1969). *A rhetoric of motives.* Berkeley: University of California Press. (Original work published 1950)

Chasin, R., Herzig, M., Roth, S., Chasin, L., Becker, C., & Stains, C. R. (1996). From diatribe to dialogue. *Mediation Quarterly, 13,* 323–344.

Cialdini, R. B. (2009). *Influence: Science and practice.* New York: Simon & Schuster.

Deutsch, M. (1969). Conflicts: Productive and destructive. *Journal of Social Issues, 25,* 7–41.

Elgin, S. H. (1995). *BusinessSpeak.* New York: McGraw-Hill.

Gabler, N. (2002, January 27). Class dismissed. *Los Angeles Times,* p. M6.

Goffman, E. (1967). *Interaction ritual.* Garden City, NY: Doubleday.

Gould, L. (1973). If your husband makes the bed, must you lie in it? *Ms., 1,* 92–95.

Ifert, D. E., & Roloff, M. E. (1998). Understanding obstacles preventing compliance: Conceptualization and classification. *Communication Research, 25*(2) 131–153.

Overton, P. (2003, March 9). *Sharp words for Yale grad students' strike.* (Hartford Courant) Retrieved January 25, 2015, from articles.Courant.com: http://articles.courant.com/2003-03-09/news/0303091716_1_graduate-employees-teaching-assistants-graduate-student

Plato. (1956). *Phaedrus* (W. C. Helmbold & W. G. Rabinowitz, trans.). New York: Liberal Arts Press. (Original work n.d.)

Reardon, K. (2009, February 12). This time I'm taking names. *Huffington Post.* Retrieved July 11, 2009, from www.huffingtonpost.com/kathleen-reardon/this-time-im-taking-names_b_166459.html

Reardon, K. K. (2004). *The skilled negotiator.* San Francisco: Jossey-Bass.

Roth, S., & Becker, C. (1992, August 15). From debate to dialogue: The Public Conversations Project. Paper presented at the annual meeting of the American Psychological Association, Peace Division, Washington, DC.

Simons, H. W. (1995). Arguing about the ethics of past actions: An analysis of a taped conversation about a taped conversation. *Argumentation, 9,* 225–250.

Smith, C. R. (1998). *Rhetoric and human consciousness.* Prospect Heights, IL: Waveland.

Smith, R. R., & Windes, R. R. (2000). *Progay/antigay: The rhetorical war over sexuality.* Thousand Oaks, CA: Sage Publications.

Weick, K. (2001). Leadership as the legitimation of doubt. In Bennis, W., Spreitzer, G., & Cummings, T. (eds), *The future of leadership.* San Francisco: Jossey-Bass, pp. 95–96.

CHAPTER 14

Leading Social Movements

- What Are Social Movements?
- Types of Social Movements
- Tactics of Social Movements
- Social Protests and Mass Media
- Leading Social Movements: The Requirements-Problems-Strategies (RPS) Approach
- Open- and Closed-Minded Movements
- The Fate of Social Movements
- Summary
- Notes
- Questions and Projects for Further Study
- Key Terms
- References

I t is April 23, 1989—early on in a sustained student protest that will eventuate in a bloody massacre on June 3 and 4 of that year. The place is Beijing's Tiananmen Square, symbolic for its history of ritual celebrations of Chinese culture and political governance; symbolic, too, because from the government buildings adjoining Tiananmen issue forth the decrees that radiate from the capital to all of China.

Beijing is to China what Washington, DC, is to the United States, and the Chinese university students have done what even American students would be forbidden to do. In direct violation of orders from the Chinese police, they have occupied the square on a continuous basis—equivalent to American students taking over the Mall surrounding the Washington monument and adjoining the Capitol building.

Quite apart, then, from what the speakers will be saying to the assembled multitudes at Tiananmen, the act of takeover sends a powerful message. Although non-violent, it is an act of massive defiance—hence, far more militant, say, than a visit to one's congressional representative armed with signatures on a petition.

One of the speakers on April 23 is a professor from Beijing University named Chen Mingyuan. "*We* are the masters of our country," he says. The "we" is important because it signals a joining of professors and students. This alone is noteworthy in a country in which professors traditionally stood well above their students in the status hierarchy and generally kept their distance from them.

"We are the *masters* of our country," says Chen. Is the professor suggesting something on the order of a takeover of the country by the educated elite? Or perhaps the "we" refers more generally and more ambiguously to "the people." In either case, the "we" is incendiary in a country not known for heeding the wishes of the intelligentsia or for Western democratic ideals.

"We are the masters of *our* country," says Chen. Is this a way of saying that Tiananmen is a grassroots protest, not something imported from foreigners? Does Chen mean that the protesters are expressing identification with the country, even as they are dis-identifying with the government's policies? On this occasion, every word takes on potential significance. Never mind that thousands, perhaps tens of thousands of those assembled at Tiananmen, were probably out of earshot of the speech. Word of the speech was distilled through the crowd.

Professor Chen Mingyuan mentions the death of Hu Yaobang, a reformer who had been removed two years earlier as party secretary. Every major protest movement has its list of heroes and legends, enemies and unmitigated evils. In the oblique language of Chinese politics, Hu had signaled his commitment to Chinese democratization and his opposition to government-tolerated corruption. Thus, the very mention of Hu Yaobang's death is a unifying expression of ideology.

Professor Chen then compliments the crowd on an earlier demonstration: "The demonstration was spontaneous, the petition peaceful, and the mourning of Comrade Yaobang very orderly. I think the students from Beijing University should feel very proud of themselves."

The takeover of Tiananmen Square was a decidedly militant act. Yet it is important that protests be construed as peaceful and orderly, if at all possible. Those who witness them, or hear about them, must be convinced that the protesters are not wildly deviant or unjustifiably rebellious. They must be seen, rather, as a habitually law-abiding aggrieved group of persons who have been unable to achieve their ends by lesser means. Thus Professor Chen's compliment to the students takes on significance, and they erupt in a chant: "Long live the students! Long live democracy! Long live freedom!" The chanting at Tiananmen is reminiscent of American protests of the 1960s for civil rights ("Freedom now! Freedom now!") and against the war in Vietnam ("Hey, hey, LBJ, how many kids have you killed today?"). There is a ritual quality to chantings of this sort, as if the crowd were speaking as one, with what Gustave Le Bon (1896) long ago called the "group mind."

Chen Mingyuan then spoke of freedom:

When I pronounced the word "freedom," some people became nervous. Some would say, "Freedom is a bad word." But I feel that freedom is the most beautiful word in the world. Why should only other people be allowed to use it? Why is it that this beautiful word is not in the vocabulary of our great motherland and our great people?

Yes, we are poor. We are backward. We are uneducated. We are living a bitter life. But we do have this ideal of freedom and democracy.

To those accustomed to Western conceptions of freedom, Professor Chen's pronouncement on the beauty of the word *freedom* may sound a bit trite. But in a country barely cutting its teeth on democratization, freedom, and especially press freedom, it must have appeared to those assembled as truly revolutionary.

Yet it would be a mistake to assume that the students wanted exactly what individuals in the West have and enjoy. This is an assumption that the Western news media may have helped popularize at the time, in part because the students and professors they talked with tended to be those whose English was especially good, and who, in general, were more Western-minded. It may come as a surprise that between chantings for freedom and democracy, the demonstrators would stand and sing the anthem of the Communist government, the "Internationale."

Indeed, much of the remainder of the speech was bland by American standards. It called for a reduction in inflation, then at 18%. It demanded that education be made a top priority on the list of government expenditures. It insisted, in strident terms, that government corruption and government-tolerated corruption be ended and severely punished.

Then Professor Chen closed:

Maybe someone will say, "You students should return [to your universities] and study quietly. You professors should simply teach your courses." But all these problems constantly wear us down. We can't accept this. We shall never accept it!

With Chen's conclusion, we see once again the "we–they" opposition that is characteristic of **social movement** rhetoric. We see the histrionic prediction, "We shall *never* accept it," that is characteristic. Not only do movement leaders prophesy continued unity and resistance, whatever the sacrifices, but also they insist that collective action is urgently needed, that victory is likely (or at least possible) if all band together, and that the leader's personal interests are linked with the group's interests.

The rhetoric of protest issues not just from the microphone or the bullhorn but from the crowd itself—it is the rhetoric of symbolic acts, not just words. Those at Tiananmen who repeatedly weathered the rain in flimsy sleeping bags were fortified by each other and by the support of friends, relatives, and strangers who braved the police to provide the students with food and drink and emotional support. Word spread of old ladies who stood in the way of trucks full of soldiers entering the city and lectured them to turn around and go back where they came from. Some city officials, not only in Beijing but in other cities where demonstrations erupted, apparently turned a blind eye to the events around them, or at least held back from the use of physical force. This, too, moved the protesters at Tiananmen, as it did Chinese and Western journalists. Having been moved, Chinese journalists provided inspiration in their own right. Timorous at first, they eventually defied censorship orders and provided a fuller accounting of what they had seen and heard. Western journalists, for their part, not only covered the events at Tiananmen and surroundings but also fed back to the protesters news of the sympathetic responses they were getting round the world.

WHAT ARE SOCIAL MOVEMENTS?

The demonstrators at Tiananmen Square were part of a *social movement,* that is, a movement that was *uninstitutionalized* or outside the mainstream. In extreme cases, as at Tiananmen, the ideas guiding members of social movements, their methods of action, and their core organizations (social movement organizations, SMOs) are all considered suspect or downright illegitimate in the larger society of which they are a part. Moreover, social movements are *cause-oriented* collectivities; they exist primarily to promote an ideology (e.g., democratization) and/or a program of action (e.g., petitioning the government to lower the rate of inflation). This is their *cause,* and they promote it through extended periods. Finally, unlike self-help organizations such as Alcoholics Anonymous, social movements see as their mission to exert influence outside their own SMOs. Formally, then, *a social movement is an uninstitutionalized collectivity that operates on a sustained basis to exert external influence in behalf of a cause.*

The civil rights movement in the United States provides another example. In the 1960s, the SMOs supporting civil rights included the Southern Christian Leadership

FIGURE 14.1   *A peaceful protest march for civil rights in the South.*
Reprinted with permission of Post-Intelligencer Collection, Museum of History & Industry

Conference (SCLC), headed by the Reverend Martin Luther King Jr., the Student Nonviolent Coordinating Committee (SNCC), the Congress on Racial Equality (CORE), and the National Association for the Advancement of Colored People (NAACP).

Not everyone who identified with the civil rights movement belonged to one or another of these core organizations, but, without them, there could not have been a movement. The cause of the civil rights movement was, minimally, the abolition of racial discrimination in law and, beyond that, the elimination of all discriminatory practices. Some might say that the ultimate goal of the civil rights movement was equality. If so, the movement is still a long way from full accomplishment.

The civil rights movement of the 1960s was uninstitutionalized in three respects: guiding ideas, modes of action, and core organizations. Its detractors in the South viewed the movement's opposition to segregation as nothing less than an assault on their traditional way of life. Its confrontational tactics, such as sit-ins at segregated lunch counters, were subjected to scorn and disapproval; even many in the North who approved of the movement's goals deplored these tactics as illegal or unnecessarily provocative. Its SMOs had varying degrees of legitimacy, with NAACP enjoying a measure of respectability because of its relatively conservative style and long tenure as an organization. By contrast, the SNCC members seemed to revel in their "upstart" status within the white South.

A collectivity may be partially institutionalized and still be a movement. For example, the National Organization of Women enjoys a measure of respectability in the larger society. Although it seldom if ever engages in practices considered deviant or outside the mainstream, its feminist agenda is far from being fully institutionalized. Likewise, the National Rifle Association is widely accepted in the larger society, but it also spearheads an anti-gun control effort that is highly controversial in American society and, in that sense, is part of a social movement. Examples of social movements from the 1960s are the movement for drug legalization, the animal rights movement, women's liberation, various people's right movements (e.g., Chicano rights, gay and lesbian rights, and Native American rights), Black Power, the environmental movement, the gun control movement, disarmament, anti-nuclear power, feminism, pro-choice, pro-life, and various *countermovements* to the right of the political spectrum.

TYPES OF SOCIAL MOVEMENTS

The goals that movements seek to realize vary considerably, and so, too, is there great variation in their means for achieving them. **Reformist movements** generally seek passage of particular laws, better enforcement of particular laws, replacement of corrupt or incompetent officials, and so on. The gun control and civil rights movements are examples. **Revolutionary movements** go even further by seeking to replace guiding ideologies, institutions, and sometimes entire regimes, on the basis of new governing principles. They are also associated with the threat or use of force (e.g., American Revolution), but there have been largely peaceful revolutions (e.g., Poland, 1989).

Resistance movements, rather than advocating change, seek to hold it back and keep the status quo, for example, the anti-gun control movement. Given the Supreme Court's decision in *Roe v. Wade* (1973), the pro-life movement would not be labeled generally as reformist, whereas the pro-choice movement is resistive. That being said, categories are not always clear. When the pro-choice movement seeks federal funding of abortions for the poor and the pro-life movement resists such funding, then pro-choice becomes the reformist movement, whereas pro-life becomes resistive. **Restorative movements** seek a return to an older and supposedly better way of life. The cause of today's Christian Identity movement echoes the rhetoric of hate toward minorities in the United States, preached in earlier days by White Citizens Councils and by the John Birch Society (Bennett, 1995; Wills, 1990). Marcus Garvey's "Back to Africa" was also a restorative movement.

Finally, **expressivist movements** try to change individuals, rather than directly trying to change institutions or laws. Theirs is a positive agenda, although they may be allied with protest groups (Jaspars, 1997). The alternative school, free clinic, and food co-op movements are examples of expressivist movements, and they share another feature: all seek to provide models of service superior to those of the institutions they oppose (Simons & Mechling, 1981). Expressivists believe that, just as institutions are created by people, so they can be changed only by changes in people. Common to the ideologies of movements for personal transformation are the themes of personal responsibility and of possible self-improvement and enlightenment.

It is not always easy to classify movements based on this or any other typology because of internal disputes about goals and methods within the movement, as well as changes in goals and strategies. For example, a conference of 1960s-style Marxist activists hit on a decidedly expressivist note when they concluded at a conference that "new social movements" such as feminism and environmentalism have

TABLE 14.1   *Types of movements*

Reformist	Seek to fix or improve the system through the passage of particular laws, better enforcement of particular laws, replacement of corrupt or incompetent officials, etc.
Revolutionary	Seek to replace guiding ideologies, institutions, and sometimes entire regimes, on the basis of new governing principles.
Resistance	Seek to hold back and keep the status quo.
Restorative	Seek to create a return to an older and supposedly better way of life.
Expressivist	Seeks to change individuals, believing that institutions are created by people, and so they can be changed only by changes in people.

demonstrated that large-scale social change "is accomplished in face-to-face relations, at the level of personal identity and consciousness … whether or not such change is enunciated in public policy" (Darnovsky, et al., 1995). Reports varied widely on what the students at Tiananmen Square wanted, although it became clear as time went on that they did *not* want the existing, hard-line regime in China. From all accounts, their demands were initially modest, but they became more radical over time.

TACTICS OF SOCIAL MOVEMENTS

Movements select from a repertoire of possibilities available to them at any given time and place (Tilly, 1979). Some tactics, such as mass demonstrations against administrative practices, are rare in autocratic societies but common in democracies. Other tactics, such as hangings in effigy, were popular for centuries in England and the United States but have largely gone out of style. Some movements rely on verbal appeals, others on a combination of exhortations and demonstrations; still others add the threat and use of force. To advance their cause, movements have characteristically relied on *confrontational tactics,* still the method of choice for street protests. But movements seeking both ideological change and resistance to ideological change are increasingly turning to *cultural politics*.

Confrontation

Consider once again the demonstrators at Tiananmen Square, some of them on hunger strikes, none of them knowing at what point the government would strike back. When it comes to making a statement, there is nothing quite like putting one's body on the line. Many years ago, Schelling, in this connection, made a distinction between speech and "moves":

> Talk is not a substitute for moves. Moves can in some way alter the game, by incurring manifest costs, risks, or a reduced range of subsequent choice; they have an information content, or *evidence* content, of a different character from that of speech. Talk can be cheap when moves are not.
>
> (1960)

The moves made by the protesters at Tiananmen were forms of confrontation. They were reminiscent of the campus sit-ins and demonstrations at colleges and universities across the United States in the late 1960s. Some of the campus confrontations were fairly mild, whereas others were quite disruptive, but all of them sought to perform attention-getting, radicalizing, and delegitimizing functions through actions that combined verbal exhortations and pressure tactics.

The confronters joined in a deliberate violation of the institution's written and unwritten code of conduct, fastening on those taboos that symbolized what the protesters took to be the institution's false ideals and inequitable practices. Representatives of these institutions were thus presented with a king-sized dilemma. Suppression of the confrontation would belie the institution's appearance of liberality and feed the flames of protest. Yet permitting violations of the code would, in effect, sanction other violations and undermine the offices of authority and discipline in the institution. And so, after promising a fair hearing and pleading in vain for a return to more moderate tactics, the institution acted to check or suppress the violations and punish the violators, frequently breaking its own rules in the process. In this way, its representatives were able, temporarily, to contain the confrontation, but, in doing so, they "completed" the rhetorical act by revealing their own "ugliness" (Scott & Smith, 1969).

Cultural Politics

Brief attention was given in Chapter 3 to the role of the schools and the mass media in the shaping of ideologies. These, together with other "culture industries" such as the arts and organized religion, have always been sources of cultural influence, but groups seeking liberalization of social values (the "cultural left") and others resisting what they see as moral decay ("social conservatives") have in recent decades been engaged in what has often been chronicled as "culture wars" (Hartman, 2015). Multiculturalists, Afrocentrists, feminists, and others on the cultural left have sought to influence educational curricula. Social conservatives have formed counter-movements of their own, pressing in some cases for textbook censorship and in others for cutbacks in federal funding of the humanities. Some social conservatives have sought to restore America to what they allege was its former greatness, before school prayer was outlawed, for example, and before abortion was legalized by the Supreme Court (Bennett, 1995; Jones, 2012). In recent years they have pressed hard for greater ideological diversity in the university (Horowitz, 2009; Neal, 2007; Ambrose, 2014; Goldberg, 2014).

These ideological battles are fought out less in the streets than in behind-the-scenes meetings of museum boards, federal funding agencies, university administrators, mental health professionals, and network news managers and, more openly, via television and in classrooms, movie theaters, churches, mental health centers, and courts. In some women's studies classrooms, for example, a concerted attempt is made to "liberate" students from the intellectual and cultural domination of patriarchal (i.e., male-oriented) ideologies. Across the hall, a socially conservative professor of philosophy declaims against postmodernism, deconstruction, cultural relativism, and other intellectual challenges to Western culture's traditional faith in logic, objectivity, meaning, and scientific method. An Afrocentric college professor counsels high school educators on how they can increase the self-esteem of inner-city youth by instilling pride in their African roots. These are but skirmishes in today's cultural wars, but they illustrate within an academic setting what is meant by cultural politics. It is an attempt by all sides to influence ideological thought via institutions such as the schools that are not often thought of as vehicles for propagandizing. The methods include not just active proselytizing but control over what gets put before students in the way of textbooks, television viewers in the way of programming, and museum goers in the way of art exhibits.

SOCIAL PROTESTS AND MASS MEDIA

Although cultural politics is highly dependent on media entertainment and schools to get its message across, the more traditional confrontational politics of social movements relies principally on news and opinion coverage, and increasingly today, on the media capabilities of the Internet to reach a wide audience with dramatic, attention-getting footage (Jones, 2012).

Media attention may inspire new adherents to join a movement and prompt sympathizers to provide increased resources and support. The larger the movement and the bigger and more spectacular its demonstrations, the more media coverage it

FIGURE 14.2   *A 2014 Demonstration in Ferguson, Missouri, protesting police actions in the shooting of 18-year-old Michael Brown, shows the intersection of traditional media and social media. An elderly protester holds up a Twitter hash tag, hoping that the traditional media will advertise his message and thereby generate more social media participation. The source of the photo is NBC News, which demonstrates the effectiveness of his strategy.*

is likely to get, thus engendering further movement support. In this respect, at least, media attention provides benefits to social movements.

That said, social movements are changing dramatically since the advent of social media. Today, participants can engage in many functions with minimal financial cost and organizational limitations via the Internet. Issues important to all social movements—public outreach, funding, recruiting, educating members, and more—can be attended to through social media. Furthermore, social media "addresses these issues in important ways—users can transcend geographical borders and easily spread ideas and information" (*Identity in flux*, 2013). Finally, social media outreach can be almost instantaneous, offering speed and interactivity that were lacking in the traditional mobilization techniques like leaflets and posters (Eltantawy & Wiest, 2007). Consequently, new media options open the doors to global outreach for social movements, with all the benefits and disadvantages that come with that outreach potential. Steven Johnson calls this "liquid democracy", where traditional hierarchies and organizational practices are weakened as participation becomes fully open to all (2012).

The question is undecided, though, as to whether social media will be a good thing for social movement activism. When we are all "untethered individual Internet *users* instead of organizational *members*" of social movements, the organization can quickly fall into anarchy or simply fade away (Schradie, 2014). "In an era of hashtag activism, clicktivism, or whatever you want to call digital politics, it still takes some level of organization to create and sustain a movement, even an online movement" (Schradie, 2014). Ultimately, commitment and connection can be very weak when all that holds the group together is the Internet.

In addition, there is an inherent contradiction in a social movement's using a corporate platform like Facebook for its central function, "with all that this implies … but they continue to use them nevertheless" (Fominaya & Cox, 2014). How can a social movement critique corporate power when it is dependent on it? This issue of being co-opted by those in power is not new. For example, a number of years ago, one of your authors was in Mexico and became involved in a protest march as part of a teacher's strike. In a true moment of intercultural enlightenment, both the Mexican strikers and the American author came to consider how odd it is that protesters in the United States secure permits before having demonstrations or marches. "Why would you ask your government permission to walk on the public streets and exercise your right of freedom of speech in critique of that very same government?" asked the strikers. It was a good question indeed, and now it is complicated even further thanks to corporate social media communication necessities like Facebook and Twitter.

Finally, we must wonder about levels of commitment when a social movement is primarily engaged in activism via the Internet. Twitter hashtag campaigns such as #BlackLifeMatters, #BringBackOurGirls, and #AllMenCan sometimes work to "animate community-based action, political debate and state agency response" (Everett-Haynes, 2014). But it is also true that "managing to get a trending topic on

Twitter does not necessarily translate into people on the streets" (Fominaya & Cox, 2014). The problem becomes when a social movement uses social media participation as a "proxy for movement participation" (Fominaya & Cox, 2014).

Social movements will continue to sort out these issues as they move forward, benefiting surely from the ability of increased public access that the Internet provides while struggling with issues of participant commitment. All that said, social media, just like traditional media, are tools to be put to use, and in the midst of new and changing opportunities, the fundamentals of organizational persuasion still apply. It is to that we now turn.

LEADING SOCIAL MOVEMENTS: THE REQUIREMENTS-PROBLEMS-STRATEGIES (RPS) APPROACH

The following is Simons's framework for leading social movements or for analyzing their moves and speech as a rhetorical critic (Simons, 1970; see also Simons, 2001; Simons, Mechling & Schreier, 1984; Simons & Mechling, 1981). Its basic assumptions are these: (a) Any movement must fulfill the same functional requirements as more institutionalized collectivities. These imperatives constitute *rhetorical requirements* for the leadership of a movement. (b) Conflicts among requirements create *rhetorical problems,* which in turn affect (c) decisions on *rhetorical strategy.* The primary test of leaders, and ultimately of the strategies they employ, is their capacity to fulfill the requirements of their movement by removing or reducing rhetorical problems.

Requirements

The basic functional requirements of a social movement are an ability to acquire and mobilize human and material resources, to exert external influence, and to mount resistance to counter-pressures (see also Oberschall, 1995; Stewart, et al., 2007; Jones, 2012). These requirements are not unlike those facing leaders of institutionalized collectivities such as business or government. For example, the managers of Ford must recruit, hire, train, motivate, and deploy personnel, and they must likewise acquire and deploy material resources for the manufacture of their cars and trucks. Likewise, the leadership of social movements must recruit, motivate, and deploy activists; the leaders need also to acquire material resources (e.g., money). Just as Ford must market its vehicles (exert external influence) and beat back its competition (mount resistance to counter-pressures), so must the leaders of social movements promote their movement's cause and deal with opposition from countermovement (e.g., pro-life versus pro-choice) and from other groups that may regard the movement as a threat.

Problems

Social movements are severely restricted from fulfilling these requirements by dint of their internal strategies and their positions in relation to the larger society. By comparison with the heads of most formal organizations (e.g., Ford), the leaders of social movements can expect minimal internal control and maximal external resistance. Although business corporations may induce productivity through tangible rewards and punishments, social movements, as voluntary collectivities, must rely on ideological and social commitments. Existing outside the larger society's conceptions of justice and reality, moreover, movements threaten and are threatened by the society's sanctions and taboos: its laws; its maxims; its customs governing manners, decorum, and taste; and its insignia of authority. Shorn of the controls that characterize formal organizations yet required to perform the same internal functions, harassed from without yet obligated to adapt to the external system (i.e., called here the larger society), leaders of social movement must constantly balance inherently conflicting demands on their positions and on the movements they represent.

Many of the foregoing problems pose dilemmas for leaders. Among the demands on any organization are that its leaders maintain a system of accurate communication up and down the line, that they operate an efficient organization and that they act in a consistent and therefore predictable manner. But in a social movement, the need to speak truthfully must be balanced against the need to inspire members and to fend off attacks on the movement by outsiders. The need for organizational efficiency must be weighed against the demands of individual volunteers (few of whom can be coerced or paid) for personal gratification or for promotion of pet projects. The need for ideological consistency must be balanced against the need for pragmatic adaptations.

There is no simple way to mobilize volunteers for sustained efforts.

A spirited, energized membership is the strength of many voluntary campaigns, yet morale cannot be secured through abdications of leadership or of leadership tasks. Members may feel the need to participate in decision making, to undertake pet projects on their own initiative, to put down leaders or other followers, to obstruct meetings by socializing, or to disobey directives. The leadership cannot ignore these needs—especially today, when members are likely to be well educated, independent, and given to "doing their own thing." Still, they cannot accede to all of them, either.

Movements are as susceptible to fragmentation from within as they are to suppression from without. Within movement organizations, factional conflicts invariably develop over questions of values, strategy, tactics, or implementation. Purists and pragmatists clash over the merits of compromise. Academics and activists debate the necessity of long-range planning. Others enter the campaign with personal grievances or vested interests. Pre-existing groups that are known to have divergent ideological positions are nevertheless invited to join or affiliate with the campaign because of the power they can wield.

These and other differences may be reflected at the leadership level as well. Rarely can one campaign leader handle all the leadership roles and tasks of the campaign. Hence the need for a variety of leadership types: theoreticians and propagandists to launch the campaign, and political or bureaucratic leaders to carry it forward. There may also be cleavages between those vested with positions of authority in the campaign, those charismatic figures who have personal followings, those who have special competencies, and those who have private sources of funds or influence outside the campaign.

These internal problems were exhibited at Tiananmen Square. Within the enormous confines of the square, said leader Chai Ling, "Anyone could form an organization and change its leaders at will. Student leaders from various organizations formed territories and proclaimed themselves commanders." By Chai's count, one organization, the Beijing Autonomous Student Union, had experienced no fewer than 182 changes in its leadership (Human Rights in China, 1990; Schell, 1989).

Strategies

Because any strategy represents an attempt to meet incompatible requirements, none is ever fully satisfactory. Each, moreover, creates new rhetorical problems in the process of resolving old ones. This section first distinguishes between *moderate* and *militant* strategies, then identifies an *intermediate* strategy, and concludes with a brief examination of the *expressivist* approach.

Moderates and Militants

As applied to protests against institutional policies or practices, moderates are the embodiment of reason, civility, and decorum. They collect petitions, send telegrams to their congressional representatives, write books, picket and march peacefully, organize voting blocs, and file lawsuits. Exuding earnestness, charm, and an aura of competence, they get angry but do not shout, issue pamphlets but never manifestos, and inveigh against social mores but always in the value language of the social order. Their "devil" is a condition or a set of behaviors or an outcast group, never the persons they are seeking to influence. Those persons are assumed to be capable of "listening to reason."

To the extent that moderates are successful at garnering mass support for their positions, their actions might well threaten those in power and might thus constitute a type of combative persuasion, but their threats are generally muted or implied, and they always operate within limits prescribed by the system. For the most part, moderates seek to reduce the psychological distance between the movement and those outside it by speaking the listeners' language, adjusting to their frame of reference, and adapting to their needs, wants, and values.

If coactive persuaders assume or pretend to assume an ultimate identity of interests between the movement and its antagonists, militant combative persuaders act on the assumption of a fundamental clash of interests. In mixed-motive conflicts, each can lay claim to a part of the truth, and each can boast support from proud philosophical traditions. The moderate's commitment to coactive persuasion is rooted in the Greco-Roman democratic tradition, in Judeo-Christian conceptions of the brotherhood of man, in Emerson's faith in human educability, and in John Stuart Mill's conviction that truth will survive any open competition of ideas. Militants, by contrast, are inclined to be mistrustful of ordinary citizens or to assume that the systems they oppose are likely to be intractable. Like Karl Marx, they are apt to believe that the masses have lost sight of their "real" interests or that those in power are unlikely to surrender it willingly. Although Machiavelli wrote for princes and not for protesters, the militant is inclined to accept that writer's view of persuasion as an adjunct to force, rather than its alternative.

Thinking It Through

After reading the descriptions of moderates versus militants, think for a moment about which style fits for you. When you want to see serious change in a situation, which framework do you think you would most likely use?

This is not to say that militants offer no appeals to shared values. They do, indeed, but in ways that call into question other widely held values. In general, the militant tends to express greater degrees of dissatisfaction than the moderate (Stewart, et al., 2007). The moderate tends to ask "how" questions, whereas the militant asks "whether" questions. The moderate sees "inefficiencies" in existing practices, whereas the militant sees "inequities." The moderate might regard authority figures as "misguided" although "legitimate," whereas the militant tends to regard these same figures as "willfully self-serving" and "illegitimate." Both might pay homage to law, but the militant is more apt to derogate human laws in the name of "higher" laws. Thus, for example, some anti-abortionists have interpreted biblical writ as justification for bombings of abortion clinics.

The actions of militants are not all of a piece by any means. The practice of classic civil disobedience, for example, borders on being intermediate between militancy and moderation. To test the constitutionality of a law, that law is violated. The law in question is violated openly and non-violently, however; no other laws are breached in the process; the rights of innocent persons are not interfered with; and, if found guilty, the law violator willingly accepts punishment.

Contrast this strategy with acts that can more clearly be labeled combative in nature: strikes, riots, political bombings, and kidnappings—all the way to organized guerrilla warfare. By means of verbal polemics and direct action techniques, protesters who practice combative persuasion threaten, harass, cajole, disrupt, provoke, intimidate, and coerce. Although the aim of pressure tactics may be to punish directly (strikes and boycotts), more frequently, they are forms of "body rhetoric," designed to dramatize issues, enlist additional sympathizers, delegitimize the established order, and—except in truly revolutionary situations—force reconsideration of existing laws and practices or pave the way for negotiated settlements.

Indeed, even the most militant acts of protesters are likely to have rhetorical elements. At the least, militants must establish the credibility of their threats and alter their target's perceptions of what is expedient under the circumstances. Beyond that, their symbolic acts of force may well engender support from those outside the movement.

So different are the rhetorical conceptions of moderate and militant strategists that it strains the imagination to believe that both approaches may work. Yet the decisive changes wrought by militant rhetoric on the left and on the right in recent years give credence to the view that coactive persuasion is not the only alternative. What, then, in general terms are the strengths and limitations of moderate and militant approaches?

Militant tactics confer visibility on a movement; moderate tactics gain entry into decision centers. Because of their ethos of respectability, moderates are invited to participate in public deliberations (hearings, conferences, and negotiating sessions) even after militants have occasioned those deliberations by prolonged and self-debilitating acts of protest.

FIGURE 14.3   *Moderate tactics: Advocates testimony before Congress on the problem of school safety and bullying.*

FIGURE 14.4 *Militant tactics: Code Pink protesters shout at the Managing Director for Insurance Ratings at Standard & Poor's Rodney Clark (C) after he testified about the AIG before the House Financial Services Committee.*

For different reasons, both militants and moderates must be ambivalent about success and failure. Militants thrive on injustice and ineptitude displayed by their targets. Should the enemy fail to implement the movement's demands, militants find themselves vindicated ideologically, yet frustrated programmatically. Should some of the demands be met, they are in the paradoxical position of having to condemn them as palliatives. Moderates, by contrast, require tangible evidence that the larger structure is tractable to hold followers in line, yet too much success belies the movement's reason for being. Not uncommonly, militants and moderates escalate their demands when faced with the prospect of success, but this makes them vulnerable to charges of bad faith. Self-proclaimed militants can avoid this problem by demanding at the outset considerably more than the system is willing to provide, but, should self-proclaimed moderates do likewise, they invite charges of being "too militant."

Militant supporters are easily energized; moderate supporters are more easily controlled. Strong identification by members with the goals of a movement—however necessary to achieve *esprit de corps*—may foster the conviction that any means are justified and breed impatience with time-consuming tactics. The use of violence and other questionable means may be prompted further by restrictions on legitimate avenues of expression imposed by the larger structure. As a result, leaders may be required to mask the movement's true objectives, publicly disclaim the use of tactics they privately advocate, promise what they cannot deliver, exaggerate the strength of the movement, and so on. A vicious cycle develops in which militant tactics invite further suppression, which spurs the movement on to more extreme methods. Having aroused their following, however, the leaders of a militant movement may become victims of their own creation, unable to contain energies within prescribed limits or to guarantee their own tenure. Leaders of moderate groups frequently complain that their supporters are apathetic. As Turner and Killian (1957) have pointed out, "To the degree to which a movement incorporates only major sacred values its power will be diffused by a larger body of conspicuous lip-service adherents who cannot be depended upon for the work of the movement."

Militants are effective with **power-vulnerables**; moderates are effective with **power-invulnerables**; neither is effective with both. Targets of protest may be labeled as power-vulnerable to the degree to which (a) they hold possessions of value and therefore have something to lose (e.g., property, status, and high office), (b) they cannot escape from a source's pressure (unlike suburbanites, for example, who could escape, physically or psychologically, from the inner-city riots of the 1960s), and (c) they cannot retaliate against a source (either because of normative or physical constraints). Such targets as university presidents, church leaders, and elected government officials are highly vulnerable—especially if they profess to be "high-minded" or "liberal"—compared with the mass of citizens who may lack substantial possessions, be able to escape, or feel no constraints about retaliating. The latter are power-invulnerables.

As leaders of institutions allocate priorities in the face of conflicting pressures from other groups, they are unlikely to act on the programmatic suggestions of protest groups—even when they are sympathetic—unless pressured to do so. Hence, coactive strategies alone are likely to be ineffectual with them, whereas combative strategies should stand a better chance of modifying their attitudes. Combative strategies are likely to be less effective with power-invulnerables than are coactive strategies, and they might well invite backlash effects.

When the movement and the larger structure are already polarized, the dilemma is magnified. However much they may wish to plead reasonably, wresting changes from those in public positions requires that leaders build a sizable power base. To secure massive internal support, leaders must at least seem militant.

Intermediate Strategies

In choosing between coactive and combative strategies of persuasion, protest leaders face a series of dilemmas: Neither approach is likely to meet every rhetorical requirement or resolve every rhetorical problem; indeed, the introduction of either approach may create new problems.

So it is that the leadership of a protest movement may attempt to resolve or avoid the aforementioned dilemmas by employing *intermediate* strategies, admittedly a catchall term for those efforts that combine militant and moderate patterns of influence. Leaders may alternate between appeals to common ground and threats of punishment, or speaking softly in private and stridently at mass gatherings. They may form broadly based coalitions that submerge ideological differences or use speakers with similar values but contrasting styles. They may stand as "conservative radicals" or "radical conservatives," espousing extreme demands in the value language of the social order or militant slogans in behalf of moderate proposals. In defense of moderation, they may portray themselves as putting on the brakes to hold back more militant followers.

Intermediacy can be a dangerous game. Calculated to energize supporters, win over neutrals, pressure power-vulnerables, and mollify the opposition, it may end up antagonizing everyone. The carefully crafted phrase may easily appear as a devilish trick, the rationale as a rationalization, the tactful comment as an artless dodge. To the extent that strategies of intermediacy require studied ambiguity, insincerity, and even distortion, perhaps the leaders' greatest danger is that others will find out what they really think.

Still, some strategists manage to reconcile differences between militant and moderate approaches and not simply maneuver around them. They seem able to convince members of the established order that bad-tasting medicine is good for them, and they seem capable, too, of mobilizing a diverse collectivity within the movement.

The key, it appears, is the leaders' capacity to embody a higher wisdom, a more profound sense of justice: to stand above inconsistencies by articulating overarching principles. Few will contest the claim that the Reverend Martin Luther King Jr. epitomized the approach. Attracting both militants and moderates to his movement, he could win respect, even from his enemies, by reconciling the seemingly irreconcilable. The heart of the case for intermediacy was succinctly stated by the Reverend King himself:

> What is needed is a realization that power without love is reckless and abusive and love without power is sentimental and anemic. Power at its best is love implementing the demands of justice, and justice at its best is power correcting everything that stands against love.
>
> (Quoted in Simons, 1970)

The major protest movements of the 1960s all seemed to require combinations of militant and moderate approaches. Militants were counted on to dramatize the Vietnam issue, moderates to plead forcefully within inner circles. Threats of confrontation prompted city and state governments to finance the building of new schools in low-income areas, but it took reasonableness and civility to get experienced teachers to volunteer for work in those facilities. Demands by revolutionary student groups for transformations of university structures helped impel administrators to heed quasi-militant demands for a redistribution of university power. Support for the cause by moderate groups helped confer respectability on the movement. Thus, however much they might have warred among themselves, militants and moderates each performed important functions.

Expressivism

As indicated earlier, many people believe that neither militant nor moderate (nor intermediate) approaches to protest are realistic. Yet if asked whether they sought significant changes in society's institutions, they would probably respond affirmatively and might even label themselves "revolutionaries." Proponents of expressivism include many holistic health people, back-to-nature advocates, religious fundamentalists, and others concerned fundamentally with matters of lifestyle. Although the expressivist approach cannot be applied to all arenas of protest, its proponents offer a significant critique of conventional approaches to protest. Here is a summary of their position as it has been argued.

In their preoccupation with strategies of persuasion, militants and moderates are really barking up the wrong tree. Institutions do not change until people change, and people do not change as a result of the machinations of movement strategists. They change when an idea is ripe for the times, and when they have come to that idea as a result of direct personal experiences.

In point of fact, moderates and militants are really cut from the same cloth, and, most ironic, they are not very different from the social order they seek to change. Scratch at the source of our society's ills, and you will find a set of dehumanizing values that are also reflected in conventional protest groups. Like the society at large, moderate and militant leaders scheme, manipulate, and exploit—even their own followers. When they get caught up in their own manipulations, their only solution is to manipulate some more. Ultimately, it is a self-defeating mentality because in addition to dominating other people and the surrounding physical environment, protest leaders begin to think of their cause as a set of cold abstractions.

That is why expressivist lifestyle movements are truly revolutionary. Their target is not so much particular laws or practices but the values giving rise to society's institutions. Only when these values are changed can the institutions of society be changed. The alternative to conventional strategies, then, is an honest, unstructured, leaderless, non-manipulative exchange of ideas and feelings among people, as demonstrated, for example, by meditation groups among Eastern religionists. The issue is not simply one of compromising between the way of the moderate and the way of the militant, but a genuine alternative.

Case Study in Strategy: The Animal Rights Movement

The case study that follows includes three parts. Part I provides background on the animal rights movement. Part II argues that animal rights has achieved its greatest gains of late by eschewing militancy in favor of coalition building. Part III offers a rejoinder by Dr. Maxim Fetissenko, a vegan who fears that these gains may have made it less likely that the movement's long-term goals will be achieved. Parts II and III both focus on the example of Proposition 2 in California, a referendum on meat and dairy farming that passed with a whopping 63.5% of the vote.

Part I Background

Sympathy for the plight of abused animals goes back to biblical times, and arguments for and against vegetarianism have ancient origins that have been ongoing until today (Shapin, 2007). A society for the prevention of cruelty to animals preceded one to protect children, but its founders had dogs and cats in mind, not sea animals or primates or cattle (Pfohl, 1977). Scores of nature documentaries have since broadened opinions, as we now have evidence of whales that empathize and chimps that symbol use, of cuddly pandas in bamboo forests and pigs that solve problems. Today, the focus on animal cruelty and animal "rights" has become the subject of much study, discussion, and even legislation. One such instance involved the passage of California's Proposition 2 in November, 2008. Specifically, it required the following:

> ... that calves raised for veal, egg-laying hens and pregnant pigs be confined only in ways that allow these animals to lie down, stand up, fully extend their limbs and turn around freely. Exceptions made for transportation, rodeos, fairs, 4-H programs, lawful slaughter, research and veterinary purposes. Provides misdemeanor penalties, including a fine not to exceed $1,000 and/or imprisonment in jail for up to 180 days.

Part II Argument for the Success that Comes from Coalition Building

Corrective efforts in the areas of animal cruelty have generally met staunch opposition. For example, early attempts by animal rights organizations to subvert the use of animals in testing the safety of new drugs or in doing crash tests of new vehicles ran counter to concerns by many people about their own safety. Significantly, it has been the Humane Society of the United States (HSUS), normally as tame as the pets its donors look after, that took the first giant step toward abolishing the worst of the meat-farming practices. Its leader, Wayne Pacelle, hit upon a strategy, a referendum on meat farming in the bellwether state of California, with sufficient resources and support to see it pass (Jones, 2008). "Prop 2," as it was called, won majorities in 47 of 58 counties, including in many top agricultural and rural counties. The measure granted producers a phase-in period of more than six years to transition to more humane housing systems, and took effect on January 1, 2015 (Humane Society, 2013, Cheeseman, 2014).

Part III Critique of the "Success" that Comes from Coalition Building (by Dr. Maxim Fetissenko)

The passage of the Proposition 2 initiative with 63.5% of the vote has been described as a major victory by leading animal protection organizations, including Farm Sanctuary, HSUS, and People for the Ethical Treatment of Animals (PETA). An alternative view, to be presented here, is that the measure makes it *less* likely that the end goal of the animal rights movement—elimination of most, if not all, animal use by humans—will ever be achieved.

Proposition 2 mandated modest improvements in the conditions in which certain farm animals are kept. The efficacy of animal welfare regulations that have a negative impact on the bottom line of industrial farms has been uneven at best, and there are documented instances of USDA inspectors being fired from their jobs for overzealous enforcement of welfare laws, which means, for example, not looking the other way when animals are skinned while still alive and fully conscious. What *is* certain is that Proposition 2 will make consumption of animal products more palatable to the public's moral sensibilities—a result that runs counter to the stated goal of the measure's major supporters.

The ambivalence some animal rights advocates feel about Proposition 2 and similar reforms highlights the difficulty of achieving significant social change through persuasion. The success of ballot initiatives promoting improved conditions for farm animals confirms that people will legislate morality of others, but only so long as they don't have to give up anything of value to *them*. Thus, we can convince voters to demand that farmers improve conditions of their animals—as long as everyone still gets to eat those animals in the end. Well-off consumers will even pay extra money for the "certified humane" label on a package of meat. But how can we convince people to give up a behavior as popular and widespread as eating animal flesh, milk, and egg products? The answer may very well be that we cannot reach this goal at all—at least not in a matter of years or decades. Between 97% and 98% of Americans consume animal food products on a regular basis—a number far larger than the number of people deriving a direct benefit from any practice ever targeted by a social movement.

What about a shift to a more militant approach? Simons's **Requirements-Problems-Strategies (RPS) model** strongly cautions against such a shift. As this chapter suggests, militant tactics are effective against power-vulnerables, but have limited impact on power-invulnerables. Most consumers and purveyors of animal products fall into the latter category. Activists can use pickets and calls for boycott to convince a chain of clothing stores that it should stop carrying a product its consumers already regard as non-essential if not downright objectionable, such as animal furs. But those same activists would likely find no success if they picketed a supermarket selling animal meat or milk products. Ultimately, until a relatively large number of people are persuaded to embrace the idea that all sentient beings deserve equal consideration, and those same people change their individual behaviors accordingly, militant approaches will remain ineffective at best and counterproductive at worst.

This leaves us with the moderate approach to persuasion, the intermediate approach, and expressivism. The rate of success in turning people to veganism one meat-eater at a time is likely to remain small, even as the growing body of scientific research supports the claims that a vegan diet provides significant health benefits to humans while dramatically reducing environmental degradation. Either way, the change will remain slow, but, as has been suggested by the authors of this book, challenging the values and beliefs that give rise to society's institutions may sometimes be the most effective way of changing those institutions. In the case of the institution of animal slavery, it is, in all likelihood, the only way.

OPEN- AND CLOSED-MINDED MOVEMENTS

This chapter has told the story of a group with whom most readers could readily identify: the demonstrators at Tiananmen Square. Yet it is important to emphasize that social movements come in a variety of shapes and sizes and that some of them are downright ugly and more than a bit scary by most Americans' standards. Vladimir Lenin led a social movement; so did Adolf Hitler.

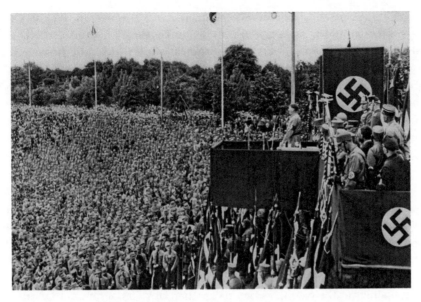

FIGURE 14.5 *Nazi Rally: Hitler speaking at Dortmund, 1933.*

FIGURE 14.6 *Martin Luther King Jr. speaking at the March on Washington, 1963.*

Protest leaders, even those of whom we approve, tend to appear most closed-minded at mass demonstrations, such as those shown in Figures 14.5 and 14.6. Still, there is a vast difference between spewers of hate, such as Adolf Hitler, and those such as the Reverend Martin Luther King Jr., who preached a doctrine of love. Moreover, King exhibited an openness to counter-arguments in his writings and in interviews with journalists—not so Adolf Hitler.

Religious cults are social movement organizations; so are right-wing militias. On the extreme right alone, one can find isolationist movements; hate groups that spew venom against blacks, Hispanics, Jews, Catholics, and immigrants of all types; and groups dedicated to bringing down government (Bennett, 1995; Domke & Coe, 2007; Wills, 1990). Timothy McVeigh, convicted and executed for the 1995 bombing of the Alfred P. Murrah Federal Building in Oklahoma City, was one such extremist; that bombing killed 168 people and shattered the lives of hundreds more. His bombing was eclipsed in its nightmarish consequences by the 9/11 Trade Tower bombings, and today the West grapples with Islamic extremist movements bent on destruction under the guise of their own vision of religious purity.

Depending on the examples one picks, then, it is easy enough to glorify social movements or to condemn them roundly. One's political sympathies will inevitably play a role in that as well.

Still, if there is one yardstick around which rhetoricians can unite in their judgment of social movements, it is open- versus closed-mindedness. Closed-minded movement organizations exhibit absolutistic, totalistic, and dogmatic thinking (Hart, 1984). Their ideological claims are offered as revealed truths and are thus presented impersonally and authoritatively. Rather than questioning these "truths," members are expected to swallow them whole and to compensate for gaps in their leaders' logic by supplying missing premises. Groups such as these are insular, xenophobic, and frequently paranoid. The world external to the movement is seen as sinister and threatening. Members, too, are seen as sinners or as prone to ideological backsliding, but there is the promise for members of redemption and salvation through acts of contrition and purification.

Clearly, not all movement groups exhibit these characteristics, not even those that one might be tempted to regard as radical or extreme. Whenever one is tempted to condemn all radicals or extremists, it is well to remember who made the American Revolution. Moderates, they were not!

THE FATE OF SOCIAL MOVEMENTS

The fate of social movement organizations varies considerably. Some ultimately achieve legitimacy in society; the once militant labor union movement in the United States is now the highly institutionalized AFL-CIO. Some movements are successful at promoting their causes; the more moderate the goal (better enforcement of traffic laws), the better the chances of success. Some movements achieve legitimacy *and* desired gains; some achieve neither (Gamson, 1990; Jones, 2012).

Militant movements have mixed effects when they engage in political activism. Typically they shore up a mainstream political party's base, but in the process they can also frighten and alienate the larger public. This happened in 1972 when a congeries of movement organizations—antiwar, civil rights, student protest and others—coalesced to become "The Movement," secured the Democratic Party nomination for their candidate, George McGovern, and then, in effect, handed an electoral landslide to the Republicans led by Richard Nixon (Simons, et al., 1973). A similar fate befell the Republicans in 1964 when Republican presidential candidate Barry Goldwater lost by a landslide after mobilizing his conservative base around a slogan proclaiming that "Extremism in defense of liberty is no vice ..."

But, among the apparent movement failures, there are often long-term positive effects. Undeveloped ideas become crystallized; new movement leaders learn from past leaders' mistakes; coalitions of kindred organizations find ways to pool their resources; publics grow accustomed to and come to accept once outlandish practices; technology makes possible solutions to problems that once seemed insurmountable; the time becomes ripe for the acceptance of previously objectionable ideas.

Often ignored are the effects, both symbolic and material, of one movement group on another. Militant groups help legitimize more moderate groups; Malcolm X's Nation of Islam did that for Martin Luther King Jr.'s Southern Christian Leadership Council. Then, the King-led civil rights movement went on to lend legitimacy to other "rights" struggles.

In other circumstances, distant movements serve as important role models. We only need to remember Martin Luther King's debts to Gandhi and Thoreau. Apparently, the students in Beijing were much influenced by revolutionary developments in Eastern Europe and by the freeing of the press in the Soviet Union. The events in turning back Soviet-style communism in turn provided a model for students in China, and the actions of the Chinese students went on to provide a model for students elsewhere in the world.

Today, Tiananmen Square is quiet, and not just because of the heavy police presence in the square. Students in Beijing today describe 1989 as "almost a historical blip, a moment too extreme and traumatic ever to repeat," said *New York Times* reporter Sharon LaFraniere (2009). When asked in an interview if students in China today might propose a pro-democracy protest, a Peking University history major responded that "People would think he was insane.... You know where the line is drawn. You can think, maybe talk, about the events of 1989. You just cannot do something that will have any public influence. Everybody knows that" (LaFraniere, 2009). For over two decades, China's government has made it abundantly clear that students and professors should stick to the books and stay out of the streets. But whether democracy still inspires them is a more complex question.

Interviews with students and teachers at Peking University, as well as with experts on China here and abroad, draw a layered portrait of today's students. They are disinclined to protest and many are disinterested in politics; they are more concerned with finding a job (Brown, 2014). A representative example is Zheng Xiaotao, who was born in 1989, the year of the protests. When interviewed concerning the twenty-fifth anniversary of the event in 2014, she said that she understands what happened. That said, she argues today that

> Tiananmen Square is in "the past, and the past is very far away from us. Our life is good now, so that I don't care about it at all. Twenty-five years ago, what the young people cared about was having enough food and keeping warm, whereas today we want to become stylish and show off our personalities."
>
> (Brown, 2014)

These young people have lived through an era of great change They are disturbed by government corruption and censorship and are still eager to study in the West, especially in the United States. That said, much like their American peers, they have other concerns, ones closer to their personal lives. Ultimately, many of China's young adults of today have decided to ignore what they label an "inconvenient" subject; they "have traded demands for political reform for greater economic freedom" (Brown, 2014).

Great movements of the past also live on in legends and myths that are invented anew by successive generations and in institutions and forms of action that are adapted to changed circumstances (McGee, 1977). One of the most tantalizing hypotheses in recent years is Timothy Garton Ash's (1999) conjecture that the peaceful revolutions of 1989 in countries formerly dominated by the Soviet Union have provided a formula of sorts for peaceful revolution. Says Ash, the 1989 model combines an absolute insistence on non-violence with the active, highly inventive use of mass civil disobedience, skillful appeals to Western media, public opinion, and governments, and a readiness to negotiate and compromise with the power-holders, while refusing to be co-opted by them.

He adds that, although this model has not been initiated in its entirety in other countries, it has had an enormous impact on the peaceful transition in South Africa, the tactics of Burmese opposition leader Aung San Suu Kyi, and the negotiations leading to peace in Northern Ireland.

Historically, opposition movements to police states, as in Burma, take generations to succeed, and then only with outside pressure and with chinks in the armor of the state, as was the case in Nepal. The fate of social movements depends as much or more on the forces of social control within a society as on the movements that seek to change it. Social control includes governments working to quell unrest by using mechanisms of socialization that persuade people to accept their situations in life; the goal is to find ways to give individuals the feeling that their lives have meaning and render them quiescent. Such socialization includes coercion and material inducements as well, but our main concern, of course, is persuasion. In Chapter 15 we focus on the ethics of persuasion by those in positions of social control: journalists, public officials, advertisers and PR professionals, religious and business leaders, and, not least, professors.

SUMMARY

This chapter has examined the rhetoric of social movements, such as the movement for democratization of China centered on Tiananmen Square in 1989. Social movements were defined as uninstitutionalized collectivities that operate on a sustained basis to exert external influence in behalf of a cause. Any given movement is likely to be coordinated by one or more social movement organizations (SMOs) and to include as well non-members of SMOs who identify with the cause and share a "we-consciousness."

Movements have been classified in myriad ways. For the purposes of this chapter we've distinguished among revolutionary, reformist, resistance, restorative, and expressivist movements, but have noted that these distinctions are muddied in practice by a movement's multiple strands and possible factionalization.

Examined here have been two main tactics of social movements: cultural politics and confrontation, the former fought out in "culture wars," the latter historically fought out in the streets and in the press (and these days, on the Internet). What Jaspars (1997) calls the "art of moral protest" is much in evidence today, particularly in its images presented via the media. Television remains the major vehicle for bringing attention to a movement's cause, with television and the other news media orchestrating how the movement will be perceived in the public's consciousness. The new media of the Internet enables movements to bypass these traditional media filters and exert considerable influence.

Featured in this chapter was Simons's Requirements-Problems-Strategies (RPS) framework for leading social movements or for analyzing its words and symbolic acts. Movements are required to perform the same essential functions as institutionalized collectivities, but are severely impeded from accomplishing them. Moreover, the strategies they employ generally create new problems in the process of resolving others.

Most strategies range on a continuum from moderate to militant. Moderates and militants differ in the degree to which they are willing to work within the system, the scope and intensity of the devils they attack, and the extent to which they rely on appeals to common ground or, on the other hand, find it necessary to bolster appeals and arguments with displays of power or delegitimizing techniques such as confrontation. Perhaps the fundamental difference between the two is in orientation. Although coactive persuaders assume or pretend to assume an ultimate identity of interests between the movement and its antagonists, militants act on the assumption of a fundamental clash of interests.

Choosing between moderate and militant approaches is far from easy. Militant tactics confer visibility on the movement and open the doors for negotiation, but it is the moderate who frequently gains entry into the actual negotiations. Militant supporters are easily energized; moderate supporters are more easily controlled. Militants are effective with power-vulnerables; moderates are effective with power-invulnerables; neither is effective with both. Some movements attempt to combine the attractive features of moderate and militant approaches by use of intermediate strategies. Other movements have looked askance at both moderate and militant approaches and have sought to develop alternative strategies that are essentially expressive in nature.

Tiananmen Square

Were the demonstrators at Tiananmen Square failures? In some respects, yes. Evidently, they were the targets of more government-initiated violence than they had bargained for. On the evening of June 3, 1989, the army moved tanks and troops onto the square and fired on demonstrators and bystanders. Hundreds, perhaps thousands, were killed.

Thus the demonstrators at Tiananmen were crushed, although not without resistance.

For a time, it appeared that in response to the massacre, the United States would deny China trade benefits. Periodically, this issue comes up, along with reports of human rights violations. But the prevailing view among government officials in the United States seems to be that maintaining China as a close trading partner does more for democracy in China than isolating it economically.

FIGURE 14.7 *The image of one lone protester blocking a parade of tanks became and remains today the symbol in the West for the Tiananmen Square protests.*

Meanwhile, many leaders of the pro-democracy movement in China were arrested, tried, convicted, and imprisoned under harsh living conditions, while others escaped to the West (Buruma, 1999).

Demonstrations commemorating the takeover of Tiananmen Square are forbidden in China, but it remains an inspiration to people everywhere, particularly among China's educated elite. Only time will tell whether it was truly a failure.

What is said and written about movements often reflects the politics of the movement analyst. Liberal and left-oriented intellectuals tend to view the movements they identify with as rational and the conservative and right-oriented movements they oppose as irrational forms of collective behavior. Conservative and right-oriented intellectuals do the reverse. Yet, in the West at least, intellectuals of all political colorations tend to prefer open-minded movements to **closed-minded movements**.

The fate of social movements can take many forms. The ideal outcome for their struggles is that the movement gains public support for their cause and acceptance for itself, leading to institutionalization. But, movements don't control their own fates and seldom achieve all that they have sought, at least not in one lifetime. Still, even "failed" movements can inspire others or provide much-needed lessons in how not to mobilize, or how not to attempt external influence, or how not to resist counter-influences. The animal rights movement was presented here as illustrative of how, over time, movement leaders overcame previous obstacles and achieved considerable gains over a relatively short period of time.

The main case study in this chapter has been the extraordinary struggle in 1989 for democracy in China, led by Chinese students in Beijing's Tiananmen Square. Was it a failure? To most outward appearances it is a historical blip in a story of economic and political liberalization in China that has come about not because of Tiananmen but despite it. But the story of China is an unfinished one. Collective memories change. Interpretations change. Fools become sages. Traitors are reconstructed as martyrs.

China has yet to have its own culture war over Tiananmen, but that day may come, and just as its earlier Cultural Revolution has been rethought, so, too, might the message of the students in Tiananmen Square. And, does what happened at Tiananmen have meaning for American students two decades later? Our answer is that we all might ponder the words of Professor Chen Mingyuan: "We are the masters of our country."

QUESTIONS AND PROJECTS FOR FURTHER STUDY

1   Read up on the movements of the 1960s. See, for example, Todd Gitlin's (1993) *The Sixties: Years of Hope, Days of Rage*. Why do you believe American campuses have been relatively free of protest demonstrations since the 1960s?

2   Find an example of what you would label a social movement, one that interests you. Analyze the rhetoric of a movement or movement leader using the RPS approach.

3   Consider that social movements often engage in "**media events**" such as large public rallies or protests that will generate media attention. Have there been any global media events since Tiananmen Square? What about American media events? What do such events do for a social movement, and why do they seems to be such a central part of the social movement arsenal?

4   Social movement groups vary from informal, grassroots undertakings to highly professionalized SMOs such as Amnesty International and the Sierra Club. Can you name other current movement organizations? Where do they fit on the continuum from grassroots to highly professionalized?

5   Analyze the confrontational tactics of militant groups like PETA and Greenpeace. What have been the effects of their more militant actions on power-vulnerables and power-invulnerables?

6   The Humane Society succeeded with Proposition 2 by forging an alliance between groups with differing interests and ideologies. But, according to Fetissenko, that success may ultimately undermine the long-term goals of the animal rights movement. Do you agree? Analyze the risks and rewards of coalition building by other groups on other issues.

7   Does what happened at Tiananmen have meaning for you today? Do you agree with Professor Chen Mingyuan: "We are the masters of our country"?

8   Working alone or with a group, develop a plan for a social movement you would start based on a concern you have about society and our world. Use the RPS model as your guide, and present your idea to the class.

KEY TERMS

- Closed-minded movements
- Expressivist movements
- Media event
- Power-invulnerables
- Power-vulnerables
- Reformist movements

- Requirements-Problems-Strategies (RPS) model
- Resistance movements
- Restorative movements
- Revolutionary movements
- Social movement

REFERENCES

Ambrose, J. (2014, December 28). *Universities need more conservatives*. Retrieved January 22, 2015, from DallasNews.com: www.dallasnews.com/opinion/latest-columns/20141228-jay-ambrose-universities-need-more-conservatives.ece

Ash, T. G. (1999, November 18). Ten years later. *New York Review of Books*, 46, 15–19.

Bennett, D. H. (1995). *The party of fear: The American far right from nativism to the militia movement* (rev. ed.). New York: Vintage.

Brown, A. (2014, June 4). *Tiananmen Square, 25 years later*. Retrieved January 22, 2015, from Aljazeera.com: www.aljazeera.com/indepth/features/2014/06/tiananmen-square-25-years-later-20146372348433611.html

Buruma, I. (1999, May 31). Tiananmen, Inc. *New Yorker*, 75, 45–52.

Cathcart, R. S. (1980). Defining movements by their rhetorical form. *Central States Speech Journal*, 31, 267–273.

Cheeseman, G. (2014, December 31). *California law banning confinement crates takes effect in 2015*. Retrieved January 22, 2015, from triplepundit.com: www.triplepundit.com/2014/12/california-law-banning-confinement-crates-takes-effect-2015/

Darnovsky, M., Epstein, B., & Flacks, R. (1995). *Cultural politics and social movements*. Philadelphia: Temple University Press.

De Luca, K. M. (1999). *Image politics: The new rhetoric of environmental activism*. New York: Guilford.

Domke, D., & Coe, K. (2007). *The God strategy: How religion became a political weapon in America*. New York: Oxford University Press.

Eltantawy, N., & Wiest, J. (2007). Social media in the Egyptian revolution: Reconsidering resource mobilization theory. *Journal of Communication*, 5, 1207–1224.

Everett-Haynes, L. (2014, September 23). *How new social movements take root* (University of Arizona, Producer). Retrieved January 25, 2015, from UANews.org: http://uanews.org/story/how-new-social-movements-take-root

Fominaya, C., & Cox, L. (2014, July 2014). *Protest and social movements: A sine qua non for democracy*. Retrieved January 25, 2015, from OpenDemocracy.net: www.opendemocracy.net/can-europe-make-it/cristina-flesher-fominaya-laurence-cox/protest-and-social-movements-sine-qua-non-

Gamson, W. (2004/1990). *The strategy of social protest* (2nd ed.). Belmont, CA: Wadsworth.

Gitlin, T. (1993). *The sixties: Years of hope, days of rage*. New York: Bantam.

Goldberg, J. (2014, February 21). *Attacking diversity of thought*. Retrieved January 22, 2015, from NationalReview.com: www.nationalreview.com/article/371625/attacking-diversity-thought-jonah-goldberg

Hart, R. P. (1984). The functions of human communication in the maintenance of public values. In Arnold, C. C., & Bowers, J. W. (eds), *Handbook of rhetorical and communication theory*. Boston: Allyn & Bacon, pp. 749–791.

Hartman, A. (2015). *A war for the soul of America: A history of the culture wars*. Chicago: University of Chicago Press.

Horowitz, D. (2009). *One party classroom: How radical professors at America's top colleges indoctrinate students and undermine democracy*. New York: Crown Publishing.

Human Rights in China (1990). *Children of the dragon: The story of Tiananmen Square*. New York: Collier.

Humane Society. (2013, August 30). *California court affirms Proposition 2's constitutionality: 2008 farm animal protection law remains on path to take effect in 2015*. Retrieved January 22, 2015, from HumaneSociety.org: www.humanesociety.org/news/press_releases/2013/08/california-court-affirms-prop2-083013.html

Identity in flux: Social media and social movements. (2013, July 9). Retrieved January 25, 2015, from Harmony-Institute.org: http://harmony-institute.org/therippleeffect/2013/07/09/identity-in-flux-social-media-and-social-movements/

Jaspars, J. M. (1997). *The art of moral protest*. Chicago: University of Chicago Press.

Johnson, S. (2012). *Future perfect: The case for progress in a networked age*. New York: Riverhead Books.

Jones, M. (2008, October 24). The barnyard strategist. *New York Times Magazine*. Retrieved November 1, 2009, from http://www.nytimes.com/2008/10/26/magazine/26animal-t.html.

Jones, V. (2012). *Rebuild the dream*. New York: Nation Books.

LaFraniere, S. (2009, May 21) Tiananmen now seems distant to China's students. *New York Times*. Retrieved November 1, 2009, from www.ny times.com/2009/05/22/world/asia/22tiananmen.html

Le Bon, G. (1896). *Psychologie des foules* [Psychology of crowds]. Paris: Alcan.

Lu, X. and Simons, H.W. (2006), Transitional rhetoric of Communist Party leaders in the post-Mao reform period: Dilemmas and strategies, *Quarterly Journal of Speech*, 92(3), 262–268.

McGee, M. C. (1977). The fall of Wellington: A case study of the relationship between theory, practice, and rhetoric in history. *Quarterly Journal of Speech*, 63, 28–42.

McGee, M. C. (1980) "Social movement": Phenomenon or meaning? *Central States Speech Journal*, 31, 233–244.

Neal, A. D. (2007, February 27). Testimony before the Higher Education Committee, Missouri House of Representatives February 27, 2007—Jefferson City, Missouri. Retrieved November 1, 2009, from www.goacta.org/publications/downloads/NealMissouri Testimony2-27-07.pdf

Oberschall, A. (1995). *Social movements: Ideologies, interest, and identities*. New Brunswick, NJ: Transaction.

Pfohl, S. J. (1977). The "discovery" of child abuse. *Social Problems*, 24(3), 310–323.

Schell, O. (1989, June 29). China's spring. *New York Review of Books*, 36, 3–7.

Schelling, T. C. (1960). *The strategy of conflict*. Cambridge, MA: Harvard University Press.

Schradie, J. (2014, November 3). *Bringing the organization back in: Social media and social movements*. (B. J. Sociology, Producer) Retrieved January 25, 2015, from BerkeleyJournal.org: http://berkeleyjournal.org/2014/11/bringing-the-organization-back-in-social-media-and-social-movements/

Scott, R. L., & Smith, D. K. (1969). The rhetoric of confrontation. *Quarterly Journal of Speech*, 55, 1–8.

Shapin, S. (2007, January 22) Vegetable love: The history of vegetarianism. *New Yorker*. Retrieved November 1, 2009, from www.newyorker.com/printables/critics/070122crbo_books_shapin

Simons, H. W. (1970). Requirements, problems, strategies: A theory of persuasion for social movements. *Quarterly Journal of Speech*, 56, 1–11.

Simons, H. W. (2001). Social movements. In Sloane, T. (ed.), *Oxford encyclopedia of rhetoric*. New York: Oxford University Press, pp. 724–732.

Simons, H. W., & Mechling, E. (1981). Political movements. In Nimmo, D., & Sanders, K. (eds), *Handbook of political communication*. Beverly Hills: Sage Publications, pp. 417–444.

Simons, H. W., Chesebro, J., & Orr, C. J. (1973). A "movement" perspective on the 1972 presidential election. *Quarterly Journal of Speech*, 59, 168–179.

Simons, H. W., Mechling, E. A., & Schreier, H. N. (1984). Functions of communication in mobilizing for collective action from the bottom up: The rhetoric of social movements. In Arnold, C. C., and Bowers, J. W. (eds), *Handbook of rhetorical and communication theory*. Boston: Allyn & Bacon, pp. 792–868.

Stewart, C. J., Smith, C. A., & Denton, R. E., Jr. (2007). *Persuasion and social movements* (5th ed.). Prospect Heights, IL: Waveland.

Tilly, C. (1979). Repertoires of contention in America and Britain, 1750–1830. In Zald, M. N., & McCarthy, J. D. (eds), *The dynamics of social movements*. Cambridge, MA: Winthrop.

Turner, R. H., & Killian, L. W. (1957). *Collective behavior*. Englewood Cliffs, NJ: Prentice Hall.

Wills, G. (1990). *Under God: Religion and American politics*. New York: Simon and Shuster 1990. (Reprinted 2007)

CHAPTER 15

More about Ethics

Questions of ethics are complicated and frustrating—no right or wrong answers, except when *we* feel wronged or believe we have been witness to unspeakable evils committed against others. We are appalled by female genital mutilation in Senegal, human rights abuses in China, and ethnic cleansing in Nigeria. We feel shock and disdain over child abuse, brainwashing of cult members, and questionable elections here at home. Then ethics become crystal clear—too clear, perhaps, because our moral certainties can blind us to complexities that need to be taken into account.

This book has identified many such complexities, deliberately muddying the waters. Well-told stories can give us examples of the truth. But they also can create falsehoods. Persuasion operates under conditions of uncertainty, time constraints, and limited information. Not surprisingly, therefore, so-called experts give contradictory advice. Highly educated people commit logical fallacies. All people—educated or not—use cognitive shortcuts. If truth is elusive—if, on some issues there seems to be no truth or no single, over-riding truth—why not lie, evade, exaggerate, or simply choose language or visuals or non-verbals that will play up your version of the truth and downplay your opponent's?

All people deceive, and some professions seem to make a virtue of it. Recall Robert Jackall's take on public relations. In that world, he said, "There is no such thing as a notion of truth; there are only stories, perspectives, or opinions" (2010). Jackall adds that in the world of public relations, as long as a story is based in the facts, it does not matter if it is "true." We can feel free to arrange these facts in a variety of ways and to put interpretations on them that suit our objectives, because "interpretations and judgments are always completely relative." The only thing limiting this process is plausibility, and insofar as it has any meaning at all, truth is what is perceived (Jackall, 2010).

Jackall's description has much in common with the critique Plato made about rhetoric generally: truth is held hostage as persuaders make the worse argument appear to be the better argument in order to achieve their goals. Thus, any study of rhetoric must confront directly the issue of the ethics of persuasion: Is persuasion inherently an unethical activity? If not, what are the ethical boundaries for the practice of persuasion?

The ancient Sophists would feel some connection to the view Jackall presents, but, being masters of rhetoric, they no doubt would have put a different spin on it. "Yes," today's sophist would declare—whether lawyer, product advertiser, political candidate, or PR professional. They would argue that they put spin on their stories, but then suggest that they are really no different in that respect from journalists, textbook writers, teachers, scientists. Don't we all provide our interpretation of situations? Isn't it the case that we all use rhetoric every day? And doesn't this even include ordinary people doing what they can to do good?

So yet again, we see that ethical questions in persuasion are often quite complicated, and this closing chapter is not about to resolve them. What it can do— what it will do—is offer some systematic ways of thinking about the issues. This chapter's focus is on institutional ethics, as opposed to private, purely personal ethics. It concerns institutional "actors" of various kinds—e.g., educators, drug manufacturers, medical researchers, business leaders, journalists, government officials—whose difficult decisions impact us as students, patients, consumers, citizens, and the like. We say "difficult" because institutional decisions tend to have far greater consequences than those of private individuals and tend also to be highly dilemma laden. We begin with the university as a site of ethical controversy.

THE ETHICS OF FACULTY ADVOCACY IN THE COLLEGE CLASSROOM

We educators don't usually talk about it in public, but we often struggle with the question of whether and when to take and defend positions on controversial issues in the classroom. Should we advocate for a side, or should we strive to appear neutral or impartial? If the former, can we advocate without intimidating or otherwise penalizing our students for their dissenting views? If the latter, can we be genuinely neutral, or will we wittingly or unwittingly smuggle in our biases by way of the questions we raise, the readings we assign, the videos we show, the assumptions we take for granted? Even assuming the possibility of appearing neutral, is it a good thing? Mightn't students benefit from our greater knowledge of the issues, our expertise as arguers, and our ability to serve as rhetorical role models? Contrariwise, even assuming the possibility of responsible and nurturing faculty advocacy, might not students benefit more by being forced to do the advocating for a side themselves? It is to those questions we now turn.

Case Study 1 Life and Liberty

Too often these issues are discussed by faculty out of earshot of their students. One of the authors of this book, Herb Simons, vividly recalls one such discussion following the showing of a video entitled *Life and Liberty for All Who Believe* at a conference of academics and journalists on the topic of the 1984 presidential election contest. The documentary is a hard-hitting critique of the religious right in the United States in the 1970s and early 1980s, complete with damning footage of leading ministers, indoctrination campaigns, censorship efforts, a book-burning ceremony, and a behind-the-scenes look at the workings of political operatives trying to promote conservative candidates. Herb was much moved by the documentary critique and decided then and there to get a copy. Still, he was unsure about how to present it to his students and even whether to show it, so he decided to ask the opinions of those who were present at the conference. Little did he anticipate the passions his question would arouse.

"A professor's job is to profess," said one professor. "A professor's job is to educate, not advocate," said another. "Your job is to teach students how to think, not what to think," said a third. "That's an indefensible distinction," said a fourth. "Criticize the video, not the religious right," said a fifth. Several in the group

FIGURE 15.1   *Jerry Falwell, founder of the Moral Majority.*
© AP Images

suggested castigating the film-maker for putting out what they considered such a one-sided, propagandistic film.

Amid all the controversy there was no doubting that *Life and Liberty* was one-sided. It certainly did not present the religious right favorably. Visuals appeared to have been selected for their damaging effect. A televangelist was captured on camera having his makeup put on, and was later shown in close-up spitting into a microphone as he thundered at his audience. Word selection seemed similarly calculated to reflect poorly on the religious right. That said, the religious right was powerful in America in that era and was seeking and gaining a strong voice in American politics and policy. Should students not be educated about the growing influence of religion in our political life?

Thinking It Through

If you were the instructor of a class on persuasion, how would you teach *Life and Liberty*, assuming you would show it at all? How, if at all, would you teach other, more recent documentaries, such as *Jesus Camp, Food Inc.* and *Capitalism, A Love Story*?

Case Study 2 NCA Town Meeting on the "Politics of Pedagogy"

Fast forward two decades to the post-9/11 era, with its "war on terror," its wars in Iraq and Afghanistan, and its political war over these wars here at home. On the stage of the Hilton Chicago's Grand Ballroom is a panel of faculty, selected for their expertise and their ideological diversity by the National Communication Association Forum (NCA-F). Questions about faculty advocacy have never been easy but the problems mount as topics like religion and politics, torture and terrorism, war and peace, engage professors' sense of obligation to speak out in the classroom, coupled with the sense that it is precisely at these moments when faculty are most in danger of going over the top. Yet leaving matters in students' hands may not be the solution either, some argue. How, wonders one panelist, can they be expected to choose sensibly among definitions of terms like terrorism and torture when the terms have been so thoroughly politicized?

Thinking It Through

At the NCA-F meeting, quarrels over meaning extended to "advocacy" and "pedagogical neutrality." What did these words about words entail?

Case Study 3 Professor Stanley Fish's Op-Eds on Faculty Advocacy

Nothing better illustrates the ethical conundrums in the faculty advocacy controversy than the seemingly contradictory op-eds on the matter by one of America's most distinguished professors, Stanley Fish. For the most part, Fish stands with those who believe faculty should refrain from classroom advocacy. "Academics," he repeatedly maintains, "are obligated to (1) introduce students to new knowledge and (2) equip students with sound analytical and other methodological skills, *'and that's it.'* " This, he says, "is the job they were trained and paid to do." His arguments for this position in *The New York Times*, including rejoinders to his critics, are collected in a book appropriately titled *Save the World on Your Own Time* (Fish, 2008). They include the following:

- The moment an instructor tries to do something more, he or she has crossed a line and ventured into territory that belongs properly to some other enterprise. It doesn't matter whether the line is crossed by someone on the left who wants to enroll students in a progressive agenda dedicated to the redress of injustice, or by someone on the right who is concerned that students be taught to be patriotic, God-fearing, family-oriented, and respectful of tradition. To be sure, the redress of injustice and the inculcation of patriotic and family values are worthy activities, but they are not academic activities. Academics are not legislators, or political leaders or therapists or ministers; they are academics, and as academics they have contracted to do only one thing—to discuss whatever subject is introduced into the classroom in academic terms.

- This does not mean that political and moral questions are banned from the classroom, but that they should be regarded as objects of study. No subject is out of bounds; what is out of bounds is using it as an occasion to move students in some political or ideological direction.

- Of course the teacher who doesn't think to declare his or her ethical preferences because it is not part of the job description might well be very active and vocal at a political rally or in a letter to an editor. Fish is not counseling moral and political abstinence across the board, only in those contexts—like the classroom—where the taking of positions on a war in the Middle East or assisted suicide or the conduct of foreign policy is extraneous to the course topic.

- Asked whether silence in the classroom in the face of evil is morally irresponsible, Fish responds that his stance is aggressively ethical:

  It demands that we take the ethics of the classroom—everything that belongs to pedagogy including preparation, giving assignments, grading papers, keeping discussions on point, etc.—seriously and not allow the scene of instruction to become a scene of indoctrination. Were the ethics appropriate to the classroom no different from the ethics appropriate to the arena of political action or the ethics of democratic citizenry, there would be nothing distinctive about the academic experience—it would be politics by another name—and no reason for anyone to support the enterprise. For if its politics you want, you might as well get right to it and skip the entire academic apparatus entirely.

(Fish, 2008)

- Contrary to those who maintain that silence of this sort is impossible, Fish declares, "it's really quite easy, a piece of cake" (Fish, 2008).

We've said that Stanley Fish's positions on issues of faculty advocacy appear to us to be contradictory. Thus far his arguments hang together admirably. But consider another blog by Stanley Fish (2007), this one reflective of his longstanding sophistic view that humans are rhetorical animals, incapable of analysis or expression that is not partisan, or, as he's put it, "partisan angled" (Fish, 1989). Says Fish, "Open-mindedness, far from being a virtue, is a condition which, if it could be achieved, would result in a mind that was spectacularly empty. An open mind is an empty mind" (Fish, 2007). Fish concludes:

Spin—the pronouncing on things from an interested angle—is not a regrettable and avoidable form of suspect thinking and judging; it is the very content of thinking and judging. No spin means no thought, no politics, no debating of what is true and what is false. The dream of improving mankind through a program of linguistic reform—a dream that dies hard and probably never will die—looks forward to a world in which everything is always and already "unspun." There is such a world; it is sometimes called heaven and it is sometimes called death. It is never called human.

(Fish, 2007)

Let us now connect the dots. It appears to us that Fish's call for non-partisanship in the classroom ("Fish One") is at odds with his position on *spin* ("Fish Two"). Fish the sophist says non-partisanship is impossible, spin inevitable. By this account, faculty, being human, cannot *not* spin; cannot *not* serve as advocates whether inside the classroom or out. Trying to do otherwise doesn't work any more than trying to be open-minded does, and, according to Fish, minds are never open; indeed, cannot be open.

Thinking It Through

Are you ready to swim with the "school of Fish"? If so, which one? If we believe the Stanley Fish who wrote the May 6, 2007, blog, can we also believe his case against faculty advocacy in the classroom? Is there a middle ground?

Case Study 4 Reed College Debate

Step outside the university classroom and you will quickly find any of a number of sites where broader ethical questions about the politics of pedagogy find expression. Inside the Administration Building the President is meeting with the Board of Trustees to discuss whether to mandate an "Academic Bill of Rights" for students, protecting their freedom to speak their minds in the classroom without fear of punishment. Also on their agenda is whether to establish professorships in conservative thought as a counter-balance to the left's alleged dominance in the university classroom. In another meeting room, a committee of students and faculty is planning to use limited funds for a university forum on terrorism with a view toward inviting a representative group of expert panelists. On the steps of the "Admin" building, students are protesting the threatened removal of a popular tenured professor. Over at the Student Activities Center, the question of removal is the occasion for a televised debate: Is faculty academic freedom an unlimited right or should faculty be disciplined and perhaps removed from their positions for plagiarism, sexual misconduct or—more to the point of this chapter—for crossing any of a number of lines: championing Muslim extremism, for example, suggesting that the bombings of the Trade Towers on 9/11 may have been an inside CIA job designed to mobilize support for war, or denying the Holocaust? All of these issues have been incendiary, occasioning media attention, and, in some cases, leading to removal of an offending faculty member. Nearly everyone endorses the view that faculty should have academic freedom of some sort, but what about students? At the center of many of these storms has been the peripatetic former leftist, David Horowitz.

David Horowitz has crisscrossed the country taking his case to college campuses and to state legislatures for his Academic Bill of Rights (ABR), designed, he says, to protect students from predominately liberal, left-oriented faculty, many of whom deviate from their assigned subject matter, using the classroom instead as a platform to indoctrinate, **proselytize**, and in some cases impose their views, punishing those who dare to dissent. On this occasion, August 28, 2006, he was at Oregon's Reed College in a public debate with Reed's Dean of Liberal Arts, Peter Steinberger. (See this book's website for a transcript of the debate.)

> *Thinking It Through*
>
> Should Horowitz's Academic Bill of Rights be adopted by more colleges and universities? Should they also hire and tenure more conservative faculty?

Putting It Together

As illustrated in these case studies, certain ethical issues reappear in debates about faculty advocacy. One of them is the *relevance* of what is taught to the course topic. There is general agreement that professors should *not* be spending class time advancing views that are irrelevant to the subjects they are hired to teach. But what counts as relevant prompts disagreement. Should torture and terrorism be matters of concern in a religion course?

Another concern is *power* that instructors have owing to their position. Instructors not only have the capacity to assign high or low grades but also can reward with high praise or punish by intimidation. They also are in a position to recommend students for scholarships, honors, and awards. What effect does this have on the ability of students to think independently and express their own views?

This raises a third consideration: What is taken as established fact, and what is a matter for legitimate discussion and criticism? For centuries Shakespeare enjoyed an exalted place atop the canon of great literature. As such his plays and poetry became required reading in college literature courses. These days Shakespeare is no longer exempt from the debate. Yale literary critic Harold Bloom engaged it in full with the publication of his book *The Western Canon* (1995). He wrote the book, he said, to beat back what he called "The School of Resentment" which included "Feminists, Historicists, Deconstructionists, and Afrocentrists, among others, all of whom wished to widen the canon so as to include works of the oppressed: blacks, Hispanics, and women" (Bloom, 1995). Bloom's case for including Shakespeare in the canon, as opposed, say, to Toni Morrison, could not be proven objectively, as he well knew; it represented his best judgment, as did the case for expanding the canon to include writers such as Morrison. Is it ethical for a professor to argue that one author's literary work is better than another? Should they then be entitled to grade students on how well they have internalized the professor's wisdom?

Let's consider an even more delicate subject. Let's apply our issues about Shakespeare and the canon to issues of religion. What about the religion professor who promotes or privileges Christianity? After all, aren't most Americans Christians, and isn't it appropriate to promote the nationally dominant religious perspective in an American religion course?

A fourth concern: Should professors refrain from knowingly *causing offense* to their students? Some students would be offended at hearing Christianity extolled over their own religion's views. A few students might, for religious or other reasons, strongly oppose genetic engineering, at least as used on human beings. How can concerns about causing offense be balanced against the need to provoke thought and perhaps overcome prejudices?

A fifth consideration is *manner of promotion.* For reasons to be discussed, some ethicists believe that professors should, where relevant, take and defend controversial positions in the classroom, even at the risk of causing offense. But they insist that professors should not do so in a one-sided, dogmatic manner. Rather, they should provide full and fair background on the controversy, including presentation (or assigned readings) of opposing positions. Only then should they profess, but even then they are obligated not to impose their views, not to reward conformity, not to preach or proselytize, and not to intimidate or otherwise coerce. Their positions need to be defended, not just pronounced from on high, and they need to subject their arguments to student criticisms (Brand, 1996; Menand, 1996; Newton, 2003). Let's call this position **limited faculty advocacy**.

A sixth concern is *cultural context*. Some educators maintain the right—indeed the obligation—to correct prevailing biases in a society under two conditions: (1) if the biases are oppressive to minorities or injurious to the society as a whole, and (2) if the corrective view is relatively unpopular and thus isn't as likely to be heard outside the classroom (Giroux, 1988). Let's call this **liberatory faculty advocacy**. Among those endorsing the *liberatory* position are women's advocates who believe that feminist teachings are a necessary corrective to what they regard as our culture's male-dominated ideology (e.g., Sowards & Renegar, 2004), and Afrocentrists and multiculturalists who believe Eurocentrism has been a force for cultural colonialism (e.g., Bizzell, 1991; Giroux, 2003; Moglen, 1996). Liberatory activists act on the basis of the belief that, historically, European social, cultural, and moral ideals have exerted total power (*hegemony*) over other possible alternatives.

But the liberatory, **counter-hegemonic position** is itself highly controversial. Critics such as David Horowitz charge that universities have run amok; that they have become overly politicized by militant feminists and other left-wing professors who have been using the academic classroom as a platform to spout their causes (Himmelfarb, 1996; Horowitz, 2006, 2007, 2009; Kimball, 2005; Newfield, 2008). Some left-oriented professors have joined in the critique of counter-hegemonic political correctness. Said Donald Lazere:

> My own political leanings are toward democratic socialism, and I believe that college English courses have a responsibility to expose students to socialist viewpoints because these views are virtually excluded from all other realms of the American cognitive, rhetorical, semantic, and literary universe of discourse. I am firmly opposed, however, to instructors imposing socialist (or feminist, or Third-World, or gay) ideology on students as the one true faith—just as much as I am opposed to the present, generally unquestioned (and even unconscious) imposition of capitalist, white-male, heterosexual ideology that pervades American education and every other aspect of our culture.
>
> (1992)

The controversy over faculty advocacy in the classroom has generated considerable debate among academics in recent years. Some activists argue that faculty advocacy is not only desirable (Giroux, 2003, 2006, 2012; Giroux et al., 2014), but that on controversial issues professors cannot help projecting their views by the readings they assign, the lectures they present, and the manner in which they conduct class discussions. Critics of this view maintain that it is at least possible to project the appearance of evenhandedness. Some go further and argue that objectivity is possible; moreover, it is the job of the professor, some argue, to teach students *how* to think, not *what* to think.

Pedagogical Talk About Pedagogical Talk and the College Experience

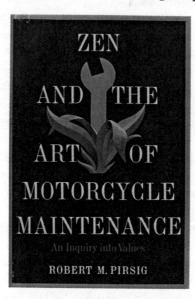

FIGURE 15.2 *Pirsig's classic book, which is less about motorcycles than it is about rhetoric and how the concept of rhetoric relates to "quality," is a must-read for any student of persuasion.*

Given the discussion here about ethics in the classroom, have you ever thought deeply about your education and your ethical stance when it comes to higher education? One man did, and his ideas are part of what is now considered a classic modern American novel: *Zen and the Art of Motorcycle Maintenance.*

Robert Pirsig describes below a classroom writing exercise that shows the persuasive power of *framing* and of *pedagogical talk about pedagogical talk.* One can only imagine what his students thought as they sat in writing class, expecting to be instructed in technique and grammar, to then find themselves in a situation that used persuasive discourse to cause them to think about the ethical attitudes that provided the framework for their behaviors as college students.

In the novel, Pirsig explains that he had been a professor at a state university in Montana. He had taught rhetoric, mostly in freshman writing courses, and, during his weeks on the motorcycle trip recounted in the book, he remembers the time he had spent engaged in this work. He reflects on the fact that, during the years when he worked as a professor, he consistently struggled to develop ideas for his classes that would help his students develop as writers.

Pirsig concluded that he needed to demonstrate the writing process in action, and so, on the chalkboard in front of his class over a number of weeks he wrote a persuasive essay. The topic of his essay was unusual: He sought to persuade his college-student audience that grades and evaluation in college should be eliminated.

Pirsig framed his argument by presenting an imaginary student, one who was "completely conditioned to work for a grade rather than for the knowledge the grade was supposed to represent" (Pirsig, 2000). The student would go to classes at first, but, since there were no grades, he would fail to turn in some assignments. There would be no penalty for this, and soon he found he'd fallen behind in the class and had difficulty understanding the lectures. Eventually, he stopped attending classes altogether, again with no penalty.

It is at this point that Pirsig's demonstrator essay made its persuasive point:

The student, with no hard feelings on anybody's part, would have flunked himself out. Good! This is what should have happened. He wasn't there for a real education in the first place and had no real business there at all. A large amount of money and effort had been saved and there would be no stigma of failure and ruin to haunt him the rest of his life. No bridges had been burned.

The student's biggest problem was a slave mentality which had been built into him by years of carrot-and-whip grading, a mule mentality which said, "If you don't whip me, I won't work." He didn't get whipped. He didn't work. And the cart of civilization, which he supposedly was being trained to pull, was just going to have to creak along a little slower without him.

(Pirsig, 2000)

Pirsig's essay was not yet complete, though, and it ended on a positive note. After quitting college, the imaginary student went to work as a mechanic. As time passed, he found that he was bored with the work, but he also learned that he was interested in mechanical engineering.

So he would come back to our degreeless and gradeless school, but with a difference. He'd no longer be a grade-motivated person. He'd be a knowledge-motivated person. He would need no external pushing to learn. His push would come from inside. He'd be a free man. He wouldn't need a lot of discipline to shape him up. In fact, if the instructors assigned to him were slacking on the job, he would be likely to shape them up by asking rude questions. He'd be there to learn something, would be paying to learn something and they'd better come up with it (Pirsig, 2000).

Consider:

- What do you make of Pirsig's ethics? Has he crossed an ethical line, where he is pushing an agenda rather than covering the material?

- What do you make of Pirsig's argument? Do you find it persuasive? What if there were no grades in college?

- What do you make of Pirsig's pedagogy? Do you find his pedagogical talk about pedagogical talk effective? How would you have responded to all of this if you'd been a student in his class?

ETHICALLY PROBLEMATIC FORMS AND STYLES OF PERSUASION

Persuasion, we have said, deals in matters of judgment rather than certainties. Says political theorist Bryan Garsten (2006), societies function best when they rely primarily on persuasion rather than force, and when the forms and styles of persuasion to which citizens are exposed foster informed, independent judgments on such practical matters as whom to vote for or which policy option to support. The kinds of judgments Garsten has in mind were exemplified in Chapter 1 by the junior high school students who decided after a debate on whether to "impeach" their school that it wasn't so bad after all. Minds were changed, some reluctantly, and it's a fair bet that the students came out of the experience with increased respect for the give-and-take of debate and with increased willingness to submit to the collective judgment of the group. On this day the classroom had become a democratic society in miniature.

It stands to reason, then, that forms and styles of persuasion that warp judgment are ethically questionable. But for these same reasons, societies reliant on persuasion to yield informed, independent political judgments are easily subverted. Says Garsten, judgment making "is an uncertain, ambiguous and fallible activity, easy to manipulate and prone to collapse into either dogmatic self-assertion or deferential submission. A politics of persuasion carries within it the potential to quickly slide into destructive forms of controversy" (2006).

The same is true of other societal institutions such as the church, the schools, the media, business, the health professions, and even the government regulatory agencies purportedly designed to protect us from the chicanery of others.

In previous chapters we identified many forms of persuasion that by Garsten's standard would have to be considered ethically questionable, or worse. They include propaganda, "brainwashing," subliminal persuasion, other forms of non-conscious or barely conscious influences such as priming in advertising, persuasion combined with other forms of influence in indoctrination campaigns, and the subversion of Cialdini's (2009) cognitive shorthands.

We will discuss in this section three forms of ethically problematic persuasion: demagoguery, duplicity, and perception management.

Demagoguery

Journalist H. L. Mencken said of the demagogue that he "preaches doctrines he knows to be untrue to men he knows to be idiots." Garsten has argued that the demagogue needn't be false to his or her beliefs. Hitler is a commonly used example of a demagogue but one who apparently believed his own anti-Jewish diatribes.

Still, demagoguery is most evident when the communicator self-indicts. David Horowitz's rhetoric again provides an example. At the Reed College debate between

Peter Steinberger and Horowitz, Steinberger quoted from one of Horowitz's many books, this one entitled *The Art of Political War and Other Radical Pursuits* (Horowitz, 2000). In politics, said Horowitz, the only thing that matters is winning. "Spin, deceit, hypocrisy and doubletalk. Unprincipled lies. Smear campaigns and other dirty tricks. In political war, argument, evidence and truth are irrelevant." He added:

> Republicans have been afraid to fight the political battle. They often pursue a passive strategy of waiting for the other side to attack. They are tentative and defensive. They lack backbone. They suffer from political timidity. Republicans are innocents abroad when it comes to political war. They don't have a clue as to how to fight the political battle. They suffer from a non-combatant attitude. While politics is war conducted by other means, Republicans are often reluctant to fire a shot.

Steinberger expressed surprise at this characterization of the Republicans:

> So, presumably when we think of people with names like ... the Swiftboat guys, Karl Rove, Rush Limbaugh, Charles Krauthammer, Bob Novak, Michael Savage, presumably we're to think of these folks as timid, non-combative, reluctant to mix it up, kindly and genial, warm and fuzzy, innocent, wide-eyed, passive, ineffectual. So, clearly we have the construction of some kind of parallel universe. Something largely unconnected with the world as we all know and recognize it.
>
> So, when Horowitz tells us, for example, that Republicans are a bunch of passive milquetoasts, we could conclude that he's just deeply and profoundly ignorant, more ignorant than almost anyone could possibly be, or we could conclude that he's crazy, radically out of touch with reality, or we could conclude what seems by far more likely that he himself is a political warrior and that he's simply doing whatever he thinks will work. So, I hypothesize, engaging in political warfare, doing and saying whatever it takes to win, this is what Mr. Horowitz does for a living. It's his job; it's his way of life. And, of course, if this is true, then clearly what it means is that it's simply impossible to take anything he says or does seriously, including anything he says today. On his own account, on his own account of political warfare, I emphasize not my account, his own account, analysis means nothing, facts mean nothing, evidence means nothing and, of course, if we know this, if we know that Mr. Horowitz himself is a political warrior, then we'd be idiots if we listened seriously to anything he says.

Horowitz might also have countered Steinberger's argument with evidence of how activists on the left have also turned mother's picture to the wall when they've deemed it necessary, indulging in forms of political warfare not much different from his own and doing so unapologetically. Community activist Saul Alinsky's *Rules for Radicals* (1971) justified his willingness to use Horowitz-like tactics if they appeared to be the only means available for redressing economic inequalities and empowering the poor. For him, to do anything less would have been the unethical stance (Perazzo,

2008). Is preaching what you know to be untrue any less demagogic if done in what you yourself believe is a worthy cause?

One of the more ambitious efforts at matching definitional criteria for demagoguery to prototypical examples is provided by Trish Roberts-Miller:

> People often use "demagoguery" simply to mean effective discourse that they don't like, or they assume that demagoguery is rhetoric used on behalf of a bad cause. (Thus, sometimes people will defend someone against the charge of demagoguery by saying, "It isn't demagoguery because he's right.") But just about any political viewpoint can be put forward in a demagogic way—it isn't restricted to one position on the political spectrum. Demagoguery is polarizing propaganda that motivates members of an ingroup to hate and scapegoat some outgroup(s), largely by promising certainty, stability, and what Erich Fromm famously called "an escape from freedom." Historically, demagoguery is a precursor to the ending of democracy—that is, when demagogues succeed, their first move is almost always to restrict the power of the people or parliaments in favor of some kind of tyrannical or totalitarian system.
>
> (2008)

Melodrama

Chief among the polarizing forms of demagogic rhetoric is **melodrama**. Melodramatic rhetoric casts issues in the simplistic terms of pure good versus pure evil. This, argue its defenders, is what mobilizes popular discontent in ways that nuanced arguments are bound to fail. Do away with melodrama in movement struggles and you might as well concede defeat (Swartze, 2006). Yet it is ethically questionable because it denies listeners the opportunity for informed judgments. It is especially questionable to us when it is used to bring a nation into war under *false* pretenses—not a real crisis, but a contrived crisis, based on crass political motives and on spurious claims (e.g., Bostdorff, 1992; Ivie, 2005; Solomon, 2005).

The two-dimensional characters of fictional melodrama and the use of exaggeration and polarization for dramatic effect find their way into political crisis rhetoric by way of a valorized "us" and a dehumanized or demonized "them" (Anker, 2005). Victims, villains, and heroes are joined together in a sanitized narrative, shorn of moral complexity. "We" have an urgent mission to perform. We must act, not just out of fear but from a clear sense of moral purpose. Good must triumph, and good will triumph, but victory will not be easy. The enemy is wily, clever, and will stop at nothing. It has already threatened (or victimized) us. By some accounts, this danger may justify borrowing a page from their book while exempting ourselves from moral standards that we impose upon others. After all, God is on our side, Satan (or the equivalent) on theirs. These narrative components may be cross-cultural and trans-historical; they are by no means confined to contemporary American militarists. Yet the themes run deep in the American psyche, and are daily reinforced in American popular culture (Simons, 2007).

Duplicity

Duplicity, defined as "the belying of one's true intentions by deceptive words or action" (Merriam-Webster Online Dictionary), is a common characteristic of institutional rhetoric arising from conflicts of interest. Duplicity doesn't rise to the level of demagoguery, but it is far more pervasive. Particularly vexing for even the most public-minded professionals are conflicts between their professional values and the institutional demands made upon them to violate those values. Here are some examples from health communication, journalism, and television entertainment.

Ethically Challenged Case 1 Health Communication

A common dilemma pits *health care* interests against business interests. For example, what would you do as CEO of Wyeth, Inc., if your company's very profitable hormone-replacement drug suddenly tanked after a huge federal study on hormone therapy concluded in 2002 that menopausal women who took certain hormones had an increased risk of invasive breast cancer, heart disease, and stroke? Would you take the drug off the market out of a sense of professional responsibility, or would you continue to hire ghost writers on the sly to write articles for medical journals that highlighted the drug's benefits and downplayed its risks? Wyeth pursued the latter course, but it was by no means alone. A lead *New York Times* editorial critiqued on this practice, noting that leading medical journals often have a difficult time disentangling themselves from the pharmaceutical industry. The *NY Times* reported, for example, on a study in the journal, *Neuropsychopharmacology*, that provided a favorable assessment of a controversial new treatment for depression resistant to conventional therapies. In fact, *Neuropsychopharmacology* failed to mention that "eight of the nine authors serve as consultants to the company that makes the device used in the therapy. The ninth works directly for the company. Just to make things particularly incestuous, the lead author of the study is the journal's editor and a consultant to the company" (*New York Times*, 2006). The editorial writers at the *New York Times* argued that medical journals should stop printing articles by scientists with close ties to these businesses, and if they cannot, they should at least force the authors to disclose their conflicts of interest publicly. That way, doctors and patients will know that the interpretations may be biased (*New York Times*, 2006).

Ethically Challenged Case 2 Journalism

Closer to home for students of mass media are ethically questionable practices in the *journalism industry*. For instance, former *Washington Post* reporter Mike Allen (2009) brought news to *Politico* that the *Post* was offering lobbyists "off-the-record dinner and discussion" with top congressional and administration officials for $25,000 a plate. A copy of the invitation reads:

> Underwriting Opportunity: An evening with the right people can alter the debate ... Underwrite and participate in this intimate and exclusive Washington Post Salon, an off-the-record dinner and discussion at the home of CEO and Publisher Katharine Weymouth.... Bring your organization's CEO or executive director literally to the table. Interact with key Obama administration and congressional leaders.

Once *Politico* printed the story, an uproar ensued about the ethics of a newsroom courting lobbyists and their money. Allen quoted online columnist Tim Graham, who criticized the *Post* by saying that the offer essentially turned the news organization into a facilitator for private lobbyist-official encounters. Graham worried that this proposed event was a "new sign of the lengths to which news organizations will go to find revenue at a time when most newspapers are struggling for survival" (Allen, 2009).

After being outed by *Politico*, Weymouth apologized for what she described as an error by her marketing department, and the event was cancelled. That said, there is no reason to think the event would not have gone on as scheduled should it not have been exposed by *Politico*. Furthermore, such ethically challenged activities are not rare; collusive arrangements between newspapers and the corporations and local governments they are supposed to cover at arm's length are commonplace. It is completely uneventful, for instance, when newspapers create entire sections of the paper designed to give advertisers a hospitable environment (Frankel, 2000).

None of this is new, or for many in the news business, particularly alarming. But nowadays there is the problem of a ratcheting-up of demands that news operations yield profits. A story written by a disgruntled media critic for *The Los Angeles Times* concerned the extent to which that venerable newspaper's reporters and editors were pressured by top management to "think corporate" as they developed their plans for news coverage. For example, the *Los Angeles Times* executives agreed to run a special issue of the Sunday magazine devoted exclusively to favorable coverage of a new downtown sports arena. Contractors and patrons were strongly encouraged to advertise. Not disclosed in the news coverage was that the *Los Angeles Times* was a secret partner in the arena project and that it was to share in the profits from the magazine advertising. Max Frankel, a longtime distinguished journalist for *The New York Times*, eloquently expressed his concerns about the ethical dangers of news-for-profit:

> A wall is needed to insulate the gathering of news, which should be a selfless public service, from the pursuit of profit, which is needed to guarantee the independence of the business. Journalism, in other words, is a costly and paradoxical enterprise: It can flourish only when profitable, but it is most suspect when it seeks a profit at all costs.
>
> (Frankel, 2000)

Ethically Challenged Case 3 Television

If ever there was a wall between entertainment programming and product advertising, it has long since been broken with the advent of modern television, with kids' shows specifically designed to promote featured products, and product displays surreptitiously inserted into most shows. But these deceptions are relatively benign when measured against reports that the government has also been attempting to persuade in the guise of entertainment (Romano, 2000). A number of years ago, the White House negotiated a deal with the television networks, forgiving them an obligation to provide so many minutes of unpaid public service advertising in return for their agreement to insert the government's pro-social messages into prime-time dramas such as *Touched by an Angel, NYPD Blue, ER, Beverly Hills 90210,* and *Chicago Hope.*

Arguably, this was a good deal for the networks. Their estimated gain would be approximately $22 million worth of added time for paid advertising. The cost would be a small reduction in their once-vaunted reputation for creative independence. Television writers would not be forced to change their scripts, and the government would not be asking television producers to promote its more controversial activities—only to insert into their prime-time scripts subtle messages about the dangers of street drugs and alcohol. Somehow, though, the ethics of this deal seem questionable.

As Georgetown University law professor David Cole pointed out, the government is not supposed to favor the content of one message over another when doling out financial benefits to facilitate private speech. They crossed the line between government speech and private speech, and basically coerced private speakers, through the public purse, into expressing government messages in a way that was designed to mislead the American public. The rights the U.S. government violated in this case were the rights of viewers and listeners not to be propagandized in an underhanded way by their leaders (Romano, 2000).

Perception Management

In order to understand perception management, we must first understand public diplomacy. *Public diplomacy* involves efforts by one government to influence the actions of another by influencing the beliefs and attitudes of its people (Rampton & Stauber, 2003). For example, the U.S. government has made great effort to win friends and influence people in the Middle East (Rampton & Stauber, 2003, 2006). In 2003, the Bush administration hired PR operatives with close connections to the administration to take over many of its public diplomacy efforts. Named the Lincoln Group, it had created radio and television outlets to compete with the popular Al Jazeera, a network considered hostile to U.S. interests. Later, the Group hired writers, translators and broadcast staff to present its stories its way, under cover of local news ownership and news management. Despite their efforts, the Lincoln Group failed to change the image of the U.S. government, which remained unpopular in the Middle

East, primarily because most of the public diplomacy stories were out of sync with the reality of peoples' daily lives (Rampton & Stauber, 2003, 2006).

But how does public diplomacy differ from perception management? Emily Goldman distinguishes public diplomacy from *perception management* as a "euphemism" for "an aspect of information warfare." Public diplomacy, she says, "does not, as a rule, involve falsehood and deception, whereas these are important ingredients of perception management; the purpose is to get the other side to believe what one wishes it to believe, *whatever* the truth may be" (Goldman, 2004). *Perception management*, sometimes called *information warfare*, is defined by the U.S. Department of Defense (DOD) as:

> actions to convey and/or deny selected information and indicators to foreign audiences to influence their emotions, motives, and objective reasoning as well as to intelligence systems and leaders at all levels to influence official estimates, ultimately resulting in foreign behaviors and official actions favorable to the originator's objectives. In various ways, perception management combines truth projection, operations security, cover and deception, and psychological operations.
>
> (Department of Defense Dictionary of Military and Associated Terms, 2001)

Although perception management is specifically defined as being limited to foreign audiences, critics of the Department of Defense charge that it also engages in domestic perception management. An example cited is the Bush-era prohibition of viewing or photographing the flag-draped caskets of dead military as they are unloaded in bulk upon arrival in the U.S. for further distribution, a policy reversed by the Obama administration.

Says Goldman (2004), the phrase "perception management" is filtering into civilian use as a synonym for "persuasion." Public relations firms now offer "perception management" as one of their services. Similarly, officials who are being accused of shading the truth are now frequently charged with engaging in "perception management." If that's the case, then perhaps the field or discipline of persuasion needs its own PR. Or perhaps the problem is that people associate persuasion with its ethically most questionable practices, including much—by no means all—of public relations.

THE MINDFUL SOCIETY

Noted psychologist Ellen Langer has done considerable research on conditions leading to what she calls **mindlessness** and **mindfulness** by persuadees. In one study, she and her colleagues (Langer, et al., 1978) found that people could be persuaded to surrender their turns at a copying machine if given just the semblance of a reason: "Because I need to make copies." This proved about as effective as giving a real reason: "Because I'm in a hurry." But mindlessness turned to mindfulness when the request was to make 20 copies or more. Then, giving the mere semblance of a reason became no more effective than a request without a reason: "Excuse me, may I use the Xerox machine?"

The Langer study further evidences what other psychologists have demonstrated as well. People act mindfully—engage in central processing—when they are motivated to think critically and have the ability to do so. People act mindlessly—engage in peripheral processing—when they are unable or unmotivated to think critically. All of us act mindlessly some of the time, and some of us seem to operate on automatic pilot—relying on cognitive shorthands—nearly all the time (Cialdini, 2009).

This book was written in part to help you engage in mindful message processing as a persuader and persuadee. The advice offered in Chapter 8 on coming to judgment prior to attempting persuasion is consistent with Langer's advice. So, too, is the advice offered on practicing an art of mistrust in attending to persuasive messages. The persuasion dialogue requires mindful speaking and listening.

Mindfulness also requires that we personally work hard to distinguish facts from assumptions and inferences. This is important because, as Reardon reminds us, in negotiations there are few facts, mostly inferences and assumptions, yet they are too often treated as facts (2004). Fact-checkers Brooks Jackson and Kathleen Hall Jamieson urged readers of *Unspun* (2007) to develop "habits of mind"—a skepticism that falls short of cynicism, a determination to seek out all the evidence, an awareness of verbal sleights of hand—that will make it less likely that one will be taken in by the next snake-oil salesman.

These habits may be helpful but they are not enough, says social psychologist Anthony Pratkanis (2007). "Know the ways of persuasion," he suggests, but don't assume that your increased awareness on its own will liberate you from the "third-person effect," discussed in Chapter 1, unless you are also mindful of your own vulnerabilities. "Monitor changes in your emotions," he adds. Look for social influence tactics as possible sources of those changes and begin asking yourself critical questions about the situation. "Also take control of your thoughts," says Pratkanis. When confronted with a causal explanation, for example, explore alternative possibilities for the same effect. Ask critical questions about the communicator's motivations in making the pitch. Finally, "have a plan for dealing with unwanted influence." You don't have to stay on the phone with the annoying telemarketer, for example, if you prepare ways to exit the conversation (Pratkanis, 2007).

Langer (1989) adds to what has been said here about the differences between mindlessness and mindfulness. She identifies repetition as one of the major causes of mindlessness. Associated with mindlessness is a tendency to create premature cognitive commitments and to allow such commitments to impose "false limits" on our competence and potential.

All of us rely on filters, or schemas, by which to process new information. But we need schemas that will allow contextual factors to enter into our judgments. The mindful message processor values the play of uncertainty, appreciates the potential of nonconformity, and welcomes the opportunity to take personal responsibility in making decisions.

Mindfulness is also less outcome-oriented than process-oriented. The mindful persuadee develops *second-order mindfulness* by thinking about the process itself. Second-order mindfulness "recognizes that there is no right answer" and "no logical stopping point" on many of the issues we confront, but assumes that gut decisions, made after specific concerns are addressed thoughtfully, will be better decisions (Langer, 1989).

Langer's (1989) insights about mindfulness are important. However, what are needed are not just mindful individuals but societal institutions that facilitate mindful message processing. Faced with mounting pressures to compete for scarce resources, the news and entertainment media, the health professions, and even higher education are becoming increasingly market-oriented (Barber, 2007). Although these institutions used to provide a check on the excesses of market economies, now they are a part of the problem.

The examples provided in this chapter of professions such as health care and journalism abrogating scholarly and journalistic integrity for the sake of the dollar are symptomatic of the threats posed by financial *dependence* on the professional *independence* of America's cultural institutions. Consider, for instance, the fate of colleges and universities, especially those unable to depend on large endowments. Will they be forced by market pressures to place increased constraints on academic freedom? To better compete, will they adopt many of the same marketing practices they used to criticize?

What's more, once colleges and universities become pawns of the market, how will they offer up the necessary critiques of that market? And once colleges no longer serve as open spaces for the transmission of knowledge, what will serve as the counterforce to excessive marketplace manipulations? Today, books such as this one offer critiques of unsavory practices by public relations professionals, product advertisers, and political campaign consultants. Will tomorrow's textbooks on persuasion eliminate the critiques and just teach the how-to of spin? And what about the students who were raised on sophisticated forms of spin from childhood and who have come to enjoy being manipulated, rather than objecting to it (Postman, 1985)?

What will happen to the digital natives who have grown up in cyberspace? The Internet offers a wondrous bounty of information. But much of this information is unreliable. Will information—sheer information—come to replace that less tangible but perhaps more valuable commodity: experienced judgment?

What's more, how will we know what to make of the information as we exercise our own judgments on the sorts of questions with which persuasion is concerned? Novelist and critic Umberto Eco has remarked that, when he enters a bookstore and glances at the spine of a book, he can make a reliable guess at its content from a number of available signs, but he is bereft of those skills when he goes on the Internet. Eco is not alone in finding the Internet baffling as a source of reliable information. But who will be the Internet intermediaries in the future to help users distinguish the accurate from the dubious?

Americans are rightly proud of their freedoms, but with freedom must come responsibility. What happens if the persuaders we trust abnegate their responsibilities? What happens when that freedom is further eroded in the civic arena by the power of the purse? Is government needed to facilitate mindful message processing? If so, how can we prevent government from also becoming part of the problem?

Government can facilitate mindful message processing by passing stiff consumer protection legislation, requiring, for example, that physicians make full disclosure to their patients about how they stand to benefit financially if their patients sign up for drug-testing programs (Eichenwald & Kolata, 1999). Government can also require networks to set aside free airtime for political advertisements as a substitute for paid advertising—this in exchange for the billions in government giveaways to the networks of increased bandwidth capacity (Frankel, 1999). Government could also reduce soft money contributions to the political parties, with a view toward leveling the playing field in political campaigns. Unfortunately, the recent U.S. Supreme Court decision *Citizens United v. Federal Election Commission* struck down legislation restricting organizations, including corporations and unions, from independent political expenditures, on the grounds that such expenditures are a form of guaranteed free speech.

But facilitating mindful message processing should not solely be a matter of government-imposed regulations. Schools need to teach critical thinking, argumentation, and the like, and television needs to provide models of it. Teenagers, not just college-age readers of persuasion textbooks, need to learn how to dissect messages at multiple levels and in multiple ways, seeing evidences, for example, of persuasion in the guises of entertainment and objectivity and of advertising's role in the shaping of ideologies. Teenagers, not just college students, need instruction in dialogue and conflict management. They need help as well in coping with the world of the Internet—learning, for example, how to evaluate its many sources of information and opinion, some trustworthy, some totally unreliable.

Television and computerized gaming are today two of the primary educators of children, and young people especially tend to learn by example. This generation, raised on television and gaming, needs also to be entertained as it is taught, and these media are in a position to teach the toughest lessons: no, "we" are not perfect; no, "they" are not all mad or bad.

Too often, young people are raised on *melodrama*: especially in computer games, forces of good end up arrayed simplistically against the sinister forces of evil. Adults, too, tend to get their information in the form of melodrama (e.g., television reality shows that have grown into melodramatic tabloid fodder); this is an extension of the childhood socialization process. How much better it would be if children and adults saw television programming that *deepened* viewers' understanding of complex social problems, rather than reinforcing simplistic us versus them thinking by way of cardboard characters in melodramatic roles.

Ironically, it seems to be animated comedy on television that is best equipping us to understand the human condition. *The Simpsons*, for example, are three-dimensional characters who make tough decisions, including bad decisions, while remaining lovable for all their foibles and eccentricities. On *South Park*, the four youngsters are often vulgar and crude, but they remain loyal friends. Each program offers a rigorous critique of our consumeristic world and ends with a sermon; from the mouths of youngsters comes what is offered up as wisdom. With instructive entertainment programming such as these, heroes display tragic flaws; villains have some redeeming characteristics. Said Kenneth Burke:

> The progress of humane enlightenment can go no further than in picturing people not as *vicious* but as *mistaken*. When you add that people are *necessarily* mistaken, that all people are exposed to situations in which they must act as fools, that *every* insight contains its own special kind of blindness, you complete the comic circle, returning again to the lesson of humility that underlies great tragedy.

(1961)

Hugh Rank's Rhetorician for Rent

How Coca-Cola can save our colleges, by Bob Greene, *Chicago Tribune*, September 10, 1991

Professor Hugh Rank, who teaches English at Governors State University, used to be appalled by how advertising had taken over virtually every area of American society. Now, though, he's ready to give up.

"Everything in my classroom is for sale," he said. "Including me. I'm inviting sponsors to apply."

The professor, like most Americans, has seen every available inch of space in our country gobbled up by advertisers. If you watched the recent U.S. Open tennis tournament, you were reminded once again that space on athletes' clothing is for sale to the highest bidder; one of the most lucrative things a person can be these days is a walking billboard.

When a private company began piping customized, commercially sponsored TV newscasts into school classrooms, Professor Rank was disgusted. "But now I've changed my mind," he said. "We're so close to the total saturation point with sponsorship that maybe my effort will put us over the top."

Thus, his idea—to allow corporations to buy advertising in college classrooms.

"If you can't beat 'em, join 'em" he said. "We at the nation's universities ought to think about selling ad space on our classroom lecterns, on the blackboards, on the walls of our classes and on our clothing."

"Everyone is always worrying about where the money is going to come from to fund higher education," he said. "This is the obvious answer. Think of all that classroom space being wasted. I'm sure that sponsors would line up to buy space in such a respected academic environment."

The professor has some specific ideas:

"There is a blackboard at the front of every classroom," he said. "The students look at it all during the lecture. You could put a Coca-Cola logo on the top of it very easily, and bring in a nice sum." "Why not let corporations sponsor the classes themselves?" he said. "At the beginning of every lecture I could remind the students, 'This class is made possible by a grant from Mobil Oil.' "

"Part of teaching involves asking questions of the students in class," he said. "It would be fairly easy to sell commercial time right before I provide the answer. For example I might say to the class: 'In John Steinbeck's *The Grapes of Wrath*,' what was the final destination of the displaced farmers?' And as the students waited to hear the answer, I could say: 'The right answer is being brought to you by Delta Air Lines.' "

"We could sell space on the front of the blue books—the blank essay books the students use to write their final exams," he said. "On the front of the blue books we could have a beer company logo, and the words: 'After the test, relax with a Schlitz.' "

"And of course we could wear advertising messages and logos on our clothing," he said. "If race car drivers can cover themselves with advertising, why not us?"

"Advertising space could easily be sold in textbooks and works of literature. At the end of a lot of paragraphs, there's blank space where the sentence doesn't fill out the whole line. The words in books are printed in black ink. So we could let sponsors use red ink to fill out the rest of the unfilled lines. A student would finish a paragraph, and then read a short message from Burger King before he starts the next paragraph."

On a basic level, of course, Professor Rank knows that his idea is ludicrous. He has long been very much against the complete commercialization of American society; he is the author of a book called *The Pitch*, which is intended to explain to people just how easily they are manipulated in our modern, ubiquitously sponsored world.

But on another level he fears that students would actually accept the idea of professors and classrooms sponsored by corporations—accept the idea, and think it was prestigious. If a student saw that his or her professor was sponsored by, say, Pepsi, the student might actually hold the professor in higher esteem. After all, if a big multinational corporation thinks enough of a teacher to stick a logo on him, then the teacher must be pretty good.

"That's the problem," he said. "You can't really make fun of this, because it has taken over our culture so completely. You have students paying $20 to buy T-shirts with the logos of big companies on the front. The students are actually paying money to walk around wearing corporate advertisements on their chests. It's hard to be satirical about something that people see as normal."

So Professor Rank's idea might conceivably catch on. And if it does, the official mottos of some of our greatest universities—"Truth Through Knowledge," "A Lamp of Wisdom" and other such sentiments—may be replaced by a much simpler slogan: "This Space for Rent."

THE ETHICS OF BEING ETHICALLY AWARE

Have you ever heard of the Eichmann phenomenon? Adolf Eichmann was an upper-middle-level manager of a large organization. In that capacity, he performed his job well, always doing what was technically efficient in accomplishing the organization's mission, always following orders from his superiors. It just so happened that Eichmann's organization was a Nazi death camp.

FIGURE 15.3   *Adolf Eichmann on trial in Jerusalem.*
© AP Images

Writing on Eichmann's trial in Jerusalem (see Figure 15.3), philosopher and political theorist Hannah Arendt (1978) was struck by how ordinary Eichmann seemed. Obedience was highly valued, expected, and required in Eichmann's organization; hence he considered himself virtuous. Operating well within the range of sanity and normality, he was simply a thoughtless man doing his job. Arendt coined the term the **banality of evil** to refer to this man without an ethical frame.

From evidence presented in Richard Nielsen's (1996) writing on organizational ethics, it appears that Eichmann was by no means alone. Organizations of every type make demands on employees to surrender their autonomy—and often their sense of ethical responsibility—in service of organizational objectives. A repeated explanation for torture of American POWs by the Japanese in World War II, for concealment of tobacco company research linking cigarettes with cancer, and for price fixing by companies has been the refrain from organizational professionals who *did* know better: "That's the way it was done in my organization." Says Gioia, organizational representatives are often not aware that they are dealing with a problem that might have ethical overtones: "If the case involves a familiar class of problems or issues, it is likely to be handled via existing cognitive structures or scripts—scripts that typically include no ethical component in their cognitive content" (1992).

Ethical behavior, then, begins with ethical awareness, the recognition that ethical considerations are present in all human interactions. Therefore, in our roles as communicators and recipients of persuasive messages, we need to recognize that every persuasive context incorporates an ethical dimension: there are no ethics-free situations. Given this, when thinking about our role in persuasion, we might ask ourselves: What ethical standards should guide our conduct in this particular case? What should we expect of others? Richard Johannesen (2001) suggests going further: Why are we adhering to these standards and not others? To whom is ethical responsibility owed? How will I feel about myself after this communicative act? Could I justify my act publicly if called on to do so? How can I judge in retrospect whether my actions were consistent with my ethical intentions? These are good questions.

COMMUNICATION ACTIVISM REVISITED

You've acquired tools for understanding, practicing, and analyzing persuasion and now we urge you to use them in creating a better world. You can do this by serving as a model for others whether among friends and family members or in the larger worlds of work and citizen action. You can also pass on what you've learned to others. Alone or in groups you can also promote needed institutional reforms.

Throughout this text, we have made every effort to define, critique, exemplify, explain, elucidate, demonstrate, and illustrate the many facets of "persuasion." We've talked about the good and the bad. As we come to our last word on the subject of persuasion, we wish to revisit a topic of vital importance. And, we wish to adopt the roles of advocates—persuaders—ourselves.

As we think back to Plato, we must admit that his critique of the Sophists is not completely unfounded. Often, persuasion is used unethically. In interpersonal situations, it is not uncommon to find persuaders who make false promises and use empty flattery to get something from another human being. In politics, it sometimes seems that honest advocacy is a practical impossibility. As we've suggested in this chapter, our media risks selling their soul to the devil and we feel more than a bit of concern about our universities. And in this book we've seen persuasion's ethically challenged business applications, where everyone from salespeople to waiters to public relations professionals seem prepared to manipulate at every turn.

That being said, we also know the positive power of ethical persuasion. America's recent history displays it forcefully. It is through persuasive activism that Martin Luther King, Jr. created a non-violent army for change that marched on Washington and shamed the nation's leaders into signing the Civil Rights Act of 1964 and the Voting Rights Act of 1965. In a book that she wrote on a yellow legal pad during stolen afternoons at the New York Public Library, Betty Friedan penned *The Feminine Mystique*, a book that opened doors for women to have more equal opportunity in the workplace and college. In San Francisco, it was through the unceasing activism of Harvey Milk that gay people organized, resisted, and challenged the status quo, and the lives of gay people were transformed. Thanks to Harvey Milk, they were able to live freely and openly in that city in ways unimagined before his campaign for gay rights. Nor can we forget evangelist Billy Graham, who started as an independent circuit preacher but who never ceased speaking out persuasively on behalf of his faith. He saw millions converted though his open-air crusades, and he then called on those millions to live lives of true dedication, following the biblical admonition to feed the hungry, give drink to those who are thirsty, and give shelter to the strangers by taking them in. And, there was Cesar Chavez, the Mexican farm worker who organized oppressed migrant workers into what is now the United Farm Workers union, thereby transforming the living conditions of millions who were so desperately in need of an advocate to fight for their basic human rights.

These are just a few of persuasion's American heroes, and they are rightly worthy of honor. But then there are also the regular people who use their persuasive powers ethically to make the world a better place. They live as advocates, involved in informed and serious engagement that enriches the communities in which they live. This is the life we both seek to live, and it is the life we wish for you. We hope that you will employ persuasion every day, not merely to get what you want, but as a force for improving our world.

SUMMARY

In keeping with the call for a mindful society, one that is especially sensitive to questions of ethics, Part III of this book has traveled a difficult path, enjoining you to see things from the perspective of the persuader one moment, from the different perspective of the persuadee the next, and, above all, to ask: What's best for society?

Chapter 9 brought to a head questions that had been lingering since Chapter 4's introduction to the coactive approach. How can persuasive speakers possibly combine expressions of genuine commitment with the impossible demands made on them to strategize, organize, and effectively use the resources of the verbal, the visual, and the non-verbal? Why should students "get real" with their audiences when they are so accustomed to being rewarded for performing mechanically?

Chapter 10 posed a number of the dilemmas for well-intentioned social activists. How do you balance the urgent need to accomplish short-term goals against the realization that your health campaign, for example, may result in long-term harm to the community you are trying to help? How do you choose between power and persuasion strategies that accomplish desirable ends versus education and facilitation strategies that are less controlling but also less likely to solve a serious problem? Normative influence is increasingly being used to tackle anti-social behaviors, but at what price? Who gets to decide what is anti-social and pro-social, propaganda or education? Groups at the margins of respectable society often use highly manipulative influence strategies, but should we condemn their efforts at "brainwashing" while being largely indifferent to the conformity pressures exerted by better respected, more entrenched organizations?

Chapter 11 took these and other such questions into the political campaign arena. Candidate Snodgrass is a worthy contender; her opponent is a self-serving opportunist. Does this justify Snodgrass using all manner of Machiavellian tactics to defeat her opponent, including, for example, a smear campaign based on rumor and innuendo? Should Snodgrass bend her professed beliefs to the whims of the voters, as well as to the demands of fat-cat contributors?

Chapter 12 posed ethical questions about product advertising. Advertisers use "puffery," no doubt about it. But why shouldn't they exaggerate, given that their competitors do it and their clients demand it? Product advertisers also play on our vanities, our insecurities, and our infantile urges. But why shouldn't they, if we consumers are foolish enough to fall for their ploys?

Chapter 13 placed us in the often ugly arena of social conflicts. Here, in the "region of the Scramble," interests are at stake, not just differences of opinion. Here, for that reason, talk can be—and often is—used to commit symbolic violence. If your room-mate, your co-worker, your best friend, or your spouse uses talk as a weapon against you, are you justified in responding in turn?

Chapter 14 brought us into an arena of asymmetrical conflict, that between protest movements and entrenched establishments. Lacking the material resources and standing in society, leaders of these social movements frequently conjure up myths of group unity, victimhood, and sacrifice, while painting their opponents as devils, fools, and puppets. Their influence strategies extend beyond peaceful petitioning to staged confrontations, civil disobedience, and guerrilla warfare. Are their more militant tactics justified, given the adverse circumstances they face?

Chapter 15 has brought all these ethical questions to a head. Its aims have been to consolidate, synthesize, and then raise some additional questions, this time about institutional ethics.

Four perspectives on ethics were introduced in Chapter 1: (1) utilitarianism, (2) universalism, (3) dialogic ethics, and (4) situational ethics. In Chapter 15 new questions were asked: Can persuaders be expected to act honestly and directly in situations where the reigning institutions of society make that type of talk risky, even self-destructive? Can persuadees be expected to make intelligent judgments when a society's reigning institutions make that difficult, if not impossible?

Chapter 15 focused upon an issue often kept under the rug in college settings: When, and under what circumstances, should instructors take and defend controversial positions in the classroom? The issues are complicated but readily identifiable. They involve conditions of relevance, power, definition of what is (and is not) controversial, manner of promotion, and cultural context. They raise additional questions, also discussed, about whether, as David Horowitz and others have argued, colleges and universities need greater ideological diversity among their faculty and greater protections for their students in the form of an Academic Bill of Rights.

Chapter 15 then drew upon political scientist Bryan Garsten's argument that democratic societies depend on persuasion of the sort that leads to informed, independent judgments, but often find their democratic aspirations subverted by forms and styles of persuasion that warp those judgments. Discussed in the section on ethically questionable forms and style of persuasion were demagoguery, duplicity, and perception management.

We returned then to a question considered in earlier chapters, particularly Chapters 7 and 8: how to produce "mindful" (as opposed to "mindless") message recipients. And we raised an additional question: How to produce "mindful" societies?

Chapter 15 concluded with the example of Adolf Eichmann and argued that his ethically indifferent stance was inherently unethical. Ultimately, we argue that, instead of such ethical indifference, the better position is toward civic engagement, where we work along and in groups as communication activists to create societies that will improve our lives and the lives of others.

QUESTIONS AND PROJECTS FOR FURTHER STUDY

1   Should professors take and defend controversial positions in the college classroom? If so, under what conditions? If not, how should they treat controversial issues? Should they strive for objectivity according to one or another definition of this troublesome term? What do you think of the idea of professors posing these problems to their students?

2   What in your view are demagoguery, melodramatic crisis rhetoric, duplicity, and perception management? Are they ever justifiable?

3   Assess the suggestions of Langer, Jackson and Jamieson, and Pratkanis. What will it take to transform a nation of couch potatoes into a mindful society?

4   In your opinion, what will be the advantages and disadvantages of cyberspace technologies on society as we seek to become more mindful?

5   What role, if any, should government play in regulating the dissemination of ideas and information? Should it require the networks to provide free television time for political candidates, for example?

6   Who is more irresponsible, an ethically insensitive killer such as Eichmann or one who is sensitive to the evil he or she commits but kills anyway?

7   Hannah Arendt has observed that the relationship between ethically thoughtless people such as Eichmann and systematically corrupt environments is mutually reinforcing. That is, environments that are corrupt reward the Eichmanns of the world, and they in turn help perpetuate such environments. Do you agree? If so, how can the vicious cycle be broken?

8   When are the news media most likely to resort to melodrama? Should we attempt to learn from television shows such as *The Simpsons* or *South Park* while being critical of most television news?

EXERCISES

1   Are you ready to "swim with the school of Fish?" Write an essay critical of an instructor you've had whose advocacy in the classroom you found objectionable. Or defend an instructor whose classroom advocacy was criticized by others.

2   Think about an instance in your life where you have been the victim of clearly unethical persuasion. Using one of the strategies provided here (mindfulness, ethical sensitivity, communication activism), work actively to confront, remedy, correct, or repair the situation. Then, write up a "lab report" on your experiment.

3   Keep a journal for one week where you catalog the ethically problematic persuasion in your life. Consider as many sources as possible: television commercials, textbooks, friends, pronouncements of politicians, etc. Create a PowerPoint presentation and share your findings with the class.

4   Take Hugh Rank's humorous discussion of placing himself up for sale as your starting place and create a research paper on how Rank's joke has become reality. Trace how corporate sponsorships have changed the way we see the world, and investigate the impact on our lives when things like sports arenas come to be named and financed by corporations.

5   Find a blog that you believe engages in demagoguery, and trace its posts for two weeks. Do a rhetorical criticism of the blog, and arrive at a conclusion as to whether the blog helps or hurts society.

6   Spend a day being fully mindful (as described in this chapter). Write a short paper describing the day, what happened, and what it was like.

KEY TERMS

- Banality of evil
- Counter-hegemonic position
- Demagoguery
- Duplicity
- Liberatory faculty advocacy
- Limited faculty advocacy
- Melodrama
- Mindfulness
- Mindlessness
- Proselytize

REFERENCES

Alinsky, S. (1971). *Rules for radicals*. New York: Vintage Books. (Republished 1989)

Allen, M. (2009, July 3). *Washington Post* cancels lobbyist event amid uproar. Retrieved November 10, 2009, from www.politico.com/news/stories/0709/24441.html

Anker, E. (2005). Villains, victims, and heroes: Melodrama, media, and September 11th. *Journal of Communication, 55*, 22–37.

Arendt, H. (1978). *The life of the mind* (M. McCarthy, ed.). New York: Harcourt Brace.

Barber, B. (2007). *Consumed: How markets corrupt children, infantilize adults, and swallow citizens whole*. New York: Norton.

Bizzell, P. (1991). Power, authority, and critical pedagogy. *Journal of Basic Writing, 10*, 54–69.

Bloom, H. (1995). *The Western canon: The books and school of the ages*. New York: Riverhead Trade Publishing.

Bostdorff, D. M. (1992). *The presidency and the rhetoric of foreign crisis*. Columbia: University of South Carolina Press.

Brand, M. (1996). The professional obligations of classroom teachers. In Spacks, P. M. (ed.), *Advocacy in the classroom*. New York: St. Martin's, pp. 3–17.

Burke, K. B. (1961). *Attitudes toward history*. Boston: Beacon. (Original work published 1937)

Burke, K. B. (1969/1950). *A rhetoric of motives*. Berkeley: University of California Press.

Cialdini, R. B. (2009). *Influence: Science and practice* (5th ed.). Boston: Pearson.

Department of Defense Dictionary of Military and Associated Terms (2001, April 12) Joint Publication 1-02 (as amended through December 17, 2003). Retrieved November 9, 2010, from http://en.wikipedia.org/wiki/Perception_management

Eichenwald, K., & Kolata, G. (1999, May 16). Drug trials hide conflict for doctors. *New York Times*, pp. A1, A34–A35.

Fish, S. (1989). *Doing what comes naturally*. Durham, NC: Duke University Press.

Fish, S. (2007, May 6). The all-spin zone. *New York Times*. Retrieved November 9, 2010, from http://fish.blogs.nytimes.com/?p=47

Fish, S. (2008). *Save the world on your own time*. New York: Oxford University Press.

Frankel, M. (1999, February 21). Save democracy first! *New York Times Magazine*, 28–29.

Frankel, M. (2000, January 9). The wall, vindicated: A sturdy barrier between news and commerce enhances both. *New York Times Magazine*, 24–25.

Friedan, B. (2001). *The feminine mystique*. New York: Norton.

Garsten, B. (2006). *Saving persuasion: A defense of rhetoric and judgment*. New Haven, CT: Yale University Press.

Gioia, D. A. (1992). Pinto fires and personal ethics: A script analysis of missed opportunities. *Journal of Business Ethics, 11*, 379–389.

Giroux, H. A. (1988). *Schooling and the struggle for public life: Critical pedagogy in the modern age*. Minneapolis: University of Minneapolis Press.

Giroux, H. A. (2003). *Public spaces, private lives: Democracy beyond 9/11*. Lanham, MD: Rowman and Littlefield.

Giroux, H. A. (2006). *America on the edge: Henry Giroux on politics, culture, and education*. New York: Palgrave Macmillan.

Giroux, H. A. (2012). *Education and the crisis of public values*. New York: Peter Lang.

Giroux, H. A., DiLeo, J., McClennen, S., & Saltman, K. (2014). *Neoliberalism, education, and terrorism: Contemporary dialogues*. Boulder, CO: Paradigm Publishers.

Goldman, E. O. (2004). *National security in the information age: Issues, interpretations, periodizations*. Oxford: Routledge.

Greene, B. (1991). How Coca-cola can save our colleges. *Chicago Tribune*. Retrieved July 13, 2009, from http://webserve.govst.edu/pa/Introduction/rent.htm

Himmelfarb, G. (1996). The new advocacy and the old. In Spacks, P. M. (ed.), *Advocacy in the classroom*. New York: St. Martin's, pp. 96–101.

Horowitz, D. (2000). *The art of political war and other radical pursuits*. Dallas, TX: Spence.

Horowitz, D. (2006). *The professors: The 101 most dangerous academics in America*. Washington, DC: Regnery.

Horowitz, D. (2007). *Indoctrination U: The Left's war against academic freedom*. New York: Encounter Books.

Horowitz, D. (2009). *One party classroom: How radical professors at America's top colleges indoctrinate students and undermine democracy*. New York: Crown Publishing.

Ivie, R. L. (2005). *Democracy and America's war on terror*. Tuscaloosa: University of Alabama Press.

Jackall, R. (2010). *Moral mazes*. New York: Oxford University Press.

Jackson, B., & Jamieson, K. H. (2007). *Unspun: Finding facts in a world of disinformation*. New York: Random House.

Johannesen, R. L. (2001). *Ethics in human communication* (5th ed.). Prospect Heights, IL: Waveland.

Kimball, R. (2005). *The rape of the masters: How political correctness sabotages art*. New York: Encounter Books.

Langer, E. (1989). *Mindfulness*. Reading, MA: Addison-Wesley.

Langer, E., Blank, A., & Chanowitz, B. (1978). The mindlessness of ostensibly thoughtless action: The role of placebic information in interpersonal interaction. *Journal of Personality and Social Psychology*, 36, 635–642.

Lazere, D. (1992). Teaching the political conflicts: A rhetorical schema. *College Composition and Communication*, 43, 194–203.

Menand, L. (1996). Culture and advocacy. In Spacks, P. M. (ed.), *Advocacy in the classroom*. New York: St. Martin's, pp. 116–125.

Mencken, H. (n.d.). Demagogy. Retrieved November 10, 2009, from www.en.wikipedia.org/wiki/Demagogy

Moglen, H. (1996). Unveiling the myth of neutrality: Advocacy in the feminist classroom. In Spacks, P. M. (ed.), *Advocacy in the classroom*. New York: St. Martin's, pp. 204–212.

Newfield, C. (2008). *Unmaking the public university: The forty-year assault on the middle class*. Cambridge, MA: Harvard University Press.

Newton, R. D., Jr. (2003). Academic advocacy. *Teaching Ethics* 3(2), 1–25.

New York Times (2006, July 23). Our conflicted medical journals. Retrieved November 9, 2010, from www.nytimes.com/2006/07/23/opinion/23sun2.html

Nielsen, R. P. (1996). *The politics of ethics*. New York: Oxford University Press.

Perazzo, J. (2008). Saul Alinksy. Retrieved November 11, 2010, from www.discoverthenetworks.org/individualProfile.asp?indid=2314

Pirsig, R. (2000). *Zen and the art of motorcycle maintenance*. New York: Harper Perennial. (Original work published 1974)

Postman, N. (1985). *Amusing ourselves to death*. New York: Viking.

Pratkanis, A. (2007). Why would anyone do or believe such a thing? A social influence analysis. In Sternberg, R. J., Roediger, III, H. L., & Halpern, D. F. (eds), *Critical thinking in psychology*. New York: Cambridge University Press, pp. 232–251.

Rampton, S., & Stauber, J. (2003). *Weapons of mass deception*. New York: Tarcher/Penguin.

Rampton, S., & Stauber, J. (2006) *The best war ever: Lies, damned lies, and the mess in Iraq*. New York: Tarcher/Penguin.

Rank, H. (1991). *The Pitch*. Park Forest, IL: Counter-Propaganda Press.

Reardon, K. K. (2004). *The skilled negotiator*. San Francisco, CA: Jossey-Bass.

Roberts-Miller, T. (2008). Characteristics of demagoguery. Retrieved 9 November, 2010, from www.drw.utexas.edu/roberts-miller/handouts/demagoguery

Romano, C. (2000, January 16). Federal review of TV scripts raises constitutional questions. *Philadelphia Inquirer*, pp. A17–A18.

Simons, H. W. (2007). From post/11 rhetoric to quagmire in Iraq. *Rhetoric and Public Affairs*, 10(2), 183–193.

Solomon, N. (2005). *War made easy: How presidents and pundits keep spinning us to death*. New York: Wiley.

Sowards, S., & Renegar, V. (2004) The rhetorical uses of consciousness-raising in third wave feminism. *Communications Studies*, 55(4), 535–552.

Swartze, S. (2006). Environmental melodrama. *Quarterly Journal of Speech*, 92, 239–261.

INDEX

Page numbers in **bold** refer to tables. Page numbers in *italics* refer to figures.
Page numbers with "n" refer to notes.